CLINICAL TRANSCUTANEOUS ELECTRICAL NERVE STIMULATION

CLINICAL TRANSCUTANEOUS ELECTRICAL NERVE STIMULATION

JEFFREY S. MANNHEIMER, M.A., R.P.T.

PRESIDENT
DELAWARE VALLEY PHYSICAL THERAPY ASSOCIATES
LAWRENCEVILLE, NEW JERSEY

GERALD N. LAMPE, B.S., R.P.T.

PRESIDENT
PROFESSIONAL PAIN MANAGEMENT SEMINARS, INC.
SHAWNEE MISSION, KANSAS

F. A. DAVIS COMPANY • Philadelphia

Library of Congress Cataloging in Publication Data

Mannheimer, Jeffrey S., 1942–
    Clinical T.E.N.S.

    Includes bibliographies and index.
    1. Transcutaneous electrical nerve stimulation.
2. Analgesia.   I. Lampe, Gerald N., 1942–   .   II. Title.
III. Title: Clinical TENS. [DNLM: 1. Electrotherapy—
Methods.   2. Pain—Therapy. WL 704 C641]
RM880.M36   1984   615.8′45   83-21020
ISBN 0-8036-5832-X

WE WOULD LIKE TO DEDICATE THIS BOOK
TO OUR WIVES AND CHILDREN
FOR THEIR UNDERSTANDING AND PATIENCE
DURING THE COMPLETION OF THIS TEXT.

MARSHA AND ZACHARY MANNHEIMER

LINDA, SUSAN, AND CHRISTIAN LAMPE

FOREWORD

At the time of this printing, pain problems in America support a multi-billion dollar industry annually. The decade of the 80s has produced more than 200 varieties of T.E.N.S. and biofeedback devices and dozens of other pain-relieving modalities and techniques. In 1982 alone, there were more than 20 million Americans with pain. An average of 200 dollars was spent on each of these individuals monthly. Of this group, approximately 250,000, or a quarter of a million, of them were T.E.N.S. users.

Similarly, hundreds of books, articles, journals, and monographs have been published addressing various aspects of the pain problem. However, the critical need for a comprehensive treatise on the evaluation and treatment of pain from the perspective of the physical therapist has continued to exist. This text presents in one volume a concise yet complete discussion of pain, both as a symptom and pathology, and methods that may be employed for its management.

In order to manage pain properly, its anatomic, physiologic, and psychologic components must be understood. A thorough knowledge of those fundamental principles is the sine qua non without which optimal results of treatment are precluded. To this end, the authors have reviewed, evaluated, and synthesized herein an exhaustive collection of current literature, both American and foreign. The foundation for sound clinical practice is established in these chapters. The magnitude and complexity of the pain problem have dictated that changes occur in how we think about that problem, what we do about it, and in what settings we might seek relief. Not uncommonly, health services for pain management are offered in a variety of nontraditional settings by a rather wide cadre of health practitioners. Nevertheless, the standard for high quality and effectiveness of treatment cannot be compromised. The trial-and-error mode of practice is extremely costly and must be minimized. This text serves as a decision guide that uses scientific analysis as the mechanism for clinical decision making. Treatment options are discussed in depth and rationale is presented in such a way that the practitioner is able to determine and manipulate the critical variables of the patient's pain problem.

Although the major emphasis of this text is on transcutaneous electrical nerve stimulation, the authors appropriately integrate the specialized orthopedic approaches to pain management with the electrophysiologic treatment strategies. Additional emphasis is given the importance of evaluating and treating the whole patient. *Clinical T.E.N.S.* is appropriate for all practitioners who offer services to pain patients or refer patients for pain management. This work is an invaluable teaching resource. Conversely, the reference value of T.E.N.S. is enhanced through the inclusion of exhaustive content on the understanding of pain syndromes. The information is carefully presented both graphically and discursively so as to appeal to all consumers—whether novice or expert. The authors are to be commended for accomplishing an apparently insurmountable task.

Lynda D. Woodruff, B.A., M.S., R.P.T.
Assistant Professor
Department of Physical Therapy
College of Health Sciences
Georgia State University
Atlanta, Georgia

PREFACE

Our purpose in writing this book is to support and enhance the utilization of transcutaneous electrical nerve stimulation (T.E.N.S.), define its role in the treatment of acute, chronic, and postoperative pain, and express our philosophy of care. The text is thus clinical in content, design, and intent, which should appeal to a multidisciplinary audience.

The book logically starts with the history of electroanalgesia with T.E.N.S. and progresses through patient evaluation guidelines, delineation of pain syndromes, and their underlying causes to provide novices a logical course of learning, and experienced practitioners a sound and extensive review. Our clinical experience produced baselines for theory, patient evaluation, T.E.N.S. applications, T.E.N.S. adjustments, and evaluation of patient responses to T.E.N.S. The contents of the book are extensively referenced and illustrated. The book also contains numerous case studies that simplify the learning process. Development of a comprehensive approach geared to treatment of the involved structure, its functional restoration, and pain control, and the prophylaxis thereof is constantly emphasized, especially in the acute stage to decrease the incidence of chronic pain. Specific chapters then can be useful separately or collectively in progression as experience grows and as problem-solving needs dictate.

Because the T.E.N.S. device is noninvasive, portable, and easy to use, T.E.N.S. therapy can play a significant role in self-treatment programs for the patient. The book discusses this role of T.E.N.S. in self-treatment and advises the professional on how it should be supervised.

Clinical T.E.N.S. is not a "cookbook" but a comprehensive text on pain management that emphasizes the adjunctive role and limitations of one modality within the available armamentarium of the informed clinician. The extensive support material contained within the text hopefully will provide all clinicians with additional ideas and techniques by which to increase the use of T.E.N.S., decrease the incidence of chronic pain, and support the acceptance of T.E.N.S. as a viable alternative to medicinal intervention.

J.S.M.
G.N.L.

ACKNOWLEDGMENTS

The authors are grateful to many people whose individual contributions add to the collective value of this book.

Lynda Woodruff reviewed the initial outline and manuscript and wrote the Foreword for this book.

Doctors Alan Hymes, Jim Kwako, and C. Norman Shealy drew upon their experiences and contributed chapters describing the postoperative applications of T.E.N.S., and the psychologic considerations of the pain experience. Doctor Steve Wolf contributed a chapter describing the theoretical postulates of pain and electroanalgesia that included thoughts for further examination of the physiologic action of T.E.N.S.

Many provided knowledge and inspiration for this book through their postgraduate courses and seminars, enlightening us on "what else" could be done to evaluate and rehabilitate persons who suffer pain: Ola Grimsby, Stanley Paris, Clifford Fowler, David Lamb, Robin McKenzie, Sandy Burkhart, Barett Dorko, Mariano Rocabado, and Doctors John Mennell, James Cyriax, C. Norman Shealy, Donlin Long, Alan Hymes, Charles Burton, Ronald Dougherty, and James L. Rowland.

Among the many others who contributed in unique ways are:

Thomas Shaw
Wayne Rath
Barbara Behrens
Marlene Kosydar
Rosemary O'Donnell
Nancy Nestlerode
Eli Glick
Kevin Koob
Regina Rosenthal
Lee Smith
Karen Weiss Freeman

Bill Shive
Richard Kader
Paula Kader
Eileen Whalen
Dawn Meyer
Bill Dunn
Carmela Jones-Calhoun
Bill Cowles
Gwen Gray
Lawrence Burton
Carl Petit
Georgia Loescher

In memory of Dorothy and LeRoy Lampe.

CONTRIBUTORS

ALAN HYMES, M.D.

CLINICAL ASSISTANT PROFESSOR OF SURGERY
UNIVERSITY OF MINNESOTA
MINNEAPOLIS, MINNESOTA

JAMES KWAKO, M.D.

HOLISTIC HEALTH
HEMET, CALIFORNIA

GERALD N. LAMPE, B.S., R.P.T.

PRESIDENT
PROFESSIONAL PAIN MANAGEMENT SEMINARS, INC.
SHAWNEE MISSION, KANSAS

JEFFREY S. MANNHEIMER, M.A., R.P.T.

PRESIDENT
DELAWARE VALLEY PHYSICAL THERAPY ASSOCIATES
LAWRENCEVILLE, NEW JERSEY

CLINICAL ASSISTANT PROFESSOR
COLLEGE OF ALLIED HEALTH PROFESSIONS PROGRAM IN PHYSICAL THERAPY
HAHNEMANN UNIVERSITY
PHILADELPHIA, PENNSYLVANIA

INSTRUCTOR
COLLEGE OF ARTS AND SCIENCES
SCHOOL OF LIFE AND HEALTH SCIENCES
ALLIED HEALTH PROFESSIONS
UNIVERSITY OF DELAWARE
NEWARK, DELAWARE

C. NORMAN SHEALY, M.D., PH.D.

DIRECTOR
SHEALY PAIN & HEALTH REHABILITATION INSTITUTE
SPRINGFIELD, MISSOURI

STEVEN L. WOLF, PH.D., R.P.T.

ASSOCIATE PROFESSOR
DEPARTMENT OF REHABILITATION MEDICINE
ASSISTANT PROFESSOR
DEPARTMENT OF ANATOMY, SURGERY, AND SCHOOL OF ALLIED HEALTH PROFESSIONS
EMORY UNIVERSITY SCHOOL OF MEDICINE
ATLANTA, GEORGIA

CONTENTS

CHAPTER 10

THE THERAPEUTIC VALUE OF POSTOPERATIVE T.E.N.S. (CASE STUDY)   497

ALAN HYMES, M.D.

LIST OF TABLES

LIST OF FIGURES

CHAPTER 7   THE PATIENT AND T.E.N.S.

CHAPTER 8   ELECTRODE PLACEMENT SITES AND THEIR RELATIONSHIP

CHAPTER 9   ELECTRODE PLACEMENT TECHNIQUES

INTRODUCTION: A REVIEW OF THE HISTORICAL USES OF ELECTRICITY

ALAN HYMES, M.D.

> The thing that hath been, it is that which shall be;
> And that which is done is that which shall be done:
> And there is no new thing under the sun.
>
> Ecclesiasticus 1:9

Although in the past 10 to 12 years there has been a resurgence of electrotherapy in various forms by allopathic physicians, one has only briefly to view the history of electrotherapy to realize the significance of the above quotation. Since the discovery of electricity, and before, current has been applied to the human flesh by a variety of methods to cure a multitude of afflictions.

Electric eels were known to the ancient Egyptians and to Hippocrates,[1] but it remained for Scribonius Largus[2] to record the use of electric eels for treatment of headache and gout in 46 AD. William Gilbert (1544–1603) was the first to classify and generalize the phenomenon of electricity.[3] Subsequently, a multitude of apparatus was made to generate and store current. During this time, current in various forms was applied to all parts of the body for all types of afflictions.[3,4]

Richard Lovett published the *Subtil Medium Proved* in 1756.[3] This was the first English-language book on medical electricity, and Lovett listed dozens of cures for many diseases. John Wesley, a religious leader and founder of the Methodist Church, became extremely enthusiastic over this method of medical treatment. He himself became a clinician and investigator in electrotherapy and in 1759 published his *Desideratum: or Electricity Made Plain and Useful by a Lover of Mankind and of Common Sense.*[3] Wesley saw the "subtile fluid" as the soul of the universe. In his book, he gave many examples of diseases that were "cured" by the use of electrotherapy. Included in the various ailments were sciatica, hysteria, headache, kidney stone, gout, cold feet (Raynaud's phenomenon), pleuritic pain, and angina pectoris.

As quoted from Calaway,[3] between the years 1750 and 1780, there were 26 publications dealing with clinical electricity. A new electrical shock machine was installed in the Middlesex Hospital in 1767.

John Birch, an English surgeon, in 1772 described the methods by which he applied electrical current and gave case reports.[5] He applied electrical current for a hand injury of an 18-year-old boy in pain and with contractures. After a few sessions, the boy regained full function of the hand and the pain disappeared. Birch also had other successes in the treatment of chronic low back pain and described cures. Moreover, he described the treatment of chronic constipation by placing a young female patient in an electrical chair. Her second treatment resulted in an evacuation of bowels in 5 minutes with the application of current. He also described apparent cures in the treatment of gout and other afflictions.

In the early 19th century, a multitude of investigators continued to apply electrical current with a variety of apparatus. James Churchill, in 1821, published *A Treatise on Acupuncture*.[4] This was followed by Sarlandiere, who applied electrical current to the acupuncture needles.[4] He described successful cures for rheumatism, nervous afflictions, and attacks of gout.

By 1875, Rockwell, Byrd, and Rockwell published the second edition of their book.[6] In this book, they summarized the history of electrotherapy. Also, there was a long description as to the application by physicians and the responsibility by physicians in the use of electrotherapy.

There were multiple chapters of specifics relating to system-related diseases, including asthma, rheumatism, gout, progressive muscular dystrophy, local motor ataxia, neuralgia, migraine, and back pain. In addition, afflictions such as alcoholism, a variety of gastrointestinal tract disorders, and skin diseases were also treated. A specific chapter on neuralgia and low back pain treated by electrical stimulation consisted primarily of case reports. Complications of chronic stimulation, such as scars and ulcerations of the skin, were also noted.

It is interesting to note that electrotherapy had little use in the mainstream of modern medicine in the past 70 years in spite of the well-documented use of this modality in previous times. As such, little clinical research and no publications have appeared in medical literature until very recently.

Basic research, however, was being conducted by numerous investigators during this time, as reviewed by Pfeiffer.[7] In 1967, Licht[8] reviewed the available historical literature and reported a comprehensive study citing more than 900 references.

Since the early 1900s, apparatus such as "Electreat" were sold directly to consumers by the manufacturer. These instruments became popular, and all imaginable types of claims, including the cure of cancer, were ascribed to these units. The FDA banned their sale in the early 1950s.

Neurophysiologic research[9–13] in the late 1950s and early 1960s led to the gate theory of pain as proposed by Melzack and Wall.[14] Without going into great detail, the gate theory states that nonpainful stimulation in the peripheral nervous system can interfere with the relay of the sensation of pain to higher centers. This block occurs within the central nervous system. Thus, the theory may explain in part why peripheral electrical stimulation may diminish or abolish the sensation of pain.

Shealy[12] reasoned that direct stimulation of the dorsal column of the spinal cord could inhibit the spread of pain impulses to higher perception areas. He experimented with cats and monkeys and found that the pain threshold was increased significantly. Subsequently, Shealy and associates reported the first clinical use of dorsal column stimulation.[15] It was described in a patient with recurrent metastatic carcinoma of the lung who had intractable pain. Since then, neurosurgeons throughout the world have implanted dorsal column and anterior column electrodes for stimulation. Recenty, Burton has implanted electrodes percutaneously on the dorsal columns of the spinal cord.

Initially, it was difficult to predict which patients would respond favorably to dorsal column stimulation. Long[16,17] and Shealy[18,19] in collaboration and independently developed means for evaluating patients for dorsal column electrode implantation by transcutaneous electrical nerve stimulation (T.E.N.S.). Many patients note that T.E.N.S. seems to reduce the perception of pain almost as well as the dorsal column implant. As such, many patients are treated successfully by this modality. It has become an important part of the pain clinics that Long established at the University of Minnesota and at Johns Hopkins University, and Shealy's clinic formerly in LaCrosse, Wisconsin, and presently in Springfield, Missouri.

The participation of private industry was an important factor in the early development of T.E.N.S. Companies such as Stim-tech, Medtronic, and Avery have made contributions in the early development of this rediscovered modality. Various clinical studies have been done on chronic and acute pain, and many of these studies were supported by the companies involved. Further, the technical features of the instruments that were developed by these companies were an extremely important part of these investigations.

The efficacy of T.E.N.S. as a modality in the treatment of pain has now been well established. T.E.N.S., however, is not a panacea for the relief of pain. I recall one patient who had a recurrent inoperable pelvic cancer, causing excruciating pain. His physician had prescribed large, frequent doses of morphine. T.E.N.S. therapy resulted in a marked reduction of pain. Yet the patient chose to leave the hospital within 24 hours of admission without a T.E.N.S. unit, preferring to suffer pain so as to continue receiving morphine.

This example is extreme, but most patients who have chronic pain have learned to use their afflictions for secondary gain such as taking drugs, receiving workmen's compensation payments, and obtaining special attention from spouses and family.

Total treatment of pain usually involves other supportive measures to change the life style that has evolved from this chronic affliction.

In 1972, Long and Shealy established pain clinics using T.E.N.S. therapeutically for chronic pain. It seemed logical to use this modality in patients with acute pain such as one sees after surgical procedures. The first postoperative patient whom I treated with T.E.N.S. was a 62-year-old obese man who had undergone a thoracotomy the previous day. He was a very cooperative and stoic patient. Within 20 minutes of applying stimulation to the posterior aspect of his wound over his right shoulder, he reported the lack of sensation of any pain. Furthermore, he could raise his arm directly overhead and touch his opposite shoulder behind his neck with no pain.

It seemed to my group that the phenomenon was most striking and deserved to be studied in more detail. The details of this investigation are reported in Chapter 10 of this book and elsewhere.[20,21]

Very early in the study, I had applied electrodes to my own back in an attempt to discover an optimal size of an electrode. In doing so, I noted an immediate hyperperistalsis resulting in a purge not unlike a high colonic irritation. Subsequent stimulation was followed by repeated peristalsis, convincing me that the observed phenomenon was indeed real. That same day, electrodes were applied to a patient who had a chronic, persistent ileus lasting 7 days following gastrectomy. By auscultation, peristalsis was strikingly increased with T.E.N.S. Within hours, the patient had expelled flatus and evacuated his bowels.

T.E.N.S. also changes the size of the pupil when applied over the stellate ganglion and causes vasodilatation in extremities distal to the site of stimulation.

There is no doubt that T.E.N.S. influences the autonomic nervous system dramatically, yet most of the basic science work dealing with this subject has not even been started. In my studies, T.E.N.S. also seemed to exhibit a local analgesic effect, which finding is supported by the work of others.[22,23]

Further, T.E.N.S. therapy may effect changes of neurohumoral mechanisms within the central nervous system itself.[24–26] Investigation in this area appears to be very exciting for future research.

It would appear that within the past decade modern medicine has rediscovered a modality that had been in the hands of various medical practitioners since 1900. Prior to that time, although electrical stimulation was commonly used in the medicine of the times, reports were anecdotal and probably would not have withstood the critical, objective analysis demanded by 20th century medical science.

The Reverend John Wesley[3] ended his *Desideratum* with the following plea:

> Before I conclude, I would beg one Thing (If it be not too great a Favour) from the Gentlemen of the Faculty, and indeed from all who desire Health and Freedom from Pain, either for themselves or their Neighbours. It is, That none of them would condemn they know not what: That they would hear the Cause, before they pass Sentence: That they would not pre-emptorily pronounce against Electricity, while they know little or nothing about it. Rather let every candid Man take a little Pains, to understand the Question before he determines it. Let him for two or three Weeks (at least) try it himself in the above-named Disorders. And then his own Senses will show him, whether it is a mere Play-thing, or the noblest Medicine yet known in the World.

Since this introduction is basically an essay, I am allowing myself latitude with at least one philosophic comment. Indeed, much of the world does suffer from physical pain, but the real pain and suffering of mankind are mental anguish as the result of distortions of the mind and emotional instability in relationship to total environment. These distortions may result in tensions; anxieties; alcohol, tobacco, or drug abuse; and faulty eating habits. This state of being plays havoc with all interpersonal relations, leading to a violent and hostile world without love. Further, most psychosomatic and organic diseases probably result from this lack of harmony.

Until mankind collectively and individually recognizes that each person must establish emotional stability in relationship to oneself and one's external environment and do away with distorted perceptions, suffering will continue. Methods such as transcutaneous electrical nerve stimulation are only stop-gap measures, for all of a human's suffering is in the end within oneself. Further, every individual is responsible for oneself and has the capacity to alleviate one's own suffering no matter what its source, if one so chooses.

REFERENCES

1. KELLAWAY, P: *The William Osler Medal essay: The part played by electric fish in the early history of bioelectricity and electrotherapy.* Bull Hist Med 20:112, 1946.
2. SCHONOCH, W: *Die Rezept Sammlung des Scribonius.* Jena, 1912–13.
3. STILLINGS, D: *A short history of electrotherapy in England to about 1880.* Museum of Electricity in Life at Medtronic, Minneapolis, Minn, 1974.
4. STILLINGS, D: *A survey of the history of electrical stimulation for pain to 1900.* Med Instrum 9:255, 1974.
5. BIRCH, J: *Essay on Electricity . . . by George Adams,* ed 4. R Hindmarsh, London, 1772, p 519. Museum of Electricity in Life at Medtronic, Minneapolis, Minn.
6. ROCKWELL, B, BYRD, GM, AND ROCKWELL, AD: *A Practical Treatise on the Medical and Surgical Uses of Electricity,* ed 2. William Wood & Co, New York, 1875. Museum of Electricity in Life at Medtronic, Minneapolis, Minn.
7. PFEIFFER, EA: *Electric stimulation of sensory nerves with skin electrodes for research, diagnosis, communication and behavioral conditioning: A survey.* Med Biol Eng 6:637, 1968.
8. LICHT, S: *Therapeutic Electricity and Ultraviolet Irradiation: History of Electrotherapy.* Physical Medicine Library 4:1. Elisabeth Licht, New Haven, Conn, 1967.
9. COLLINS, WF AND RANDT, CT: *Evoked central nervous system activity relating to peripheral unmyelinated or "C" fibers in the cat.* J Neurophysiol 21:345, 1958.

10. HAGBARTH, KE AND DERR, DIB: *Central influences on spinal afferent conduction.* J Neurophysiol 17:295, 1954.
11. POGGIO, GF AND MOUNTCASTLE, VB: *A study of the functional contributions of the lemniscal and spinothalamic systems to somatic sensibility.* Bull Johns Hopkins Hosp 106:266, 1960.
12. SHEALY, CN: *The physiological substrate of pain.* Headache 6:101, 1966.
13. WALL, PD: *The laminar organization of dorsal horn and effects of descending impulses.* J Physiol (Lond) 188:403, 1967.
14. MELZACK, R AND WALL, DW: *Pain mechanisms: A new theory.* Science 150:971, 1965.
15. SHEALY, CN, MORTIMER, JT, AND RESWICH, JB: *Electrical inhibition of pain by stimulation of the dorsal column: Preliminary clinical reports.* Anesth Analg (Cleve) 45:489, 1967.
16. LONG, DM: *Recent advances in the management of pain.* Minn Med 56:705, 1974.
17. LONG, DN: *External electrical stimulation as treatment of chronic pain.* Minn Med 57:195, 1974.
18. SHEALY, CN: *Transcutaneous electroanalgesia.* Surg Forum 23:419, 1973.
19. SHEALY, CN: *Six years' experience with electrical stimulation for control of pain.* Adv Neurol 4:775, 1974.
20. HYMES, AC, ET AL: *Electrical surface stimulation for treatment and prevention of ileus and atelectasis.* Surg Forum 25:223, 1974.
21. HYMES, AC, ET AL: *Acute pain control by electrostimulation: A preliminary report.* Adv Neurol 4:761, 1974.
22. CAMPBELL, JM AND TAUB, A: *Local analgesia from percutaneous electrical stimulation.* Arch Neurol 28:347, 1973.
23. IGNELZI, RJ AND NYQUIST, JK: *Direct effect of electrical stimulation on peripheral nerve evoked activity: Implications in pain relief.* J Neurosurg 45:159, 1976.
24. ANDERSSON, SA: *Pain control by sensory stimulation: Second World Congress on Pain, Montreal, Canada.* Pain Abstracts 1:97, 1978.
25. HOSOBUCHI, Y, ADAMS, J, AND LINCHITZ, R: *Pain relief by electrical stimulation of the central gray matter in humans and its reversal by naloxone.* Science 197:183, 1977.
26. SHEALY, CN, KWAKO, JL, AND HUGHES, W: *Effects of transcranial neurostimulation upon mood and serotonin production: A preliminary report.* Il dolore 1:13, 1979.

CHAPTER 1

PAIN AND T.E.N.S. IN PAIN MANAGEMENT

JEFFREY S. MANNHEIMER, M.A., R.P.T.,
AND GERALD N. LAMPE, B.S., R.P.T.

The phenomenon known as pain, whether it be acute, chronic, superficial, deep, visceral, somatic, or referred, has numerous etiologies but generally falls into three categories: physical, physiologic, and psychologic (Fig. 1-1). The pathophysiology of various pain syndromes may be simple or quite complex. The high degree of neuromodulation throughout the central nervous system (CNS) or autonomic nervous system (ANS) may frequently produce misinterpretation and make diagnosis difficult.

Pain is the primary factor that causes the patient to seek medical attention. Because pain is a symptom that can provide both helpful and misleading information, it is imperative that the patient provide as much information as possible and that the clinician conduct a thorough evaluation so the cause or pathology behind the pain can be established. Consequently, it is also imperative that health-care practitioners, regardless of their specialty, have a thorough understanding of the character, nature, and mechanisms of pain. The majority of education concerning pain pertains merely to methods of alleviating it symptomatically. Far too little time is spent on its value as a diagnostic aid and the necessity for determining the pain-producing structure. Frequently, treatment is solely of a symptomatic nature with no attempt to rehabilitate the structure that has given rise to the symptoms. Determination of the cause of pain thus should allow for the initiation of a comprehensive treatment program designed to correct the pathology, control or alleviate the pain, and prevent its recurrence.

THE PAIN CYCLE

When trauma (either physical or psychologic) is sustained, a painful response is frequently noted. This pain precipitates measures by the body to protect itself by guarding, frequently noted as muscle spasms (Fig. 1-2). Guarding promotes subsequent dysfunction of the soft tissue and the joints of the area being guarded. The pain cycle is accompanied by certain internal changes that tend to compound the element of pain (Fig. 1-3). The

7

PHYSICAL

Trauma
Heat
Cold

STRESS

Congenital
Infectious
Environmental
Neoplastic

Vascular
Degenerative
Immunologic
Chemical
   -Potassium ions
   -Lactic Acid
   -Bradykinin
   -5-Hydroxytryptamine
   -Histamine

Irritation
Compression
Distraction
Distention
Abrasion
Contusion
Laceration
Psychosomatic

PHYSIOLOGIC

Spasm
Inflammation
ANS Dysfunction
Sensory Deprivation

PSYCHOLOGIC

Emotional

FIGURE 1-1. A general classification of the causes of pain.

process of guarding, which the body has initiated in response to pain, produces a state of muscle tension that results in a diminished blood supply within the area, or a state of ischemia. Also, since guarding is performed by tonic muscle activity, there is an increased production of metabolites as by-products of the muscle contractions. In a muscle contraction, it is estimated that 20 percent of the energy produces mechanical movement or stabilization, whereas 80 percent of the energy produces heat with the by-products of increased metabolites. Concomitant with the state of ischemia produced by guarding and the increased production of metabolites, there tends to be an increased accumulation of these metabolites. The microscopic responses to trauma may also include the production and concentration of endogenous pain-producing substances, such as:

1. Peptides, that is, bradykinin (BK)
2. Amines, that is, serotonin (5-HT) and histamine (HIS)
3. Substance P
4. Prostaglandin E (not a potent allogenic, but can intensify or elicit inflammation and potentiate the effects of pain producing peptides)

With prolonged guarding, discomfort also tends to occur as a result of fatigue of the muscle fibers involved in the guarding response. The resultant ischemia and retention of the

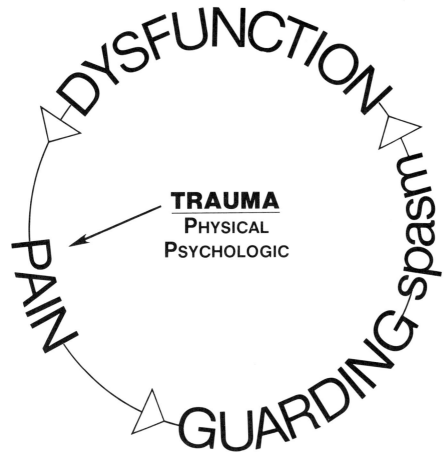

FIGURE 1-2. Primary typical acute/chronic pain cycle.

metabolites tend, as internal factors, to produce more pain. Ischemia also reduces the supply of oxygen and other elements essential to the healing processes.

Therefore, it can be seen that macroscopically there is a pain cycle that tends to perpetuate and compound the painful symptoms and that there are microscopic, internal changes that also tend to compound the pain factor.

Therefore, it is evident that effective management of the pain response is a very important, perhaps essential, element in resolution of the pain cycle. It is our premise that transcutaneous electrical nerve stimulation (T.E.N.S.) is an effective, noninvasive, nonaddictive method of managing this pain and that it adds dimensions that have not been previously available to the medical team. These factors make T.E.N.S. a very logical adjunctive procedure to other forms of therapy. It should be noted that in attempts at managing patients experiencing acute pain, the emphasis is on prevention, because if pain can be effectively managed in the acute phase, the guarding and dysfunction that may result tend to be avoided or at least reduced. Preventing progressive amplification of the pain cycle thereby permits the body's normal healing processes to occur without the encumbrances created by secondary pain factors. In management of patients with chronic pain, the emphasis is obviously not on prevention since the pain cycle is already well established. Instead, emphasis is placed on trying to "break" the pain cycle.

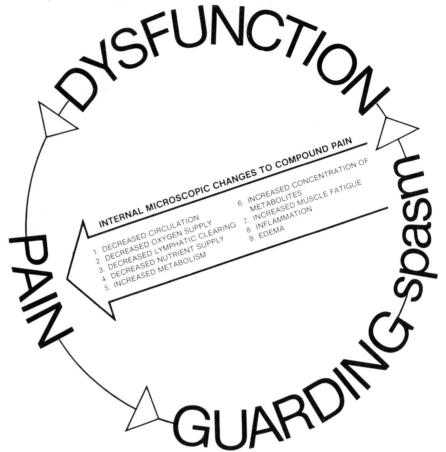

FIGURE 1-3. Primary pain cycle and associated internal changes.

ACUTE VERSUS CHRONIC PAIN

Differentiation between acute and chronic pain is necessary at this juncture to better explain the value of a comprehensive approach to the management of pain. Acute pain is most commonly caused by an accident or trauma resulting in localized tissue damage to the neuromusculoskeletal system. Obviously, visceral irritation can also give rise to acute pain, but for the purposes of this comparison, visceral pain will be discussed separately in Chapter 5.

Acute pain, if diagnosed properly and treated comprehensively, is often easily resolved. However, such acute pain can become chronic if the treatment consists solely of pain modulation, whether it be via T.E.N.S., heat, ice, or medication. However, in many instances, the initiation of comprehensive treatment early in the acute phase can prevent the development of chronic pain.

A general comparison of the characteristics of acute and chronic pain can be seen in Table 1-1. Sternbach[10] categorizes patients with acute pain as having autonomic changes indicative of increased muscular tension, blood pressure, heart rate, and sweating, and patients with the vegetative nature of chronic pain as having decreased interests, libido, appetite, and sleep.

TABLE 1-1. Characteristics of Acute and Chronic Pain

ACUTE*	CHRONIC
Sudden onset/short duration	Onset usually weeks or months (6) after acute
Usually easily diagnosed, treated, and resolved	Pain persists for months or years
Usually able to be localized by patient at or near lesion	Frequently referred away from lesion
	Serves no useful biologic purpose or meaning
Serves a biologic purpose: protective mechanism or danger sign	*Further Characterization*
	Usually extreme abuse of medications
	Multiple surgical procedures may have been performed
	Extent of pain seems much greater than organic pathology
	Patients may become depressed, hypochondriacal, and hysterical
	Pain games may predominate in patients' behavior patterns
	Symptoms and complaints may be compounded or prolonged in the presence of ongoing litigation

*If not adequately diagnosed and properly treated, can lead to chronicity

The chronic pain process obviously involves the patient both physically and psychologically. The psychologic aspects are discussed in detail in Chapter 2. Figure 1-4 illustrates the chronic pain cycle. Chronic pain is pain that persists for 6 months or more.[1–3,11] However, we feel that an acute pain problem such as tendinitis, bursitis, or low back strain becomes chronic if it persists beyond 3 to 6 weeks without improvement. This is frequently encountered when a patient with one of the aforementioned conditions is treated solely by a symptomatic approach (medication, T.E.N.S., diathermy or moist heat, and ultrasound). The lack of specific techniques designed to treat the cause, to correct the involved structure, and to prevent weakness, hypomobility, and resultant dysfunction leads to adhesive capsulitis or intractable low back pain and immobility.

The longer pain persists, the greater is the chance that it will be referred away from the lesion. This can promote involvement of other areas and mislead the clinician into treatment of a secondary manifestation of the problem instead of the primary cause (see Chapter 5, Trigger Points). Patients with chronic pain may frequently abuse medications, may undergo multiple surgical procedures without benefit, and may become depressed, hypochondriacal, and hysterical.[10,12] Pain games may begin to dominate their behavior patterns, and the extent of suffering seems to become much greater than the original pathology.[13,14] All of the previous manifestations of chronic pain may be compounded if ongoing litigation exists.

As illustrated in Figure 1-4, stress can lead to physical as well as psychologic disturbances, all of which are most commonly treated in today's society by medication. Medications may be tranquilizers, muscle relaxants, sleeping pills, stimulants, antidepressants, and mood enhancers. Some of these medications can become addictive and may also interfere with the effectiveness of T.E.N.S., as discussed in Chapter 11.

Generally, a stressor may be congenital, vascular, immunologic, environmental (including accident and trauma), infectious, neoplastic, chemical, degenerative, emotional, or psychologic. Without being specific to a distinct pain syndrome, the cycle indicative of the physical component of chronic pain is easily understood, but the psychologic component, often overlooked, is not (Fig. 1-5).

Psychologically, the feeling or attitude of the patient toward pain or illness can impart positive (helpful) or negative (destructive) thoughts that have become known as imagery. Positive imagery is transmitted to the patient by the clinician who provides comprehensive

PSYCHOLOGIC   PHYSICAL

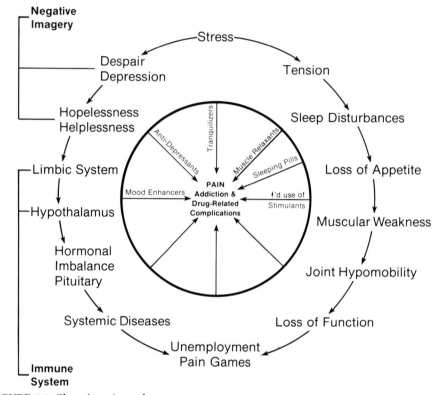

FIGURE 1-4. Chronic pain cycle.

care and has the patient participate in his or her own rehabilitation. Home use of a T.E.N.S. unit by the patient, specific exercises to perform, proper body mechanics and nutritional habits, and so forth assure patient participation. Specific suggestions to enhance the healing effect are presented in Chapter 2.

In comparison, negative imagery will most likely occur when the clinician fails to demonstrate an interest in the patient's complaint, is unwilling or unable to take the time to adequately evaluate the patient, and provides treatment that is directed solely for pain relief and not to the etiology. A patient receiving such care without improvement may easily begin to feel that there is no hope of recovery. This is especially true if more than one practitioner has imparted similar feelings to the patient. Such feelings may lead to depression and hopelessness, which directly affect a part of the brainstem known as the limbic system.[15-16] The limbic system responds to thoughts, suggestions, past experience, and emotions, and thus is also known as the emotional brain. The limbic system has neural connections with the hypothalamus, the autonomic nervous system regulator, and thus exerts a profound effect on all autonomic mechanisms. Papez, in 1937, first described a so-called emotional circuit consisting of the hypothalamus, anterior thalamus, cingulate gyrus, and hippocampus.[15,16] The function of the limbic system is part of the central biasing mechanism of the gate control theory (see Chapter 4).[17]

The concept of negative imagery may conceivably disrupt normal hormonal, metabolic, immunologic, and other homeostatic mechanisms. This obviously provides a primary or secondary impetus behind not only the complications of chronic pain but also various systemic diseases. Cancer and rheumatoid arthritis, among other disorders, have been so implicated. The use of visual imagery techniques as an adjunct to therapeutic measures, such as relaxation, biofeedback, and autogenic training in combination with chemotherapy and radiation therapy, has shown great clinical promise in the treatment of many diseases, including cancer and pain syndromes.

A complete discussion of the process of imagery is not appropriate for the purposes of this text; however, the enormous impact of the psychologic component in chronic pain is important. Kwako and Shealy have had a great deal of experience in this area and present a strong case for consideration and appropriate utilization of the behaviorial and psychologic factors in any pain treatment program (see Chapter 2). Fordyce[12] and Sternbach[10] have made outstanding contributions regarding the role of behavior modification in comprehensive pain management.

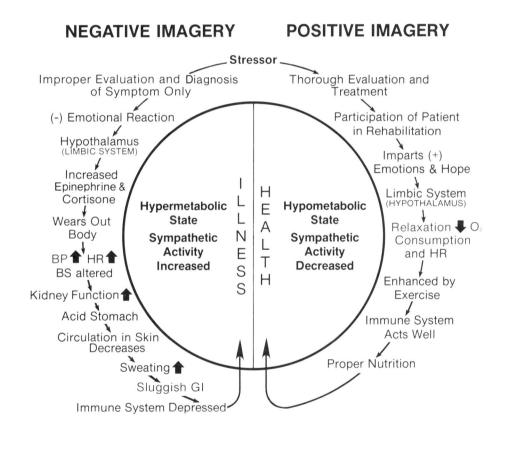

FIGURE 1-5. Patient feelings or attitudes toward illness.

PAIN CLINICS

As a result of the merging of many disciplines in the study of pain, a new medical specialty, *dolorology*, has been developed (see Chapter 2). Dolorologists are few in number and deal exclusively with the treatment of patients with chronic pain in comprehensive pain clinics.

The first truly comprehensive and multidisciplinary pain clinic was founded by Bonica at the University of Washington in 1961.[1-3] A directory of pain clinics is available from the American Society of Anesthesiologists, and clinics are listed by state (national) and country (international) and are designated as to their status (Fig. 1-6).[4] For example, syndrome-oriented clinics treat only specific conditions, such as low back pain or headaches.

It is important at this point to differentiate between single-modality and comprehensive pain clinics. In single-modality clinics, one modality—such as acupuncture, biofeedback, faith healing, hypnosis, nerve block, or T.E.N.S.—is used. The use of a single modality cannot adequately rehabilitate a patient with chronic pain. Even in the acute stage, treatment that consists solely of pain modulation, regardless of the mode, frequently does not prevent chronicity.

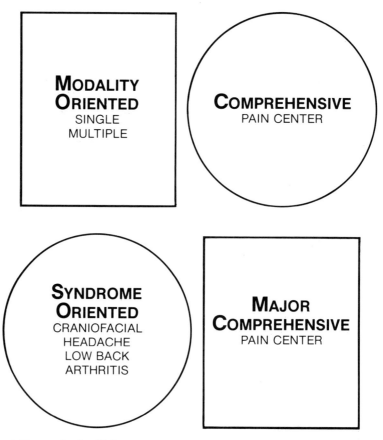

FIGURE 1-6. Types of pain clinics.

If all single modalities were incorporated into one clinic, the basis for a multidisciplinary and comprehensive clinic would be obtained. The components of a comprehensive clinic are outlined in Table 1-2. At present, there are few such clinics in the United States.

Single-modality or modality-oriented pain clinics probably comprise the abundance of listed pain clinics. Many hospital-based pain clinics use nerve blocks as the sole treatment technique. Specific modulation, however, is beneficial in the alleviation or modulation of pain for periods of time but usually makes no attempt to deal with correction or rehabilitation of the cause of pain, with the noted exception of biofeedback clinics. Biofeedback, along with autogenic/biogenic and visual imagery techniques (Chapter 2), has been shown

TABLE 1-2. Components of Comprehensive Pain Clinic

Treatment and rehabilitation directed toward the physical and psychologic components.

I. Treatment provided on either an inpatient or outpatient basis.
   Programs run from 2 weeks to 2 months with daily home practice on the part of the patient. Patient must participate in his or her own rehabilitation.
II. Screening and clarifying evaluation
   A. Performed prior to initiation of treatment
   B. Psychological testing (MMPI, etc.)
   C. Pain questionnaire
   D. Report from referring physician
   E. Consultant examinations
III. Multidisciplinary staff
   A. Orthopedist
   B. Neurologist/neurosurgeon
   C. Anesthesiologist
   D. Radiologist
   E. Oral surgeon/dentist
   F. Internist
   G. Psychiatrist/psychologist
   H. Physical therapist
   I. Physical therapist assistant
   J. Social worker/vocational counselor
   K. Nutritionist
   L. Pharmacist
   M. Pastoral counselor
   N. Biofeedback therapist
   O. Nurse
IV. Treatment and pain modulation
   A. General physical therapy
   B. Acupuncture
   C. Biofeedback (EMG, TEMP, GSR, EEG)
   D. T.E.N.S.
   E. Nerve blocks
   F. Psychotherapy
   G. Behavior modification
   H. Relaxation training
   I. Therapeutic exercise
   J. Nutritional counseling (headaches, etc.), habit regulations
   K. Weaning from medication
   L. Facet rhizotomy
   M. Group lectures and vocational counseling
   N. Joint mobilization/manipulation
   O. Autogenics, biogenics, visual imagery
   P. Health maintenance
V. Follow-up
   A. Patient visit
   B. Mail
   C. Research
   D. Teaching

TABLE 1-3. Pain Statistics*

1. On any given day, chronic pain can disable one million American workers.
2. Thirty-five to 50 million people have chronic pain in one form or another. About 25% of all chronic pain patients are also severely disabled. Thirty-five percent of the severely disabled in the 20- to 64-year-old age bracket have various musculoskeletal disorders in which pain alone is the major factor.
3. There are approximately 20 to 40 million physician office visits per year for back pain alone.
4. Twenty-five million Americans suffer from one form or another of recurrent headaches. As a result, about 180 million work days are lost at a cost of about $10 million.
5. Twelve million hours of physician time per year are given to the management of migraine headaches.
6. Approximately 21 million Americans are afflicted by arthritis, and the majority are disabled by pain. About 600,000 new cases occur each year.
7. In 1976, the Georgia Board of Workers Compensation reported that 2 million work days were lost, one third of which were for minor accidents where pain was the only disabling factor.
8. The state of California spent $200 million in 1973 for the treatment of chronic low back pain.
9. Annually, $50 billion is spent for medical expenses and compensation benefits for chronic pain.
10. Each year, $1 billion is spent by Americans for over-the-counter analgesic medication. This does not take into consideration the purchase of narcotics such as Darvon, Darvocet, Percodan, and Empirin with Codeine.
11. Each year, $10 billion is spent to cover the cost of prescription drugs and surgical procedures in the management of chronic pain.
12. Many patients take five or more different pain-relieving medications. Half of these patients frequently see more than one physician for prescriptions and concurrently also take over-the-counter drugs; 25% of these individuals develop addiction to medication.
13. At least 100,000 Americans are hospitalized each year for the treatment of addiction and other drug-related complications. This figure may be much higher, as many cases are unreported. A significant number of patients who die in hospitals die of complications as a result of drugs.
14. Many patients treated at the University of Washington Pain Clinic have already spent more than $40,000 for health care.

*Statistics were obtained from references and bibliography listed at the end of this chapter.

in numerous clinical and experimental studies to be an extremely effective means of aborting or preventing the onset of pain. Specifically, patients with migraine headaches can effectively learn to abort the onset of a headache after completing a temperature biofeedback and relaxation training program. Patients with muscle contraction headaches can gain increased awareness of the cervical musculature that gives rise to such headaches and then be taught proper postural corrective exercises and positions. Electromyographic biofeedback plays a significant role in such retraining programs. The use of autogenic and biogenic techniques as a means of teaching stress reduction and relaxation (emotional and physical) also is an excellent method of reducing pain. Chapter 2 provides information relative to the role of the aforementioned techniques in the rehabilitation of the patient with pain.

The number of pain clinics is growing rapidly.[5-8] Their need is expressed by the profound statistics concerning pain listed in Table 1-3. The cost of treatment prior to rehabilitation is striking. Medication and loss of work time add to the overall cost factor. Perhaps the need for such clinics stems in large part from the improper care provided to the patient with pain in the acute stage.[9]

THE ROLE OF T.E.N.S.

Transcutaneous electrical nerve stimulation (T.E.N.S.) is the procedure of applying controlled, low-voltage electrical pulses to the nervous system by passing electricity *through* the skin via electrodes placed *on* the skin. This therapy has found broad applications because physicians and physical therapists have rapidly accepted the ease of application, efficacy, and lack of undesirable side effects of T.E.N.S.

The indications for the use of T.E.N.S. seem almost limitless. An attempt to list the clinical conditions for which T.E.N.S. therapy is indicated would be exhaustive. Instead, the best indications for T.E.N.S. are embodied in statements made by C. Norman Shealy. "Taken all in all," Shealy believes, "T.E.N.S. is completely safe and it can be used universally, subject to instruction and the caution that it not be used in cases of persistent pain without medical advice. Most certainly, it should be standard in every emergency room facility. My feeling is that it should be used in every single pain state and it should be the very first treatment for acute pain, even before any drugs."[17]

The efficacy of T.E.N.S. is strongly dependent on who administers it and the role that it plays in a comprehensive treatment program. The physician, although required to prescribe the use of T.E.N.S., does not always have the time to instruct the patient in its proper use, or to adequately determine optimal electrode placement sites or the most effective stimulation mode.[18] The aforementioned constitutes the T.E.N.S. evaluation, which is discussed in detail in Chapters 7, 8, 9, and 11. Physical therapists, registered nurses, and physicians, who have received specific postgraduate training in the administration of T.E.N.S., are the clinicians with the proper background to use this new modality. Physical therapists specifically are trained to treat with electrotherapy and have a strong background in neuromusculoskeletal anatomy. The nature of the treatment provided by physical therapists in the rehabilitation of a patient with pain and disability provides an atmosphere that is most conducive to the administration of T.E.N.S. Physical therapists commonly spend at least 30 to 60 minutes with a patient in a hands-on fashion, and this type of approach is imperative to obtaining proper benefit from T.E.N.S.

T.E.N.S. is not perceived as a panacea since no single therapy can provide complete and effective management and solution of all pain. Although T.E.N.S. therapy alone may provide adequate symptomatic pain relief, it is not usually used as an independent alternative to drug treatment or any other therapy for pain. The role of T.E.N.S. is adjunctive to what should be a comprehensive rehabilitation program consisting of evaluation, treatment of the causes, modulation of pain, and prevention of recurrence.

T.E.N.S.: "AN ADJUNCTIVE THERAPY"

Most commonly, the successful clinical management of pain requires a synergism of therapeutic procedure and modalities. Such an approach provides symptomatic pain relief adjunctively to treatment that is provided to correct or eliminate the cause of those symptoms. To examine this adjunctive role of T.E.N.S., it will be helpful to review other therapies as well.

As the phenomenon of pain is more fully understood, a multidisciplinary approach is necessary for a better understanding of the neuroanatomy, neurochemistry, neurophysiology, and psychodynamics involved in the pain process. Perhaps the most frequently recognized intervention for the management of pain involves the field of clinical pharmacology. Medications with analgesic properties may be prescribed for a patient experiencing pain. Frequently, these analgesic agents are supplemented with anti-inflammatory agents, muscle relaxants, and/or psychotherapeutic drugs.

More and more, psychologic and psychiatric evaluation and interventions are employed in the protocol for management of a patient with pain. Such psychiatric and/or psychologic behavioral interventions may be provided in several modes of therapy, for example:

1. Traditional psychotherapy
2. Behavioral modification techniques
3. Relaxation techniques

4. Autogenic training
5. Stress management techniques
6. Therapeutic applications of guided imagery
7. Biofeedback

Use of these processes often provides important intervention in the cognitive and affective domains. It is our opinion that most patients experiencing chronic pain can receive substantial benefit from one or more of these interventions.

Although its history dates back more than 5000 years, acupuncture for the management of pain is not readily available in the United States because of the limited number of skilled practitioners. We have studied acupuncture and have observed the beneficial results afforded to patients when this technique is provided by learned and skilled practitioners. As is the case with any treatment intervention, acupuncture is not appropriate for all patients experiencing pain.

Historically, neurosurgical intervention has been available to the patient who experiences intractable, chronic pain. Neurosurgical procedures may be employed to modify input from the peripheral nervous system by such procedures as peripheral neurectomy and rhizotomy. More central neurosurgical intervention may be employed when indicated by spinal cord modification in the form of tractotomy or cordotomy. Various neurosurgical procedures have also been employed to modify sensorial events in the higher centers of the central nervous system. Most recently, the procedure of stereotaxic insertion of electrodes into deep brain regions such as the periaqueductal gray has been developed for the management of severe, intractable, chronic pain (electroanalgesia).

The procedures listed above are frequently supplemented with physical therapy. Traditionally, physical therapy employs hyperthermia (application of heat) and cryotherapy (application of cold) as part of the treatment regimen. Usually, not but always, massage is employed after hyperthermia or cryotherapy has been applied for an appropriate period of time. Massage usually precedes specific exercise and traction procedures used to maintain or increase soft-tissue or joint function. Physical therapy is discussed in more detail later in this chapter.

In the early 1970s, the use of T.E.N.S. was initiated as an adjunctive procedure to the modalities listed above. The original theoretical premise, the gate control theory of Melzak and Wall,[19] which caused renewed interest in electrical stimulation for the relief of pain, resulted in the development of dorsal column implants for dorsal column stimulation and peripheral nerve implants for peripheral nerve stimulation. Since each procedure required surgery, patients experiencing *chronic pain* became the initial target population for these interventions. The use of T.E.N.S. occurred subsequent to the investigation and utilization of dorsal column and peripheral nerve stimulation, but the T.E.N.S. system was developed parallel and concomitantly with these therapies. Consequently, T.E.N.S. also received its initial use and evaluation in the population of patients with chronic pain. Even though the earliest investigators noted that T.E.N.S. therapy might be more valuable for patients experiencing acute rather than chronic pain, because of the developmental history of T.E.N.S., the primary use of this therapy continues to be for patients experiencing chronic pain.

With this utilization pattern, it is frequently oberved that T.E.N.S. therapy is called for as an intervention "after everything else has failed." Figure 1-7, labeled "The Pain Game" and seen as a funnel with several layers of "filters," illustrates a frequently observed program of intervention for the management of pain.

In Level 1, a common initial intervention program is outlined. After medical evaluation, a physician commonly prescribes analgesic medication. Often, the patient is instructed to rest as much as possible. The patient may be referred to physical therapy for heat or cold applications followed by massage and perhaps traction and therapeutic exercise. The pa-

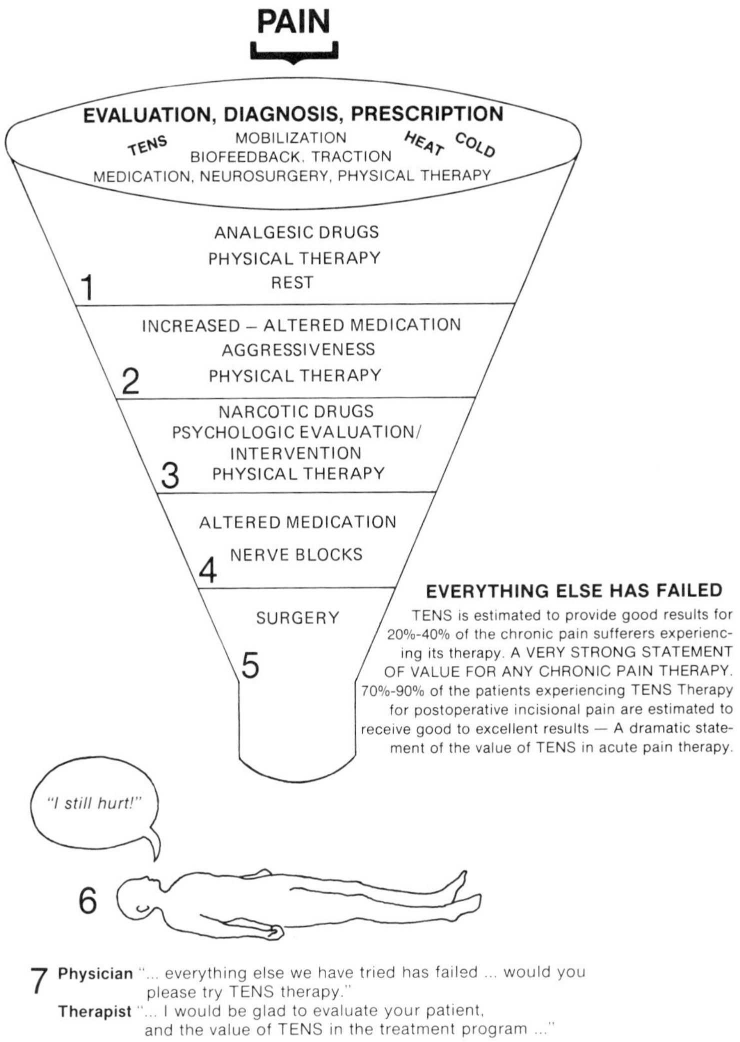

FIGURE 1-7. The pain game.

tient is instructed to take the medications as prescribed and to receive physical therapy for a specified period before returning to the physician for re-evaluation. In Level 2, the patient returns to the physician with continued complaints of pain. The medication level may be increased and the physical therapy will be continued for another specified period. In Level 3, the patient returns after the second specified period with continued pain. Again the medication level may be increased, perhaps with the addition of a narcotic. Physical therapy will be continued, and psychologic or psychiatric evaluation and/or treatment may be employed. In Level 4, the medication dosages and types may again be altered. With the persistence of the pain, nerve blocks may be attempted in an effort to improve the patient's response. At this point, it may be determined that physical therapy has not been beneficial and may be discontinued. Level 5 outlines the continuing modification of the treatment program in response to the patient's refractory condition to previous treatment. Searching for the intervention that will benefit the patient, the patient may be referred to a surgeon.

Often, even when a primary physician does not recommend surgical intervention, a patient may seek this on his or her own. Level 6 shows the patient waking up from the surgical procedure with the all-too-frequent experience that "I still hurt." Level 7 relates a conversation of the primary physician or the surgeon with a practitioner involved in T.E.N.S. therapy.

Physician: "I have this patient that I would like you to see. I want you to try T.E.N.S. therapy. The patient has previously experienced interventions of multiple medications, psychologic intervention, nerve blocks, and surgery, and everything has failed."

T.E.N.S. practitioner: "Doctor, I would be glad to see the patient and to utilize T.E.N.S. in a complete program. It will take approximately five visits to evaluate the effectiveness of the T.E.N.S. device. We will carry out our full treatment program and advise you of the patient's response."

Physician: "That will be fine. I hope that the patient will benefit from your services because there doesn't appear to be much else that I can do."

It has been our experience that even in these worst patient circumstances, after all else has failed, 20 to 40 percent of these patients will receive significant pain relief from the T.E.N.S. therapy. Although 20 to 40 percent good results may not initially appear to be significant, this percentage of favorable responses is a very positive statement regarding the effectiveness of T.E.N.S. therapy.

Perhaps if T.E.N.S. had been effectively used early in the intervention efforts, the favorable responses would be greater than the 20 to 40 percent presented, and the more aggressive, invasive procedures might have been avoided.

The request is made to all clinicians involved in the management of pain to *initiate the use of T.E.N.S. therapy early and aggressively to improve early management of the pain cycle and thus reduce or prevent the occurrences of exacerbating involvement of compounding problems that are frequently observed to be part of progressive pain.*

PHYSICAL THERAPY AND T.E.N.S.

The physical interventions that are employed are directed at a portion of the component parts of the pain cycle in an effort to interrupt the collective cycle.

One modality employed in physical therapy is hyperthermia (application of heat), which can be shortwave, microwave, or ultrasound diathermy; hot, moist packs; paraffin baths; whirlpools; hubbard baths; and infrared radiating sources. This application of heat creates a hyperthermia in the tissue and a secondary hyperemia, which results in increased vasodilation and improved circulation within the area. The increased circulation provides an improved transport system so that valuable nutrients required for the healing process may be brought to the injured area. The state of improved circulation also results in increased lymphatic clearing and reduced metabolic concentration within the injured area. Thus, the local state of edema is improved. The endogenous pain-producing substances also will be more effectively resolved.

Another significant benefit of locally applied heat to human tissue is sedation. The sedation obtained from heat applications helps to reduce the guarding action and muscle tension that initially promoted ischemia. Heat also reduces the production of metabolites within the region.

It is generally recognized that the physiologic effects of cryotherapy are essentially the same as those of hyperthermia except for the initial phases of vasoconstriction experienced with applications of cold. Cryotherapy can be in the form of ice packs, ice massage, cold whirlpool, and vapocoolant sprays such as ethyl chloride and fluorimethane. The application of cold also provides a sedative effect in response to the applications (greater with cryotherapy than with hyperthermia).

However, the point must be made that the primary effects of these therapies are to reduce guarding and the internal microscopic changes (Fig. 1-8). The secondary benefit is some degree of analgesia. Also, it must be noted that the analgesic effects tend to be transient.

Another frequent component of physical therapy intervention is *massage*, which usually follows the application of heat and/or cold. The primary purpose of massage is mechanical, to move body fluids. The therapeutic massage is in a centripetal direction to aid in clearing the exudate from the local region. There is an associated reflex response to massage, probably from the repetitive tactile stimulation, that tends to provide some degree of analgesia and sedation. This is a secondary benefit similar to that of heat and cold applications.

Efforts to maintain or improve soft-tissue and/or joint mobility are frequently provided in the form of cervical and/or lumbar traction, range-of-motion exercises, joint mobilization procedures, soft-tissue friction massage, and regimens of therapeutic exercise. A glance at the pain cycle makes it obvious that these measures are primarily provided to improve the

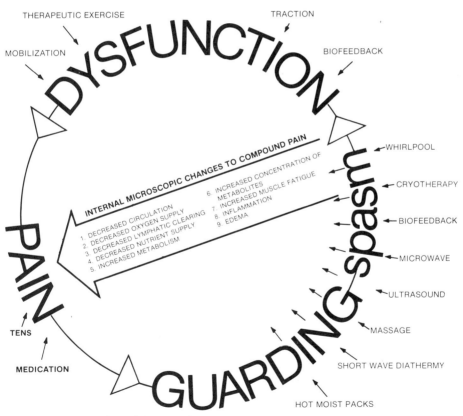

FIGURE 1-8. Pain cycle and interventions.

functional capacity of the soft tissues and joints in the affected area. If improvement of mobility is produced, then secondary gains are obtained toward the reduction of discomfort.

This cursive review of physical therapy shows that such therapy has provided valuable benefit in managing the pain cycle and promoting the healing process. However, only two of the three components of the pain cycle have received primary attention and effective management.

The purpose of T.E.N.S. is to reduce the symptom of pain. Although secondary benefits such as sedation and increased tissue temperature (probably a sympathetic response to stimulation) are often noted, the primary effects are to produce an analgesia and reduction of pain. By the unique role of T.E.N.S. in managing the pain cycle, analgesia for pain, it can be concluded that in comparison with other forms of physical therapy, T.E.N.S. provides us with the ability to manage all three components of the pain cycle. Thus continues the persuasive suggestion that T.E.N.S. should be a routine part of managing patients experiencing pain, in both the acute and the chronic pain phases, as an adjunctive procedure to complement the more traditional forms of therapy.

On many occasions, clinicians have found that after the more traditional forms of physical therapy have been provided without T.E.N.S., the subjective response to the treatment has been disappointing to both the patient and the clinician. When these treatment forms are carried out in a series, an eventual resolution of the total pain cycle may occur by the accelerated healing process and increased mobility provided by such treatment. However, resolution of the total pain cycle will occur more extensively and more quickly when T.E.N.S. is implemented adjunctively. However, if further modification of the traditional treatment program is not made, the extent and duration of this early favorable response can be diminished or negated.

If all active physical intervention ceases with the conclusion of a particular treatment session, the patient will often return for the next treatment session reporting that the benefit gained from the previous treatment lasted only a few hours, and the patient's clinical condition returned essentially to the pretreatment level. Such a response pattern is illustrated in Figure 1-9 as a peak-and-valley pattern. In this schematic, zero is the pretreatment level of discomfort. The first ascending arc indicates progressive benefits obtained from the treatment to its maximum, at which time treatment is interrupted and the patient, as indicated by the first downsloping arc, tends to return to the pretreatment level of pain. This peak-and-valley pattern repeats itself over and over until, sometime in the future, the problem is slowly resolved. By the presence of patients with chronic pain, we are reminded that sometimes recovery may never occur. By including T.E.N.S. as an adjunctive procedure, this profile of peaks and valleys may be modified in two ways. First, as seen in Figure 1-9, the maximum benefit from therapy tends to be increased by the adjunctive use of T.E.N.S., and thus a greater degree of analgesia is experienced within each treatment period. Second, T.E.N.S. can be used as an extension of the clinical facility and of the professional providing service. By permitting the patient to retain a T.E.N.S. system to continue "self-treatment" in the hospital room or in the home, the state of enhanced analgesia may be sustained throughout the periods between treatments. In this manner, the peak-and-valley profile can be modified to appear as a series of an escalation of benefits and maintenance of these benefits at a plateau between treatments. Then the ensuing series of treatments provides progressively higher plateaus of benefit. By using the T.E.N.S. to produce the plateau effect as described, a patient's problem may often be resolved faster.

Modern T.E.N.S. systems are very safe, compact, portable, and easy to operate for patients under professional supervision and guidance. Such therapy is noninvasive and

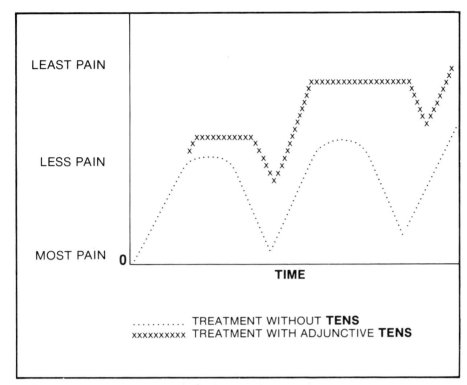

FIGURE 1-9. Response pattern to clinical treatment.

nonaddictive and does not produce any adverse, irreversible changes in the body. Detailed guidance for employing the T.E.N.S. system in this manner is provided in Chapters 6, 7, and 9.

ANALGESIC MEDICATION AND T.E.N.S.

An assessment of the comparative role of T.E.N.S. in the management of pain would be incomplete without observing its relationship with medications. The combined effects of drugs and T.E.N.S. therapy may provide the best clinical results. Thus far, instances have been noted in which some medications appear to diminish the effectiveness of T.E.N.S. It has been our experience that patients who are taking drugs such as diazepam, codeine, and narcotics tend to have a diminished response to T.E.N.S. Even though the response is diminished, T.E.N.S. has been found to be very valuable in the withdrawal of these drugs from a patient's therapy.

Since in some instances medications tend to diminish the effectiveness of T.E.N.S. by antagonistic function, other medications should probably be expected to interact synergistically to potentiate T.E.N.S. therapy. Both of these areas deserve evaluation and are discussed in more detail in Chapter 11.

A brief review of the generalized role of medication in pain relief will provide some further guidelines regarding the comparative role of T.E.N.S. therapy. In order to provide

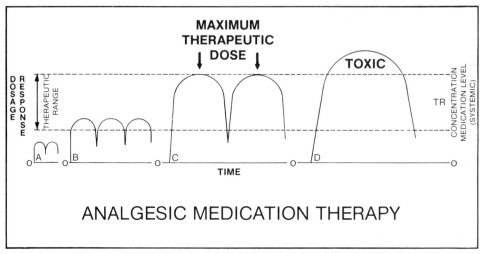

FIGURE 1-10. Analgesic medication therapy profile.

significant pain relief for a patient, medication must be administered at a dosage sufficient to enter the patient's therapeutic range. Figure 1-10 depicts four different dosage levels of medication and four different levels of patient responses. The horizontal baseline marked zero indicates a zero level of concentration of a medication in the patient's system. The first arc, A, indicates that a dose is administered to a patient and is absorbed into the patient's system. Even at peak concentrations provided by this dose, the therapeutic range is not reached. Therefore, the patient response indicates no pain relief in response to this therapeutic dose. The second arc, B, indicates the therapeutic range is reached but only minimally. In this instance, the patient may report some minor relief of short duration only. The third arc, C, illustrates a dosage that results in the therapeutic range being obtained and peak dosage reaching the maximum of the patient's therapeutic range. This would be an ideal situation. The dosage could be *titrated* so the patient receives the exact dosage required to meet the upper limits of the therapeutic range, and the resulting analgesia would persist for a period of 4 hours or longer. This ideal titration is very difficult, if not impossible, to obtain in most clinical settings. The fourth arc, D, illustrates a common clinical occurrence—a dosage that provides maximum therapeutic benefit but overshoots the maximum into a range of toxicity. This profile thereby results in the often-noted deleterious side effects such as dizziness, nausea, and tinnitus associated with medication provided for pain management.

This marks another contrast between the analgesia provided with medications and the analgesia provided with T.E.N.S. No such adverse side effects are associated with T.E.N.S. therapy.

Use of T.E.N.S. in conjunction with medication therapy may perhaps reduce the dosage of medication required for effective analgesia and thereby reduce or abate the associated adverse, deleterious side effects of medication. There are no such adverse side effects associated with T.E.N.S. therapy. The adjunctive use of T.E.N.S. may also permit the state of analgesia to be increased and sustained so that, again, a plateau response pattern may be produced, thus preventing the episodic recurrence of substantial pain symptoms.

A review of the comparative role of T.E.N.S. in the management of patients with pain will tend to support our recommendation that T.E.N.S. should be used early in the attempts at intervention and aggressively as an adjunctive procedure to more traditional forms of therapy. The role of T.E.N.S. is *not* viewed as a singular panacea. Rather, T.E.N.S. is seen as an invaluable adjunctive procedure to enhance the effectiveness of already existing therapies.

T.E.N.S.: "A FREE-STANDING THERAPY FOR ANALGESIA"

There are clearly instances in the management of clinical conditions when rapid and complete recovery will occur simply because of the remarkable recuperative, curative powers of the human body. In such instances, the normal, spontaneous processes of "healing" may be augmented or accelerated by effective symptomatic reduction or abatement of pain. This observation is well established in medical experience; physicians have frequently prescribed analgesic medication for patients (as the only exogenous therapy), and a full and complete recovery has been achieved by the endogenous powers of the body.

In this context, T.E.N.S. has proven to be a viable alternative therapy for analgesia. Perhaps most notably, this has been observed in the management of postoperative pain. Some, but certainly not all, patients experience successful pain management with T.E.N.S. postoperatively to the extent that no adjunctive medications are required. Other clinical problems that may respond to T.E.N.S. therapy in similar manner and degree are as follows:

1. Fractured ribs
2. Intercostal soft-tissue sprains and strains
3. Casted fractures with in-cast electrodes
4. Acutely sprained or strained soft tissues (preventing development of full pain cycle responses)
5. Pain following some dental procedures
6. Initial pain associated with trauma that may be seen in patients seeking medical care in emergency rooms or family physicians' offices. This type of pain cannot be treated with medications pending further medical evaluation to determine the full treatment plan, that is, a suspected or determined fracture may require orthopedic procedures, prior to which drug therapy would not be indicated.

Experience has demonstrated also that T.E.N.S. therapy may be used successfully as the only analgesia to permit certain therapeutic procedures to be applied more comfortably. In physical therapy, it is observed that friction massage and certain types of therapeutic exercises can be performed more efficiently and more comfortably if T.E.N.S. is used before and/or during the procedures. Postoperatively, patients can frequently move a body segment more effectively and more comfortably in conjunction with T.E.N.S. therapy, that is, deep breathing and coughing. Some wounds that require bandaging and taping may produce significant pain when the dressings are removed. Sometimes, as in severely injured digits, drugs may be administered to facilitate removal of dressings. We have successfully used T.E.N.S. as an alternative analgesia for this purpose by placing electrodes at or around the volar aspects of the affected fingers and at appropriate proximal locations along the innervating nerve(s).

These are only a few examples illustrating the use of T.E.N.S. as a "free-standing therapy for analgesia." They are included to focus attention on the ever-increasing experience and awareness that T.E.N.S. is significantly more effective for managing acute pain symptoms. Because of the safe, noninvasive, nonaddictive characteristics of this therapy, the clinical application of T.E.N.S. for acute pain conditions is expanding rapidly, and the applications that may be helpful for readers will be as diversified as their clinical specialties and interests.

REFERENCES

1. BONICA, JJ, PROCACCI, P, AND PAGNI, CA: *Recent Advances on Pain: Pathophysiology and Clinical Aspects.* Charles C Thomas, Springfield, Ill, 1974, p 274.
2. BONICA, JJ: Neurophysiologic and pathologic aspects of acute and chronic pain. Arch Surg 112:750, 1977.
3. BONICA, JJ: *Basic principles in managing chronic pain.* Arch Surg 112:783, 1977.
4. AMERICAN SOCIETY OF ANESTHESIOLOGISTS: *Pain Center/Clinic Directory.* American Society of Anesthesiologists, Park Ridge, Ill, 1980.
5. NEAL, H: *The Politics of Pain.* McGraw-Hill, New York, 1978.
6. CHERRY, L: *Solving the mysteries of pain.* New York Times Magazine, Jan 30, 1977, p 12.
7. CLARK, M, GOSNELL, M, AND SHAPIRO, D: *The new war on pain.* Newsweek, April 25, 1977, p 48.
8. DREW, C: *Alleviating aches: At new pain clinics groups of specialists aid chronic sufferers.* Wall Street Journal 51:1, Sept 13, 1976.
9. CAILLIET, R: *Chronic pain: Is it necessary?* Arch Phys Med Rehabil 1:4, 1979.
10. STERNBACH, RA: *Pain Patients: Traits and Treatment.* Academic Press, New York, 1974.
11. BERGMAN, JJ AND WERBLUN, MN: *Chronic pain: A review for the family physician.* J Fam Pract 7:685, 1978.
12. FORDYCE, WE: *Behavioral Methods for Control of Chronic Pain and Illness.* CV Mosby, St Louis, 1976.
13. SHEALY, CN: *The Pain Game.* Celestial Arts, Millbrae, Calif, 1976.
14. SHEALY, CN: *The pain patient.* Am Fam Physician 9:130, 1974.
15. CHUSID, JG: *Correlative Neuroanatomy and Functional Neurology,* ed 16. Lange Medical Publications, Los Altos, Calif, 1976, p 9.
16. WARWICK, R AND WILLIAMS, PL: *Gray's Anatomy,* ed 35. WB Saunders, Philadelphia, 1973, p 930.
17. SHEALY, CN: *A new approach to pain.* Emergency Medicine 1:6, 1974.
18. LOESER, JD, BLACK, RG, AND CHRISTMAN, A: *Relief of pain by transcutaneous stimulation.* J Neurosurg 22:308, 1975.
19. MELZACK, R AND WALL, PD: *Pain mechanisms: A new theory.* Science 150:971, 1965.

BIBLIOGRAPHY

ACHTERBERG, J AND LAWLIS, GF: *Imagery of Cancer (Image-Ca): An Evaluation Tool for the Process of Disease.* Institute for Personality and Ability Testing, Champaign, Ill, 1978.
BENSON, H: *The Relaxation Response.* William Morrow & Co, New York, 1975.
BENSON, H: *The Mind/Body Effect.* Simon & Schuster, New York, 1979.
BRESSLER, DE: *Free Yourself From Pain.* Simon & Schuster, New York, 1979.
BROWN, BB: *New Mind, New Body.* Bantam Books, New York, 1974.
BROWN, BB: *Stress and the Art of Biofeedback.* Bantam Books, New York, 1977.
GREEN, E AND GREEN, A: *Beyond Biofeedback.* Robert Briggs Associates, San Francisco, 1977.
KRUSEN, FH, KOTTKE, FJ, AND ELWOOD, PM: *Handbook of Physical Medicine and Rehabilitation,* ed 2. WB Saunders, Philadelphia, 1971.
LAZARUS, A: *In the Mind's Eye.* Rawson Associates, New York, 1977.
OYLE, I: *The Healing Mind.* Celestial Arts, Millbrae, Calif, 1975.
PELLETIER, KR: *Mind as Healer, Mind as Slayer.* Delta Books, New York, 1977.

Physicians Desk Reference, ed 33. Medical Economics, Oradell, NJ, 1979.

SELYE, H: *Stress Without Distress.* Signet, New York, 1974.

SELYE, H: *The Stress of Life.* McGraw-Hill, New York, 1976.

SHEALY, CN: *Health: A Manual of Biogenic Exercises.* CN Shealy, La Crosse, Wis, 1975.

SHEALY, CN: *Occult Medicine Can Save Your Life.* Dial Press, New York, 1975.

SHEALY, CN: *Biogenic Health Maintenance.* Self-Health Systems, La Crosse, Wis, 1976.

SHEALY, CN: *Ninety Days to Self-Health.* Dial Press, New York, 1977.

SIMONTON, OC, SIMONTON, SM, AND CREIGHTON, J: *Getting Well Again.* St Martins Press, New York, 1978.

SOMMER, R: *The Mind's Eye.* Dell Publishing, New York, 1978.

CHAPTER 2

PSYCHOLOGIC CONSIDERATIONS IN THE MANAGEMENT OF PAIN

JAMES KWAKO, M.D., AND C. NORMAN SHEALY, M.D.

> Your pain is the breaking of the shell that encloses your understanding. Much of your pain is self chosen. It is the bitter portion by which the physician within you heals your sick self.
> —Kahlil Gibran[1]

Pain is the awareness of irritation with varying degrees of physical and psychologic distress. Although an uncomfortable stimulus to the sensory system, pain is also what the patient feels, an event experienced. Objective aspects of pain are detectable by physical examination and testing; however, one's reaction to pain is entirely subjective and very personal. Pain may be acute, predominantly physical, and thus more a warning of bodily dysfunction; or it may be chronic, lasting longer than a reasonable time for repair and healing, at least 6 months.[2]

Whether acute or chronic, pain is a signal from the organism that a tissue-damaging stimulus is occurring and that change is necessary. If pain is acute, nature plays its role and soon brings relief. If pain is chronic, there is an opportunity for conditioning or learning to occur, whether to the patient's advantage or disadvantage. Indeed, chronic pain is referred to as a disease in its own right.[3]

The perception of pain is influenced by physiologic, emotional, and mental factors.[4] Certainly, physiologic models predominate because of the greater ease of measurement, objectivity, and reproducibility. The specificity, pattern, and gate theories are the most popular and reasonable physiologic explanations. To determine the nature and dimensions of pain, investigators have devised complex studies in which volunteers are subjected to such stimuli as electric shocks, cold immersions, radiant heat, and pressors delivered at varying intensities to different body levels—cutaneous, somatic, and visceral. The subjects' responses yield data concerning pain threshold, drug request point, pain tolerance, and pain sensitivity range. Factor analysis of these variables may produce a significant factor called *pain endurance*, a relatively stable characteristic, little influenced by environment.[5]

Even basic physiologic measurement is in question, however. Variations in the methods of recording latency and distance between stimulating and pick-up electrodes have been noted.[6] Excellent studies show that the sensory threshold measurements for electrical stimulation of the digits appear variable with repeated measurements over time.[7] The time-honored tourniquet pain test has failed to detect differences in the analgesic potency of morphine, codeine, aspirin, and placebo in a double-blind, counterbalanced design.[8] In addition, pain threshold tolerance may vary widely in a single person.[9]

The stimulation of peripheral or central nerve receptors is not the beginning of the pain process. Rather, the stimulation is only adding further impulses to an already active nervous system. An active selection and integration process is at work, influenced and patterned by previous experience, culture, and the present focus of attention.[10]

Cultural factors have long been recognized as significant modifiers of the pain complex.[11,12] Initial transcultural studies indicated differing pain thresholds among various European groups. However, Zborowski discovered that cultural approval for public expression is the predominant factor. Older Americans have a phlegmatic, matter-of-fact, physician-helping orientation. Jews express a concern for the meaning and implications of the pain, distrusting palliatives. Italians express a desire for immediate relief, part of their outcry designed to bring family and professional support. The Irish attitude involves deliberate suppression of suffering and concern for the implications of pain; the Irish have significantly lower pain tolerance to electric shocks. Interestingly, there is a significant correlation among thresholds and heart rate, skin resistance, and skin potential levels that parallels the culturally acquired attitudinal sets toward pain.[13]

The present focus of attention, anxiety, and suggestion alters the intensity of the pain experienced. Boxers, football players, and other athletes can sustain severe injuries during the excitement of the sport without being aware that they have been hurt. Almost any situation that attracts a sufficient degree of intense, prolonged attention may allow stimuli to go unnoticed, including wounds that cause considerable suffering under normal circumstances. A group of civilians was compared with a group of soldiers in a war zone. Although both groups were paired by similarity of surgical wounds, more than twice as many civilians (80 percent) pleaded for morphine injections.[14] A similar comparison is provided by patients with chronic pain when asked whether the pain is worse when alone, at night, and when thinking about it, or when on the telephone involved in a very interesting conversation.[15]

Previous experience as a modifier of the pain sensation is the basis of learning theory. Especially in the definition of chronic pain, length of time implies opportunity for conditioning and learning to occur. Learning is automatic, and pain is influenced by learning. Older people may define pain differently from younger subjects.[16] Older subjects require stronger stimulation from radiant heat before reporting pain, although the data indicated there was no reduction in ability to perceive the stimulation as such.

It is evident from physiologic and psychologic sources that pain is not generated in a fixed, direct-line nervous system. Indeed, anatomic pathways correlate with physical, emotional, and mental levels of the pain experience.[17] Sensations are described in terms of time, space, pressure, and heat. Affective qualities of pain associated with limbic activity include tension, fear, and anger. In addition, the subjective readout is processed and screened through cerebral processes. Each of these levels of experiences is probably influenced by past, present, and cultural influences. A panoramic view seems to confirm Artistotle's definition of pain as "quale—a quality (sensation) of the soul, a state of being."[18]

PSYCHOLOGIC TESTING

The psychology of pain refers to the wide perspective of the individual beyond the physical aspect. It includes observable behavior, posture, and movement; the emotional status and expressions; and the thinking patterns—positive and negative. In addition, if

taken etymologically, the psychology (knowledge of the soul) of pain should also deal with the spiritual or transpersonal side of the individual.

The psychology of pain has recently taken on new dimensions in fully understanding and treating the patient with pain. In fact, because of the prominent psychologic aspects of pain management, it has been referred to as an area beyond the realm of the physician alone.[19] Comprehensive pain clinics routinely employ psychologists, social workers, counselors, ministers, and physicians.

Psychology of pain has traditionally referred only to the malingerer and hysteric with pain. Malingering generally meant "laziness," a desire not to work. It may even start at a young age with the grade-school child who complains of a headache to avoid a school day. However, this problem is rarely seen in patients with chronic pain.[20] When it does occur, it is the result of a very complex condition, and objective physical signs may be present. There are usually many more important reasons, conscious and unconscious, why people are unable to become well enough for employment.

There is an hysterical component in over 70 percent of patients with chronic pain.[21] Although specifically an overreaction to situations and people, an hysterical reaction is usually thought to mean that "it is all in your head." The false assumption that follows is that the patient could easily eliminate the problem and be healthy. Even the "pure" hysteric, however, has serious subconscious conflicts requiring long-term psychotherapy for adequate control.

The application of psychology to the medical specialty of dolorology (the study of pain) may be simply classified into its use in diagnosis and its use in treatment. In diagnosis, organic and functional components can be more clearly assessed; in almost every case, elements of both occur. Personality strengths and weaknesses are delineated to clarify "no-win" and destructive thought and action patterns as well as the lack of healthy qualities. Delineating the reactions of frustration, tension, self-doubt, and depression that preceded the disease can many times add insight and self-assurance. If indeed the condition occurred as a result of destructive reactions, one can choose the opposite of these to reverse the process to stimulate the repair potential.

The diagnostic element should include a history of basic personality, mental alertness, major relationships, suicidal ruminations, and any psychotic elements. The family background and position in the family can help to establish basic patterns of major relationships and the trends toward disease or health. Some of this information can be gained from psychologic testing.

Traditionally, the Minnesota Multiphasic Personality Inventory (MMPI) is used for psychologic assessment. In patients with chronic pain, more than 91 percent have at least one abnormality.[21] The average person has one abnormality only 5 percent of the time. Approximately 70 percent exhibit the neurotic triad of depression, hysteria, and hypochondriasis.[21] Upon relief of pain, these symptoms usually subside. Although helpful in delineating various types and degrees of neuroses and psychoses, the MMPI does not provide practical therapy guidelines.

The Fuchtran Limitation and Activity Scale indicates that patients with low back pain have little involvement in virtually all social activities, even in comparison with patients with other chronic illness.[22] When measured by self-evaluation (Stewart), hopelessness scale (Beck), marital scale (Locke and Wallace), and symptom checklist 90 (Derogatis), 80 percent of patients with chronic pain report significant hopelessness, low self-image, depression, somatization, and unrealistic expectations for therapy.[23] Patients with chronic facial pain may be anhedonic rather than depressed and may even exhibit features of borderline psychosis.[24]

The California Psychological Inventory (CPI) is especially interesting and practical in assessing personality characteristics important in everyday life.[25] As a group, when com-

pared with norms, patients with chronic pain are poorly adjusted and shallow. They score low in socialization, empathy, and intellectual efficiency. They are more likely to be dependent, withdrawn, indifferent to the feelings of others, confused, and poorly organized, and they have difficulty with social interactions. The CPI not only is beneficial diagnostically but also clarifies areas of weakness that can be easily understood and discussed as therapeutic goals.

Another diagnostic tool with practical therapeutic value is the Social Readjustment Rating Questionnaire (SRRQ) developed by Holmes and Rahe.[26] Forty-three major life events were scaled according to the degree of stress. The number of points accumulated correlates with the potential and time of disease onset. The SRRQ not only is applicable to common psychosomatic ailments but also predicts the onset of organic disease, such as infection,[27] diabetes mellitus,[28] and accidental injury.[29] When applied to patients with chronic pain, the SRRQ showed that patients with facial pain have the same relative order of the changing event as the nonpatient group.[30] However, major differences appeared in 21 items, especially those concerned with object loss and personal or family matters. The patients perceived those events as requiring more of a change than did the normal group.

Psychologic testing differentiates personality characteristics of the individual in pain. However, this may be more a reflection of the state of psycho-emotion at the time of testing rather than deeper-seated, self-destructive, subconscious elements, which may be the real source of the problem. To date, no psychologic test accurately determines potential for improvement. For these reasons, an individual clinical history is necessary.

A LIFE STYLE OF PAIN

Pain is more than a hurt; for many, it is a devastating way of life. Initial physical impairment is usually followed by emotional debilitation. Anger, hurt, loneliness, depression, and hopelessness become the only feelings expressed. Medical and surgical failures lead to rejection of or by the medical community. Strained relationships lead to family rejection and divorce 70 percent of the time; emotionally bankrupt, 20 percent of patients attempt suicide.[3] An acute illness or injury can be so serious that even over a period of a few weeks, one's life's savings can be wiped out. Afflicting millions of individual lives and families, the financial drain of chronic illness to society is alarming. Requiring 20 million physician visits per year, chronic pain costs Americans 35 to 50 billion dollars annually in health services, drugs, and lost work days.[32] Most tragic of all, it is not necessary.

Patterns of behavior largely determine the reaction to pain problems.[33] Medication and surgical procedures to relieve pain may be only the first steps in a series of unnecessary and unsatisfactory attempts to find relief. More insidious but less evident are the games of disease played by patient and physician. Not to imply a conscious choice of disease or to deny the need for compassion, suffering becomes a game when healthy alternatives are available but not chosen.

The first choice to relieve illness may be to reach for the pain-relieving medication. However, analgesics and tranquilizers do not always promote healing. They may caus' addiction, depression, and a host of other complications.[34] Also, analgesic medications ï tranquilizers can interfere with the secretion of endorphins and natural processes of regulation.[35]

The most common pain game is based on the attitude that "I'll just have to l' it." All attempts clearly to diagnose and treat have failed, and both the phys' patient are discouraged. Unknowingly, friends and acquaintances contribute t' with each repetition of "I don't know how you do it." These patients are the "

pain, and once on their way, they rapidly run through every effort or suggestion given to help. The most recent medication, vitamin, or exercise in fact may well help—but only for a short time. Intense behavior modification and saturation by positive affirmation are especially helpful tools in redressing with health.

The Somatizers regard their bad health as the biggest problem of their lives. They know the various ways it changes and have elaborate descriptions for ways that it has spread to other parts of their bodies. They complain that the pain disturbs sleep and all their daily activities. Convinced of the seriousness of their illness, they display little anxiety, irritation, or sadness, describing their situation rather mildly. Too often, these patients are merely refusing to recognize emotional difficulties or to see the effects of the condition on family members. Fear is their basic attitude; so suppressed, they deny fear of any kind.

The Tyrants are angry at physicians who have failed them, employers who don't want them back, the person who caused the accident, and the world itself. Although these patients can make most dramatic recoveries, until they do, there are stormclouds of chaos and hostility with every thought. At times, getting them to laugh at themselves, with the support of a group, can turn them around 180 degrees.

Certainly, there are many games, types of players, and combinations of both.[36] Identifying the type provides a direction for therapy. Patients taking medication may respond to vitamins and nutritional supplements; these are rarely harmful and have been shown to be beneficial. Patients more attuned to surgery may have to be approached with physical modalities such as T.E.N.S., massage, mobilization, acupuncture, and others. The Streakers need reinforcement for healthy behavior; the Somatizers, courage to face fears; and the Tyrants, a clear picture of their effect on themselves and others.

Patients with severe, chronic pain will most likely require a comprehensive approach. Comprehensive pain clinics do not emphasize the traditional approaches of nerve block, surgery, and psychotherapy, although specialized aspects of these may occasionally be helpful. These clinics do offer drug withdrawal, increasing physical activity, transcutaneous electrical nerve stimulation, behavior modification, and psychophysiologic rebalancing. The primary goal is first to establish healthy habits of thinking, feeling, eating, and acting. With direction, these people can be reconditioned to expect health, to want it to happen, and to let it happen. In one such clinic, a five-scale pain profile reveals at least 50 percent improvement in over 90 percent of the patients after a 2-week outpatient session.[37]

Comprehensive approaches are not restricted to chronic pain conditions. Since we are now realizing that the roots of illness behavior are largely independent of chronicity and are already established at the onset of pain,[38] it is becoming apparent that the best treatment of acute pain states may also be a comprehensive approach. For this reason, the following sections should be viewed from the perspective of establishing greater healthy behavior whatever the state of illness or health.

THE PLACEBO EFFECT

The placebo effect is the response of a patient to an inert substance or alternate therapeutic procedure. It is used as the standard by which all new medications must be measured to verify effectiveness. The placebo response controls symptoms about 35 percent of the time in postoperative pain, diabetes mellitus, colitis, chronic headache, and several other diseases.[39]

Recently, cimetidine (Tagamet) achieved popularity as an effective treatment of duodenal ulcers.[40] In a multicenter, double-blind, controlled United States study on endoscopically diagnosed duodenal ulcers, at the end of 6 weeks Tagamet was found to be associated with healing in 76 percent of those studied. However, in the placebo group, there was a 63 percent positive response within the same period.

How does the placebo work? What allows it to have a profound effect consistently on one third or more of people regardless of the illness or severity of disease? The patient's acceptance of the therapy offered, desire to be well, self-image, and support system all influence the development of a positive reaction to the placebo. There is also evidence that the placebo response can induce the production of endorphins—the body's own morphine-like chemical,[41] which may also induce a positive response. There can be complications or side effects with placebos as well.[42] Nausea, vomiting, headache, dizziness, and weakness have all been recorded.

Placebo studies with surgical procedures have been conducted in which the responses to the technically correct procedures were compared with alternate or placebo procedures. The percentage of improvement appeared similar in both groups.[43] Almost 100,000 coronary bypass procedures and 400,000 laminectomy procedures are performed annually in this country, and a large number of positive responses may in fact be due to a placebo reaction. Again, the patient's acceptance and desire to be well could be the major cause of this response.

MODIFYING BEHAVIOR

The second major step in health development is establishing healthy behavior. Behavior refers to observable and potentially measurable actions. The expression or display of pain, a moan, grimace, verbalized complaint, or posturing is behavior. As such, it is vulnerable to influence by factors that influence all behaviors. Activity or inactivity can stem from a pain problem or can be the cause of it. Muscle tension or deficient circulation also strongly influences behavior. Likewise, nutritional behavior can contribute to the spiral of disease or hasten a rapid recovery. All of these factors are interrelated and therefore deserve comment.

Behavior modification is derived from operant conditioning (trial-and-error learning). It is a technique in which the individual learns to change the intensity or frequency of behavior by means of the outcome produced. Its application to pain behavior means that healthy bodily movements are reinforced and signs of pain behavior ignored or negated, verbally or nonverbally. Essentially, one presents a model for normal behavior, realizing that we are very sensitive to what is going on around us and that our behavior is influenced by it.

Such an approach was introduced into the first behavior modification or operant conditioning pain program in 1965.[44] Carefully screened, only 25 percent of the applicants were admitted to the 8-week operant conditioning program. In a limited series of 100 patients treated over a 5-year period, 60 percent were markedly improved. Although only about one third maintained pain relief, behavior modification is clearly an important therapeutic technique.

When behavior modification is used in combination with several other approaches, its value is more difficult to assess. However, comments from patients and early observable improvement reveal its effect. During the initial interview, many patients attest to the fact that talking about the pain makes it worse. Most people do not want to be thought of as crippled or diseased and yet do not realize that their behavior invites sympathy. This awareness alone motivates many to participate in modifying their own verbal and nonverbal expressions of pain.

Modifying behavior can also refer to performing healthy movement, such as physical exercise. Inability to pass a test of minimal muscle strength and flexibility is indeed a cause of back pain.[45] More than 5000 people with back pain whose cause could not be diagnosed were evaluated by the Kraus-Weber test.[46] Eighty percent were unable to perform six basic movements: touching toes; sitting up with knees bent, then straight; straight leg raise; upper body raise; and lower body raise for 10 seconds. They were instructed to follow a series of exercises and were observed over a period of 7 years. Eighty percent became pain-free.

A similar survey of 6- to 16-year-olds was conducted in the United States, Austria, Italy, Switzerland, and England.[47] Children in the United States had a much higher percentage of failures than in the other, generally less mechanized, countries. British children were 27 percent more fit than children in the United States.

More vigorous exercising can follow once minimal strength is established. Brisk walking, cycling, swimming, and jogging can ensure physical health.[48] In addition, psychologic benefits are also noticed. Depression, hysteria, and hypochondriasis can be replaced by optimism, enthusiasm, and a better body image.

Nutritional habits also influence behavior. Depressive psychosis, schizophrenia, personality disorders, and affective illnesses have all been related to nutrient deficiencies.[49] Deficiencies of thiamin, riboflavin, pyridoxine, biotin, niacin, calcium, magnesium, and vitamins B_3 and B_{12} result in physical and emotional abnormalities.[50] Seventy-seven percent of hyperactive children have abnormal glucose tolerance test results.[51]

The influence is apparent and most people are aware of the relationship between diet and health.[52] The key to proper nutrition habits may well be the method of delivering the message. When information is simply made available, people are not persuaded.[53,54] Techniques that arouse fear are unsuccessful, unless accompanied by specific recommendations for action.[55] The approaches used in commercials work well; they are simple, colorful, and humorous, and are repeated over and over, but in many cases they are promoting junk food. Most importantly, nutrition requires the attention of the medical and teaching professions, so that sound, tested guidelines can be given.

Basic guidelines for healthy nutritional habits were outlined in the 1979 Surgeon General's Report on Health Promotion and Disease Prevention.[56] It stated that Americans would probably be healthier, as a whole, if they maintained ideal weight; emphasized fresh fruit, vegetables, and grains; substituted fish, poultry, and legumes for red meat; and consumed less fat, sugar, and salt.

BIOFEEDBACK AND BIOGENICS

The use of electronic devices to send and register internal physiologic parameters dates back to 1888.[57] A galvanic skin resistance (GSR) device was used to measure the body's electrical resistance, which at that time was associated with emotional distress. The GSR was developed into the standard lie detector and was also a prototype of the present voluminous array of biofeedback machines. With the monitoring of muscle tone, temperature, brain waves, and heart beat, biofeedback training is being successfully applied to a wide range of illnesses.[58] Voluntary self-regulation has helped approximately 80 percent of patients treated for chronic pain, especially migraine and tension headaches, low back pain syndromes, hypertension, asthma, colitis, and epilepsy.

How does biofeedback training relieve pain? Since pain is similar to most stress diseases in that it is a nonspecific reaction to stress, nonspecific training in generalized relaxation may be quite therapeutic. The first step in biofeedback training is relaxation. Physiologic changes during relaxation begin the relief process. Decrease in muscle tone, respiratory rate, heart rate, blood pressure, and blood lactic acid level help relieve abnormally tightened muscles. The parasympathetic nervous system is activated, while the action- and tension-producing sympathetic system is relaxed. In addition, frustration, anxiety, and depression are neutralized.

There are many methods of facilitating the relaxation response. In the 1920s, Edmund Jacobson developed a technique of muscle contraction-relaxation progressing from the hands to the rest of the body. He documented a high rate of response in many stress disorders.[59] During the same time, J. H. Schultz developed Autogenic Training (AT)—verbal and self-regulation exercises emphasizing heaviness and warmth.[60] The benefits of AT in a variety of disease states have been confirmed by more than 2400 scientific studies.

One method developed especially for use in patients with pain[61,62] is biogenics. Biogenics is a progressive series of mental exercises incorporating biofeedback training, auto-suggestion, Gestalt, jungian guided imagery, and psychosynthesis plus progressive relaxation and autogenic training. Defined as "life generating," biogenics facilitates psychophysiologic balancing. It emphasizes complete physiologic relaxation, then focuses on neutralizing emotional excesses. Upon achieving physical and emotional balance, one is then encouraged to reprogram the desired goal—a previously arranged positive phrase associated with an image of the condition desired. Further stages of insight and attunement begin to occur spontaneously with consistent practice.

With biogenics, the improvement accelerates rapidly. Although many modalities are responsible for the 90 percent improvement after a 2-week session, the most significant factor after 6 months is the continuation of the mental exercises.[63] Eighty-four percent of patients practicing biogenics 5 to 30 minutes, 6 to 16 times per day achieve significant, lasting relief.

The successful use of biogenics is illustrated in the following case histories:

J. W. is a 46-year-old man with arachnoiditis, presented to us with chronic low back and leg pain. Two years previously, while throwing some luggage into an airplane, he felt a "popping" sensation in his back. Myelograms, two operations, and three epidural nerve blocks followed. His condition worsened, and severe arachnoiditis developed—the most difficult to treat organic cause of chronic pain. The various physical modalities were extensively tried, at times aggravating his pain. Physical activity was encouraged, and he was given biogenics exercises to practice 10 times per day. Because of the inherent, organic nature of scarring, he was frankly told of the difficulty of controlling his condition—that it would probably take 2 years to control it adequately. Being very persistent, however, he followed all of the suggestions and, in fact, did more than given. Initially having a pain profile of 100-75-75-75-0 (maximum 100-100-100-100-100), he showed improvement to 0-25-25-25-0 after 6 months. Within 21 months he was running up to 20 miles a day, jogging 436.8 miles in 1 month. His MMPI revealed a return to normal after an initial abnormal elevation of 6 of the 10 measured scales. By December 1977, less than 2 years later, he was working as a full-time airline pilot.

M. L. came to the Pain and Health Rehabilitation Center in 1975. She had had severe rheumatoid arthritis for 6 years. Having tried high doses of aspirin, cortisone, and gold, she was still in chronic pain. However, in the first week, following a biogenics exercise, she stated that she no longer had pain and, furthermore, no longer had arthritis. Indeed, her joints became more flexible and less swollen. She remained pain-free the rest of the session. Three months later, her physician's report confirmed dramatic improvement of her condition. At the end of the 2-week session, she related what had occurred during the biogenics exercise preceding her dramatic change. She recognized that for many years she had held a tremendous amount of resentment toward her husband. She decided that she had chosen to build these feelings and this had caused her arthritis. She decided to change her relationship with her husband. As they subsequently reached a workable agreement, she has remained free of arthritis 4 years later.

T. H., a 37-year-old man, had severe chronic abdominal pain for 6 years and a history of five major abdominal operations before his visit to the Pain and Health Rehabilitation Center. He had been unemployed for 4 years, and his irritability and depression were tearing his family apart. His pain profile was initially 100-75-75-75-75. The third day of the program, he began noticing relief of pain during the biogenics exercises. By the fifth day, this relief was complete and continued after the exercises. He was without pain the entire second week and completed the program with a pain profile of 0-0-0-0-50, still slowly withdrawing from his high drug intake.

The final stage of biogenics is attunement to one's highest self. Attunement is a means of contacting a universal source of order and harmony. Psychologically, it may be translated as the meaning and purpose of major aspects of our lives. At times, it appears as though a serious disease is much more than secondary gain. It may be a sign to change one's course in life, to renew one's interest and responsibility as a parent, companion, or contributing member of society.[64]

One such example is H. B., an electrical engineer who enjoyed his work and supported his family well. While at work, he lifted a heavy object, "tearing" his lower back. After several months of disability, he returned to photography, a previous hobby abandoned because of his busy schedule. He participated in a rehabilitation program. During the program, he became aware of the new direction he was being given, that photography was bringing the beauty of nature and people to life in ways he had not always perceived. He realized he had abandoned photography partly because he felt it could not provide a sufficient income. Soon after, he was invited to exhibit his work publicly, and he discovered that although the remuneration was less than that of an electrical engineer, it was sufficient and certainly much more enjoyable and fulfilling.

Obviously, many methods are available that can facilitate the healing process. The important thing is not which method is chosen but that at least one comprehensive method is fully learned and practiced. Such a comprehensive approach should include a means to rebalance the individual physically, emotionally, mentally, and spiritually.

ENHANCING THE RESPONSE TO TREATMENT

Compliance can be problematic for any patient. With compliance averaging less than 50 percent for a wide variety of illnesses, health professionals no longer expect all patients, or even a majority, to adhere to the medical and therapeutic regimens they prescribe.[65] Noncompliance poses a problem regardless of the severity of the disorder in terms of painfulness, disability, or threat to life. It is particularly high when the disorder is asymptomatic or psychiatric.[66,67] Social class, age, sex, education, occupation, income, and marital status have little relationship with patient compliance. It is not necessarily increased with knowledge about the illness and prescribed regimen. The most consistent predictors of compliance have been found to be health-related beliefs of the patient, various characteristics of the regimen, and some aspects of the interaction between physician and patient.[68]

The health-related beliefs implicated in compliance are perceptions of the severity of the illness, susceptibility to future attacks or complications, and the costs and benefits associated with the treatment plan. The strategies selected to improve compliance must be based on the beliefs and needs of the individual patient. There is no universally effective method. Possible interventions to promote compliance include fully informing the patient about the illness and the regimen, using emotional appeals and social supports, and pointing out inconsistencies in the patient's belief system. In addition, simplifying the regimen and tailoring it to the patient's daily activity pattern can be helpful.

Most importantly, the attitudes of patients about themselves determine response to treatment. Trust in oneself, the physician, and the procedure hastens healing. Belief in oneself is also the most important reason to differentiate the placebo effect; even the most dramatic documented cures of serious disease treated by essentially nonphysiologic substances fail to last when exposed to public and professional negation.[69]

The following specific suggestions can be used to enhance the healing process psychologically.

1. Expressing sincerity, caring, and compassion.
2. Explaining how the modality can and has worked successfully.
3. Encouraging hopefulness and a positive response by clarifying the goal in a phrase-and-image form such as "Every day in every way, I am better and better" while picturing oneself healthy and well.
4. Deciding on a good reason to be well, determining the highest needs of fulfillment for an enjoyable, active, healthy life.
5. Discouraging unnecessary painful behavior and negative thoughts and feelings.
6. Relaxing well 10 to 30 minutes 2 to 12 times per day depending on the severity and chronicity of the problem.
7. Exercising major muscle groups, major joints, and the cardiovascular system as outlined in *The New Aerobics* by Kenneth Cooper.[48]
8. Establishing good eating habits, emphasizing fresh foods and high-quality protein.
9. Avoiding nicotine, caffeine, salt, fat, and processed sugars.
10. Follow-up reinforcement allowing for life changes and belief changes.

REFERENCES

1. GIBRAN, K: *The Prophet.* Alfred A Knopf, New York, 1923, p 60.
2. SHEALY, MC AND SHEALY, CN: *Behavioral techniques in the control of pain—A case for health maintenance versus health treatment.* In WEISENBERG, M AND TURSKY, B (EDS): *Pain: New Perspectives in Therapy and Research.* Plenum Press, New York, 1976.
3. SHEALY, CN: *Editorial: Principles of treatment of chronic pain.* Headache 16:35, 1976.
4. MELZACK, R: *Puzzle of Pain.* Basic Books, New York, 1973, p 16.
5. WOLFF, D: *Can pain be measured.* Current Concepts on Pain and Analgesia 5:11, 1978.
6. LIEBERSON, WT, ET AL: *Comparison of conduction velocities of motor and sensory fibers determined by different methods.* Arch Phys Med Rehabil 47:17, 1966.
7. WOLFF, SL AND COHEN, BA; *Sensory threshold measurements for electrical stimulation of the digits.* Arch Phys Med Rehabil 58:127, 1977.
8. STERNBACH, RA, ET AL: *On the sensitivity of the tourniquet pain test.* Pain 3:105, 1977.
9. WORTMAN, CB: *Some determinants of perceived pain.* J Pers Soc Psychol 31:282, 1975.
10. MELZACK, R: *Puzzle of Pain.* Basic Books, New York, 1973, p 21.
11. STERNBACH, RA: *Pain: A Psychophysiological Analysis.* Academic Press, New York, 1968, p 74.
12. FORDYCE, WE: *Behavioral Methods for Chronic Pain and Illness.* CV Mosby, St Louis, 1976, p 23.
13. TURSKEY, B AND STERNBACH, RA: *Further physiological correlates of ethnic differences in response to shock.* Psychophysiology 4:67, 1967.
14. BEECHER, HK: *Measurement of Subjective Responses.* Oxford University Press, London, 1959.
15. WARD, RC: Personal communication, 1978.
16. HARKINS, SW AND CHAPMAN, CR: *Detection and decision factors in pain perception in young and elderly men.* Pain 2:253, 1976.
17. MELZACK, R: *Puzzle of Pain.* Basic Books, New York, 1973, p 153.
18. BONICA, J: *Pain—its definition, its effects and its mechanisms.* Modern Medicine, Sept 16, 1974, p 26.
19. FORDYCE, WE: *Some implications of a behavioral perspective on evaluation, treatment and measurement in chronic pain.* Second World Congress on Pain, International Association for the Study of Pain, Vol 1, 1978, p 218.

20. SHEALY, CN: *The Pain Game.* Celestial Arts, Millbrae, Calif, 1976, p 39.

21. DEALS, RK AND HICKMAN, NW: *Industrial injuries of the back and extremities.* J Bone Joint Surg 54-A:1593, 1972.

22. YELLIN, A, COHEN, M, AND MOK, MS: *Personality profiles of patients with chronic pain in comparison with patients with other chronic illness.* Second World Congress on Pain, International Association for the Study of Pain, Vol 1, 1978, p 285.

23. KHATAMI, M AND CHRISTENSEN, HD: *Psychological profile on chronic pain patients.* Second World Congress on Pain, International Association for the Study of Pain, Vol 1, 1978, p 286.

24. MARBACH, J, LUND, P, AND VAROSCAK, J: *Anhedonia and depression measures in chronic facial pain patients.* Second World Congress on Pain, International Association for the Study of Pain, Vol 1, 1978, p 287.

25. VIERNSTEIN, MC, ET AL: *Personality characteristics of patients with chronic pain.* Second World Congress on Pain, International Association for the Study of Pain, Vol 1, 1978, p 285.

26. RAHE, RH AND HOLMES, T: *Social stress and illness onset.* J Psychosom Res 8:35, 1964.

27. RAHE, RH: *Life change measurement as a predictor of illness.* Proc R Soc Med 61:1124, 1968.

28. KIMBALL, CP: *Emotional and psychosocial aspects of diabetes mellitus.* Med Clin North Am 55:1007, 1971.

29. BRAMWELL, ST, MASUDE, M, AND WAGNER, NN: *Psychosocial factors in athletic injuries.* J Human Stress 1:6, 1975.

30. MARBACH, AJ AND LIPTON, HA: *Perception of life events by chronic pain patients.* Second World Congress on Pain, International Association for the Study of Pain, Vol 1, 1978, p 289.

31. McCLEARY, EH: *Chronic pain.* Family Health, August 1977.

32. LEFF, DN: *Management of chronic pain—medicine's new growth industry.* Medical World News, Oct 18, 1976, p 54.

33. FORDYCE, WE: *Behavioral Methods for Chronic Pain and Illness.* CV Mosby, St Louis, 1976.

34. BRADSHAW, JS: *Doctors on Trial.* Paddington, New York, 1978, p 61.

35. PUIG, MM, GASCON, P, AND MUSACCHIO, JM: *Electrically induced opiate-like inhibition of the guinea-pig ileum: Cross-tolerance to morphine.* J Pharmacol Ther 206:289.

36. STERNBACH, RA: *Pain Patients.* Academic Press, New York, 1974.

37. SHEALY, CN: *From pain treatment to health maintenance.* Holistic Health Review, Winter 1978.

38. PILOWSKI, I AND SPENCE, MD: *Is illness behavior related to chronicity in patients with intractable pain.* Pain 2:167, 1976.

39. BEECHER, HK: *The powerful placebo.* JAMA, Dec 24, 1955.

40. BINDER, HJ, ET AL: *Cimetidine in the treatment of duodenal ulcer.* Gastroenterology 74:380, 1978.

41. LEVINE, JD, GORDON, NC, AND FIELDS, HL: *Evidence that the analgesic effect of placebo is mediated by endorphins.* Second World Congress on Pain, International Association for the Study of Pain, Vol 1, 1978, p 18.

42. WOLF, S AND PINSKY, RH: *Effects of placebo administration and occurrence of toxic reactions.* JAMA 155:339, 1954.

43. DIAMOND, EG, KITTLE, CF, AND CROCKETT, JE: *Comparison of internal mammary artery ligation and sham operation for angina pectoris.* Am J Cardiol 5:483, 1960.

44. LEFF, DN: *Management of chronic pain—medicine's new growth industry.* Medical World News, Oct 18, 1976, p 54.

45. KRAUS, H: *Clinical Treatment of Back and Neck Pain.* McGraw-Hill, New York, 1970.

46. KRAUS, H: *Diagnosis and treatment of low back pain.* Gen Pract, April 1952, p 55.

47. KRAUS, H AND HIRSCHLAND, RP: *Minimal muscular fitness test in school children.* Res Q 25:178, 1954.

48. COOPER, KH: *The New Aerobics.* Bantam Books, New York, 1970.

49. CHERASKIN, E AND RINGSDORF, WM: *Psychodietetics.* Bantam Books, New York, 1974.

50. WILLIAMS, RJ: *Nutrition Against Disease.* Bantam Books, New York, 1971.

51. LEISMAN, G: *Basic Visual Processes in Learning Disability.* Charles C Thomas, Springfield, Ill, 1975.

52. WINIKOFF, B: *Changing public diet.* Human Nature, January 1978, p 60.

53. BERGMAN, AB AND WERNER, RJ: *Failure of children to receive penicillin by mouth.* N Engl J Med 268:1334, 1963.

55. SACKETT, D, ET AL: *A randomized clinical trial of strategies for improving medication compliance in primary hypertension.* Lancet 1:1205, 1975.
55. DAVIS, M: *Variations in patient compliance with doctor's advice.* Am J Public Health 58:274, 1968.
56. *Healthy People: The Surgeon General's Report on Health Promotion and Disease Prevention.* Department of Health, Education and Welfare, Public Health Service, Washington, DC, 1979.
57. BROWN, BB: *New Mind, New Body.* Harper & Row, New York, 1974, p 54.
58. BARBER, T, ET AL: *Biofeedback and Self-Control.* Aldine-Atherton, Chicago, 1971.
59. JACOBSON, E: *Progressive Relaxation.* University of Chicago Press, Chicago, 1929.
60. SCHULTZ, JH AND LUTHE, W: *Autogenic Therapy,* Vol 1. Grune & Stratton, New York, 1969.
61. SHEALY, CN: *The Pain Game.* Celestial Arts, Millbrae, Calif, 1976.
62. SHEALY, CN: *90 Days to Self Health.* Dial Press, New York, 1977.
63. SHEALY, CN: *Biofeedback training in the physician's office: Transfer of pain clinic advances to primary care.* Wis Med J 77:000, 1978.
64. LEICHTMAN, RR AND JAPIKSE, C: *Coping With Stress.* Ariel Press, Columbus, Ohio, 1978.
65. HAYNES, R: *A critical review of the determinants of patient compliance with therapeutic regimens.* In SACKETT, DL AND HAYNES, R (EDS): *Compliance With Therapeutic Regimens.* Johns Hopkins University Press, Baltimore, 1976.
66. MARSTON, M: *Compliance with medical regimens: A review of the literature.* Nurs Res 19:312, 1970.
67. MITCHELL, J: *Compliance with medical regimens: An annotated bibliography.* Health Edu Monogr 2:75, 1974.
68. ROSENSTOCK, I: *Why people use health services.* Milbank Mem Fund Q 44:94, 1966.
69. FRANK, JD: *The medical power of faith.* Human Nature 1, August 1978.
70. SIMONTON, C AND MATTHEWS, S: *Stress, Psychological Factors and Cancer.* New Medicine Press, 1976.

CHAPTER 3

NEUROPHYSIOLOGIC MECHANISMS IN PAIN MODULATION: RELEVANCE TO T.E.N.S.

STEVEN L. WOLF, Ph.D., R.P.T.

Any surgical, pharmacologic, or modality-oriented approach to the amelioration of clinical pain presumes that the efficacy of a procedure resides in well-established protocols. These protocols should be based on a firm comprehension of the physiologic and psychologic factors that will impact upon the patient. In the case of transcutaneous electrical nerve stimulation (T.E.N.S.), little definitive information is available concerning how this modality interacts with the human central nervous system to effect changes in pain perception. Perhaps it is this paucity of knowledge that accounts for the broad diversity in treatment approaches and the high degree of variability reported for outcomes among patients exposed to T.E.N.S.

With these realities in mind, the purpose of this chapter is to review some basic neurophysiologic tenets necessary for an appreciation of how T.E.N.S. may affect ongoing activity within the central nervous system and, hence, modulate that experience labeled uniquely by each of us as "pain." The manner by which noxious input is delivered to the central nervous system, the mechanisms proposed for conveying this information through the neuraxis, and possible ways of modulating pain information and the role of T.E.N.S. in effecting pain relief will be discussed. Chapters 5 and 8 cover specific anatomic considerations of importance such as cranial and peripheral nerve anatomy; dermatomal, sclerotomal, and myotomal distributions; the autonomic nervous system; and spinal nerve orientations. For further information, a number of texts are listed in the references at the end of this chapter.[1–13]

AFFERENT INPUT: RECEPTORS AND THEIR AXONS

A receptor is an anatomic entity capable of detecting information from an organism's internal or external environment for the purpose of conveying this input as a transduced signal to the nervous system. Such receptors may have specialized functions such as taste, temperature, vision, and audition, and may reside superficially, deep, or within viscera.

Those receptors transducing information that the organism can construe as painful are commonly referred to as nociceptors.

With the advent of satisfactory systems for recording electrophysiologic events, investigators were able to initiate detailed examination of receptor behavior patterns (Table 3-1). Credit is given to Adrian and Zotterman[14] for their pioneering analysis of sensory receptor activity in 1926. Zotterman[15,16] was soon able to discern that single A-delta and C fiber impulses (see Table 3-1) within multifiber recordings could be linked to noxious stimuli. The progression of events in sensory physiology then permitted the discrimination of unique nociceptor categories. Mechanosensitive nociceptors are receptors responding to mechanical stimuli but are designated as noxious when applied to man. These receptors transmit noxious input applied to single-spot receptive fields along C fibers or from multiple fields along group III fibers.[17–19] They respond to pinch or pinprick but not to moderate pressure.

Thermal nociceptors are receptors that most typically respond to noxious heat, with discharge thresholds generally placed between skin temperatures of 40° and 45°C. This form of stimulation is interpreted as "hot" by humans[20] but will provoke escape behavior in animals. The input from these receptors is conveyed over C fibers.[21] In addition, certain receptors, called polymodal nociceptors, respond to both thermal and mechanical stimuli. They convey information along C fibers more frequently than along group III fibers. Nociceptors have also been located within viscera and may signal pain in response to distention, chemical irritation, and ischemia[22] in an attempt to induce homeostatic-oriented responses. Muscle nociceptors probably convey their information to the central nervous system along group III and IV fibers and may be activated by combined repetitive contraction and ischemia.[23]

The development of microneurographic recordings from single peripheral nerve fibers in conscious humans has enabled clinicians to correlate axon responses with subjective interpretation of noxious stimuli.[24–27] From these studies, it has been ascertained that A-delta activation is associated with feeling of first or fast, well-defined pain, whereas C fiber activation is correlated with second or slow, diffuse, long-duration pain. Thus, these microelectrode recording techniques have established that human experiences of induced peripheral pain are initiated by inputs along A-delta and C fibers, and that, indeed, each fiber category transmits different interpretive noxious experiences (as well as other sensory information such as temperature and pressure).

TABLE 3-1. Physiologic Classification of Afferent Fibers*

Type	Group	Subgroup	Diameter (μ)	Conduction Velocity (m/sec)	Presumed Function
A	I	Ia	12–20	72–120	Signal muscle velocity and length change
A	I	Ib			Signal muscle shortening of rapid speed
A	II	Muscle	6–12	36–72	Signal muscle length changes
A	II	Skin			Convey information from touch receptors or pacinian corpuscles
A	III	Muscle	1–6	6–36	Convey information from pain-pressure receptors
Aδ	III	Skin			Convey information from pain, temperature, or touch receptors
C	IV	Muscle	1	0.5–2	Convey information from pain receptors
C	IV	Skin			Convey information from pain, temperature, or touch receptors

*Adapted from Willis and Grossman.[11]

TABLE 3-2. Sensory Receptor Characteristics*

Anatomical Distribution	Receptor	Adaptation Speed	Presumed Function
Dermis of glabrous (nonhairy) areas	Free endings	Slow	Pain, temperature, touch
	Krause end-bulbs	Probably rapid	Cold, touch
	Ruffini endings	Slow	Touch, pressure
Glabrous dermal papillae	Meissner's corpuscles	Rapid	Vibration (higher frequencies), touch
Glabrous—deep dermis and subcutaneous	Pacinian corpuscles	Rapid	Vibration (higher frequencies), touch
Glabrous—epidermis	Merkel's disks	Slow	Touch
	Free endings	Slow	Pain, temperature, touch
Dermis of hairy areas	Free endings	Slow	Pain, temperature, touch
Epidermis of hairy areas	Hair follicle endings	Rapid	Touch
	Merkel's disks	Slow	Touch
	Free endings	Slow	Pain, temperature, touch
Muscle spindles	Primary endings	Slow	Stretch reflex or tendon jerk
	Secondary endings	Slow	Flexion reflex
Fascial planes of muscle	Pacinian corpuscles	Rapid	Vibration (higher frequencies)
	Pain-pressure endings	Slow	Pain or pressure within muscle
Tendon	Golgi tendon organs	Slow	Fast length change or length change of sufficient excursion
Joint capsule	Paciniform ending	Rapid	Change in joint position, particularly extremes of motion
Ligaments and joint	Ruffini endings	Slow	Joint position
	Free endings	Slow	Joint pain

*Adapted from Willis and Grossman.[11]

The morphology of exteroceptors and proprioceptors that transduce information into electrical signals has been known for some time.[28] Table 3-2 briefly summarizes the essential characteristics of receptors. The primary receptor type that transduces nociceptive information in skin, ligaments, joints, and muscle is the free nerve ending. Compared with other known receptors with more precisely defined cytoarchitecture, free nerve endings convey noxious input far more slowly.

SENSORY SIGNAL TRANSMISSION

How does an end-organ receptor convey its series of signals through the nervous system to ultimately result in a sensory perception? Throughout the past century, many scientists have advocated specific theories to account for this biologic phenomenon. In 1895, Max Von Frey postulated that each identified end-organ transmitted information for unique stimuli.[29] Each stimulus-specific end-organ would be connected to a specific brain location according to Von Frey's *specificity theory*. Thus, pain was assigned to free nerve endings, warmth to Ruffini endings, cold to Krause end-bulbs, and touch to the endings of hair follicles or to Meissner corpuscles. This theory has been challenged repeatedly. For example, Geldard[30] argued that the wide distribution of "pain spots" among thermoreceptors would suggest that the latter are also sensitive to pain stimuli, and any receptor stimulated with enough intensity could produce pain. Alternatively, Goldscheider[30] had developed a *summation theory* that suggested that pain resulted from summated impulses within the nervous system after temperature or pressure stimuli were applied to the skin. The Von Frey theory further fails to account for qualities of sensations, to explain the function of receptor types other than the four originally assigned to specific sensations, to explain polymodal receptors, and to account for modality convergence[31] within the neuraxis. Furthermore, whereas the variations among receptors within skin on the human back are limited, humans are still capable of discriminating most stimuli alternatives applied to this area.[32]

At the turn of the century, Henry Head[33,34] developed a concept of hierarchic control over sensation predicated upon two distinct systems, protopathic and epicritic. The former system subserved pain and temperature, whereas the latter governed light touch, temperature discriminations, and tactile location. Following recovery from denervation, the protopathic system would first regenerate. Unfortunately, much of the work underlying this theory could not be replicated.[35] The Head theory has recently been revived[36] by virtue of clear distinctions regarding the quality of sensations conveyed along the spinothalamic and lemniscal systems, with the former governing general aspects of sensation and the latter addressing stimulus-specific aspects of sensory experiences.

In 1929, Nafe,[37] making use of the electrophysiologic data developed by Adrian and Zotterman, hypothesized that a sensation is based not on specific receptors, but on the temporal and spatial pattern of a number of impulses. This hypothesis subsequently became known as the *pattern theory* and was unique because there was no need for specific fibers with a sensation—only a shifting of impulses arriving at the brain. The integration of time for the number of fibers active and their concomitant frequencies would dictate the sensation. An alternative to this theory, which fails to account for stimulus-specific receptor input, has been advocated by Melzack and Wall.[38] Their *eclectic theory* incorporates the pattern theory, which can be modified to accommodate both the notion of stimulus specificity and the absence of same. With respect to noxious inputs, the predominance of contemporary information would favor the adoption of a specificity approach with some modification.[39] The situation can best be summarized in the words of Kerr and Wilson:[40]

> . . . The long-debated issue of specificity vs. pattern theory appears to be inclining progressively toward a specific system in which nociceptors with corresponding afferent fibers activate nociceptive neurons in the CNS. Some of the latter are pure high-threshold units, i.e., responding only to noxious stimuli, but a considerable degree of convergence between noxious and non-noxious input on certain neurons tends to obscure some of the specificity. However, this issue appears to be resolved for such units by their increase in firing rate in response to noxious stimulation.

But where does T.E.N.S. fall within the realm of cutaneous input? Certainly anyone who has experienced this form of skin stimulation can attest to the clear "tingling" sensation. To answer this question presumes knowledge of both the receptor types responsive to T.E.N.S. and the physiologic classification of those axons emanating from these receptors. Surprisingly, this question has gone unanswered. Clinicians have presumed that T.E.N.S. activates large-diameter afferents subserving the skin fields stimulated by the modality[41] and that this input is primarily responsible for altering pain perception (see Theories of Pain Modulation below). The possibility that T.E.N.S. activates sympathetic vasomotor responses which, in turn, may have an effect upon entero-nociceptor activity cannot be excluded.

CENTRAL PROCESSING OF NOXIOUS INPUT

The gray matter of the spinal cord can be divided into ten segments or laminae (Fig. 3-1, A). This laminar organization is based on the cytoarchitectural differentiations and is oriented according to the original detailed work of Bror Rexed.[42] Laminae I through V reside

A

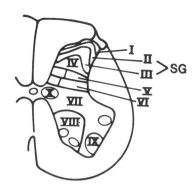

B

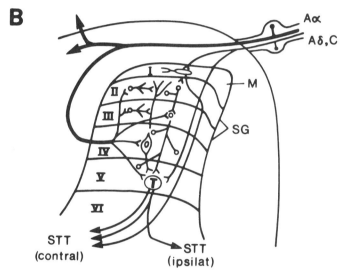

FIGURE 3-1. *A*, Typical organization of laminae within gray matter of the spinal cord. *B*, A schematic representation of primary afferent fiber projections into the dorsal horn. SG = substantia gelatinosa, M = marginal zone (lamina I), T = location of transmission cells (lamina V), STT = spinothalamic tract. (Adapted from Heavner, JE: *Jamming spinal sensory input: effects of anesthetic and analgesic drugs in the spinal cord dorsal horn.* **Pain 1:239, 1975.**)

in the dorsal horn. Lamina VI and part of laminaVII are located in the intermediate zone. Much of lamina VII and all of lamina VIII are within the ventral horn. Most motoneurons are arranged in functional groups (motor nuclei) as lamina IX. The area near the central canal comprises lamina X.

In the present discussion, attention is directed to the dorsal horn components.[43] Lamina I, also called the marginal zone, contains small, medium, and large cells ranging from 5 to 30 μm in diameter. In contrast, lamina II houses tightly packed small cells (many interneurons) measuring between 5 and 10 μm. Cells in lamina III are slightly less packed than those in lamina II and are 8 to 12 μm in diameter. Collectively, laminae II and III are called the substantia gelatinosa (see Fig. 3-1, A). Cells in lamina IV vary between 7 and 45 μm and give the appearance of being loosely packed. Lamina V contains fewer cells than any of the more dorsally located laminae but becomes reticulated in appearance because of numerous fiber groupings running through it.

Numerous primary afferent fibers project to the dorsal horn (Fig. 3-1, B) By penetrating this area with a microelectrode, it is possible to record the location of neurons responding to specific inputs from well-defined stimuli applied to the appropriate peripheral (limb or trunk) area. These neurons have been classified according to the receptors activated by specific stimuli and the axons conveying input to them.[44] Class 1 nociceptive neurons respond to specific noxious or near-noxious stimuli and are located primarily in the marginal layer (lamina I) of the dorsal horn in the cat[45] and monkey.[46] Similarly, inputs have been noted from projections to the spinal nucleus of the trigeminal nerve.[47]

Nociceptive cells comprising the class 2 category are located chiefly in laminae IV through VI and are characterized by low-level responsiveness to peripheral mechanical inputs with increased and prolonged discharge rates as these stimuli are increased to noxious levels.[48–50] Class 2 cells also show afterdischarges of long duration following applications of noxious heat.[51] In addition, somatic and visceral inputs appear to converge upon class 2 interneurons. With repetitive activation of C fibers, these cells undergo considerable temporal summation. This neurophysiologic phenomenon might account for hyperalgesia in clinical syndromes such as causalgia or post-herpetic neuralgia wherein large-diameter efferents are selectively deactivated.[52]

Clinical data from Mayer and associates[53] and Price and Mayer[54] seem to indicate that activation of class 2 spinal cord neurons can lead to the experience of pain. These observations do not preclude the possibility of class 1 neurons mediating pain transmission in humans. Finally, the reader should note that spinal cord neuron classifications exist for all types of inputs[40,44] in addition to those noted as exclusively responsive to noxious or potentially noxious inputs.

ASCENDING PROJECTIONS OF PATHWAYS CONVEYING NOXIOUS INFORMATION

But what about the fate of pain input following activation of spinal cord neurons? To which areas along the neuraxis do such neurons project? Figure 3-2 represents a simplification of ascending systems known to transmit pain information. The spinothalamic tract, also called the neospinothalamic tract (NSTT), is a phylogenetic modification and adaptation to improve on the direct transmission of pain inputs to conscious levels. Such inputs appear to originate from laminae I, IV, V, VI, and VII[55,56] and project directly to the ventrolateral posterior and posterior thalamic nuclei, from whence they are relayed to the somatosensory cortex. This pathway is thought to transmit information regarding the discriminative aspects of the pain experience.[57]

Other pathways capable of transmitting noxious information also exist. One such pathway is the paleospinothalamic tract (PSTT) (see Fig. 3-2). The course of this pathway typifies many of the ascending systems known to convey pain inputs. This tract, as well as the spinoreticular system and the spinotectal tract, may well originate from class 1 or 2 cells and traverse the anterolateral quadrant of the spinal cord.[58] Other pathways, such as the dorsal column and the spinocervical tract, convey noxious data by way of the dorsal funiculi of the spinal cord. Whereas some tracts travel along the medial aspects of the neuraxis and others along the lateral portion,[59] all are multisynaptic in nature. As a result, it becomes particularly difficult to gather conclusive anatomic and physiologic comprehension about the brainstem areas receptive to these systems. Nontheless, present knowledge

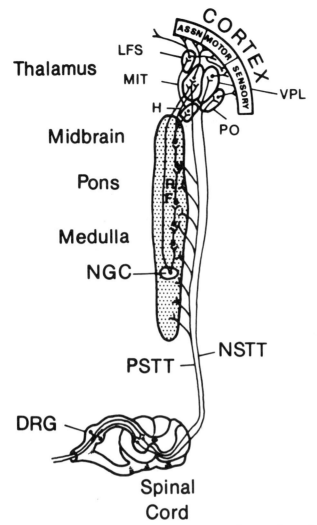

FIGURE 3-2. Generalized conceptualization of projections from pain pathways traversing the neuraxis. NSTT = neospinothalamic tract, PSTT = paleospinothalamic tract, DRG = dorsal root ganglion, NGC = nucleus gigantocellularis, RF = reticular formation, H = hypothalamus, PO = posterior thalamus, VPL = ventral posterolateral thalamus, MIT = medial and intralaminar thalamic group, LFS = limbic forebrain structures. (Adapted from Bonica, JJ: *Introduction: Pathophysiology of pain*. In *Current Concepts in Postoperative Pain, Hospital Practice*. HP Publishing, New York, 1978.)

about the diffuse areas to which these systems project and detailed behavioral and lesion studies permit speculation that these pathways are concerned with motivational and affective qualities of pain. Undoubtedly, the multiplicity of ascending systems and their courses through the spinal cord and neuraxis help to explain why such procedures as anterolateral spinal cordotomies for pain relief[60] provide, at best, only transient benefits. Furthermore, electrical stimulation studies involving sensorimotor cortex,[61] midbrain,[62] and medulla[63] suggest additional evidence that pain pathways project to these areas since their activation can modulate noxious input.

THEORIES OF PAIN MODULATION

Very rarely does the patient who has endured chronic pain suddenly receive complete relief as a result of surgical, physical, or behavioral interventions. More often than not, this patient is subjected to a comprehensive pain management regimen that, at best, enables him or her to cope more effectively with discomfort and, by so doing, sustain a more meaningful and productive life style. Given that this depiction is realistic, it can be surmised that pain-alleviating measures, whether they be modality-oriented or psychologic, act by modifying or modulating a long-lasting behavior that may have an organic basis.

It is little wonder then that considerable basic and clinical research over the past decade has been devoted to the study of pain-modulating mechanisms. Unquestionably, the greatest impetus in this direction evolved from the gate control theory of pain proposed by Melzack and Wall in 1965.[64] Since that time, several theories of pain control have been presented. Although the neural substrates and biochemical interactions ascribed to these ideas have varied, they all share one common element—pain, in whatever prevalent form, must be modulated at some neural level or levels by pharmacologic, psychologic, and/or physical intervention. It is, therefore, a disappointment that in an era characterized by an unprecedented bulging of literature on pain modulation, many clinicians still persist in blindly ascribing pain-relieving techniques to the original gate control theory.[65]

Melzack and Wall based their theory on well-established clinical data and contemporary knowledge of dorsal horn neurophysiology. The gate control theory of pain proposed a constant and dynamic interaction between large-diameter (A fiber) inputs and smaller-diameter (A-delta and C fiber) inputs at the segmental level of the spinal cord (Fig. 3-3). The larger fibers convey input responding to pressure or touch stimuli, whereas the smaller fibers send input governing specific or diffuse pain. The terminals of these fibers interact within the substantia gelatinosa (laminae II and III). These substantia gelatinosa[56] cells serve as inhibitory interneurons that exert a presynaptic inhibition on both large- and small-diameter afferent terminals as the latter synapse on transmission (T) cells presumably located within lamina V. The larger fibers send collaterals to these interneurons to excite (facilitate) them, thus further promoting presynaptic inhibition and, in effect, closing the gate. Collaterals from smaller-diameter afferents are inhibitory to the SG interneurons and would reduce presynaptic inhibition, thus opening the gate. Whether the gate would be opened or closed would depend on the predominating input from these two sources. For transmission cells to convey noxious stimuli to the level of consciousness would require an inhibition of SG interneurons and a substantially greater input from pain-conveying fiber systems. T cells could also be influenced in an excitatory or inhibitory manner from descending brainstem influences acting on them.

During the past several years, this theory has been subjected to numerous variations at the spinal cord segmental level. For example, Kerr[66] has proposed that large-diameter afferents inhibit nociceptive cells in the marginal layer (lamina I), but nociceptive inputs excite these cells. The mode of action for this central inhibitory balance theory is dependent on a postsynaptic inhibitory mechanism.

In noting that pain relief assumed the form of either immediate alleviation of pain or gradual improvement during repeated therapeutic trials, Melzack[67] suggested that certain forms of stimulation might activate a "central biasing mechanism" that would inhibit pain signals of pathologic origin. These chronic pain signals are implicated in a pattern-generating mechanism[63] based on any combination of tonic or phasic sensory inputs, autonomic activity, personality, cultural variables, anxiety, expectation, and brainstem inhibitory pathways. Presumably, this novel form of stimulation would mobilize inherent neurohumoral and neurophysiologic pain-inhibitory mechanisms to retard the memory-like pathologic processes emanating from distant or peripheral loci.

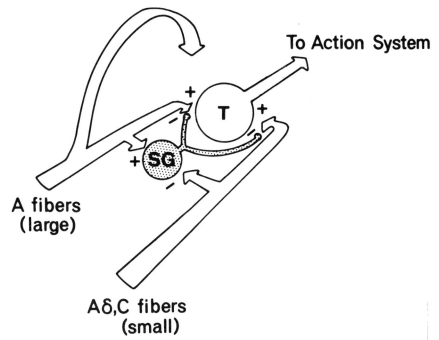

FIGURE 3-3. Schematic representation of primary afferent and interneuronal interactions implicated in gate control theory. SG = substantia gelatinosa, T = transmission cells, − = inhibitory synapse; + = facilitatory synapse. (Adapted from Sindou, M, et al: *Connaissances actuelles sur la physiologie de la douleur: Le controle medullaire.* CML [French] 49:445, 1973.)

An additional theory that has been expounded by European and Soviet clinicians deals with the role of the cortex in modulating pain perceptions. In general, the cortical inhibitory surround theory proposes that counterirritants can suppress cortical responses to noxious inputs by mechanisms that have not as yet been elucidated. Suffice it to say that cortical areas responsive to counterirritant stimulation are located in close proximity to cells engaged by pain input; in fact, these cells may be one and the same. Until more sound scientific data have emerged, this concept should be regarded with cautious scrutiny. Chapter 8 also provides information relative to this theory.

By far the greatest barrage of investigative effort into understanding pain modulation mechanisms has been in the field of neuropharmacology. This rapidly developing area has been integrated with neurophysiologic and behavioral techniques to produce one of the most productive and prolific areas of research in the past half century. With the demonstration of opiate receptors to which opiate compounds could bind stereospecifically,[69] investigators sought to find endogenous compounds with potent analgesic action.

In 1975, Hughes[70] isolated two natural, endogenous, morphine-like pentapeptides: methionine and leucine-enkephalin. Since that time, larger peptides (endorphins) such as β-endorphin (a portion of the pituitary hormone β-lipotropin) have been identified and isolated in numerous locations within the central nervous system.[71]

One area of copious endogenous opiate receptor location is the periaqueductal gray (PAG). Stimulation of this midbrain area had been known to yield considerable analgesia in experimental animal models subjected to noxious presentations to the periphery or to viscera.[72] This stimulus-produced analgesia (SPA) yields behavioral consequences similar to those observed during morphine administration (Table 3-3).[72,73]

TABLE 3-3. Common Responses Between Morphine Analgesia and Periaqueductal Gray (PAG) Stimulus-Produced Analgesia (SPA) to Pain Perception

Event	PAG Stimulus	Morphine Admin.
Site of action	PAG	PAG
Pharmacologic antagonist	Naloxone	Naloxone
Crosstolerance	With morphine	With PAG
Pain transmission suppression	Spinal cord lamina IV and V	Spinal cord lamina IV and V
Raphe magnus activity	Augmented	Augmented
Spinal cord lesion	Nociceptive reflexes abolished	Nociceptive reflexes abolished

Since SPA of the PAG will inhibit spinal reflexes, it stands to reason that this inhibitory influence must descend into the spinal cord. Elaborate lesion studies by Basbaum and associates[75] have shown that the dorsolateral funiculus (DLF) conveys this descending input since only lesions in this spinal cord quadrant will eliminate SPA. These lesions will also abolish opiate analgesia. Furthermore, the rich serotonergic pathways associated with the nucleus raphe magnus (NRM) are intimately involved in pain modulation[77] since stimulation of this nucleus will produce analgesia.[78] Autoradiographic studies[79] have revealed that descending fibers from NRM run through the spinal cord DLF and synapse on cells known to receive noxious peripheral inputs. Interestingly enough, the ventrolateral PAG also projects to the NRM. The nucleus reticularis gigantocellularis (RGC), known to receive ascending pain-transmission pathways, also projects to the NRM.[80]

These and other data have prompted Basbaum and Fields[81] to combine contemporary neuropharmacologic and physiologic findings to propose an endorphin-mediated negative feedback loop (Fig. 3-4). According to this theory, small-diameter fibers conveying noxious input would ascend the neuraxis (see Fig. 3-4, far left) and convey input to RGC in the

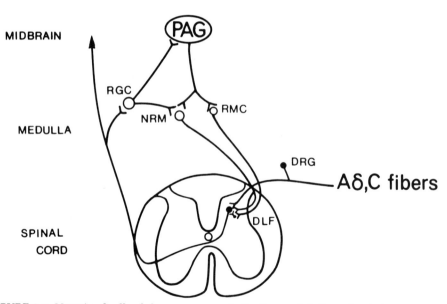

FIGURE 3-4. Negative feedback loop components for the modulation of pain inputs. DLF = dorsolateral funiculus, DRG = dorsal root ganglion, NRM = nucleus raphe magnus, RMC = nucleus reticularis magnocellularis, RGC = nucleus reticularis gigantocellularis, PAG = periaqueductal gray. See text for details. (Adapted from Basbaum, AI and Fields, HL: *Endogenous pain control mechanisms: review and hypothesis.* Ann Neurol 4:451, 1978.)

medulla. Output from this nucleus would travel to PAG, which, in turn, sends axons to both NRM and RMC. Efferents from these nuclei would descend through the DLF to terminate among neurons receptive to pain inputs in laminae I and V of the spinal cord and inhibit subsequent noxious inputs to these laminae from the periphery. Thus, small-diameter visceral or peripheral inputs (possibly mediating nociception) are necessary and responsible for activating a negative-loop, endogenous opiate brainstem response network.

In conjunction with this mechanism, enkephalins have been localized within the spinal dorsal gray, presumably in a region that on electrophysiologic testing corresponds to an area showing heightened extracellular field potential activity during appropriate peripheral noxious stimuli.[81] Inhibition of pain transmission at a spinal segmental level could be the result of the release of endogenous opiates within lamina V or within the spinal cord from supraspinal activation or through both modes of action, but further research is required.

PRESENT NEUROPHYSIOLOGIC CONCEPTUALIZATIONS AND T.E.N.S.

At present, there is a paucity of scientifically valid data on T.E.N.S. and the mechanism(s) underlying neural responsiveness to this modality. As noted earlier, an argument[41] has been provided for the gate control theory of Melzack and Wall[64] to account for pain modulation with T.E.N.S. Numerous clinicians have, in fact, subscribed to this theory, the modus operandi of T.E.N.S. However, the theory works on a segmental basis, and if T.E.N.S. activates large-diameter afferent systems, then it must be exposed to the criticisms[32,82] voiced against the gate theory—criticisms that cite pain modulation in the absence of large-diameter axons.

For those compelled to believe that T.E.N.S. operates on a large-diameter system to modulate small-fiber pain-transmission inputs, perhaps the "central control trigger" theory described by Melzack and Casey[83] might be more appealing. This modification of the original gate control theory more vividly implicates dorsal column transmission of large-fiber input to activate central inhibitory mechanisms that descend to modulate pain-transmission neurons within the dorsal horn.

Several alternative proposals are available. An informal report[84] suggested that certain nuclear regions within the nervous system may possess neurons that discharge after a fixed latency and in synchrony with T.E.N.S.-stimulating frequencies. Although these data provide no useful information regarding mechanism, additional studies along these lines may prove valuable in developing neural linkages leading to mechanistic interpretations.

Another avenue worthy of investigation is derived from the belief that T.E.N.S. may operate via a peripheral blocking mechanism[85] in which T.E.N.S. produces an antidromic blocking of pain impulses. This mechanism would have implications for comprehending the action of T.E.N.S. if the origin of pain-producing impulses indeed resided at peripheral locations and would help to explain some specific clinical findings.[86]

The role of the autonomic nervous system in response to T.E.N.S., in terms of either visceral-somatic reflex activation or direct vasomotor action, has yet to be explored in earnest despite the fact that T.E.N.S. is capable of reducing sympathetic tone.[87] Thus, autonomic activity and its relative impact on alterations in pain perception following T.E.N.S. remain open-ended questions worthy of significant exploration.

By far the most promising evidence of central nervous system responsiveness to T.E.N.S. comes from work by Mayer and associates,[88] who demonstrated that naloxone, an opiate antagonist, blocks the action of acupuncture. Combining this information with the suggestion by Fox and Melzack[89] that acupuncture and T.E.N.S. may possess a similar mode of action, one is directed toward opiate-rich brainstem areas, particularly PAG. Recently, Mayer (in a personal communication) noted areas within the PAG that are responsive to certain skin stimulation parameters. Finally, recent data[90,91] have revealed that electrical stimulation through silver chloride electrodes using constant current stimuli in 1-mA increments will elevate endorphin levels within the cerebrospinal fluid of patients with high pain threshold levels. The location of endorphin release is not known, although there is reported evidence[92] that electroacupuncture will cause elevated endorphin levels at lamina V of the cat. Collectively, however, the above data provide the strong suggestion that pain modulation with T.E.N.S. may definitely occur within the brainstem and may well mobilize endogenous opiates. Further, definitive data on sites of T.E.N.S. action and pharmacologic agents capable of antagonizing benefits derived from the modality will be required. For the perpetuation and development of this modality as a viable (and reimbursable) treatment tool, the continued scientifically validated research to reveal the complex intricacies of its interaction with biologic systems is necessary.

REFERENCES

1. NETTER, FH: Nervous System, Vol 1, The CIBA Collection of Medical Illustrations. CIBA, Summit, NJ, 1968.
2. ANDERSON, JE: Grant's Atlas of Anatomy, ed 7. Williams & Wilkins, Baltimore, 1979.
3. GRAY, H: Anatomy of the Human Body, ed 28, Goss, CM (ED). Lea & Febiger, Philadelphia, 1969.
4. BRODAL, A: Neurological Anatomy in Relation to Clinical Medicine, ed 2. Oxford University Press, New York, 1968.
5. WILLIAMS, PL AND WARWICK, R: Functional Neuroanatomy of Man. WB Saunders, Philadelphia, 1975.
6. BOURNE, GH (ED): Structure and Function of Nervous Tissue, Vol 1. Academic Press, New York, 1968.
7. TRUEX, RC AND CARPENTER, MB: Human Neuroanatomy, ed 6. Williams & Wilkins, Baltimore, 1969.
8. BOSSY, J: Atlas of Neuroanatomy and Special Sense Organs. WB Saunders, Philadelphia, 1970.
9. BARR, ML: The Human Nervous System, ed 2. Harper & Row, New York, 1974.
10. GUYTON, AC: Structure and Function of the Nervous System. WB Saunders, Philadelphia, 1972.
11. WILLIS, WD JR AND GROSSMAN, RC: Medical Neurobiology. CV Mosby, St Louis, 1973.
12. GARDNER, E: Fundamentals of Neurology, ed 6. WB Saunders, Philadelphia, 1975.
13. LANGMAN, J AND WOERDEMAN, MW: Atlas of Medical Anatomy. WB Saunders, Philadelphia, 1978.
14. ADRIAN, ED AND ZOTTERMAN, Y: The Impulses produced by sensory nerve endings, Part 3: Impulses set up by touch and pressure. J Physiol (Lond) 61:465, 1926.
15. ZOTTERMAN, Y: Specific action potentials in the lingual nerve of cat. Arch Physiol Scand 75:105, 1936.
16. ZOTTERMAN, Y: Touch, pain and tickling: An electrophysiological investigation on cutaneous sensory nerves. J Physiol (Lond) 95:1, 1939.
17. BECK, PW, HANDWERKER, HO, AND ZIMMERMANN, M: Nervous outflow from the cat's foot during noxious radiant heat stimulation. Brain Res 67:373, 1974.
18. BURGESS, PR AND PERL, ER: Myelinated afferent fibers responding specifically to noxious stimulation of the skin. J Physiol (Lond) 190:541, 1967.
19. BESSOU, P AND PERL, ER: Response of cutaneous sensory units with unmyelinated fibers to noxious stimuli. J Neurophysiol 32:1025, 1969.
20. HARDY, ID, WOLFF, HD, AND GOODELL, H: Pain Sensations and Reactions. Williams & Wilkins, Baltimore, 1972.
21. ZIMMERMANN, M: Neurophysiology of nociception. In PORTER, R (ED): International Review of Physiology, Neurophysiology II, Vol 10. University Park Press, Baltimore, 1976.

22. Neil, E (ed): *Handbook of Sensory Physiology, Vol 2, Enteroceptors.* Springer, New York, 1972.
23. Mense, S: *Muscular nociceptors.* J Physiol (Paris) 73:233, 1977.
24. Murthy, KSK: *Vertebrate fusimotor neurons and their influences on motor behavior.* Prog Neurobiol 11:249, 1978.
25. Torebjörk, HE and Hallin, RG: *Perceptual changes accompanying controlled preferential blocking of A and C fibre responses in intact human skin nerves.* Exp Brain Res 16:321, 1973.
26. Torebjörk, HE and Hallin, RG: *Identification of afferent C units in intact human skin nerves.* Brain Res 67:387, 1974.
27. Van Hees, J and Cybels, JM: *Pain related to single afferent C fibers from human skin.* Brain Res 48:397, 1972.
28. Kenshalo, DR (ed): *The Skin Senses.* Charles C Thomas, Springfield, Ill, 1968.
29. Sinclair, D: *Cutaneous Sensation.* Oxford University Press, New York, 1967.
30. Geldard, FA: *The Human Senses.* John S Wiley & Sons, New York, 1953.
31. Wall, PD: *Cord cells responding to touch, damage, and temperature of skin.* J Neurophysiol 23:197, 1960.
32. Nathan, PW: *The gate-control theory of pain: A critical review.* Brain 99:123, 1976.
33. Head, H: *The afferent nervous system from a new aspect.* Brain 28:99, 1905.
34. Rivers, WHR and Head, H: *A human experiment in nerve division.* Brain 31:323, 1908.
35. Walshe, FMR: *The anatomy and physiology of cutaneous sensibility: A critical review.* Brain 65:48, 1942.
36. Mountcastle, VB: *Some functional properties of the somatic afferent system.* In Rosenblith, WA (ed): *Sensory Communication.* Oxford University Press, New York, 1961.
37. Nafe, JP: *A quantitative theory of feeling.* J Gen Psychol 2:199, 1929.
38. Melzack, R and Wall, PD: *On the nature of cutaneous sensory mechanisms.* Brain 85:331, 1962.
39. Perl, ER: *Is pain a specific sensation?* J Psychiat Res 8:273, 1971.
40. Kerr, FWL and Wilson, PR: *Pain.* Annu Rev Neurosci 1:83, 1978.
41. Howson, DC: *Peripheral neural excitability: Implications for transcutaneous electrical nerve stimulation.* Phys Ther 58:1467, 1978.
42. Rexed, B: *The cytoarchitectonic organization of the spinal cord in the cat.* J Comp Neurol 96:415, 1952.
43. Heavner, JE: *The spinal cord dorsal horn.* Anesthesiol 38:1, 1973.
44. Iggo, A: *Peripheral and spinal "pain" mechanisms and their modulation.* In Bonica, JJ and Albe-Fessard, D (eds): *Advances in Pain Research and Therapy, Vol. 1.* Raven Press, New York, 1976.
45. Christensen, BN and Perl, ER: *Spinal neurons specifically excited by noxious or thermal stimuli: Marginal zone of the dorsal horn.* J Neurophysiol 33:293, 1970.
46. Willis, WB, et al: *Responses of primate spinothalamic tract neurons to natural stimulation of hindlimb.* J Neurophysiol 37:358, 1974.
47. Mosso, JA and Kruger, L: *Receptor categories represented in spinal trigeminal nucleus caudalis.* J Neurophysiol 36:472, 1973.
48. Besson, JM, et al: *Modifications of dorsal horn cell activities in the spinal cord after intra-arterial injection of bradykinin.* J Physiol (Lond) 221:189, 1972.
49. Hillman, P and Wall, PD: *Inhibitory and excitatory factors influencing the receptive fields of lamina 5 spinal cord cells.* Exp Brain Res 9:284, 1969.
50. Wall, PD: *The laminar organization of dorsal horn and effects of descending impulses.* J Physiol (Lond) 188:403, 1967.
51. Handwerker, HO, Iggo, A, and Zimmermann, M: *Segmental and supraspinal actions on dorsal horn neurons responding to noxious and non-noxious skin stimuli.* Pain 1:147, 1975.
52. Price, DD and Wagman, IH: *Physiological roles of A and C fiber inputs to the spinal dorsal horn of Macaca mulatta.* Exp Neurol 29:383, 1970.
53. Mayer, DJ, Price, DD, and Becker, DP: *Neurophysiological characterization of the anterolateral spinal cord neurons contributing to pain perception in man.* Pain 1:59, 1975.
54. Price, DD and Mayer, DJ: *Neurophysiological characterization of the antero-lateral quadrant neurons subserving pain in M. mulatta.* Pain 1:59, 1975.

55. TREVINO, DL, COULTER, JD, AND WILLIS, WD: *Locations of cells of origin of spinothalamic tract in lumbar enlargement of the monkey.* J Neurophysiol 36:750, 1973.

56. TREVINO, DL AND CARSTENS, E: *Confirmation of the location of spinothalamic neurons in the cat and monkey of the retrograde transport of horseradish peroxidase.* Brain Res 98:177, 1975.

57. CASEY, KL: *The neurophysiologic basis of pain.* Postgrad Med 53:58, 1973.

58. WOLF, SL: *Perspectives on central nervous system responsiveness to transcutaneous electrical nerve stimulation.* Phys Ther 58:1443, 1978.

59. DENNIS, SG AND MELZACK, R: *Pain-signalling systems in the dorsal and ventral spinal cord.* Pain 4:97, 1977.

60. MEHLER, WR: *Central pain and the spinothalamic tract.* In BONICA, JJ (ED): *International Symposium on Pain: Advances in Neurology.* Raven Press, New York, 1974.

61. COULTER, JD, MAUSZ, RA, AND WILLIS, WD: *Effects of stimulation of sensorimotor cortex on primate spinothalamic neurons.* Brain Res 65:351, 1974.

62. OLIVERAS, JD, ET AL: *Behavioral and electrophysiological evidence of pain inhibition from midbrain stimulation in the cat.* Exp Brain Res 20:32, 1974.

63. BEALL, JE, ET AL: *Inhibition of primate spinothalamic tract neurons by stimulation in the region of the nucleus raphe magnus.* Brain Res 114:328, 1976.

64. MELZACK, R AND WALL, PD: *Pain mechanisms: A new theory.* Science 150:971, 1965.

65. WALL, PD: *The future of attacks on pain.* In BONICA, JJ (ED): *International Symposium on Pain: Advances in Neurology.* Raven Press, New York, 1974.

66. KERR, FWL: *Pain: A central inhibitory balance theory.* Mayo Clin Proc 50:685, 1975.

67. MELZACK, R: *Prolonged relief of pain by brief, intense transcutaneous somatic stimulation.* Pain 1:357, 1975.

68. MELZACK, R AND TAENZER, P: *Concepts of pain perception and therapy.* Geriatrics 32:44, 1977.

69. SYNDER, SH AND MATTHYSSE, S (EDS): Neurosci Res Program Bull 13(1), 1975.

70. HUGHES, J, ET AL: *Identification of two related pentapeptides from the brain with potent opiate agonist activity.* Nature 258:577, 1975.

71. MATSUKURA, S, ET AL: *The regional distribution of immunoreactive β-endorphin in the monkey brain.* Brain Res 159:228, 1978.

72. GEISLER, GJ JR AND LIEBESKIND, JC: *Inhibition of visceral pain by electrical stimulation of the periaqueductal gray matter.* Pain 2:43, 1976.

73. LIEBESKIND, JC AND PAUL, LA: *Psychological and physiological mechanisms of pain.* Annu Rev Psychol 28:41, 1977.

74. FIELDS, HL AND BASBAUM AI: *Brainstem control of spinal pain-transmission neurons.* Annu Rev Physiol 40:217, 1978.

75. BASBAUM, AI, CLANTON, CH, AND FIELDS, HL: *Opiate and stimulus produced analgesic: Functional anatomy of a medullospinal pathway.* Proc Natl Acad Sci USA 73:4685, 1976.

76. BASBAUM, AI, MARLEY, NJE, AND O'KEEFE, J: *Reversal of morphine and stimulus-produced analgesia by subtotal spinal cord lesions.* Pain 3:43, 1977.

77. PROUDFIT, HK AND ANDERSON, EC: *Morphine analgesia: Blockade by raphe magnus lesions.* Brain Res 98:612, 1975.

78. SIMANTOV, R, JUHAR, MJ, AND UHL, GP: *Opioid peptide enkephalin: Immunohistochemical mapping in the rat central nervous system.* Proc Natl Acad Sci USA 74:2167, 1977.

79. BASBAUM, AI, CLANTON, CH, AND FIELDS, HL: *Three bulbospinal pathways from the rostral medulla of the cat: An autoradiographic study of pain modulating systems.* J Comp Neurol 178:209, 1978.

80. MEHLER, WR: *Some neurological species differences—a posteriori.* Ann NY Acad Sci 167:424, 1969.

81. BASBAUM, AI AND FIELDS, HL: *Endogenous pain control mechanisms: Review and hypothesis.* Ann Neurol 4:451, 1978.

82. NATHAN, PW AND RUDGE, P: *Testing the gate-control theory of pain in man.* J Neurol Neurosurg Psychiat 37:1366, 1974.

83. MELZACK, R AND CASEY, KL: *Sensory motivational and central control determinants of pain.* In KENSHALO, DR (ED) *The Skin Senses.* Charles C Thomas, Springfield, Ill, 1968.

84. *Hypothesis: An informal interpretation of how the pain suppressor works.* Pain Suppressor Labs, Clifton, NJ, 1977.

85. CAMPBELL, JN AND TAUB, A: *Local analgesia from percutaneous electrical stimulation: A peripheral mechanism.* Arch Neurol 28:347, 1979.

86. WALL, PD AND GUTNICK, M: *Ongoing activity in peripheral nerves: The physiology and pharmacology of impulses originating from a neuroma.* Exp Neurol 43:580, 1974.

87. OWENS, S, ATKINSON, ER, AND LEES, DE: *Thermographic evidence of reduced sympathetic tone with transcutaneous nerve stimulation.* Anesthesiol 50:62, 1979.

88. MAYER, DJ, PRICE, DD, AND RAFII, A: *Antagonism of acupuncture analgesia in man by the narcotic antagonist naloxone.* Brain Res 121:368, 1977.

89. FOX, EJ AND MELZACK, R: *Transcutaneous electrical stimulation and acupuncture: Comparison of treatment for low back pain.* Pain 2:141, 1976.

90. VON KNORRING, L, ET AL: *Pain perception and endorphin levels in cerebrospinal fluid.* Pain 5:359, 1978.

91. SJÖLUND, B, TERENIUS, L, AND ERIKSSON, M: *Increased cerebrospinal fluid levels of endorphins after electro-acupuncture.* Acta Physiol 100:382, 1977.

92. POMERANZ, B AND CHENG, H: *Suppression of noxious responses in single neurons of cat spinal cord by electroacupuncture and its reversal by the opiate antagonist naloxone.* Exp Neurol 64:307, 1979.

CHAPTER 4

SOME LIMITATIONS OF T.E.N.S.

GERALD N. LAMPE, B.S., R.P.T., AND
JEFFREY S. MANNHEIMER, M.A., R.P.T.

There are limitations to the usefulnes of T.E.N.S., as there are for all forms of therapy, but there are guidelines that can be followed in determining the role of T.E.N.S. therapy.

CONTRAINDICATIONS

Although no documentation of adverse effects exists, the use of T.E.N.S. would be contraindicated in two instances:

1. In a patient with a cardiac pacemaker, particularly a demand pacemaker.

In 1978, Ericksson, Schuller, and Sjolund[1] reported that T.E.N.S. is contraindicated in patients with cardiac pacemakers of synchronous type (ventricular inhibited, ventricular triggered, and atrial synchronous), but T.E.N.S. could be used without risk to patients with asynchronous fixed-rate pacemakers. Their work suggested that problems existed both with stimulation rates less than 6 Hz as well as with higher frequencies, depending upon the type of pacer.

2. T.E.N.S. stimulation should not be applied over the carotid sinuses where a hypotensive response might occur secondary to the vagovagal reflex that might also produce cardiac arrest.

PRECAUTIONS

There are some clinical conditions in which the use of T.E.N.S. would not be contrain-dicated, but care should be taken in its application.

1. Pregnancy. The effects on pregnancy are unknown at this time, but it appears that this warning is consistent with the warning extended to the use of ultrasound, microwave

diathermy, and shortwave diathermy. There are several reports describing the successful use of T.E.N.S. for labor and delivery without complications. We have also experienced success in managing pain in the sacral and coccygeal regions in pregnant women who sustained injury as a result of falling. This therapy was administered under the close observation of the obstetrician, without adverse side effects or complications.

2. Over the eyes. Electrodes should not be placed on the eye, but no deleterious effects have been noted when stimulating the cutaneous areas over the bony orbit of the skull surrounding the eye.

3. Internal use. T.E.N.S. electrodes should not be applied internally. The mucosal linings of internal structures probably would not tolerate, without some damage, prolonged stimulation with T.E.N.S. (output in milliamperage).

4. Anterior chest wall in cardiac problems. Electrodes should not be applied on the anterior chest wall of patients with histories of cardiac problems. Although no known complications have arisen from such application, it is our opinion that until more is known about the effects of such stimulation, T.E.N.S. to this region under these circumstances should be administered only after proper notification to the physician so patient monitoring may be increased.

5. Cerebrovascular accident (CVA), transient ischemic attacks (TIA), and/or epilepsy and other seizure disorders. Until more definitive information is available regarding the effects of stimulation to the head or upper cervical spine regions, such applications should be accompanied by appropriate patient monitoring.

6. The incompetent patient. In the presence of senility or other complications that render a patient incompetent to manage the device adequately, precautions should be exercised to ensure the patient's safety, that is, taping or otherwise securing all output parameters so they cannot be adjusted incorrectly.

SKIN CARE

No deaths or complications of existing diseases or conditions have been reported with the use of T.E.N.S.; however, there have been reports of slight skin reactions at the electrode sites. The incidence of such adverse skin reactions has been quite low, slightly higher than the 1.6 percent incidence of adverse skin reactions to cosmetics reported by the FDA.[2]

The clinical experience with T.E.N.S. may be made even more enjoyable and problem-free for both the patient and the clinician if certain characteristics are understood and application protocols followed.

Skin is the largest organ of the body, and, as such, its primary function is to seal off and protect the essential internal fluids from the external environment. Human skin is normally almost totally impermeable to gases and most liquids. There is some degree of excretion by the sebaceous and sweat glands.

The protective function of the skin is complemented by its other essential functions:

1. To regulate body temperature through vasodilation-vasoconstriction activities so more or less blood is allowed to radiate its heat to the outside and through controlled sweat secretion for heat loss by evaporation.

2. As a sense organ with its abundant innervation from the cranial and spinal nerves. Because it forms the outside surface of the body, the skin is a particularly important sense organ through which much information concerning the environment is obtained. T.E.N.S. has its basic value because of this function.

The skin is the only effective body part that performs vital protective and regulatory functions and yet provides the structure to allow T.E.N.S. stimulation to interact with the nervous system.

As noted previously, slight adverse skin reactions may be caused by some factors, such as the electrical current, the composition of the electrodes, the substance of the coupling gel, the adhesives used to secure the electrodes in place, or more commonly, the techniques employed in fastening the electrodes in place. In other words, the skin problems associated with T.E.N.S. may be:

1. Electrical.
2. Chemical.
3. Allergic.
4. Mechanical.

ELECTRICAL REACTIONS

In addressing the electrical nature of possible trauma, consideration should be given to several factors.

1. Constant current versus constant voltage. Generators that are constant-current sources tend to be more effective than those with constant voltage because the constant-current stimulus supplies a greater amount of electrical charge to the underlying neurologic structures than does a constant-voltage source. The possibility of adverse skin reaction is minimized with a constant-current source. The waveform that is generated is grossly affected by the output impedance of the T.E.N.S. pulse generator when driving the impulses across the skin. It seems that the skin impedance appears as a resistor shunted by a capacitor. The skin and electrode–skin interface have significant capacitive components, and, therefore, constant-current sources tend to largely remove the possibility of skin burns from the electrical impulses. The electrical impulses are biphasic to further reduce the potential of injury secondary to the flow of electrical current both on the long- and short-term effects.

2. The potential for electrical burns exists if one or both of the following errors of application is made.

a. Skin burns may occur with excessive stimulation with small-area electrodes. The heat produced beneath the electrodes must be less than 250 $mcal/cm^2/sec^3$. This means that to ensure safety of stimulation, the electrode surface area must be equal to or greater than 4 cm^2. Electrodes of this size will ensure safe current densities for clinical applications of T.E.N.S., and if applied correctly, skin burns will not result.

b. Care must be exercised to avoid placing electrodes too close to one another. If the distance between the electrodes is less than the cross-sectional diameter of the electrodes, then the current density between the electrodes is greater than that beneath either electrode. Thereby, the heat produced may exceed the safe limits and a skin burn may result.

3. Another type of clinical error may result in micropunctate burns. This may occur secondary to poor electrical contact between the skin and the stimulating electrode. Such burns may be observed when inadequate or improper "gelling" of the electrodes occurs or when electrodes are not properly conformed to the body contour. These clinical oversights result in a current distribution pattern that is not spread over the total, wide surface of the electrodes. Instead, the current may be concentrated in large volumes at small, punctate areas such as at the hair follicles. This may produce current densities within small areas sufficiently high to produce true thermal damage—burns to the skin.

It is helpful to note that thermal damage as described is not necessarily an inherent complication of T.E.N.S. therapy. This thermal damage results instead from errors of application, and knowledge of these restrictions will prevent these complications.

CHEMICAL REACTIONS

If the current generated by the T.E.N.S. system were of the direct current (DC) type, there would be electrochemical reactions that could cause chemical injury to the skin. However, the electrical impulses generated by most T.E.N.S. systems are balanced biphasic pulses with equal energy above and below the zero baseline. As such, they produce no net unbalanced ionic shift in the tissues, and, therefore, no acid-base concentrations are produced within the tissues as a result of the applied electrical stimulation. This, along with the fact that modern T.E.N.S. systems generate pulses with very short pulse durations, in microseconds, makes chemical reactions within the skin structures improbable contributors to irritation or inflammation.

ALLERGIC REACTIONS

Adequately sized electrodes and proper application may, on rare occasions, result in skin irritation with prolonged use of T.E.N.S. unless stimulation sites are periodically altered. Patients must be taught a good program of skin hygiene, and compliance with the program is important with prolonged use of T.E.N.S. to avoid areas of erythema and inflammation. Proper care should be given to both the skin and the electrodes. Electrodes are commonly molded from an elastomere such as carbon-impregnated silicone rubber to conform to the body. These electrodes, like the skin, should be periodically washed and thoroughly rinsed before being reapplied to the skin. *Note:* Carbon-silicone electrodes may not change in appearance with time, but the spread of the generated impulses over the entire surface of the electrode is progressively lessened, thus tending to produce the potential for large volumes of current to concentrate in small areas with possible skin irritation. It is therefore suggested that carbon-silicone electrodes be replaced at approximate 6-month intervals.

Very few irritation or allergic reactions have been attributed to the rubber-type electrodes. Allergic reactions caused by rubber are probably a result of the component substance mercaptobenzothiazole. Most carbon-impregnated silicone electrodes used with T.E.N.S. therapy do not contain mercaptobenzothiazole.

Occasionally, a patient may be sensitive to nickel, which may be a component of the metal snap projection in the center of an electrode. Although these factors have been reported, they constitute a very small clinical population, consistent with the FDA's findings on allergic responses to cosmetics.

Adhesive Tape Reactions

Often, the stimulating electrodes are fastened to the skin with adhesive patches or strips. Very rarely, in less than 1.6 percent, patients will demonstrate an allergic reaction or irritation to the pressure-sensitive adhesives on the tape.[3] When this situation presents itself clinically, these persons may be able to use a paper- or cloth-backed adhesive tape. If continued irritation or allergic reaction is experienced with acrylic tapes, patch testing may be useful to determine the cause of the reaction. Place the electrode on the body away from the irritated area and fasten to the skin *without* adhesive tape. Place a strip of adhesive tape alone in another body area. Observe the areas for reactions to the substances applied.

Irritation From Electrode Gels

Some conducting media used as electrode–skin interfaces, whether electrolyte gels or otherwise, contain chemical or abrasive irritants that are present to improve electrical contact. With these gels, an adverse skin reaction is probably not an allergic reaction but an irritant, follicular reaction. One of the irritating substances may be silicone oxide.

Instances have been reported in which true allergic reactions have occurred with gels containing propylene glycol. The hypersensitivity to propylene glycol seems to be specific, and an alternative coupling substance may be tolerated by these persons.

Some clinicians have used substances on the skin to reduce the shearing stresses between the adhesive tape and the skin or to increase the adhesiveness of the tape. If these spray-on or wipe-on substances are used, special care should be exercised in their application; only the skin area beneath the tape is coated or covered. If the skin directly beneath the electrode is also coated, the chemicals of this "special" substance may be driven into the skin tissues by the stimulating current, and skin irritation may result. To avoid this, properly position the electrodes and then apply the solution to the skin immediately surrounding the electrodes. When the tape is placed on the skin, the dried solution is beneath the tape, not the electrodes.

MECHANICAL REACTIONS

The most common adverse skin reactions are due to the mechanical stresses created by shearing forces between the tape and the skin. These forces, or stresses, may be created by several application errors. It must be noted that the incidence of skin reactions is really quite small, and when such reactions do occur, they most likely are *not* the result of *allergic* responses. We propose that a significant amount of the adverse skin reactions are caused by the manner in which clinicians apply the tape.

If one end of the strip is applied first and the remainder of that strip is adhered progressively from the fixed end toward the opposite end, the skin may be stretched in the process, causing an immediate shearing force between the skin and the tape. Even brief applications done in this manner may produce erythema or other evidence of skin irritation. Instead, the tape should be applied center first, with sequential fastening from the center toward one end, then toward the other. When tape is removed from the skin, it should be removed in the direction that the hair in the region lies.

When applying tape, consideration should be given to the movement patterns of the area in relation to the body movement. For example, when applying adhesive tape to the lumbar spine region to fasten the electrodes in place, consideration must be given to the flexion requirements of the region for sitting and bending forward. If long strips of tape are placed parallel to the spinal column, bending forward and sitting will produce very strong shearing stresses between the skin and the tape.

Even when the tape is properly applied, shearing stresses may be exerted at the tape–skin interface by the patient's movement patterns. The lead wires attached to the electrodes constitute effective lever arms that tend to shear the tape from the skin as a result of the tugging action on the lead wires with body movement. This may be minimized by looping the lead wires about 6 to 10 inches from the electrode and taping that "tension loop" to the skin, similar to the procedure used to protect indwelling catheters from inadvertent removal by a sudden tug.

These mechanical problems may be reduced or eliminated by alternative fastening techniques. At times, the electrodes may be held in place with elastic bandages or Coban (3M Company). Less commonly, articles of clothing may be used to secure electrodes.

Recent developments in electrode design have significantly helped reduce the problems of electrode application and skin response. Specially treated karaya electrodes permit good conformation of electrodes to body contours while providing good electrical contact. They also provide adhesive properties within the conducting medium, thus reducing the requirement for adhesive tape to hold the electrodes in place.

Conductive polymer electrodes have been developed that permit excellent conformability and electrical contact with the skin. The conductive medium is the only adhesive required, so adhesive tape, except for the remote "tension-loop" anchor previously described, may be omitted completely.

The impedance of karaya and polymer electrodes tends to be a little higher than that of the gel-tape systems, but the power of the T.E.N.S. generators offers more than adequate compensation for this factor. The ease of application, the diminished adverse skin responses, the convenience of these systems, and the comparative cost ratio for repeated applications make the polymer and karaya systems excellent alternatives to the gel-tape systems. To ensure maximum benefit with these electrodes, the proper method of application and removal must be followed. With some types, the skin must be moistened prior to application of the electrode; with others, the electrode must be moistened before its application to the skin. All must be removed by rolling back the edges toward the center of the electrode and perhaps moistening the undersurface of the electrode as it is rolled back. Removal in this manner will minimize skin response to the removal process and will preserve the integrity of the electrode construction so it may be reapplied over and over.

SUMMARY

Awareness of the contraindications, precautions, and adverse reactions will promote procedures and techniques that will improve the safety and efficacy of clinical T.E.N.S. The patients we serve will benefit directly, and we will benefit indirectly.

REFERENCES

1. ERIKSSON, MBE, SCHULLER, H, AND SJOLUND, BH: Letter: *Hazard from transcutaneous nerve stimulators: In patients with pacemakers.* Lancet 1:1319, 1978.
3. *FDA Drug Bulletin,* July–August 1975.
3. FISHER, AA: *Dermatitis associated with transcutaneous electrical nerve stimulation.* Current Contact News 21:24, 1978.

CHAPTER 5

DIFFERENTIAL EVALUATION FOR THE DETERMINATION OF T.E.N.S. EFFECTIVENESS IN SPECIFIC PAIN SYNDROMES

JEFFREY S. MANNHEIMER, M.A., R.P.T., AND GERALD N. LAMPE, B.S., R.P.T.

Pain must first be thought of as being an indicator of pathology. Characteristics of pain such as location, quality, intensity, and chronology provide information that can be used in part to decide on the origin and appropriate treatment of the discomfort. However, pain existing by itself, without objective signs, is not a reliable indicator of the nature of the pathology, especially one considered to be neurologic.[1] Varied testing procedures must be performed as part of a comprehensive evaluation of the patient to properly determine the specific structure in the neuromusculoskeletal or visceral system that is giving rise to the perceived pain.

PAIN AS AN INDICATOR OF PATHOLOGY

One value of pain is that it can function as a biologic protective system, providing a warning signal to prevent impending damage.[79] However, the flaw in this protective pain mechanism is the variance in onset of the pain, which can make it an unreliable indicator of pathology or of the pain-producing structure.[2]

Pain is frequently referred from the involved structure and may not be perceived at its point of origin. For example, pain produced locally by tendinitis or bursitis differs in quality from that referred by the diaphragm, gallbladder, or apex of the lung. All these distinctly different structures can produce pain perceived at the shoulder. Cervical spine involvement may add to the diagnostic problem since nerve root irritation can also result in referred pain to the shoulder.

Pain may occur from non-noxious stimuli, as in trigeminal neuralgia and shingles. The mechanism behind this process may be confusing to the clinician who is unaware of the nature of pain due to sensory deprivation resulting from the disruption of the normal balancing relationship among large and small fibers. Normal balancing occurs in minor mechanical traumatic episodes when mechanoreceptors and nociceptors are activated simultaneously.[32] The resultant large-fiber activity balances out the small (pain) fiber activity so that pain is not perceived. Pain of acute onset from a facet or sacroiliac joint hypomobility may be misinterpreted as arising from an intervertebral disk. This is in direct opposition to the slow onset of pain due to malignancy.[79]

Severe pain resulting in causalgia may occur from a relatively minor lesion such as a wrist sprain. Functional limitation or weakness due to pain may mislead the practitioner into considering neurologic involvement. This is clearly demonstrated by a patient's inability to adequately flex the elbow against resistance because of pain, which commonly signifies the presence of a bicipital tendinitis as opposed to a cervical spine or musculocutaneous nerve injury.

Pain usually precedes the onset of weakness, as in the case of sciatic nerve irritation that may progress to compression. Pain may then disappear, giving the impression of improvement, but further evaluation may reveal weakness of sciatic-innervated musculature indicative of nerve root compression. On the other hand, a pain-free patient unable to adequately dorsiflex the ankle as a result of nerve root compression may complain of sciatic pain after a few days of lumbar traction designed to relieve compression. The clinician should not conclude that the patient is getting worse. This change from little or no pain to significant discomfort is actually a sign of progress.

Pain provides only a portion of the information needed for proper diagnosis and appropriate treatment regimen. To use pain as the sole criterion in the development of a diagnosis without delineating its characteristics is totally unjustified. A thorough evaluation of each patient should be conducted prior to initiating treatment. Treatment given prior to the evaluation or when no evaluation is contemplated may eliminate the information the pain itself may provide.

A thorough description of the characteristics and location of the pain, as described by the patient, is warranted in all cases where T.E.N.S. or any pain treatment modality is indicated. In order to delineate pain, the clinician must be familiar with those structures that are capable of producing an afferent impulse resulting in nociception. A description and discussion of pain receptors were presented in Chapter 3.

Recent articles present the interesting assumption that pain is not a primary sensation resulting from specific pain endings or receptors, but the result of the whole pattern of central input initiated at the dorsal horn level.[3,4,39] Unspecialized free nerve endings (polymodal) as well as mechanoreceptors and thermoreceptors (unimodal) may contribute to a perception of pain when the proper threshold has been reached. Thus, the term nociceptor must be placed in a more specific context, such as a high-threshold mechanoreceptor or thermoreceptor. The quailty of pain that is perceived depends on the class, size, and arrangement of nerve fibers in a particular structure as well as its depth.[39] Figure 5-1 illustrates these concepts.

STRUCTURES IN THE NEUROMUSCULOSKELETAL SYSTEM THAT PRODUCE PAIN

Zohn and Mennell[5] review seven structures in the neuromusculoskeletal system that need to be considered in any pain evaluation. These are bone and periosteum, hyaline cartilage, joint capsule, ligament, muscle (tendon and tendon sheath if present), intra-articular menisci, and bursa. Since we are not solely concerned with the musculoskeletal

PAIN

 NOT A PRIMARY SENSATION FROM SPECIFIC NERVE ENDINGS OR RECEPTORS

RESULT OF WHOLE INPUT PATTERN (PERIPHERAL AND CENTRAL)

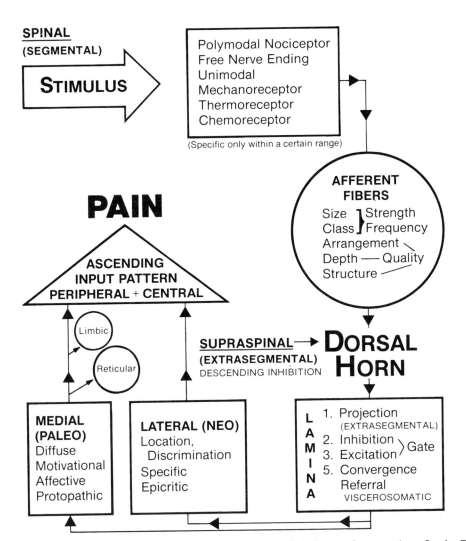

FIGURE 5-1. Factors involved in the transmission, modulation, and perception of pain. The ultimate quality and location of pain depend on the nature of the stimulus, size of the excited afferent fibers, depth and arrangement of the involved structure, dorsal horn interactions, and ascending pathways. Receptors are specific only within a certain range. A thermoreceptor provides information on temperature change. However, if heat greater than 45°C or cold lower than 10°C comes in contact with the skin, the thermoreceptor becomes a nociceptor. Strong mechanical pressure or deformation can also be perceived as pain.

system, the following additional structures need to be considered: skin, fascia, fat, nerve, dura mater, and visceral structures. The characteristics of the pain produced by each of these structures, primarily based on experimentation, will be discussed (Fig. 5-2). Specific pathologies affecting each structure and the nature of the pain will be discussed later in this chapter.

The detailed discussion of sensory endings (free nerve endings and specific end-organs) relative to each specific tissue or structure is beyond the scope of this text. Information concerning sensory receptors can be found in Chapter 3. However, it should be mentioned that free nerve endings are present in the skin, fascia, ligaments, tendons, blood vessel sheaths, joint capsules, periosteum, muscle endomysium, and the haversian system of bone, which contains a neurovascular bundle.[25] Also, every hair follicle is innervated by the deep dermal cutaneous plexus of nerves via myelinated fibers, some of which terminate as free nerve endings and others as specialized end-organs (see Table 3-2).

SKIN

Skin possesses the greatest density of free nerve endings of any body tissue. The skin and subcutaneous tissue are densely innervated by a subepithelial meshwork of thin unmyelinated nerve fibers. Smaller nerve endings pass upward to the skin surface to branch out between the epithelial cells.[32] The surfaces of the face, hands, and feet are the most highly sensitive skin areas. These factors account for the easy localization of skin pain.

Brief stimulation of the skin, intense enough to be noxious, yields a pricking sensation that will change to a burning nature when the stimulus is prolonged.[6] This is characteristic of the phenomenon of first and second pain mediated by the faster-conducting A-delta and slower-conducting C fibers, respectively.[7–9,436]

Referral of pain does not occur with noxious stimulation of the skin, but it has occurred with non-noxious stimulation. Sterling and Bean delved into this phenomenon.[10,437] They illustrated examples of extrasegmental cutaneous referral perceived in an ipsilateral dermatome different from that in which the stimulus originated.[10,26,437] The resultant referred sensation is sharp and easily localized by the patient, which is consistent with the characteristics of skin pain. Referred cutaneous sensation as discussed by Sterling and Bean differs from that of visceral pain, which is referred to related dermatomes. Sterling's hypothesis for this referred cutaneous sensation is possibly a process of convergence in the spinal cord, nervous system errors related to embryology, or some type of altered impulse pattern. Additional information has been presented relative to the fact that there are three distinct skin layers each yielding different pain sensations to stimulation. Itching and burning are produced by the epidermis, superficial bright pain by the dermis, and aching pain by the subcutaneous tissue.[39]

FASCIA

Fascia is fibrous tissue and may be superficial (loose areolar tissue) or deep (compact tissue).[17,25] The superficial fascia serves to facilitate movement between muscles as well as acting as a body insulator. Neurovascular bundles (peripheral nerves and blood and lymph vessels) travel within the superficial fascia, with their main trunks located at deeper levels.

Adipose tissue forms a significant part of superficial fascia between skin and muscle and thus plays a role in pain syndromes such as panniculitis.[5,28,30] Panniculitis may or may not be associated with joint dysfunction. Zohn and Mennell consider panniculitis to be a

CAN A DEFINITIVE DIAGNOSIS BE MADE BY PAIN ALONE?

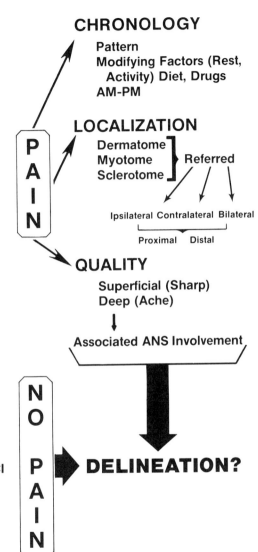

HAVE NOCICEPTIVE AFFERENTS

SKIN
FASCIA
TENDON
LIGAMENT
BURSAE
PERIOSTEUM
MUSCLE
JOINT
JOINT CAPSULE
DURA MATER
NERVE ROOT
NERVE TRUNK
PERIPHERAL NERVE
VISCERA

LACK NOCICEPTIVE AFFERENTS

ARTICULAR CARTILAGE
INTRA-ARTICULAR MENISCI
NUCLEUS PULPOSUS OF
  INTERVERTEBRAL DISK
SYNOVIAL MEMBRANE
LIVER PARENCHYMA
LUNG ALVEOLI
SESAMOID OR
  COMPACT BONE

CHRONOLOGY
Pattern
Modifying Factors (Rest,
  Activity) Diet, Drugs
AM-PM

LOCALIZATION
Dermatome
Myotome   Referred
Sclerotome

Ipsilateral Contralateral Bilateral
Proximal   Distal

QUALITY
Superficial (Sharp)
Deep (Ache)

Associated ANS Involvement

DELINEATION?

FIGURE 5-2. A schematic of the various somatic and visceral structures. Note that certain tissues do not have nociceptive innervation. Thus, evaluation must depend not only on the characteristics but on tests and procedures that aim to increase, decrease, or recreate pain. Many musculoskeletal structures give rise to pain of similar quality and distribution.

form of fibrositis representing adherence of the skin and superficial fascia to the deep fascia and interstitial tissue of muscle frequently seen at the spine as a result of joint dysfunction. Panniculitis is also found at the iliotibial band and over muscle acting upon rheumatic joints.[5] This finding is supported by Stoddard with the addition of diffuse thickening and tenderness in other body regions such as the upper medial condyle of the tibia, glutei, deltoids, and cervicothoracic junction (dowager's hump).[30] Encapsulated fatty nodules may be found in the sacroiliac and gluteal regions, which may be palpable, tender, and produce local pain, but differ from those nodules considered to be trigger points for fibrositis.[30] This seems to be consistent with what Maigne termed "cellulalgia," causing local pain and tenderness.[19] Another related condition may be nonsuppurative nodular panniculitis (Weber-Christian disease) as noted by Cyriax.[28]

Deep fascia consists of compact collagen fibers quite similar to those of aponeurotic tissue. Fascia, aponeuroses, and tendons seem to have similar afferent innervations via nerves of associated muscle and branches from adjacent cutaneous or deep nerves.[257–258] Squeezing normal fatty tissue is not painful, but squeezing adipose tissue involved in panniculitis is painful.

Fascial pain must be differentiated between superficial (subcutaneous) and deep (intermuscular fascial planes). Subcutaneous fascia gives rise to the same pain characteristics as does skin. Fascial planes that separate adjacent muscle groups give rise to a diffuse, aching type of pain similar to that of muscle. However, the pain arising from subcutaneous fascia is relatively local—not as localized as skin, but definitely not diffuse.[6,11,14]

TENDON

Tendon pain is usually characterized as being poorly localized, referred distally, and of a dull, achy nature.[257] Upon active movement of the involved muscle and tendon, as in the case of tendinitis, the pain may become better localized and sharper.[30] Severe tendon pain can result in a spread of discomfort within the corresponding myotome. This is clearly illustrated in patients with supraspinatus tendinitis in which pain is referred through the C5 and occasionally the C6 dermomyotome.[6] A detailed discussion of the dermatome, myotome, and sclerotome is presented in Chapter 8.

Tendon sheaths located at the wrist, hands, shoulder, and ankle produce local pain that may become diffuse with increased severity.[5,6,11] The pain arising from superficial tendon sheaths is much easier to localize and is sharp. Tendons have a poor vascular supply, and nerve innervation is primarily afferent. Golgi tendon organs located chiefly at the musculotendinous junction (proximal end) are excited by active or passive stretch.[25] Periosteal tendinous insertions contain a large density of free nerve endings.[257]

The specific innervation of a tendon is via nerves from its attached muscle as well as communications from cutaneous or deep nerves dependent on the depth of the tendon. Tendons of the hand and foot are innervated by nerves arising from the cutaneous plexus penetrating to the tendon. These nerves have been termed "paratendinous" since they extend along the whole length of the tendon before anastomosing with digital branches of major nerves in the palm and dorsal surface of the hand and related regions of the foot. The implications of these anatomic arrangements are important since they may account for pain referral along the tendon distally as well as the maintenance of tactile sensation of the fingers following complete median and ulnar nerve lesions at the wrist.

BONE

Compact bone is not innervated, but cancellous bone is.[11,30,32] Cancellous bones of vertebral bodies and arches, the sacrum, and the ilium are innervated by a perivascular nociceptive system.[32] Periosteum, however, is highly innervated.[5,6,11,12,257,258] Periosteum that is relatively superficial (tibia, sternum, spinous processes, acromion, olecranon) gives rise to well-localized pain. Deeply situated periosteum produces a dull, diffuse, and referred pain when stimulated.[11] In direct contrast, sesamoid bones primarily embedded in tendons (quadriceps, adductor longus, flexor pollicis brevis, flexor hallucis brevis) are devoid of periosteum. Periosteal pain may be referred proximal or distal to the site of stimulation. The distance of referral and the presence of associated vasomotor disturbances (sweating, skin blanching, nausea) increase with the strength of the stimulus. This type of pain follows a sclerotomal distribution usually differing from that of the overlying dermatome and running continuously throughout the length of the limb (see Chapter 8).[12] Joint pain is commonly referred to the muscles acting on it and is deep, diffuse, and achy. The nerve supply of joints is via specific articular nerves from separate branches of adjacent peripheral nerves, nerves of articular blood vessels, and nonspecific articular branches of nerves innervating the muscles acting upon the joint.[13] Long-bone periosteal innervation is quite dense at muscle, tendon, and ligament attachments.[257,258]

Experimental studies were carried out to determine the nature and location of pain from the spinal facet joints. The injection of 1 to 3 ml of 5 percent hypertonic saline solution into the facet joints of the lumbar spine produced an initial deep, dull, vague discomfort that became increasingly uncomfortable within 20 seconds. Pain that was considered indistinguishable from that of intervertebral disk syndromes was referred into the lower extremity.[24]

Unmyelinated nerve fibers densely innervate the periosteum of the vertebral bodies, which is continuous with that of fascia, aponeuroses, and tendon attachments.[32]

MUSCLE

Pain arising from muscle is classically described as being dull, achy, deep, and diffuse.[6,14] Experimental studies conducted by Feinstein and associates describe pain as a gripping, boring, heavy, lumpy, and crampy sensation.[15] Referred muscular pain also differs from that of the dermatome and depends somewhat on the shape and location of the muscle. Muscles such as the triceps exhibited varied pain distributions depending on which head was stimulated. In addition, muscles such as the trapezius, pectoralis major, and deltoid, which are permeated by superficial fascial planes, can give rise to a more locally perceived pain.[14] The referral patterns found by Feinstein differ somewhat more from the classic dermatomes than do those established by Kellgren, primarily due to the experimental procedure (see Chapter 8).[15] Similar patterns were seen when single muscles with related segmental innervation were injected with a 6 percent saline solution. A high degree of segmental overlap was observed, with an increase in the size of the referral pattern directly related to the strength of the stimulus. Areas of deep tenderness within the muscles were found to be smaller than the referral area. As with bone, concomitant ANS reactions were most commonly seen with injection in the thoracic region. Related muscle spasm and trigger points will be discussed later in this chapter.

LIGAMENT

Ligament pain is very similar to that of muscle. Experiments conducted by Kellgren on the interspinous ligaments showed that the pain distribution was different from that of the conventional dermatomes but was usually referred in a segmental scleratogenous pattern.[6,11,259] Pain was described as an ache and perceived as being deeply situated with associated hyperalgesia and tenderness.[6,11] It should be noted that ligaments that are relatively superficial (subcutaneous) can yield pain that is relatively easily localized.[6,30] Ligaments are highly innervated, containing all major types of nerve endings (free, unencapsulated, and encapsulated).[257,258] In paraspinal ligaments, the greatest density of innervation exists in the posterior longitudinal, less in the anterior longitudinal, and least in the flaval and interspinous.[31,32]

Zohn and Mennell state that palpation of a normal ligament will not produce any tenderness, whereas palpation of an injured ligament (sprain, tear, or rupture) or one associated with a dysfunctional joint will.[5] Stoddard also states that an irritated ligament becomes tender to pressure.[30]

ARTICULAR (HYALINE) CARTILAGE

It is generally agreed that hyaline cartilage is devoid of nerve innervation and is avascular.[5,6,11,17] Experimental studies of articular cartilage were performed during aspiration of joints. When the needle pierced the cartilage, "tapping or pressure," not pain, was the perceived sensation.[6,11] Thus, noxious input cannot be mediated from articular cartilage, but damage to it (displacement, swelling, loose body) can result in periarticular or capsular changes as well as joint dysfunction that may be the structural source of pain.[5,6,30]

INTRA-ARTICULAR MENISCI

The meniscus is devoid of nerve supply. Intra-articular menisci definitely exist in the knee, ulnotriquetral, temporomandibular, sternoclavicular, and radiohumeral joints. Small meniscoid structures may be present at all intervertebral joints.[18,24]

Menisci are basically avascular only in the center; the peripheral aspect receives blood supply via capillary loops from the joint capsule and synovium.[22,25] However, structures known as meniscoids, possibly representing synovial fringes, are innervated at the central region.[19] Since these structures are lacking in sensory nerve endings, they cannot by themselves initiate the pain impulse.[13] However, their role in producing joint dysfunction can result in the onset of a pain syndrome.

JOINT CAPSULE

The fibrous capsules of joints have a dense sensory innervation.[13,22,31,33,42] Innervation of the spinal facet joints and capsule is via the medial branch of the posterior primary ramus.[24,31–33] Innervation of the capsules of the extremity joints is via nerves innervating the musculature that acts upon each respective joint.[13,17,31–37] Numerous sensory end-organs are found in joint capsules. A plexiform system of unmyelinated nerve fibers is found in the capsules of extremity, sacroiliac, and spinal facet joints.[32] A review of the action of sensory end-organs and innervating nerve fibers is beyond the scope of this text but can be found in the work of Wyke and others.[27,38,39,257,258] The sensory end-organs of joint capsules respond strongly to stretching, causing discomfort as experienced in adhesive capsulitis. The region of the fibrous capsule that lies near its bony attachments is particularly sensitive.[12]

The synovial membrane that lines the joint has a dense vascular supply, but sensory innervation is not as diffuse as that in the capsule.[26,257,258] Cyriax and Wyke[13,28] consider the synovium to be devoid of sensory nerve supply. Sympathetic nerve fibers occur in all blood vessels, and the dense vascular supply of the synovium may in part account for the mediation of an afferent impulse indicative of pain.[17] Ralston and associates have seen free nerve endings in synovial membrane.[258]

According to Zohn and Mennell, a normal synovial joint capsule cannot be palpated even though excess fluid is retained. Disease or serious pathology resulting in hemarthosis or pyarthrosis may allow for palpable distinction of the capsule.[5]

Pain of capsular origin is characterized as diffuse and poorly localized.[26] In many joints, the capsule is continuous with that of tendons and ligaments, and the resultant pain may represent a composite of these structures. Numerous receptors are present in synovial joint capsules.[13,31–33]

BURSAE

Bursae are lined with and composed of synovium interspersed with superficial fascia, and are located primarily near joints. In some cases, the synovial membrane of the bursa may be continuous with that of the joint and hence is known as communicating bursa.[25] The purpose of bursae is to reduce the friction of movement between two differing structures and allow for freedom of movement between the tissues. Bursae are found between skin and bone, two tendons, tendon and ligament, two ligaments, muscle and bone, and bone and aponeurotic areas, and are called subcutaneous, subtendinous, interligamentous, submuscular, and subfascial bursae, respectively.[25]

Bursae are not present in the back, but adventitious bursae may develop as a result of soft-tissue trauma in the lumbar spine from spinous process impingement (kissing spines) and between the angles of the ribs and vertebral border of the scapula.[5] Adventitious bursae have no endothelial lining and therefore are not considered to be true bursae, but can give rise to local tenderness and pain.[6]

The vascular and nervous system supply to bursae is, like that of synovium, dense and highly sensitive to trauma, inflammation, and possibly neoplasm.[5,6] Swelling may or may not produce redness of the skin and palpable warmth but will result in tenderness to pressure.

The location of bursae at or near other structures that are capable of initiating pain makes it difficult in some cases to differentiate this pain from that of a joint or tendon problem. Bursae can also result in referred pain. This was illustrated by Cyriax in a patient with an acute subdeltoid bursitis where, after 3 days, pain was referred from the shoulder through the C5–6 dermatomes to the wrist. The primary means of differentiation must be by manual tests of all the involved structures (active, passive, and resistive) and not solely by pain characteristics.[28]

A comparative summary of musculoskeletal structures giving rise to pain is presented in Table 5-1.

INTERVERTEBRAL DISK

The innervation of the intervertebral disk is presented in detail in Chapter 8. The important factor concerning the intervertebral disk is that the outer annulus, not the nucleus

TABLE 5-1. Musculoskeletal Structures Giving Rise to Pain as a Result of Noxious Stimuli

Structure	Depth	Quality	Chronologic and Variant Factors	Localization	Referral Pattern
SKIN	Epidermis → Dermis	Itching, prickling Burning	Brief stimulus (noxious) Prolonged stimulus	Excellent	None
		Sharp	Non-noxious stimulus	Good	Extrasegmental (dermatomal) Ipsilateral referral
FASCIA Loose	Subcutaneous (adipose)	Sharp		Good	None
Compact	Intermuscular (deep) Septa + retinacula	Achy		Poor (diffuse)	Segmental (myotomal)
TENDON	Superficial	Sharp	Pain ↑ with movement and becomes diffuse with ↑ severity	Good	Segmental to distal extent of dermomyotome or tendon
TENDON SHEATH		Burning, boring Achy, dull		Poor	
MUSCLE	Deep	Boring Achy, dull	Shape of muscle	Poor to fair (diffuse)	Segmental (myotomal)
	Superficial	Sharper	Permeated by superficial fascial planes	Fair to good	
LIGAMENT	Superficial	Sharp	Pain ↑ with stretch	Fair	Segmental (sclerotomal)
	Deep	Achy, tender		Poor	
BURSAE	Subcutaneous Subfascial Subtendinous Submuscular	Sharp → Achy	Pain ↑ with movement (pinching) of communicating bursae (synovial membrane continuous with that of joint)	Fair	Segmental (sclerotomal)
FIBROUS CAPSULE	Deep	Ache	Bony attachment may be continuous with tendons & ligaments	Poor (diffuse)	Segmental (myotomal, sclerotomal)
PERIOSTEUM	Superficial	Sharp	Referral may be proximal or distal	Good	Segmental (myotomal)
BONE JOINT	Deep	Dull		Poor (diffuse)	Segmental (sclerotomal)

pulposus, is innervated primarily at its posterolateral margin via the sinuvertebral nerve.[19,25,28,31,32,41–46] Wyke states that the annulus is devoid of nerve endings but there are free and plexiform nerve fibers embedded in the fibroadipose tissue that connects the posterior longitudinal ligament to the outermost posterior annulus.[32] The periphery of the disk has a vascular supply throughout life.[47] Cloward conducted experiments in the cervical region with diskography and suggested, from his results, that both the right and left sinuvertebral nerves pass around the disk, each supplying one half of it. This would imply that the entire circumferential periphery of the disk has sensory innervation.[42,48,49]

Pain arising from the disk itself has been termed diskogenic. Diskogenic pain is characterized as being deep, nagging, dull, and poorly localized. When the posterolateral aspect of the annulus is stimulated, pain is ipsilateral to the side of stimulation.[19,48,49,51] Anterolateral annular stimulation is similar to that obtained by stimulation of the ventral root. There may also be associated ANS reactions such as sweating, nausea, and decreased blood pressure due to involvement of the sympathetic component of the sinuvertebral nerve. Since the sinuvertebral nerve innervates more than one intervertebral level, localization of pain by the patient may not be specific to the exact segment.

Back pain will be discussed in greater detail later in this chapter. However, for this discussion, our concern is solely with pain brought about by peripheral annular fiber injury possibly due to penetration by the nucleus pulposus or vertebral end-plate fractures causing fissures or distraction.[47] This can be termed a minor herniation not yet severe enough to result in referred pain or to press on and irritate the posterior longitudinal ligament, dura mater, or nerve root. The type I acute back sprain of Charnley is consistent with this type of injury.[46]

DURA MATER

The anatomy and innervation of the dura mater are discussed in detail in Chapter 8. The dura mater actually consists of two sections—cerebral and spinal. Our concern at this juncture is with the spinal portion innervated on its anterior aspect by the sinuvertebral nerve.[25] The posterior aspect of the dura mater has been shown to be devoid of sensory innervation.[25,28,42] Evidence has been presented that only free unmyelinated nerve endings are found innervating the anterior dura and dural sleeve.[32,42] Epidural fibroadipose tissue, which is innervated by a plexiform system of unmyelinated nerve fibers, is found between the dura and vertebral column. The density of this innervation is greater in the cephalad than in the caudal vertebral column.[32]

Pain arising from irritation or pressure on the dura mater is poorly localized and referred extrasegmentally.[28,30,42] Pressure on the dura in the low lumbar area can cause groin and thoracic pain and even unilateral or bilateral headache pain.[28] Such a pain distribution can result in the clinician concluding that the patient is malingering or misinterpreting the diagnosis. The characteristics of dural pain, similar to that of the PLL, are deep and achy.[42] Anterior dural impingement from traumatic posterior vertebral dislocation, bone fragments from lumbar or upper sacral vertebral fractures, and posterolateral osteophytes usually give rise to pain at or close to the midline.[32]

NERVE ROOT

The anatomy of the nerve root is described in detail in Chapter 8. The nerve root and its highly sensitive dural sheath are subject to irritation, compression, stretch, and even

TABLE 5-2. Nervous System Structures Giving Rise To Pain as a Result of Noxious Stimuli

Structure	Depth	Quality	Chronologic and Variant Factors	Localization	Referral Pattern
Dura mater	Deep	Dull, achy, boring, referred, paresthesia	Unilateral or bilateral	Poor to fair	Extrasegmental
Dural sleeve	Deep	Sharp, electric shock-like, lancinating	Varies with foraminal encroachment	Fair	Segmental (dermatomal)
NERVE ROOT Ventral	Deep	Irritation Tenderness, ache, cramp	Compression no tenderness or pain, paralysis	Poor to fair	Segmental (myotomal)
Dorsal	Superficial	Pins and needles, paresthesia	Numbness	Fair	Segmental (dermatomal)
Sympathetic component		↑ ANS signs	↓ ANS signs	Poor	Sympathetic dermatome
Nerve trunk ↓ Peripheral nerve	Superficial ↓ Deep	Pins and needles Hyperesthesia Burning Background ache	Neurapraxia ↓ Axonotmesis Neurotmesis Numbness and paralysis	Fair to good	Course of nerve distally, sensory and/or motor loss
Spinal cord	Deep	Paresthesia, not pain	irritation or compression (Babinski, spasticity)	Poor	Bilateral extrasegmental

severance within the intervertebral foramen.[5,6,19,24,25,28–33,41–49] The dural sheath is continuous with the epineurium of the nerve but does not extend beyond the intervertebral foramen.[28,52,54]

For an adequate description of the character of pain emanating from the nerve root, it must be divided into its component parts—dorsal and ventral roots plus sympathetic component. Pain arising from irritation or stretch of the dural sleeve is neuralgic and characterized as shock or electric-like and severe.[28] It is usually fairly well localized within the corresponding dermatome.[19,28,30] Involvement of the ventral root yields a myalgic pain and is characterized as deep, crampy, or achy with a distribution within the related myotome similar in character and distribution to that resulting from intervertebral disk stimulation (Table 5-2).[19,28,30,49]

Irritation of the dorsal root results in the sensation of "pins and needles," termed paresthesia and perceived at the distal extent of the dermatome (hands and feet). Major pressure severe enough to result in complete blockage of nerve transmission will result in loss of sensation. Compression of the ventral root results in weakness or paralysis of the related myotome, depending on the degree of compression. Mixed signs indicative of stages between irritation and full compression are frequently encountered; therefore, these explanations are by no means as clear-cut as described. Recent experimentation on persistent pain after anterolateral cordotomy and dorsal rhizotomy has implicated other afferent pathways that may mediate nociceptive input.[57–59] The ventral spinothalamic tract previously thought to mediate only touch and light pressure was suggested by Kerr to be involved also in mediating pain.[57,58]

Hosobuchi has confirmed the findings of Coggeshall and others that unmyelinated fibers are present in human ventral roots, comprising perhaps as much as 25 percent of ventral root axons.[59]

Furthermore, Melzack and Loeser present evidence for the existence of pain even after total spinal cord transection as well as sympathetic blocks or sympathectomy in paraplegic patients.[60] These authors propose the existence of pattern-generating mechanisms above the level of the lesion developed in part by the loss of sensory input to the brainstem inhibitory systems.[60]

Direct pressure on the spinal cord will yield bilateral and extrasegmental paresthesia but no distinct pain.[28] Cloward states that midline disk protrusions resulting in spinal cord compression give rise to a myelogenic pain when the involved disk is injected. This results in a shock-like pain down the spine that may spread into one or all extremities for a brief period.[49] Cloward further states that a midline lesion encroaching upon the spinal cord will result in bilateral Babinski signs and lower extremity spasticity.[48]

Involvement of the sympathetic component of the spinal nerve will result in autonomic disturbances such as sweating, nausea, and decreased blood pressure.

NERVE TRUNK

It is generally agreed that complete compression of a nerve trunk results in a blockage of conduction distal to the lesion.[55,56] Therefore, complete loss of motor and sensory function ensues. However, partial or intermittent pressure (compression) will result in paresthesia as opposed to numbness at the onset and release of the compression.[53] This is the release phenomenon discussed by Cyriax.[28] Paresthesia may be considered irritating enough to be classified as painful, but it is important to differentiate paresthesia from sensory loss. A dense system of ascending and descending articular branches of nerve trunks connects adjacent dorsal roots and facet joints in the lumbosacral region.[32] This may result in pain that is not segmentally related to the involved nerve root. Directly related to this is the anatomic distribution of the afferent branch of L2, which descends within the posterior longitudinal ligament to the level of L5.[32] Thus, pain at the L5 level may arise from an L2 lesion.

Minor irritation of a nerve trunk produces distal paresthesia along the distribution of the nerve.[28,52–54] Partial injuries or lesions of peripheral nerves resulting in actual mechanical damage but not complete severance usually give rise to burning pain classified as causalgia with associated vasomotor and sudomotor changes.[55]

Injuries to nerves are variable, depending on the extent of damage. Nerve injuries have been categorized as simple neurapraxia, axonotmesis, and neurotmesis.[56] Neurapraxia represents a transitory, localized block of nerve transmission. This usually produces temporary motor paralysis but little, if any, sensory or sympathetic involvement. Stimulation of the nerve can still elicit a response above or below the block.[5] In axonotmesis, wallerian degeneration distal to the lesion occurs. There is associated loss of motor, sensory, and sympathetic functions. Recovery from axonotmesis takes considerably longer than from a neurapraxia. Neurotmesis represents complete severance of the nerve with total conduction loss.

The vascularity of nerve sheaths is denser than that of ligaments, tendons, and aponeuroses.[53] Thus, sympathetic involvement is not uncommon.

The distribution of peripheral nerves makes them susceptible to entrapment as they course through narrow tunnels; between muscle, fascia, and ligaments; and against bony prominences. Various degrees of irritation and/or compression can occur at numerous areas.

Finally, nerves are susceptible to damage from plexus injuries, traction, root avulsion, and neuropathy stemming from neuromuscular and systemic diseases or toxic substances. The pain resulting from a diabetic neuropathy is perhaps the most well known. A comparative summary of the pain characteristics related to nervous system tissue is presented in Table 5-2.

VISCERA AND PERITONEUM

The anatomic arrangement of the autonomic nervous system (ANS), its connections, and its relationship to the central nervous system (CNS) are presented in Chapter 8. Generally, afferent fibers from the hollow viscera travel via the vagus, splanchnic, or pelvic nerves of the ANS to the CNS by three pathways: parasympathetic, sympathetic, and somatic nerves.[8,25,50,61,62] Viscera are considered to be sparsely innervated with a resultant poor sensation of visceral events.[8,50,62,126] Visceral damage that is well localized to specific areas usually does not produce severe pain. It therefore requires a strong stimulus or one resulting in excitation of a large section of viscera (ischemic irritation) in order to recruit enough nociceptors to give rise to an impulse that results in pain perception. Thus, stimuli sufficient to result in visceral pain can occur from obstruction, distention, inflammation, spasms or strong contractions, ischemia, hyperacidity, formation and accumulation of pain-producing substances, and traction or compression of ligaments, mesentery, and vessels.[8,25,50,63] Stimuli arising from viscera or visceral peritoneal structures consisting of localized pinching, cutting, clamping, or burning are usually not perceived by the conscious patient.[8,25]

The quality of visceral pain is generally quite similar to that of deep somatic pain, namely, vague, poorly localized, aching, dull, and referred.[6,8,50,61–64] Visceral irritation as a result of pathology produces not only pain but hyperalgesia, hyperesthesia, sweating, piloerection, and muscular rigidity in segmentally related areas.[62,63]

Visceral pain can be further broken down into that which results from stimulation of the inner surfaces of a body wall (quasivisceral pain) and that which arises from the viscera themselves. Quasivisceral pain is actually pain arising from the thorax and abdomen. Visceral pathology spreading to the parietal peritoneum, for example, can result in inflammation, pressure, friction, or invasion, creating nociceptive stimuli mediated by somatic nerves.

The peritoneum consists of a complex serous membrane lining the deep surface of the abdominal wall and peripheral surfaces of the viscera, including the pericardium. The membrane has a smooth, moist surface to allow for freedom of movement of the viscera within the confines of their attachments.[25] Extraperitoneal tissue (areolar connective tissue) lies between the parietal peritoneum and abdominal wall. Experimental studies of pain sensitivity show parietal serous membranes to have the lowest threshold, followed by hollow visceral walls, and then parenchymatous organs with the highest threshold.[63]

Visceral peritoneum is considered to be part of the viscera, and its innervation is via the sympathetic nerves that innervate the viscera. Visceral pain is referred to the dermatomal region consistent with the segmental embryologic development of the involved organ. Table 8-1 lists the segmental innervation of the viscera. A knowledge of the dermatomal mapping of the body is helpful in the evaluation of visceral pain (see Chapter 8).

Innervation of the parietal peritoneum is via segmental spinal nerves from the thoracic and upper lumbar region of the cord as well as by the phrenic nerve. The phrenic nerve (C3–5) innervates the central zone of the diaphragm, portions of the pericardium, and the biliary tract. Somatic afferent fibers (thoracic and upper lumbar) innervate the parietal pleura and peritoneum, diaphragmatic borders, and roots of the mesentery (peritoneal folds of the small intestine, mesoappendix, and transverse and sigmoid mesocolon).[25,62]

The parietal peritoneum and its corresponding dermatome and myotome are innervated by the same somatic nerves. The thoracic/abdominal area is the only region truly consistent with the segmental relationship among skin (dermatome), muscle (myotome), and bone (sclerotome). Sufficient irritation of the parietal peritoneum will result in reflex muscle contractions, tenderness, and rigidity in the region overlying the involved structure. This is considered to be one aspect of referred pain, a visceromotor reflex.[6,8,25] According to Fulton, this is known as a parietoskeletal reflex involving the body wall but not hollow organs.[62] Parietal pain is usually sharp and pricking. A diffuse parietal nociceptive stimulus will produce burning and aching pain.[263]

The undersurface of the diaphragm is parietal peritoneum and is innervated by both the phrenic nerve (centrally) and the lower six intercostal and subcostal nerves (peripherally). Pain referred from the diaphragm can be perceived at the shoulder or lower anterior abdominal wall, depending on the irritated area of the diaphragm.[25,50,61,62] The parenchyma of the liver, lung, and visceral pleura are considered to be almost insensitive to any nociceptive stimulus.[263]

Blood vessels are also considered to be viscera since they supply all bodily structures in company with the main nerve trunks. Thus, there may be no such entity as a pure somatic (peripheral) nerve.[61,65] Visceral motor and sensory nerves innervate muscle of peripheral blood vessels, hair, and glands and can also accompany cranial nerves (trigeminal, facial, and glossopharyngeal as well as the vagus).[25,61]

Free nerve endings are present in walls of blood vessels and hollow viscera. Pacinian corpuscles have been found in walls of many organs and large arteries. Small groups of pacinian corpuscles are also present at the bifurcation of major vessels (brachial into radial and ulnar, common femoral into the superficial and deep femoral arteries).[61] The vertebral venous system is in communication with the large mass of chest, abdominal, and pelvic veins. Any elevation in thoracic or abdominal pressure can directly affect the vertebral

TABLE 5-3. The Characteristics of Superficial, Deep Somatic, and Visceral Pain

Superficial (first, epicritic)	Deep Somatic (second, protopathic)	Visceral
Sharp	Dull ache	Dull ache
Easily localized by patient	Fairly well localized; tendency to be referred	Hard to localize by patient
Perceived at point of origin	*STRUCTURES*	Perceived away from point of origin, referred to embryologically related dermatomes
Easily palpated	Sensitivity Threshold	Difficult to palpate
May result in loss of strength, reflexes, and sensory changes	HIGH Periosteum LOW ↑ Ligaments ↑ ⋮ Fibrous capsules ⋮ ⋮ of joints ⋮ Tendons ⋮ ↓ Fascia ↓ LOW Muscle HIGH	Rarely results in loss of strength, reflexes, sensation, but may cause segmental sudomotor, visceromotor, viscerocutaneous changes (rigidity, tenderness, hyperalgesia)
STRUCTURES Skin, superficial fascia, ligaments, tendon sheaths, and periosteum	Segmental reflexive changes can occur, indicative of ANS involvement such as cutaneous hyperalgesia	*STRUCTURES* Parietal serous membranes Threshold Hollow visceral walls LOW Parenchymatous organs ↑ ⋮ ↓ HIGH

veins, resulting in distention. The nerve endings on vertebral blood vessel walls will be excited from the resultant mechanical irritation and give rise to deep back pain.[32]

Venous pressure may also be periodically elevated by weightlifting, coughing, vomiting, parturition, constipation, and obstructed micturition due to enlargement of the prostate.[32] Persistent elevation of venous pressure resulting in backache can occur in chronic emphysema, congestive heart failure, and the final stages of pregnancy.[32] A diffuse headache may accompany the backache since similar distention can occur in the intracranial veins and sinuses that communicate with the vertebral system.

Pain arising from visceral structures can become complex. In light of all the above factors, the distinction between visceral and deep somatic pain syndromes is often difficult. A detailed explanation of visceral pain, which can differ in acute and chronic situations, will be presented in the section on referred pain.

The delineation of the involved structure or source of pain therefore cannot be determined by pain alone and can easily lead to confusion or misinterpretation. A comparative analysis of pain characteristics from superficial, deep somatic, and visceral structures is presented in Table 5-3. Table 5-4 presents a summary of the aforementioned facts based on experimental research and clinical findings.

WHY EVALUATE?

In order to obtain the greatest degree of success with T.E.N.S., the source of the pain must be found. It therefore becomes important to perform a thorough evaluation of each patient. The characteristics of pain, such as nature, quality, and location, comprise only a small part of the evaluation, but this delineation of the pain can provide the clinician with information necessary for treatment or further testing. Effectiveness depends on application to the proper structure.

The evaluation/examination process is optimally performed by all medical personnel treating the patient. By working together, one clinician may determine information not found by another.

TABLE 5-4. The Confusing Nature of Pain

1. Pain may be referred from both visceral and somatic structures.
2. The severity of the pain and the distance of referral away from the involved structure are directly proportional to the strength of the stimulus.
3. The determination as to whether or not referred pain is diffuse or localized depends upon the depth of the involved structure more than its type.
4. Superficial structures give rise to well-localized dermatomal pain and deep structures to pain that is more difficult to localize.
5. When deep pain is of a chronic nature, it is easier to localize and may also possess the qualities of superficial pain.
6. Referred pain from somatic structures follows a myotomal or sclerotomal segmental pattern of distribution not indicative of nerve root or peripheral nerve distribution.
7. Associated autonomic and reflexive disturbances may occur with deep pain.
8. Pain may be referred proximal or distal to the involved structure.
9. Pain that arises from a joint may be easily confused with that arising from the muscles acting upon that joint. The reverse can also occur.
10. Referred pain from various deep somatic structures may be similar and difficult to differentiate.
11. Pressure on the spinal cord as well as the dura mater produces extrasegmental paresthesia.
12. All pain is not the same. Its quality, intensity, location, and chronology, along with the effects of modifying factors, must be determined if information on pain is to be of value.

Adequate time must be allotted for the patient to sufficiently describe the discomfort and locate it as distinctly as possible. Since pain is always subjective and directly related to the emotions, the patient must be asked pertinent questions about the problem.

Table 5-5 lists specific terms describing pain. These definitions have been developed by the subcommittee on taxonomy of the International Association for the Study of Pain (IASP) and represent diverse specialized medical disciplines.

PAIN: NATURE AND DELINEATION VIA ITS CHARACTERISTICS

The basic differences between acute and chronic pain have been presented in Chapter 1. Further differentiation of pain is by its chronology, quality and nature, intensity, location, modifying factors, and associated physiologic disturbances. Physiologic disturbances such as autonomic nervous system involvement are discussed where appropriate.

The myriad pain syndromes, diagnostic tests, and treatment techniques constitute a great body of literature, and it is beyond the scope of this text to present all there is to know about pain. Our chief concern is to present relevant information on pain and discuss in some detail the common syndromes and afflictions in which T.E.N.S. has been shown to be beneficial.

CHRONOLOGY

At the start of any evaluation, it is obviously important to learn the nature of the etiology (car accident, fall, twist, fracture, or unknown) and the specific date of onset. If the date of onset is recent, questions pertaining to treatment and change in signs and symptoms that have taken place between the date of onset and the present are of minor concern. A long-standing problem requires a more extensive history and consideration of the possibility of a chronic pain cycle (see Chapters 1 and 2).

TABLE 5-5. Pain Definitions*

PAIN	An unpleasant sensory and emotional experience associated with actual or potential tissue damage, or described in terms of such damage.
	Note: Pain is always subjective. Each individual learns the application of the word through experiences related to injury in early life. Biologists recognize that those stimuli which cause pain are liable to damage tissue. Accordingly, pain is that experience which we associate with actual or potential tissue damage. It is unquestionably a sensation in a part or parts of the body, but it is also always unpleasant and therefore also an emotional experience. Experiences that resemble pain, e.g., pricking, but are not unpleasant, should not be called pain. Unpleasant abnormal experiences (dysesthesia) may also be pain but are not necessarily so because, subjectively, they may not have the usual sensory qualities of pain.
	Many people report pain in the absence of tissue damage or any likely pathophysiologic cause; usually this happens for psychologic reasons. There is no way to distinguish their experience from that due to tissue damage if we take the subjective report. If they regard their experience as pain and if they report it in the same ways as pain caused by tissue damage, it should be accepted as pain. This definition avoids tying pain to the stimulus. Activity induced in the nociceptor and nociceptive pathways by a noxious stimulus is not pain, which is always a psychologic state, even though we may well appreciate that pain most often has a proximate physical cause.
ALLODYNIA	Pain due to a non-noxious stimulus.
	Note: This is a new term that is intended to refer to the situation where otherwise normal tissues that may have abnormal innervation or may be referral sites for other loci give rise to pain on stimulation by non-noxious means. "Allo-" means "other" in Greek and is a common prefix for medical conditions that diverge from the expected. "Odynia" is derived from the Greek word "odune" or "odyne," which is used in "pleurodynia" and in "coccydynia," and is similar in meaning to the root from which we derive words with -algia or -algesia in them. Allodynia is suggested following discussions with Professor Paul Potter of the Department of the History of Medicine and Science at The University of Western Ontario.
ANALGESIA	Absence of pain on noxious stimulation.
ANESTHESIA DOLOROSA	Pain in an area or region that is anesthetic.
CAUSALGIA	A syndrome of sustained burning pain after a traumatic nerve lesion combined with vasomotor and sudomotor dysfunction and later trophic changes.
CENTRAL PAIN	Pain associated with a lesion of the central nervous system.
DYSESTHESIA	An unpleasant abnormal sensation, whether spontaneous or evoked.
	Note: Compare with pain and with paresthesia. Special cases of dysesthesia include hyperalgesia and allodynia. A dysesthesia should always be unpleasant and a paresthesia should not be unpleasant, although it is recognized that the borderline may present some difficulties when it comes to deciding whether a sensation is pleasant or unpleasant. It should always be specified whether the sensations are spontaneous or evoked.
HYPERALGESIA	Increased sensitivity to noxious stimulation.
	Note: This represents a lowered threshold to noxious stimulation or an increased response to a suprathreshold stimulation. It should not be used to refer to a response to non-noxious stimulation.
HYPERESTHESIA	Increased sensitivity to stimulation, excluding special senses.
	Note: The stimulus and locus should be specified. The word has often been used to indicate not only diminished threshold but also increased response to noxious stimulation and pain after non-noxious stimulation. Hyperalgesia should now be used for pain when there is an increased response to noxious stimulation. The new term allodynia is suggested for pain after non-noxious stimulation. Hyperesthesia may also refer to other modes of cutaneous sensitivity including touch and thermal sensation without pain.
HYPERPATHIA	A painful syndrome, characterized by delay, overreaction, and aftersensation to a stimulus, especially a repetitive stimulus.
	Note: It may occur with hypoanesthesia, hyperesthesia, or dysesthesia. Faulty identification and localization of the stimulus, delay, radiating sensation, and aftersensation may be present, and the pain is often explosive in character.
HYPOALGESIA	Diminished sensitivity to noxious stimulation.
	Note: Hypoalgesia is a particular case of hypoesthesia (q.v.).
HYPOESTHESIA	Decreased sensitivity to stimulation, excluding special senses.
	Note: Stimulation and locus to be specified.

*From IASP Subcommittee on Taxonomy: Pain 6:249, 1979, and Pain 14:205, 1982, with permission.

TABLE 5-5. Pain Definitions—*continued*

NEURALGIA	Pain in the distribution of a nerve or nerves. *Note:* Common usage often implies a paroxysmal quality. This is especially the case in Europe. More often, neuralgia is used for non-paroxysmal pains. The technical usage is as given, and neuralgia should not be reserved for paroxysmal pains.
NEURITIS	Inflammation of a nerve or nerves. *Note:* Not to be used unless inflammation is thought to be present.
NEUROPATHY	A disturbance of function or pathologic change in a nerve; in one nerve, mononeuropathy; in several nerves, mononeuropathy multiplex; symmetric and bilateral, polyneuropathy. *Note:* Neuritis is a special case of neuropathy and is now reserved for inflammatory processes affecting nerves. Neuropathy is not intended to cover cases like neurapraxia, neuronotmesis, or section of a nerve.
NOCICEPTOR	A receptor preferentially sensitive to a noxious or potentially noxious stimulus. *Note:* Avoid use of terms like pain receptor, pain pathway, etc.
NOXIOUS	A noxious stimulus is a tissue-damaging stimulus.
PARESTHESIA	An abnormal sensation, whether spontaneous or evoked. *Note:* Compare with dysesthesia. After much discussion, it has been agreed to recommend that paresthesia be used to describe an abnormal sensation that is not unpleasant whilst dysesthesia be used preferentially for an abnormal sensation that is considered to be unpleasant. The use of one term (paresthesia) to indicate spontaneous sensations and the other to refer to evoked sensations is not favored. There is a sense in which, since paresthesia refers to abnormal sensations in general, it might include dysesthesia, but the reverse is not true. Dysesthesia does not include all abnormal sensations, but only those that are unpleasant.
PAIN THRESHOLD	The least stimulus intensity at which a subject perceives pain. *Note:* The above has been the common usage for most pain research workers. In psychophysics, thresholds are defined as the level at which 50% of stimuli are recognized. In that case, the pain threshold would be the level at which 50% of stimuli would be recognized as painful. Pain here serves as a measure of the stimulus. The stimulus is not pain (q.v.) and cannot be a measure of pain.
PAIN TOLERANCE LEVEL	The greatest intensity causing pain that a subject is prepared to tolerate.

Specific considerations to the chronology of pain are its effects during a 24-hour period, changes in severity, and time patterns. Visceral pain may be present constantly, as in the advanced stages of cancer, but it is more frequently associated with attacks in relation to breathing, eating, exercise, and peristalsis.[64,66,68]

If pain is constant, it is imperative to investigate whether the pain can be altered by movement or changes in posture and position, as should occur with most somatic pains. Does the pain have a reproducible pattern or does it occur at any time? Is the pain associated with a time-intensity curve illustrating speed of onset, duration, and smoothness at its most intense level and speed of decline?[6] Pain from simple joint dysfunction or tendinitis may be apparent only upon certain movements, whereas the pain of acute bursitis may be present almost constantly but increased with movement.

Other general chronologic considerations relate to changes in pain according to the degree of humidity, temperature, menstrual cycle, and after eating certain foods. The onset of pain from arthritis and migraine headaches may fall into such a classification.

Guidelines for the development and implementation of a thorough clarifying evaluation of the patient with pain are presented in Table 5-6. Specific examples relative to each topic are included. The compilation of this section is based in large part on the knowledge and clinical experience gained from numerous postgraduate courses given by the clinicians listed in the preface as well as numerous texts and articles. They were initially developed as a handout for courses on "T.E.N.S. and pain" given by us and sponsored by Professional Pain Management Seminars.

TABLE 5-6. A Guide to Conducting a Thorough Clarifying Evaluation*

Pain is an indication of pathology, and its location and characteristics provide the medical professional with information related to the etiology of the problem as well as in determining the proper course of treatment. The practitioner is, therefore, encouraged to conduct a clarifying evaluation, and if possible attempt to eliminate the cause of the pain rather than simply resorting to symptomatic treatment. Equal weight should be given to the information derived from the evaluation to avoid the possibility of masking the pain of a progressive pathology.

A determination of the structure from which pain is arising is of utmost importance in the formulation of a treatment plan as well as in deciding on optimum sites for electrode placement.

I. Observation of Patient
  A. Limp or shuffle—unilateral pain or weakness
  B. Sitting on one leg or side—sciatica
  C. Slow sitting may signify an acute twinging pain
  D. Facial expression
II. History
  This should be as complete as possible. Many times, the problem may become apparent from the history, but this should not take the place of a thorough physical evaluation. Give the patient adequate time to answer your questions so that the responses will be clear. Questions should be developed in relation to the following topics or parameters:
  A. Cause of the pain or condition
    1. Accident, surgery, disease, unknown
    2. Onset: sudden—facet, gradual—disk
  Many conditions can occur without an obvious precipitating event.
  B. Length of time that pain has been present—distinguish between acute vs a chronic condition
    1. When pain does occur, consider its duration
      a. Frequent recurrences—mechanical instability
      b. Continuous but fluctuating in intensity—muscular
      c. Rhythmic pulses—headache or toothache
      d. Long and less rhythmic phases—intestinal colic
      e. Increasing in frequency and severity—possible disk herniation
      f. Occurring every few months—loose disk fragment
      g. Consider family or environmental problems as source of stress or tension that may affect pain intensity.
  C. Is the condition worsening, remaining the same, or getting better
    1. A pain that disappears and then is replaced by numbness and weakness is not indicative of improvement
    2. Compare pain at present to that at time of onset
  D. Do activities or postures influence the pain
    1. Sleeping, work, sports
    2. Pain-free position or activities
    3. Painful positions or activities
      a. Visceral pain is unrelated to posture
      b. Once a nerve root swells and neuritis sets in, relief will not occur with any posture
      c. If standing on the involved leg causes increased pain, consider possibility of SI joint involvement
    4. What is the effect of rest upon the pain? Pain alleviated by rest is not so significant, but pain that increases or is not relieved by rest is important. This could signify a malignancy or other serious pathology.
    5. AM vs PM
      a. Carpal tunnel and thoracic outlet syndromes produce paresthesia at night
  E. Have the patient describe the pain
    1. Where did it start
    2. Where is it now? A central backache that has changed to a unilateral leg pain may be significant of a disk problem.
    3. Sharp—superficial pain
    4. Dull, sore, achy—deep pain
    5. Tiring, suffocating, punishing—signs of chronic problem
        Sensory loss vs paresthesia
    6. Draw or color in area of pain on a body diagram
      a. Mark the beginning and end of painful area
      b. Darken most intense region
      c. Place an X on very sensitive spots (possible trigger points)
      d. Differentiate between kidney and L-S area, hip and SI area, and anterior vs lateral thigh
    7. Bilateral (cord, dura mater), unilateral (sciatic, facet), back only (may be visceral)
    8. Hard to localize pains (sclerotogenous) may be indicative of visceral or dura mater involvement

*Adapted from notes of numerous post-graduate courses along with material from orthopedic, osteopathy, manual therapy, and pain management texts.

CLINICAL T.E.N.S.

  9. Does pain originate in the neck or shoulder
 10. Is the pain referred—where, how far, which fingers?
 11. Does the pain follow the pathway of a peripheral nerve, dermatome, myotome, sclerotome, or trigger point pattern of referral
 12. Have the patient rate the intensity of the pain on a scale of 0 to 10
 F. Severity of pain
    1. Neuralgic (radiculitis, neuritis, or causalgia) is severe. Muscular from fatigue backache is achy, dull, and not too unbearable.
    2. Malignancy may be severe and constant
    3. Signs of serious pathology
       a. Vague pain reference
       b. Gradual progressive worsening
       c. Onset of fresh symptoms
       d. Pain unaffected by treatment
       e. Weight loss, hunger
       f. Constant pain (24 hr/day)
 G. Any associated symptoms
    1. Weakness
    2. Bowel or bladder problems—cauda equina, involvement S3-4
    3. Coughing or sneezing increases intracranial pressure, puts pressure on weight-bearing structures (facets, disks), and may also distract the SI joint causing unilateral buttock pain.
 H. Does the patient do anything to the involved area that relieves the pain
    1. They may point to a specific area or give a clue to treatment approach
 I. Prior treatment
    1. Do not repeat that which already has been unsuccessful
 J. Diet
    1. In relation to headaches, certain substances are vasodilators and may contribute to headaches (MSG, sodium nitrite, etc.), Constant low-grade achyness may be due to dietary deficiencies.
 K. Medication (certain drugs may interfere with actual treatment by increasing awareness to pain)
    1. Type and amount may provide information relating to severity of pain. Is medication taken regularly even when pain is not present? Is medication helpful and what percentage of pain is relieved by it?
 L. Consider other information such as x-rays, general health history, related conditions, and prior occurrences
 M. Conclude by allowing the patient to mention anything else that he or she may consider to be in any way related

The Malingerer

Helpful Hints
  1. Observe patient when he is unaware that you are looking
  2. Usually no coherent pattern emerges
  3. They tend to interpret effort as pain so that everything hurts
  4. Present varying responses to the same test performed in different ways
  5. They resent being asked for the exact site of their pain

Physical Evaluation

   Correlation of subjective pain complaint and what the examiner finds. Pain may be referred to a specific area where pain is perceived, but its origin frequently can be a distant structure.
 I. Structural
    A. Pelvic levels (ASIS, PSIS)
    B. Spinal curvature (scoliosis, loss of lumbar lordosis)
    C. Leg length (may be changed by SI joint torsion)
    D. Muscular guarding or atrophy
    E. Hip or knee flexion contracture
II. Active movements
    A. Spine—individual segments
       1. Related spinal segments should be checked prior to evaluating peripheral joints or body regions
    B. Extremities—check proximal and distal to suspected joint
       1. Contractures—is limitation by joint or muscle
       2. Look for capsular pattern
       3. ROM (may be helpful to do repeated movements)
       4. Crepitation
       5. Compare involved and uninvolved side
       6. Painful arc

III. Passive movements

To determine extent of hypomobility or hypermobility and if pain occurs from these movements. This is a test of the noncontractile tissues (capsule, synovium, ligaments, cartilage, bursae, nerves, and dura mater)

    A. Spinal and extremity joints

        1. Compare active and passive range

            a. If restricted and painful in same direction, consider arthogenic involvement

            b. If restricted or painful in the opposite direction, consider soft tissue and/or contractile structure

            c. A capsular pattern is indicated with relative restriction of passive movements in various directions

            d. Pain with limited movement in some directions but not all for a particular joint—consider possibility of ligamental strain, capsular, adhesion, internal derangement, bursitis

            e. Painless limitation of movement (symptomless osteoarthritis)

        2. Check joint play and component motions (gliding, oscillation)

        3. Check end-feel

        4. Overstretch for ligamental involvement

        5. Compare effects of passive compression and distraction

        6. Perform specific orthopedic tests related to individual spinal and peripheral joints

IV. Resistive movements

To determine involvement of contractile elements. Test is by isometric contraction of muscle groups related to a specific joint or vertebral segment. Test all muscles innervated by a specific root if one is found to be weak or painful. Consider plexus involvement with multisegmental weakness.

        1. Consider the following strength and pain patterns

            a. Strong and painful—local involvement of muscle or tendon

            b. Weak and painful—major lesion of muscle or tendon

            c. Weak and painless—rupture of tendon or neurologic involvement

            d. Strong and painless—normal, any tenderness is probably referred (visceral)

        2. Look for specific sites of tendinitis: long and short heads of biceps, supraspinatus, infraspinatus, subscapularis, etc. in regard to the shoulder. Check resisted movements involving tendons acting on other peripheral joints.

V. Palpation

        1. Normal ligaments are never tender to palpation

        2. Normal capsules are never palpable even with excess fluid. If it can be palpated, then synovial pathology exists. Therefore, fluid can never be palpated in a normal synovial joint.

        3. Perform the following tests:

            a. Skin rolling (trigger points, fibrositic nodules, boggy)

            b. Spring test is normally painless. Sharp, short well-localized pain = simple joint dysfunction. Deep, achy, sometimes throbbing pain = serious pathology. Sharp, short pain causing referral = disk prolapse.

            c. Palpate tendons for tendinitis

            d. Palpate for trophic changes, edema, spasm, inflammation

            e. Check sensation within dermatomes—allodynia, hyperpathia, etc.

            f. Palpate for tender acupuncture, motor, or trigger points in painful region that may supply information toward the involved spinal segmental level. (Tender points existing in muscles of the anterior and posterior primary rami of one root may signify the segmental level of involvement.)

VI. Neurologic

    A. Reflexes—not reliable (can be absent in the presence of normal strength). Test in different positions. They may be inhibited or increased by voluntary effort and are dependent on the state of relaxation.

    B. Tinel's sign (peripheral nerve injury)

    C. Nerve stretch tests

        1. SLR (sciatic nerve) can be misleading and may be limited or painful due to tight hamstrings, hip, SI joint, or facet pathology

        2. ELY test (femoral nerve)

        3. Dura mater

    D. Cranial nerves may need to be considered (facial pain)

    E. Upper vs lower motor neuron lesion.

    F. Adson's maneuver, etc. (thoracic outlet)

The points presented in this outline generally are applicable to every pain patient, but are not inclusive of the enormous range of pain syndromes. Obviously, there are numerous other procedures that can be performed, and the necessary expertise can be gained only by further education through postgraduate courses, seminars, and conventions.

QUALITY, NATURE, AND INTENSITY

The general quality and nature of pain derived from specific structures of the body have already been discussed. The complexity of various pain syndromes that result in irritation of more than one structure may, of course, alter the normal quality. The severity or intensity of pain may be helpful in differentiating between pain of neuralgic and myalgic origin. Neuralgic pain related to causalgia or a radiculopathy is more severe than pain of muscular origin, which is perceived as dull, achy, and bearable.[6]

Immediately after an acute injury or accident, pain may be too severe to adequately differentiate its location or determine how it is affected by various movements and tests. It is thus necessary to evaluate as much as possible from the history and pain distribution and provide noninvasive pain modulation (we have excellent results with T.E.N.S. immediately after whiplash injuries) and then re-evaluate after a day or two and institute restorative treatment to the involved structure.

It is also not uncommon that severe pain from one lesion masks that of another lesion. Elimination of the more severe problem frequently brings out the less intense pain.

Cyriax states that intense pain is more difficult for the patient to localize. As pain increases in severity, its distribution increases.[28] Severe pain can result in increased pulse and respiratory rates, sweating, and blood pressure; and, at times, nausea and vomiting.[30] Visceral pain, however, may initially be vague and difficult to localize but becomes severe and easier to localize in a long-standing involvement.

Differentiation between pins and needles or tingling sensations (paresthesia) and actual loss of sensation (anesthesia) is important. The majority of patients use the word numb to describe a sensation of paresthesia. Paresthesia is usually a sign of nerve irritation, whereas anesthesia is indicative of complete compression. Paresthesia may also occur from vascular pathology, as in temporary ischemia. If paresthesia exists and the peripheral circulation is intact, the tingling is probably neurologic.[30]

Paresthesia in the lower extremities, occurring without root pain, may be indicative of diabetes, disseminated sclerosis, or pernicious anemia.[28] However, paresthesia usually is related to spinal cord pressure such as a central disk protrusion at the cervical or thoracic level, with the exception being a spondylolisthesis at the lumbar region.[28]

Tenderness must be differentiated between hyperesthesia of the skin from pinching, compression, or rolling friction (superficial tenderness) and hyperalgesia of the underlying muscle, ligament, or tendon that occurs when the skin is pressed against soft tissue or bone (deep tenderness).[6,30]

Certain areas of the body are always somewhat tender to palpation because of their anatomic location and therefore can be misleading as to the source of pain. Tissues lying directly over or against bone, the heelcord, and the upper trapezius muscle are prime examples. The first rib, clavicle, and midthoracic spinous processes are usually tender in young females. Such tenderness existing without other objective signs is unreliable.[70] Cyriax[28] and Maigne[19] noted the misleading nature of associated tenderness occurring at the styloid process of the radius due to tenovaginitis of the abductor pollicis longus, extensor pollicis brevis, greater trochanter of the femur in sciatica, and the posterior aspect of the lateral epicondyle of the humerus in tenoperiosteal tennis elbow. These areas may exhibit a great deal of tenderness, yet the lesion may involve the tendons or spine and not bone.[19,28] It is therefore important to test the related spinal segments and not just the extremity joint complex. Also misleading, according to Cyriax, is referred tenderness in the scapular region as a result of dura mater irritation from a small intervertebral disk herniation impinging on the posterior longitudinal ligament.[28] This is quite true, as the lesion is at the cervical spine and not the scapular region, but to the experienced clinician it can be a valuable piece of information.

Maigne illustrates this well in his discussion of the nature of the interscapular point.[19] Resisted isometric contraction of the rhomboids and trapezius muscles usually has no effect on the pain or tenderness when the etiology is from the cervical spine. Occasionally, the medial branch of the large dorsal ramus of T2 supplies an innervating twig to the rhomboid or trapezius that will result in pain on contraction and/or palpation. Maigne states that the location of the interscapular point (2 cm adjacent to T5 or T6 whether the etiology is C6, C7, or C8) is quite consistently very tender to palpation and is confirmed by the anterior cervical doorbell pushbutton sign.[19] This sign, consisting of moderate pressure segment by segment at the anterolateral lower cervical spine, will, according to Maigne, reproduce the dorsal pain when the involved cervical segment is tested. If such reproduction does not occur, the scapular pain is not considered to be of cervical origin.

The physiologic nature of the interscapular point is based in part on anastomoses between the posterior branches of the lower cervical and upper thoracic nerves found by Maigne via anatomic research. The work of Cloward explains the interscapular point as occurring from an intervertebral disk herniation with resultant irritation of the sinuvertebral nerve and secondary reflex transmission to the ventral root.[48,49] The sinuvertebral nerve arises from a sympathetic branch as well as a spinal branch (see Chapter 8). Pain similar in location and character (deep, dull ache) has been elicited by cervical diskography of the anterior portion of the annulus as well as mechanical stimulation of the ventral roots.[48,49] The myalgic nature of this tenderness has been investigated electromyographically, demonstrating abnormal action potentials in the scapular musculature in the presence of cervical disk pathology.[19,48,49] As previously stated, Cloward considers the sinuvertebral nerve to innervate the entire periphery of the outer annulus.

Maigne makes extensive use of palpation in his examination process. In the presence of spinal segmental lesions, he palpates for a tender point one finger's breadth lateral to the spinous processes. The location of the most tender point (paramedian posterior point) should also reveal greater tenderness than at adjacent superior and inferior levels as well as at the corresponding level on the opposite side. Tenderness of the supraspinous ligament is also evaluated by the use of the head of a key (key sign). In addition to thorough movement testing and neurologic evaluation, it is necessary to perform skin rolling to determine the presence of cellulitis, trigger points, or fibrositic nodules.

Gentle pressure on the spinous processes in an axial or lateral direction is of value in localizing the level of a mechanical derangement. The goal is to reproduce or intensify the exact pain as described by the patient. However, this can also be misleading, since spinous processes may become extremely tender as a result of apophysitis.[19] This occurs commonly from repeated superficial trauma such as rubbing the spine on the back of a chair. The quality of pain in the presence of apophysitis is more like a hyperesthesia as compared with the deep tenderness that results from pressure or oscillation of the spinal segment. Posterior-anterior glides as well as springing of the vertebral segment can provide similar information. A sharp, localized discomfort of relatively short duration is indicative of simple joint dysfunction. Pain from springing or percussion that is deep, achy, or throbbing may signify a more serious pathology. Resultant or referred pain may point to the intervertebral disk.[5,116]

Tenderness always occurs in chronic pain syndromes. It is imperative to look for the maximal site of tenderness, always compare the right and left sides, and be aware that very strong pressure will always produce some degree of tenderness. Tenderness can exist at many structures: skin, ligaments, tendons, muscles, and bone. Differentiation is thus difficult, and its difficulty is compounded by the fact that reflexive tenderness can occur in the presence of visceral involvement.[30] However, evaluation for tenderness can provide information related to the origin and segmental level of a spinal lesion when used as part of a comprehensive examination.

Pain questionnaires or scales have been developed to help assess the nature of pain as described by patients. The most notable of these is the McGill-Melzack Pain Questionnaire (MPQ) developed for use with patients suffering from diverse pain syndromes and of variable environmental backgrounds (Fig. 5-3). [71–73] Three classes of descriptive words—sensory, affective, and evaluative—were grouped into 20 descriptor subclasses. Other investigators have expanded the word list and classes.[74,75]

In a study of 72 admissions to a psychiatric hospital, it was found that patients with an underlying physical reason for their pain described their discomfort in terms of physical measures. Those with psychologic etiologies described physical as well as emotional factors. The most frequently used adjective was achy or sore.[76]

Patients with chronic pain may exemplify the emotional aspect of their pain more than the physical component. Their descriptions are usually more complex and the location of pain more diffuse.[76–78] Patients with psychologic disturbances with nonorganic causes of low back pain describe pain in a more specific and limited manner.[78] The results of studies on patients with chronic pain have supported the necessity for a multidisciplinary approach to their treatment and rehabilitation.[74,79]

Inherent variables such as the patient selection processes, differences in the severity of functional disabilities, the effects of previous treatment approaches, cultural factors, and the overall complex nature of the chronic pain process have resulted in some criticism of the MPQ.[74,77] However, recent studies of the results obtained with the MPQ in a population of patients with low back, dental, and cancer pain provide support for the MPQ and also discuss factors related to variance in patient responses.[80,115,127]

The manner in which a patient describes pain may provide insight into its precipitating factors. The use of intensity as the sole means of assessing the description of pain is unjustified. Intensity characterizations may be described in an effective-evaluative, as opposed to sensory, mode.[74,82,438]

The enormous complexity and resultant problems concerned with the evaluation of pain, such as the differences between experimental and clinical pain, signify the problem of gaining universal agreement.[63,83–86,93]

PAIN MEASUREMENT

The most suitable method for measuring the intensity of pain experimentally has largely consisted of studies using radiant heat or electrical stimulation, and recording the intensity of a liminal stimulus.[63,86,112] The use of stimuli beyond the threshold range brings on other reactions among the subjects that interfere with the clarity of the subjective rating.[63,86] Sternbach developed the torniquet pain test (TPT), which was adapted from the submaximal effort torniquet test developed by Smith and associates[110,111] as a means of closely relating experimental pain to clinical pain.[87–90] The use of ischemia as a means of studying pain has several disadvantages in that it first produces paresthesia, progressive sensory deprivation, and a decrease in temperature, all of which may interfere with the subjective evaluation.[86] The inherent advantages, however, are that the test is reliable, simple, and relatively easy to use without the end result being subjected to influence by the experimenter.[112] This test, which measures the time it takes for ischemic pain to match the severity or intensity of a patient's clinical pain (clinical pain level) as well as the length of

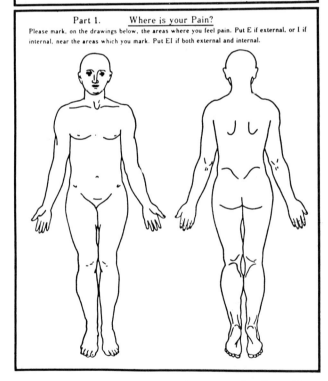

McGill-Melzack
PAIN QUESTIONNAIRE

Patient's name _____   Age _____
File No. _____   Date _____
Clinical category (eg. cardiac, neurological, etc.):

Diagnosis : _____
_____
_____

Analgesic (if already administered):
    1. Type _____
    2. Dosage _____
    3. Time given in relation to this test _____
Patient's intelligence: circle number that represents best estimate
    1 (low)   2   3   4   5(high)

★★★★★★★★★★★★★★★

This questionnaire has been designed to tell us more about your pain. Four major questions we ask are:
    1. Where is your pain?
    2. What does it feel like?
    3. How does it change with time?
    4. How strong is it?

    It is important that you tell us how your pain feels now. Please follow the instructions at the beginning of each part.

© R. Melzack, Oct. 1970

Part 1.   Where is your Pain?

Please mark, on the drawings below, the areas where you feel pain. Put E if external, or I if internal, near the areas which you mark. Put EI if both external and internal.

FIGURE 5-3. McGill-Melzack Pain Questionnaire. (From Melzack,[73] with permission.)

Part 2. What Does Your Pain Feel Like?

Some of the words below describe your present pain. Circle ONLY those words that best describe it. Leave out any category that is not suitable. Use only a single word in each appropriate category—the one that applies best.

1	2	3	4
Flickering	Jumping	Pricking	Sharp
Quivering	Flashing	Boring	Cutting
Pulsing	Shooting	Drilling	Lacerating
Throbbing		Stabbing	
Beating		Lancinating	
Pounding			

5	6	7	8
Pinching	Tugging	Hot	Tingling
Pressing	Pulling	Burning	Itchy
Gnawing	Wrenching	Scalding	Smarting
Cramping		Searing	Stinging
Crushing			

9	10	11	12
Dull	Tender	Tiring	Sickening
Sore	Taut	Exhausting	Suffocating
Hurting	Rasping		
Aching	Splitting		
Heavy			

13	14	15	16
Fearful	Punishing	Wretched	Annoying
Frightful	Gruelling	Blinding	Troublesome
Terrifying	Cruel		Miserable
	Vicious		Intense
	Killing		Unbearable

17	18	19	20
Spreading	Tight	Cool	Nagging
Radiating	Numb	Cold	Nauseating
Penetrating	Drawing	Freezing	Agonizing
Piercing	Squeezing		Dreadful
	Tearing		Torturing

Part 3. How Does Your Pain Change With Time?

1. Which word or words would you use to describe the pattern of your pain?

1	2	3
Continuous	Rhythmic	Brief
Steady	Periodic	Momentary
Constant	Intermittent	Transient

2. What kind of things relieve your pain?

3. What kind of things increase your pain?

Part 4. How Strong Is Your Pain?

People agree that the following 5 words represent pain of increasing intensity. They are:

1	2	3	4	5
Mild	Discomforting	Distressing	Horrible	Excruciating

To answer each question below, write the number of the most appropriate word in the space beside the question.

1. Which word describes your pain right now? _____
2. Which word describes it at its worst? _____
3. Which word describes it when it is least? _____
4. Which word describes the worst toothache you ever had? _____
5. Which word describes the worst headache you ever had? _____
6. Which word describes the worst stomach-ache you ever had? _____

time during which a patient can endure such pain (maximum pain tolerance), has been shown to be both reliable and valid. However, in a study using the TPT in patients with chronic pain after the injection of oral medication (placebo-aspirin, codeine, and morphine), test scores were so variable that discrimination among the different potency levels of such analgesics could not be determined by the test.[91] The subjective pain estimates by the participating patients also were not sufficient to significantly differentiate among the analgesics. Sternbach discusses the fact that this may be due to the long-standing chronic pain and previous use of narcotic medication, which could have interfered with the patients' discriminability. Studies using the same analgesics in acute states did not present similar problems.

The TPT has also been used to study the effectiveness of T.E.N.S. Results showed that T.E.N.S. is able to provide long-term pain modulation, especially in patients who have not undergone surgery. T.E.N.S. is able to decrease clinical pain levels but has only a slight effect on maximum pain tolerance.[92] Sternbach infers that this is related to the peripheral blocking effects of T.E.N.S., instead of a central effect. However, this may depend on the stimulation parameters employed. Conventional T.E.N.S. seems to have a peripheral or local segmental effect, whereas high-amplitude modes of T.E.N.S. may also produce central effects. It would be most interesting to repeat the aforementioned study using all three types of T.E.N.S. as explained in Chapters 9 and 12.

Chapter 2 discusses other factors concerning pain measurement such as cultural and emotional influences, and the lack of agreement pertaining to the measurement of pain threshold, tolerance, pain sensitivity range (difference between threshold and tolerance), and the smallest perceptible distinction between successive levels of pain called the just-noticeable difference.[84] Merskey considers pain threshold to be based more on physiologic determinants and pain tolerance to be based more on psychologic factors.[112]

Further studies on pain threshold have brought out some interesting factors distinctly related to this text. Notermans, in studies on the determination of pain threshold by electrical stimulation, found pain threshold to be relatively constant over the whole body, varying by no more than 15 to 20 percent. Measurement in milliamperes (mA) showed threshold in normal persons to always be below 1 mA, with the difference between right and left corresponding dermatomes less than 0.1 mA. Pain thresholds of more than 1 mA and/or a difference of 0.2 mA between corresponding dermatomes was considered to be pathologic. Threshold was lowest on the face and neck and highest on the sole and palm.[94] Murray and Hagan determined that the feet are less sensitive to pain than the hands, with sensitivity being greater on the left than right.[97]

A recent study has shown that hypertensive individuals have a higher than normal threshold for pain sensation, as determined by the tooth-pulp test.[440] Notermans initially determined that there was no significant difference in threshold between males and females. However, in a later study, he concluded that males can tolerate pain better than females in an experimental pain situation, but there was no significant difference in pain threshold.[95,98] Other studies have shown the cutaneous pain threshold to be significantly lower in females than in males.[86]

Notermans found no significant diurnal variation in pain threshold. There is no agreement in the literature concerning this, but other researchers, as reported by Notermans, found pain threshold to be higher in the afternoon and evening than in the morning; yet Rodgers and Vilkin found the threshold to be higher in the morning than in the early evening.[94,99] The questions pertaining to diurnal or circadian rhythm that have been shown to affect pain threshold need further study, but the existence of these fluctuations has been confirmed.[86,99,449]

Notermans also infers, on the basis of his studies, that fear and fatigue may slightly decrease the pain threshold. Cooling of the skin below 20°C produces an increase in pain threshold. Distraction of the subject or stimulation of other areas of the body can substantially increase pain threshold.[94] This has definite implications for T.E.N.S., relating to stimulation of unrelated areas.

The aging process seems to result in an increase of the skin threshold to pricking pain, as well as to thermal pain.[89,100,101] Notermans did not find such an influence.[86,96,98]

More recent experimentation based on use of the sensory decision or signal detection theory directly relates to the previous reports as well as to T.E.N.S. This theory uses sensory sensitivity (absolute sensitivity of the subject to the noxious stimulus) and response bias (the criteria used by the subject for emitting particular responses) in the determination of pain threshold by the patient.[63,100–106]

Clark found that variations in criteria for reporting pain were more important than the differences in sensitivity.[100,101] Harkins and Chapman acknowledge the previous reports on age and pain threshold performed with radiant heat tests but were unable to support them in a study of pain threshold with electrical stimulation of tooth pulp as measured by the sensory decision method. They did find elderly men to be less accurate than younger males in discriminating between two suprathreshold tooth pulp shocks.[102] In another study employing sensory decision analysis to compare the analgesic effects of acupuncture, T.E.N.S., and placebo acupuncture, the T.E.N.S. group showed a slightly greater increase in pain threshold than the acupuncture group.[103] The group that received placebo acupuncture did not show a positive response. Additional research by Chapman and coworkers in the area of dental pain threshold and evaluation by the sensory decision theory elucidated the efficacy of intrasegmental stimulation as opposed to extrasegmental stimulation.[104] An in-depth review of segmental versus extrasegmental stimulation as related to T.E.N.S. can be found in Chapter 7.

Rollman reviewed the sensory decision or detection theory and concluded that it measures discrimination instead of pain. Chapman has defended the use of the theory as one reliable method but not the final solution to the problem of the measurement of pain.[105–107]

Considering all the confusing and varied results obtained from pain measurement experiments, one factor—the subjective nature of pain—stands out. Apart from verbal scales of measurement, other means of determining the intensity of one's discomfort and assessing the effects of pain modulation via T.E.N.S. or other modalities thus exist.

Perhaps the simplest approach is merely asking the patient to grade the pain at the present moment on a scale of 0 to 10 or 0 to 100, the former scale being generally well accepted.[84,438] Various other rating scales exist, such as those that require the patient to match the degree or intensity of the pain to sound, colors, or previous painful experiences.[84,112]

Merskey is of the opinion that the estimation of the degree to which a patient winces, jumps, or objects is unsatisfactory.[112] However, we have needed to use observations of behavioral and affective responses such as facial expressions or changes in personality to analyze the effects of T.E.N.S. in a few senile or aphasic patients. In such cases, it is recommended that the clinician ensure the presence of a family member who is familiar with the patient's actions and responses while in pain and when pain-free, in order to make any valid assessment at all. Change or improvement in range of motion, ambulatory ability, pulse rate, and respiratory rate has also been used by the authors to assess the effectiveness of T.E.N.S. A log of daily activity (sitting, walking, and reclining) can also be helpful.[113] Figure 5-4 highlights pertinent factors in the measurement of pain.

PAIN MEASUREMENT

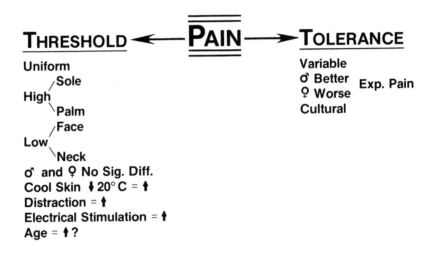

THRESHOLD — Perception Point 〉 Physiologic Sensitivity Range
TOLERANCE — End Point   Psychologic

LOW INTENSITY 〉 Smallest Degree — Just Noticeable
HIGH INTENSITY   of Discrimination   Difference

THRESHOLD ←— **PAIN** —→ TOLERANCE

Uniform   Variable
  /Sole   ♂ Better   Exp. Pain
High   ♀ Worse
  \Palm   Cultural
  /Face
Low
  \Neck
♂ and ♀ No Sig. Diff.
Cool Skin ↕ 20° C = ↑
Distraction = ↑
Electrical Stimulation = ↑
Age = ↑ ?

RATING SCALES

SUBJECTIVE   TPT   **OBJECTIVE**

Numerical   Facial Expression
Simple Description   ROM
Visual Analog   Function
Color   Personality
Previous Exp.
  (Sensory Matching)

FIGURE 5-4. A summary of the results obtained from experimental studies of the measurement of pain. *Note:* Experimental pain may differ from clinical pain.

LOCATION

The successful use of T.E.N.S. obviously depends on the definitive location of the patient's pain, which is not a simple matter when dealing with referred or radiating pain. An essential part of the clarifying evaluation is to have the patient outline or color the exact area of pain on views of the body (anterior, posterior, and lateral). Instructing the patient to make an X on areas of extreme sensitivity or where pressure increases or decreases pain is very beneficial since the patient may indicate areas such as trigger points that can be used for specific treatments or pain modulation. Having the patient place one finger instead of the whole hand on the exact area of pain is helpful in differentiating between superficial and deep pain. Superficial pain is easy to localize, while the pain from deep somatic or visceral structures is more difficult to pinpoint.[8,30,63,68]

The location of the pain at the time of the initial evaluation should be compared with that which existed at the onset of the problem. A change in location may be indicative of progression or regression of the pathology. Low back pain initially present in the lumbosacral region that has referred down the sciatic distribution of one leg indicates a progressing lesion. The reverse process would indicate a decreasing lesion. Pain that initially is perceived in the loin, moving to the iliac fossa and then genitals, may be indicative of a renal calculus.[28]

What effect does a change in position have on the pain? Visceral pain is unchanged by movement, but musculoskeletal pain changes. Can the pain be eliminated or intensified by changes in posture? A positive response signifies that the etiology is probably mechanical. The distribution of pain will increase as the lesion worsens.[28]

Studies concerning the lateralization of pain found that most patients experience pain on the left side of the body as compared with the right, except in trigeminal neuralgia.[81,114] An excellent paper concerned with referred pain of cardiac origin showed a predominance of trigger points sensitive to pressure and pain on the left side of the body.[142] The phenomenon of lateralization of pain exists both in physical and psychosomatic conditions. The explanation provided by Merskey and Watson[114] is that the right hemisphere may be less efficient in the integration and discrimination of sensory input but dominant for emotional expressions. Lower thresholds in the nondominant side of the body (obviously left more often than right) may also play a role in the lateralization of pain. Hall and associates tested Merskey and Watson's hypothesis in 264 patients and found that pain occurred with equal frequency on the right and left sides of the body.[452] Their results may be due to differences in patient population and testing procedures.

It is important to delineate the location of pain when patients state that pain is in the hip, back, kidney region, or sacroiliac area. Many patients may state that the pain is in the hip but point to the sacrum. Pain located at the posterior-superior iliac spine (unilaterally) as opposed to the lumbar spine may indicate sacroiliac joint dysfunction, not lumbar spine pathology. This is again best determined by having the patient use one finger instead of the whole hand to pinpoint the pain.

It is not uncommon for the patient to relate "sciatica"—a symptom, not a causative lesion—to any pain distribution in the lower extremities. We have had patients referred for T.E.N.S. with "sciatic pain" who actually had a femoral or lateral femoral cutaneous nerve pain distribution. Low back and sciatic pain can be caused by numerous etiologic factors, which will be discussed later in this chapter.

The shoulder is another area where the location of the perceived pain is frequently misleading. An attempt should be made to differentiate whether the pain is in the anterior, posterior, lateral, or superior aspects, as well as the scapula, since each may relate to involvement of different structures (somatic or visceral). Pain arising from an acute subdeltoid bursitis or supraspinatus tendinitis cannot be differentiated solely by the location of pain at the lateral aspect of the shoulder, as shown by the patient. Active, passive, and resistive movement testing, outlined by Cyriax, can easily confirm the diagnosis.[28] When pain is referred to an extremity, its pathway must be determined. Does the distribution relate to the course of a particular peripheral nerve, root, trigger point pattern, acupuncture meridian, dermatome, myotome, or sclerotome? Is the distribution segmental or extrasegmental? When pain or paresthesia is perceived in the hand, it is important to determine which fingers are involved. Root irritation resulting in paresthesia is an indicator of the involved segment only at the distal extent of the dermatome.[70]

Pain is not always perceived at its point of origin. The only way to determine the location of the pain and the structure from which it is arising is to have a thorough knowledge of all the misleading and confusing facts concerning pain. Expertise must be developed to differentiate structure from structure and to perform evaluative techniques that aim to reproduce, increase, and/or decrease the *exact* pain that each individual is experiencing.

Information relative to the difference between the dermatome, myotome, and sclerotome is important when discussing the location of pain. We have already alluded to the fact that the relationship among the dermatome, myotome, and sclerotome is not totally uniform. Illustrations and extensive research concerning this relationship as it pertains to electrode placement are presented in Chapter 8.

The segmental relationship of the body is generally thought of in terms of the dermatomal map and primarily relates to superficial structures such as the skin. Visceral pain referral is also delineated via dermatomes, partly because of sparse innervation and the dominance of skin perception. Pain referral from viscera travels along the general visceral afferents (see Chapter 8) into the dorsal horn of the spinal cord where various physiologic interchanges occur, resulting in referral. This has been termed the dermatomal rule and will be discussed later in greater detail.[62]

Pain patterns that previously could not be explained via dermatomal distribution, especially those originating from spinal injury, may indeed follow a sclerotomal pattern.[70] The irritation of dorsal root fibers can cause pain referral to the innervated periosteum.[55] Other deep somatic structures refer pain along a myotomal or sclerotomal distribution. Considerable overlap of referred pain was found with the injection of saline solution into the facet joints of the upper and lower lumbar spine. This was considered to be against the existence of sclerotomes.[140] The myotome and sclerotome correspond better with each other than with the dermatome. Thus, the referral of pain arising from muscle closely resembles that of other deep somatic structures. Trigger point referral patterns previously related to the dermatome map may be better explained via the myotomal distribution.

Sclerotomal pain may radiate proximal or distal from its origin. It is not infrequent to see infragluteal pain associated with irritation of the L4 and L5 nerve roots.[35] Pain referral from sacroiliac joint pathology may be perceived in the lumbar spine, sciatic nerve distribution, groin, and anterior thigh.[178] When pain syndromes involve the autonomic nervous system, the resultant pain distribution is diffuse and poorly localized.[8,30] Reflex sympathetic dystrophy (shoulder-hand syndrome) may involve all the major peripheral nerves of the upper extremity. The term sympathetic dermatome has been employed to define the cutaneous segmental distribution of sympathetic nerves. There is little correspondence between sympathetic and somatic dermatomes, the former being quite irregular and asymmetric.[126]

The extensive overlapping of dermatomal segments, differences in segmentation based on experimental variables, and the knowledge that deep somatic structures refer pain differently from superficial and visceral structures point to the futility of using the dermatomes as the sole means of determining the origin of pain (see Chapter 8).

MODIFYING FACTORS

Pain can be increased or decreased by factors such as food, medication, posture, movement, activity, rest, friction, coughing, sneezing, straining, and pressure.[8,64] The effects of some of these factors have been previously discussed. The others that should be considered as part of the evaluative process will be highlighted.

The ingestion of certain foods with a high fat content may cause the gallbladder to release bile, resulting in referral of pain to the tip of the shoulder or scapula region, as in cholecystitis.[8,64] Migraine headaches may be triggered by eating foods that contain a high concentration of monosodium glutamate or tyramine.[8,118,119] Pain from a duodenal ulcer may be relieved by the ingestion of milk or alkaline medicine.[8,64] The effects of medication in relieving pain are well known, but the side effects, mixing of drugs, and, of course, addiction can result in increased pain or accidental death.[120-124]

The actions of narcotics are not localized to one specific site. They can produce constipation as a result of decreased gastrointestinal motility, depress the respiratory center, cause nausea and vomiting, cause difficulty in urination (increased tone or spasm of urinary sphincter muscle), and result in some degree of cutaneous vasodilation, pruritus, and sweating.[120] The chronic use of aspirin in high dosages for a period of time may cause epigastric distress, tinnitus, headache, sweating, tachycardia, and tachypnea.[121] One or more of these side effects may serve to mask the actual symptomatology of a pain syndrome, produce confusing or false signs, and, of course, alter the effectiveness of T.E.N.S. as well as other therapy. The use of small doses of barbiturates, such as secobarbital, pentobarbital, and phenobarbital, for sedation may serve to increase pain (cause hyperalgesia) rather than promote relaxation or sleep in musculoskeletal pain syndromes.[441] Barbiturates decrease the normal inhibitory action of higher centers. The descending reticulospinal pathways to the dorsal horn are affected and may result in an increase in the severity of the pain.[32]

Small amounts of alcohol and caffeine and the use of drugs, such as benzedrine, marijuana, and lysergic acid diethylamide, enhance cortical action. The net result is stimulation of the reticular system, which increases awareness of all sensation, emotions, and pain.[32] Cortical activation can be decreased and pain diminished by the practice of relaxation and biogenic techniques, sleep, and large amounts of alcohol and drugs, such as meperidine.[1,32] Tricyclic antidepressants (amitriptyline) enhance brain serotonin, which has been shown to promote sleep, increase the pain threshold, and decrease depression and anxiety without being habituating.[260,441] Tryptophan, a serotonin precursor, is also very helpful.[260] Drugs of this nature are most beneficial to the pain patient, whereas diazepam and lorazepam inhibit serotonin activity.

Posture and activities of daily living are very important factors in relation to pain. The effect of changes in posture on pain may help to delineate the etiology as being one of mechanical origin. Changes in posture from physiologic to unphysiologic can result in abnormal forces exerted upon joints, viscera, blood vessels, and nerves.[30] Headaches, tinnitus, and vertigo can result from a forward position of the head, accentuating the cervical lordosis and tightening the small suboccipital musculature. Afferent impulses that help to regulate positions of the head in space come from the dorsal roots of C1–3, originating in part from the musculature and ligaments of the cervical vertebral joints, primarily the occipitoatlantal joint.[30] An accentuated cervical lordosis decreases the foraminal opening and may precipitate radiculopathy and degenerative spondylosis.[17] The occipital nerves originate from the upper cervical spine. Irritation of these nerves by foraminal narrowing as a result of postural abnormalities (forward head) can result in occipital headaches.[6,17,19,28,30,45] Pain syndromes of the shoulder-girdle complex and cervicothoracic junction can arise from postural faults resulting in round shoulders, upper thoracic kyphosis, alar scapulae, and so forth. In turn, round shoulders and an increased thoracic kyphosis can result in a loss of active range of motion (ROM) and increase the possibility of supraspinatus tendon entrapment under the acromion.[17] The performance of postural maneuvers, resulting in an increase or decrease of pressure on the subclavian artery and lower trunk of the brachial plexus, can aid in the determination of neurovascular compression syndromes such as cervical rib, scalenus anticus, and thoracic outlet.

The thoracic and lumbar spine should be observed closely for scoliosis, increased thoracic kyphosis, flat thoracic spine, increased or decreased lumbar lordosis, and pelvic symmetry. It is always wise to check for a leg length discrepancy, which can either be a precipitory factor or occur as a result of sacroiliac joint dysfunction.[448] The patient should be questioned about sleeping posture, size and number of pillows, firmness of the mattress, and method of getting in and out of bed. Pain syndromes can also result from faulty posture when sitting (home, work, or driving), standing, lifting, bending, and exercising.

Lumbar intradiskal pressure is greatest while bending forward in the sitting position and least when sitting erect with maintenance of the normal lumbar lordosis.[17,125] The type of shoes and resiliency of the heelcord may increase or decrease the lumbar lordosis. High heels cause hip and knee flexion and increase the lordosis, whereas an elongated heelcord will decrease the lordosis.[5,116] Posture may also be indicative of specific pathology. In a patient with acute low back pain, standing or sitting with a lateral shift toward the side of pain may be indicative of a disk protrusion medial to the nerve root.[51] Sacroiliac joint involvement may be suspected in a patient who stands with the weight on one leg and the opposite knee flexed.

A complete evaluation must include the effects of movement and activity upon pain. With information provided by the patient as to the movements or positions that aggravate or alleviate particular pain, the clinician should try to reproduce the same effects. If such information is unobtainable, it must be determined whether or not pain is arising from an inert, movable, or contractile structure. Pain that arises in a moving part should be reproducible by a particular movement or posture. If pain is reported as being constant, determine if any movement will alter it. Constant pain unaffected by anything at any time may signify severe pathology such as a neoplasm or visceral involvement.[30,438] There is usually some constant background soreness in post-herpetic neuralgia.[8]

An excellent scientific and systematic method for the examination of the neuromusculoskeletal system has been developed by Dr. James Cyriax. A major portion of the information that follows stems from his text and various postgraduate seminars.[28]

The assessment of the active range of a particular joint or section of the spine provides information relative to the ability and willingness of the patient to move the structure. Active movements of a joint may produce a painful arc, indicating pinching of a sensitive structure, such as an inflamed subdeltoid bursa between the acromion and humeral head. Active movements of the spine may produce pain as a result of stretching or compression. Low back pain brought on by bending forward after a short delay may indicate ligamental involvement as well as hypermobility. Immediate stretch pain may result from adhesions and can cause hypermobility.[30]

A capsular pattern may also be evident on assessment of the active ROM of a joint. Capsular patterns occurring only at joints controlled by muscles indicate the presence of some type of arthritis. The sacroiliac, acromioclavicular, and sternoclavicular joints are not controlled by muscles; thus pain occurring only at the extreme end range may indicate their involvement. The capsular pattern of each joint and section of the spine differs. Specific aspects of synovial lining and joint capsule resist stretch to different degrees in varied directions depending upon the involved joint. Ligamental adhesions, internal derangement, or extra-articular lesions are suspected when a joint does not exhibit a capsular pattern. There may be a large loss of range in one direction, as seen with abduction in acute subdeltoid bursitis.

Passive ROM is used to test the inert structures. Experience is a necessity in this test to determine the end feel. A springy block may indicate internal derangement as occurs with a torn meniscus at the knee. A vibrant twang at end range may indicate an acute or subacute arthritis, whereas a hard restriction with some resiliency prior to full range is indicative of nonacute arthritis. If considerable discomfort occurs before end range and there is no block or resistance to further movement, an acute bursitis, extra-articular abscess, or neoplasm may be present. This is characterized as having an empty end feel. It is imperative to compare passive ROM with active ROM to confirm the existence of a capsular or noncapsular pattern. Pain produced in the same direction by both active and passive movement near end range along with painless resisted movements is indicative of involvement of an inert structure. If both passive and active movements produce pain in opposite directions, the involved structure is contractile (muscle or tendon).

Resistive testing must be performed isometrically in midrange of motion to relax the inert structure. Resistive testing provides information relative to pain and strength of the contractile tissues. A tendinitis is indicated when the muscle is strong but pain to resistance occurs in one direction only with full passive ROM present. However, passive ROM may become limited in the presence of a long-standing tendinitis that was either not treated or treated improperly. The classic example is the patient with chronic shoulder pain who received no treatment other than heat and developed adhesive capsulitis. Tendinitis can also be present simultaneously in two tendons acting on one joint. This results in two motions that exhibit pain to resisted movement.

A muscle that is weak yet does not produce pain with resistance is indicative of a muscle or tendon rupture or neurologic involvement. Serious pathology, such as a fracture, may exist if testing indicates a muscle that is weak as well as painful. When all resistive movements prove to be painful, there is usually an emotional overlay. Intermittent claudication is suspected when repeated testing, although initially strong and painless, begins to hurt. Movement testing should be performed bilaterally and the related spinal segments evaluated prior to extremity assessment.

During the performance of movement testing various auditory signs such as snaps, cracks, clicks, pops, grating, and grinding may occur. These are frequently painless but may relate to the presence of a loose body, chondromalacia of the patella, various forms of arthritis, the snapping of a tendon, and so forth.[5]

The assessment of neurologic involvement should include resistive testing of at least one major muscle primarily innervated by each spinal cord segment. There are, however, no muscles that are innervated solely by one nerve root because of the high degree of segmental overlap.[25,55] The performance of such a quick scan of the myotomes may provide initial insight into the existence of a neurologic problem. If a particular muscle related to the C6 spinal cord segment tests weak, its strength should obviously be compared with that of the opposite side, and musculature of the adjacent segments must be retested. Unilateral weakness involving all muscles primarily innervated by one nerve root as well as those innervated by adjacent spinal cord segments may signify a nerve root compression syndrome or plexus lesion, respectively. The presence of muscle atrophy should be checked and then determined if the atrophy is due merely to disuse or to actual neurologic involvement. The possibility of a malignancy should also be suspected. In differentiating between a disk lesion and malignancy, several additional factors become evident. Pain is usually unilateral and more intense, and involves one root; and strength of the related myotome is somewhat diminished in disk involvement. In the presence of a malignant process, pain may not be as severe but weakness is more pronounced, usually involving two to three segments, and frequently is bilateral.[28] Neoplastic syndromes result in constant pain that is worse at night and unrelieved by rest but may be somewhat relieved by activity.[30] Pain that occurs at night may imply the presence of a bone tumor, an early sign of ankylosing spondylitis, or spinal cord tumor.[5] The entrapment and neurovascular compression syndromes produce night pain that frequently awakens the patient.[5,6,28,30] An increase in intra-abdominal pressure via coughing, sneezing, straining, and to some degree taking a deep breath or laughing can result in dura mater irritation with secondary extremity pain. Intervertebral disk prolapse, displaced vertebral fractures, or intraspinal tumor can irritate the sinuvertebral nerve or dorsal nerve roots, causing partial distention of the epidural veins. The addition of venous pressure from coughing to the already distended blood vessels can cause a further increase in back or leg pain.[32] A positive response from the patient when inquiring about these bodily functions can steer the clinician to the possibility of intervertebral disk pathology or involvement of the sacroiliac joints. Distraction of the sacroiliac joints can occur from coughing, sneezing, and so forth.[28]

Tables 5-7 and 5-8 present the muscles that are most commonly employed for a quick bilateral myotome scan utilizing strong isometric resistance. Further neurologic testing, such as reflex, sensation, nerve root stretch, peripheral nerve signs, and upper motor neuron involvement as well as the results of electromyography, blood tests, and x-rays must be adapted to the individual syndrome.

It is, however, beyond the scope of this text to cover all the facets of an extensive neurologic evaluation. Guidelines have been presented that should be sufficient to perform a comprehensive evaluation. Pain, however, is a multidimensional experience and often presents a confusing picture for the clinician. Therefore, we will summarize various sections, discuss others in more detail, and cover some of the common pain syndromes in which T.E.N.S. is adjunctively used.

TABLE 5-7. Muscles to Test for a Quick Scan of the Cervical Myotomes*

Cord Segment	Muscle	Innervation	Action
C1	Rectus Capitis Anterior . . . . Longus Capitis	Anterior Primary Rami	Tuck chin in
C2	Rectus Capitis Posterior Major & Minor. . . . . Obliquus Capitis Superior	Posterior Primary Rami	Push chin up
	Masticators	Spinal Trigeminal.	Jaw motion
C3	Scaleni (all).	Anterior Primary Rami	Press head lateral
	Erector Spinae	Posterior Primary Rami	Press head posterior
C4	Levator Scapulae	Branches C3 & C4.	Elevate shoulder
	Trapezius.	Spinal Accessory	girdle
C5	Deltoid.	Axillary (C5, C6)	Abduct arm
C6	Biceps	Musculocutaneous (C5, C6)	Flex elbow
	Extensor Carpi Radialis Longus & Brevis.	Radial (C6)	Extend wrist
C7	Triceps.	Radial (C7)	Extend elbow
	Flexor Carpi Radialis	Median (C7)	Flex wrist
C8	Extensor Pollicis Longus and Brevis.	Radial (C7)	Extend thumb
	Flexor Digitorum Profundus . . . . . . and Superficialis	Median (C7, C8, T1).	Flex fingers
		Ulnar (C8, T1).	Flex fingers
T1	Intrinsics	Ulnar (C8, T1).	Abduct & adduct fingers

*From HUNT, J (ED): *Fundamentals of Manual Therapy: A Course Workbook.* Sorlandets, Fysikalske Institutt, Yagsbyd, Norway, 1980, with permission.

TABLE 5-8. Muscles to Test for a Quick Scan of the Lumbar Myotomes*

Cord Segment	Muscle	Innervation	Action
L2	Iliopsoas	Femoral (L1,L2,L3)	Flex hip
L3	Quadriceps	Femoral (L2,L3,L4)	Extend knee
L4	Tibialis anterior	Deep peroneal (L4)	Dorsiflex and invert foot
L5	Tibialis posterior	Tibial (L5)	Plantarflex and invert foot
	Extensor Hallucis longus . . . . Extensor Digitorum longus and brevis	Deep peroneal (L5)	Extend toes
S1	Peroneus longus and brevis	Superior peroneal (S1)	Evert foot
	Hamstrings	Sciatic (L5,S1)	Flex knee
S2	Gastrocnemius . . . . Soleus	Tibial (S1,S2)	Tip toe
S3–4	Somatic—Bladder and genital functions		
S2–3–4	Parasympathetic— Bladder and genital functions		

*From HUNT, J (ED): *Fundamentals of Manual Therapy: A Course Workbook*. Sorlandets, Fysikalske Institutt, Yagsbyd, Norway, 1980, with permission.

SUPERFICIAL VERSUS DEEP PAIN

The initial physiologic assessment of pain concerns delineating its characteristics. Pain can first be classified as to its superficial or deep nature. Such a classification also incorporates terminology such as fast and slow pain, first and second pain, and epicritic and protopathic pain (see Chapter 4).[7–9,30,39,62,63,107,129,130,136,138,436]

Superficial pain is considered to represent a sensation such as pricking that is sharp and well localized, occurs almost instantaneously after the irritating stimulus, and is perceived at its point of origin (little if any referral).[7–9,30,39,62,63,107] The patient should be able to pinpoint pain of superficial origin with one finger. Superficial pain is basically synonymous with cutaneous pain, mediated primarily by myelinated A-delta fibers through the rapidly conducting lateral ascending system in the CNS (see Chapter 4). Furthermore, because of its rapid transmission, superficial pain is considered to be the first pain resulting from a stimulus capable of initiating a nociceptive impulse and serves as a biologic warning system indicative of the extent and location of the injury.[107] Such a biologic warning system is considered to be poor since pain may occur after the acute injury.[2]

Analogous with superficial pain are brief irritants such as sharp objects, bee stings, pinching, pulling of hair, heat, or electricity, which can later give rise to deep or second pain if prolonged.[62] Various tissue structures give rise to superficial pain (skin, superficial ligaments, fascia, tendon sheaths, and periosteum). There may be a secondary loss of strength from disuse as a result of tendinitis or development of hyperalgesia in pathologic states such as post-herpetic neuralgia.

Deep pain is a sensation characterized as being dull, achy, diffuse, hard to localize, and frequently perceived away from its point of origin. The patient will tend to use the whole hand rather than one finger to localize the pain. It is necessary at this juncture to differentiate between deep pain of visceral origin and of somatic origin. Characteristics of deep visceral and deep somatic pain are the same, but these types of pain may be differentiated by their referral patterns. Deep visceral pain will refer pain in a dermatomal distribution embryologically related to the involved organ.[6,8,28,32,61,62,64,66,68–70,116,126] Deep somatic pain will be referred in a myotomal or sclerotomal pattern.[6–8,11,12,14–16,28,32] The referred pain from viscera is generally considered harder to localize than that originating from deep somatic structures (see Table 5-3 and Fig. 5-5).

Deep pain is analogous to second pain, as it is transmitted primarily by nonmyelinated C fibers through the slower-conducting medial ascending system in the CNS (Table 5-9). Deep, or second, pain continuously propagated as in myofascial and visceral syndromes

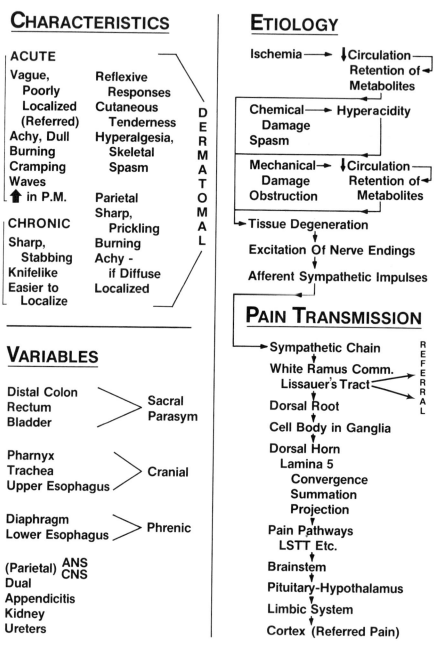

CHARACTERISTICS

ACUTE

Vague,	Reflexive
Poorly	Responses
Localized	Cutaneous
(Referred)	Tenderness
Achy, Dull	Hyperalgesia,
Burning	Skeletal
Cramping	Spasm
Waves	
↑ in P.M.	Parietal
	Sharp,

CHRONIC

	Prickling
Sharp,	Burning
Stabbing	Achy -
Knifelike	if Diffuse
Easier to	Localized
Localize	

D E R M A T O M A L

VARIABLES

Distal Colon
Rectum   Sacral
Bladder   Parasym

Pharnyx
Trachea   Cranial
Upper Esophagus

Diaphragm
Lower Esophagus Phrenic

(Parietal) ANS
Dual   CNS
Appendicitis
Kidney
Ureters

ETIOLOGY

Ischemia → ↓Circulation
            Retention of
            Metabolites

Chemical → Hyperacidity
Damage
Spasm

Mechanical → ↓Circulation
Damage   Retention of
Obstruction   Metabolites

→ Tissue Degeneration
↓
Excitation Of Nerve Endings
↓
Afferent Sympathetic Impulses

PAIN TRANSMISSION

→ Sympathetic Chain
↓
White Ramus Comm.
Lissauer's Tract ⇄
↓
Dorsal Root
↓
Cell Body in Ganglia
↓
Dorsal Horn
Lamina 5
Convergence
Summation
Projection
Pain Pathways
LSTT Etc.
↓
Brainstem
↓
Pituitary-Hypothalamus
↓
Limbic System
↓
Cortex (Referred Pain)

R E F E R R A L

FIGURE 5-5. The characteristics and mechanisms of visceral pain.

TABLE 5-9. Ascending Pain Transmission Systems

Superficial Pain	Deep Pain
Exteroreceptors	Interoreceptors
A-delta fibers (CNS)	B and C fibers (ANS and CNS)
Fast conduction via late-developing pathways (neospinothalamic)	Slow conduction via early pathways (paleospinothalamic)
Lateral ascending system	Medial ascending system
Postsynaptic dorsal column	Diffuse polysynaptic propriospinal system
Spinocervical tract	
Few synapses (3)	Spinoreticular system (diffuse limbic and reticular connections)
Projects to lateral thalamic nuclei and localized by SSC	Numerous synapses
	Projects to midline
	Intrathalamic regions
	Also conveys psychologic and motivational aspects of pain

serves as a reminding system to the brain.[107] Deep pain may exist concomitantly with segmental reflex changes (sudomotor, visceromotor, viscerocutaneous). A loss of strength, reflexes, or sensation rarely occurs with deep visceral pain, except in malignancy of the spinal cord or other CNS involvement and in pathology of peripheral nerves such as diabetic neuropathy.

The various deep somatic structures—periosteum, ligaments, joint capsules, tendons, fascia, and muscle—demonstrate increasing threshold to noxious stimuli[12] (see Table 5-3). This is also seen in visceral structures where parietal serous membranes have a low threshold and parenchymatous organs a high threshold. The walls of hollow viscera have a moderate threshold to noxious stimuli.

The terms protopathic and epicritic were originated by Head, Rivers, and Sherren in 1905 in the study of nerve regeneration.[7,9,30,63,129] Protopathic sensibility referred to the initial phase of returning sensation that was unpleasant, diffuse, and hard to localize, and was considered to represent crude sensation. This is related to the fact that regeneration of unmyelinated and thin myelinated fibers occurs first. The last stage of nerve regeneration results in the return of two-point discrimination, light touch, and temperature distinction as well as improved localization of sensory stimuli indicative of the large myelinated fibers. Thus, protopathic and epicritic sensations refer to deep and superficial pain, respectively. Normal sensation cannot be apparent without both small- and large-fiber innervation.

Superficial pain mediated by large myelinated fibers and deep pain mediated by small fibers have different implications for modulation via T.E.N.S. The response characteristics of the afferent nerve fibers relate to their size. The threshold of activation is inversely proportional to the diameter of the fiber. Therefore, large myelinated fibers are excitable at a low threshold (intensity or amplitude of electrical stimulation), and small myelinated plus unmyelinated fibers require stronger stimuli for excitation. Some of the small myelinated A-delta fibers will not be activated until frank tissue damage occurs, and C fibers originating from smooth skin have very high-pressure thresholds.[131] Large myelinated fibers have large internal cores of axoplasm that allow for more efficient transport of the internal current through the nerve membrane and along its axon, thereby allowing for a lower threshold of excitation and higher conduction velocity.[131] Therefore, conduction velocity is directly proportional to the diameter of the fiber.[135]

The application of electricity transcutaneously initially activates the large myelinated fibers, resulting in a mild tingling sensation often described as pins and needles. As current intensity is increased, greater numbers of small fibers are excited, and the sensation becomes one of sharp burning or pricking to intense pain.[131-133] The recruitment of A-delta fibers is necessary for the experience of sharp pain. Repetitive stimulation of C fibers produces poorly localized, unbearable pain after a 2- to 4-second latency period.[132,136] Thus, second pain demonstrates the process of summation. The intensity and duration of second pain increase if intense electrical stimulation of C fibers is given at a frequency greater than one every 3 seconds.[132,133,138] A decrease in first pain, however, occurs with increasing frequency of stimulation, possibly indicative of accommodation.[138]

Myelinated A-delta fibers have punctate receptive fields.[129] They may thus play a role in the localization of a pinprick type of pain. Unmyelinated C fibers have larger and overlapping receptive fields and may be unable to adequately conduct information concerning the location of a stimulus to the cortex.[9,132,136] In addition, the different ascending pathways (see Chapter 3) also influence localization of sensation. The lateral ascending (neospinothalamic) system basically consists of only three synapses (dorsal horn, lateral thalamic nuclei, and somatosensory cortex).[151] In comparison, the medial ascending (paleospinothalamic) system has diffuse connections in the hindbrain and thalamus, particularly throughout the limbic and reticular systems.[151] Thus, C fibers convey nociceptive information that is effectively dampened by convergent and divergent synapses in the thalamus. They are subject to summation mechanisms in the dorsal horn, which can result in a more intense sensation and the perception of a larger area of pain.[107] C fibers also play a role in the emotional aspect of pain.[8] Therefore, other factors besides the depth of the structure determine the ability to localize superficial and deep pain.

Generally, it can be stated that various forms of counterirritation, which include T.E.N.S., are effective modalities in the modulation of superficial pain. Conventional T.E.N.S., which selectively activates the large myelinated A fibers (see Chapter 6), is the method of choice. Deep pain, however, responds best to the administration of opiates and strong, low-rate T.E.N.S. Strong, low-rate (acupuncture-like) T.E.N.S. activates all sizes of nerve fibers but is specifically designed to excite C fibers, as does high-amplitude pulse-train or burst T.E.N.S. (see Chapters 3 and 6).

Itching, as well as the sensation of tickling, is considered to be derived from a specific combination of the four primary sensations of the skin (touch, pain, heat, and cold),[129] is closely associated with pain, and may occur at a point between the waxing and waning of pain in the inflammation process or as an after-action.[8,62] Itching disappears completely in the presence of analgesia but not in cases of touch anesthesia.[62] Itching is believed to be mediated by C fibers and as a result is easily modulated by large A-fiber activation from rubbing or scratching.[8,62,129,444] Histamine is implicated as the causative agent of itching. Its release stimulates related sensory receptors, causing the itching sensation.[62] T.E.N.S. has been shown to be very effective in relieving itching from various disorders with short periods of stimulation (1 to 2 minutes), 0.2-msec pulse duration, a frequency of 60 Hz, and an intensity just below pain threshold, although some patients required only subliminal stimulation. These parameters are consistent with those needed to selectively stimulate the large-diameter A fibers.[137]

REFERRED VERSUS RADIATING PAIN

The terms referred pain and radiating pain have been used interchangeably throughout the literature. Many clinicians and researchers consider both words to mean the same thing. In our opinion, a definite distinction exists between referred and radiating pain.

Cyriax considers referred pain to be an error in perception. He believes that referred and radiating (root) pain are the same entity but states that referred pain does not necessarily follow a peripheral nerve distribution.[28] Zohn and Mennell basically agree with Cyriax, differentiating radiating pain as related to nerve involvement and referred pain as a pattern arising from irritable trigger points.[5] In an excellent study of dorsal root ganglia, Howe, Loeser, and Calvin reported that radicular pain can result from activation of nerve fibers appropriate to the region of pain and need not be a referred phenomenon. They also support the notion that referred extremity pain can occur from stimulation of paraspinal, intra-spinal, and visceral structures separate from the nerve root.[139] Fisk differentiates referred and nerve root pain according to quality.[45] He considers referred pain to be deep, poorly defined, and patchy in distribution. Localization by the patient is with the hand rather than a finger. Root pain has a sharper quality and greater intensity, and spreads down an extremity along the course of the related nerve in an unbroken fashion, possibly associated with paresthesia. Root pain is able to be localized by the fingers. Fisk infers that root pain is synonymous with radiating pain.

These distinctions are not common throughout the literature. Therefore, the concepts of referred and radiating pain need to be clarified, which can best be done by using a definition proposed by Cyriax that *referred pain is any pain felt elsewhere than at its true site.*[28] This definition eliminates the need to use the term radiating pain. Two mechanisms of referred pain can occur. Direct irritation of a structure such as a nerve root can result in pain referral along its peripheral distribution. A second mechanism involves the processes of summation and convergent and divergent afferent influences on common interneurons in the dorsal horn, resulting in an indirect referral of pain. Both mechanisms of pain referral can ultimately lead to segmental or extrasegmental pain distribution perceived in related dermatomal, myotomal, or sclerotomal segments. In the former instance, direct irritation can occur in a structure such as the dura mater, which has been known to result in extrasegmental pain referral. In the latter instance, various forms of irritation (mechanical, chemical, and so forth) can result in continuous abnormal or nociceptive input to a related spinal cord segment, producing a spread of input along pathways such as Lissauer's tract to other segments.

It should now be apparent that the location of referred pain can provide misleading information as to the origin of the pathology unless the whole pattern of objective and subjective findings is considered. Furthermore, referred pain may be superficial, as in the burning pain of causalgia, and also may be a deep ache or tenderness when referred from visceral or deep somatic structures. Associated ANS involvement is also not uncommon.

A few important concepts concerning physiology and anatomy must be presented prior to a discussion of the spinal cord mechanism of referred pain. A review of the laminar structure of the dorsal horn, as discussed in Chapter 3, and the anatomic relationship between the ANS and CNS, as discussed in Chapter 8, is imperative. All sensory input arrives at the dorsal horn by the way of afferent nerve fibers that make synaptic connections with neurons in various dorsal horn layers.[3,4,50,57–59,131,136,141,147–152] There are two classes of dorsal horn neurons that respond optimally to nociceptive input from the skin—high-threshold and wide dynamic-range neurons.[147–152] The latter neurons also receive a convergent input from deep somatic (muscle) and visceral afferents.[7,31,39,147–152,160]

Early theories of referred pain suggested that such interactions among visceral and cutaneous structures must occur, but it was not known exactly where and how this took place. Two theories of referred pain remain prominent—the convergence-facilitation theory of MacKenzie and the convergence-projection theory of Ruch.[7–8,62,68,129,142–146]

MacKenzie's theory was based on the development of facilitation or excitation of the normal skin afferent input by the addition of visceral afferent input arriving into the same spinal cord segment. Appenzeller states that the awareness of visceral pain can be facili-tated by afferent impulses from the skin that enter the dorsal horn at the same segment simultaneously with input from a viscus.[126] This would create what was termed an "irritable focus," or high region of activity. It has been shown that such summation or facilitation does indeed occur but does not necessarily result in referred pain but can cause segmental hyperalgesia and viscerosomatic reflexes.[126] This has been explained in detail and shown experimentally by Livingston, Denslow, and Korr.[129,153,154]

The convergence-projection theory presents a clear explanation of the referral process.[450,451] The convergent mechanism, as outlined previously, is further hypothesized to indicate that such convergence occurs not only in the same segment of the spinal cord but also on some of the same interneurons, resulting in a projection of visceral pain to the related dermatome. Based on past experience during one's lifetime, the brain learns to recognize cutaneous stimuli easily since they are constantly occurring.[145,146] Visceral stimuli are basically unlearned because intense irritation of visceral structures must occur to stimulate the sparsely innervated organs before a perceptible threshold is obtained. The visceral threshold to noxious stimulation, however, can be lowered by ongoing or prior irritation.[126] In comparison, the skin, being so densely innervated, can perceive very mild stimuli and localize them quite easily. Unlike the representative cortical projection areas for cutaneous and deep somatic structures, the cortical representation of the viscera is far from specific.[167] Thus skin referral seems to predominate over visceral pain unless an intense and prolonged (chronic) pathology such as a progressive malignancy occurs. Interneurons that are activated only by visceral afferents can mediate true visceral pain localized to the region of the involved organ.[145]

In actuality, the referral of visceral pain to the skin is an example of misinterpretation by the brain. The dermatomal map of the body is basically the brain's interpretation of ongoing segmental input patterns. Therefore, the area or dermatome in which pain is perceived by the patient merely depends upon the spinal cord segment or segments that are producing ascending impulses to the brain. Thus, even though pain is perceived in the skin, it may be originating in a deep somatic or visceral structure, all of which may be segmentally related. The only difference in the perceived pain may be that it is felt more deeply if it is arising from a visceral or deep somatic structure. Associated ANS reactions can also occur.

Further support for misinterpretation is based on the work of Woolsey, as outlined in a text by Cyriax.[28] Electroencephalographic recordings using monkeys have shown electrical activity in a fixed region of the somatosensory cortex from stimulation of specific skin regions. Cortical representation of the viscera, however, is not as specific as that of cutaneous and somatic structures. When the intensity of such cutaneous stimuli increases, there is a corresponding increase in the number of cortical cells excited. This will result in the perception by the patient (based on interpretation of the brain) of pain in a more diffuse region.

Previous research based on somatosensory evoked potentials and more recently on spinal evoked potentials may prove to be a means of verifying the exact segmental level or locations of pathology.[107,155–159] One recent study performed with recording electrodes in the epidural space and transcutaneous stimulation of the median nerve showed that it was possible to diagnose the level of the lesion in patients with cervical spondylotic myelopathy.[157]

As previously mentioned, the convergence of cutaneous, deep somatic, and visceral input can occur on specific neurons. Research by Pomeranz, Wall, and Weber[144] and by Selzer and Spencer[145,146] provides information as to where this takes place. Their experiments showed that cells distinctly in lamina V of the dorsal horn of the spinal cord respond to both high threshold myelinated and unmyelinated fibers from skin, muscle and viscera. Lamina V is one of the three large cell regions of the dorsal horn.[144]

Lamina V cells physiologically take part in referred pain as well as sympathetic reflex activity. This region also receives descending input from the higher centers such as the brainstem which can also facilitate or inhibit activity of sympathetic preganglionic neurons.[160] In addition, dendrites from neurons in lamina V ascend into laminae I and II, thus having connections with the tract of Lissauer.[149] Furthermore, neurons in the substantia gelatinosa (laminae II and III) descend into lamina V.[150,160] Neurons in lamina V send axons via ascending pathways to the higher centers where the appreciation and localization of pain take place (see Chapter 3). Thus, there are extensive projections within, into, and out of lamina V in the dorsal horn.

VISCERAL PAIN

The region to which viscera refer pain is, of course, dependent on the segmental innervation of the organ or structure. There are, however, some specific variables that commonly occur (see Fig. 5-5). These are well illustrated in the case of pain referred to the shoulder, scapula, and upper extremity from diaphragm, gallbladder, and lung and heart pathology (Figs. 5-6 through 5-9).

The mechanism causing diaphragmatic pain referral to the shoulder has been previously discussed. Some fibers of the right phrenic nerve may reach the gallbladder in the hepatic plexus.[25] This can account for pain referral specifically to the right shoulder. Sympathetic innervation of the gallbladder is T7–9, which accounts for pain at the inferior angle of the right scapula.[261] Gallbladder pain can also be perceived in the upper abdomen or right upper quadrant.

Cancer of the lung as evidenced by a tumor in the apical portion can result in arm pain and is known as the brachial syndrome. Invasion into the lower roots of the brachial plexus causes pain down the ulnar distribution of the affected arm. This pain is severe and may involve a Horner's syndrome if the cervical sympathetic chain is involved.

We have seen two patients whose conditions were ultimately diagnosed by the physician as Pancoast's syndrome.[8] One patient was referred for strengthening of the right upper extremity secondary to weakness (with minimal pain) of unknown etiology. Initial evaluation determined strength to be within the poor to fair range throughout the C5–T1 myotomes only on the right. Muscular function of the left upper extremity and both lower extremities was within normal limits. There were no ROM deficits. The referring physician was contacted and electromyography (EMG) suggested prior to the initiation of any therapy. EMG findings indicated a brachial plexus lesion. Results of x-rays of the chest, shoulder girdle, and cervical spine confirmed a diagnosis of Pancoast's syndrome. The patient was subsequently referred to a neurosurgeon.

Initially, the second patient did not reveal a clear-cut picture, but with ongoing evaluation of his response, the pain pattern pointed to greater involvement. The following is a complete case history.

Case History

Clarifying Evaluation: Patient was a 74-year-old male referred on 7/16/79 with a diagnosis of cervical spondylosis. Patient stated that onset of cervical and right upper extremity pain began 5 months earlier, first noticed while plastering a wall. He developed right scapula and extremity pain that had been steadily increasing and was now constant.

Pain was described as knife-like in quality and present in the right cervical spine, axilla, shoulder, ulnar distribution of the hand, upper anterior chest, and vertebral border of scapula.

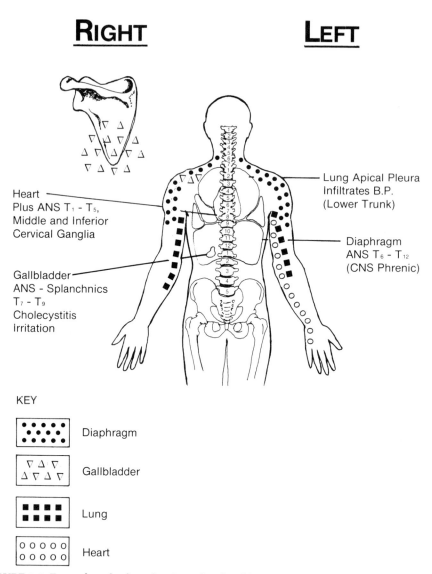

RIGHT   LEFT

Heart
Plus ANS T₁ - T₅,
Middle and Inferior
Cervical Ganglia

Lung Apical Pleura
Infiltrates B.P.
(Lower Trunk)

Diaphragm
ANS T₆ - T₁₂
(CNS Phrenic)

Gallbladder
ANS - Splanchnics
T₇ - T₉
Cholecystitis
Irritation

KEY

::::::	Diaphragm
▽ Δ ▽ / Δ ▽ Δ ▽	Gallbladder
■■■■ ■■■	Lung
○ ○ ○ ○ ○ / ○ ○ ○ ○ ○	Heart

FIGURE 5-6. Examples of referred pain to the shoulder.

The patient was unable to find any position of comfort and frequently jumped from sudden episodes of shooting pain. He had difficulty sleeping at night and complained of being constipated for the past 2 months. Pain was intensified by moist heat but relieved by ice. He had been on pain medication since onset.

Active ROM of the cervical spine was severely limited in all directions except forward bending. Backward bending, side bending, and rotation were limited by 75 percent. Rotation produced the greatest degree of discomfort. Active ROM of both shoulders was within normal limits. Strength of the C1–T1 myotomes revealed weakness of at least one grade of the ulnar-innervated musculature. Passive movement testing of the cervical and upper thoracic spine revealed significant hypomobility. Cervical x-ray films taken at a local hospital revealed evidence of foraminal encroachment at the right C5–6 and C6–7 levels.

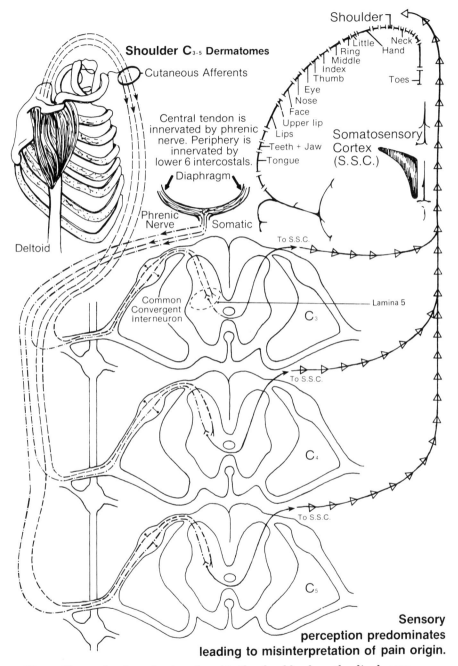

Shoulder C₃₋₅ Dermatomes

Cutaneous Afferents

Central tendon is innervated by phrenic nerve. Periphery is innervated by lower 6 intercostals.

Diaphragm

Phrenic Nerve   Somatic

Deltoid

Shoulder
Little
Ring
Middle
Index
Thumb
Neck
Hand
Toes
Eye
Nose
Face
Upper lip
Lips
Teeth + Jaw
Tongue

Somatosensory Cortex (S.S.C.)

To S.S.C.

Common Convergent Interneuron

Lamina 5

C₃

To S.S.C.

C₄

To S.S.C.

C₅

Sensory perception predominates leading to misinterpretation of pain origin.

FIGURE 5-7. The mechanism of pain referral to the shoulder from the diaphragm.

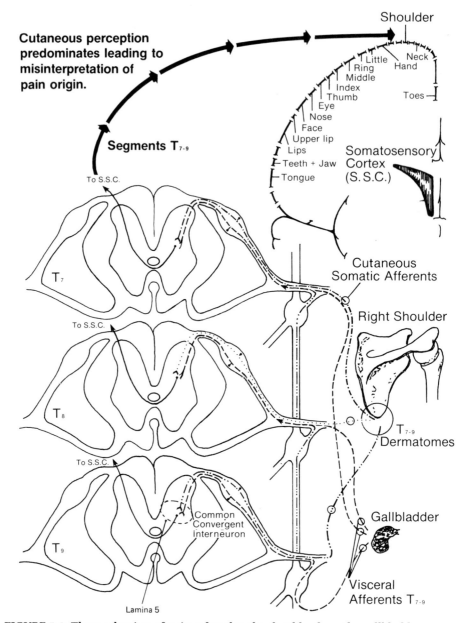

Cutaneous perception predominates leading to misinterpretation of pain origin.

Segments T₇₋₉

To S.S.C.

Shoulder

Little
Ring
Middle
Index
Thumb
Eye
Nose
Face
Upper lip
Lips
Teeth + Jaw
Tongue

Neck
Hand

Toes

Somatosensory
Cortex
(S.S.C.)

Cutaneous
Somatic Afferents

T₇

To S.S.C.

Right Shoulder

T₈

T₇₋₉
Dermatomes

To S.S.C.

Common
Convergent
interneuron

Gallbladder

T₉

Lamina 5

Visceral
Afferents T₇₋₉

FIGURE 5-8. The mechanism of pain referral to the shoulder from the gallbladder.

Palpation revealed a hypersensitive region at the superior aspect of the vertebral border of the right scapula. Skin rolling was painful paravertebrally at the right upper thoracic and low cervical spine. Manual cervical compression increased pain, whereas traction decreased pain.

Goals: Decrease pain and increase cervical spine mobility.

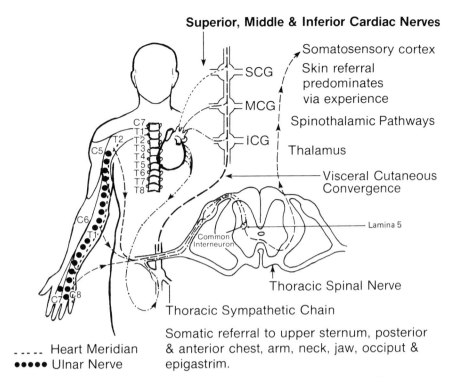

Superior, Middle & Inferior Cardiac Nerves

- SCG
- MCG
- ICG

Somatosensory cortex

Skin referral predominates via experience

Spinothalamic Pathways

Thalamus

Visceral Cutaneous Convergence

Lamina 5

Common Interneuron

Thoracic Spinal Nerve

Thoracic Sympathetic Chain

Somatic referral to upper sternum, posterior & anterior chest, arm, neck, jaw, occiput & epigastrim.

- - - - - Heart Meridian
●●●●● Ulnar Nerve

Visceral cardiac afferents enter spinal cord from T_1 - T_5.

FIGURE 5-9. Referred pain from cardiac pathology, according to the convergence-projection theory. Cardiac pain is referred to the upper sternum, posterior and anterior chest walls, and ulnar distribution of the arm (primarily left side). Pain referral to the occiput, jaw, and neck may occur via sympathetic ganglionic connection (gray rami communicans) to cervical spinal nerves.

Treatment Plan: High-voltage galvanic stimulation followed by gentle joint mobilization, manual cervical traction, and therapeutic exercise 3 times per week. The patient was instructed in a home exercise program.

After six treatments, there was no decrease in pain, but a definite increase in active ROM of the cervical spine was evident. Transient pain relief was obtained by strong manual cervical traction. Conventional T.E.N.S. was added, providing 90 percent pain relief, according to the patient, which persisted for 1 hour after a 30-minute application.

Ongoing evaluation showed persistent pain in the lower cervical and upper thoracic spine with referral to the axilla and ulnar distribution of the hand. Intrinsic musculature on the right was at least one grade below that on the left. The referring physician was unavailable when contacted by phone. The patient was given a typed progress report to present to the physician (8/9/79).

This report expressed concern about the patient's failure to respond to treatment, continuous pain in the aforementioned region, weakness of the intrinsic musculature, and inability to sleep through the night. The patient had been instructed in resting positions to gap the right cervical foramina but stated that he was unable to relieve pain in any position. The patient also now reported that he recently lost 10 lb and had been experiencing dryness of the throat.

These findings, along with the previously noted objective signs, prompted the inclusion of the following in the report: "I am wondering about the possibility of visceral referral such as is seen in a Pancoast neoplasm which may not show up early on an x-ray. I have previously seen a patient with this problem who had marked brachial plexus weakness. I have not in my experience seen a patient in such discomfort that he literally jumps from pain without any provocation except, of course, in post-herpetic neuralgia, causalgia, or a malignancy. Hopefully, the problem is solely due to the severe degenerative changes. Please let me know the results of your examination and recommendations."

The patient was not scheduled for further treatment after 8/9/79 pending word from the referring physician, but a request for a written prescription for a T.E.N.S. unit at home was made. Following the patient's visit to the physician, a return call was received stating that x-rays and blood tests were ordered.

The patient initially refused to go for the additional tests but eventually was persuaded to do so. A prescription for a T.E.N.S. unit was never received, and the patient did not return to the referring physician. The patient continued to deteriorate. When he would not return to the physician, suggestions as to another physician were given. The second physician was seen on or about 9/21/79. No treatment had been given since 8/9/79. A final diagnosis obtained from the second physician was that of inoperable Pancoast syndrome. The patient passed away a few months later.

The importance of continued reassessment of each patient is exemplified by the preceding case history. Clinicians such as physical therapists who observe the patient on a more personal and frequent basis must report unusual signs, deterioration, or lack of progress to the referring physician, who in turn should take appropriate action.

Turnbull has classified six pain syndromes that may accompany cancer of the lung.[161] There may be *no pain* at all, or *substernal pain* that occurs early in onset characterized by tightness, dull soreness, or mild burning that is aggravated by exertion. Pain in the substernal syndrome can also spread to the neck with involvement of tissues around the esophagus. *Sharp pain* is initiated during coughing with possible associated dysphagia.

The *deep unilateral syndrome* is characterized by a steady ache, little affected by the coughing. Rapid breathing may intensify discomfort on the involved side. The *costopleural syndrome*, the most common and serious, is evidenced by invasion of the chest wall. This gives rise to a constant dull ache, periodic sharp pain aggravated by coughing, and tenderness at the painful site. Pain as a result of the *peripheral syndrome* may not become evident until just prior to death. Metastatic involvement of nearby organs such as the liver and pancreas result in severe constant pain. A knowledge of these syndromes is important since the lung is insensitive. Pain from lung pathology becomes apparent only with involvement of the parietal plexus or other innervated structure.[61] Other than the case history just presented, we have no clinical experience in the use of T.E.N.S. with patients suffering from the above syndromes. A related case of a patient with substernal pain as a result of emphysema is reviewed in Chapter 9.

The role of cardiac involvement in arm pain is well known, but its mechanism is not. The heart receives sympathetic innervation from the T1–5 spinal cord segments. Visceral and cutaneous convergence can occur within these segments, giving rise to referred pain in the T1–5 dermatomes. This primarily occurs in the ulnar distribution of the arm on the left side as well as the upper anterior and posterior left thorax. One reason for the greater incidence of left-sided involvement is that pathology of the heart occurs with greater frequency on its left side.[61,142] Another factor is that the left sympathetic trunk provides more sensory input.[61] The heart also receives innervation via the superior, middle, and inferior cardiac nerves from the cervical sympathetic ganglia as high as C3. This would account for cardiac involvement to refer pain to the neck and even the face (see Fig. 5-9). Travell presents information relative to three stages of cardiac pain following an infarction.[174] Stage 1 does not contain a somatic component but consists of noxious-visceral afferent impulses transmitted directly to the brain, resulting in what has been called true visceral pain.[145] Stage 2 is termed viscerosomatic since somatic trigger points become evident in related thoracic myotomes, which can be only temporarily relieved by local treatment since noxious afferent impulses continue to bombard the related spinal cord segment. Kennard and Haugen have published an excellent study relating to this stage.[142] Stage 3, termed somatic stage, is characterized by the remaining trigger points, which may be the cause of the postinfarction syndrome. These trigger points can be effectively treated with injection or ethyl chloride spray. Figure 5-6 summarizes the visceral structures that may refer pain to the shoulder.

Cardiac pain may be confused with intercostal neuralgias, esophagitis, and indigestion. Exercise and anxiety can bring about attacks of angina pectoris.[8] Esophagitis produces heartburn perceived behind the sternum or at the xiphoid process.[64] Generally, when a patient is referred for pain modulation with T.E.N.S. and the clarifying evaluation shows normal strength and range of motion, no signs of spinal involvement, and no abnormal neurologic findings, but the pain is constant, possibly worse at night, unchanged by movement or posture, and unable to be localized with one finger, the possibility that the pain is referred from some visceral structure should be considered. If this occurs, the following should be considered as part of a more extensive history.[64]

1. Greasy, fatty, or fried foods can result in gallbladder or pancreatic pain, but eating can relieve the pain of an ulcer. Pancreatic pain may ocur near the umbilicus or occasionally in the chest with referral to the low thoracic and upper lumbar region (T12–L2); mild pancreatitis may solely cause abdominal tenderness. Persistent vomiting for 24 hours or more may be indicative of acute pancreatitis.[261]

2. Painful defecation can be a sign of referral from the colon.

3. Vomiting may relieve gallbladder but not pancreatic pain.[261]

4. Standing up can relieve the pain of esophagitis or a hiatal hernia; such pain is intensified by lying down.

5. Involvement of the abdominal and chest wall produces sharp stabbing and burning pain that may be secondary to pathology of the esophagus, stomach, or duodenum.

6. Cramping, twisting, or gripping pain in waves is indicative of intestinal or biliary obstruction. Pain of this nature increases in intensity over 10 to 20 seconds, is maintained for 1 minute, and then subsides, only to be repeated with each peristaltic wave.[85]

7. When pain is unable to be pinpointed, its exact dimensions may be helpful. The pancreas can result in pain high in the left upper abdomen and back. Involvement of the liver gives rise to epigastric and right upper quadrant pain. Distention of the small intestine and colon produces pain around and below the umbilicus, respectively.

8. Pain just above the pubis in the lower abdomen may be related to sigmoid colon and rectal disease. In addition, the colon can result in pain across the whole abdomen.

9. Chronic pain due to gynecologic pathology can be referred no higher than the anterior-superior iliac spine and dorsally to the upper half of the sacrum and gluteal region.[167]

10. Pathology involving the heart, pericardium, aorta, esophagus, or other mediastinal structures produces substernal chest pain.[263]

Figure 5-5 summarizes the nature of visceral pain, and Figure 5-10 illustrates the mechanism of a viscerosomatic reflex.

MYOFASCIAL PAIN

Myofascial pain syndromes occurring in part as a result of "trigger points" also cause referred pain. A trigger point is considered to be a small hypersensitive region in muscle,

MYOCARDIAL INFARCTION

Lamina 5. Convergence

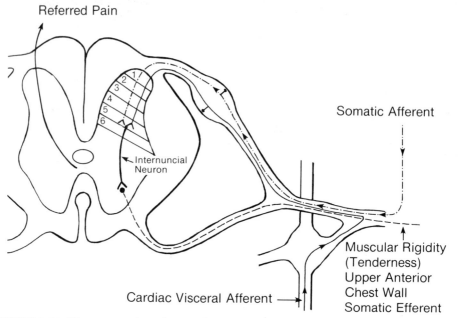

FIGURE 5-10. Viscerosomatic reflex mechanism (myocardial infarction). Somatic (muscle) rigidity and tenderness as a result of a visceral lesion.

ligament, fascia, or joint capsules from which impulses bombard the CNS, causing referred pain.[175] The histologic aspects of trigger points and information pertaining to their relationship to acupuncture and motor points are covered in Chapter 8. Therefore, this section will deal with the pathophysiology and mechanisms of trigger points as related to myofascial pain syndromes.

Before embarking on a discussion of myofascial syndromes, it is necessary first to mention fibrositis, myositis, and related terms since they frequently are lumped into the myofascial category.[5,46,187,194] Neufeld prefers the term "fibropathic syndrome" in place of fibrositis to indicate the pathologic complexes of arthritic or nonrheumatic syndromes.[168] Kraus defines fibrositis as a condition of exquisite tenderness of the skin and myositis as tenderness to touch existing in muscle.[169] Sola and coworkers prefer the term "myofasciitis" in place of muscular rheumatism, fibrositis, myositis, fasciitis, and myalgia.[170,173] Fibromyositis is defined by Awad as acute or chronic inflammation of the fibrous tissue in muscle that results in pain and stiffness.[171] He further states that interstitial myofibrositis is more descriptive since it indicates an inflammatory disorder in the fibrous tissue of muscle.

Disagreement exists, however, when biopsy findings are used to support the statements about histologic cellular changes (see Chapter 8).[186,187] According to Simons, Wyke, and Cyriax, the term fibrositis was originally coined by Gowers in 1904 as an explanation for backache caused by the inflammation of fibrous tissue.[28,32,186,187] Wyke states that inflammatory changes in the connective tissue related to back muscles have not been demonstrated even by biopsy. He feels that the terms fibrositis and fasciitis should not be used in regard to backache. Cyriax equates fibrositis with referred tenderness also characterized by trigger points. He dismisses fibrositis as a secondary phenomenon of intervertebral disk impingement against the posterior longitudinal ligament and dura mater. Gunn and Milbrandt also equate the presence of trigger points with radiculopathy.[199] Fibrositis applied to other areas undergoes an excellent critique by Cyriax at the beginning of his classic text.[28] He eliminates fibrositis as too general a term, opting instead to use more distinctive terminology such as tendinitis, rupture, scarring, and the names of infectious diseases.

The second related term is myositis. Wyke defines myositis as nonsuppurative inflammation of muscle. Cyriax concurs, and agreement exists that myositis is rarely painful and is basically a result of infectious conditions. Closely related in usage throughout the literature is the term "rheumatism," again considered to be too vague a term.[28,32] Cyriax does, however, consider generalized fibrositis to apply to rheumatoid arthritis. Bonica also states that myofascial syndromes have been described in terms of myalgia, myositis, fibrositis, fibromyositis, fasciitis, myofasciitis, muscular rheumatism, and muscular strains.[194]

There are numerous causes of myofascial pain syndromes, and the trigger point is sometimes considered to be the primary causative factor. Clinically, we believe that in many cases the trigger point is secondary yet frequently overlooked as a compounding and/or prolonging agent in various pain syndromes.

Numerous articles have been published concerning the ramifications of trigger points.[168–201] It is generally agreed that excitation of an active trigger point produces the characteristic "jump sign," consisting of a flinch by the patient, shortening of the involved muscle, and/or visible fasciculation. Recent studies have confirmed the existence of increased motor unit activity at rest in some abnormally tender muscle regions as well as an increase in pain from stretch (active or passive) or isometric contraction of the related structure.[445] Concomitant pain referral to the joint acted upon by the involved muscle also occurs.[178,186–188,197,207]

Even more descriptive of an active trigger point is the concomitant pattern of pain consisting of a localized deep, dull ache; a surrounding hyperalgesia; and referral of discomfort.[174–176,179–181,188,191,194]

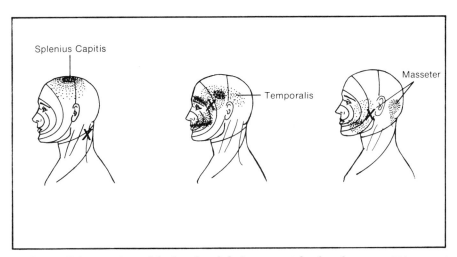

FIGURE 5-11. Trigger points of the head and their segmental referral pattern. Trigger points are delineated by an "X." (Adapted from Travell, J and Rinzler, SH: *The myofascial genesis of pain.* Postgrad Med 11:425, 1952.)

Examples of the most commonly occurring trigger points are illustrated in Figures 5-11 through 5-15. The pattern of referral is generally considered to be extrasegmental, thus not following a dermatomal (nerve root) or peripheral nerve distribution, but such a description is incorrect. Since trigger points occur in deep somatic structures, the referral pattern should also be equated with that of the myotomes and dermatomes. A comparison with the patterns established by Kellgren, via intramuscular saline injection, shows a significant similarity.[11,14] Chapter 8 contains illustrations of Kellgren's work. The comparison, however, is not exact due to some interesting variables. Kellgren's work was done under experimental conditions that do not simulate the whole clinical entity of the trigger point. Pain was of short duration via saline injection but is prolonged with resultant opportunity for increased segmental facilitation and more widespread pain referral in an ongoing myofascial syndrome. Myofascial chronicity can also lead to sympathetic involvement and increased pain referral. A chronically active trigger point may, in fact, produce such strong afferent noxious input that involvement may include a composite of dermatomal, myotomal, and sclerotomal patterns.[199] It should also be noted that, as with the dermatomes, there is overlapping innervation of muscles. This fact, as well as the particular portion of the muscle that was injected and the location of a trigger point within a specific muscle, can account for an incomplete comparison or a different referral pattern.[177,178,181]

Figures 5-11 and 5-14 illustrate trigger points that refer pain in a segmental and/or single dermatomal or myotomal distribution. The vastus medialis and soleus trigger points are prime examples. It is noteworthy to state, however, that pain referral from trigger points can cross the midline and give rise to the bilateral or contralateral discomfort clearly evident in the case of the sternocleidomastoid muscle.[176–178] Kellgren's work did not illustrate midline crossover.

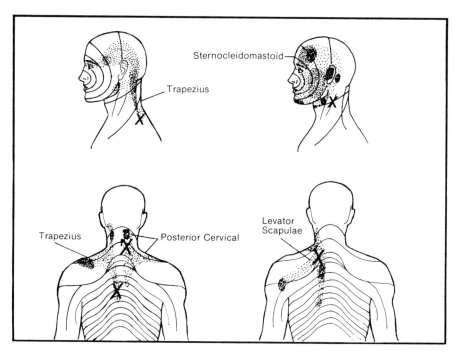

FIGURE 5-12. Trigger points of the neck and upper back. Referral patterns are basically extrasegmental. Trigger points are delineated by an "X." (Adapted from Travell, J and Rinzler, SH: *The myofascial genesis of pain.* Postgrad Med 11:425, 1952.)

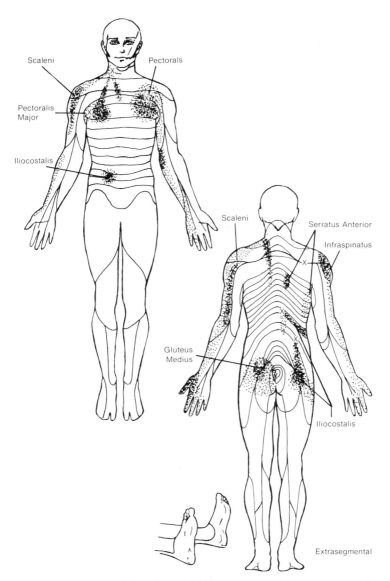

FIGURE 5-13. Trigger points of the thoracolumbar region and upper extremity. Referral patterns are extrasegmental. Trigger points are delineated by an "X." (Adapted from Travell, J and Rinzler, SH: *The myofascial genesis of pain.* Postgrad Med 11:425, 1952.)

Myofascial pain syndromes can arise from a myriad of causes and predisposing factors (Table 5-10). The simplest and least complex etiology is that of a joint sprain.[5] Postural, emotional, and traumatic stresses and strains are also common and give rise to trigger points and related pain syndromes in areas of greatest mechanical stress, such as the neck, shoulder girdle, and low back.[177–179,182,183,185,190,192,194,199]

Exposure to cold, chronic infection, generalized fatigue, arthritis, and visceral disease have also been implicated.[175,182,183,190,194,199] Predisposing factors may be mild anemia; low metabolic rate; deficiencies of potassium, calcium, vitamins C and B complex, and estro-

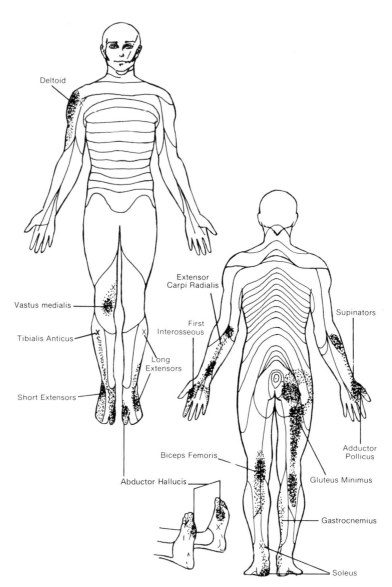

FIGURE 5-14. Trigger points of the extremities and their segmental referral patterns. Trigger points are delineated by an "X." (Adapted from Travell, J and Rinzler, SH: *The myofascial genesis of pain.* **Postgrad Med 11:425, 1952.)**

gen;[178,182,183,188] hypothyroidism; creatinuria; localized circulatory disturbances; peripheral nerve injury; and spinal complex (nerve root, facet, disk involvement) pathology.[182,183,194,199]

An active trigger point when pressed, massaged, pinched, needled, stretched, or subjected to intense heat or cold will produce the previously mentioned symptomatic triad (localized deep pain and hyperalgesia, fasciculations, and referred pain). Diathermy, although a commonly used therapeutic modality for myofascial pain, is considered controversial and may indeed increase pain.[178,186,187,194] However, pressure over a trigger point that

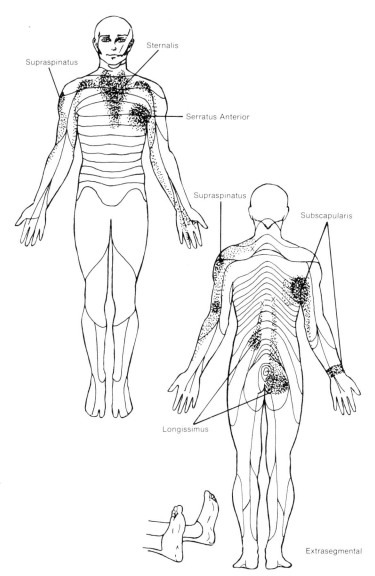

Supraspinatus

Sternalis

Serratus Anterior

Supraspinatus

Subscapularis

Longissimus

Extrasegmental

FIGURE 5-15. Trigger points of chest, posterior thoracic region, and upper extremities. Referral patterns are extrasegmental. Trigger points are delineated by an "X." (Adapted from Travell, J and Rinzler, SH: *The myofascial genesis of pain.* **Postgrad Med 11:425, 1952.)**

is maintained (with patient tolerance) for at least 2 to 3 minutes may result in a decrease in pain.[178,186,187] Prolonged ice application will have the same effect as heat. The most commonly used treatment mode, fluorimethane spray and stretch, will not freeze the tissue and is employed for a rather short time.[176,184,185,188,191,192] Fluorimethane, being nonvolatile, nonflammable, and nontoxic, has replaced ethyl chloride as the vapocoolant spray of choice.[174,175,177–183,194] Dry needling and/or injection have recently been shown to be extremely effective (see Table 5-10).[195,196,200] Evaluation of desensitization can be done by pressure-threshold measurements.[201]

TABLE 5-10. Etiologic Factors in the Onset and Approaches to the Treatment of Trigger Points

Travell --
Bonica ---
Kraus -------------
Sola
Kennard & Haugen --
Mennell --
Cyriax --

Definitions
Irritable focus

Histologic changes
Inflammation
Hyperactive sensory end organ
Disk fragment impingement on
    dura mater

Etiology
Localized injury to muscle, ligament, joint capsule, or nerve
Improper body mechanics
Spinal involvement
Emotional stress or tension
Joint dysfunction
Visceral disease
Endocrine imbalance
Chronic infection
Prolonged exposure to cold
Fatigue
Vitamin and mineral deficience
Anemia
↓ BMR
Frequently Seen
Areas of mechanical stress
Muscle, ligament, connective tissue, joint capsule
Site of previous injury or disease
Treatment
Comprehensive (The trigger point may be only a symptom, not the cause)
    Spray and stretch
    Pressure and ice
    Electrical stimulation
        Neuroprobe
        T.E.N.S.
        High volt
    Ultrasound
    Needling
    Injection
    Biofeedback
    Joint mobilization
    Massage
    Ethyl chloride vs fluorimethane
Follow-up
    Sinusoidal stimulation
    ↑ Normal proprioceptive input
    Postural correction
    Therapeutic exercises
    Mandibular appliance
    Relaxation training
    Stress reduction
    Nutrition

Prolonged presence of active trigger points can result in muscle spasm, loss of normal rest length, weakness, and even contracture due to fibrosis.[5] Joint dysfunction can also compound the syndrome. Neurologic signs will not be present unless nerve entrapment occurs, as seen in the piriformis and scaleni syndromes, compressing the sciatic nerve and lower trunk of the brachial plexus, respectively.[182,183,188,202,203]

Associated ANS signs may occur with persistent trigger points. Vasoconstriction, pallor, sweating, decreased skin resistance, and temperature may be seen with intense pain.[172,174,176–179,181,188,194,199] Desensitization of the trigger point usually results in vasodilation.[196]

Trigger points that remain active for a long time can also lead to the development of satellite, or secondary, trigger points within the area of referred pain.[188,199,445] They may also result from visceral involvement, causing deep tenderness in the somatic reference zone indicative of a visceromotor reflex. Satellite trigger points may compound the syndrome and cause confusion as to the source of pain since they give rise to pain patterns that overlap that of the primary trigger point[445] and are also capable of exhibiting the characteristics of the primary trigger point.

Trigger points of long duration may remain latent after the causative mechanism has been successfully treated and may even be present after surgery, particularly those occurring as a result of spinal complex involvement.[181–183,194] Incomplete desensitization of a trigger point or repetitive minor stresses and strains of related tissue may result in the reactivation of latent trigger points, which are responsible in part for the prolongation of many common myofascial pain syndromes. Latent trigger points can exhibit a positive jump sign and localized deep tenderness when sufficiently stimulated but will not result in referred pain unless actual penetration by a needle occurs.[181,194] Table 5-11 lists the characteristics of active, satellite, and latent trigger points.

It should be apparent that trigger points and/or myofascial pain syndromes not only may be overlooked but can mislead the clinician into false diagnoses by mimicking symptom complexes indicative of other specific pathologies (Table 5-12). But the fact remains that these trigger points may develop as a result of the pathology they mimic, or the pathology in some cases may be nothing more than the pain and dysfunction created by an active trigger point, which began as a minor stress or strain.

It has been shown that cardiac disease gives rise to the development of trigger points in the anterior and posterior upper thoracic musculature.[142,178,194] Also, the development of these same trigger points from somatic trauma or other pathology distinct from viscera has been shown to mimic cardiac pain.[7,178,194]

TABLE 5-11. The Characteristics of Active, Satellite, and Latent Trigger Points

Active	Satellite	Latent
Localized deep tenderness	Secondary points within area of referred pain	Localized deep tenderness
Hyperalgesia		Positive jump sign
Positive jump sign	Cause overlapping pain patterns	No referred pain with sustained pressure but via needle insertion
Referred pain from sustained pressure	Occur when trigger points are active for long periods	
Weakness and shortening of related muscle may result in joint dysfunction	Occur in the somatic reference zone of involved viscera (visceromotor reflex)	May remain after causative pathology is resolved
Diffuse deep tenderness within pain referral area	May exhibit all characteristics of an active trigger point	Reactivation by minor stresses and strains
Increased motor unit activity at rest of related muscle		May become apparent as a result of incomplete eradication or desensitization of active point
ANS changes occur		Common in over-40 age group
Vasoconstriction		
Pallor		
Sweating		
Coldness of skin		
Piloerection		
Skin resistance ↓		
No neurologic signs		

TABLE 5-12. Trigger Points—Are They Primary or Secondary Manifestations of Specific Syndromes or Pathology?

Cause	Effect
SCM, temporalis, splenius ◁----------------------------------▷ capitis, masseter, trapezius, pterygoids	Ear infections, migraine headaches, Ménière's syndrome, occipital neuralgia, trigeminal neuralgia, cerebellar ataxia, torticollis, petit mal seizures, toothaches, hypersensitivity, tinnitus, stuffiness of ear, tearing eyes, ↑ salivation, vertigo
Scaleni ◁---▷	Peripheral nerve injury
Infraspinatus, supraspinatus, ◁ -------------------------▷ deltoid, levator scapulae, rhomboids	Tendinitis, bursitis, cervical spondylosis, disk pathology
Pectorals, sternalis ◁-------------------------------------- ▷	Cardiac disease
Serratus anterior ◁--- ▷	Rib fracture
Iliocostalis, longissimus, ◁---------------------------------▷ multifidus, quadratus lumborum	Disk pathology, spondylolisthesis
Gluteus medius, gluteus minimus, ◁----------------------- ▷ piriformis	Sciatica
Vastus medialis ◁ -- ▷	Chondromalacia
Biceps femoris ◁-- ▷	Baker's cyst
Soleus ◁ -- ▷	Heel spur
ABD hallucis ◁ --- ▷	Gout
Tibialis anterior ◁-- ▷	Diabetic neuropathy
Supinator, extensor carpi radialis ◁ ----------------------- ▷	Tennis elbow
Gastrocnemius ◁ -- ▷	Intermittent claudication

An injury to the vastus medialis muscle may produce a trigger point resulting in referred pain to the patella, mimicking chondromalacia and even producing buckling of the knee.[187] It seems apparent that chondromalacia may cause a change of function of the vastus medialis, resulting in abnormal trauma and the subsequent development of a trigger point. Ligamentous trigger points are most commonly present at the sacroiliac joint, sacrum, iliac crest, and spinous processes.[182,183] These trigger points, as well as those occurring at joint capsules, are related to posture and activities of daily living. They may result in dysfunction of the related joint or occur as a result of such dysfunction. The interaction between visceral and somatic structures as well as two distinct somatic structures makes it quite difficult to determine the actual pathology or primary causative factor by pain alone.

A few specific trigger points need special mention because of the wide-ranging symptomatology that occurs from them. The sternocleidomastoid (SCM) gives rise to vertigo, lacrimation, ptosis and/or reddening of the eye, headache, nausea, syncope, tinnitus, hearing and visual (blurring) impairment, and ataxia.[176–178,186,187] Distinction between the sternal and clavicular heads of the sternocleidomastoid (SCM) is necessary. A trigger point in the sternal region results in unilateral facial and, at times, throat pain with eye symptomatology in the affected side. The clavicular portion gives rise to dizziness, imbalance, and headache in the occipital and frontal areas and the mastoid unilaterally. Intensification of headache can result in a midline crossover of pain. A trigger point of the clavicular head can produce contralateral forehead pain.

The SCM has a dual innervation—cranial (accessory nerve) and ventral rami of C2 and C3. The accessory nerve innervates the upper trapezius muscle via a plexus formed with C3 and C4 ventral rami and has a branch that joins the vagus nerve. Compound nerves have more than one nucleus of origin and termination.[25] There are anastomoses between the accessory nerves and the hypoglossal, which joins the sensory nuclei of the trigeminal nerve.[25,286] The proximal fibers of cranial nerves 5, 7, 9, and 10 are associated with the sensory nucleus of the trigeminal nerve and have sympathetic connections with the upper cervical spine via the nucleus caudalis.[228] A significant percentage of the fibers from the sensory nucleus of the trigeminal nerve crosses the midline, while a smaller amount remains ipsilateral.[25,288] The resultant anatomic relationship and transmission pathways can account for the many effects of the SCM as well as the upper trapezius trigger points (Fig. 5-16).

Scapulocostal syndrome is in part characterized by the presence of a trigger point in the levator scapulae muscle.[6,204–205] The scapulocostal syndrome may have a postural, cervical spine, or upper extremity etiology. The symptom complex includes hemicrania (posterior) and pain referral to the scapula joint, anterior chest (fourth and fifth intercostal

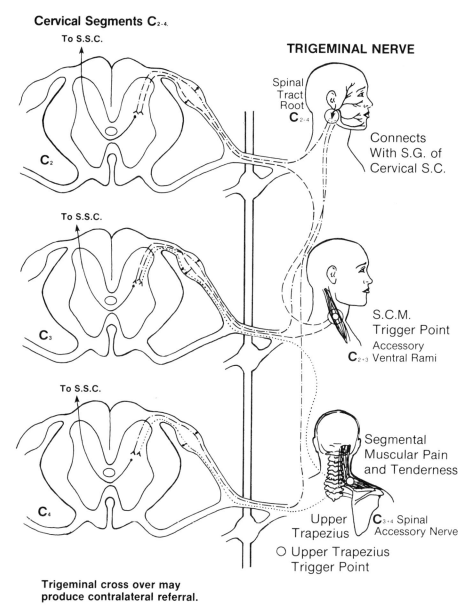

Cervical Segments C$_{2-4}$.

To S.S.C.

TRIGEMINAL NERVE

Spinal Tract Root C$_{2-4}$

Connects With S.G. of Cervical S.C.

C$_2$

To S.S.C.

C$_3$

S.C.M. Trigger Point

Accessory C$_{2+3}$ Ventral Rami

To S.S.C.

C$_4$

Segmental Muscular Pain and Tenderness

Upper Trapezius

C$_{3+4}$ Spinal Accessory Nerve

O Upper Trapezius Trigger Point

Trigeminal cross over may produce contralateral referral.

FIGURE 5-16. Anatomic relationship between SCM and upper trapezius trigger points.

nerves), and down the ulnar distribution of the arm. Paresthesia of the fourth and fifth fingers, arm and shoulder weakness, and a hypersensitive trigger point at the superior-medial angle of the scapula (palpated optimally with the scapula abducted) are quite common. Syndromes such as the scapulocostal will be discussed separately under entrapment syndromes.

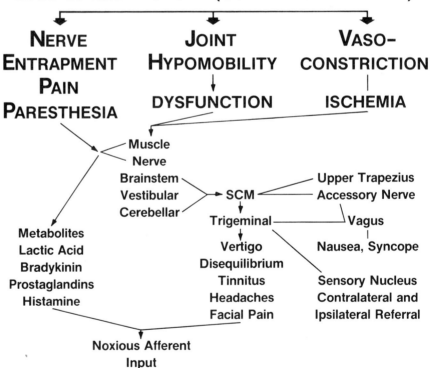

FIGURE 5-17. Trigger point mechanisms. Factors giving rise to the onset of trigger points and their resultant signs and symptoms.

The temporomandibular joint (TMJ) syndrome was until recently relatively unknown, and its symptom complex masks many other pathologic considerations. Trigger points of the masseter, temporalis, and external and internal pterygoids all may be involved, resulting in a multiplicity of pain referral patterns to the cheeks, jaw, ears, TMJ, teeth, eyes, head, and neck.[181,187,198,206,267–270] Associated signs and symptoms include vertigo, tinnitus, joint crepitation, burning and pricking of one side of the tongue and roof of mouth, sore throat,

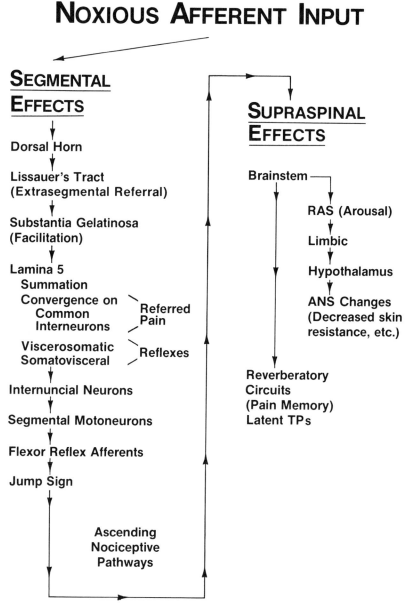

FIGURE 5-18. Trigger point mechanisms. The transmission of noxious mechanisms. The transmission of noxious afferent input to the CNS and resultant actions.

swallowing problems, impaired hearing, clogged ears, and decreased oral aperture. In long-standing cases, TMJ syndrome may result in widespread muscular tension throughout the body.[181,198,206] It is important to note that the vertigo seen in TMJ syndrome is similar to that in the SCM syndrome inasmuch as nystagmus is not present (Fig. 5-17). [181,206]

The mechanisms of trigger point pain, both local and referred, are quite complex (Fig. 5-18). Regardless of whether the trigger point is the primary or secondary component of a specific pathology or symptom complex (pain syndrome), its physiologic mechanisms should be the same. The wide-ranging nature of myofascial pain syndromes, however, makes them quite difficult to delineate.

The simplest explanation of how a trigger point can cause pain is the cycle of pain-spasm-pain. The trigger point results in muscle guarding or spasm, which gives rise to pain. However, such a simplistic explanation cannot be accepted since it does not explain the referred pain process, the jump sign, and associated ANS involvement. It is generally agreed that the trigger point is responsible for a continuous noxious input into the CNS.

A possible CNS scenario resulting from active trigger points obviously would involve decreased muscular resting length and joint hypomobility. Muscular spasm could promote vasoconstriction, causing localized ischemia to adjacent muscle fibers and nerve. Ischemia would cause metabolite production, leading to further nerve fiber irritation. Thus, afferent noxious impulses could arise from mechanoreceptors (muscle, joint capsule) and chemoreceptors (nerve), all of which would enter into the dorsal horn at related segments.

Fibers carrying nociceptive input will synapse either in the marginal layer of the dorsal horn where extrasegmental referral can occur or in the substantia gelatinosa, resulting in an "opening of the gate." Summation mechanisms and/or convergence upon common interneurons in lamina V are the likely origins of viscerosomatic and somatovisceral reflexes as well as referred pain characteristics of the trigger point. Further activation of motoneurons and flexor reflex afferents may be the mechanism behind the jump sign.

Impulses ascending via nociceptive pathways (Chapter 4) and subsequently synapsing in various brainstem centers responsible for hypothalamic modulations could be the impetus behind the associated ANS signs. Reverberatory brainstem circuits may develop, producing the pain memory process behind latent trigger points. A schematic representation of the physiologic effects of an active trigger point is shown in Figure 5-18. A trigger point of a muscle that is solely or partially innervated by a cranial nerve would result in additional manifestations. Involvement of the sternocleidomastoid could result in ischemia of brainstem, vestibular, or cerebellar structures, producing vertigo, equilibrium changes, and head, facial, and TMJ pain.

HEADACHE

The adjunctive use of T.E.N.S. for myofascial pain and headaches necessitates evaluation of the causative factors to prevent continuous recurrence of the pain-spasm-pain cycle. Therefore, there is no way to justify the use of T.E.N.S. as the only intervention. T.E.N.S. can serve only to relieve the headache symptomatically and thus is unable to prevent it from recurring.

The effectiveness of T.E.N.S. and acupressure for the relief of headache pain seems to be closely related to the type of headache and when it is employed. Acupressure has been touted as being an effective means of self-modulation in the treatment of headache pain.[208,209,239] However, in our experience, its value is significant only when employed immediately at or just after onset of the headache. We have obtained relief (partial to complete) of headache pain with T.E.N.S., but success is most apparent when applied close to onset.

Our use of T.E.N.S. for headaches is entirely adjunctive. We may use T.E.N.S. and acupressure for symptomatic relief of headache that is present as part of a specific symptom complex such as a cervical strain or temporomandibular joint pathology.

The optimal treatment of headaches centers around determining their classification and training the patient to prevent their recurrence, thus negating the need for T.E.N.S. The determination of the specific variety of headache is necessary to implement an appropriate and comprehensive treatment program. However, the simple tension headache that many people acquire at one time or another during stressful situations, fever, hangover, or sinus conditions can be alleviated by acupressure or T.E.N.S. techniques.[208]

Electromyographic (EMG) biofeedback training in conjunction with instruction in postural and body mechanics can be very effective in preventing tension headaches of a purely physical nature. EMG biofeedback training can increase awareness of the involved musculature. Patients can be taught to sense the onset of tension, correct postural abnormalities, and thus prevent the onset of headache. If the headache can be prevented, T.E.N.S. is obviously unnecessary. During attempts to train a patient in relaxation with or without biofeedback, the presence of a headache can make it difficult for the patient to concentrate. T.E.N.S., acupressure, or noninvasive point stimulation by devices such as the Neuroprobe* may be helpful in decreasing or eliminating the headache so that effective training can ensue.

Temperature biofeedback training is now widely used in the treatment of vascular headaches. The hypothesis that increasing hand or finger temperature via peripheral vasodilation will result in a shunting of blood from the head to the arms, however, is still considered conjectural.[219,220,232,234,235,237,240,245] The hand temperatures of patients with migraine headaches are usually below the normal range of 85° to 96°F, commonly in the 70° to 80°F range and as low as the 60° to 70°F range. Recent reports have shown that temperature biofeedback training does result in changes in the cerebral circulation.[251] It is interesting to note that patients who have been trained to increase hand temperature autogenically can abort a migraine attack but that the lowering of hand temperature in some patients can also be effective.[251]

The literature supports the fact that merely training headache patients in the principle of relaxation without the aid of biofeedback may be equally effective.[220,244,246,248]

T.E.N.S. has been shown to be effective in providing symptomatic pain relief during migraine, cluster, and tension headaches, and it has been reported that attacks of headache did not occur after successful treatment for periods of up to 8 months.[1,238,252–254] Electroacupuncture and Ryodoraku (see Chapter 8) have also been successfully used in the treatment of headache.[225,226] However, there is a paucity of documentation to support the primary and sole use of these modalities.

Diamond classifies headaches into three categories: traction and inflammatory, vascular, and psychogenic.[210] Traction and inflammatory headaches are a result of mass lesions; eye, ear, nose, and throat pathology; allergies; infections; cranial neuralgia; arteritis; and musculoskeletal (TMJ, osteoarthritis, myositis) causes. Vascular headaches include migraine, cluster, ophthalmoplegic, hemiplegic, toxic, and hypertensive. Psychogenic headaches occur as a result of depression, conversion, delusion, and anxiety reactions.

Friedman classifies headaches according to time factors.[211] A patient seeking initial medical attention for a headache representative of a new problem would fall into the acute category. Examples of acute headaches are those stemming from sinusitis, glaucoma, iritis, dental origin, neuritis or neuralgia, infection, neoplasm, trauma, and musculoskeletal etiol-

---

*Medical Research Laboratories and Joanco Medical Electronics Ltd.

ogy. Some of these can, of course, become chronic. Acute headaches may also occur in cyclic fashion in the case of cerebral aneurysms, angioma, or subarachnoid hemorrhage. Headaches as a result of pituitary tumors, intracranial lesions, chronic nasal conditions, and vascular and occipital tension fall into the subacute and chronic category. Markovich states that 2 percent of all headaches are of the traction-inflammatory mode; 8 percent are vascular, which includes both migraine and cluster varieties; and 90 percent consist of the muscle-contraction type.[227]

For the purpose of this text, headaches will be classified as muscle contraction, vascular, cluster, and other headaches of infrequent appearance. As with all pain syndromes, delineation must occur in relation to etiology as well as the location, intensity, pattern, duration, modifying factors, chronologic variables, and associated symptoms affecting the subjective pain complaint.

Graham lists various mechanisms that can give rise to pain in and about the head:[224] hysteria; intrinsic disorders of pain pathways such as demyelination; direct pressure or traction on nerves or pain-sensitive structures; intracranial or extracranial arterial dilation; inflammation of meninges or cranial blood vessel walls; prolonged muscle contraction of scalp, face, or neck musculature; and endocrine imbalances.

MUSCLE-CONTRACTION HEADACHES

The most common type of headache, more common in females, is the muscle-contraction or tension headache.[215,229,238,239] It occurs bilaterally most of the time in the occipital, occipitofrontal, or temporal lobe or in a circumscribed pattern. Pain is a dull, achy, non-throbbing sensation usually from the head to the upper trapezius muscles, with possible tightness, pressure, or weight. The headache usually lasts for 1 to 4 hours.

Muscle-contraction headaches are subdivided into acute and chronic.[215,232,238] The acute form usually begins as a result of tension, fatigue, eyestrain, improper neck posture, or bruxism. Depression, anxiety, and related psychologic factors that may yield a constant dull pain of long duration and variable intensity (months or years) represent the chronic form. Alcohol can provide relief from tension headaches.[220] Such patients usually awaken with a headache that increases in intensity during the day and can become severe one to three times each week (Table 5-13). There may be associated throbbing, nausea, and increased irritability to light (photophobia) and sound (sonophobia) relating closely to the migraine headache.

Other muscle-contraction types of headaches are the anticipatory, post-traumatic, and conversion cephalalgia, all with emotional or neurotic etiology. These so-called psychogenic headaches are mild to moderate in intensity, continuous, worse in the morning, decreased in the afternoon, increased in the evening, and decreased at the end of the day. They are thus manifested by a waxing and waning pattern. Further delineation by location is that of a sand-like sensation in a depression headache, and a slowly moving (crawling) sensation inside the skull (delusion) and a spread of pain to the involved side with an inability to vocalize at a normal pitch in patients with conversion headache.[210,219,249]

Contraction of scalp muscles may be such that it can be painful to comb or brush the hair or place the head on a pillow. The sternocleidomastoid, upper trapezius, temporalis, scalenes, masseter, levator scapulae, and suboccipital muscles such as the splenius capitis and posterior cervical are commonly involved. The patient may have been involved in an auto accident prior to onset.[249]

TABLE 5-13. The Characteristics of Muscle Contraction (Tension) Headaches

	Variables	
Onset	Age—any	
	Sex—females more than males	
	Family history (−)	
Location	Bilateral occipital, frontal, temporal	Splenius capitis, SCM, upper trapezius, temporalis, masseter, scalenes, levator scapulae
Intensity	Not as severe as migrane or cluster	Psychogenic, mild to moderate
Quality	Non-throbbing, dull, achy	Tight, pressure, heavy weight
		Delusion—crawling
		Depression—band-like
Pattern	No prodromal symptoms, slow	
	onset	Chronic—awaken with headache, ↑ + ↓ continuously throughout the day
Duration	Acute—1–4 hr.	
	Chronic—with ongoing psychologic problems, months to years	
	Anticipatory ↔ psychogenic	
Associated Symptoms	Irritability	10% also have migrane, throbbing, nausea
Aggravating/Easing Factors	Relaxation ↓, alcohol ↓, anxiety ↑, poor posture ↑	
Precipitating or Triggering Factors	Posture, work, auto accident, tension, fatigue, eyestrain, emotional stress, bruxism, joint dysfunction (TMJ)	

VASCULAR HEADACHES

There seems to be a link between some tension headaches and migraine headaches. About 10 percent of patients with tension headaches also suffer from migraines.[220] One possible physiologic explanation is that the scalp arteries constrict during the tension headache, which may result in a rebound vasodilation at night. The patient may thus awaken with a vascular-type headache.[215,220] Contraction of the aforementioned musculature can lead to ischemia, hypoxia, lactic acidosis, and the liberation of catabolites.

A further correlation between some tension and vascular headaches has been determined as a result of EMG studies.[236,240,248] Increased action potentials (muscle activity) were shown to occur in patients with both migraine and tension headaches during relaxation. This seems to imply that muscle contraction may in part cause the headache.

Vascular headaches, most commonly of the migraine type, have a more involved physiologic mechanism.[241] Migraine headaches are thought to occur as a result of noxious stimuli from a neurogenic vasomotor disorder involving the internal and external carotid arterial beds. Constriction of the internal carotid arterial bed caused local tissue acidosis, loss of vessel tone, and vasodilation of the external carotid arterial bed. This then may produce periarterial inflammation and capillary permeability, giving rise to subsequent edema, stretching, and increased pulse amplitude. The scenario culminates in the pulsing, throbbing, migraine pain.[241]

Blau considers migraine to arise from the meningeal blood vessels, particularly the venous sinuses, and to be of two types, constriction and dilation.[236] He does not agree it is due to extracranial vasodilation.

Speer divides migraine into two stages.[221] Stage 1 is an aura or premonitory stage, thought to consist of cerebral artery constriction causing a decrease in circulation and oxygen to the sensory areas of the cortex, specifically the tactile, visual, auditory, and vestibular functions. The circulatory deficit may account for the visual and sensory disturbances that precede the headache.[220,221] Stage 1 is thus characterized by a scintillating scotoma, a disturbance of flashing lights or lines, and visual deficit to the opposite half of the body. This usually does not produce complete blindness in one eye, but a spasm of the basilar artery and its branches or constriction of the ophthalmic artery may cause temporary blindness for a few minutes. The scintilating scotoma may last for up to 20 minutes. Ophthalmoplegic migraine may be the cause of weak eye muscles or double vision.[239] Basilar migraine will result in instability and visual symptoms.[239,249] Hemiplegic migraine can produce slurred speech. Retinal migraine is implicated by visual hallucinations, partial or complete unilateral loss of sight, and a dull ache behind the eye.[239] Repeated vomiting and abdominal pain are consistent with abdominal migraine.[8,239] Another chronologic variant is the weekend sufferer. Persistent constriction during the week may give way to vasodilation when relaxation occurs.[239] Associated symptomatology of stage 1 migraine involves paresthesia in the fingers (possibly as proximal as the elbow), noises perceived as originating in the center of head, and dizziness (Table 5-14).

Rebound vasodilation signals the onset of stage 2, characterized by pain in any part of the head except the lower jaw. Onset of pain is usually unilateral, frequently at the temple or low forehead. Pain may then involve the occiput, neck, and shoulder and may be perceived as encompassing the whole head, but one side is usually more painful. Migraine is considered to be unilateral in 70 to 80 percent of cases, but Olesen considers bilateral pain to be almost as frequent.[210,221,232,233] Signs associated with stage 2 migraines include increased urination, abdominal pain, diarrhea, profuse sweating, pallor, fever, redness and dullness of eyes, sleepiness, and exhaustion.[221] The lower-half headache, or facial migraine,

TABLE 5-14. The Characteristics of Vascular or Migraine Headaches

Onset	Childhood → puberty, plus family history
Location	70–80% temple or forehead
	Unilateral, spread to occiput, neck, shoulder
	Whole head; one side more painful
Intensity	Mild to severe
Quality	Throbbing, pulsing
Pattern	Stage I—Prodromal (aura) Stage II—Headache
	Scintillating scotoma
	Visual disturbances
	Paresthesia
	Dizziness
	Head noises
Duration	Stage I, 20–30 min; stage II, 12–24 hr
Frequency	Several times per day, week, or year
Associated symptoms	↑ urination, nervousness, colitis, abdominal pain, nasal symptoms, dyspepsia, diarrhea, constipation, sweating, exhaustion, pallor, fever, red, dull eyes, awaken 3–4 AM
Chronology	3–9% of population; onset as early as 8 months; in children females and males are equal; 12% onset before 40 years; more common in females
Aggravating/easing factors	Menstruation ↑, contraceptives ↑
	Pregnancy ↓, tryptophan ↓
Precipitating factors	Food additives: MSG, caffeine, alcohol, tyranine, sodium nitrite, calcium propionate, histamine
	Glare, dust, odors, temperature changes, barometric pressure and humidity changes, stress—physical and psychologic, lack of O_2, hunger, smoking, ↓ in blood serotonin

TABLE 5-15. Types of Headaches Related to the Vascular or Migraine Variety

Variables

Ophthalmoplegic	Weak ocular muscles, double vision
Basilar	Instability
Hemiplegic	Slurred speech
Retinal	Visual hallucinations, unilateral visual loss, dull ache behind eye
Abdominal	Vomiting, GI pain
Tension Headache	Symptoms in 30–40%
Common	Less severe, bilateral pain, minor associated symptoms: blurred vision, dizziness, instability, vague, nausea
Classic	10%, sharp prodrome for 30 min, more severe pain, nausea, vomiting, anorexia
Lower Half Headache (Facial)	Unilateral, pain spreading to cheek, nostril, ear, and jaw
Childhood	Vomiting, little or no headache
	↑ 6–7 yr of age
	Puberty—prodromal symptoms
	Middle age—vomiting ↓, mild nausea ↑, appetite ↓, headaches ↑
Menopause	Menopause = ↓ in frequency

can present with infraorbital pain spreading to the cheek, nostril, ear and jaw unilaterally.[220,239]

Migraine may also be classified as common or classic. The classic variety occurs in 10 percent of patients. This is characterized by a sharp prodrome with visual sensations that may last for 30 minutes contralateral to the painful side. Pain is more severe than in the common variety with associated nausea, vomiting, and anorexia (Table 5-15). The term hemicrania was originally applied to this type of migraine. Common migraine is not as severe, may be bilateral, and can last for hours or days. Associated disturbances are blurred vision, dizziness, irritability, and vague nausea.[214,220,221,232,233,235,239,249]

Migraine is not uncommon in children and has been reported as early as 8 months. In 92 percent of migraine patients, symptoms develop before age 40, and 5 percent during childhood.[232] Fifty percent of children who develop migraines have parents who were also affected. The incidence in males and females is nearly equal in childhood but is more prevalent in females, as high as 5 to 1, later in life. Migraine in a young child is characterized by attacks of vomiting with little or no headaches.[239] Headaches as a rule are uncommon in young children and, if present, may signify serious pathology. Cerebellar tumors may initially give rise to headaches in children. Directly associated with such involvement will be behavioral changes such as irritability and lack of energy, along with vomiting and papilledema.[287] Headaches become more prominent at ages 6 to 7. Prodromal visual symptoms usually have their onset at puberty. In middle age, vomiting subsides, but mild nausea and loss of appetite occur. Migraine seems to decrease in frequency at menopause and may even stop completely.[220]

However, menstrual migraine frequently has its onset at menarche. A decrease in estrogen levels has been implicated but is controversial.[213] The incidence increases among users of birth control pills, which produce a prolonged elevation in the level of estrogen with the headache occurring upon withdrawal.[213] Menstrual migraine decreases during pregnancy as estrogen levels are maintained.[220] The release of prostaglandins (E or F) before or during menstruation may cause vasodilation (E) or constriction and uterine contractions (F). A similar means of vasoconstriction may occur in the brain by circulating prostaglandins causing menstrual migraine.[220,234] Prostaglandins given to nonmenstruating volunteers produced vasodilation, headache, abdominal pain, nausea, and a pale or flushed appearance.

Birth control pills are considered to be contraindicated in women who have speech difficulty, paresthesia, unilateral weakness, or visual loss associated with migraine.[8,220,232,234,239]

Transient ischemic attacks may mimic prodromal symptoms of migraine. Headache is a common sign in the developing stages of a cerebral vascular accident.[218]

Migraine may occur only once; however, it commonly afflicts about 3 to 9 percent of the population several times a year, week, or day. Migraine sufferers may be awakened by pain at 3 to 4 AM. This factor was researched with the aid of an EEG monitor that determined that attacks coincide with rapid eye movements (REM) sleep.[217,220]

Symptoms mentioned as being associated with migraine headaches include blockage, discharge, sneezing, or itching of the nose (usually ipsilateral to the side of pain); postnasal drip; redness of the eye; and profuse sweating. Gastrointestinal effects consist of colitis, constipation, diaphragmatic irritation, diarrhea, dyspepsia, and frequency of urination.[212,221,239] Nervousness is also common.[221]

Numerous precipitating factors have been implicated in triggering migraines. Allergies, such as hay fever or asthma, are rarely considered to be related. However, glare, dust, odors, cold, heat, humidity, dry air, physical and psychologic stress, hunger, caffeine, alcohol, barometric pressure changes, and certain drugs such as indomethacin and reserpine are commonly mentioned.[220,221,242] The most frequently discussed causative factors are specific foods or additives. Table 5-16 lists substances suspected of causing headaches primarily of the vascular variety. There is controversy as to whether such substances cause migraine headaches.[220–222,224,234,239]

Chemical substances known to be nociceptive and vasoneuroactive have been mentioned as being involved in the mechanism of migraine.[220,223,226,242] Histimine, serotonin, and bradykinin fall into this category. The intravenous administration of histamine has been shown to produce headaches in migraine patients but not in normal persons.[242] Serotonin is released from normal blood platelets and the intestinal wall during the onset of migraine, which may be a causative factor of diarrhea and/or vomiting.[220,243,235,239] Bradykinin and serotonin seem to potentiate each other and can sensitize arteries, resulting in vasodilation.[220] Administration of a serotonin precurser, l-tryptophan, has been shown to decrease the frequency of migraine headaches.[223] Below-normal levels of serotonin result in an increase in pain and depression.[223] Blood serotonin is not increased in cluster headaches, but blood histamine is.[220] There is a small increase in histamine at the end of the migraine attack.[220,221] Migraine headaches may occur in the morning simply from sleeping in a room with poor ventilation. A lack of sufficient oxygen will result in vasodilation as well as an increase in the level of CO_2 in the bloodstream.[220]

Migraine patients are considered to be compulsive, obsessive, meticulous, anxious, depressed, ambitious, and sensitive.[214,234,239]

CLUSTER HEADACHES

The most painful variety of headache is the cluster type.[216,220,221,249] Cluster headaches have also been termed Horton's or histamine headaches and periodic migrainous neuralgia.[216,239,239] Pain is usually unilateral, is located deep behind or around one eye, and may spread to the forehead, cheek, or jaw, but remains unilateral. Onset is quite rapid without a prodrome except for occasional burning pain in the forehead for about 5 minutes.[216,239] The headache is usually of short duration, ranging from 10 minutes to about 4 hours.[210,214,220,230,232,239]

TABLE 5-16. Headache-causing Substances

I. Avoid Potential Headache-Causing Substances:
1. Caffeine: Occurs naturally in tea, coffee, and cola nuts. Caffeine is added to many nonalcoholic carbonated beverages. An example: a 12-ounce can of Coke has 64.7 mg. of caffeine.
   Side Effects: Produces nervousness, insomnia, and tachycardia. Caffeine contracts blood vessels and relieves vascular headaches; however, victims of tension headaches who continually take caffeine as a part of APC tablets may develop headaches as the effects wear off. Similarly, going cold turkey with tea or coffee will cause withdrawal headaches.
2. Sodium Nitrite: Used extensively as preservatives and "color fixatives" in cured meats, meat products, and in certain cured fish.
   Side Effects: Nitrites dilate blood vessels and even the tiny amount found in cured meats can cause headaches in some people.
3. MSG (Monosodium Glutamate): Is a "flavor enhancer" and is manufactured from corn or wheat gluten or from sugar beet by-products. MSG is used by restaurants to restore the flavor and maintain the fresh-cooked quality of canned and re-heated foods.
   Side Effects: Symptoms develop 15 to 20 minutes after eating. Victims complain of numbness to both arms and the back, general weakness and palpitations. Other symptoms include "profuse, cold sweat," "tightness on both sides of the head," and a "viselike pounding, throbbing sensation in the head." The ensuing headache is a pressure or throbbing type over the temples with a sensation of a tight band across the forehead. People who react to MSG usually are susceptible to migraine and other vascular headaches.
4. Alcohol and Histamine: Both substances will severely dilate blood vessels. Red wine, in particular, may have a high histamine content, and can trigger migraine and cluster headaches in susceptible individuals. The hangover headache the morning after is the result of acetaldehyde and acetate breakdown products of alcohol circulating in the blood and affecting the arteries in the skull.
5. Calcium or Sodium Propionate: A chemical preservative used as mold and rope inhibitor in bread, rolls, and other baked goods; in poultry stuffing; in chocolate products; in processed cheeses; in cakes and cup cakes; in artificially sweetened fruit jelly and preserves; in pizza crust and in food packaging materials.
   Side Effects: Moderate allergic reactions have been reported 4 to 18 hours after ingestion. Disturbances commenced in the upper gastrointestinal tract and ended with partial or total migraine headaches. The gastrointestinal distress symptoms are similar to gallbladder attacks, and can be especially severe in individuals where there is a combined allergy and gallbladder ailment. When the calcium propionate is used, it destroys the enzyme that normally makes it possible for the body to assimilate any calcium present naturally, or added through enrichment in bread.
6. Tyramine: Is a food chemical that dilates blood vessels and may be considered a potential allergenic headache-triggering substance. This compound is found primarily in red wines and aged cheeses. Some tyramine-high foods are: Dairy Products—sour cream, ripened or aged cheese, cheddar, gruyere, stilton, emmentabo, brie, camembert, gouda, mozzarella, parmesan, provolone, romano, roquefort, Swiss, edam, and yogurt; Meats and Fish—pickled herring, summer sausage, fermented sausage and other varieties, salami, bologna, pepperoni, salted fried fish, beef and chicken liver; Vegetables—avocados, Italian broad beans with pods (fava beans), sauerkraut, Chinese food, onions and lima beans; Alcoholic Beverages—beer, wine yeast extract, ale, red wines (chianti is the worst!), riesling, sauterne, champagne, and sherry; Miscellaneous—yeast and yeast extracts, chocolate, vanilla, soy sauce, and anything pickled or marinated.
7. Drugs: Ninety percent of the drugs listed in the *Physician's Desk Reference (PDR)* have headaches listed as one of their side effects. One must consider any medication presently being taken as a possible triggering substance. However, caution must be exercised because headaches must be listed as a side effect even if a very small percentage of test patients experience the symptom.
   Victims of chronic headaches, or those with frequent tension headaches, may be creating their own head pain by abusing the analgesics being consumed. Withdrawal headaches very often can be attributed to the rebound effect of the caffeine present in aspirin compounds. Caffeine, like nicotine, constricts blood vessels. Going cold turkey, either from stopping smoking or discontinuing your headache relief pills, will result in the blood vessels dilating, thus triggering a headache.
   Heavy consumption of coffee, tea, and/or cigarettes, on a daily basis, maintains the blood vessels in a constricted state. Failure to meet your daily quota may trigger a rebound headache when the blood vessels dilate.
8. Birth Control Pills: The "Pill" changes the female hormone balance. As a result, migraine-prone women suffer more severe headaches, while migraine-free women become more susceptible to headache pain than non-pill users.
II. Other Headache-Causing Food Candidates:
1. Beverages: Coke, Pepsi, coffee, tea, Dr. Pepper, Mountain Dew, and root beer, all have a high caffeine content.
2. General Group: Chicken*, fish*, shellfish*, onions or onion powder, hot fresh breads, peanut butter, spices and spicy foods, hot dogs, Chinese foods*, all fresh fruits, pizza, pork, lard, and legumes.
   NOTE: Restricting your diet by eliminating or reducing meat and salt intake may help reduce your migraine headaches.

---

*These foods are listed because they are usually seasoned with MSG (monosodium glutamate). Also included are Japanese teriyaki, kosher chicken soup, matzo-ball soup, and green pea soup.
Reproduced with permission of Gerald H. Smith, D.D.S., Newtown, Pa.

Attacks come in clusters of 1 to 10 per day, lasting for weeks or months and then stopping for months or years at a time. Chronic cluster headaches may occur in 20 percent of cases and recur regularly like migraine.[230]

Cluster headaches, unlike tension and migraine headaches, are almost exclusively (85 percent) present in males (Table 5-17).[214,216,220,230,239] Onset may occur during the teenage years and generally between ages 10 and 30. Females known to suffer from cluster headaches seem to exhibit masculine characteristics. Affected males frequently are meek and dependent on females, which has led to the use of the term leonine mouse syndrome to describe such individuals.[216,228] Cluster headache patients also show an exaggerated response to pain demonstrated by unusual behavior during an attack.

Causative or trigger factors are nitroglycerin, histamine, tyramine, smoking, drinking, glare, sleeping late (naps), skipping a meal, emotional upsets, and allergies such as hay fever.[216,220,239] The intensity of pain is excruciating and described as sharp, burning, knife-like, penetrating, deep, piercing, tearing, or boring.[210,214,216,220,230,232,239] Attacks are common at night during REM sleep.[214,216,220,221] There are numerous associated symptoms such as reddening of the eye and forehead, tearing, ptosis, drooping of the upper eyelid, sweating, skin hypersensitivity, nasal blockage or rhinorrhea, visible dilation of the temporal artery, and an ipsilateral Horner's syndrome in 20 percent of patients.[214,216,220,230,239] Horner's syndrome is due to interruption of the sympathetic input to the orbital structures and is manifested by miosis, ptosis, enophthalmos (sinking of eyeball into orbit), pupillary vasodilation, and conjunctival redness.[55] Nausea and vomiting may occur but are not common.[239] Less is known about the causes of cluster headaches, although they are considered by some to be a variant of migraine and have been confused with trigeminal neuralgia.[216,221,228,239] There is no measurable decrease in blood serotonin during cluster headache, but the level of histamine increases significantly. Twenty-five percent of cluster headache sufferers have peptic

TABLE 5-17. The Characteristics of Cluster Headaches

		Variables
Onset	Adulthood (10–30) Family history Males more than females	
Location	Unilateral	Small cold spots on forehead, ipsilateral to side of pain
Intensity	Most severe Excruciating	
Quality	Sharp, burning, knife-like Penetrating—piercing, deep Tearing—boring, no prodrome	
Pattern	PM Attacks daily for 1–3 months	
Duration	Abrupt onset and termination 2 hours	Chronic paroxysmal hemicrania, daily attacks, 6–30/day, less in PM, 15–45 min duration
Frequency	Paroxysmal	
Associated Symptoms	Reddening of forehead, nasal blockage, rhinorrhea, lacrimation, peptic ulcer, visible dilation of temporal artery sweating, skin hypersensitivity, 20% ipsilateral Horner's, miosis, ptosis, enophthalmos, conjunctival redness, pupillary vasodilation (nausea and vomiting are rare)	
Precipitating or Triggering Factors	Nitroglycerin ↑ Histamine ↑ Tyramine ↑ Smoking ↑ Alcohol ↑ Glare ↑ Sleeping late ↑	Missing meals ↑ Emotional stress ↑ Hayfever ↑

ulcers, which may implicate a vasoactive substance in the stomach or upper gastrointestinal tract.[216,230] The ingestion of vasodilating substances during a cluster headache period immediately triggers an attack.[230] Small forehead cold spots ipsilateral to the side of pain interspersed between areas of warmth have been found.[230] The circulation of the involved eye may be affected during cluster headaches as opposed to intracerebral circulation in migraine. Significant increases in corneal temperature, intraocular pressure, and corneal pulse amplitude have been recorded during a cluster headache attack.[230] Seasonal changes and family history are not significant factors.[230]

Chronic paroxysmal hemicrania is considered to be a variant of cluster headache.[228,232] It is characterized by frequent daily attacks (6 to 30 per 4-hour period). The duration of the headache is short, lasting only 15 to 45 minutes. Pain is unilateral and excruciating, with associated lacrimation, nasal symptoms, and bradycardia. There are no visual prodromes, nausea, or vomiting. Headache resulting from glaucoma is also similar to that of the cluster variety. Pain is severe and perceived as being deep in the eye or brain, or around the ocular orbit.[220,250] Chronic paroxysmal hemicrania differs from true cluster headache in that it occurs daily, less frequently at night, and it seems more common in females. However, there is little information on this type of headache to verify a definite trend.

All headaches cannot be easily categorized. The inhalation of a vasodilating substance has been shown to intensify tension headaches, which may relate more to migraines.[244] Of patients with migraine headaches, 30 to 40 percent also have symptoms of tension headaches at different times or simultaneously.[217,229,240,244] It is common to have daily tension headaches interspersed with vascular headaches, which may occur at the time of menstruation or stress.[217] Stiffness and ache of the cervical spine may, of course, occur after a migraine.[217] Headaches of this nature have thus been classified as being mixed.

HEADACHES OF INFREQUENT APPEARANCE

There are other headaches that may fall into the aforementioned groups but deserve separate mention. Temporal arteritis usually occurs after ages 50 to 55. It involves the temporal artery, which is a branch of the external carotid anastomosing with branches of the internal carotid ipsilaterally as well as contralaterally.[218,220] Headaches due to temporal arteritis may be present on one or both sides of the head and are caused by a low-grade inflammation (redness, swelling, tenderness) of the arteries that usually manifests itself first in the scalp. Pain is described as excruciating, worse at night, and boring with periods of stabbing pain along the distribution of the temporal artery. Involvement of the temporal artery may spread intracranially and involve the ophthalmic artery, resulting in blindness.[250] Decreased circulation may result in an achy pain of masticatory muscles as well as intermittent claudication.[218] If this occurs, the patient may exhibit loss of weight.

Intracranial pathology can also result in headaches. A subarachnoid hemorrhage can produce excruciating pain of abrupt onset that remains relatively constant.[211,220] Pain is primarily nuchal, producing cervical stiffness. Changes in consciousness may signify the need for a more intensive workup. Cerebellar hemorrhage can give rise to occipital or frontal headache 50 percent of the time. Brainstem compression can result in coma. Ataxia, vertigo, deviation of the eye, weakness, and lower extremity paralysis may also occur.[211]

Any increase in intracranial pressure increases arterial tension, which can cause headache. Pituitary tumors, nasopharyngeal neoplasms, and posterior fossa lesions can produce pain in the frontal or occipital regions as well as the whole head. Headaches occurring as a result of intracranial hypertension usually begin in the morning and may be relieved by vomiting. Pain is described as throbbing or bursting and may be intensified by coughing, sneezing, or straining; quick movements; and forward bending or jarring of the head.[220,287] As intracranial pressure increases, neurologic signs, which can be as minor as a loss of the sense of smell and difficulty in hearing, may gradually become apparent.

Trauma to the skull from concussion, fracture, and whiplash injuries is a common cause of headache that may slowly intensify over a period of weeks or months due to a subdural hematoma.[220] Infectious diseases such as meningitis and encephalitis can also cause vasodilation secondary to inflammation.[220]

There are very specific headaches related to one distinct etiology. These include the ice cream, hot dog, Chinese food, hangover, fasting, withdrawal, exercise, and benign sex headaches.[220] The direct application of cold to the palate and throat results in vasoconstriction and a reflex vasodilation. Sodium nitrite in hot dogs and other cured meats, monosodium glutamate in Chinese food, and histamine in red wine are vasodilators.[220] Fasting or missing a meal can lower blood sugar and set off a migraine headache. Caffeine and nicotine cause vasoconstriction that may persist with continued use; withdrawal can result in vasodilation. Exercise and sexual intercourse increase blood pressure and pulse rate, resulting in vasodilation. During intercourse, other factors such as contraction of facial and neck muscles may produce a tension headache.

Changes in cerebral spinal fluid (CSF) pressure can result in headaches. After myelograms, there is a decrease in the CSF pressure. The floating level of the brain may be changed, causing a strain on the intracranial veins. Hydrocephalus as a result of ventricular blockage of CSF can increase pressure and cause a headache.[220]

Sinusitis results in a headache at the related sinus. Pain is moderate but constant, and palpable tenderness exists.[225] The frontal sinus commonly refers pain to the forehead, but the headache can be referred to the frontal region from any sinus.

Systemic diseases also take part in the production of headache.[224] Rheumatoid arthritis may result in cranial arteritis with headache symptoms. The renin-angiotensin system of the kidney functions to raise blood pressure. During renal disease, this homeostatic mechanism dysfunctions and a decrease in blood pressure results in headaches. Tightening of the scalp muscles or collagenous impairment of circulatory vessels may cause constant headaches secondary to scleroderma. Systemic lupus erythematosus may cause headaches as a result of circulatory damage. Endocrine imbalances such as hyperthyroidism and pituitary and adrenal dysfunction can also give rise to headaches. The importance of evaluating the whole patient and not just treating the headache symptomatically may uncover disorders resulting in Cushing's syndrome or Addison's disease.

Relaxation and biofeedback training have been shown to be very beneficial in the prevention of tension and vascular headaches provided the patient continues to follow the home program.[246,247]

TEMPOROMANDIBULAR JOINT SYNDROME

Pathology involving the cervical spine can also result in headaches, and temporomandibular joint (TMJ) and upper extremity pain. TMJ involvement commonly occurs in patients with sustained cervical strains as a result of an automobile accident. Following a comprehensive rehabilitation program designed to restore normal cervical spine active ROM and to eliminate muscle guarding and pain, a significant number of these patients continue to experience a low-grade chronic discomfort of the face, neck, shoulder girdle, and occasionally the upper ipsilateral extremity. There may be associated complaints of headache, dizziness, nasal congestion, burning of one side of the tongue, dryness of the mouth, and auditory disorders. This complex commonly occurs when the normal function and smooth articulation of the TMJs are disturbed.[206,290,453] The TMJ syndrome may be precipitated by causes other than direct trauma from a whiplash injury or blow to the head.[275] Congenital joint defects, postural abnormalities, degenerative osteoarthritis, malocclusion, systemic conditions such as hypothyroidism, bruxism, and fatigue have been implicated as contributing to TMJ syndrome.[206,267–271,453] The syndrome is primarily unilateral and occurs most frequently in females (80 percent of the reported cases) between ages 30 and 60, although cases have been reported in children below age 10.[269]

Innervation of the TMJ is complex. Posterior and lateral innervation is via the auriculotemporal nerves. The masseteric, deep temporal, and lateral pterygoid nerves supply accessory articular branches from the mandibular musculature.[272] Sensory branches of the trigeminal nerve, motor distribution of the facial nerve, and autonomic fibers of the otic ganglion play a role in supplying the TMJ. This extensive innervation accounts for the large array of symptoms as well as referred pain. The spinal tract of the trigeminal nerve is one means by which the referral of TMJ-related pain to the neck, shoulder girdle, and upper extremity can occur. Biomechanical relationships can also account for pain referral. The anatomic connections between the trigeminal nerve and the upper cervical spine are fully described in Chapter 8.

The TMJ is the most active joint in the body, constantly in motion during breathing, talking, eating, and swallowing. The constant movement of the joint can easily account for the chronicity of symptoms. A synopsis of the TMJ pain cycle can be seen in Figure 5-19. The loss of normal and smooth joint articulation can lead to structural changes and displacement of the disk, giving rise to a grating sound, clicking, and crepitation.[453] The use of a stethoscope is invaluable in determining this sign. The joint surfaces may flatten, restricting mobility and causing pain. Clicking on opening the mouth, stemming from changes in the position of the superior articular eminence and the anterior head of the condyle of the mandible, can be heard.[206,268] Anterior displacement of the disk leads to a posterior and superior position of the mandibular condyle, placing it in what is known as the close-packed position.[453] This leads to significant pain since the anterior and posterior edges of the condyle are densely innervated. A loose-packed position of the mandibular condyle in its fossa or a position that is slightly anterior to and facing the middle one third of the eminentia articularis and the biconcave surface of the disk is the desired relationship.[453] Clicking on closing the mouth may signify a loss of normal vertical dimension ipsilateral to the side of the click.[269] Muscle guarding or spasm will obviously ensue, producing circulatory disturbances and trigger points, causing referred pain and local tenderness. The medial (internal) pterygoid muscle most commonly goes into spasm, followed in order of frequency by the masseter, temporalis, sternocleidomastoids, lateral pterygoid, posterior cervicals, and the digastricus.[198,270] Resultant referred pain patterns are illustrated in Figures 5-11, 5-12, and 5-20.[181]

Evaluation of the TMJ should be incorporated into any head, neck, or shoulder examination. The patient should be observed for facial deviation. The lips, eyebrow, and ear may be higher on the side of the joint that has the greater loss of vertical dimension. The ipsilateral shoulder may be lower and scoliosis present.[273] The extremity musculature ipsilateral to the side of dysfunction may test weaker.[274] Muscular weakness due to TMJ dysfunction is controversial, however. The oral aperture should be measured and movement observed for deviation on opening or closing. Males of average height have a normal aperture of 5.0 to 7.3 cm, and females 4.5 to 6.5 cm. A vertical opening less than 5.0 cm in males and 4.5 cm in females is considered abnormal.[181] The "rule of knuckles" can also be used to measure aperture.[181] Individuals with normal apertures should be able to place the knuckles of the second to fourth proximal interphalangeal joints (one on top of the other) into the mouth between the incisors.

TMJ

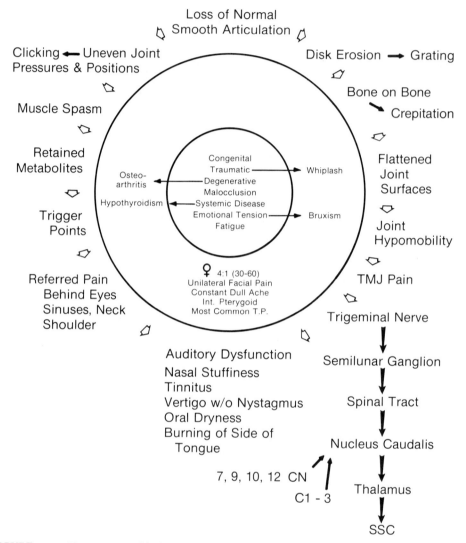

FIGURE 5-19. Temporomandibular joint syndrome: etiology, biomechanical factors, and symptomatology.

Palpation is of utmost importance in performing a comprehensive TMJ evaluation. The fingers can determine trigger points, spasm, and joint mobility. The use of the index fingers to palpate and determine abnormal movement of the TMJ external to the joint and within the external auditory meatus is simple to perform.[285]

Treatment of the TMJ syndrome must be comprehensive. The clinician can employ joint mobilization to increase mobility and stretch soft tissue. The adjunctive use of fluori-

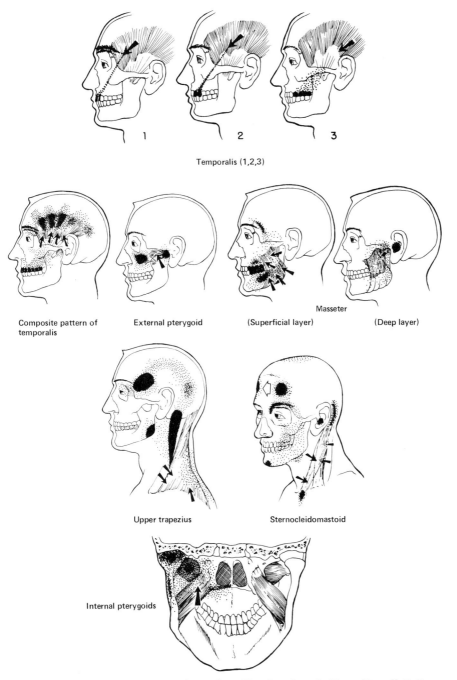

Temporalis (1,2,3)

Composite pattern of temporalis

External pterygoid

Masseter

(Superficial layer)

(Deep layer)

Upper trapezius

Sternocleidomastoid

Internal pterygoids

FIGURE 5-20. Pain referral pattern of muscles of head and neck. (From Travell, J: *Temporo-mandibular joint pain referred from muscles of head and neck.* J Prosthet Dent 10:745, 1980, with permission.)

methane spray and stretch to masseter, temporalis, upper trapezius, scaleni, sternocleidomastoid, suboccipital musculature, and so forth is very beneficial. High-voltage galvanic stimulation and T.E.N.S. have been used to decrease pain and muscle guarding.[227,276,281,282] Cryotherapy in the form of ice packs has also been employed.[276] Proper postural mechanics must not be overlooked.

In most cases, rehabilitation of the TMJ cannot be accomplished without the aid of a dentist. It may be necessary for the patient to wear orthopedic mandibular appliances for 3 to 12 months to establish optimal repositioning and remodeling of the joint.[206,269,390,443] The majority of our patients have achieved an almost immediate, profound decrease in pain after obtaining such an appliance.[274]

CRANIOMANDIBULAR AND CERVICAL SPINE DYSFUNCTION

The innervation of the spinal or vertebral complex is quite involved with multiple overlap among adjacent segments as well as contralateral connections via the sinuvertebral nerve (see Chapter 8). Headaches can therefore arise from a myriad of traumatic episodes resulting in disk derangement, facet malalignment, and other mechanical faults. In addition, congenital and postural anomalies, osteoarthritis, rheumatoid arthritis, Paget's disease, ankylosing spondylitis, multiple myeloma, osteomyelitis, and neoplasm may give rise to headaches.[277] Cyriax mentions irritation or kinking of the vertebral artery by osteophytes as one cause of headaches. He particularly relates dura mater impingement by a cervical disk as a cause of extrasegmental pain referred to the head.[28] A detailed discussion of all pain syndromes arising from the cervical spine is beyond the scope of this text; therefore, a general discussion of factors giving rise to headaches of cervical origin will be presented.

Involvement of the upper cervical facet joints C1–3 results in irritation of the occipital nerves that originate from the C2–3 segments. The C1 root is not considered to have a cutaneous distribution.[28] However, the C1 root may provide some sensory innervation to the anterior half of the head since stimulation of C1 rootlets during posterior fossa surgery produced orbital, frontal, and vertex pain.[277] The common distribution of the postwhiplash occipital headache from the occiput to the vertex of the head follows the course of the occipital nerves. Directly related is the splenius capitis trigger point that produces a vertex headache (see Fig. 5-11). The distribution of the supraorbital nerves from the forehead to the vertex of the skull can account for the referral of occipital pain to the forehead, as can the anastomosis between the spinal tract of the trigeminal nerve and the upper cervical spine. Occipital neuralgia may result in referred temporal or retro-orbital headache as well as pain to the shoulders.[287] The patient with occipital neuralgia may relate sensory changes on half of the scalp, which are noticeable when combing or brushing the hair. Maigne states that the supraorbital headache occurs most frequently and is usually unilateral.[19] A simple pinch and skin roll test of the eyebrow will reveal a thickening and discomfort on the side of the headache. Similar pinch tests can be performed over the mandibular and temporal regions to delineate occipitomandibular and auriculotemporal headaches, respectively.[19] Palpation of the upper cervical spine should reveal tenderness on the side corresponding to the headache.

A severe flexion-extension or whiplash injury can result in damage (tear or stretch) to both posterior and anterior ligaments and muscle. The immediate result is muscle guarding and soreness with pain spreading from the suboccipital to frontal regions. Discomfort is obviously increased by cervical motion, which is hindered by guarding and if prolonged will cause joint hypomobility. The normal cervical lordosis may be lost, and palpation will reveal tenderness and spasm. Muscle spasm and interstitial edema may entrap and irritate the upper cervical nerve roots.[17,277] Information regarding the pain syndrome resulting from whiplash injuries is fully covered in many texts; however, the craniomandibular relationship is ignored.[17,19,28,278,279] Many patients with myofascial pain and TMJ dysfunction due to whiplash injuries are referred solely for T.E.N.S., often as a last resort, when proper treatment based on the work of Rocabado may correct such a craniomandibular syndrome.

Rocabado has clearly established that malocclusion and abnormal TMJ mechanics are not the sole causes of craniomandibular pain.[453] A comprehensive evaluation of such patients must include observation of head, neck, and shoulder girdle posture along with function of the related musculature and joint ROM. The position of the head in space must be determined. A change in the so-called orthostatic or balanced head position can result in mechanical disruption of the mandible, cervical spine, thoracic outlet, and shoulder girdle. Bilateral guarding of the SCM will cause extension of the occiput on atlas-axis resulting in forward bending of the lower cervical vertebrae on the thorax. This is one cause of a forward head posture. The SCM muscles undergo an angulation change from 45 degrees to 90 degrees, with increased hyperactivity and shortening.

A forward head position can lead to round shoulders and compression of occiput on the upper cervical spine, resulting in tension on the suprahyoid and infrahyoid muscles. The hyoid bone, which has no bony articulation, attaches to the mandible via the suprahyoids and to the clavicle, sternum, and rib cage via the infrahyoids. The mandible is under control of the masticatory muscles and articulates with the cranium via the teeth (occlusion) and TMJ. Increased spasm of the anterior cervical musculature can lead to tightness of the throat, resulting in swallowing problems and voice changes. The position of the mandible can be altered, producing increased posterior occlusion and "close-packed" position of the TMJ.

Cervical dysfunction and/or guarding of lateral musculature, such as the scalenes, can lead to a side-bent position of the head and neck with rotation of the head to the opposite side. This can result in deviation of the mandible to the opposite side, causing occlusion on the buccal cusps in the premolar and molar areas on the contralateral side.

A prolonged forward or side-bent head posture will produce shoulder girdle abnormalities that can result in thoracic outlet syndrome, scapulocostal syndrome, tendinitis, nerve root entrapment, neurovascular compression, and TMJ dysfunction. The shoulder girdle cannot remain in its normal position if there is a prolonged forward head posture. It will migrate forward as well as causing round shoulders, alar scapulae, and changes in clavicular angulation and position of the mandible, hyoid bone, and even the tongue. Medial entrapment of the dorsal scapular nerve that innervates the rhomboids and levator scapulae can occur, causing pain referral to the shoulder and upper thoracic region. Elevation of the hyoid bone can alter the normal resting position of the tongue, causing it to drop down from the palate.

Rocabado has clearly established that the head, neck, and shoulder girdle must be evaluated and treated as a functional unit. Treatment for restoration of normal mobility and a pain-free state must consist of postural corrections, diaphragmatic breathing and tongue exercises, soft-tissue stretching, and joint mobilization as well as pain modulation techniques.

Lewit describes a syndrome of the posterior arch of the atlas that results in headaches.[280] Signs and symptoms reveal pain and limitation of motion on retroflexion and rotation to one side and tenderness to palpation of the posterior arch of the atlas just lateral to the midline and occasionally to the transverse process. Tender points correspond to the course of the occipital nerves. Successful treatment techniques consisted of manipulation and dry needling.

Cyriax, Maigne, Stoddard, and Lewit feel some migraine headaches are related to cervical spine dysfunction. They report relief with cervical manipulations to the mid and lower cervical spine. Migraine of cervical origin always occurs on the same side during each episode. There is usually a history of trauma to the cervical spine and dysfunction.

The posterior cervical sympathetic syndrome, also known as the Barre Lieou syndrome, causes headaches due to cervical pathology that have been compared with migraine.[19,130,277,283] The syndrome is thought to occur as a result of irritation of the sympathetic fibers surrounding the vertebral artery from an osteophyte arising from the uncovertebral joints.[130,278,283] Any lesion or anomaly of the cervical spine that irritates or compresses the posterior cervical sympathetic network can result in intracranial vasoconstriction affecting the cranial nerves that give rise to the widespread symptomatology.[283] The posterior cervical sympathetic syndrome is most common in patients over the age of 50.[19] The symptom complex involved in this syndrome includes pain anywhere in the head and neck, impaired hearing, tinnitus and vestibular problems, blurred vision (a feeling of dust in the eyes), hoarseness, nasal irritation, tearing of the eye, hot flashes, sweating, and psychologic disturbances. Pain is frequently continuous, with periods of intensification as though the head is being hit by a hammer or squeezed by tongs. Patients with this syndrome describe the pain as throbbing, burning, stinging, pricking, or creeping.[283] Aggravating or precipitatory factors include cervical movement, sneezing, coughing, mental activity, emotional disturbances, atmospheric changes, and gastrointestinal problems. Involvement of the eye can shift from side to side, but the suboccipital and nuchal areas exhibit constant tenderness.

Delineation of the cervical sympathetic syndrome from migraines requires evaluation to determine the presence of cervical spine involvement. Mobility will be impaired, and certain movements will intensify or bring on the symptoms. Treatment of all headaches of cervical origin must include appropriate restoration of cervical spine function. Traction has been shown to be effective.[283]

Edmeads lists seven signs to delineate the origin of a headache as coming from the cervical spine:[277]

1. Persistent suboccipital or occipital pain, usually intense and unilateral.
2. Cervical movements bring on or change the headache.
3. Abnormal head and neck posture such as a forward head.
4. Tenderness in the suboccipital or nuchal region, particularly if unilateral headache is produced by deep suboccipital pressure.
5. Significant and painful hypomobility.
6. Craniocervical dysfunction.
7. Symptomatology indicative of the upper cervical spine and nerve roots.

SENSORY DEPRIVATION PAIN SYNDROMES

These pain syndromes share the following general characteristics:

1. Loss of or damage to either large or small fibers.
2. Cutaneous hyperesthesia (increased sensitivity to touch) and hyperpathia (continued irritation after a stimulus).
3. Precipitation of pain as a result of non-noxious somatic stimuli (allodynia) or emotional upsets.
4. May be activated by summation mechanisms.
5. Severe, intractable pain.
6. Involvement of the autonomic nervous system.[6–8,66,129,130,292]

A loss of or damage to either the large or small fibers stops the normal relationship or balancing of afferent input between the proprioceptive and nociceptive systems. The result is a reversal or lowering of the normal high threshold of activation inherent in the small fibers so that non-noxious stimuli may give rise to pain or summate with other continuous non-noxious input (sweating and so forth) to raise the total amount of afferent activity to the threshold level of perception. Repetitive sympathetic stimulation results in an increase of afferent input, causing facilitation of internuncial neurons and a decrease in the threshold of excitation.[308]

Sensory deprivation pain syndromes may also damage small myelineated and non-myelineated fibers in comparison with just-selective attacks of large myelineated fibers.[56,325,340] Peripheral neuropathies that involve only destruction of the small fibers have caused severe pain, and other neuropathies that involve destruction of large fibers may not cause pain. This phenomenon occurs in thallium neuropathy.[39] Thus, numerous neuropathies can be caused by disease processes as well as circulatory disturbances, chemical

TABLE 5-18. Characters of Common Sensory Deprivation Pain Syndromes

Neuralgia	Causalgia	Phantom Limb

mild
Trigeminal moderate   mandibular
    severe   maxillary
Hyperesthesia
Females 60–80 (non-noxious ↑)
Unilateral
Little function loss (no
   neurologic signs)
Paroxysmal—fast onset and
   decline (1–3 min)
Sharp, shooting, jabbing,
   burning, lancinating
   (segmental)
Rare in PM
Facial
Glossopharyngeal
Vagus
 	
Atypical facial neuralgia
Unilateral → bilateral
Not within cranial nerve
   distribution
Not paroxysmal
Worse in PM
Deep, dull ache, throbbing,
   burning
Gradual onset and decline
Non-noxious stimuli do not
   trigger pain
More common in females
 	
Post-herpetic
Spinal and cranial—trigeminal
   (ophthalmic division)
Burning, stabbing, shooting
   pains
Spontaneous onset
Background soreness
Hyperesthesia
Non-noxious stimuli increase
   pain
	Median, ulnar, sciatic, brachial
	   plexus
	Blood vessels
	Pain distal to lesion
	Hyperesthesia
	Non-noxious stimuli increase pain
	Constant
	Severe burning
	Associated deep ache
	Persist for 6 months
	Spontaneously ends
	Trophic changes
	
	Minor causalgia
	Lack of damage to one or more
	   peripheral nerves
	Onset—minor trauma
	RSD (shoulder-hand syndrome)
	Sudeck's atrophy
	Post-traumatic osteoporosis
	Extrasegmental
	Burning and achy discomfort
	Non-noxious stimuli increase
	   pain
		30–35% of amputees
		5–10% severe—history
		Shooting, crushing, twisting,
		   cramping
		Periodic
		Non-noxious and noxious input
		   triggers pain

deficiencies, toxic substances, and so forth. T.E.N.S. has been reported to be beneficial in the modulation of pain due to neuropathies.[331,332] Biofeedback and relaxation training have recently been shown to be effective,[314,342] as well as the use of sympathetic blocks early in the course of a sensory deprivation pain syndrome.[6,8,130]

Three categories of syndromes that possess the above characteristics are neuralgia, causalgia, and phantom limb (Table 5-18). The effectiveness of T.E.N.S. in these related syndromes has been well documented.[60,72,123,166,289,303,306,313,344–351,354,357]

NEURALGIA

The term neuralgia encompasses a wide range of specific syndromes. A neuralgia usually implies that pain follows the distribution of a peripheral, spinal, or cranial nerve.[289] Causative factors include sinusitis, viral infections, sclerotic plaques, mechanical pressure from neoplasms or the petrous ridge of the temporal bone, circulatory problems, diabetes, vitamin deficiency, inflammation, metabolic disturbances, trauma, and toxicity.[8,66,287,293–300]

Pain is characterized as severe with intense paroxysmal episodes but may differ somewhat depending on the etiology and type of nerve fiber damaged. Neuralgic syndromes involving specific areas of the body that are more representative of central pain states will be briefly discussed later. These include the thalamic syndrome, multiple sclerosis, tabes dorsalis, and paresis or paralysis.

Trigeminal neuralgia, also known as "tic douloureux," is perhaps the most common cranial nerve neuralgia and is manifested by facial tics or grimaces. This extremely irritable condition is most common in females between ages 60 and 80.[130] Pain is most often unilateral and is not accompanied by a loss of motor function or sensation, or other neurologic signs (see Table 5-18).[287,289] The pain is characterized as shooting, jabbing, electric or lightning-like, sharp, lancinating, and burning.[7,8,287,289,291] A relatively constant but less intense background ache that is quite bearable when compared with the severe paroxysmal pain that lasts only a few minutes also exists. Trigeminal neuralgia can be mild, moderate, or severe depending on the frequency of attacks. Attacks occurring with intervals of days or weeks are considered mild. Daily or more frequent attacks are moderate. Attacks lasting throughout a 24-hour period with as many as 40 occurrences are termed severe.

Patients with trigeminal neuralgia frequently state that their pain is worse than any other pain they have experienced. It may be triggered by various non-noxious stimuli such as light touch, eating, swallowing, shaving, talking, chewing gum, washing the face, sneezing, emotional upsets, or for no apparent reason (allodynia).[7,8,287,291] As a result of this phenomenon, patients may be unshaven, quiet, weak from not eating, and obviously extremely depressed. Pain usually does not occur at night, and these patients learn to sleep with the involved side up to eliminate stimulation from the bed, blanket, or pillow. Noxious stimuli, such as pressure, pinching, needling, and extremes of heat or cold, commonly do not produce an attack.

Involvement is usually of the maxillary division of the fifth cranial nerve, with the right side affected more frequently than the left.[8] The mandibular division is also commonly involved.[287,293] A sensitive trigger point or zone is usually found at the infraorbital region (below the eye to the side of the nose and angle of the mouth).[8,60,130] Obviously, this will change depending on which of the three trigeminal divisions is involved.

There is no general consensus concerning the physiologic mechanisms of trigeminal neuralgia.[291,300] Obviously, many of the mechanical, toxic, and infectious conditions that result in irritation of the trigeminal nerve or its spinal tract can result in fiber damage, demyelination, and a lowering of the excitation threshold, resulting in pain from non-noxious stimuli.[7,293,298,308] The presence of three categories of trigeminothalamic neurons (nociceptive-specific, wide-dynamic, and low-threshold mechanoreceptive) in the trigeminal nucleus caudalis also needs to be considered.[299,301] Nociceptive-specific neurons are activated only by intense mechanical and/or thermal stimuli. Wide-dynamic range neurons respond to mild mechanical forces, hair movement, and maximally to noxious pinch or heat. Low-threshold mechanoreceptive neurons respond to light touch, pressure, or hair movement. Consequently, neurons within the primary trigeminal modulation region (nucleus caudalis) can be activated by summation mechanisms, influenced by convergent input, and result in inhibition or facilitation.[293] Summation mechanisms definitely occur in trigeminal neuralgia, as is evidenced by gentle touch or rubbing of the involved skin. A 15- to 30-second lapse of period of stimulation may be required, after which severe pain will occur for 1 to 3 minutes and then terminate abruptly (hyperpathia). Another theory concerns the formation of ephapses (abnormal synaptic connections between sympathetic efferents and somatic afferent fibers at a lesion) and the resultant "cross-talk" of impulses that may cause increased excitation similar to summation.[7,130,135,293,306,308] This, however, is considered to be controversial and not yet confirmed.[320] The release of chemical irritants at the site of injury may also cause a lowering of the threshold.[130]

Sensory end-organs decrease in number with age. In the later years, 80 percent of tactile corpuscles are no longer present or functional. The innervation of these receptors via nerve fibers is also reduced.[25,32] Gardner states that by age 65, 30 percent of the myelineated fibers degenerate.[7] This physiologic factor, which results in a decrease of large-fiber afferent input, may also play a role in trigeminal neuralgia, which is most common in elderly females.

Differential diagnosis is imperative as somewhat similar pain complaints may be caused by multiple sclerosis (demyelination of the spinal tract of the trigeminal nerve), TMJ syndrome, neuralgia of other cranial nerves, atypical facial pain syndromes, myofascial pain syndromes or headaches (muscle contraction, cluster and migraine), and cervical spine dysfunction, which may also cause headaches and facial pain.[129,287] Particular concern should be shown if motor and/or sensory neuralgic signs exist, symptoms persist in someone under the age of 50, and pain is bilateral or referred to the neck.[287] These symptoms may be due to medullary neoplasm, infection, syringomyelia, thalamic syndrome, or an aneurysm.[287,291] Cancer of the nasopharynx will give rise to severe trigeminal pain, but it will be constant, not paroxysmal, and described as deep and boring.[130,287] Nosebleeds (epistaxis) and forward projection or displacement of the eyeball (proptosis) may occur prior to pain.[287,291]

Other cranial neuralgias involving the seventh, ninth, and tenth cranial nerves may be thought of as primary trigeminal neuralgia.[7,8,66,287,289,291] The sensory portion of the facial nerve (nervus intermedius) and the geniculate ganglion can be affected by the herpes zoster virus and produce the Ramsey-Hunt syndrome or geniculate neuralgia.[8,287,289] Associated facial involvement (Bell's palsy) may also occur. Etiology is usually due to shingles of the ear, and pain is perceived as being deep inside the ear. Differentiation from other neuralgias is that pain is usually constant, not paroxysmal, yet severe.

The glossopharyngeal nerve and vagus may also exhibit tic-like symptomatology.[8,66] The glossopharyngeal nerve innervates the base of the tongue and soft palate.[139,286] A burning or stabbing pain of a paroxysmal nature similar to that of trigeminal neuralgia can thus occur. Pain, however, is felt at the back of the tongue, throat, and middle ear.[8,66,130] Some sensory components of the glossopharyangeal nerve run with that of the vagus entering the brainstem by the uppermost region of the medulla.[130] They then descend via the spinal tract of the trigeminal nerve. Glossopharyngeal neuralgia is also precipitated by touch, swallowing, and talking.

Involvement of the vagus nerve may produce superior laryngeal neuralgia. This form of neuralgia has characteristics similar to those of glossopharyngeal, producing pain at the base of the tongue as well as the glottis, and may also be referred to the upper thorax.

All of the cranial neuralgias except trigeminal are considered to be rare and obviously may involve other lesions of the medulla and gasserian ganglion. Such a lesion may give rise to trigeminal pain and hyperesthesia in all three divisions of the nerve.[287] Accurate diagnosis becomes difficult and may be further complicated by the presence of atypical facial neuralgias of unknown origin.

Atypical Facial Neuralgia

The pain associated with atypical facial neuralgias is usually not within or along the distribution of one of the cranial nerves.[297] It is nonparoxysmal, more frequent at night, and a deep, dull ache that throbs and may burn.[294,297] Atypical facial neuralgia has a slow onset, lasting for hours, days, or months with a gradual decline in discomfort, as opposed to sudden termination. There are no obvious neurologic signs.[287] Atypical facial pain is usually unilateral but may spread bilaterally over the face and to the cervical spine. Touching the face does not trigger pain, as in trigeminal neuralgia.[130,287] Atypical facial neuralgias are most common in females, but the average age range is below that of trigeminal neuralgia.[8] Etiology may be emotional or pychologic with associated ANS symptoms of vascular origin.[297] Depression is common.[289] Other causes may be tumors, headaches, toxic neuropathies, TMJ syndrome, temporal arteritis, sinusitis, glaucoma, or ophthalmoplegic migraine.[287,297]

Post-herpetic Neuralgia

Post-herpetic neuralgia (shingles) is the result of a virus (herpes zoster) that attacks one or more dorsal root ganglia and corresponding sensory nerves (see Table 5-18). The virus can attack the anterior horn cells, but this is rare.[6,8,62] Involvement is primarily of the larger myelinated fibers and may involve spinal (usually intercostal) as well as cranial nerves.[8,130] Post-herpetic neuralgia of the trigeminal nerve usually involves the ophthalmic division as opposed to the maxillary and mandibular divisions commonly affected in other neuralgias.[8,287,293] The herpes zoster virus is related to one causing chickenpox, and a previous history of chickenpox may aid in the diagnosis.[6,8,289]

Diagnosis is initially difficult when skin eruptions (vesicles or blisters) are not yet apparent and the only complaint is pain.[8,289] This initial phase commonly lasts for 2 to 5 days prior to the appearance of the skin rash.[8] The skin rash follows the involved nerve as well as its sensory (dermatomal) area and may last for up to 6 weeks.[6–8,130] The acute phase is characterized by a painful burning that frequently decreases as regeneration of new fibers occurs. Periods of burning, stabbing, and shooting pains occurring spontaneously day and night persist for months or years after the acute phase.[6,8]

A tolerable background soreness or ache may be present constantly. The involved area becomes hyperesthetic, and non-noxious stimuli can cause a painful response.[7,8,66,130] The severe pain of post-herpetic neuralgia may be triggered by light touch, clothing rubbing against the skin, noise, temperature changes, sweating, and emotional upsets.[7] There is frequently a delay of a few seconds in the onset of pain following non-noxious stimuli, as occurs in trigeminal neuralgia.[7] This phenomenon may be due to the slow regeneration of the faster-conducting, large A fibers, the process of summation, and delayed conduction velocity.[56]

CAUSALGIA

Causalgia is intense, burning pain and is caused by a partial or incomplete injury to a peripheral nerve, most commonly from bullets or metal fragments.[6,7,8,66,129,130,302,303] Involvement is usually of a mixed nerve or the brachial plexus, most commonly the median, ulnar, and sciatic (see Table 5-18).[7,8,53,303–306] A complete section of the nerve rarely produces causalgia. The pain syndrome may begin at the time of injury, but more frequently within a week when healing commences and less frequently after several weeks.[7,53,129,306]

Patients with causalgia may have sensory, neurovascular, and trophic disturbances. Pain is relatively constant with periods of exacerbation (severe burning pain) but is not paroxysmal. There may be an associated deep, achy pain. Pain is perceived distal to the wound or lesion, usually in the palmar surface of the hand or dorsum of the foot depending on nerve involvement.[53,129] The pain of causalgia does not follow a dermatomal distribution but occurs almost throughout the whole extremity.[126]

Causalgic pain may persist for 6 months or longer and usually ends spontaneously.[7,8,53,66,129,136,328] Approximately 25 percent of causalgic pain lasts for a year or more.[7,53,129] The involved area is usually very sensitive to touch and other non-noxious stimuli (hyperesthesia) such as noise, air, heat, and emotions. Patients may protect the involved extremity by wrapping it in cool or wet material.[71,126,304,306]

In the acute stage, the area of involvement may exhibit a local hyperthermia and may appear as red, dry, and edematous, which usually changes to being cool, cyanotic, and sweaty. The longer the condition persists, the greater the chances of developing trophic changes: thin, hairless, tight skin; muscle atrophy; long nails; osteoporosis (Sudeck's atrophy); joint hypomobility; and possibly paralysis.[6,126,306,308] Occasionally, similar symptoms may develop in the contralateral extremity.[6,129] These conditions result from sympathetic involvement and a loss of normal proprioceptive input because of protection and lack of use by the patient.

Minor Causalgia

In minor causalgia, there is a lack of definitive damage to one or more peripheral nerves (see Table 5-18).[305] Onset usually follows a sprain, fracture, amputation, postoperative scar, simple bruise, burn, infection, or crush injury. The pain of minor causalgia is similar in description (burning and achy) and intensity to that of major causalgia. Differentiation between the two is that in minor causalgia, pain spreads or is referred throughout the involved extremity, proximal and/or distal to the lesion or injury, without necessarily involving a major peripheral nerve. It is not uncommon to see such a condition after a Colles' fracture or digital fractures of the long bones.[6,310] Included in this category are reflex sympathetic dystrophy (shoulder-hand syndrome), Sudeck's atrophy, and post-traumatic osteoporosis. Etiology may also stem from visceral and vascular pathology such as CVA, myocardial infarction, and thrombophlebitis.[6,8,17,129,309]

T.E.N.S. has been used adjunctively with patients who developed reflex sympathetic dystrophy (RSD) following Colles' fractures. These patients complained of pain and dysfunction from the fingertips to the shoulder and ipsilateral cervical spine (see Chapter 9). RSD following angina or an infarction will affect the shoulder initially and then the hand. The hand may resemble and possibly be confused with one involved in an ongoing arthritic process as it becomes edematous and red.[6,8,309–311] RSD following a CVA can result in a painful, sweaty, clammy hand that may also develop trophic changes and atrophy. RSD may also involve the lower extremity after a CVA, and contralateral manifestations may also occur.[6]

All variations of causalgia have a sympathetic component and are characterized by vascular and trophic changes of skin, soft tissue, and bone. Pain may be intractable and obviously may lead to various degrees of disability. Sympathetic blocks performed at the first sign of RSD have proved very beneficial.[6,8,66,288,307–311]

Reflex Sympathetic Dystrophy

A Colles' fracture resulting in reflex sympathetic dystrophy may cause a myriad of pain complaints. The fracture obviously results in tissue damage to adjacent neuromuscular and vascular structures. An inflammatory reaction begins, causing a local temperature rise and edema.[320] Damage to tissue results in the interstitial release of endogenous pain-producing substances such as histamine and bradykinin that can be potentiated by prostaglandin E.[308,309,317–327] In addition, other substances such as potassium ions, acetylcholine, serotonin, and norepinephrine are released as a result of damage to erythrocytes, nerves, platelets, and sympathetic fibers. Many of these substances are considered to be vasoneuroactive and capable of increasing small-vessel permeability and exciting nociceptors in superficial and deep tissues.[8,50,320,321,327]

Nerve fibers that are damaged as a result of neurapraxia or axonotmesis develop denervation hypersensitivity.[317–320] The injury, such as a Colles' fracture, may press on, cut, or injure adjacent nerve fibers of the main branch of the nerve. The larger myelinated fibers are usually involved.

The ensuing damage, continuous noxious stimulation, inflammation, and partial denervation may bring on a loss of large-fiber inhibition, causing a juxtaposition in threshold activities.[7,288] Small fibers and sensory end-organs will now exhibit an increased sensitivity to non-noxious stimuli, neurotransmitters, and pain-producing substances.

Damage to the nerve, which need not be major, obviously can involve the motor, sensory, and sympathetic components. In the case of a Colles' fracture, the close proximity of the superficial radial, musculocutaneous, and median nerves to the distal radius frequently results in nerve damage. Depending upon the degree of damage, a neuroma may form. Nerve fibers sprouting from a neuroma exhibit an increased sensitivity to pressure, are easily excited by vasoneuroactive substances, and are prone to receive alien (nerve fiber other than its own) innervation.[317,318]

Damage to a mixed nerve can cause motor, sensory, and sympathetic disturbances. Irrespective of the immobilization to the area as a result of the fracture, disuse atrophy and metabolite retention, which can cause achy pain plus the release of acetylcholine, can increase the size of the surface membrane of denervated muscle fibers. This results in hypersensitivity of the whole muscle fiber, not just at the neurovascular hilus, producing fibrillations as determined by EMG studies.[56,317,318,330] Tenderness to pressure (myalgic hyperalgesia) results, being most prominent at the motor point.[317,318]

Involvement of the sensory components of the nerve gives rise to the burning pain of causalgia. Endogenous pain-producing substances excite A-delta and C fiber receptors, which now have a lowered threshold, producing hyperesthesia. Histamine and serotonin excite thermal nociceptors, which are also excited by nerve pressure.[50,80,321] Such excitation may in part give rise to the sensation of burning. Autonomic nervous system fibers are involved wherever there has been neurovascular damage; vasomotor and trophic changes of bone, skin, fingernails, and soft tissue may ensue. The development of ischemia can result in the lowering of the pH and facilitation of the action of bradykinin.[322]

The following phases outline the progression of the syndrome:[6] Phase 1—initial burning pain, increased skin temperature, and a dry, red, edematous appearance of the involved region. Phase 2—increasing pain and edema, decreasing temperature with associated sweating, coldness, and cyanosis. Osteoporosis, muscle atrophy, and contractures ensue. Phase 3—pain may become intractable and atrophy and osteoporosis progress, along with trophic changes (loss of hair, shiny then taut skin).

In the case of a Colles' fracture, objective and subjective signs could spread from the hand and wrist to the elbow, shoulder, and ipsilateral cervical spine. In our experience, such patients have the greatest degree of discomfort and dysfunction at the shoulder and hand, followed by the elbow. Treatment must be directed to the whole extremity (see Case Study 10, Chapter 9).

All of the pain mechanisms described send a constant afferent barrage to the CNS that can keep the internuncial pool in a state of facilitation. Such facilitation lowers the stimulus threshold to the point where non-noxious input may produce paroxysmal pain (the sharp, shooting pain of a pressure-sensitive neuroma) as well as a constant, deep ache.[288,308,309]

PHANTOM LIMB PAIN

Pain that occurs after amputation of an extremity or body part and is perceived in the region of the missing limb is known as phantom limb pain. It generally occurs in about 30 to 35 percent of amputees but is severe in only up to 10 percent, depending on the source.[7,309,312] Severe phantom limb pain is characterized as a shooting, crushing, twisting, telescoping, and/or cramping sensation that is periodic.[7] Frequently, changes in temperature, heaviness, itching, tingling, and movement of the limb are described but are not painful (see Table 5-18). Severe phantom limb pain is considered more common in patients with histories of chronic pain in the extremity prior to amputation.[7,8]

There are numerous explanations for the phenomenon of phantom pain. The presence of neuromas causing nerve fiber irritation and trigger zones is considered a common cause. Such trigger zones may occur in the stump, other body regions, or the contralateral limb.[7,316] The loss of proprioceptive input, resulting in an imbalance between large and small fibers, pain memory, and psychologic and emotional factors have also been implicated. Altered input patterns may also occur from denervated skin flaps, pressure on the end of the stump, or muscle atrophy.[7] Continuous sympathetic input from sweating, decreased circulation, and coldness may also result in pain via summation mechanisms.[329] Any of these forms of afferent stimuli can bombard the appropriate spinal cord segments with input that can facilitate and disrupt the internuncial pool. Phantom pain may therefore be triggered by non-noxious as well as noxious stimuli.

A recent explanation by Melzack pertains to an advancement of Livingstone's theory of self-sustaining reverberatory circuits.[7,129,338] These circuits are formed by deafferented neuron pools at the spinal cord level that ultimately can excite higher CNS centers, causing pain perception. Such circuits could be initiated by injury, amputation, or the growth of pain fibers into the stump. Nerve fibers sprouting at or near the lesion demonstrate increased sensitivity to various neurotransmitters and mechanical stimuli.[309] The presence of a neuroma is common when the distal end of the nerve has been removed. The neuroma has sensory innervation, and its sprouting ends are very sensitive to mechanical and chemical stimuli (epinephrine, norepinephrine).[288,317–319,324,329] This hypothesis can also be applied to phantom pain in paraplegic patients where such a reverberatory circuit may exist above the level of spinal cord injury or at the supraspinal level.[60,329]

Phantom pain following the removal of the bladder in which a patient had sensations of a full bladder with periods of sharp, burning, acute pain has also been reported.[314] Successful alleviation of phantom pain has been accomplished by the use of sympathetic blocks, T.E.N.S., and relaxation training (see Chapter 9).

CENTRAL PAIN SYNDROMES

The reports of the effectiveness of T.E.N.S. in modulating pain in central pain syndromes are minimal. The thalamic syndrome falls into this category. This syndrome is characterized by a slight hemiplegia, constant superficial hemianesthesia or hyperesthesia, astereognosis, mild hemiataxia, paroxysmal pain, and choreoathetoid movements ipsilateral to the hemiplegic (hemiparetic is more appropriate) side.[8,243] Pain is severe and is described as burning or stabbing. The thalamic syndrome is a result of pathology such as CVA of the posterior cerebral artery.[8,343] A lesion in this area seems to block all inhibiting input to the limbic system and its functions, which may account for the intense reactions to pain demonstrated by patients with the syndrome.[8,343] T.E.N.S. has not been shown to be beneficial in this pain syndrome.[349–351,354]

T.E.N.S. has been reported to be effective in the reduction of pain and spasticity in multiple sclerosis. Winter attributes the benefit of T.E.N.S. in this demyelinating disease to an enhancement of polarization and depolarization of the involved nerves.[356]

Another syndrome characterized by demyelination is tabes dorsalis. This end-stage result of syphilis attacking the dorsal roots and column is characterized by paroxysmal sharp pains that occur a few seconds after stimuli generally considered to be non-noxious.[7,8] The pain response elicited from the patient seems to be exaggerated in light of the stimulus strength.[7] There are no reports on the use of T.E.N.S. for this condition, which would obviously be extremely difficult to treat.

Syringomyelia resulting in cavitation or lesions of the spinal cord may initially produce deep pain in the shoulder girdle and upper extremities. Progression into an advanced stage usually results in a loss of pain and temperature sensation. Motor function becomes impaired, spasticity develops, and the pathology spreads from the dorsal to ventral horn of the spinal cord, cervical to lumbar.[8,56] Picaza and associates report the beneficial use of T.E.N.S. in one case of syringomyelia.[357]

Patients with spinal cord injuries have benefited from the use of T.E.N.S. Although the CNS is directly affected, it is as a result of direct trauma rather than a disease process. Patients with paresis or paralysis involving either the lower extremities or the upper extremities or both may develop painful radicular, visceral, or phantom pain below the level of the lesion.[60,352,353,355] Pain of this variety does not affect all spinal-cord-injured patients, but estimates run as high as 30 percent and are generally 5 to 10 percent.[60] Pain may be described as tingling, burning, crushing, or knife-like, and has been reported in cases of complete spinal cord transection as well as after the surgical removal of one or more cord segments (cordectomy).[60] The sympathetic chain was considered to be a likely remaining pathway for impulse transmission, but sympathetic blocks and sympathectomy do not always bring relief. Pattern-generating mechanisms have been proposed as a possible explanation.[60]

T.E.N.S. has also been used to reduce the incidence of ileus and related complications with excellent results.[358,359] The application was similar to that employed for postoperative use (see Chapters 10 and 11). T.E.N.S. has also been used to modulate pain resulting from Guillain-Barré syndrome.[365]

ENTRAPMENT SYNDROMES

Nerves and/or blood vessels can become compressed or impinged upon at many areas throughout the body. Entrapment usually occurs from muscle spasm; passage through an osseofibrous tunnel or a channel within fibrous tissue; trauma, producing scar tissue or a hematoma that may press upon the nerve; neoplasms; congenital defects; fractures; exostoses; and systemic diseases such as hypothyroidism, rheumatoid arthritis, myxedema, acromegaly, and tuberculosis.[5,6,8,28,53,55,56,330,361,362] Pregnancy may be implicated since the uterus can compress the lateral femoral cutaneous nerve as it crosses the iliacus muscle, giving rise to meralgia paresthetica.[8]

Entrapment that produces irritation of the peripheral nerve will cause a subjective sensation of distal paresthesia, tenderness of innervated musculature, possible hyperesthesia, and burning or shooting pain which may become worse at night. Objectively, edema may occur at the site of entrapment due to inflammation. Vascular symptoms will occur if the entrapment involves blood vessels.

Profound irritation causing partial or complete compression of the nerve will yield signs of weakness or paralysis, atrophy, and sensory loss. Nerve conduction velocity and electromyography are extremely helpful in evaluating the site of the entrapment and the extent of compression.[5,56,330,361,363]

Numerous entrapment syndromes involve the major peripheral nerves, some of which are listed in Table 5-19. Perhaps the most common is carpal tunnel syndrome. This involves the median nerve as it courses through the carpal tunnel in conjunction with the tendons of the finger flexors under the transverse carpal ligament. Symptomatology may be motor, sensory, and/or sympathetic since the median nerve is a mixed nerve. Irritation of the

TABLE 5-19. Characteristics and Mechanisms of Peripheral Nerve and Nerve Root Entrapment

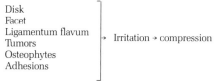

| Impingement irritation Compression Spasm → | Burning or shooting pain, increased in PM
Paresthesia
Tenderness
Edema
Associated weakness
Sensory loss | **Commonly seen**
Carpal tunnel
Meralgia paresthetica
Anterior interosseus
Canal of Guyon
Saturday night palsy
Posterior interosseus syndrome
Piriformis
Tarsal tunnel
Posterior primary ramus (medial branch) |

Foraminal narrowing via:

| Disk
Facet
Ligamentum flavum
Tumors
Osteophytes
Adhesions → | Irritation → compression |

Intervertebral disk degeneration
H$_2$O content ↓ → slack of annular fibers → tissue breakdown → histamine
Bradykinin → excitation of free nerve endings in annulus → local segmental pain

tendon (tendinitis or tenosynovitis) resulting in swelling or edema may compound the symptoms that are primarily distal to the site of entrapment but can give rise to a referral of pain proximally to the shoulder and cervical spine.[56]

Differentiation between a cervical and peripheral origin is imperative since similar pain can occur from C5–6 compression.[19,28,30] A complete cervical spine evaluation plus electromyography is necessary to determine the etiology and optimal treatment.[19,28,30,56] The presence of Tinel's sign (tapping the nerve) and Phelan's sign (forced wrist flexion) is helpful when both are positive for carpal tunnel involvement, if distal paresthesia occurs.[8] Further differentiation is needed in the presence of bilateral paresthesia of the fingers and toes (acroparesthesia). This frequently occurs in the morning, with edema and stiffness, which subside later in the day. ANS dysfunction may be the etiology. This is most common in women at menopause.[19,30]

Entrapment of the nerve root may also occur at the intervertebral foramen. Foraminal narrowing may irritate or compress the roots and their branches, such as the medial branch of the posterior primary ramus, as a result of intervertebral disk, facet, or osteophyte pathology. Impingement may also occur from tumors, scarring, and adhesions or sclerosing of the ligamentum flavum.[19,32,44,52,364,388]

NEUROVASCULAR COMPRESSION SYNDROMES

The neurovascular compression syndromes include thoracic outlet, scapulocostal, costoclavicular, scalenus anticus, and hyperabduction.[5,6,8,17,19,28,56,66,278,365–367] All of these syndromes involve compression of the subclavian artery and/or vein and the lower trunk of the brachial plexus.

Etiology is usually congenital (cervical rib); postural (forward head, alar scapula, scoliosis, dowager's hump), trauma, and infrequently, hypertrophy of the scalenes or compression via soft tissue. These syndromes, although not common, occur most frequently between ages 20 and 40 in females.[366] Table 5-20 summarizes the various neurologic and vascular signs and the influence of modifying factors. Neurologic signs will vary from paresthesia as a result of irritation to weakness and sensory deficit from compression. Complete vascular compression may lead to ischemia, discoloration, trophic changes, Raynaud's disease, and even gangrene.[6] The patient may be awakened frequently at night by pain that can intensify up to the morning. Nocturnal paresthesia occurs when the lower trunk of the brachial plexus is lifted off the first rib. While sleeping, compression is decreased and pain impulses can travel beyond the lesion to the supraspinal appreciation centers. While upright, in positions of improper posture, compression occurs and pain decreases. Vascular signs may become more prominent during the day.

It is quite difficult to differentiate one specific neurovascular compression syndrome from another solely by pain quality and distribution. However, by observation of posture and the performance of movement tests, differentiation can be accomplished.[6,17,366,367] Cyriax states that pain that occurs in the hands after a minute of scapula elevation is indicative of a thoracic outlet syndrome.[28] Adson's maneuver has been advocated to determine the presence of scalenus anticus involvement. This test involves hyperextension of the cervical spine, rotation to the involved side, and a deep breath during which the radial pulse should be checked for obliteration, which indicates a positive sign. The military posture is used to test for costoclavicular involvement. The shoulders should be back and down, the chest out, and a deep breath taken, which decreases the costoclavicular space. This has the net effect of neurovascular compression between the clavicle and first rib. To test for the hyperabduction or pectoralis minor syndrome, the patient performs full elevation of the

TABLE 5-20. The Characteristics of Neurovascular Compression Syndrome

Scalenus anticus
Scapulocostal
Thoracic outlet
Hyperabduction
  (pectoralis minor)
Costoclavicular
All involve compression of subclavian artery, vein, and lower cord of brachial plexus.
  Interscalene space
  Costoclavicular space
  Axilla, pectoralis minor tendon, and coracoid process

Neuro	**Vascular**	**Symptoms**	
Weakness (ulnar)	Ischemia	Intermittent or chronic, ↑ by:	
Numbness	↓ temperature	Movement	Emphysema
Heaviness	Discoloration (cyanosis)	Inspiration	Posture—round
Paresthesia	Trophic changes	Hypertrophy	shoulders, alar
	Edema	Trauma	scapulae
	Claudication		
	↓ pulse		

Peripheral vascular disease
Ischemia → cramping pain (claudication)
  (relieved by rest)

Venous insufficiency

Varicosities ⎫   Pain
Stasis   ⎬ Achy, heavy   Pallor
Ulcers   ⎭ ↑ prolonged standing   Pulselessness
             ↓ rest and elevation   Paresthesia
                                             ⎫ Paralysis
Occlusive (chronic)   ⎬→ ↓
                                             ⎬ Ulceration
Arteriosclerosis obliterans   ⎬ ↓
Buerger's disease—elderly males   ⎬ Gangrene
Raynaud's—young females   ⎭

arm behind the head, which compresses the neurovascular components between the taut pectoralis minor tendon and underlying costal borders. The test for scapulocostal involvement is performed by palpating the superior medial angle of the scapula while the examiner pulls the arm into hyperextension, depression, and internal rotation. The cervical and thoracic spine is also tested. The innervation of the scalenes is via the C3–C8 segments.[55] Cervical spine dysfunction can result in scalene spasm, producing neurovascular compression. The extensive innervation of the scalenes can account for pain referral into the upper extremity (primarily C5–6 distribution to the thumb and index finger) regardless of entrapment of the lower trunk of the brachial plexus. The pain referral pattern of the scalene trigger point corresponds to its myotomal innervation (see Fig. 5-13).

Frequently associated with the scapulocostal syndrome is a trigger point of the levator scapulae at the superior medial angle of the scapula.[6,204,205] As previously discussed, this syndrome can cause a widespread pain pattern resulting in occipital headaches, and neck, shoulder, arm (ulnar distribution), and even anterior chest pain to the level of T4–5. The referral pattern of the scaleni also encompasses the pectoral region. A pectoralis trigger point can lead to ulnar distribution referral. The pectoralis minor is innervated by C7–T1 and the pectoralis major by C5–T1.

In order to properly establish the etiology of neck, shoulder girdle, and upper extremity pain, a comprehensive evaluation of the cervical and thoracic spine, shoulder girdle, and sites of entrapment must be performed. There is a close overlap of pain from all of these structures, and the quality and locations of pain may be very similar. Proper treatment

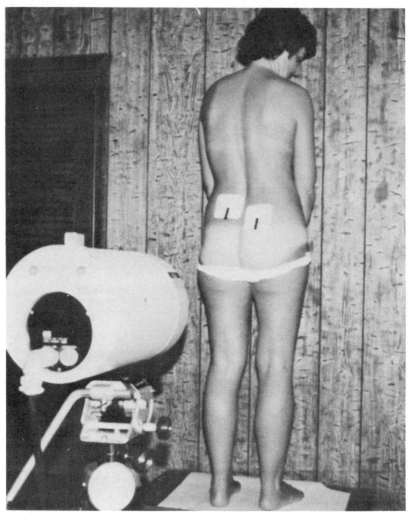

FIGURE 5-21. *A,* Patient in standing position in thermography laboratory with infrared AGA scanning camera focused on the low back. Note electrode placement over the bilateral lumbar area. Patient has a history of chronic low back pain, improved after disk surgery. She also has right sciatic referral that is significantly improved by T.E.N.S. therapy. (Courtesy of Delaware Pain Clinic.) *B,* Thermogram, low back, showing both lower extremities. Black is cool, and white is warm on the scale. This is an abnormal thermotome, consistent with a sympathetic dystrophy, and represents a pre-T.E.N.S. pattern. Note the distribution of the white and black on the right. (Courtesy of Delaware Pain Clinic.) *C,* Post-T.E.N.S. stimulation employing bilateral lumbar-placed electrodes (see *A*). Low-amplitude alternating pulse stimulation at 10 mV, 10 pulses per second for 15 minutes' stimulation. Note the normalizing to a warmer temperature due to a vasodilatation effect of the T.E.N.S. therapy. At threshold, the patient reports a pleasant sensation in the leg and significant improvement of pain. (Courtesy of Delaware Pain Clinic and P. Leroy, M.D.)

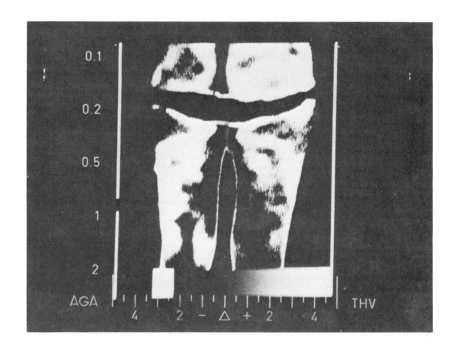

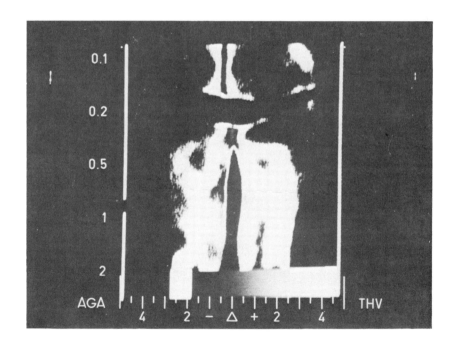

aimed at the cause, as well as pain modulation, depends entirely on a definitive evaluation that should include circulatory, radiologic (cervical rib), and electromyographic studies.

Peripheral vascular disease, venous insufficiency, and occlusive vascular disorders may also exist in the upper and lower extremities. These syndromes yield symptomatology that is similar to that of neurovascular compression. Insufficiency of the superior gluteal artery can cause claudicant pain in the buttock and/or sciatic referral. Pain in this instance will be increased by ambulation and decreased by standing still.[386] Pain will not increase on bending forward, thus practically eliminating the possibility of its origin from a lumbar mechanical abnormality.

Raynaud's disease is one of the vasoconstrictive disorders with an emotional etiology. It is most common in young to middle-aged females and frequently associated with systemic conditions such as rheumatoid arthritis, scleroderma, and polyarteritis nodosa.[6,17,66] Associated paresthesia and severe discomfort can occur.

Raynaud's disease is more common in the upper extremities, whereas occlusive arterial disease is seen more often in the lower extremities. Raynaud's disease may effect the hands, feet, edge of the ears, or tip of the nose. Occlusive arterial disease produces claudicating ischemic pain that increases with activity but decreases with rest. Burning pain at rest or in bed with paresthesia may be more indicative of a neuritis (peripheral neuropathy). The higher threshold of thin nerve fibers provides greater resistance to anoxia than the large myelinated fibers, thus relating to the sensory deprivation category.[8]

Peripheral vascular disease resulting in ischemia will give rise to the characteristic intermittent claudication during activity that is relieved by rest.[5,6,8] The "five P's" (pain, pallor, pulselessness, paresthesia, and paralysis) resulting from venous insufficiency or occlusive vascular disease can lead to ulceration and finally gangrene (see Table 5-20).[5,8]

Various exercises and temperature biofeedback have been employed with varying degrees of success in the treatment of vascular disorders.[369,374] Temperature changes possibly indicative of vasodilation have been reported with T.E.N.S.[375,378] It has been inferred that T.E.N.S. must stimulate the antidromic fibers in the dorsal roots and sympathetic fibers. Dooley states in his report that Foerster in 1933 noted vasodilation in the related dermatome following faradic stimulation to the distal part of a divided posterior root.[375] Thermographic evidence of increased temperature following T.E.N.S. is illustrated in Figure 5-21, A through C.

BONE AND JOINT PAIN

A stress fracture causes pain that comes on with activity and is relieved by rest. Although the discomfort may be perceived at the fracture site (point tenderness, edema), pain referred either proximal or distal is quite common and can be misleading. A femoral shaft fracture may refer pain to the hip and knee.[379] Pain is thus referred in a sclerotomal manner not conducive to the dermatomal distribution. The correlation between the myotome and sclerotome can easily mislead the clinician to think of a soft-tissue involvement. X-ray and bone scan studies may be necessary to delineate the fracture from that of a soft-tissue injury.

Systemic pathology (metastatic and rheumatic) involving bone gives rise to a deep, achy, throbbing sensation that is relatively constant and may be worse at night.[5,6,28,30] Table 5-21 summarizes these various conditions. Pain involving fractures or resulting from glandular and vitamin disturbances may become sharp or lancinating in quality.[5,6] Specific joint pathology and dysfunction, discussed previously, are also summarized in Table 5-21.[5,37]

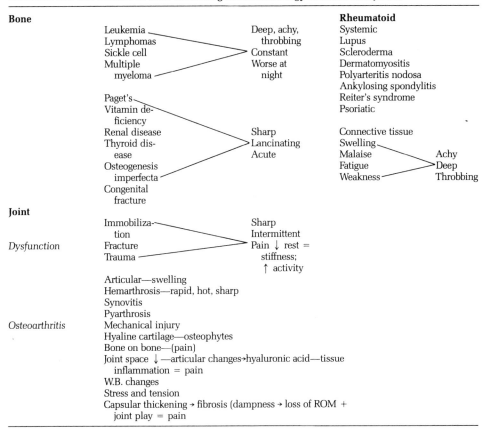

Bone

			Rheumatoid	
Leukemia	Deep, achy,		Systemic	
Lymphomas	throbbing		Lupus	
Sickle cell	Constant		Scleroderma	
Multiple myeloma	Worse at night		Dermatomyositis	
			Polyarteritis nodosa	
			Ankylosing spondylitis	
Paget's			Reiter's syndrome	
Vitamin deficiency			Psoriatic	
Renal disease	Sharp		Connective tissue	
Thyroid disease	Lancinating		Swelling	
	Acute		Malaise	Achy
Osteogenesis imperfecta			Fatigue	Deep
Congenital fracture			Weakness	Throbbing

Joint

Dysfunction

Immobilization	Sharp
Fracture	Intermittent
Trauma	Pain ↓ rest = stiffness; ↑ activity

Osteoarthritis

Articular—swelling
Hemarthrosis—rapid, hot, sharp
Synovitis
Pyarthrosis
Mechanical injury
Hyaline cartilage—osteophytes
Bone on bone—(pain)
Joint space ↓ —articular changes→hyaluronic acid—tissue
  inflammation = pain
W.B. changes
Stress and tension
Capsular thickening → fibrosis (dampness → loss of ROM +
  joint play = pain

Metastases involving bone may not be painful. One study has shown that one third of breast cancer patients with bone metastases did not have pain.[380] Pain in this case may arise only when distortion or traction irritates periosteal or endosteal nociceptive endings.[5,69,381] Osseous pain can occur from irritations of the perivascular receptor system of cancellous bone in the vertebral bodies and sacrum. This may occur from fractures, vertebral body collapse, osteomalacia, postmenopausal osteoporosis, or neoplasm.[32] It has been recommended that bone scintigraphy should be performed periodically on all patients with breast cancer. T.E.N.S. has been used successfully to modulate pain from rheumatoid arthritis.[384]

BACK PAIN

It has been estimated that 60 to 80 percent of the population experience back pain to some degree in their lifetimes.[391] Many patients with low back pain develop chronic problems, undergo numerous surgical procedures, and become addicted to or dependent on medication. Intervertebral disk surgery is considered to be one of the most frequent procedures in the United States; this is not true in Europe.[1,392–396] The causes of back pain are numerous; consequently, resolution of the problem is difficult. As a result, treatments are given that are purely symptomatic, mainly consisting of medication, various types of heat, and/or electrical stimulation, which give only transient relief. In addition, surgery is performed when the only symptom may be pain. T.E.N.S. should not be the sole means of treating back pain. It should be an adjunctive part of a comprehensive program designed to correct the cause of pain and dysfunction. Figure 5-22 illustrates numerous factors that may give rise to low back and/or sciatic pain. A standard procedure for treatment of all patients with low back pain is unjustified when the etiology is so varied and poorly delineated.[397,398] It has been estimated that 50 to 90 percent of the diagnoses made for low back pain are relatively imprecise, using words such as muscle strain, ligamentous sprain, or lumbago.[385,391]

Nociceptors are located in many tissue structures that comprise the spinal complex.[31,32] Loeser states that "no amount of knowledge about the physiologic, anatomic, and biochemical substrates of pain receptors will suffice to fully explain the common chronic syndrome of low back pain (LBP)."[397]

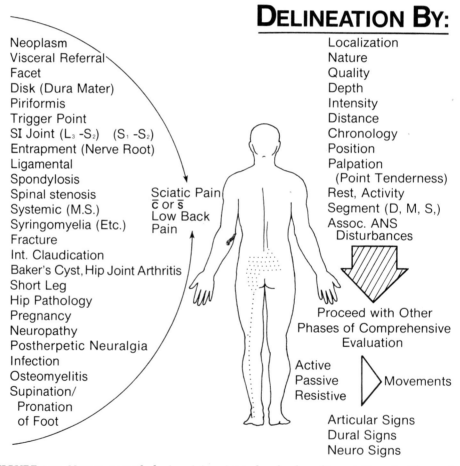

DELINEATION BY:

Neoplasm
Visceral Referral
Facet
Disk (Dura Mater)
Piriformis
Trigger Point
SI Joint (L₃ -S₂)   (S₁ -S₂)
Entrapment (Nerve Root)
Ligamental
Spondylosis
Spinal stenosis
Systemic (M.S.)
Syringomyelia (Etc.)
Fracture
Int. Claudication
Baker's Cyst, Hip Joint Arthritis
Short Leg
Hip Pathology
Pregnancy
Neuropathy
Postherpetic Neuralgia
Infection
Osteomyelitis
Supination/
  Pronation
  of Foot

Sciatic Pain
c̄ or s̄
Low Back
Pain

Localization
Nature
Quality
Depth
Intensity
Distance
Chronology
Position
Palpation
  (Point Tenderness)
Rest, Activity
Segment (D, M, S,)
Assoc. ANS
  Disturbances

Proceed with Other
Phases of Comprehensive
Evaluation

Active
Passive   Movements
Resistive

Articular Signs
Dural Signs
Neuro Signs

FIGURE 5-22. Numerous pathologies giving rise to low back and/or sciatic pain. The varied etiology necessitates thorough delineation if a rehabilitation program designed to treat the cause rather than the symptom is to be initiated.

In order to attempt to delineate the causes of back pain, a review of the innervation of the spinal complex is pertinent. Figure 5-23 illustrates the nerves that innervate spinal structures. The sinuvertebral nerve (SVN) and medial branch of the posterior primary ramus provide for spinal innervation. Basically, the sinuvertebral nerve, also known as the recurrent meningeal nerve, is formed by branches from the mixed spinal as well as a sympathetic component.[19,23,25,28,41–43,49,399,400] The SVN via various branches innervates the periosteum of the vertebral body, outer annular fibers, posterior longitudinal ligament, dura mater, meninges, and blood vessels. There are also reports of the SVN innervating the anterior longitudinal ligament and the entire periphery of the disk.[48,49] The SVN anastomoses with its contralateral counterparts, innervating the above structures at its level of origin as well as the one below. The medial branch of the posterior primary ramus innervates the inferior facet and capsule at its level of origin as well as the superior facet and capsule of the level below. Therefore, all of the spinal structures receive innervation from at least two segmental levels. In addition, the contralateral connections of the SVN allow for the referral of pain from one side of the spine to the other. In comparison, the facet joints on one side of the spine receive only ipsilateral innervation since no contralateral connections have been noted.[24,259,399] The composition, origin, and distribution of these nerves are fully described in Chapter 8. Table 5-22 lists some of the anatomic discrepancies that make the diagnosis of low back pain difficult.

Certain anatomic variables also need to be presented. The cutaneous branches of the posterior rami of L1–3 and possibly as high as T10–12 may descend to the iliac crest, buttock, and greater trochanter.[19,25,265] An afferent branch of L2 descends to the level of the L5 segment embedded within the posterior longitudinal ligament.[399] Cloward cites Von-Buskirk who states that longitudinal strands of the SVN extend along the entire spine, anastomosing with other strands above, below, and contralateral.[49] Soft-tissue structures, namely, the posterior longitudinal ligament, dura mater, and paraspinal musculature, are capable of pain referral. Irritation of the dura mater can give rise to extrasegmental referral. Trigger points of facet joint capsules or paraspinal musculature may compound the referral pattern. The sympathetic component of the SVN should not be overlooked as a source of pain referral in light of the differences between the somatic and sympathetic dermatomes. A continuous, ongoing afferent barrage into the dorsal horn may account for pain referral via Lissauer's tract for up to six segments.

Other than the classic Travell and Rinzler trigger points (see Figs. 5-11 through 5-15), involvement of the piriformis muscle must be considered.[202,203,388,400] The piriformis is an abductor and external rotator of the hip and may even play a small role in hip extension. The muscle originates from the anterior aspect of the sacroiliac joint capsule and sacrum (spinous process levels S2–4) and inserts at the medial side of the greater trochanter of the femur. Innervation of the piriformis is via the anterior primary rami of S1 and S2. The sciatic nerve runs under the piriformis and, in 10 to 15 percent of cases, runs through it.[202,203] In close approximation to the superior border of the piriformis are the superior gluteal nerves and blood vessels. The pudendal, inferior gluteal, sciatic, and posterior femoral cutaneous nerves and blood vessels are close to the inferior border. Obviously, entrapment of nerve and/or blood vessels can occur from piriformis pathology, producing signs of neurovascular compression (see Table 5-20). Involvement of the pudendal nerve may be a factor behind sexual dysfunction (painful intercourse or impotency).

Objectively, patients with piriformis involvement may exhibit a limp (dragging of involved leg), persistent external rotation of the hip due to spasm, and tenderness over the sciatic notch (trigger point). There will be subjective complaints of pain at the hip, buttock, coccygeal, and sacroiliac regions. Low back pain with referral to the popliteal space is quite common. Pain is intensified by squatting and resisted abduction plus external rotation of

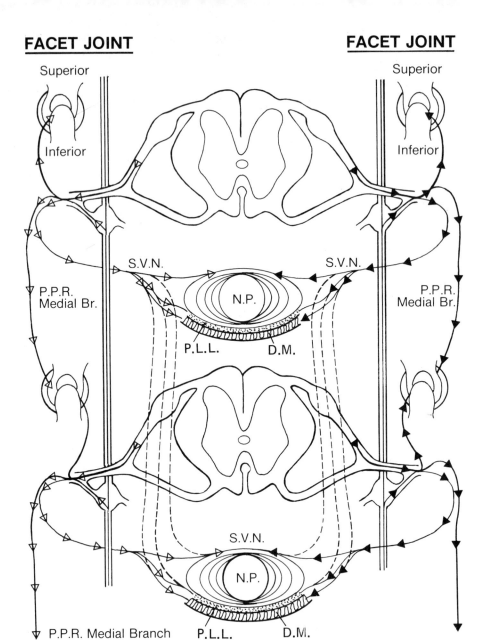

FACET JOINT   **FACET JOINT**

FIGURE 5-23. Distribution of the sinuvertebral nerve (SVN) and the medial branch of the posterior primary ramus (PPR). In the lumbar spine, the SVN innervates the outer annular fibers, posterior longitudinal ligament (PLL), dura mater (DM), vertebral body, and blood vessels at its level and the level below. Cloward hypothesizes that the outer annulus is innervated circumferentially. The SVN anastomoses contralaterally. The medial branch of the PPR innervates the facet joint and its capsule at its level and the one below. Hatched lines indicated ascending and descending branches of the SVN.

TABLE 5-22. Discrepancies in Delineation of Low Back Pain

1. Most spinal structures and tissues are densely innervated and refer pain in a similar manner.
2. All structures innervated by the SVN and medial branch of the PPR receive fibers from at least 2 levels.
3. The SVN anastomoses contralaterally.
4. The dura mater refers pain extra segmentally.
5. Many visceral organs refer pain to the lumbar and sacral regions, lower abdomen, and groin.
6. Cutaneous branches of the dorsal rami; of T12–L3 descend to the iliac crest, buttock, and greater trochanter of the femur.
7. An afferent branch of L2 descends embedded in the PLL to L5.
8. The sacroiliac joint is innervated anteriorly by L3–S2 and posteriorly by S1–S2.
9. Whenever there is derangement of the disk, the facets are also involved and vice versa.
10. SI joint dysfunction may cause intervertebral disk derangement.
11. The facet and SI joints are frequently overlooked as a source of pain.
12. Minor intervertebral derangements are usually overlooked as a source of pain yet can cause paravertebral hyperesthesia, tenderness of specific points, localized dull ache, ↓ ROM due to pain.
13. The pattern of pain may be confusing due to lack of correspondence between dermatome and myotome.

the hip, which may also reveal unilateral weakness. Passive internal rotation of the involved hip may also cause pain (Freidberg sign). There should be no neurologic signs; ROM and SLR are usually normal. A contracture of the piriformis may produce a short leg on the involved side, rotoscoliosis, increased lordosis, and deeper sacral sulcus unilaterally.

Predisposing factors to the piriformis syndrome include prolonged hip external rotation or crossing of one leg while in a car. Stretch or tears of the muscle causing protective guarding (spasm), incomplete fall, osteoarthritis of the hip, and improper positioning during obstetric or urologic surgery are also implicated.

Treatment includes various contract-relax and manual pressure techniques, nerve blocks, and ultrasound (vaginal or rectal). T.E.N.S. should be used merely as an adjunctive technique.

Table 5-23 depicts the relationship of pain location and objective and neurologic signs for common low back pain syndromes. A simple muscle or ligamentous strain will give rise to a dull achy pain that is localized to the area of involvement but may spread if a trigger point develops. Wyke equates back strain with the term primary fatigue backache.[32] Fatigue of a specific region causes localized pain and tenderness. This may be brought about by improper posture, activity, work, or recreational habits. The interesting aspect of this type of backache is that pain will intensify during rest as blood flow decreases, waste products accumulate, and large afferent fiber input declines. Poor posture can stress the spinal ligaments, producing ligamentous pain.[32] Regardless of the tissue, direct irritation of inherent nociceptors can occur from mechanical or chemical irritation, producing localized pain.

The pain of primary backache can be of cutaneous origin such as from a laceration, burn, cellulitis, abscess, and contusion. There will be little if any pain referral in these instances. A tear or rupture of paraspinal muscle fibers or the fascial sheath will yield a sharp, intense, stabbing pain of short duration followed by the characteristic deep, dull ache and guarding perceived paraspinally. Prolonged achy discomfort is produced by excitation of chemoreceptors from lactic acid and other metabolites that accumulate in the interstitial fluid.[32] Primary backache may occur during the last trimester of pregnancy, degenerative disk disease, rheumatoid arthritis and osteoarthritis, osteoporosis, visceral pathology, and constant wearing of high-heeled shoes or pronation of the foot.[448] Primary backache should not produce any neurologic signs. There may be articular signs of pain upon certain motions. The symptomatology of primary backache correlates well with category 13 of White's classification of low back pain.[46]

TABLE 5-23. Symptomatology Indicative of Common Low Back Pain Syndromes

	Location of Pain	True Neurologic Signs	Objective Signs
Strain Muscle + ligament	Localized → referred several segments uni or bilateral. Trigger point = referral, point tenderness	None	Point tenderness, no pain upon springing Rest = stiffness, movement-1st pain, then decreased-dull achy, S.L.R. ↓
Sprain facet	Localized → referred unilateral, dermatomal	None	Twinge, catch, springing—localized pain Rest ↓ pain, movement ↑ pain, SLR ↓, point tenderness step or rot malalignment
Hypermobility Spondylolisthesis	Localized	None unless impingement	Pain ↑ activity, point tenderness palpable step, forward bending may improve alignment + ↓ pain
Spondylosis	May be pain-free	None unless impingement	Rest = stiffness
Spinal stenosis	Back and bilateral leg	Numbness/weakness, paresthesia, burning	Elderly ♂, amb = weakness, pain ↑ claudication, forward bending and rest ↓ pain, backward bending ↑ pain
Cord compression cauda equina	Bilateral back + leg pain If complete = no pain	Bowel/bladder dysfunction, bilateral paresthesia, extrasegmental	Pain ↑ by backward bending
Sacroiliac	Baer's point, pain at PSIS, unilateral referral ↑ or ↓	None unless results in mechanical problem at lumbar spine	Dull, pain ↑ movement, point tenderness, SLR ↓, leg length differential
Compression fx.	Localized—adjacent segments	None	Sharp pain, forward bending ↑ pain, backward bending ↓ pain

The syndrome of the facet joint is considered a controversial entity. Cyriax argues against the facet joint syndrome as being a primary clinical entity, whereas others have supported its importance in back pain.[1,5,19,24,29,30,32,45,47,70,116,265,279,386,388,395,402] The problem may arise from the fact that any facet dysfunction could directly affect the disk, and disk derangement affect the facet.[19,24,386,399–401,403,404,407,409] As a synovial joint, the facet joint is prone to degeneration, arthritic changes, and the possibility of meniscoid inclusions precipitating synovial pinching.[45] Inflammation of joint tissues can give rise to articular pain, reflex spasm of paravertebral musculature, cutaneous hyperesthesia, point tenderness, loss of ROM, and decreased SLR, but there are no neurologic signs unless the nerve root is involved.[24,402] A facet joint sprain can result in swelling within or external to the joint capsule. It is possible that edema may be enough to cause pressure upon the nerve root from foraminal narrowing.[30]

Spondylosis is associated with facet or disk degeneration, but it may not result in any sensory or motor loss. Ankylosing spondylitis may cause bilateral low back pain, but as the condition progresses, pain may decrease with joint fusion.[429]

Spondylolisthesis results from a defect in the lamina or neural arch. Palpation of the spine may reveal a step between the spinous processes. This can be pain-free or predispose to disk herniation at the level above.[28,46,386,405]

Saline injection into the facet joints and capsule primarily shows a pattern and quality of pain similar to that of the disk. One distinct difference is that the pain referral is rarely below the knee, as it may commonly be with a posterolateral disk.[24,140,259] A recent study has shown overlap of pain referral from intracapsular and pericapsular injections at the L1–2 and L4–5 levels.[140] The results of this study do not support the specific segmental referral patterns that were established by earlier investigators.[11,12,14–16] Furthermore, Farfan states that at any given spinal level, the disk, ligaments, and facets are part of the same somite and, therefore, may all refer pain in a similar manner.[47,404] Cloward claims that it is difficult to differentiate involvement of the disk and facet joints.[48,49] The vertebral complex is composed of three movable structures, the two facet joints and the disk. Derangement of one structure, such as a loss of the normal vertical dimension of the disk, can lead to approximation and possible dysfunction of the facets (Table 5-24).[386,402,404,405]

Biomechanical factors point to an inseparable relationship between the disk and facet joints at each segmental level.[24,45–47,402,404,405,407] Other than with direct involvement of the nerve root or spinal cord, it may be difficult to delineate disk pathology from that of the facet solely by an evaluation of local and referred pain. There are many stages of disk

TABLE 5-24. A Comparison of the Objective and Subjective Signs of Disk and Facet Pathology

DISK (Lumbar)	Versus	FACET (Lumbar) Med. br. P.P.R.
Fast onset: lifting, forward bending Slow onset: gradual, hours, days, months	Etiology	Trauma, sudden movement, rotation/forward bending
Unilateral or bilateral	Pain	Unilateral (adjacent segments)

Extrasegmental-dural
  unilateral → nerve root
  bilateral → dura mater
Can be below the knee
	Referral	Upper lumbar to iliac crest, buttock, GI, (L2 afferent branch ↓ embedded in PLL to L5) overlap L1 ↔ L5, unilateral, never below the knee

Bilateral—(one side greater) erector spinae	Tenderness, Springing	Over facet joint between T.P.'s, interspinous and supraspinous ligaments, local pain unilateral
Possible repeated movements more frequent	Lateral shift or sciatic scoliosis	Less frequent
Deviate to involved side (disk fragment medial to root) Deviate away from involved side (disk fragment lateral to root upon forward bending)	Active ROM	Deviate to hypomobile side upon forward bending
↓ due to dural impingement	S.L.R.	May be ↓ due to hamstring spasm
Yes	Neuro signs	None

DELINEATION IS NOT CLEAR CUT.
Clinical and experimental findings show that objective and subjective signs are not totally distinct.
The disk and facet are part of the same somite.
Diskal degeneration or derangement can directly effect the facet and facet dysfunction the disk.
Further clinical evaluation (designed to ↓, ↑, or reproduce the exact pain) and the response to specific treatment may be helpful in determining the intervertebral structure and related segment.

herniation (bulge) and protrusion prior to an actual annular prolapse resulting in nerve root or spinal cord irritation or compression. These have been well delineated by Cyriax,[28] McKenzie,[413,447] and White.[46] Unfortunately, this is primarily not well recognized by many clinicians. Herniation of an intervertebral disk is immediately viewed as an irreparable or irreducible lesion that requires surgical intervention. Becoming familiar with the various degrees of derangements of the disk will show that many pain patterns are commonly not related to irritation of the sciatic nerve. Figures 5-24 and 5-25 illustrate the most common progressive stages of disk herniation.

Most mechanical disorders of the lumbar spine occur from a forward bent position. The position of forward bending at the lumbar spine, especially when sitting, produces the greatest degree of intradiskal pressure and creates a force component that causes the nucleus to track backward against the annulus.[28,45–47,391,392,399,401,404–409,411,447] An annular tear or fissure can occur from sudden, forceful movement or repeated (gradual onset) stresses resulting in derangement. Objectively, one of the first signs of posterior displacement of the nucleus is a loss of the normal lumbar lordosis.[28,46,47,386,447] Many clinicians are unaware of this fact and continue to order back-flexion exercises for an already flat lumbar spine. Back flexion is indicated when there is a hyperlordosis. The injury in most cases is one of forward bending, which causes the nucleus to move toward the highly innervated posterior tissues, resulting in pain. The protruding nucleus causes an enlargement of the posterior intervertebral space, forcing the lumbar spine into forward bending and flattening the low back. Further forward bending, such as with back-flexion exercises, may serve to exert further posterior pressure and increased pain. The work of McKenzie and Cyriax advocates treatment geared to regaining the normal lordosis.[28,434,447] Electromyographic studies have shown the slightly extended lumbar spine to be represented by less paraspinal activity.[46] The use of back support pillows to maintain the lumbar lordosis while sitting also decreases intradiskal pressure.[409] Pain of a diskogenic nature will occur at the midline if the nuclear protrusion is central, and lateral to the midline if the protrusion is off center at least 2 to 3 mm lateral to the midline.[48,49] There should be no pain referral beyond two or three adjacent spinal segments, and no sciatica, scoliosis, or neurologic signs with such a central protrusion. This state is difficult to differentiate from primary backache. Involvement is solely of the sinuvertebral nerve. The bulging outer annular fibers may excite mechanoreceptors, which are terminal endings of the sinuvertebral nerve. Chemoreceptors may also be excited by interstitial metabolites, such as histamine, potassium, and bradykinin, liberated as a result of tissue breakdown.

Further backtracking of the nucleus resulting in irritation of the posterior longitudinal ligament will cause an increase in the intensity of pain and possibly referral throughout additional spinal levels.

The posterior longitudinal ligament is more densely innervated than that of the outer annular fibers, and therefore is capable of causing a more intense pain when irritated. At this stage, any lateralization of the protrusion will result in forward bending and lateral deviation of the trunk away from the side of the prolapse. This occurs as a result of a space-occupying lesion, not muscle guarding, due to posterolateral tracking of the nucleus. The patient is thus unable to stand up straight, as the space-occupying herniation prevents side bending to the involved side as well as backward bending. Muscle guarding will be most evident on the side of the prolapse and thus serves to counteract the lateral shift away from pain.

Continued posterior bulging of the nucleus, pushing the annulus and posterior longitudinal ligament against the anterior dura mater, can result in extrasegmental pain and paresthesia. This may be perceived bilaterally in the back as well as the lower extremities. Irritation of the spinal cord will produce what is called myelogenic pain (Fig. 5-24). Pares-

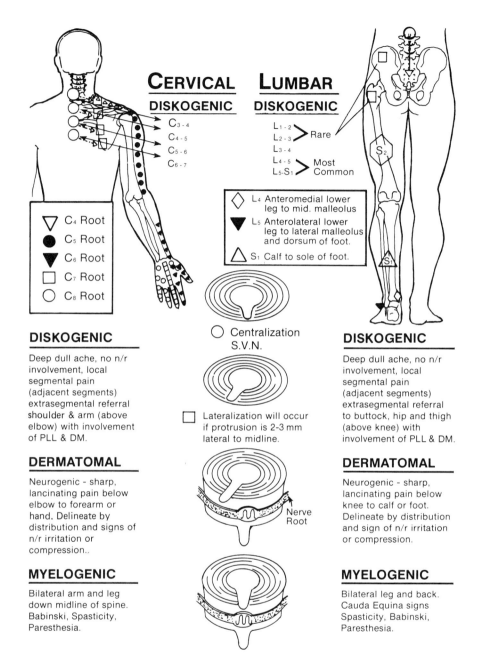

CERVICAL

DISKOGENIC

C₃₋₄
C₄₋₅
C₅₋₆
C₆₋₇

LUMBAR

DISKOGENIC

L₁₋₂
L₂₋₃ } Rare
L₃₋₄
L₄₋₅
L₅-S₁ } Most Common

▽ C₄ Root
● C₅ Root
▼ C₆ Root
□ C₇ Root
○ C₈ Root

◇ L₄ Anteromedial lower leg to mid. malleolus
◆ L₅ Anterolateral lower leg to lateral malleolus and dorsum of foot.
△ S₁ Calf to sole of foot.

DISKOGENIC

Deep dull ache, no n/r involvement, local segmental pain (adjacent segments) extrasegmental referral shoulder & arm (above elbow) with involvement of PLL & DM.

DERMATOMAL

Neurogenic - sharp, lancinating pain below elbow to forearm or hand. Delineate by distribution and signs of n/r irritation or compression..

MYELOGENIC

Bilateral arm and leg down midline of spine. Babinski, Spasticity, Paresthesia.

○ Centralization S.V.N.

□ Lateralization will occur if protrusion is 2-3 mm lateral to midline.

Nerve Root

DISKOGENIC

Deep dull ache, no n/r involvement, local segmental pain (adjacent segments) extrasegmental referral to buttock, hip and thigh (above knee) with involvement of PLL & DM.

DERMATOMAL

Neurogenic - sharp, lancinating pain below knee to calf or foot. Delineate by distribution and sign of n/r irritation or compression.

MYELOGENIC

Bilateral leg and back. Cauda Equina signs Spasticity, Babinski, Paresthesia.

A clear distinction is difficult due to involvement of facets and possible active trigger points which can increase distal extent of referral.

FIGURE 5-24. The pattern and characteristics of pain resulting from intervertebral disk pathology. Diskogenic pain is not referred below the elbow or knee. Neurogenic pain may be referred to hands or feet.

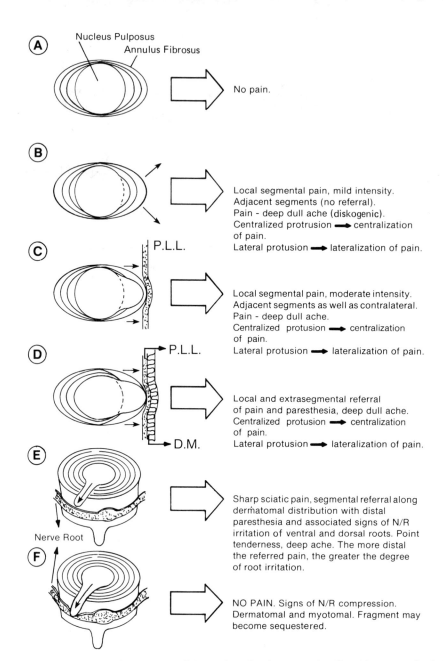

FIGURE 5-25. Position, character, and intensity of pain occurring from intervertebral disk herniations. *A,* Normal disk—no bulging, fissures, or tracts and therefore no pain. *B,* Herniation into annulus. Periphery of annulus remains intact. *C,* Annular bulge or herniation has irritated the posterior longitudinal ligament. The annulus remains intact, and pain is intensified. *D,* Annular bulge as a result of posterior tracking of nucleus now impinges on the dura mater, giving rise to local and extrasegmental pain referral. *E,* Posterolateral protrusion resulting in nerve root irritation. Pain is sharp and referred in a dermatomal pattern. *F,* Complete root compression, which would result in sensory loss (no pain) and unilateral paralysis.

thesia as well as upper motor neuron signs (Babinski, spasticity) will occur. In the cervical region, involvement will include the arms and legs bilaterally. Lumbar involvement will include the back and both legs as well as causing bowel and bladder dysfunction (cauda equina signs).[28,405] Spinal cord compression (spinal stenosis) as a result of a central disk protrusion can ultimately cause complete paralysis and sensory loss distal to the lesion. Spinal stenosis occurs to the greatest extent in elderly persons, frequently due to lumbar spondylosis. Pain can occur in one or both legs with associated weakness, coldness, or burning sensations depending on the degree of stenosis. Symptoms are increased by standing and ambulating and decreased by reclining.[46,386,388,428,429]

Spinal stenosis may also occur in the cervical spine due to disk protrusion, osteophytes, and folding or bulging of the ligamentum flavum, resulting in encroachment upon the spinal cord. Neurologic signs may mimic multiple sclerosis. Paresthesia, pain, and motor weakness may occur. Backward bending increases the symptoms of spinal stenosis.

Neurogenic pain perceived in the related dermatome with distal paresthesia will occur when the nerve root is irritated. Pain is then referred down the related extremity in a distinctive pattern. Neurogenic symptoms can involve either the dorsal or ventral root when irritated within the foramen. Upon exit from the foramen, the nerve is mixed and can produce symptoms indicative of each component (dorsal, ventral, and sympathetic). Neurogenic pain can also result from root irritation due to an osteophyte, producing a radiculopathy. The onset in this case is very slow (months or years); consequently, pain may not be severe and weakness will occur gradually. Progressive weakness will produce a concomitant decrease in pain as a result of impending compression. The characteristics of neurogenic pain are presented in Table 5-25.

Cloward has demonstrated that irritation of the C3–4 disk caused diskogenic pain at the level of the C7 spinous process. Pain will be perceived at the midline from central irritation or herniation and at the same level but alongside the vertebral border of the scapula with lateralization. Pain will be felt at the T3, T5, and T7 levels with pathology of the C4–5, C5–6, and C6–7 disk respectively.[48,49]

It is important to note that pain from the above cervical disk derangements is felt in the thoracic dermatomes. The pain, however, is not superficial; it is dull, deep, and achy and will produce myalgic or trigger points in the scapular musculature that are innervated by the cervical spine. Therefore, the location of the pain may mislead the clinician to suspect a thoracic pathology, but delineation of pain quality establishes the lesion at the cervical level.

Intervertebral disk derangement is much more common in the lumbar spine, particularly at the L4–5 and L5–S1 levels.[28,32] Rarely does this occur in the upper lumbar spine. There are other variations in disk pathology, degeneration, or derangements, but they are rare and may not be painful. Anterior (mushroom phenomenon) and vertical protrusions (Schmorl's nodes) occasionally occur.[28] The mushroom phenomenon produces pain when standing or walking for a few minutes but can be relieved by sitting or reclining. Schmorl's nodes resulting from vertical displacement of disk material may cause transient pain as a result of end-plate fracture but frequently becomes painless.[28]

Minimal intervertebral derangements can occur as a result of facet, ligament, disk, and capsule lesions.[19,265,403] A lesion in any of these structures can cause dysfunction in another. Such derangement at the low thoracic or upper lumbar region, T11–L3, can result in a referral of pain to the iliac crest, buttock, and greater trochanter via the cutaneous branches of the dorsal rami (Fig. 5-26). The pain reference may be misinterpreted as originating from a low lumbar disk, sacroiliac joint dysfunction, trochanteric bursitis, hip pathology, or a viscus. Delineation of the related segments giving rise to the painful region must begin with an analysis of the cutaneous innervation. Referral from the low thoracic

TABLE 5-25. Review of the Characteristics of Diskogenic, Myogenic, and Neurogenic Pain

LUMBOSACRAL AND SCIATIC PAIN OF SPINAL ORIGIN

No Nerve Root Involvement

Discogenic
Sclerotogenous pain
Deep, dull, nagging ache
Poorly localized
ANS reactions

Pain referral (extra segmental)
Bilateral lumbar and/or to
buttock, greater trochanter, S.I. region
(rarely below knee)

Etiology → *Herniation*-minor bulge
         = outer annulus
         = PLL
         = Dura mater (sheath)

         = Vertebral body
         = End plate fracture

→ Nerve Root Involvement ←

	DORSAL	→pain←	VENTRAL	SYMPATHETIC
I R R I T A T I O N	neurogenic		myogenic	
	sharp, electriclike ←	→	dull, achy, boring	
	superficial ←	→	deep	
	distal paresthesia ←	→	tenderness of	
	(hyperesthesia)		specific points	
			↑ muscle tone	ANS reactions
			(guarding)	sweating
	fairly well localized ←	→	moderately well localized	nausea
	dermatomal distribution ←	→	myotomal/sclerotomal	
	(below knee)		distribution (below knee)	

↑ reflexes

C O M P R E S S I O N	loss of sensation		weakness → paralysis	ANS reactions
		↓ reflexes no tenderness		
		POSTEROLATERAL PROTRUSION		
		EMG Findings:		
		↑ insertional activity		
		polyphasics		
		fasciculations		
		fibrillations and		
		sharp waves		

and upper lumbar segments will be primarily cutaneous since the upper buttock and posterolateral thigh are the T11–L3 dermatome. The same segments, however, innervate musculature that acts on and originates from the iliac crest (iliocostalis and quadratus lumborum). Therefore, the clinician may expect to find cutaneous hypersensitivity of the related dermatome inferior to the iliac crest distinct from motor point tenderness superior to the iliac crest depending on the degree of derangement.[19,265,403]

Involvement of the L4–S1 segments could produce tenderness of motor points over the buttock and posterolateral thigh since innervation is to the gluteal group and tensor fascia lata. However, the respective dermatomes are far removed to the lower leg. Confirmation of the origin of pain may be obtained by palpating for tender motor points of the respective erector spinae muscles.[414] Further evaluation should, of course, be performed to confirm the site of pathology. Central and lateral pressures or oscillation along with mobility testing of the related spinal segments, hip, and sacroiliac joints are suggested. (See Figs. 8-19 to 8-26, Chapter 8.)

Pain referral to iliac crest, buttock and greater trochanter can mimic low lumbar disk involvement, trochanteric bursitis, sacroiliac dysfunction, hip pathology, visceral referral, etc.

DELINEATION

T₁₁-L₃ • Cutaneous supply to iliac crest, upper buttock, greater trochanter and groin
• Joint hypomobility
• Localized pain at T_{11} - L_3 segments to central & lateral pressures, skin rolling

L₄ - S₁ • No cutaneous supply from P.P.R.
• Joint hypomobility
• Localized pain at L_4 - S_1 segments to central & lateral pressures, skin rolling, at lower leg only

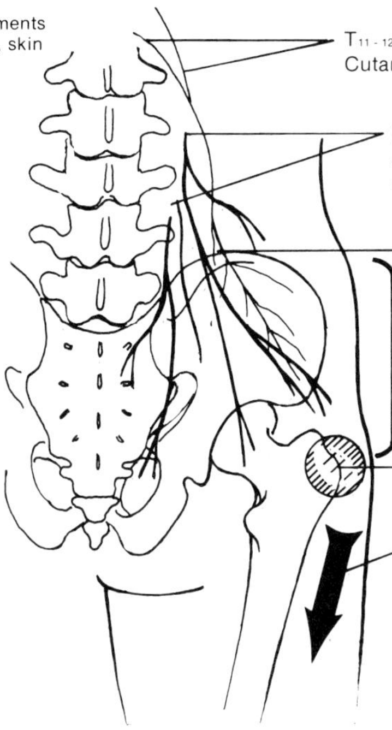

T₁₁ - ₁₂, L₁
Cutaneous branches

Posterior rami of L_{1-3}, cutaneous branches

Hypersensitive cutaneous band

DERMATOME

T_{11} - L_3 hypersensitivity inferior to iliac crest, motor point tenderness superior to iliac crest.

Tenderness of specific points

Tenoperiosteal pain

MYOTOME

L_4 - S_1 Point tenderness over buttock and posterolateral thigh inferior to iliac crest.

Referred pain from greater trochanter to knee laterally along iliotibial band (fascia lata)

FIGURE 5-26. An example of pain referral to the low back and lateral thigh that can mimic various types of pathology. (Adapted from Maigne.[19])

A related study by Gunn and Milbrandt concerned cervical radiculopathy as a cause of pain described as tennis elbow.[41] Pain existed at the lateral or medial epicondyle, along with tenderness of related motor points. Treatment directly to the cervical spine instead of the elbow proved effective in the majority of patients.

Minimal intervertebral derangement (MID) may mislead the clinician who uses only the location of pain to determine the site or etiology of the lesion. A referral of pain as a result of MID, whether it be from the disk or facet, usually will not be manifested below the elbow or knee. Pain perceived below the elbow or knee may represent involvement of the nerve root, peripheral nerve, or spinal cord.

Palpation of motor points will reveal tenderness of varying degrees depending on the stage of pathology in patients with spondylosis but not necessarily those with intrinsic peripheral problems or dysfunction. Tenderness of motor points in the distribution of the anterior and posterior rami of one segment may confirm the level of involvements reported by Glover.[403] In addition, palpation and observation of the skin may reveal the "peau d'orange" effect, pilomotor erection, sweating, trophic changes, tenderness, and hyperesthesia indicative of denervation supersensitivity (ANS dysfunction). These signs may be evident in the dermatome, myotome, or sclerotome.[199,317,318,414–421]

The lumbar spine is commonly a source of pain referral as a result of sacroiliac joint dysfunction. The sacroiliac joint is a mobile synovial joint and is frequently the source of unilateral groin, buttock, lumbosacral, and upper posterolateral thigh pain.[30,70,117,386,422,426] According to Stoddard, a lumbosacral strain or disk lesion can result in central back pain as well as pain over the sacroiliac joints, but a sacroiliac lesion never produces central back pain. However, unilateral erector spinae guarding may be noticeable.[30] The innervation of the sacroiliac joint, L3–S2 anterior and S1–S2 posterior, can account for this distribution. Dysfunction may have its etiology from falling on the buttock, bending forward without adequate pelvic support, parturition, contraceptive pills (causing ligamental laxity), and unilateral or rotational movements and activities. Point tenderness is at the posterior superior iliac spine as well as at Baer's point (2 inches from the umbilicus to the anterior superior iliac spine and pubic symphysis) (Table 5-26).[424]

In approximately 10 percent of the patient population with mechanical low back pain, the sacroiliac joint is involved. Probably the most common dysfunction of this joint

TABLE 5-26. The Objective and Subjective Signs of Disk and Sacroiliac Pathology

(post. lat.) Low Lumbar Disk	Versus	Sacroiliac
↑ male laborers 30–50, desk workers	Sex	↑ young females
Forward bending, lifting, rotational	Etiology	Torsional and/or forward bending
Unilateral (leg)/bilateral (back)	Pain	Unilateral (pelvic, thigh)
Extrasegmental (dural) or segmental (dermatomal)	Referral	Ventral L3–S2 Dorsal S1–S2
Erector spinae bilateral (one side more than the other)	Tenderness	S.I. joint (PSIS) Symphysis ⟩ unilateral
Common, very pronounced	Lateral shift or scoliosis	Less common, less pronounced
No	Pelvic asymmetry	Yes
Articular signs, deviation upon forward bending	Active ROM	Usually relatively normal
Signs of root irritation or compression ↓ SLR, etc.	Neuro signs	None (may have slight ↓ in SLR on involved side)
↑ pain due to intra-abdominal pressure	Cough, sneeze	↑ pain due to spread of innominates

DELINEATION IS NOT CLEAR CUT

Clinical and experimental findings show that objective and subjective signs are not too distinct, but are more distinct than between the disk and facet.

SI dysfunction can give rise to disk derangement.

Disk derangement can give rise to SI dysfunction.

Innervation of the low lumbar spine is via the same segments as the sacroiliac joints.

TABLE 5-27. A Biomechanical Explanation of Sacroiliac Joint Dysfunction

Posterior Rotation of the Right Ilium on Sacrum
1. Right PSIS lower than left
   Right ASIS higher than left
2. Pull of iliolumbar ligament rotates L5 to the right, resulting in lateral flexion to the left → scoliosis + increased lordosis
3. Acetabulum forced anterior and superior—functionally shorter leg in standing or supine, lengthens in long sitting
4. Femur forced into external rotation, ↑ adductor and internal rotator tone.

Anterior Rotation of Right Ilium on Sacrum
1. Right PSIS higher than left
   Right ASIS lower than left
2. Acetabulum forced posterior and inferior—functionally longer leg in standing (supine), shorter in long sitting
3. Decreased lordosis and may have scoliosis due to functionally longer leg
4. Femur forced into internal rotation, ↑ external rotator tone → possible piriformis syndrome, sciatic pain

is either an anterior or posterior rotation of one innominate (ilium) on the sacrum. It appears that a posterior rotation is the more frequent problem. In the case of rotation of one ilium, several clinical signs may delineate the sacroiliac joint as the source of dysfunction.[427] One important sign is obtained by the long-sitting test in which there is an obvious fluctuation of leg length on the affected side. Measurement must be done in the supine and long-sitting positions. Given a patient with equal anatomic leg length in the supine position, a posterior rotation of the right ilium will result in the right leg becoming shorter than the left. However, in the long-sitting position, the right leg will be longer than the left. It is important to note that at least 10 percent of the population have structural leg length discrepancies of 1 cm or more.[431]

This explanation is an important consideration to the unaware clinician who may treat such a patient with T.E.N.S. for pain and a heel lift. When the ilium rotates posteriorly, the acetabulum of the affected side shifts anteriorly as well as superiorly since the acetabulum has moved in a circular path instead of linear with the sacroiliac joint as the center of rotation.

In a supine or standing position, the patient will have a functionally shorter leg on the affected side due to cephalic movement of the acetabulum. On assuming a long-sitting position, the short leg will appear longer than the unaffected one due to anterior movement of the acetabulum. The opposite movement takes place in the case of an anterior rotation. In a patient with unequal anatomic leg length, there will still be an obvious fluctuation of leg length, but the direction of change will depend on which leg is short and the side plus direction to which the ilium has rotated.

The fluctuation must be consistently reproduced in order for the test to be valid. Elimination or control of other pelvic, trunk, or shoulder motion is imperative. The test is not valid on a patient with a structural scoliosis (Table 5-27, Fig. 5-27)

Many visceral organs can refer to the lumbar spine, waist, groin, and perineum. Figure 5-28 illustrates sites of visceral referral.

Referred pain to the low back most frequently arises from gynecologic problems such as endometriosis or dysmenorrhea.[32,45] Referral can be to the low back with or without suprapubic pain and may commence immediately before or on the first or second day of menstruation. Referral may also occur from ovarian lesions, uterine prolapse, cancer of the cervix, or involvement of fallopian tubes.[32]

Pain may be referred to the back from the esophagus, heart, aorta, gallbladder, gastrointestinal tract, or pancreas.[30,45,429] Pancreatic cancer may cause pain in the upper left lumbar region.[69] Pain in this instance is described as dull and intermittent, which can become

POSTERIOR ROTATION ® ILIUM

SUPINE   LONG SITTING

Ilium and Acetabulum Move

SUPERIOR   **AND**   ANTERIOR

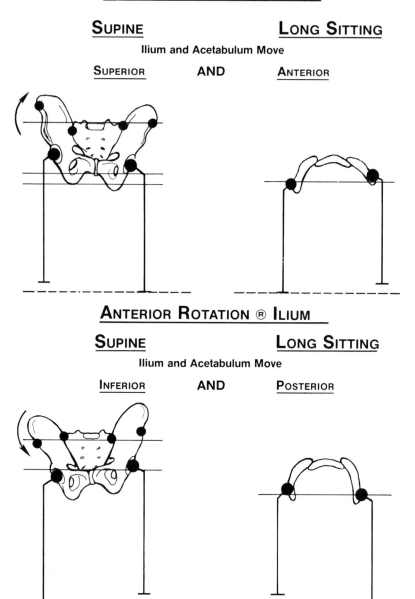

ANTERIOR ROTATION ® ILIUM

SUPINE   LONG SITTING

Ilium and Acetabulum Move

INFERIOR   **AND**   POSTERIOR

FIGURE 5-27. A diagrammatic representation of changes in leg length due to sacroiliac joint torsion.

constant and intractable as the condition progresses. Such patients are frequently awakened from pain. A progression of pathology increases pain and makes localization more accurate.

Pain perceived in the right lumbar region can occur from an inflamed retrocecal appendix with *prostitis*, a frequent source of referred pain to the sacrum.[32] A dull ache in the flank as a result of a renal calculus can become excruciating as the calculus enters the

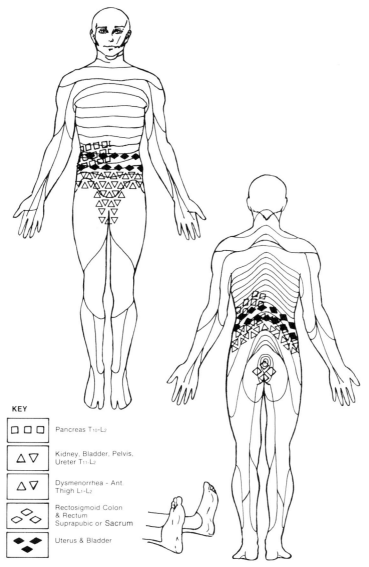

KEY

□ □ □	Pancreas T$_{10}$-L$_2$
△ ▽	Kidney, Bladder, Pelvis, Ureter T$_{11}$-L$_2$
△ ▽	Dysmenorrhea - Ant. Thigh L$_1$-L$_2$
◇ ◇ ◇	Rectosigmoid Colon & Rectum Suprapubic or Sacrum
◆ ◆	Uterus & Bladder

FIGURE 5-28. The sites of visceral referred pain to the lumbar spine. Note the overlap.

ureter. This results in pain referral to the lower abdomen, groin, bladder, urethra, genitals, and inner thigh.

The delineation of visceral and somatic pain is imperative when T.E.N.S. has been prescribed for low back pain. Pain of visceral origin should be unrelated to changes in position, posture, activity (including rest), and even coughing resulting in increased intra-thoracic pressure.[28,30,32,386,429,430] Somatic back pain should be able to be intensified, relieved, or reproduced by the aforementioned factors, thus necessitating the need for a comprehensive evaluation.

The malingerer should be able to be weeded out by the clinician who is familiar with the basis for a thorough subjective and objective back evaluation. The patient should be observed in the waiting room for objective signs such as facial expression and body mechanics. If a jovial patient acts morose and depressed once the evaluation begins, the clinician should note this and consider it when correlating all findings. The patient who fills out the admittance form or other questionnaire in a seated, forward bent position but yet is unable to tolerate 30 degrees of SLR during the evaluation may not be providing the clinician with a true response.

Observation of the patient with cervical spine involvement should be performed by the clinician (without the knowledge of the patient) for the extent of active ROM that the patient exhibits. If the patient freely rotates the cervical spine to talk to someone in the waiting room yet demonstrates severe restriction during the evaluation, the possibility of malingering must be considered. It is extremely beneficial for the clinician to stand to each side of the patient when asking questions during the evaluation. The patient may unconsciously turn to talk to the clinician, demonstrating greater active ROM than that observed during the actual ROM test.

Waddell and Mennell have written excellent articles relating to testing procedures and patient reactions that may be used to spot the patient with either visceral or nonorganic back pain.[410,430]

A thorough evaluation of the back must include tests to assess articular, dural, and neurologic signs (Table 5-28). The results of each test, however, must be viewed as one spoke in the wheel and not as a definitive diagnosis. Many of the articular signs have previously been discussed. It is necessary, however, to state that a lateral deviation resulting from intervertebral disk herniation may not always occur away from the side of nuclear lateralization. The nucleus may be lodged medial to the nerve root, which will cause deviation of the trunk toward the involved side to relieve irritation.[386] Deviation of the trunk may not occur or become evident unless forward bending is performed. Increased pressure and posterior displacement as a result of forward bending can result in lateral deviation. This should also be tested with the patient's eyes closed as correction will automatically occur with the eyes open.

TABLE 5-28. The Implications of Various Signs and Tests Involving the Lumbar Spine

OBJECTIVE AND SUBJECTIVE FINDINGS

True Neurologic Signs	Non-neurologic Signs
Dermatomal sensory loss (numbness)	Hyperalgesia or hypoalgesia
Definitive weakness or paralysis	Weakness due to pain
Bowel and/or bladder changes	ANS signs such as sweating, circulatory changes, piloerection
SLR 30°–60° (↓ 30° very +)	SLR above 60°
(Dural) Reproducible–D.F. of ankle	Posterior thigh }
Contralateral back pain	Low back } PAIN
Forward bending of head	Buttock, greater trochanter
Medial rotation of hip	Referred pain
Babinski—spasticity	Point tenderness
IMPLICATIONS	Muscle guarding
Posterolateral disk protrusion	ROM loss
Central disk	Postural deviation
SC tumor	Stretch pain
	IMPLICATIONS
	Facet Visceral
	SI joint Tight hamstrings
	Trigger points Short leg

Dural signs may be misleading to the unaware clinician. The dura mater runs uninterrupted from the foramen magnum to the base of the spine. Any stretch of this tissue over a region of impingement by the posterior longitudinal ligament from annular protrusion can result in extrasegmental referral. Forward bending of the head may intensify low back pain.[28,431] Any thorough evaluation of SLR should include forward bending of the head to assess the possibility of increasing discomfort in the lumbar spine. Passive dorsiflexion of the foot is also valuable if performed 5 to 10 degrees below the SLR angle that brings on low back pain. This may serve to further stretch the dura mater from its caudal extent, as forward bending of the head does from the cephalad extent. Medial rotation of the hip may also serve to reproduce or intensify low back pain.[432,446] The addition of active cervical forward bending, passive ankle dorsiflexion, and medial rotation of the hip to the standard SLR test may increase its efficacy. The so called "well leg raising test" is considered to be a reliable indicator of sciatic irritation. This test is considered to be positive when SLR of the nonpainful leg produces contralateral low back pain as a result of lateral tension on the involved nerve root.[432,446]

Decreased SLR due to low back pain is not necessarily indicative of nerve root involvement. Pain may occur from sacrospinalis guarding, spasm of the glutei and hamstrings, and hip and sacroiliac joint pathology.[433,446] Estimates of positive ranges with SLR run from a low of 15 degrees to a high of 60 to 70 degrees. The important point is that a positive SLR may not be indicative of definitive nerve root irritation, as a positive Ely test (femoral nerve stretch test) may merely be due to tight quadriceps or an increased lumbar lordosis. There are numerous other tests including x-ray and myelography that may also be false-positive.[1,32]

SUMMARY

This chapter has provided the reader with an understanding of pain and how it differs according to chronology, quality, nature, intensity, and location among the somatic and visceral structures of the body. The production, transmission, modification, and perception of pain, along with the means by which to evaluate it, have been discussed. The information presented was then incorporated into an analysis of common pain syndromes that the clinician may encounter as well as in the implications for the use of T.E.N.S. It was emphasized that pain cannot be separated from each patient and treated symptomatically without considering the physical, physiologic, and psychologic factors that modify it.

T.E.N.S. is rapidly becoming one of the initial treatment modalities for back pain with very good efficacy.[435] The clinician should again bear in mind that T.E.N.S. is providing only symptomatic relief and a comprehensive approach necessitates treatment of the cause and prevention of re-injury. Instruction in proper body mechanics and a therapeutic exercise program specifically designed for each patient are adjunctive to the use of T.E.N.S. and provide the groundwork for the development of a comprehensive treatment program. Even though T.E.N.S. can be looked upon as a means of decreasing pain and muscle guarding, thus allowing for increased active ROM or mobility of the patient, it should not be considered as a definitive treatment in all pain syndromes.

The evaluation forms on pages 190 to 197, developed and used by the Delaware Valley Physical Therapy Associates, have been included to assist the clinician in the assessment of the type, location, and distribution of the patient's pain.

REFERENCES

1. SHEALY, CN: *The Pain Game*. Celestial Arts, Millbrae, Calif, 1976.
2. WALL, PD: *On the relation of injury to pain: The John J. Bonica Lecture.* Pain 6:253, 1979.
3. CRUE, BL, KENTON, B, AND CORREGAL, EJA: *Review article—Neurophysiology of pain—peripheral aspects: Speculations concerning the possibility of a unitary peripheral cutaneous input system for pressure, hot, cold and tissue damage.* In CRUE, BL (ED): *Chronic Pain: Further Observations from City of Hope National Medical Center.* SP Medical and Scientific Books, New York, 1979, p 59.
4. BISHOP, B: *Pain: Its physiology and rationale for management: Part I. Neuroanatomical substrate of pain.* Phys Ther 60:13, 1980.
5. ZOHN, DA AND MENNELL, JM: *Musculoskeletal Pain.* Little, Brown & Co, Boston, 1976, p 15.
6. TARSY, JM: *Pain Syndromes and Their Treatment.* Charles C Thomas, Springfield, Ill, 1953, p 32.
7. MELZACK, R: *The Puzzle of Pain.* Basic Books, New York, 1973.
8. HANNINGTON-KIFF, JG: *Pain Relief.* JB Lippincott, Philadelphia, 1974, p 23.
9. MUMFORD, JM AND BOWSHER, D: *Pain and protopathic sensibility: A review with particular reference to the teeth.* Pain 2:223, 1976.
10. STERLING, P: *Research note: Referred cutaneous sensation.* Exp Neurol 41:451, 1973.
11. KELLGREN, JH: *On the distribution of pain arising from deep somatic structures with charts of segmental pain areas.* Clin Sci 4:35, 1939.
12. INMAN, VT AND SAUNDERS, JMB: *Referred pain from skeletal structures.* J Nerv Ment Dis 99:660, 1944.
13. WYKE, B: *The neurology of joints.* Ann R Coll Surg Eng 41:25, 1967.
14. KELLGREN, JH: *Observations on referred pain arising from muscle.* Clin Sci 3:175, 1938.
15. FEINSTEIN, B, ET AL: *Experiments on pain referred from deep somatic tissues.* J Bone Joint Surg [Am] 36:981, 1954.
16. LEWIS, T AND KELLGREN, JH: *Observations relating to referred pain, visceromotor reflexes and other associated phenomena.* Clin Sci 4:47, 1939.
17. CAILLIET, R: *Soft Tissue Pain and Disability.* FA Davis, Philadelphia, 1977.
18. LEWIT, K: *The contribution of clinical observation to neurobiological mechanisms in manipulative therapy.* In KORR, IM (ED): *The Neurobiologic Mechanisms in Manipulative Therapy.* Plenum Press, New York, 1978, p 6.
19. MAIGNE, R: *Orthopedic Medicine: A New Approach to Vertebral Manipulations.* Charles C Thomas, Springfield, Ill, 1972.
20. KOS, J AND WOLF, J: *Intervertebral menisci and their possible role in intervertebral blockage.* Translated by BURKART, S. Bulletin of the Ortho and Sports Med Section of the APTA 1(3):4–5, 1976.
21. SAUNDERS, HD: *Classification of musculoskeletal spinal conditions.* Journal of Orthopaedic and Sports Physical Therapy 1(1):3, 1979.
22. HETTINGS, DL: *II. Normal joint structures and their reaction to injury.* Journal of Orthopaedic and Sports Physical Therapy 1(2):83, 1979.
23. CARMICHAEL, SW AND BURKART, SL: *Clinical anatomy of the lumbosacral complex.* Phys Ther 59:966, 1979.
24. MOONEY, V AND ROBERTSON, J: *The facet syndrome.* Clin Orthop 115:149, 1976.
25. WARWICK, R AND WILLIAMS, PL: *Gray's Anatomy,* ed 35. WB Saunders, Philadelphia, 1973.
26. HETTINGS, DL: *I. Normal joint structures and their reaction to injury.* Journal of Orthopaedic and Sports Physical Therapy (1):16, 1979.
27. LAMB, DW: *The neurology of spinal pain.* Phys Ther 59:971, 1979.
28. CYRIAX, J: *Textbook of Orthopaedic Medicine. Vol I: Diagnosis of Soft Tissue Injuries.* Bailliere Tindall, London, 1975.
29. PARIS, SV: *Mobilization of the spine.* Phys Ther 59:988, 1979.
30. STODDARD, A: *Manual of Osteopathic Practice.* Harper & Row, New York, 1969.
31. WYKE, BD: *The neurological basis of thoracic spine pain.* Rheumatol Phys Med 10:356, 1967.

32. WYKE, BD: *Neurological aspects of back pain.* In JAYSON, M (ED): *The Lumbar Spine and Back Pain.* Grune & Stratton, New York, 1976, p 189.

33. WYKE, BD: *Articular neurology: A review.* Physiotherapy 58:94, 1972.

34. GARDNER, E: *The innervation of the shoulder joint.* Anat Rec 102:1, 1948.

35. GARDNER, E: *The innervation of the knee joint.* Anat Rec 101:109, 1948.

36. GARDNER, E: *The innervation of the hip joint.* Anat Rec 101:353, 1948.

37. GARDNER, E: *The innervation of the elbow joint.* Anat Rec 102:161, 1944.

38. GOWITZKE, BA AND MILNER, M: *Understanding the Scientific Bases of Human Movement,* ed 2. Williams & Wilkins, Baltimore, 1980.

39. NATHAN, PW: *The gate control theory of pain: A critical review.* Brain 99:123, 1976.

40. GRANIT, R: *Receptors and Sensory Perception.* Yale University Press, New Haven, 1955.

41. BRADLEY, KC: *The anatomy of backache.* Aust NZ J Surg 44:227, 1974.

42. EDGAR, MA AND GHADIALLY, JA: *Innervation of the lumbar spine.* Clin Orthop 115:35, 1976.

43. PEDERSEN, HE, BLUNCK, CFJ, AND GARDNER, E: *The anatomy of lumbosacral posterior rami and meningeal branches of spinal nerves (sinuvertebral nerves).* J Bone Joint Surg [Am] 38:377, 1956.

44. CULBERSON, JL: *Origins of low-back pain—the intervertebral foramen.* In KENT, B (ED): *Third International Seminar on Manual Therapy.* Proceedings of the International Federation of Orthopaedic Manipulative Therapists. IFOMT, Hayward, Calif, 1977, p 21.

45. FISK, JW: *The Painful Neck and Back.* Charles C Thomas, Springfield, Ill, 1977, p 15.

46. WHITE, AA AND PANJABI, MM: *Clinical Biomechanics of the Spine.* JB Lippincott, Philadelphia, 1978, p 277.

47. FARFAN, HF: *Mechanical Disorders of the Low Back.* Lea & Febiger, Philadelphia, 1973, p 24.

48. CLOWARD, RB: *Cervical diskography: A contribution to the etiology and mechanism of neck, shoulder and arm pain.* Ann Surg 150:1052, 1959.

49. CLOWARD, RB: *The clinical significance of the sinu-vertebral nerve of the cervical spine in relation to the cervical disc syndrome.* J Neurol Neurosurg Psychiat 23:321, 1960.

50. IGGO, A: *Pain receptors.* In BONICA, JJ, PROCACCI, P, AND PAGNI, CA (EDS): *Recent Advances on Pain: Pathophysiology and Clinical Aspects.* Charles C Thomas, Springfield, Ill, 1974, p 3.

51. KESSLER, RM: *Acute symptomatic disk prolapse: Clinical manifestations and therapeutic considerations.* Phys Ther 59:978, 1979.

52. SCHAUMBERG, HH AND SPENCER, PS: *Pathology of spinal root compression.* In GOLDSTEIN, M (ED): *The Research Status of Spinal Manipulative Therapy.* DHEW Publication # (NIH) 76-998, Bethesda, Md, 1975, p 141.

53. MITCHELL, SW: *Injuries of Nerves and their Consequences.* Dover Publications, New York, 1965.

54. SUNDERLAND, S: *Traumatized nerves, roots and ganglia: Musculoskeletal factors and neuropathological consequences.* In KORR, IM (ED): *The Neurobiological Mechanisms in Manipulative Therapy.* Plenum Press, New York, 1978, p 137.

55. HAYMAKER, W AND WOODHALL, B: *Peripheral Nerve Injuries,* ed 2. WB Saunders, Philadelphia, 1953, p 17.

56. GOODGOLD, J AND EBERSTEIN, A: *Electrodiagnosis of Neuromuscular Diseases,* ed 2. Williams & Wilkins, Baltimore, 1978.

57. KERR, FWL: *The ventral spinothalamic tract and other ascending systems of the ventral funiculus of the spinal cord.* Comp Neurol 159:335, 1975.

58. KERR, FWL: *Segmental circuitry and spinal cord nociceptive mechanisms.* In BONICA, JJ AND ALBE-FESSARD, D (EDS): *Advances in Pain Research and Therapy,* Vol I. Raven Press, New York, 1976, p 75.

59. HOSOBUCHI, Y: *The majority of unmyelinated afferent axons in human ventral roots probably conduct pain.* Pain 8:167, 1980.

60. MELZACK, R AND LOESER, JD: *Phantom body pain in paraplegics: Evidence for a central "pattern generating mechanism" for pain.* Pain 4:195, 1978.

61. GILLIAN, LA: *Clinical Aspects of the Autonomic Nervous System.* Little, Brown & Co, Boston, 1954.

62. FULTON, JF: *Textbook of Physiology.* WB Saunders, Philadelphia, 1963, p 358.

63. PROCACCI, P, ZOPPI, M, AND MARESCA, M: *Experimental pain in man.* Pain 6:123, 1979.

64. WHITE, TT: *Visceral pain.* Postgrad Med 53:199, 1973.

65. SWEET, WH: *Autonomic contributions to pain syndromes.* Clin Neurosurg 25:603, 1978.

66. FINNESON, BE: *Diagnosis and Management of Pain Syndromes.* WB Saunders, Philadelphia, 1969.

67. HALE, MS: *A Practical Approach to Arm Pain.* Charles C Thomas, Springfield, Ill, 1971.

68. JACOX, AK: *Pain: A Source Book for Nurses and Other Health Professionals.* Little, Brown & Co, Boston, 1977.

69. FERGUSON, RH: *Medical evaluation of backache and neckache.* In GURDJIAN, ES AND THOMAS, LM (EDS): *Neckache and Backache—Proceedings of a Workshop Sponsored by the American Association of Neurological Surgeons in Cooperation with the National Institute of Health.* Charles C Thomas, Springfield, Ill, 1970, p 120.

70. GRIEVE G: *Mobilisation of the Spine.* Churchill Livingstone, Edinburgh, 1979.

71. MELZACK, R AND TORGESON, WS: *On the language of pain.* Anesthesiology 34:50, 1971.

72. MELZACK, R: *Prolonged relief of pain by brief, intense transcutaneous somatic stimulation.* Pain 1:357, 1975.

73. MELZACK, R: *The McGill Pain questionnaire: Major properties and scoring methods.* Pain 1:277, 1975.

74. CROCKETT, DJ, PRKACHIN, KM, AND CRAIG, KD: *Factors of the language of pain in patient and volunteer groups.* Pain 4:175, 1977.

75. LEAVITT, F, ET AL: *Affective and sensory dimensions of back pain.* Pain 4:273, 1978.

76. BOYD, DB AND MERSKEY, H: *A note on the description of pain and its causes.* Pain 5:1, 1978.

77. FORDYCE, WE, ET AL: *Relationship of patient semantic pain descriptions to physician diagnostic judgements, activity level measures and MMPI.* Pain 5:193, 1978.

78. LEAVITT, F AND GARRON, DC: *Psychological disturbance and pain report differences in both organic and non-organic low back pain patients.* Pain 7:187, 1979.

79. DEGENAAR, JJ: *Some philosophical considerations on pain.* Pain 7:281, 1979.

80. PRIETA, EJ, ET AL: *The language of low back pain: Factor structure of the McGill pain questionnaire.* Pain 8:11, 1980.

81. AGNEW, DC AND MERSKEY, H: *Words of chronic pain.* Pain 2:73, 1976. Reprinted with a follow-up in CRUE, BL (ED): *Chronic Pain: Further Observations from the City of Hope National Medical Center.* SP Medical and Scientific Books, New York, 1979, p 29.

82. BAILEY, CA AND DAVIDSON, PO: *The language of pain: Intensity.* Pain 2:319, 1976.

83. WEISENBERG, M: *Pain: Clinical and Experimental Perspectives.* CV Mosby, St Louis, 1975.

84. STEWART, ML: *Measurement of clinical pain.* In JACOX, AK (ED): *Pain: A Source Book for Nurses and Other Health Professionals.* Little, Brown & Co, Boston, p 107.

85. JOHNSON, M: *Assessment of clinical pain.* In JACOX, AK (ED): *Pain: A Source Book for Nurses and Other Health Professionals.* Little, Brown & Co, Boston, 1977, p 139.

86. PROCACCI, P, ET AL: *Pain threshold measurements in man.* In BONICA, JJ, PROCACCI, P, AND PAGNI, CA (EDS): *Recent Advances on Pain—Pathophysiology and Clinical Aspects.* Charles C Thomas, Springfield, Ill, 1974, p 105.

87. STERNBACH, RA: *Pain: A Psychophysiological Analysis.* Academic Press, New York, 1968.

88. STERNBACH, RA: *Pain Patients: Traits and Treatment.* Academic Press, New York, 1974.

89. STERNBACH, RA, ET AL: *Measuring the severity of clinical pain.* In BONICA, JJ (ED): *Advances in Neurology,* Vol 4. Raven Press, New York, 1974, p 281.

90. STERNBACH, RA: *Psychological factors in pain.* In BONICA, JJ AND ALBE-FESSARD, D (EDS): *Advances in Pain Research and Therapy,* Vol I. Raven Press, New York, 1976, p 293.

91. STERNBACH, RA, ET AL: *On the sensitivity of the tourniquet pain test.* Pain 3:105, 1977.

92. STERNBACH, RA, ET AL: *Transcutaneous electrical analgesia: A follow-up analysis.* Pain 2:35, 1976.

93. LUTTERBECK, PM AND TRIAY, SH: *Measurement of analgesic activity in man.* In WEISENBERG, M (ED): *Pain: Clinical and Experimental Perspectives.* CV Mosby, St Louis, 1975, p 67.

94. NOTERMANS, SLH: *Measurement of the pain threshold determined by electrical stimulation and its clinical application.* In WEISENBERG, M (ED): *Pain: Clinical and Experimental Perspectives.* CV Mosby, St Louis, 1975, p 72.

95. NOTERMANS, SLH AND TOPHOFF, MMWA: *Sex difference in pain tolerance and pain appercep-tion.* In WEISENBERG, M (ED): *Pain: Clinical and Experimental Perspectives.* CV Mosby, St Louis, 1975, p 111.

96. PROCACCI, P, ET AL: *The cutaneous pricking pain threshold in old age.* In WEISENBERG, M (ED): *Pain: Clinical and Experimental Perspectives.* CV Mosby, St Louis, 1975, p 117.

97. MURRAY, FS AND HAGAN, BC: *Pain threshold and tolerance of hands and feet.* In WEISENBERG, M (ED): *Pain: Clinical and Experimental Perspectives.* CV Mosby, St Louis, 1975, p 121.

98. WOODROW, KM, ET AL: *Pain tolerance: Differences according to age, sex and race.* In WEISENBERG, M (ED): *Pain: Clinical and Experimental Perspectives.* CV Mosby, St Louis, 1975, p 133.

99. RODGERS, EJ AND VILKIN, B: *Diurnal variation in sensory and pain thresholds correlated with mood states.* J Clin Psychiatry 39:431, 1978.

100. CLARK, WC AND MEHL, L: *Thermal pain: A sensory decision theory analysis of the effect of age and sex on various response criteria and 50% pain threshold.* J Abnorm Psychol 78:202, 1971.

101. CLARK, WC: *Pain sensitivity and the report of pain: An introduction to sensory decision theory.* Anesthesiology 40:272, 1974.

102. HARKINS, SW AND CHAPMAN, CR: *Detection and decision factors in pain perception in young and elderly men.* Pain 2:265, 1976.

103. CHAPMAN, CR, WILSON, ME, AND GEHRING, JD: *Comparative effects of acupuncture and trans-cutaneous stimulation on the perception of painful dental stimuli.* Pain 2:265, 1976.

104. CHAPMAN, CR, CHEN, AC, AND BONICA, JJ: *Effects of intrasegmental electrical acupuncture on dental pain: Evaluation by threshold estimation and sensory decision theory.* Pain 3:213, 1977.

105. ROLLMAN, GB: *Signal detection theory measurement of pain: A review and critique.* Pain 3:187, 1977.

106. CHAPMAN, CR: *Sensory decision theory methods in pain research: A reply to Rollman.* Pain 3:295, 1977.

107. CHAPMAN, CR: *Pain and perception: Comparison of sensory decision theory and evoked poten-tial methods.* Res Publ Assoc Res Nerv Ment Dis 58:111, 1980.

108. WOLFF, BB: *Measurement of human pain.* Res Publ Assoc Res Nerv Ment Dis 58:173, 1980.

109. BEECHER, HK: *Quantification of the subjective pain experience.* In WEISENBERG, M (ED): *Pain: Clinical and Experimental Perspectives.* CV Mosby, St Louis, 1975, p 56.

110. SMITH, GM, ET AL: *An experimental pain method sensitive to morphine in man: The submax-imum effort tourniquet technique.* J Pharmacol Exp Ther 154:324, 1966.

111. SMITH, GM, ET AL: *Experimental pain produced by the submaximum effort tourniquet tech-nique: Further evidence of validity.* J Pharmacol Exp Ther 163:468, 1968.

112. MERSKEY, H: *Assessment of pain.* Physiotherapy 60:96, 1974.

113. STERNBACH, RA: *Evaluation of pain relief.* Surg Neurol 4:199, 1975.

114. MERSKY, H AND WATSON, GD: *The lateralization of pain.* Pain 7:271, 1979.

115. VANBUREN, J AND KLEINKNECHT, RA: *An evaluation of the McGill pain questionnaire for use in dental pain assessment.* Pain 6:23, 1979.

116. MENNELL, JM: *Back Pain.* Little, Brown & Co, Boston.

117. ERHARD, R AND BOWLING, R: *The recognition and management of the pelvic component of low back and sciatic pain.* Bulletin of the Ortho Section, APTA 2:4, 1977.

118. LANCE, JW: *Headache: Understanding. Alleviation with a Special Section on Migraine.* Charles Scribner's Sons, New York, 1975.

119. APPENZELLER, O: *Pathogenesis and Treatment of Headache.* Spectrum Publications, New York, 1976.

120. MALANGA, CJ: *Analgesic Pharmacology.* Presented at Clinical TENS Seminar, Emory University, March 14–16, 1980.

121. HALPERN, LM: *Analgesic drugs in the management of pain.* Arch Surg 112:861, 1977.

122. LARKIN, TJ: *Mixing medicines? Have a care.* FDA Consumer, DHEW Publication # 76-3020, March, 1976.

123. DOUGHERTY, RJ: *TENS: An alternative to drugs in the treatment of chronic pain.* Presented at 30th Annual Scientific Assembly American Academy of Family Physicians, San Francisco, September 25–28, 1978.

124. WALKER, I: *Iatrogenic addiction and its treatment.* Int J Addict 13:461, 1978.

125. NACHEMSON, A: *Lumbar intradiscal pressure.* In JAYSON, M (ED): *The Lumbar Spine and Back Pain.* Grune & Stratton, New York, 1976, p 257.

126. APPENZELLER, O: *Somatoautonomic reflexology—normal and abnormal.* In KORR, IM (ED): *The Neurobiologic Mechanisms in Manipulative Therapy.* Plenum Press, New York, 1978, p 179.

127. GRAHAM, C, ET AL: *Use of the McGill Pain Questionnaire in the assessment of cancer pain: Replicability and consistency.* Pain 8:377, 1980.

128. MELZACK, R: *Psychologic aspects of pain.* In BONICA, JJ (ED): *Pain, Research Publication of the Association for Research in Nervous and Mental Disease* 58:143, 1980.

129. LIVINGSTON, WK: *Pain Mechanisms: A Physiologic Interpretation of Causalgia and Its Related States.* Plenum Press, New York, 1976.

130. PAWL, RP: *Chronic Pain Primer.* Yearbook Medical Publishers, Chicago, 1979.

131. WALL, PD: *Physiological mechanisms involved in the production and relief of pain.* In BONICA, JJ, PROCACCI, P, AND PAGNI, CA (EDS): *Recent Advances on Pain—Pathophysiology and Clinical Aspects.* Charles C Thomas, Springfield, Ill, 1974, p 36.

132. TOREBJORK, HE AND HALLIN, RG: *Responses in human A and C fibers to repeated electrical intradermal stimulation.* J Neurol Neurosurg Psychiat 37:653, 1974.

133. IGNELZI, RJ AND NYQUIST, JK: *Observations on fast axoplasmic transport in peripheral nerve following repetitive electrical stimulation.* Pain 7:313, 1979.

134. HOWSON, DC: *Peripheral neural excitability.* Phys Ther 58:1467, 1978.

135. GRUNDFEST, H: *Discussion of excitation and conduction in traumatized nerves.* In KORR, IM (ED): *The Neurobiologic Mechanisms in Manipulative Therapy.* Plenum Press, New York, 1978, p 167.

136. WILSON, ME: *The neurological mechanisms of pain.* Anesthesia 29:407, 1974.

137. CARLSON, CA, ET AL: *Electrical transcutaneous nerve stimulation for relief of itch.* Experientia 31:191, 1975.

138. PRICE, DD, ET AL: *Peripheral suppression of first pain and central summations of second pain evoked by noxious heat pulses.* Pain 3:57, 1977.

139. HOWE, JF, LOESER, JD, AND CALVIN, WH: *Mechanosensitivity of dorsal root ganglia and chronically injured axons: A physiological basis for the radicular pain of nerve root compression.* Pain 3:25, 1977.

140. MCCALL, IW, PARK, WM, AND O'BRIEN, JP: *Induced pain referral from posterior lumbar elements in normal subjects.* Spine 4:441, 1979.

141. HANDWERKER, HO, IGGO, A, AND ZIMMERMAN, M: *Segmental and supraspinal actions on dorsal horn neurons responding to noxious and non-noxious skin stimuli.* Pain 1:147, 1975.

142. KENNARD, MA AND HAUGEN, FP: *The relation of subcutaneous focal sensitivity to referred pain of cardiac origin.* Anesthesiology 16:297, 1955.

143. DORAN, FSA: *The sites to which pain is referred from the common bile-duct in man and its implication for the theory of referred pain.* Br J Surg 54:599, 1967.

144. POMERANZ, B, WALL, PD, AND WEBER, WV: *Cord cells responding to fine myelinated afferents from viscera, muscle and skin.* J Physiol 199:511, 1968.

145. SELZER, M AND SPENCER, WA: *Convergence of visceral and cutaneous afferent pathways in the lumbar spinal cord.* Brain Res 14:331, 1969.

146. SELZER, M AND SPENCER, WA: *Interactions between visceral and cutaneous afferents in the spinal cord: Reciprocal primary afferent fiber depolarization.* Brain Res 14:349, 1969.

147. WILLIS, WD: *Neurophysiology of nociception and pain in the spinal cord.* In BONICA, JJ (ED): *Pain, Research Publication of the Association for Research in Nervous and Mental Disease* 58:77, 1980.

148. PERL, ER: *Afferent basis of nociception and pain: Evidence from the characteristics of sensory receptors and their projections to the spinal dorsal horn.* In BONICA, JJ (ED): *Pain, Research Publication of the Association for Research in Nervous and Mental Disease* 58:19, 1980.

149. KERR, FWL AND FUKUSHIMA, T: *New observations on the nociceptive pathways in the central nervous system.* In BONICA, JJ (ED): *Pain, Research Publication of the Association for Research in Nervous and Mental Disease* 58:47, 1980.

150. WALL, PD: *The role of substantia gelatinosa as a gate control.* In BONICA, JJ (ED): *Pain, Research Publication of the Association for Research in Nervous and Mental Disease* 58:205, 1980.

151. DENNIS, SG AND MELZACK, R: *Pain-signalling systems in the dorsal and ventral spinal cord.* Pain 4:97, 1977.

152. KERR, FWL: *Neuroanatomical substrates of nociception in the spinal cord.* Pain 1:325, 1975.

153. DENSLOW, JS, KORR, IM, AND KREMS, AD: *Quantitative studies of chronic facilitation in human motoneuron pools.* Am J Physiol 150:229, 1947.

154. KORR, IM: *The Neurobiologic Mechanisms in Manipulative Therapy.* Plenum Press, New York, 1978.

155. MYKLEBUST, JB: *Selected bibliography on evoked potentials.* Neuroelectric News 8:1, 1979.

156. CARMON, A: *Considerations of the cerebral response to painful stimulation: Stimulus transduction versus perceptual event.* Bull NY Acad Med 55:313, 1979.

157. HATTORI, S, SUIKI, K, AND KAWAI, S: *Diagnosis of the level and severity of cord lesion in cervical spondylotic myelopathy: Spinal evoked potentials.* Spine 4:478, 1979.

158. REGER, SI, ET AL: *Spinal evoked potentials from the cervical spine.* Spine 4:495, 1979.

159. STOWELL, H: *Event related brain potentials from somatosensory nociceptive stimulation.* In CRUE, BL (ED): *Chronic Pain—Further Observations from City of Hope National Medical Center.* Spectrum Publications, New York, 1979, p 105.

160. COOTE, JH: *Somatic sources of afferent input at factors in aberrant autonomic, sensory and motor function.* In KORR, IM (ED): *The Neurobiologic Mechanisms in Manipulative Therapy.* Plenum Press, New York, 1978, p 91.

161. TURNBULL, F: *The nature of pain that may accompany cancer of the lung.* Pain 7:371, 1979.

162. WILSON, RE: *The Management of Pain in Surgical Practice: Part II—Pain in Advanced Neoplastic Disease.* Chirurgecom Division of Appleton-Century-Crofts, Plainfield, NJ, 1979.

163. ROBERTS, HJ: *Transcutaneous electrical nerve stimulation in the management of pancreatitis pain.* South Med J 71:396, 1978.

164. OSTROWKSI, MJ AND DODD, VA: *Transcutaneous nerve stimulation for relief of pain in advanced malignant disease.* Nursing Times, August 11, 1977, p 1233.

165. LONG, D: *External stimulation as a treatment of chronic pain.* Minn Med 57:195, 1974.

166. LOESER, JD, BLACK, RG, AND CHRISTMAN, A: *Relief of pain by transcutaneous stimulation.* J Neurosurg 42:308, 1975.

167. RENAER, M AND GUZINSKI, GM: *Pain in gynecologic practice.* Pain 5:305, 1978.

168. NEUFELD, I: *Pathogenic concepts of fibrositis.* Arch Phys Med Rehabil 363, 1952.

169. KRAUS, H: *Evaluation and treatment of muscle function in athletic injury.* Am J Surg 98:353, 1959.

170. SOLA, AE, RODENBERGER, ML, AND GETTYS, BB: *Incidence of hypersensitive areas in posterior shoulder muscles.* Am J Phys Med 34:585, 1955.

171. AWAD, EA: *Interstitial myofibrositis: Hypothesis of the mechanisms.* Arch Phys Med Rehabil 54:449, 1973.

172. SOLA, AE AND KUITERT, JH: *Myofascial trigger point pain in the neck and shoulder gridle.* Northwest Med 54:980, 1955.

173. TRAVELL, J AND BIGELOW, NH: *Referred somatic pain does not follow a simple "segmental" pattern.* Pro Fed Amer Soc Exp Biol & Med 5:106, 1946.

174. TRAVELL, J: *Basis for the multiple uses of local block of somatic trigger areas (procaine infiltration and ethyl chloride spray).* Miss Valley Med J 71:13, 1949.

175. TRAVELL, J AND RINZLER, SH: *The myofascial genesis of pain.* Postgrad Med 11:425, 1952.

176. WEEKS, UD AND TRAVELL, J: *Postural vertigo due to trigger areas in the sternocleidomastoid muscle.* J Pediatr 47:315, 1955.

177. TRAVELL, J: *Referred pain from skeletal muscle: The pectoralis major syndrome of breast pain and soreness and the sternomastoid syndrome of headache and dizziness.* NY State J Med 55:331, 1955.

178. TRAVELL, J: *Pain mechanisms in connective tissue.* In RAGAN, C (ED): *Connective Tissues: Transactions of the Second Conference.* Josiah Macy Jr. Foundation, New York, 1952, p 86.

179. TRAVELL, J: *Ethyl chloride spray for painful muscle spasm.* Arch Phys Med 33:291, 1952.

180. TRAVELL, J: *Rapid relief of acute "stiff neck" by ethyl chloride spray.* J Am Med Wom Assoc 4:89, 1949.

181. TRAVELL, J: *Temporomandibular joint dysfunction: Temporomandibular joint pain referred from the head and neck.* J Prosthet Dent 10:745, 1960.

182. KRAUS, H: *Clinical Treatment of Back and Neck Pain.* McGraw-Hill, New York, 1970, p 92.

183. KRAUS, H: *Triggerpoints.* NY State J Med 73:1310, 1973.

184. MENNELL, JM: *"Spray and stretch" treatment for myofascial pain.* Hospital Physician, December 1973, p 1.

185. MENNELL, JM: *The therapeutic use of cold.* JAOA 74:1146, 1975.

186. SIMONS, DG: *Muscle pain syndromes: Part I.* Am J Phys Med 54:289, 1975.

187. SIMONS, DG: *Muscle pain syndromes: Part II.* Am J Phys Med 55:15, 1976.

188. TRAVELL, J: *Myofascial trigger points: Clinical view.* In BONICA, JJ AND ALBE-FESSARD, D (EDS): *Advances in Pain Research and Therapy,* Vol I. Raven Press, New York, 1976, p 919.

189. BERGES, PU: *Myofascial pain syndromes.* Postgrad Med 53:161, 1973.

190. MELZACK, R, STILLWELL, DM, AND FOX, EJ: *Trigger points and acupuncture points for pain: Correlations and implications.* Pain 3:3, 1977.

191. NIELSEN, AJ: *Spray and stretch for myofascial pain.* Phys Ther 58:567, 1978.

192. BROWN, BR: *Diagnosis and therapy of common myofascial syndromes.* JAMA 239:646, 1978.

193. WYANT, GM: *Chronic pain syndromes and their treatment. II: Trigger points.* Can Anaesth Soc J 26:216, 1979.

194. BONICA, JJ: *Management of myofascial pain syndromes in general practice.* JAMA 164:732, 1957.

195. LEWIT, K: *The needle effect in the relief of myofascial pain.* Pain 6:83, 1979.

196. DORIGO, B, ET AL: *Fibrositic myofascial pain in intermittent claudication: Effect of anesthetic block of trigger points on exercise tolerance.* Pain 6:183, 1979.

197. MACDONALD, AJR: *Abnormally tender muscle regions and associated painful movements.* Pain 8:207, 1980.

198. SCOTT, DS AND LUNDEEN, TF: *Myofascial pain involving the masticatory muscles: An experimental model.* Pain 8:207, 1980.

199. GUNN, CC AND MILBRANDT, WE: *Utilizing trigger points.* Osteopathic Physician 44:29, 1977.

200. PACE, JB: *Treatment of "muscle contraction headache" by a combination of cervical facet injection and muscle trigger point injection.* Scientific Program Abstracts, First Annual Meeting of American Pain Society, 1979, p 56.

201. FISCHER, AA: *Pressure threshold measurements in diagnosis and treatment of myofascial pain.* Scientific Program Abstracts, First Annual Meeting of American Pain Society, 1979, p 32.

202. RETZLAFF, EW, ET AL: *The piriformis muscle syndrome.* JAOA 73:799, 1974.

203. PACE, JB AND NAGLE, D: *Piriform syndrome.* West J Med 124:435, 1976.

204. MICHELE, AA AND EISENBERG, J: *Scapulocostal syndrome.* Arch Phys Med 49:383, 1968.

205. SHULL, JR: *Scapulocostal syndrome: Clinical aspects.* South Med J 162:8956, 1969.

206. GELB, H: *Clinical Management of Head, Neck and TMJ Pain and Dysfunction.* WB Saunders, Philadelphia, 1977.

207. SIMONS, DG: *Electrogenic nature of palpable bands and "jump sign" associated with myofascial trigger points.* In BONICA, JJ AND ALBE-FESSARD, D (EDS): *Advances in Pain Research and Therapy,* Vol I. Raven Press, New York, 1976, p 913.

208. KURLAND, HD: *Quick Headache Relief Without Drugs.* William Morrow & Co, New York, 1977.

209. KURLAND, HD: *Treatment of headache pain with auto-acupressure.* Diseases of the Nervous System 37:127, 1976.

210. DIAMOND, S AND MEDINA, JL: *The headache history—key to diagnosis.* In APPENZELLER, O (ED): *Pathogenesis and Treatment of Headache.* Spectrum Publications, New York, 1976, p 1.

211. FRIEDMAN, AP: *An approach to the patient with headache.* In APPENZELLER, O (ED): *Pathogenesis and Treatment of Headache.* Spectrum Publications, New York, 1976, p 9.

212. ZIEGLER, DK: *Epidemiology and genetics of migraine.* In APPENZELLER, O (ED): *Pathogenesis and Treatment of Headache.* Spectrum Publications, New York, 1976, p 19.

213. KUDROW, L: *Hormones, pregnancy and migraine.* In APPENZELLER, O (ED): *Pathogenesis and Treatment of Headache.* Spectrum Publications, New York, 1977, p 31.

214. FRIEDMAN, AP: *Migraine*. In APPENZELLER, O (ED): *Pathogenesis and Treatment of Headache*. Spectrum Publications, New York, 1976, p 69.

215. KUDROW, L: *Tension headache (scalp muscle contraction headache)*. In APPENZELLER, O (ED): *Pathogenesis and Treatment of Headache*. Spectrum Publications, New York, 1976, p 81.

216. GRAHAM, JR: *Cluster headache*. In APPENZELLER, O (ED): *Pathogenesis and Treatment of Headache*. Spectrum Publications, New York, 1976, p 93.

217. KUNKEL, RS: *Mixed headache*. In APPENZELLER, O (ED): *Pathogenesis and Treatment of Headache*. Spectrum Publications, New York, 1976, p 109.

218. APPENZELLER, O: *Headache in temporal arteritis and cerebral vascular disease*. In APPENZELLER, O (ED): *Pathogenesis and Treatment of Headache*. Spectrum Publications, New York, 1976, p 115.

219. DIAMOND, S: *Psychogenic headache: Treatment, including biofeedback techniques*. In APPENZELLER, O (ED): *Pathogenesis and Treatment of Headache*. Spectrum Publications, New York, 1976, p 131.

220. LANCE, JW: *Headache: Understanding/Alleviation, With a Special Section on Migraine*. Charles Scribner's Sons, New York, 1975.

221. SPEER, F: *Migraine*. Nelson-Hall, Chicago, 1977.

222. MOFFETT, A, SWASH, M, AND SCOTT, DF: *Effect of tyramine in migraine: A double-blind study*. J Neurol Neurosurg Psychiat 35:496, 1972.

223. APPENZELLER, O: *Monoamines, headaches and behavior*. In APPENZELLER, O (ED): *Pathogenesis and Treatment of Headache*. Spectrum Publications, New York, 1976, p 43.

224. GRAHAM, JR: *Headache related to a variety of medical disorders*. In APPENZELLER, O (ED): *Pathogenesis and Treatment of Headache*. Spectrum Publications, New York, 1976, p 49.

225. RYAN, RE AND RYAN, SR: *Acute nasal sinusitis*. In APPENZELLER, O (ED): *Pathogenesis and Treatment of Headache*. Spectrum Publications, New York, 1976, p 159.

226. SICUTERI, F, ET AL: *Headache and cardiac pain*. In BONICA, JJ, PROCACCI, P, AND PAGNI, CA (EDS): *Recent Advances on Pain: Pathophysiology and Clinical Aspects*. Charles C Thomas, Springfield, Ill, 1974, p 148.

227. MARKOVICH, SE: *Pain in the head: A neurological appraisal*. In GELB, H (ED): *Clinical Management of Head, Neck and TMJ Pain and Dysfunction*. WB Saunders, Philadelphia, 1977, p 125.

228. SJAASTAD, O: *So-called "vascular headache of the migraine type": One or more nosological entities?* Acta Neurol Scand 54:125, 1976.

229. SJAASTAD, O AND DALE, I: *A new (?) clinical headache entity "chronic paroxysmal hemicrania" 2*. Acta Neurol Scand 54:140, 1976.

230. HORVEN, I AND SJAASTAD, O: *Cluster headache syndrome and migraine—ophthalmological support for a two-entity theory*. Acta Ophthalmol (Copenh) 55:35, 1977.

231. SJAASTAD, O: *Pathogenesis of the cluster headache syndrome*. Res Clin Stud Headache 6:53, 1978.

232. KUDROW, L: *Managing migraine headache*. Psychosomatics 19:685, 1978.

233. OLESEN, J: *Some clinical features of the acute migraine attack: An analysis of 750 patients*. Headache 18:268, 1978.

234. SAPER, JR: *Migraine II: Treatment*. JAMA 239:2480, 1978.

235. FRIEDMAN, AP: *Migraine*. Med Clin North Am 62:481, 1978.

236. BLAU, JN: *Migraine: A vasomotor instability of the meningeal circulation*. Lancet 11:1136, 1978.

237. COHEN, MJ: *Psychophysiological studies of headache: Is there similarity between migraine and muscle contraction headaches*. Headache 18:189, 1978.

238. DIXON, HH AND DICKEL, HA: *Tension headache*. Northwest Med 66:817, 1967.

239. FEHLER, BM: *Headaches—Fact or fantasy*. S Afr Med J 55:138, 1979.

240. ZIEGLER, DK: *Tension headache*. Med Clin North Am 62:495, 1978.

241. SOVAK, M, ET AL: *Current investigations in headache*. In BONICA, JJ (ED): *Pain*. Raven Press, New York.

242. KRABBE, AA AND OLESEN, J: *Headache provocation by continuous intravenous infusion of histamine: Clinical results and receptor mechanisms*. Pain 8:253, 1980.

243. DVILANSKY, A, ET AL: *Release of platelet 5-hydroxytryptamine by plasma taken from patients during and between migraine attacks.* Pain 2:315, 1976.

244. MARTIN, PR AND MATHEWS, AM: *Tension headaches: Psychophysiological investigation and treatment.* J Psychosom Res 22:389, 1978.

245. PECK, CL AND KRAFT, GH: *Electromyographic biofeedback for pain related to muscle tension.* Arch Surg 112:889, 1977.

246. BLANCHARD, HB, ET AL: *Temperature biofeedback in the treatment of migraine headaches.* Arch Gen Psychiatry 35:581, 1978.

247. DIAMOND, S, ET AL: *The value of biofeedback in the treatment of chronic headache: A five year retrospective study.* Headache 19:90, 1979.

248. JESSUP, BA, NEUFELD, RWJ, AND MERSKEY, H: *Biofeedback therapy for headache and other pain: An evaluative review.* Pain 7:225, 1979.

249. DIAMOND, S: *Psychogenic headache: Treatment, including biofeedback techniques.* In APPENZELLER, O (ED): *Pathogenesis and Treatment of Headache.* Spectrum Publications, New York, 1976, p 131.

250. CARLOW, TJ: *Ophthalmic causes of headache.* In APPENZELLER, O (ED): *Pathogenesis and Treatment of Headache.* Spectrum Publications, New York, 1976, p 131.

251. FERGUSON, M (ED): *Hand-warming increases cerebral blood flow.* Brain-Mind Bulletin 5:1, 1980.

252. APPENZELLER, O AND ATKINSON, R: *Transcutaneous nerve stimulation for the treatment of migraine and other head pain.* Munch Med Wochenschr 117:1953, 1975.

253. APPENZELLER, O AND ATKINSON, R: *Transcutaneous nervous stimulation in the treatment of hemicrania and other forms of headache.* Minerva Med 67:2023, 1976.

254. RUTKOWSKI, B, NIEDZIALKOWSKA, T, AND OTTO, J: *Electric stimulation in chronic headache.* Anaesth Resusc Intensive Ther 4:257, 1976.

255. CHENG, ACK: *The treatment of headache employing acupuncture.* Am J Chin Med 3:181, 1975.

256. OKAZAKI, K, ET AL: *Ryodoraku therapy for migraine headache.* Am J Chin Med 3:61, 1975.

257. STILLWELL, DL: *The innervation of tendons and aponeuroses.* Am J Anat 100:289, 1957.

258. RALSTON, HJ, MILLER, MR, AND KASAHARA, M: *Nerve endings in human fasciae, tendons, ligaments, periosteum and joint synovial membrane.* Anat Rec 136:137, 1960.

259. HOCKADAY, JM AND WHITLY, CWM: *Patterns of referred pain in the normal subject.* Brain 90:481, 1967.

260. HENDLER, N: *Chronic pain patients: Diagnosis and treatment.* In *Psychobiological Issues in Psychiatry.* Schering Corp, 1979.

261. SPIRO, HM: *Acute pancreatitis.* Chest Pain: Problems in Differential Diagnosis 3(5):1, 1978.

262. MELZACK, R: *The McGill pain questionnaire: Major properties and scoring methods.* Pain 1:277, 1975.

263. INGRAM, RH JR: *Diagnosing chest pain caused by pulmonary disease.* Chest Pain: Problems in Differential Diagnosis 3(4):1, 1978.

264. KOIZUMI, K: *Autonomic system reactions caused by excitation of somatic afferents: Study of cutaneo-visceral reflex.* In KORR, IM (ED): *The Neurobiologic Mechanisms in Manipulative Therapy.* Plenum Press, New York, 1978, p 219.

265. MAIGNE, R: *Manipulation of the spine.* In ROGOFF, JB (ED): *Manipulation, Traction and Massage,* ed 2. Williams & Wilkins, Baltimore, 1980, p 59.

266. MAIGNE, R: *Manipulations and mobilization of the limbs.* In ROGOFF, JB (ED): *Manipulation, Traction and Massage,* ed 2. Williams & Wilkins, Baltimore, 1980, p 121.

267. GELB, H, ET AL: *The role of the dentist and the otolaryngologist in evaluating temporomandibular joint syndrome.* J Prosth Dent 18:497, 1967.

268. GALTON, L: *The great imposter.* Emergency Medicine, May 1975, p 182.

269. GELB, H AND TARTE, J: *A two-year clinical dental evaluation of 200 cases of chronic headache: The craniocervical-mandibular syndrome.* J Am Dent Assoc 91:1230, 1975.

270. GELB, H AND ARNOLD, GE: *Syndromes of the head and neck of dental origin.* AMA Archives of Otolaryngology 70:681, 1959.

271. COSTEN, JB: *A syndrome of ear and sinus symptoms dependent upon disturbed function of the temporomandibular joint.* Ann Otol Rhinol Laryngol 43:1, 1934.

272. KLINEBERG, I: *Structure and function of TMJ innervation.* Ann R Coll Surg Engl 49:268, 1971.

273. SMITH, SD: *Muscular strength correlated to jaw posture and the temporomandibular joint.* NY State Dent J 44:278, 1978.

274. VERSCHOTH, A: *Weak? Sink your teeth into this.* Sports Illustrated, June 2, 1980, p 37.

275. WEINBERG, LA: *The etiology, diagnosis and treatment of TMJ dysfunction-pain syndrome. Part III: Treatment.* J Prosthet Dent 43:186, 1980.

276. GELB, H: *Effective management and treatment of the craniomandibular syndrome.* In GELB, H (ED): *Clinical Management of Head, Neck and TMJ Pain and Dysfunction.* WB Saunders, Philadelphia, 1977, p 288.

277. EDMEADS, J: *Headaches and head pains associated with disease of the cervical spine.* Med Clin North Am 62:533, 1978.

278. CAILLIET, R: *Neck and Arm Pain.* FA Davis, Philadelphia, 1964.

279. JACKSON, R: *The Cervical Syndrome.* Charles C Thomas, Sprinfield, Ill, 1971.

280. LEWIT, K: *Pain arising in the posterior arch of the atlas.* Eur Neurol 16:263, 1977.

281. JACH, ET: *Relief of myo-facial pain: Treatment of 5 patients.* Dental Survey, June 1975, p 44.

282. JANKELSON, B, ET AL: *Neural conduction of the myo-monitor stimulus: A quantitative analysis.* J Prosthet Dent 34:245, 1975.

283. GAYRAL, L AND NEUWIRTH, E: *Oto-neuro-ophthalmologic manifestations of cervical origin: Posterior cervical syndrome of Barré-Lieou.* NY State J Med 54:1920, 1954.

284. LIEB, MM: *Oral orthopedics.* In GELB, H (ED): *Clinical Management of Head, Neck and TMJ Pain and Dysfunction.* WB Saunders, Philadelphia, 1977, p 32.

285. GELB, H: *Patient evaluation.* In GELB, H (ED): *Clinical Management of Head, Neck and TMJ Pain and Dysfunction.* WB Saunders, Philadelphia, 1977, p 73.

286. BRODAL, A: *The Cranial Nerves: Anatomy and Anatomicoclinical Correlation, ed 2.* Blackwell Scientific, Oxford, 1965.

287. NEEDHAM, CW: *Major cranial neuralgias and the surgical treatment of headaches.* Med Clin North Am 62:545, 1978.

288. BONICA, JJ: *Neurophysiologic and pathologic aspects of acute and chronic pain.* Arch Surg 112:750, 1977.

289. LOESER, JD: *Neuralgia.* Postgrad Med 53:207, 1973.

290. HELLAND, MM: *Anatomy and function of the temporomandibular joint.* J Ortho Sports Phys Ther 1:144, 1980.

291. HASSLER, R AND WALKER, AE: *Trigeminal Neuralgia.* WB Saunders, Philadelphia, 1970.

292. MASPES, PE AND PAGNI, CA: *A critical appraisal of pain surgery and suggestions for improving treatment.* In BONICA, JJ, PROCACCI, P, AND PAGNI, CA (EDS): *Recent Advances on Pain: Pathophysiology and Clinical Aspects.* Charles C Thomas, Springfield, Ill, 1974, p 201.

293. CALVIN, WH, LOESER, JD, AND HOWE, JF: *A neurophysiological theory for the pain mechanism of tic doloureux.* Pain 3:147, 1972.

294. LOESER, JD: *The management of tic douloureux.* Pain 3:155, 1977.

295. GREGG, JM, ET AL: *Radiofrequency thermoneurolysis of peripheral nerves for control of trigeminal neuralgia.* Pain 5:231, 1978.

296. SMITH, DG AND MUMFORD, JM: *Petrous angle and trigeminal neuralgia.* Pain 8:269, 1980.

297. KERR, FWL: *Facial neuralgias: Mechanisms, diagnosis and treatment.* In Pain Abstracts, Vol I. Second World Congress on Pain, International Association for the Study of Pain, Montreal, 1978, p 87.

298. CALVIN, WH: *Facial neuralgias: What do normal and pathophysiological mechanisms suggest?* In Pain Abstracts, Vol I. Second World Congress on Pain, International Association for the Study of Pain, Montreal, 1978, p 88.

299. PRICE, DD: *Peripheral and central mechanisms of trigeminal pain.* In Pain Abstracts, Vol I. Second World Congress on Pain, Montreal, 1978, p 89.

300. YOKOTA, T: *Trigeminal nociceptive neurons in the trigeminal subnucleus caudalis and bulbar lateral reticular formation.* In Pain Abstracts, Vol I, Second World Congress on Pain, Montreal, 1978, p 90.

301. DUBNER, R, HAYES, RL, AND HOFFMAN, DS: *Neural and behavioral correlates of pain in the*

trigeminal system. In Bonica, JJ (ed): Pain, Research Publication of the Association for Research in Nervous and Mental Disease 58:63, 1980.

302. Whidden, A and Fidler, SMB: *Pathophysiology of pain.* In Jacox, AK (ed): *Pain: A Source Book for Nurses and Other Health Professionals.* Little, Brown & Co, Boston, 1977, p 27.

303. Meyer, GA and Fields, HL: *Causalgia treated by selective large fiber stimulation of the peripheral nerve.* Brain 95:163, 1972.

304. McDonnell, D: *Surgical and electrical stimulation methods for relief of pain.* In Jacox, AK (ed): *Pain: A Source Book for Nurses and Other Health Professionals.* Little, Brown & Co, Boston 1977, p 169.

305. Homans, J: *Minor causalgia: A hyperesthetic neurovascular syndrome.* N Engl J Med 222:870, 1940.

306. Steinschein, MJ, et al: *Causalgia.* Arch Phys Med Rehabil 56:58, 1975.

307. Thompson, JE: *The diagnosis and management of post-traumatic pain syndromes (causalgia).* Aust NZ J Surg 49:299, 1979.

308. Korr, IM: *Sustained sympathicotonia.* In Korr, IM (ed): *The Neurobiologic Mechanisms in Manipulative Therapy.* Plenum Press, New York, 1978, p 229.

309. Nathan, PW: *Involvement of the sympathetic nervous system in pain.* In Kosterlitz, HW and Terenius, LY (eds): *Pain and Society: Report of the Dahlem Conference on Pain and Society, Life Science Report 17.* Verlag Chemie, Deerfield Beach, Fla, 1980, p 311.

310. Cooney, WP, Dobyns, JH, and Linscheid, RL: *Complications of Colles' fractures.* J Bone Joint Surg [Am] 62:613, 1980.

311. Cailliet, R: *The Shoulder in Hemiplegia.* FA Davis, Philadelphia, 1980.

312. Russell, WR: *Neurological sequelae of amputation.* Br J Hosp Med 4:607, 1970.

313. Melzack, R: *Phantom limb pain: Implications for treatment of pathologic pain.* Anesthesiology 35:409, 1971.

314. Brena, SF and Sammons, EE: *Phantom urinary bladder pain—case report.* Pain 7:197, 1979.

315. Feinstein, B, Luce, JC, and Langton, JNK: *The influence of phantom limbs.* In Klopsteg, P and Wilson, P (eds): *Human Limbs and Their Substitutes.* McGraw-Hill, New York, 1954, p 79.

316. Melzack, R: *Phantom limbs.* Psychology Today, October 1970, p 64.

317. Gunn, CC: *Causalgia and denervation supersensitivity.* American Journal of Acupuncture 7:317, 1979.

318. Gunn, CC: *"Prespondylosis" and some pain syndromes following denervation supersensitivity.* Spine 5:185, 1980.

319. Wall, PD and Gutnick, M: *Ongoing activity in peripheral nerves: The physiology and pharmacology of impulses originating from a neuroma.* Exp Neurol 43:580, 1974.

320. Wall, PD: *Physiological mechanisms involved in the production and relief of pain.* In Bonica, JJ, Procacci, P, and Pagni, CA (eds): *Recent Advances on Pain: Pathophysiology and Clinical Aspects.* Charles C Thomas, Springfield, Ill, 1974, p 36.

321. Arcangeli, P and Galletti, R: *Endogenous pain producing substances.* In Bonica, JJ, Procacci, P, and Pagni, CA (eds): *Recent Advances on Pain: Pathophysiology and Clinical Aspects.* Charles C Thomas, Springfield, Ill, 1974, p 82.

322. Hermanssen, L and Osnes, JB: *Blood and muscle pH after maximal exercise in man.* J Appl Physiol 32:304, 1972.

323. Bonica, JJ: *Causalgia and other reflex sympathetic dystrophies.* In Pain Abstracts, Vol I. International Association for the Study of Pain, Montreal, 1978, p 11.

324. Wall, PD: *Sensory physiology after various types of peripheral nerve injury.* In Pain Abstracts, Vol I. International Association for the Study of Pain, Montreal, 1978, p 10.

325. Thomas, PH: *Painful neuropathies.* In Pain Abstracts, Vol I. International Association for the Study of Pain, Montreal, 1978, p 9.

326. Ochoa, J and Noordenbos, W: *Pathology and disordered sensation in local nerve lesions: An attempt at correlation.* In Pain Abstracts, Vol I. International Association for the Study of Pain, Montreal, 1978, p 8.

327. Handwerker, HO: *Pain producing substances.* In Kosterlitz, HW and Terenius, LY (eds):

Pain and Society: Report of the Dahlem Conference on Pain and Society, Life Science Report 17. Verlag Chemie, Deerfield Beach, Fla, 1980, p 325.

328. TASKER, RR, ORGAN, LW, AND HAWRYLYSHYN, P: *Deafferentation and causalgia.* In BONICA, JJ (ED): *Pain.* Raven Press, New York, 1980, p 305.

329. LAWRENCE, RM: *Phantom pain: A new hypothesis.* Medical Hypotheses 6:245, 1980.

330. LIVESON, JA AND SPIEHOLZ, NI: *Peripheral Neurology: Case Studies in Electrodiagnosis.* FA Davis, Philadelphia, 1979.

331. GERSH, MR, WOLF, SL, AND RAO, VR: *Evaluation of transcutaneous electrical nerve stimulation for pain relief in peripheral neuropathy.* Phys Ther 60:49, 1980.

332. MEHTA, JM, NIMBALKAR, ST, THALAYAN, K: *A new approach in the relief of pain of leprous neuritis.* Lepr India 51:459, 1979.

333. MILES, J AND LIPTON, S: *Phantom limb pain treated by electrical stimulation.* Pain 5:373, 1978.

334. LOESER, JD, BLACK, RG, AND CHRISTMAN, A: *Relief of pain by transcutaneous stimulation.* J Neurosurg 42:308, 1975.

335. BOHM, E: *Transcutaneous electrical nerve stimulation in chronic pain after peripheral nerve injury.* Acta Neurochir 40:277, 1978.

336. THORSTEINSSON, G, ET AL: *Transcutaneous electrical stimulation: A double-blind trial of its efficacy for pain.* Arch Phys Med Rehabil 58:8, 1977.

337. LONG, DM: *Electrical stimulation for relief of pain from chronic nerve injury.* J Neurosurg 39:718, 1973.

338. STILZ, RJ, CARRON, H, AND SANDERS, DB: *Case history number 96, Reflex sympathetic dystrophy in a 6 year-old: Successful treatment by transcutaneous nerve stimulation.* Anesth Analg (Cleve) 56:438, 1977.

339. GYORY, AN AND CAINE, DC: *Electric pain control (EPC) of a painful forearm amputation stump.* Med J Aust 2:156, 1977.

340. NOORDENBOS, W: *Sensory findings in painful traumatic nerve lesions.* In Pain Abstracts, Vol I. International Association for the Study of Pain, Second World Congress on Pain, Montreal, 1978, p 7.

341. ERIKSSON, MBE AND SJOLUND, BH: *Pain relief from conventional versus acupuncturelike TNS in patients with chronic facial pain.* In Pain Abstracts, Vol I. International Association for the Study of Pain, Montreal, 1978, p 128.

342. SHERMAN, RA, GALL, N, AND GORMLEY, J: *Treatment of phantom limb pain with muscular relaxation training to disrupt the pain-anxiety-tension cycle.* Pain 6:47, 1979.

343. WILKINS, RH AND BRODY, IA: *The thalamic syndrome.* Arch Neurol 20:559, 1969.

344. NATHAN, PW AND WALL, PD: *Treatment of post-herpetic neuralgia by prolonged electrical stimulation.* Br Med J 3:645, 1974.

345. INDECK, W AND PRINTY, A: *Skin application of electrical impulses for relief of pain.* Minn Med 58:305, 1975.

346. LONG, D AND HAGFORS, N: *Electrical stimulation in the nervous system: The current status of electrical stimulation of the nervous system for relief of pain.* Pain 1:109, 1975.

347. CAUTHEN, JC AND RENNER, EJ: *Transcutaneous and peripheral nerve stimulation for chronic pain states.* Surg Neurol 4:102, 1975.

348. THURIN, E, MEEHAN, PF, AND GILBERT, BS: *Treatment of pain by transcutaneous electric nerve stimulation in general practice.* Med J Aust 1:70, 1980.

349. GYORY, AN: *Transcutaneous electric nerve stimulation (TENS) analgesia.* Med J Aust Jan 26, 1980.

350. KIRSCH, WM, LEWIS, JA, AND SIMON, RH: *Experiences with electrical stimulation devices for the control of chronic pain.* Med Inst 9:217, 1975.

351. LONG, DM: *External electrical stimulation as a treatment of chronic pain.* Minn Med 57:195, 1974.

352. HACHEN, HJ: *Psychological, neurophysiological and therapeutic aspects of chronic pain: Preliminary results with transcutaneous electrical stimulation.* Paraplegia 15:353, 1977–78.

353. HEILPORN, A: *Two therapeutic experiments on stubborn pain in spinal cord lesions: Coupling melitracen flupenthixol and the transcutaneous nerve stimulation.* Paraplegia 15:368, 1977–78.

354. SERRATO, JC: *Pain control by transcutaneous nerve stimulation.* South Med J 72:67, 1979.

355. BANERJEE, T: *Transcutaneous nerve stimulation for pain after spinal injury.* N Engl J Med 291:796, 1974.

356. WINTER, A: *The use of transcutaneous electrical nerve stimulation (TNS) in the treatment of multiple sclerosis.* J Neurosurg Nurs 8:125, 1976.

357. PICAZA, JA, ET AL: *Pain suppression by peripheral nerve stimulation.* Surg Neurol 4:105, 1975.

358. RICHARDSON, RR, MEYER, PR, AND RAIMONDI, AJ: *Transabdominal neurostimulation in acute spinal cord injuries.* Spine 4:47, 1979.

359. RICHARDSON, RR, MEYER, PR, AND CERULLO, LJ: *Transcutaneous electrical neurostimulation in musculoskeletal pain of acute spinal cord injuries.* Spine 5:42, 1980.

360. McCARTHY, JA AND ZIEGENFUS, RW: *Transcutaneous electrical nerve stimulation: An adjunct in the pain management of Guillain-Barre syndrome.* Phys Ther 58:23, 1978.

361. GOODGOLD, J: *Anatomical Correlates of Clinical Electromyography.* Williams & Wilkins, Baltimore, 1974.

362. LEWIT, K: *The contribution of clinical observation to neurobiologic mechanisms in manipulative therapy.* In KORR, IM (ED): *The Neurobiologic Mechanisms in Manipulative Therapy.* Plenum Press, New York, 1978, p 3.

363. NELSON, RM AND CURRIER, DP: *Anterior interosseus syndrome: A case report.* Phys Ther 60:194, 1980.

364. SUNDERLAND, S: *Anatomical perivertebral influences on the intervertebral foramen.* In GOLDSTEIN, M (ED): *The Research Status of Spinal Manipulative Therapy.* DHEW Publication # (NIH) 76-998, Bethesda, Md, 1975, p 129.

365. BRITT, LP: *Nonoperative treatment of the thoracic outlet syndrome symptoms.* Clin Orthop 51:45, 1967.

366. CAILLIET, R: *Shoulder Pain.* FA Davis, Philadelphia, 1966.

367. SMITH, KF: *The thoracic outlet syndrome: A protocol of treatment.* J of Ortho and Sports Physical Therapy 1:89, 1979.

368. WOLF, SL: *Perspectives on central nervous system responsiveness to transcutaneous electrical nerve stimulation.* Phys Ther 58:1443, 1978.

369. GREEN, E AND GREEN, A: *Beyond Biofeedback.* Robert Briggs Associates, San Francisco, 1977.

370. JACOBSON, AM, ET AL: *Raynauds phenomenon: Treatment with hypnotic and operant technique.* JAMA 225:739, 1973.

371. SAPPINGTON, JT, FIORITO, EM, AND BREHONY, KA: *Biofeedback as therapy in Raynauds disease.* Biofeedback and Self-regulation 4:155, 1979.

372. BROWN, B: *Stress and the Art of Biofeedback.* Bantam Books, New York, 1977.

373. GAARDER, KR AND MONTGOMERY, PS: *Clinical Biofeedback: A Procedural Manual.* Williams & Wilkins, Baltimore, 1977.

374. OLTON, DS AND NOONBERG, AR: *Biofeedback Clinical Applications in Behavioral Medicine.* Prentice-Hall, Englewood Cliffs, NJ, 1980.

375. DOOLEY, DM AND KASPRAK, M: *Modification of blood flow to the extremities by electrical stimulation of the nervous system.* South Med J 69:1309, 1976.

376. ABRAM, SE: *Increased sympathetic tone associated with transcutaneous electrical stimulation.* Anesthesiology 45:575, 1976.

377. ABRAM, SE, ASIDDAO, CB, AND REYNOLDS, AC: *Increased skin temperature during transcutaneous electrical stimulation.* Anesth Analg (Cleve) 59:22, 1980.

378. LeROY, PL: *Personal communication, 1980.*

379. NORFRAY, JF, ET AL: *Early confirmation of stress fractures in joggers.* JAMA 243:1647, 1980.

380. FRONT, D, ET AL: *Bone metastases and bone pain in breast cancer: Are they closely associated?* JAMA 242:1747, 1979.

381. KOTTKE, FT: *Bone pain from metastases.* JAMA 243:2397, 1980.

382. COOPER, NS: *Arthritis and the rheumatic diseases.* In LAMONT-HAVERS, RW AND HISLOP, HJ (EDS): *Arthritis and Related Disorders.* APTA, Washington, DC, 1965, p 11.

383. CALABRO, JJ: *Clinical aspects and medical management of chronic arthritides.* In LAMONT-

HAVERS, RW AND HISLOP, HJ (EDS): *Arthritis and Related Disorders.* APTA, Washington, DC, 1965, p 35.

384. MANNHEIMER, C, LUND, S, AND CARLSSON, C: *The effect of transcutaneous electrical nerve stimulation on joint pain in patients with rheumatoid arthritis.* Scand J Rheumatol 7:13, 1978.

385. BENN, RT AND WOOD, PHN: *Pain in the back: An attempt to estimate the size of the problem.* Rheumatol Rehabil 14:121, 1975.

386. MCNAB, I: *Backache.* Williams & Wilkins, Baltimore, 1977.

387. SIM, FH, ET AL: *Primary bone tumors simulating lumbar disc syndrome.* Spine 2:65, 1977.

388. KIRKALDY-WILLIS, WH AND HILL, RJ: *A more precise diagnosis for low-back pain.* Spine 4:102, 1979.

389. ROCABADO, M: *Relationship of the temporomandibular joint to cervical dysfunction.* In KENT, BE (ED): *Proceedings of the International Federation of Orthopaedic Manipulative Therapists.* International Federation of Orthopaedic Manipulative Therapists, Hayward, Calif, 1977, p 103.

390. WEINBERG, LA: *Treatment prosthesis in TMJ dysfunction—pain syndrome.* J Prosthet Dent 39:645, 1978.

391. NACHEMSON, AL: *The lumbar spine: An orthopedic challenge.* Spine 1:59, 1976.

392. POPE, MH, ET AL: *The relation between biomechanical and psychological factors in patients with low back pain.* Spine 5:173, 1980.

393. FEILD, JR AND MCHENRY, H: *The lumbar shield: A progress report.* Spine 5:264, 1980.

394. SPENGLER, DM, ET AL: *Low-back pain following multiple lumbar spine procedures. Failure of initial selection?* Spine 5:356, 1980.

395. FAGER, CA AND FREIDBERG, SR: *Analysis of failures and poor results of lumbar spine surgery.* Spine 5:87, 1980.

396. SHEALY, CN: *Facet denervation in the management of back and sciatic pain.* Clin Orthop 115:157, 1976.

397. LOESER, JD: *Low back pain.* In BONICA, JJ (ED): *Pain.* Raven Press, New York, 1980, p 363.

398. WIESEL, SW, ET AL: *Actue low back pain: An objective analysis of conservative therapy.* Spine 5:324, 1980.

399. REILLY, J. ET AL: *Pathological anatomy of the lumbar spine.* In HELFET, AJ AND GRUBELLEE, DM (EDS): *Disorders of the Lumbar Spine.* JB Lippincott, Philadelphia, 1978, p 26.

400. CAILLIET, R: *Low Back Pain Syndrome.* FA Davis, Philadelphia, 1981.

401. WHITE, AH, DERBY, R, AND WYNNE, G: *Epidural injections for diagnosis and treatment of low-back pain.* Spine 5:78, 1980.

402. HICKEY, RFJ AND TREGONNING, GD: *Denervation of spinal facet joints for treatment of chronic low back pain.* NZ Med J 85:96, 1977.

403. GLOVER, JR: *Back pain and hyperesthesia.* Lancet:1165, 1960.

404. FARFAN, H: *Pathological basis for manipulative therapy.* In KENT, B (ED): *Third International Seminar on Manual Therapy. Proceedings of the International Federation of Orthopaedic Manipulative Therapists.* International Federation of Orthopaedic Manipulative Therapists, Hayward, Calif, 1977, p 135.

405. HELFET, AJ AND GRUEBEL LEE, DM: *Disorders of the Lumbar Spine.* JB Lippincott, Philadelphia, 1978.

406. NACHEMSON, A AND MORRIS, JM: *In vivo measurements of intradiscal pressure.* J Bone Joint Surg [Am] 46:1077, 1964.

407. FARFAN, HF: *The application of biomechanics to the treatment of lumbar intervertebral joint derangements.* Clin Neurosurg 25:284, 1978.

408. ANDERSSON, GBJ, ET AL: *The influence of backrest inclination and lumbar support on lumbar lordosis.* Spine 4:52, 1979.

409. HICKEY, DS AND HURKINS, DWL: *Relation between the structure of the annulus fibrosus and the function and failure of the intervertebral disc.* Spine 5:106, 1980.

410. WADDELL, G, ET AL: *Non-organic physical signs in low-back pain.* Spine 5:117, 1980.

411. KAPANDJI, IA: *The Physiology of the Joints. Vol 3: The Trunk and the Vertebral Column.* Churchill Livingstone, Edinburgh, 1974.

412. HASUE, M, ET AL: *Post-traumatic spinal stenosis of the lumbar spine: Report of a case caused by hyperextension injury; review of literature.* Spine 5:259, 1980.
413. MCKENZIE, R: Personal communication, 1980.
414. GUNN, CC AND MILBRANDT, WE: *"Bursitis" around the hip.* American Journal of Acupuncture 5:53, 1977.
415. GUNN, CC AND MILBRANDT, WE: *Tennis elbow and the cervical spine.* Journal of the Canadian Medical Association 114:803, 1976.
416. GUNN, CC, MILBRANDT, WE, AND LITTLE, A: *Peripheral nerve injuries mimicking lumbar disc herniations.* Med J of British Columbia 19:350, 1977.
417. GUNN, CC AND MILBRANDT, WE: *Tenderness at motor points: An aid in the diagnosis of pain in the shoulder referred from the cervical spine.* JAOA 77:196, 1977.
418. GUNN, CC AND MILBRANDT, WE: *Shoulder pain, cervical spondylosis and acupuncture.* American Journal of Acupuncture 5:121, 1977.
419. GUNN, CC AND MILBRANDT, WE: *Tennis elbow and acupuncture.* American Journal of Acupuncture 5:61, 1977.
420. GUNN, CC AND MILBRANDT, WE: *Tenderness at motor points: A diagnostic and prognostic aid for low-back injury.* J Bone Joint Surg [Am] 58:815, 1976.
421. GUNN, CC AND MILBRANDT, WE: *Early and subtle signs in low-back sprain.* Spine 3:267, 1978.
422. FRIGERIO, NA, STOWE, RR, AND HOWE, JW: *Movement of the sacro-iliac joint.* Clin Orthop 100:370, 1974.
423. STODDARD, A: *Conditions of the sacro-iliac joint and their treatment.* Bulletin of the Ortho Section APTA 3:18, 1978.
424. DON TIGNY, RL: *Dysfunction of the sacro-iliac joint and its treatment.* J Ortho & Sports Phys Ther 1:23, 1979.
425. LE BARR, MM, ET AL: *Symphyseal and sacro-iliac joint pain associated with public symphysis instability.* Arch Phys Med Rehabil 59:470, 1978.
426. MENNELL, JM: *Back Pain.* Little, Brown & Co, Boston, 1960.
427. SHAW, TE: Personal communication, 1980.
428. DYCK, P, ET AL: *Intermittent cauda equina compression syndrome: Its recognition and treatment.* Spine 2:75, 1977.
429. DIXON, A ST J: *Diagnosis of low-back pain.* In JAYSON, M (ED): *The Lumbar Spine and Back Pain.* Grune & Stratton, New York, 1976, p 77.
430. MENNELL, JM: *Differential diagnosis of visceral from somatic back pain.* Journal of Occupational Medicine 8:477, 1966.
431. YATES, A: *Treatment of back pain.* In JAYSON, M (ED): *The Lumbar Spine and Back Pain.* Grune & Stratton, New York, 1976, p 341.
432. BRIEG, A AND TROUP, JDG: *Biomechanical considerations in the straight-leg-raising test: Cadaveric and clinical studies of the effects of medial hip rotation.* Spine 4:242, 1979.
433. FISK, JW: *The straight-leg-raising test: Its relevance to possible disc pathology.* NZ Med J 81:557, 1975.
434. MCKENZIE, RA: *Prophylaxis in recurrent low back pain.* NZ Med J 89:22, 1979.
435. ERSEK, RA: *Low-back pain: Prompt relief with transcutaneous neuro-stimulation. A report of 35 consecutive patients.* Ortho Rev 5:27, 1976.
436. BOWSHER, D: *Pain pathways and mechanisms.* Anesthesia 33:935, 1978.
437. BEAN, WB: *A curious double reference of mild pain produced by scratching the skin: With a note on the gentle art of snoring.* Trans Am Clin Climatol Assoc 91:147, 1979.
438. SWANSON, DW AND MORUTA, T: *Patients complaining of extreme pain.* Mayo Clin Proc 55:563, 1980.
439. DOMZAL, T, ET AL: *Diurnal rhythm of pain in sciatica. Preliminary report.* Neurol Neurochir Pol 14:253, 1980.
440. ZAMIR, N AND SHUBER, E: *Altered pain perception in hypertensive patients.* Brain Res 201:471, 1980.
441. LONG, DM: *The comparative efficacy of drugs vs. electrical modulation in the management of chronic pain.* In LEROY, PL (ED): *Current Concepts in the Management of Chronic Pain.* Symposia Specialists Medical Books, Miami, 1977, p 53.

442. NORDEMAR, R AND THORNER, C: *Treatment of acute cervical pain—a comparative group study.* Pain 10:93, 1981.

443. GOHARIAN, RK AND NEFF, PA: *Effect of occlusal retainers on temporomandibular joint and facial pain.* J Prosthet Dent 44:206, 1980.

444. Editorial: *Itch.* Lancet 2:568, 1980.

445. SIMONS, DG AND TRAVELL, J: *Myofascial trigger points, a possible explanation.* Pain 10:106, 1981.

446. URBAN, LM: *The straight leg raising test: A review.* Journal of Orthopedic and Sports Physical Therapy 2:117, 1981.

447. McKENZIE RA: *The Lumbar Spine: Mechanical Diagnosis and Therapy.* Spinal Publications, Waikanae, New Zealand, 1981.

448. BOTTE, RR: *An interpretation of the pronation syndrome and foot types of patients with low back pain.* J Am Podiatry Assoc 71:243, 1981.

449. RODGERS, EJ: *Pain threshold neuromodulation.* Illinois Medical Journal 159:153, 1981.

450. FORERMAN, RD, HANCOCK, MB, AND WILLIS, WD: *Responses of spinothalamic tract cells in thoracic spinal cord of the monkey to cutaneous and visceral inputs.* Pain 11:149, 1981.

451. MILNE, RJ, ET AL: *Convergence of cutaneous and pelvic visceral nociceptive inputs onto primate spinothalamic neurons.* Pain 11:163, 1981.

452. HALL, W, HAYWARD, L, AND CHAPMAN, CR: *On "the lateralization of pain."* Pain 10:337, 1981.

453. ROCABADO, M: *Course Notes—Head, Neck and TMJ Joint Dysfunctions.* Rocabado Institute for Craniomandibular and Vertebral Therapeutics, Tacoma, Wash, 1981.

PAIN ASSESSMENT FORM

Name: _____ Age: _____ Date: _____
Occupation: _____ Injured at work: _____ Presently working: _____
Date of injury: _____ or Onset of pain: _____ Gradual _____ Sudden _____
Description of accident: _____
_____
_____
_____

PAIN DESCRIPTION

What does your pain feel like? _____
Is it present constantly? _____ periodically? _____
Is it present at certain times during the day? _____ night? _____
When your pain is present, how long does it last? _____
What positions, movements, or activities increase or bring on pain? _____
_____
What positions, movements or activities decrease your pain? _____
_____
Are you able to sleep at night without pain? _____
Do you have a firm mattress? _____ Are you awakened by pain? _____
What is your primary sleeping position? _____
_____
What pain medications, if any are you taking? _____
_____ How frequently? _____
How long have you been taking this medication? _____
How much pain relief does the medication provide? _____
Does anything else affect your pain? _____

_____ Food	_____ Coughing or sneezing	$\oplus$ = Increase
_____ Weather changes	_____ Exertion	$\ominus$ = Decrease
_____ Finger pressure	_____ Noise	
_____ Menstruation	_____ Light	
_____ Heat		
_____ Ice		

Since the onset of pain, has it been: decreasing _____ , increasing _____ , or remaining the same _____ .
Have you had a similar problem in the past? If so, when? _____
What treatment if any did you receive at that time? _____
_____ Was it helpful? _____
Have you already received treatment elsewhere for your present problem? _____ If so,
specify the type of treatment which you received _____
Was it beneficial? _____
Place an "X" next to the statements that apply to you.

_____ Grinding your teeth	_____ Visual disturbances
_____ Facial or head pain	_____ Gastrointestinal discomfort
_____ Vomiting _____ Frequency _____ Does this ↓ or ↑ pain _____	
_____ Pain during or after eating	_____ Pain upon chewing

PAIN LOCATION

Where did your pain start? _____

Has it changed location or spread to other areas? _____

_____

Are there any areas where discomfort is most intense? _____

Where? _____

Are there any areas where you don't feel any sensation? _____

_____

      Use the diagrams on the back of this page to draw the distribution and quality of your pain. Try to be as specific as possible in regard to the exact type or quality of pain.

COMPLETING THE DIAGRAMS

      First decide which of the following words best describes your pain or discomfort . . .

      Achy, sharp, shooting, burning, tingling (pins and needles or numbness), sensitive to touch.

      Use the following pages to show areas of pain that may intensify only while standing, sitting, or lying down. We would like you to rate your pain on a scale of 10 as it exists in each position.

Pain Rating Scale

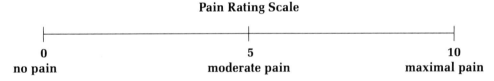

<table>
<tr><td>0</td><td>5</td><td>10</td></tr>
<tr><td>no pain</td><td>moderate pain</td><td>maximal pain</td></tr>
</table>

      Thank you for your cooperation in filling out this form for us. It will further help to clarify your complaints of pain and aid us in your evaluation.

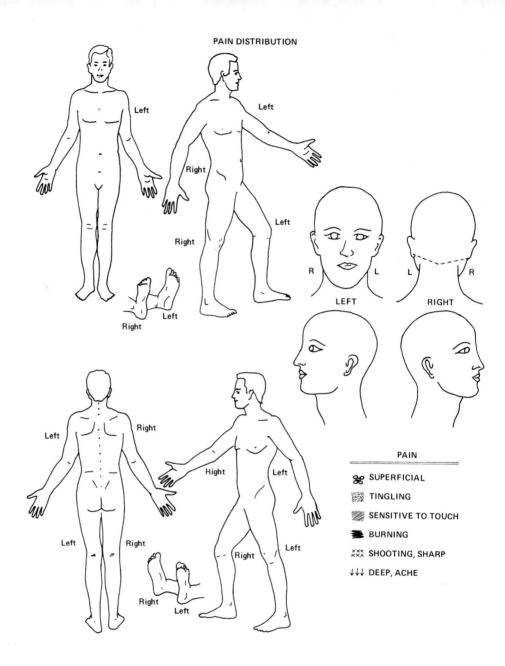

PAIN DISTRIBUTION

PAIN

�֍ SUPERFICIAL

▒ TINGLING

▨ SENSITIVE TO TOUCH

▰ BURNING

XXX SHOOTING, SHARP
XXX

↓↓↓ DEEP, ACHE

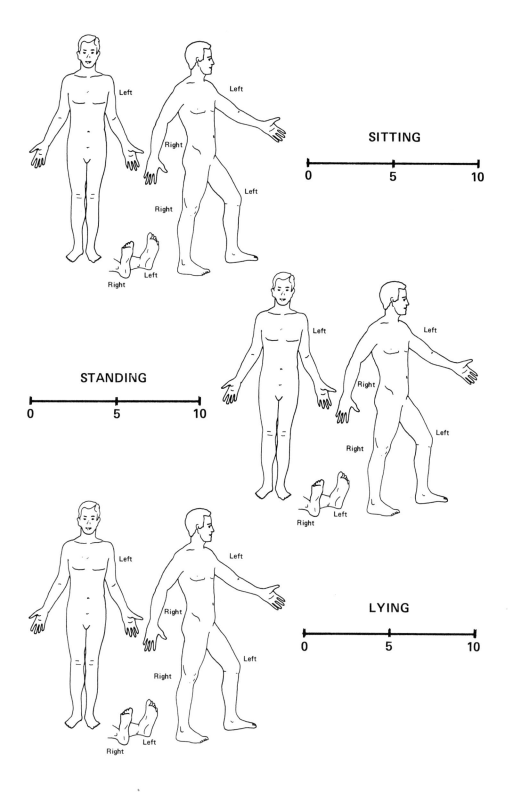

SITTING

STANDING

LYING

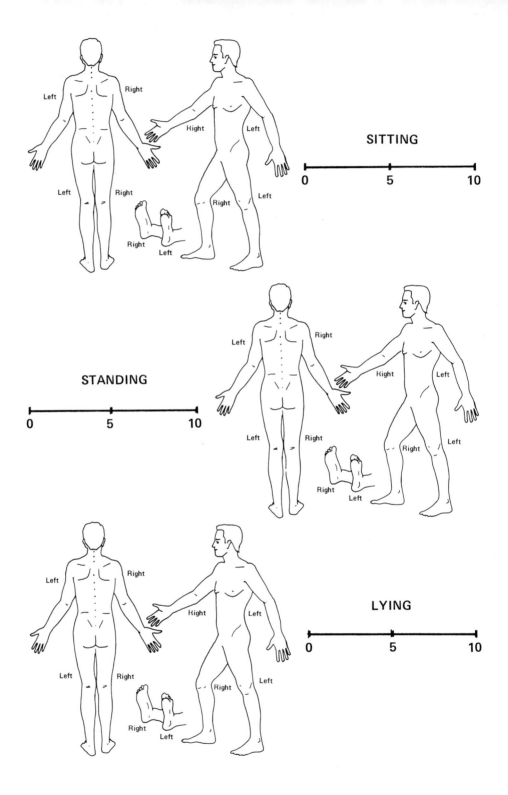

SITTING

STANDING

LYING

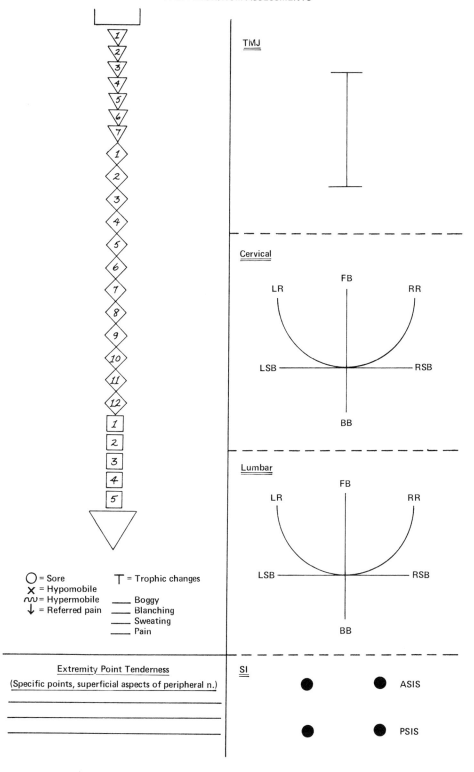

TMJ

Cervical

FB

LR   RR

LSB —————————— RSB

BB

Lumbar

FB

LR   RR

LSB —————————— RSB

BB

○ = Sore   ⊤ = Trophic changes
✗ = Hypomobile
∿ = Hypermobile   ___ Boggy
↓ = Referred pain ___ Blanching
                   ___ Sweating
                   ___ Pain

Extremity Point Tenderness
(Specific points, superficial aspects of peripheral n.)

SI

● ● ASIS

● ● PSIS

DETERMINATION OF T.E.N.S. EFFECTIVENESS IN SPECIFIC PAIN SYNDROMES 195

POSTURE

_____ Forward head
_____ Dowager's hump
_____ Alar scapula
_____ Round shoulders
_____ Kyphosis
_____ Scoliosis
_____ Lordosis
_____ Contractures
_____ Atrophy
_____ Leg length
_____ Edema
_____ Pronation/supination of foot

MYOTOME ASSESSMENT

Cervical _____

_____

Lumbar _____

_____

B&B signs _____

NEUROLOGIC ASSESSMENT

Sensation _____
Reflexes _____
Dural signs _____
                    DF   FB   Med Hip Rot
SLR Ⓛ _____
     Ⓡ _____
Ely _____
Ober _____
Tinel _____
Adson's _____
Other tests: _____

_____

_____

_____

_____

_____

_____

_____

Gait _____
Sitting posture _____
Walking posture _____
     Aids _____
Facial expression _____

MOBILITY (peripheral)

TMJ _____
AC _____
SC _____
Shoulder _____
Elbow _____
Forearm _____
Wrist _____
Hand _____
Hip _____
Knee _____
Ankle _____
Foot _____
Painful arc _____
Capsular pattern _____
Pain with resistance _____
   Upon _____
   End feel _____
   Compression _____
   Distraction _____
Crepitation _____

REPEATED (SPINAL) MOTIONS

	Standing	**Lying down**
FB		
BB		
LSG		
RSG		
Compression		
Distraction		

CHAPTER 6

STIMULATION CHARACTERISTICS OF T.E.N.S.

GERALD N. LAMPE, B.S., R.P.T., AND
JEFFREY S. MANNHEIMER, M.A., R.P.T.

The use of electricity as a form of therapy is a well-established procedure in medicine but also has as part of its history some "crude" forms of application. As long ago as 400 BC, the torpedo fish, or electric eel, was used to impart electric shocks to persons standing in water to treat gout, headaches, asthma, hemorrhoids, and many other medical maladies. Later, names like Kratzenstein, Volta, Galvani, Faraday, and Bordet became important through their development of concepts and devices that generated and/or measured "electric shocks" for therapeutic purposes. Current technology and medical electronic devices, especially transcutaneous electrical nerve stimulators, present stark contrasts to the concepts and instrumentation of that early period.

TRANSCUTANEOUS ELECTRICAL NERVE STIMULATION (T.E.N.S.)

There is still skepticism about the use, safety, and effectiveness of T.E.N.S. The "currents" generated in T.E.N.S. are extremely safe, reliable, and controlled. The sophistication of T.E.N.S. is demonstrated by the fact that it has successfully passed the scrutiny of medical device regulations, which are imposed on all medical instrumentation. T.E.N.S., in passing that FDA scrutiny, became a Class II device restricted to prescription by a licensed physician in its distribution and application to patients, similar to other medical electronic devices.

INDICATIONS

While the technology has advanced as described, it is helpful to contrast modern T.E.N.S. therapy with its historic counterparts. The claims for early "electric shocks" included the widest list of *indications* imaginable. Pain control was only one of the benefits. Other claims for such treatment included weight/fat loss, curling of the hair, enlargement of the bust, revitalization of vital organs including reproductive organs, improvement of hearing, and "recalling to life" persons who had just died.

There is but one valued, singular claim or indication offered for T.E.N.S.: *to symptomatically relieve pain*. This indication is qualified by the prudent guidelines that pain relief should not be attempted until appropriate diagnostic and evaluation procedures are exercised to assess the etiology of the pain and thereby the appropriateness of pain management procedures. In this manner, acute pain can serve its important biologic function as a warning system alerting the patient to seek proper attention and evaluation.

These guidelines also cover the use of T.E.N.S. analgesia and all other forms of analgesia. If acute pain does serve the biologic function as a warning system, certain measures must be employed to ensure patient safety when pain is effectively managed during the acute phase. Careful instructions must be given to establish the level and type of activity that would safely be tolerated by a patient.

The early efforts were supported primarily by patient testimonial, and there was a significant absence of scientific and clinical documentation of safety and efficacy. In stark contrast, modern T.E.N.S. has undergone extensive evaluation in research and development settings and in many of the most traditional and respected clinical facilities. Publication of the results has occurred extensively, reporting and supporting the safety and efficacy of T.E.N.S. therapy. Although the exact mechanism by which analgesia within the nervous system occurs secondary to external stimulation with T.E.N.S. is not fully understood, it is well established that such analgesia does occur safely and effectively for many patients. Proper perspective may be maintained by remembering that the exact mechanism(s) by which aspirin produces analgesia for many patients is also not fully understood.

STIMULATION: THE EXCITABILITY OF THE NERVOUS SYSTEM

In physical therapy, the most extensive application of the principles of "electric shock" has been low-voltage stimulation of peripheral nerves and associated efferent motor units. The application of low-voltage neuromuscular stimulation to restore or improve the function of the neuromuscular unit is extensive and is supplemented by direct-current stimulation of denervated muscle structures. Many of the physiologic principles observed in low-voltage currents for neuromuscular stimulation are the same as the physiologic principles of T.E.N.S. Neuromuscular stimulation, by name, describes the basic unit of function as the nervous system. It emphasizes the principle that "stimulation" must produce altered activity within the nervous system first and then a motor unit will respond consistent with the patency level of the neuromuscular junction.

The phrase *transcutaneous electrical nerve stimulation* specifically describes the process of passing electricity across the skin to effect nervous system responses. In this observation, the similarity between neuromuscular stimulation and T.E.N.S. is shown to illustrate that both have, as their basis, the excitability of nerve tissue. The types of current used are similar, but there are important differences. In neuromuscular stimulation, the "target" nerve population is the *efferent, motor* nerve structures. In T.E.N.S., since pain is a *sensory* phenomenon within the *afferent* structures of the nervous system, the *sensory* nerve structures are the "target." Except for low-rate, acupuncture-like T.E.N.S., this form of therapy for managing pain occurs at low amplitudes within sensory threshold ranges only. Intentionally, sustained muscular contractions that obviate recruitment of the efferent, motor units are avoided.

Direct current (DC), often referred to as galvanic current, is useful in supplementing alternating-current (AC) sources for direct muscle stimulation in the presence of denervated muscles. DC is also useful for ion transfer techniques by iontophoresis. Few principles of low-voltage direct-current stimulation are helpful or appropriate for nerve stimulation.

All references to the generators for T.E.N.S. and the electrical impulses produced by the generators will suggest biphasic, balanced current types and the modified waveforms that may be observed. Exceptions will be specifically noted.

COST-QUALITY REVIEW

Because of the variety of systems available and the medicolegal liability a practitioner assumes when prescribing or applying a T.E.N.S. system, it strongly behooves the practitioner to carefully scrutinize the generators for overall safety and quality. The cost-quality evaluation is also important to the relative cost-value relationships. In this evaluation process, it frequently becomes apparent that, in some instances, the higher-priced, higher-quality devices will also be the best cost-value system.

Where possible, an initial comparison should be made. The quality of materials, the engineering elements, and the assembly process should be assessed. Other characteristics may become apparent only through more specific investigations. Where all objective factors are essentially equal, the intangible factor of service is important. Perhaps an adequate but lesser-quality device, as assessed in the evaluation process, may distinguish itself as better or best overall because of this essential factor—service. Some manufacturers provide instruction manuals to facilitate the general and component investigative processes. With such a manual, it is rather easy to evaluate units being considered. Such an evaluation process may include but not be limited to these considerations:

1. When the waveform image on the oscilloscope is viewed, is it the same as that described in the product specifications? This is *not* a given truth as one may assume.

2. As the variable output parameters are viewed, is the observable range for minimum to maximum consistent with that on the list of specifications?

3. As each output parameter is increased, what relationship exists between the dial settings and the actual internal quantitative changes? That is, if the variable range of rate (R) is 10 to 100 pps and the dial settings range from 0 to 10, one can assess only that a zero (0) dial setting will equal 10 pps and a ten (10) dial setting will equal 100 pps. It cannot be correctly assumed that a five (5) setting will equal 50 ± pps. It must first be established whether the output distribution is linear, front-end-loaded, or back-end-loaded.

a. In linear distribution, a five (5) dial setting may be 50 pps ±. With linear devices, the degree of subjective and objective, changes will be essentially equal throughout the entire excursion of the dial within the sensory range. Linear distribution appears to be preferred over front-end-loaded.

b. In front-end-loaded systems, more than 50 percent of the output is generated within the dial range of 0 to 5, and sensory changes are reported very early in the movement of the dial. Therefore, slight dial movements in the early ranges precipitate proportionately greater subjective sensory changes. The crossover from sensory fiber stimulation to include efferent motor stimulation may occur with the least fractional change of the dial setting.

c. Conversely, in the back-end-loaded systems, more than 50 percent of the output is distributed in the dial range of 5 to 10, and early movement of the dial may not produce direct, significant, sensory, subjective changes. Thus, unawareness or impatience may cause more rapid advancement of the dial into the higher ranges beyond five (5) where internal changes occur more rapidly. This may "surge" the output and initiate a startle reflex by the patient.

Many clinicians report that once the output distribution is understood, linear and back-end-loaded systems permit a "fine tuning" capability in adjustment, thus indicating a preference over front-end-loaded systems.

It is important to acquire a reference chart for each unit/model correlating the dial settings with the internal output ranges.

4. Are the channels separate and independently variable in amplitude? In some units, the amplitudes of a dual-channel unit may function inversely; that is, if both channels are operating, the amplitude of one channel may decrease if the amplitude dial of the other is increased, and vice versa. While this is easily assessed on an oscilloscope, it also may be noted in the clinical setting. If a patient is receiving T.E.N.S. therapy with both channels operating simultaneously and the clinician terminates stimulation in one channel without altering the amplitude setting of the second channel, a startle response may be observed. This startle response may occur because part of the energy used by the first channel is transferred suddenly to the second channel when the first is turned off. Poor separation of channels indicates either a defect in the unit or a poorly designed and assembled unit. Crossover dependence should be a factor of 5 percent or less.

5. Are the externally variable parameters independent of one another? If all output parameters are initiated at a predetermined value, it should be possible to adjust one parameter singularly without causing changes greater than 5 to 10 percent in the other parameters. Failure to observe these constants within the parameters may indicate relatively poor quality of design and assembly.

6. By inquiring about the performance specifications of one or more internal components, general system quality can be assessed. In this way, the performance specifications can be applied as a relative or comparative unit of measure from model to model and manufacturer to manufacturer. One component that may be evaluated is the potentiometer. By convention, a potentiometer is a device for controlling electric potential. On a T.E.N.S. device, the potentiometer is the knob or dial by which the electric potential is altered. The amplitude dial (A), the pulse width dial (W), and pulse rate dial (R) are potentiometers, each being separate from the others. The potentiometer rating, or POT rating, is the rated number of rotations a potentiometer will probably sustain before breaking. The maximum value, and thus the highest-quality rating, is approximately 15,000 rotations. Potentiometers with a rating of 15,000 rotations may perform in excess of the rating but no less than the rating. In contrast, some units have POT ratings of only 200 rotations. The differences in these ratings are only one example of the importance of assessing component-part quality. Singular component evaluations are excellent measures but are admittedly sometimes difficult to perform or obtain. Therefore, summary component evaluation may then be made by assessing the failure rate of the generator (excluding batteries). It is our opinion that a variable failure rate of less than 5 percent is very good and less than 3 percent is excellent. These qualitative differences may or may not be evidenced by a price difference of the respective devices. Final determination of cost-value comparison may vary with different circumstances. Manufacturers are required to "track" each unit produced, and therefore a quantitative record of failure rate is readily available. If a company refuses to answer such an inquiry, one must ask, "Why?"

ENERGY SOURCE

Most, but not all, T.E.N.S. units have batteries as the energy source. Those with AC 60-cycle current sources are usually referred to as "clinical" models. They are not usually taken home or to the hospital room for self-treatment by the patient. Consequently, portability is not a major advantage.

The batteries used in most T.E.N.S. "patient" models make portability a major benefit. These models accommodate either an alkaline battery source or a rechargeable nickel-cadmium system. Alkaline batteries have a single period of usefulness; thus they are disposable rather than rechargeable. The energy-use profile (capacity) of the disposable battery is a slow, linear decay from maximum to discharge. The battery life of an alkaline system tends to be longer than that of the rechargeable system. The per-use cost of the T.E.N.S. system using the alkaline battery tends to be higher. This factor contributes to the tendency to view the rechargeable system as preferred. However, there are also some factors that might make the alkaline system the preferred system, such as:

1. The constant, 24-hour per day stimulation required in early management of post-operative incisional pain.

2. The general nuisance factor of recharging.

3. A possible logistic difficulty posed by the rechargeable system, for example, in its use by a cross-country truck driver.

The pattern of battery life and usefulness of alkaline battery sources is readily reviewed by recounting that:

1. New, full "capacity" alkaline batteries are inserted into the generator.

2. A gradual, linear discharge phase follows.

3. The completely discharged batteries are disposed.

The linear decay process is not usually observed with the rechargeable nickel-cadmium (NICAD) cell system because of its unique characteristics. As in the alkaline system, the full capacity of a NICAD battery is the total amount of electrical energy that can be obtained from a fully charged battery. The "capacity" of a NICAD battery may vary over time partly because of its design and partly because of the charge-discharge cycles.

First, a NICAD battery is composed of a number of cells connected in series. To charge each of these cells fully so the battery reaches full "capacity" generally takes more than 12 hours. As the battery discharges, each cell discharges in series. Therefore, the battery delivers peak or near-peak currents until the last cell is discharged. Thus, the discharge is not linear with time as in the alkaline cells. Also, the rate of discharge may vary from cell to cell, and a "careless" charge-discharge protocol may result in cellular damage that reduces the total "capacity" of the battery. It is frequently observed that these batteries are not permitted to discharge fully prior to being recharged. If this shallow discharge-recharge cycle is repeated frequently, it tends to reduce the "capacity" of the battery to a narrower range. Once this occurs, the internal changes cannot be reversed. It is also frequently observed that after full discharge of a NICAD battery, a short, shallow recharge cycle may follow. This will result in similar loss of "capacity" if carried out repeatedly. The following recommendations may help avoid building this "memory," or "diminished capacity," into a NICAD battery:

1. The batteries should be allowed to *fully discharge* a minimum of once a week. Ensure that the batteries are *fully charged* at least once a week. The more frequently the batteries are fully cycled, the closer they will perform to the projected 1000 recharges expected before permanent failure. We prefer that the "fast-charge" battery chargers *not* be used regularly. Instead, a slow, trickle charger is recommended.

2. A fully discharged battery should *not* be stored before it is fully recharged. Failure to fully recharge before storage will increase the possibility of permanent battery failure.

3. A fully charged battery tends to retain its charge longer if stored in a cool place, such as a refrigerator.

Specific recommendations that may improve battery life during patient use will be presented later in this chapter. General points are discussed here.

First, intermittent stimulation periods will require less energy drain than constant stimulation for prolonged periods. Second, battery life will be improved, except for the spike waveform that does *not* have an externally, independently variable pulse width, if the pulse width is maintained at its *minimum effective* width. Third, if the pulse rate is sustained at the *lowest effective* rate for each mode of T.E.N.S., battery life will be similarly improved.

The energy sources may be used to provide, through the generator, stimulation through one channel in a single-channel unit or through one or both channels in a dual-channel unit. Selecting a single-channel or dual-channel unit is probably best based on need rather than on cost. If pain relief is adequate with two electrodes (one channel), then a dual-channel unit would not be necessary. However, if pain has multiple locations on the same patient either because of multiple sites of injury or because of a primary pain site with radiating or referred pain symptoms, the dual-channel unit should be selected. For clinical applications and multiple patient use, it is generally best to purchase a dual-channel unit because of the additional versatility provided in meeting the multiple needs of multiple patients.

It should be stated that many manufacturers offer systems that permit bifurcating the lead wires so multiple electrodes can be used on each channel if required. Also, it is easy to splice bifurcating wires into primary lead wires if commercial modifications are not available. As long as the T.E.N.S. generator has the power to provide stimulation through the multiple electrodes, this practice is acceptable.

LEAD WIRES

The electric potential, or electric current, generated by a T.E.N.S. unit must be transmitted to the patient before it can cause nervous system modulation secondary to its effects. At this time, the current must be transmitted from the T.E.N.S. generator by way of lead wires interposed between the T.E.N.S. generator and electrodes on the skin.

Many different lead wire systems are available, varying in thicknesses, tensile strengths, degrees of flexibility, and lengths. Some of the cable lead wires manufactured are illustrated in the appendix. It is not possible to state which system is most preferable; therefore, the various systems should be investigated to identify which lead wire, cable system best meets the needs of one's patient population.

ELECTRODES

The electrode systems have been perhaps the greatest problem area in a T.E.N.S. system. Initial T.E.N.S systems provided sponge electrodes for the conducting surface at the electrode–skin interface. The sponge electrodes tend *not* to conform to body contours and the conducting fluids used for electrode-skin interface evaporate rather quickly. These characteristics limit the usefulness of this system to the "search phase" for electrode placement, if used at all. Improvements in electrode systems centered on the carbon-silicone electrode with a gel medium to provide the electrode–skin interface. These systems provide excellent conformation of electrodes to body contour and perhaps the lowest impedance of all systems currently available.

Electrode impedance is a topic occasionally discussed to cite contrasts between systems. It is generally regarded that the lower the impedance of a system, the better it is and vice versa. While theoretically this may be true, the clinical features of an electrode system may or may not support these postulates. If a given T.E.N.S. generator has the "power" to drive the stimulating current through the electrodes to the body, it can be deduced that the electrode impedance will require more power to accomplish "adequate stimulation." The most tangible *negative* result is some reduction of battery life. It could be argued that higher-impedance electrodes tend to modify waveform more by attenuation than do lower-impedance electrodes. This has not been translated into significant clinical changes. Some electrodes with higher impedance ratings demonstrate other factors significantly benefiting the patient. For example, they may be worn for several days and may be affixed to the skin surface with little or no tape, thus facilitating application and reducing or abating the adverse skin responses noted with tape-gel systems. The carbon-silicone electrodes should be replaced every 6 months, even though no visible changes are noticed. The loss of electrical conductance of this electrode system over time will not be apparent but is always present.

Electrode systems of the 1980s provide self-conductive tape strips, karaya gum electrodes, and various synthetic polymer electrodes. They conform well and adhere without extensive taping; conducting substances tend not to evaporate; and some electrodes can be worn for extended periods, including active movement phases by a patient. Initial cost and electrode impedance may be higher than with other systems. However, these systems should be evaluated by practitioners and patients to assess the value of the alternatives they provide.

WAVEFORM: T.E.N.S. PARAMETER ADJUSTMENT

Assessing the quality and performance characteristics of the T.E.N.S. generators, cable-lead wires, and electrode systems is an important process that, to date, has not been properly exercised.

Product support literature presents descriptions of different waveform types and recommendations for "how to adjust a T.E.N.S. device." Many practitioners have supplemented these recommendations with their own recommendations. The process of evaluating the level of effectiveness of T.E.N.S. has been impaired by the fact that within this multitude of recommendations, there is *no baseline* that can be used as a standard or reference point. Therefore, there is very little standardization of protocol for T.E.N.S. parameter adjustment. The result is that it is not possible, with a high degree of reliability, to compare clinical results. The following proposals represent a conscious effort to establish baseline reference settings. These proposals are based on the didactic and clinical knowledge obtained by us since 1973.

Previously, it was cited that T.E.N.S. has as its basis the excitability of nerve tissue. It was also described that T.E.N.S. generators produce and control electric potentials or current. The essential guidelines for T.E.N.S. parameter adjustment can be established by combining these issues to note that it is the externally applied electric potential from the

T.E.N.S. generator that, when properly applied, causes evoked potentials in the underlying peripheral nerve structures.

By first focusing on the basic nature of the peripheral nervous system at rest, the essential requirements that an externally applied electric impulse must meet to alter activity in the nervous system can be outlined.

The resting potential of peripheral nerve membrane is negative inside versus outside because of the action of the sodium pump (Fig. 6-1, A). If an adequate stimulus is applied to the resting nerve structure, the capacity of the sodium pump will be exceeded and an explosive influx of sodium ions will result. This event will be followed by a change in membrane potential, with the internal potential passing from negative to zero and finally to a positive potential inside versus outside. At this instant, the nerve action potential (NAP), the message or signal unit of the nervous system, is evoked (Fig. 6-1, B). The NAP complies with the all-or-none law and is conducted within and along a nerve fiber by its own metabolic inertia independent of further increases of stimulus.

Figure 6-2 illustrates nerve fiber responses to graded intensities leading up to the events of evoked potentials with "adequate stimuli." Subthreshold stimuli A and B cause minor deviations in membrane potential. The magnitude of change is not adequate to evoke a NAP. Stimulus D exceeds the magnitude required for adequate stimulus (threshold), and although it does evoke a NAP, the amplitude of the NAP is not greater than that produced by stimulus C. This is dictated by the all-or-none law and is not arguable. Why then does

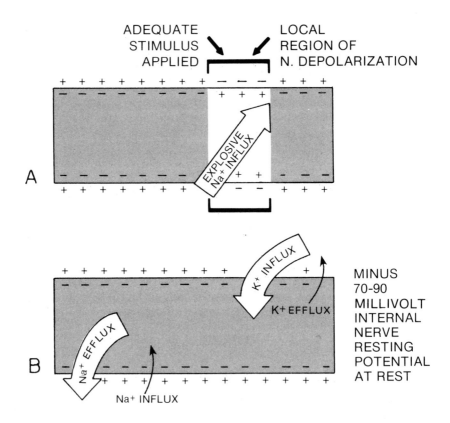

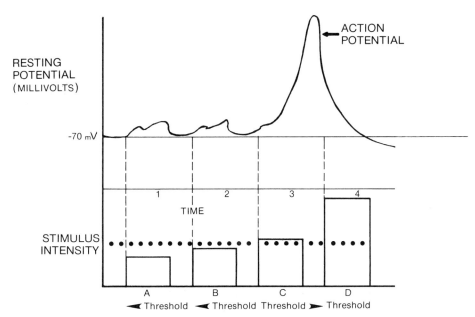

FIGURE 6-2. Stimulus intensity needed to evoke an action potential.

an increase in impulse amplitude beyond threshold levels produce the perception of increased strength of stimulus and clinical response? While this is not a new concept, it may be helpful to acknowledge, for review, that a "stronger" sensation and response are noted as a result of progressive recruitment of nerve fibers involving increasing populations of nerve structures (Fig. 6-3, A through C).

Electrodes placed on the skin must "radiate" the electric current into the underlying structures to initiate stimulus-induced ionic migration. When the "current" reaches the underlying nerve structure, it "enters" that structure on the side nearest the skin surface where the electrodes are placed. As ionic migration of adequate amplitude occurs between the positive and the negative electrode, the larger, coarsely myelinated nerve fibers on the side of entry of electric current are recruited first. Hyperpolarization of these nerve fibers beneath the positive electrode will occur, whereas depolarization (NAP) will occur beneath the negative electrode as the "current" exits the nerve fibers (Fig. 6-3, A).

Figure 6-3, B illustrates that increased amplitudes of the generated "current" will spread across the nerve structure, progressively recruiting the larger, densely myelinated nerve fibers first. This produces a stronger sensation and clinical response. At these higher settings, further increases of the amplitude begins to recruit the smaller, less densely myelinated nerve fibers nearest the side of entry (Fig. 6-3, C). Therefore, it is imperative that upper limits of stimulation be established if selective, large, afferent nerve fiber recruitment is desired for the management of pain. This underscores the reason for carefully designating and demonstrating the strength of stimulation that is best for each patient and each mode of T.E.N.S. stimulation. *Whereas a little bit is good . . . more may not be better.*

The previous discussion sited an "adequate stimulus" as the agent that may produce a NAP. What is an adequate stimulus? A definition of a stimulus as it pertains to externally applied electric stimulation of the nervous system follows.

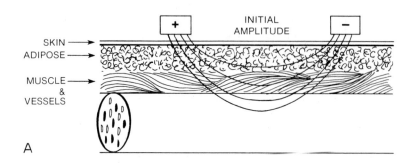

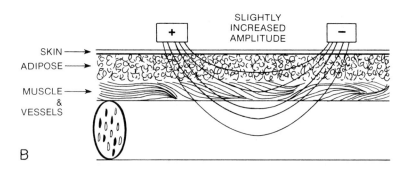

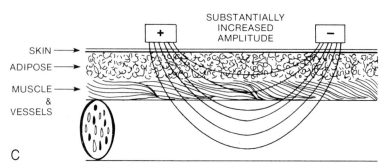

FIGURE 6-3. Stimulus strength and nerve fiber recruitment.

STIMULATION

A stimulus is any change in the environment of excitable tissue which causes it to react—a stimulus source may be mechanical, chemical, thermal, or electric.

Conditions a stimulus must fulfill to be effective:

1. A certain *intensity*.

2. A certain *duration.*
3. It must *rise to its final intensity* with a *minimum* certain *speed.*

(Rheobase) Intensity = threshold = amplitude
(Chronaxie) Duration = utilization time = width
Speed of rise = must reach full strength with adequate speed (rise time)

Noting the conditions a stimulus must fulfill to be effective will provide guidelines for adjustment of the amplitude and pulse width variables of a T.E.N.S. device. These guidelines will be meaningful it we recall the strength-duration curve, which represents clinical correlation of "a certain intensity" and "a certain duration" (Fig. 6-4). Application of these observations is useful in attempting either to selectively recruit certain nerve fiber classes or to simultaneously recruit multiple fiber classes.

The variable rate (R) adjustment is useful in two ways. First, Class I afferent nerve fibers can selectively be recruited by impulses at relatively low amplitude, high frequencies, and short durations.

The characteristics of the Class I afferent fibers are:

1. Densely myelinated.
2. Fast conducting.
3. Low threshold.
4. Short refractory period.
5. Short chronaxie values.

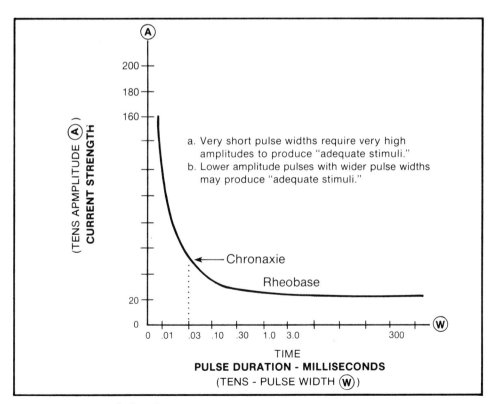

FIGURE 6-4. Strength-duration curve.

With this as a guide, we attempted to establish baseline parameter settings to selectively recruit the large, densely myelinated afferent nerve fibers to exercise some afferent control of pain. Consistent with the gate control theory and its revisions, we instituted conventional, high-rate T.E.N.S. to assess the clinical effectiveness experienced from T.E.N.S. generally set to meet the high-rate, low-amplitude definitions. We attempted to refine these settings to more objectively defined ranges. Our work led to the first recommended baseline settings for conventional T.E.N.S., as follows:

HIGH-RATE, CONVENTIONAL T.E.N.S.

1. Preset the (R) setting between 75 and 150 pps.
2. Preset the pulse width (W) at less than 200 miscroseconds.
3. Adjust the amplitude (A) settings to assure that sensory stimulation is maintained but that sustained muscle contraction is avoided.

Continued refinement of this procedure to maintain excellent clinical benefit while providing the best battery life during stimulation resulted in the following recommendations:

1. Preset the rate (R) at about 80 ± pps.
2. Preset the pulse width (W) at about 60 microseconds.
3. Adjust the amplitude (A) intensity to first produce a "change of sensation" within the area of the electrodes and/or distal to them. Then slowly increase the amplitude further until slight discomfort or muscle contraction is experienced and reported. These two steps establish the minimum and maximum limits of the sensory threshold. The proper amplitude that should be sustained is approximately in the middle of this range.

With all T.E.N.S. experiences, it is *perceived* that the strength of stimulation diminishes over the first 5 to 10 minutes of stimulation. In fact, the output of the generator remains unaltered; *only the perception* of the amplitude of stimulation is altered. The desired perception of stimulation as described above should be restored by slightly advancing the amplitude knob. This initial change in perception probably occurs because of the initial changes in skin resistance/impedance in response to the flow of the current across that skin. Generators that exhibit constant current characteristics rather than constant voltage tend to minimize this event and reduce the amount of "corrective" amplitude adjustment required over prolonged stimulation periods. Also, constant-current devices minimize the possibility of micropunctate burns that may occur with the passage of current across the skin. Thus, based on this information, we prefer constant-current devices to constant-voltage devices.

4. Slowly advance the pulse width (W) knob to assess:
   a. Is the perceived change a stronger stimulation? (Every patient will describe the stimulation as stronger, but the question causes the patient to focus on the change being created.)
   b. Is the sensation perceived as stronger *and* as going deeper, wider, or spreading?

If the perception is that of *spreading, getting wider,* or *going deeper,* then *SUSTAIN STIMULATION* at the higher pulse width (W) setting. If it is *ONLY STRONGER,* reduce (W) to preset value.

5. If after a single period of stimulation, or a series of stimulation periods, some residual discomfort persists, the energy delivered to the CNS from the PNS can be increased by slowly advancing the pulse rate (R) dial. This demonstrates a second benefit derived from an externally variable pulse rate. Recall that the amplitude of response by each nerve fiber *cannot* be increased by advancing the amplitude beyond threshold settings. However,

the total energy conducted per time unit by each nerve fiber can be modified by the rate of stimulation, demonstrating a directly proportional relationship. The recommended preset rate adjustment is 80 ± pps. This represents the lower portion of an effective range and provides good relief at lesser energy expense to the battery than a setting at the upper limit of 150 ± pps.

If T.E.N.S. generators with a spike waveform energy source are used, the external variables may be limited to pulse rate (R) and amplitude (A). The above procedure thus requires modification with this generator source. These modifications are as follows:

1. Preset rate (R) at 80 ± pps.

2. Slowly advance the amplitude (A) to initial sensory changes and then to the upper limits of the sensory range where discomfort and/or muscle contractions are reported.

3. Decrease the amplitude (A) to midsensory range and sustain stimulation for several minutes.

4. Make a "fine tuning" adjustment by slowly advancing the amplitude (A) setting to assess:

a. if the perceived stimulation is only stronger, or

b. is the sensation perceived as being stronger, and deeper, wider, or spreading (pulse width increases as a direct function of amplitude)?

If the sensation is altered in the former instance, return to a lower setting. If the latter changes are described, persist with stimulation at the higher setting.

LOW-RATE, ACUPUNCTURE-LIKE T.E.N.S.

Recent theories regarding the existence and variable concentrations of endogenous opiate substances have given advent to an alternate mode of stimulation and alternate baseline settings. This type of low-rate stimulation does *not* require selective recruitment of afferent nerve fiber classes. In fact, it is an explicit requirement that motor nerve fibers be recruited and that visible muscle twitches be produced. The chronaxie of motor nerve structures is approximately 200 to 300 μsec and higher. The neurochemical changes that are the goal of low-rate stimulation occur best with settings between 1 and 4 pps. The pps *must be* less than 10. This range is not available on some older units with minimum rates of 10 to 20 pps when the rate (R) dial setting is zero.

Recommendations for baseline settings for low rate, "acupuncture-like" T.E.N.S. are:

1. Preset the rate (R) at 1 to 4 pps.

2. Preset the width (W) at 200 to 300 μsec (external adjustment may not be available. May compensate by increasing amplitude).

3. Adjust the amplitude (A) to produce visible muscle twitches within the tolerance levels of the patient.

4. In contrast to conventional T.E.N.S., this mode should not continue for longer than 30 to 45 minutes because of possible residual muscle fatigue and soreness from prolonged muscle twitching. Also, the onset of analgesia may be latent (15 to 30 minutes).

Note: Impulses per second may also describe bursts per second (bps) as well as individual pulses per second (pps). See below.

SINGLE PULSE VERSUS PULSE BURST/CHAIN

Low-rate, acupuncture-like T.E.N.S. (2 to 4 pps) is a common, easily conceptualized application. A more recent development in providing this mode of stimulation is the pulse burst concept. This pulse burst has at least the same net effect quantitatively and qualitatively as the single pulse at the same rate. The engineering difference is that instead of generating a single impulse at 2 to 4 pps, bursts of 5 to 7 (most common) or more pulses are generated each at 2 to 4 bursts per second. Schematically, the difference may appear as shown in Figure 6-5.

In the case of the pulse bursts, what the nervous system recognizes is probably the carrier wave, *burst*, as a whole as well as its component parts. Thus, they may be functionally observed as shown in Figure 6-6.

The clinical effect of the pulse burst feature is that muscle twitches will tend to occur at lower amplitude settings, and thus this feature tends to provide a more comfortable sensation for patients using low-rate, acupuncture-like T.E.N.S. therapy.

BRIEF, INTENSE T.E.N.S.

Some procedures, such as friction massage, wound debridement, and gentle extremity joint mobilization may benefit more from brief, intense stimulation. This form of stimulation should not persist for periods longer than 15 minutes but may be repeated in series with a 2- to 3-minute off period between each series.

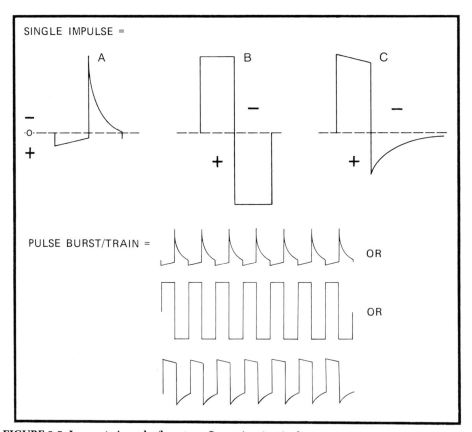

FIGURE 6-5. Low-rate impulse/burst configuration (typical).

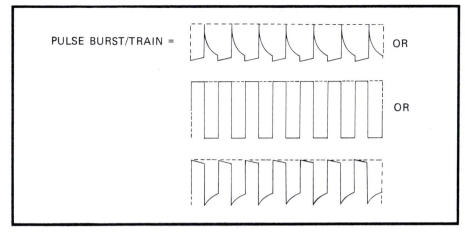

FIGURE 6-6. Low-rate carrier-wave and internal impulse components: burst/pulse train.

Recommended baseline settings are:

1. Preset rate (R) at 150 pps (or highest available).

2. Preset pulse width (W) at 150 microseconds ±.

3. Increase amplitude (A) to level at early range of muscle fasciculations or to tolerance.

4. Stimulation periods, 15 minutes or less, may be performed in series with off periods of 2 to 3 minutes.

The sensory changes that occur with variations of each individual stimulus parameter are described in Chapter 7.

WHICH WAVEFORM IS BEST?

Thus far, "impulse" has been a term used to describe electric potential without specific reference to any particular waveform. This has been followed purposefully because there has been no definitive work or publication to support that one waveform is better than all others for T.E.N.S. therapy. This being the case, the sales promotions based on more effective waveform hypotheses are poorly based. So too is the rather significant amount of attention that clinicians may have devoted to this topic as a criterion for qualifying or disqualifying the use or purchase of a particular device. We do, however, recommend that a clinician have access to two waveform options. We do this because occasionally, with unpredictable frequency or reason, a patient who receives incomplete benefits from one waveform may receive better pain relief from an alternate waveform energy source. This may be observed with a variety of primary and alternative waveform combinations, so no definitive judgment can be made regarding waveform superiority.

Figure 6-7 illustrates some of the waveforms produced by T.E.N.S. units.

The waveform illustrated in Figure 6-7, B is biphasic and balanced with a zero net DC component. The area of the positive wave portion is equal to the area within the negative portion. Therefore, there are no net polar effects to cause long-term positive-negative ion concentrations within the tissues beneath either electrode. Alkalosis and acidosis are avoided within the tissues beneath the electrodes, and thus the adverse skin reaction to polar concentrations are avoided. Also avoided are iontophoretic tendencies, which might other-

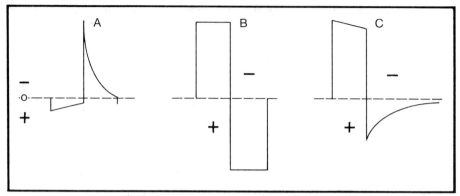

Figure 6-7. T.E.N.S. waveforms: Each is balanced-biphasic with zero net DC component. *A,* Spike. *B,* Asymmetric rectangular/square. *C,* Symmetric biphasic rectangular.

wise impel ionic gel substances and metallic substances of some electrodes into the body tissues.

The waveform in Figure 6-7, C is the most common produced by T.E.N.S. generators. Figure 6-7, A depicts the second most common waveform.

A rapid recall of the S-D curve reminds us that an "adequate stimulus" is determined by the interdependent relationship of amplitude (A) and pulse width (W). Thus, the important description of an adequate stimulus, amplitude, and adequate duration, can be sketched as shown in Figure 6-8.

Applying this sketch to the waveforms in Figure 6-7, it can easily be noted that the essential component, as sketched, is present in each (Fig. 6-9).

This observation illustrates that the essentials of an "adequate impulse" are inherently contained within each of the waveforms and probably accounts for the grossly similar clinical performances. This observation is also helpful in understanding the conclusion that one waveform does not possess constant superiority in clinical efficacy over all the others.

With a biphasic waveform, the positive portion or phase of that waveform is emitted at one electrode of a two-electrode system (one channel), and the negative portion is emitted at the other. It should also be noted that even though a zero net DC current is produced, one electrode may be more "active" than the other. The potential of an impulse varies

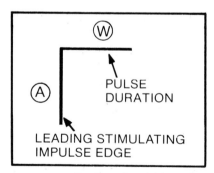

FIGURE 6-8. Impulse components: amplitude and width correlate with rheobase and chronaxie, respectively.

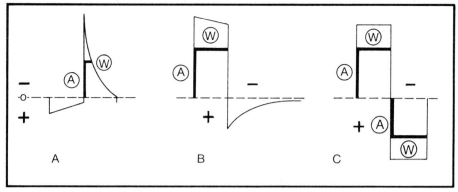

FIGURE 6-9. "Adequate stimulus" component of each waveform as indicated by amplitude (A) and duration (W) as described in S-D relationships governing nerve fiber stimulation.

directly with the degree of vertical deviation of the impulse from the zero baseline and is not altered by changes along the horizontal axis. Thus, if an asymmetric, biphasic rectangular waveform (Fig. 6-10, A) undergoes an amplitude increase, an increase in potential, the waveform will differ in its shape (Fig. 6-10, B). The potential of wave portion X is increased to $X + X^1$ secondary to increased vertical movement. The potential of wave portion Y is unchanged in amplitude along the vertical axis. However, a zero net DC component continues to be present because the wave portion Y reveals an increase (Y^1) along the horizontal axis to compensate for the increased surface area within the opposite wave portion (Fig. 6-10, B). Because of these changes, the electrode receiving the rectangular wave portion will display increased potential and will become more "active."

Similar and yet different observations can be made by following the same exercise with the spike waveform (Fig. 6-11, A).

As previously discussed, the waveform will change with externally increased amplitude (Fig. 6-11, B).

In this example, the potential of the "spike" portion X of the waveform was increased (X^1) by greater movement along the vertical axis. The potential of segment Y^1 was un-

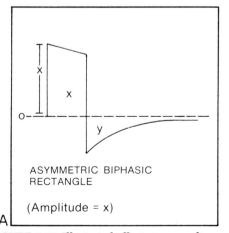

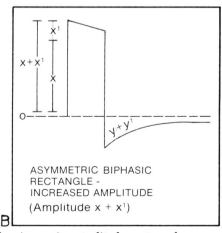

FIGURE 6-10. Illustrated effects on waveshape when increasing amplitude: rectangular wave.

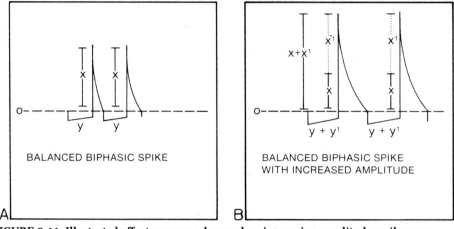

FIGURE 6-11. Illustrated effects on waveshape when increasing amplitude: spike wave.

changed from Y, but by increased horizontal excursion of Y^1, the area within each wave portion remains equal and a zero net DC condition is sustained ($X = Y$; $X^1 = Y^1 \rightarrow$ constant 0 net DC component). The electrode receiving the "spike" portion of the waveform thus becomes more "active."

These examples illustrate the alteration along the vertical axis of a typical waveform as the amplitude is increased.

Continuing with the same two waveforms as examples, changes in the pulse width or duration can be recognized.

Generators that produce the asymmetric biphasic waveform usually, but not always, have a pulse width (W) knob that permits independent external control of pulse width. If

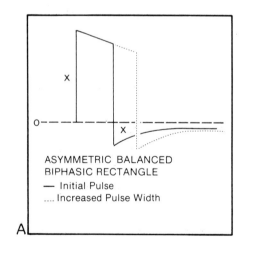

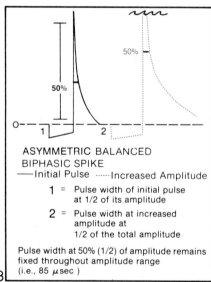

FIGURE 6-12. Illustrated changes of waveform when increasing width: independently A as a function of amplitude B.

TABLE 6-1. Summary of Recommended Baseline Settings for Modes of Stimulation

High-Rate Conventional Mode	Low-Rate, Acupuncture-like Mode	Brief, Intense Mode
A = strong, comfortable sensory stimulation	A = visible muscle twitches	A = strong sensory stimulation; muscle fasciculations may occur
W = less than 200 μsec; 40–60 μsec base	W = 200–300 μsec	W = 150 ± sec
R = 70–150 pps; 80/85 pps base	R = 1–4 pps (single impulse) or 7 pulses each at 2–4 burst/sec (pulse burst/chain) (no longer than 45 min)	R = 150 pps (no longer than 15 min each period with 2–3 min off/rest period, 15 min may be repeated. Sequence until procedure completed

the pulse width setting is increased, the energy within the pulse is increased by an increase in surface area along the *horizontal axis only* (Fig. 6-12, A).

Generators that produce the "spike" waveform may not have a pulse width (W) knob. Thus, the pulse width could not be independently, externally controlled. Such a device would, by the conventions of physics and engineering, be described as having a fixed pulse width. In a spike wave, pulse width is measured at 50 percent of its amplitude and reported as fixed. Figure 6-12, B shows that in spite of the substantial change in appearance with increased amplitude, the recorded pulse width remains unchanged. Thus, a fixed pulse width is an inherent part of a spike wave by conventional recording and reporting methods. However, recalling the previous discussion of S-D curves and the interdependent function of amplitude and pulse width/duration, the fixed pulse width concept may be modified. Because of the exponential appearance of the falling portion of the spike wave, it may be observed that within functional definitions the *effective pulse* width of a spike wave *is not fixed*—it varies as a direct function of amplitude within certain limits.

SUMMARY

The gross evaluation of devices and accessory quality is possible on visual inspection. Our professional responsibilities dictate that a more focused scrutiny be exercised to help ensure safety and a relative cost-value profile. Basic considerations of the interaction of externally applied electric potentials with the targeted nervous system permits that guidelines for parameter adjustment be set forth. The strength-duration curve and its general principles further reinforce visualization of the internal changes (within the unit) that occur as the knobs are adjusted. Adjustment of the devices must occur based on sound principles (Table 6-1). If these things occur, the clinical efficacy of T.E.N.S. will be improved and the ability to record more objective data and the basis to compare clinical results will concomitantly be enhanced. Treating patients can be enjoyed rather than dreaded with the successes of a rational protocol for treatment.

BIBLIOGRAPHY

BRAZIER, MAB: *Electical Activity of the Nervous System*, ed 4. Williams & Wilkins, Baltimore, 1977.
BUKSTEIN, EJ: *Introduction to Biomedical Electronics*. Howard W Sams & Co, Indianapolis, 1973.
THE BURDICK CORP: *Syllabus*, ed 6. The Burdick Corp, Milton, Wis, 1966.

CROMER, AH: *Physics for the Life Sciences*, ed 20. McGraw-Hill, New York, 1976.

LICHT, S: *Therapeutic Electricity and Ultraviolet Radiation*, ed 2. Elizabeth Licht, New Haven, 1961.

RUSK, HA: *Rehabilitation Medicine*, ed 4. CV Mosby, St Louis, 1977.

RYAN, CW: *Basic Electricity*. John Wiley & Sons, New York, 1976.

TUTTLE, WW AND SCHOTTELIUS, BA: *Textbook of Physiology*, ed 14. CV Mosby, St Louis, 1961.

CHAPTER 7

THE PATIENT AND T.E.N.S.

GERALD N. LAMPE, B.S., R.P.T., AND
JEFFREY S. MANNHEIMER, M.A., R.P.T.

Foremost in the process of introducing the patient to transcutaneous electrical nerve stimulation (T.E.N.S.) is to remember that the pain is not treated with the modality. Instead, the person who is experiencing pain is treated. A person in pain demonstrates at least three interdependent components: physical, emotional, and rational. Attention to each of these interdependent factors provides a great deal of insight into the patient's perception of the probability of his or her recovering to a normal state. Therefore, the emotional and rational needs of the patient must be considered in the evaluation and treatment of the physical component.

INITIAL PATIENT-CLINICIAN INTERVIEW

During the patient interview, the history of the onset and present condition is obtained. The clinician should assess the accuracy of the communication before recording it on the permanent medical record. Pain is a subjective phenomenon, and the description of its onset and presence varies with each patient. Therefore, it must be clearly established that:

1. The patient has adequately expressed what he or she intended.
2. The clinician has accurately heard and interpreted what the patient reported..

It is helpful to follow the history given by the patient with the clarifying process that begins with the statement,"Let me make sure I understand you correctly." This statement is followed by a synopsis of what the clinician "thinks" the patient has told him or her. This permits confirmation and/or clarification of the history of the injury or illness. When this is completed, it assures an accurate entry into the medical records. This also allows the person to recognize that the clinician respects and is interested in the *person* as well as the presenting symptoms.

As an extension of the verbal history, an indirect verbal probe, such as "Tell me how this makes you feel," may reveal the patient's emotional and rational responses to the painful experience. If this probe elicits one or more response indicating a sense of:

1. helplessness
2. hopelessness
3. frustration
4. fear and anxiety
5. anger

the inquiry should continue with verbal probing to assess the basis for these reactions and institute appropriate measures to reduce or remove these feelings. In our opinion, this is a significant part of the patient-clinician interaction, and efforts to deal with these feelings constitute a positive measure in reducing the probability that the "acute pain patient" will become a "chronic pain patient." If the person is already a chronic pain patient, the probing often discloses many of the dominant issues that must be dealt with if resolution of the overall condition is to occur.

Anger is one response we observe as a cue to evaluate the presence of overt or covert secondary gain mechanisms. When anger is projected, it is often helpful to guide the patient to realize that the object of the anger is usually not "hurt by his or her pain" and that the patient really suffers alone. Also, if the patient indicates that a monetary gain is the object of punishing another, pointing out the problems and limitations of this goal may be helpful. It should be understood that a clinician can do a great deal toward helping the patient deal with these feelings without possessing all of the answers. Simply through effective listening and continued verbal probing by the clinician, the patient "discovers" the solution to the underlying feelings as a result of the introspection and "talking it out."

It is also important to ask the patient at the outset what expectations exist relative to the treatment. It is our opinion that if the patient demands immediate 100 percent relief of the pain, the patient-clinician relationship (for effective pain management) is predisposed to failure. If the patient retains this expectation steadfastly, he or she will most probably be refractory to treatment and a poor candidate for T.E.N.S. therapy. A more realistic expectation is that the therapy may produce partial relief, total relief, or perhaps no relief. When some level of relief is obtained, it probably will occur progressively rather than immediately.

A concept embraced when introducing a patient to T.E.N.S. is that management of the painful clinical condition will be performed by a *partnership* between the patient and the clinician. Patients most frequently seek out the health-care providers with the overt or covert expectations that the clinician must do everything *to* them and/or *for* them to "make them well." Having the patient take a shared responsibility in the act of getting well will result in a much better recovery. (It would be helpful for every clinician to read *The Pain Game* by C. Norman Shealy, M.D., for more insight into patient-clinician interactions.) The responsibilities of the clinician in the partnership-in-care are as follows:

1. To explicitly advise the patient of the activities permitted and those prohibited in the treatment program. This includes a contracted responsibility by the patient to participate as instructed.

2. To instruct the patient as to the normal responses to injury, the changing processes of recovery, and the patient's current position within the injury-response-recovery cycle.

3. To permit the patient to perform some part of the treatment and evaluation activities.

When evaluation procedures result in the recommendation that T.E.N.S. should be employed, there may be fear and skepticism on the part of the patient that must be considered.

A primary concern is the reality that very few people do not harbor some anxiety or fear of electricity. Since the person being introduced to the T.E.N.S. system is already experiencing discomfort, it should be no surprise that the suggestion that transcutaneous *electrical* nerve stimulation is about to be applied to his or her body is met with the thought or verbalization of, "That will hurt me, not help me." To encourage patient compliance and cooperation without creating anxiety, it has been our experience that modifying the introductory description can be effective. A patient can readily understand that pain is a sensory phenomenon that is mediated by the nervous system. Therefore, the initial explanation that T.E.N.S. will be applied to cause a *neuromodulation* is an accurate description. Although the patient may not really understand the term neuromodulation, it is an adequate initial explanation and, more importantly, it does not sound like it hurts (as does the term electricity). After the stimulation has ensued and the patient senses that it is a comfortable sensation, then an appropriate electrical description can be offered without accompanying anxiety.

In keeping with the partnership concept, the patient should assume an active role in the therapy, beginning with the initial experience with T.E.N.S. Following the guidelines for adjusting the output parameters of the T.E.N.S. generator (described in Chapter 6), patient participation is extremely easy and safe. (*Note:* If conditions exist that prohibit adequate mental understanding, this participation by the patient would obviously be precluded. In these instances, adjustment should be performed by the clinician and care taken to prevent inadvertent adjustment by the incompetent patient.)

When the electrodes are in place (described in Chapters 8 and 9) and after the introduction of the T.E.N.S. generator, instruct the patient to turn the unit on and very, very slowly advance the amplitude. (Very slow advancement of the output should be encouraged because many of the T.E.N.S. generators are "front-end-loaded" in their output and a significant change can be experienced in the early movements of the amplitude knob. However, in back-end-loaded units, more rapid changes in the output occur from numbers 4 to 10.) The amplitude advancement should continue until a *slight change of sensation* in the region of the electrodes is experienced and reported. Particular note should be given to this instruction/inquiry phase. Do not instruct the patient to report when a tingle or buzz is perceived. Instead, permit the patient the latitude to describe in his or her own words the altered sensations produced by the T.E.N.S. system. Valuable information may be obtained by following this procedure.

1. Clues regarding the subjective acceptability of the sensations perceived by the patient can be obtained.

2. The competence of the electrode–skin interface can be determined if the patient describes a "prickly," "pins and needles," or "burning" sensation at this electrode–skin interface. This is undesirable. The coupling should be checked by removing the electrodes for inspection after the unit is turned off. This "prickly," "pins and needles," or "burning" sensation is similar to that experienced with improperly applied ultrasound therapy.

3. The electrode placements can be evaluated and qualified. If one of the above undesirable sensations is described even when the coupling medium is adequate and the electrodes conform to the body contour with total electrode–skin contact, this may suggest that the electrodes are not on *trigger points* over "neural junctions." This observation is similar to neuromuscular stimulation when the active electrode is placed on the skin above a muscle but not accurately on the motor point. In this instance, there will be described a

prickly, pins and needles, or burning sensation beneath the active electrode accompanying a significantly depressed motor response. Very slight movement of the electrode, so it is accurately over a motor point, will improve the objective quality of the muscle response and the subjective quality of the sensation beneath the electrode. In T.E.N.S. just as in neuromuscular stimulation, the burning, prickly, or pins and needles sensation at the electrode–skin interface will be absent when the electrodes are accurately located on *trigger points*. Accurately placed electrodes are located at skin sites with lowered impedance secondary to their integrated relationship with the peripheral nervous system (see Chapter 8).

4. In contrast to the above undesirable descriptors, other descriptors will indicate that the electrodes are on proper skin sites at neural junctions (trigger points.) The most common of these are tingling, vibration, buzzing, or tapping; not at the electrode–skin interface but within the deeper tissue.

With the electrodes properly placed and the initial quality of sensations assessed, the patient should be instructed to advance the amplitude in the same slow manner as before. As this is accomplished, ask the patient, "Where do you feel the sensation as you advance the amplitude?" The proper objective is that the buzzing or tingling is perceived *within the body part* being stimulated. The sensation may be between the electrodes or distal to them or both. For the best results, the sensation should be perceived specifically at the site or region of pain and/or along any radiating pathway. Failure to produce a "paresthesia within the area of pain" may indicate that alternate electrode sites should be considered (see Chapters 8 and 9). Changes in stimulus sensation among the different parameters (amplitude, pulse rate, and pulse width) are best illustrated by varying one parameter while keeping the other two constant at fixed levels. Tables 7-1 to 7-4 highlight such changes in the perceived sensation, using the same electrode placement arrangement.

The following clinical guidelines may help to determine whether the correct processes of electrode site selection has been employed.

With the conventional mode of T.E.N.S., it is often possible to determine the presence or absence of the sense of stimulation "deep within the body" or within the area of described pain after only several minutes of stimulation (we suggest that evaluation always begin with this mode). Also, it is often possible to recognize after 5 to 10 minutes whether or not the painful symptoms have been altered by the T.E.N.S. stimulation. Practicing clinicians frequently note that patients may indicate that the strength of stimulation has diminished after 5 or 10 minutes with the conventional T.E.N.S. mode, even with units

TABLE 7-1. Changes in the Perceived Sensation as Intensity (Amplitude) Is Increased

Assuming a fixed pulse rate of 100 Hz and pulse width of 100 μsec with a single-channel electrode array (brachioradialis to dorsal web space), the following changes in perception would occur:

60–80 mA	Uncomfortable and intolerable, producing complete muscle tetany and paresthesia, strong pressure sensation under electrode
40–60 mA	Very strong paresthesia between electrodes, may become uncomfortable, can produce muscle tetany, and a pressure sensation under electrode
20–40 mA	Stronger tingling but still comfortable under and between electrodes, occasional nonrhythmic muscle fasciculation
10–20 mA	Moderate tingling, some spreading of electrical paresthesia between electrodes
5–10 mA	Barely perceptible tingling, locally under each electrode

5–40 mA	Comfort range for conventional T.E.N.S.
40–80 mA	Range for brief, intense T.E.N.S.

Note: Electrode size and type of transmission medium, skin impedance, and interelectrode distance will produce variability in the perceived sensation.

TABLE 7-2. Changes in the Perceived Sensation as Pulse Width (Duration) Is Increased

Assuming a fixed pulse rate of 100 Hz and amplitude of 40 mA with a single-channel electrode array (brachioradialis to dorsal web space) the following changes in perception would occur:

220 μsec	Muscle tetany; strong paresthesia may become uncomfortable
160 μsec	Moderately strong muscle fasciculation, may produce tetany and profound paresthesia within stimulation area
120 μsec	Deeper penetration of current begins to excite motor fibers. Produces mild, nonrhythmic muscle fasciculation and good paresthesia (tingling) between electrodes
80 μsec	Penetration of tingling is deeper and begins to get stronger with a spread between the electrodes
40 μsec	Barely perceptible tingling locally under electrodes

Note: Individual pulse width controls offer an excellent means by which to fine-tune the penertration and distribution of the stimulation.

having constant current (amperage) characteristics. When this is indicated, direct the patient to increase the amplitude to renew the strong, comfortable sense of stimulation. Concurrently ask if the sense of stimulation is perceived within the body part or if the painful symptom has begun to diminish. If neither the sense of "deep stimulation" nor diminished pain is reported, rather than complete the following 20 to 30 minutes with the same electrode sites, alternative sites for electrode placement should be selected.

It should be remembered that there will be many points that are locally tender within the painful region. These are not all true functional *trigger points*. *All trigger points are locally tender, but all locally tender points are not trigger points* (see Chapters 5 and 8). The difference is that a *trigger point* is locally tender, but it also possesses the characteristics that deep palpation will cause discomfort to be radiated from the trigger point. Selecting the trigger points that relate to the pain location and syndrome peculiar to each patient may be guided initially by palpation. Palpation of appropriate trigger points may cause duplication of the pain initially described by the patient or may precipitate radiating patterns that extend into the area or areas implicated in the patient's painful complaint.

Placing electrodes over the correct trigger points will usually result in a general perception that the "stimulation" is within the body rather than on the skin surface and in a specific perception of stimulation within the site or region of pain. This perception of

TABLE 7-3. Changes in the Perceived Sensation as Pulse Rate (Frequency) Is Increased

Assuming a fixed amplitude of 20 mA and pulse width of 100 μsec utilizing a single-channel electrode array (brachioradialis and dorsal web space), the following changes in perception would occur:

5–10 kHz*	Produces a flickering sensation of the eyes when modulated at a lower rate (40–50 Hz) with an intensity up to only 5 mA and pulse width of 40 μsec. At higher amplitude and pulse width, strong muscle contraction and/or paresthesia will occur.
150 Hz	Significant paresthesia (tingling) throughout the stimulation area and into fingers. Can produce erythema as well as a burning sensation under the electrodes if stimulation is prolonged and muscle tetany at high intensity occurs. Good for brief, intense T.E.N.S.
50–100 Hz	Smooth, comfortable tingling paresthesia between electrodes, best for conventional T.E.N.S. Will also produce muscle tetany at high intensity.
20–50 Hz	Significant tingling begins, producing paresthesia that is relatively smooth. Muscle tetany will occur at high intensity.
10–20 Hz	Increased speed of muscle contractions, greater difficulty discriminating individual pulses. Mild tingling sensation begins under electrodes.
5–10 Hz	Increased speed of muscle contraction or pulsing dependent upon intensity.
1–5 Hz	Individual pulses can be perceived easily. A jerky sensation producing rhythmic muscle contractions if amplitude and pulse width is increased. Best for use with acupuncture-like T.E.N.S.

*This example specifically relates to electrode placement on the head (frontal or temporal fossa) for use in the management of headaches.

TABLE 7-4. Pulse-Train (Burst) (100 Hz Modulated at 2 Hz)

Tested With a Brachioradialis to Dorsal Web Space Channel (Two Electrodes)

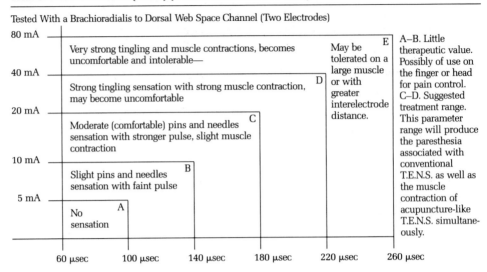

internal stimulation results in a paresthesia within that area or body part. *Assessing the presence or absence of this paresthesia is perhaps the most useful process in predicting the symptomatic response of the patient to T.E.N.S.* When T.E.N.S. does produce this modified sensory condition, the patient will almost always have at least temporary improvement of the pain symptom.

During the initial instruction phase in the use of T.E.N.S., we also instruct the patient to advance the amplitude slowly until muscle contractions are observed. This is done to demonstrate to the patient that this response is not harmful when using conventional T.E.N.S., but that sustained *neuromuscular stimulation is not desirable.* Whereas brief periods of stimulus-induced muscle tetany are not harmful, they may reduce the benefit of stimulation with T.E.N.S. if sustained for long periods. It is important that the patient understand that with T.E.N.S. a little bit may be good, but a lot more may not be better! In fact, long periods of sustained stimulus-induced tetany can cause soreness and perhaps an exacerbation of painful symptoms. Therefore, it is stressed that the patient maintain strong sensory stimulation but avoid concomitant sustained tetanic neuromuscular stimulation. (Note: This is true for the conventional mode of T.E.N.S., but not for the low-rate acupuncture-like, pulse-train or burst, and brief, intense T.E.N.S.)

Although it may appear harsh, the patient should be instructed (in the initial instruction period *only*) to turn the amplitude all the way up for a very, very brief instant to experience the worst possible thing that could happen should the amplitude adjustment accidentally be advanced to its highest level. Failure to do this has been found to leave the patient with an anxious apprehension about "what if. . . .?" Further, it demonstrates that although this is not comfortable, such an advancement would not induce real harm. *Caution:* Good judgment should be exercised, however, to assess if this step of instruction would be well tolerated. In instances where T.E.N.S. is applied to a patient experiencing pain associated with acute trauma, this step may be tempered or omitted. Similarly, the output knobs should be adequately protected to avoid accidental advancement when a T.E.N.S. device is worn for extended periods during the acute phase of pain.

ISSUES IN T.E.N.S. THERAPY

After completing the initial introduction of the T.E.N.S. therapy, the following issues specifically related to T.E.N.S. therapy must be addressed.

1. Is it appropriate to take away the patient's pain?
2. For this patient, will T.E.N.S. therapy provide symptomatic relief? If so, how much relief will be obtained, how quickly will it occur, and how long will it last?
3. Should the T.E.N.S. therapy be provided only in the clinical setting?
4. How often should T.E.N.S. therapy be repeated?
5. How long should each stimulation period be?
6. How many days, weeks, or months will this therapy be required?
7. Should the patient rent or buy a unit?
8. How much should the patient be charged?
9. What evaluation procedures other than those already used might be useful in charting the patient's progress?
10. What should be the protocol for follow-up observation and supervision?

Every clinician using T.E.N.S. therapy or contemplating its use recognizes the problem areas of output parameter adjustment of the pulse generators and electrode placement site selection. These are obvious important considerations. The questions listed above are less obvious at the beginning of one's experience with T.E.N.S. therapy, but they become major questions as experience continues and are important to the effective use of T.E.N.S. therapy.

When we began employing T.E.N.S. therapy, a data base to answer these questions did not exist and still does not exist. However, this need not be a source of frustration now as it has been in the past. We have accepted that inherent in the nature of pain and the individual responses to pain is a variability that virtually precludes rigid answers to these questions. As a result of this acceptance, perhaps the most reasonable answers have evolved. Do not accept the responsibility of offering a rigid, definitive answer at the outset when in reality one does not exist. Instead, allow the patient's clinical symptoms and responses to provide the boundaries and guidelines to answer these questions. Rationale for this position follows as each question is answered. The following information assumes that appropriate evaluation of the patient has occurred and that instruction in the use of the T.E.N.S. unit has been completed.

1. Is it appropriate to take away the patient's pain?

The obvious goal of treatment is to relieve the patient's painful symptoms and to help the patient recover from the illness or injury. The painful response to an acute injury has a valuable biologic function as a warning system. The fact that the patient has sought medical attention indicates that the pain has served that purpose. The medical team initiates interventions to remediate or abate these symptoms and instructs the patient in what activities are appropriate and inappropriate so that the healing process will be unencumbered and further injury and more pain are avoided. When T.E.N.S. is recommended as part of the therapy, it is a valid consideration to ask if "taking away the pain" is appropriate. This may be put in perspective by recognizing that frequently after a physician has initially evaluated the patient and assessed the problem, he or she may prescribe analgesic medications for that patient. It is our opinion that if the physician determines that it is appropriate to use analgesic medication, then it is most often appropriate for T.E.N.S. therapy to be utilized adjunctively with the same consideration given to the patient's welfare as presented above. It has been our experience that, in contrast to some drugs, T.E.N.S. does not cause central nervous system depression, which could impair the patient's ability systemically to recognize "too much activity." Instead, T.E.N.S. therapy can be administered at amplitudes adequate to relieve the local painful symptoms with the patient in a relatively inactive, resting state and at the same time permit local "breakthrough pain" to be experienced if the patient enters an activity phase that may exceed safe limits. In this way, T.E.N.S. demonstrates a marked advantage over drug-induced analgesia.

The answer to the posed question requires different considerations when T.E.N.S. therapy is contemplated for a patient experiencing chronic pain. Chronic pain, in our opinion, does not exhibit the characteristic of a biologic warning system as does acute pain. Instead, the initial tissue responses to the acute injury have probably been resolved, and the continued pain probably results from persistent peripheral noxious stimuli (e.g., microscopic interstitial edema, scar tissue, reduced extensibility and elasticity of the muscular tendinous unit, shortening of fascia, or impaired joint function) and/or from central neuraxis origin. When treating patients experiencing chronic pain, instead of considering pain singularly as a stimulus acting as a biologic warning, pain should be viewed as the "disease" of primary concern. With this foundation, it is very appropriate to reduce or abate the painful symptoms so that rehabilitation toward a more normal life style can occur. T.E.N.S. therapy for the management of chronic pain symptoms frequently diminishes the painful symptoms, allowing the patient to participate in physical rehabilitation processes that would otherwise be limited by discomfort, and may reduce the discomfort produced as a result of the increased activity. In this manner, T.E.N.S. has a twofold function: it reduces the primary pain response to noxious peripheral input, and it reduces perpetuation of a central pain engram.

2. For this patient, will T.E.N.S. therapy provide symptomatic relief? If so, how much relief will be obtained, how quickly will it occur, and how long will it last?

One obvious means of assessment is to simply ask the patient if relief has occurred or to observe the changes in the patient's pain behavior. An asessment can be made after the trial treatment periods, which generally last 20 to 30 minutes. However, if after a trial period of 20 to 30 minutes, little or no symptomatic relief has occurred, a decision is required to determine whether to resume treatment for another 20 to 30 minutes using alternate electrode sites or output parameters. Sometimes, it will be necessary to wait until the next scheduled treatment to evaluate T.E.N.S. treatment with these alternate variables. Both of these assessment processes require valuable time. It is our opinion that if stimulation is initiated with the conventional mode of T.E.N.S. as a matter of routine, several clinical responses are often helpful in condensing this initial assessment. Beginning stimulation in this mode may help assess initial accuracy of electrode placement. Continuation of this mode in the initial treatment period results in a gradual decrease in the strength of stimulation perceived by the patient within the first 5 to 10 minutes even though the amplitude is not altered. This may occur secondary to nerve accommodation or, more probably, as a result of altered skin impedance precipitated by the initial stimulation. (As noted earlier, this may be diminished when a T.E.N.S. generator with constant current/amperage characteristics is used.) When this diminished perception occurs, the amplitude should be slightly increased to restore strong, comfortable sensory perception. Then inquire to assess the early response(s):

a. Consider your present level of discomfort. "Is it the same as, greater than, or less than before stimulation began?"

If the patient indicates that the discomfort is diminished or absent, then make no changes at that time. If, however, the patient states that the discomfort is worse, then consider decreasing the amplitude or pulse width adjustment. Very infrequently, this response may suggest that alternate electrode sites should be selected. We hasten to report that exacerbation of discomfort is very, very rare. It is so infrequent that we initially become suspicious of secondary gain factors when it is reported. If the patient does not report relief of discomfort at this time juncture, ask a second question.

b. "After you increased the amplitude output, was the sensation of stimulation (tingling, buzzing, etc.) present in the region of discomfort?"

If the response to this question is "yes," then complete the stimulation period originally intended. In most instances, the patient will have significant symptomatic improvement at the conclusion of the stimulation period.

If the response to each of the questions is "no," then probably the remaining treatment time would be best used if electrode placement sites were altered immediately. It has been our experience that if both questions have been answered with a negative response at the 5- to 10-minute juncture, almost always it will follow that the same response will be present after 30 minutes or even 1 hour. This results in better use of the valuable time spent with the patient in the initial period of evaluation.

When a patient has responded favorably to the initial period of stimulation and reports symptomatic relief, then the clinical consideration of how much relief occurred, how quickly it occurred, and how long it will last come into focus.

By recording the interval between the start of stimulation and the onset of pain relief, "how quickly relief did occur" can be established.

Long-term evaluation of the patient over several days will be the final answer to how much relief was obtained as the comparative requirements for medication, range of motion, and strength and sensory integrity are evaluated, and the patient's overall clinical picture is reviewed. However, initially one might judge the degree of relief obtained by the patient through the use of a subjective analog (Fig. 7-1). By using a horizontal line that is unmarked except at its beginning and end, a subjective rating of the patient's discomfort can be accomplished. The patient is asked if he or she can best rate the pain in relation to inches of a ruler or in percentages. A scale in inches or percentages is given to the patient to rate his or her pain by placing a mark along the horizontal line. Zero indicates the perception of no pain, and the highest number represents the worst pain imaginable. After the mark has been placed on the horizontal line, the appropriate transparent overlay with gradations from 0 to 12 or 0 to 100 is applied to determine the subjective pain rating. This "quantified" subjective rating is then entered on the patient's record. If this is administered prior to treatment and immediately after treatment, it gives some early feedback regarding the patient's perceived response to the therapy. By repeating this evaluation process each time the patient visits the treatment center, an accumulated comparison can be made. This may be further augmented in developing a profile of response by having the patient repeat this exercise in the hospital room or at home at assigned periods throughout the day or night. Such an accumulation of the evaluation in comparing the subjective response can provide valuable information in comparing the subjective response by the patient with the objective signs obtained by other clinical measurements traditionally used to evaluate patient progress. This evaluation process requires very little time on the part of the clinician and the patient, and the insight gained can be very valuable to both.

Upon evaluating an accumulated, chronologic series of responses by the patient, it will be noted that the responses will tend to vary from day to day, but that the responses will be closely aligned and tend to cluster (see Fig. 7-1, B). In this instance, the variability simply measures a phenomenon that has long been recognized, that discomfort varies from time to time and day to day in each individual patient. However, when a patient improves, it will be noted that the *clusters* of responses will tend to move closer to zero, indicating progressive resolution of the problem. This response is illustrated in Figure 7-1, C.

It has been our experience that this subjective analog and the evaluation it provides have several significant indicators beyond what we initially expected. On repeated occa-

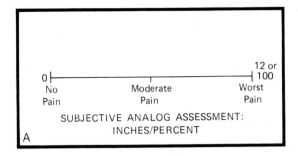

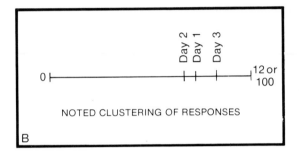

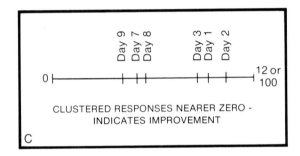

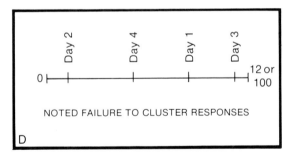

FIGURE 7-1. *A,* Subjective analog scale for patient to use for indicating magnitude of perceived discomfort. *B,* Subjective analog showing typical clustering of sequential markings made by a patient. *C,* Subjective analog ratings of two separate 3-day periods by the same patient. The clustering of day 7, 8, and 9 markings suggests "improvement" by its location closer to the zero (no pain) indicator. *D,* Sequential assessments by subjective analog do *not* cluster or indicate a trend of improvement or other responses: Does this accurately relate response to treatment, or does it suggest reflections of secondary gain motivations?

sions, after a patient had experienced a series of treatments, the question was raised by the patient as to whether or not there was improvement. By simply asking oneself, "How bad was the headache that I had two weeks ago?," we can readily recognize how difficult it is to remember and rate accurately the pain experienced in the past. When this question has been initiated by a patient, it has been helpful for both the clinician and the patient to review the accumulated responses from the subjective analogs and to simultaneously observe that the clusters of responses have in fact moved closer to zero. For the patient, particularly, this is helpful, since any pain he or she might still be experiencing could lead to the honest feeling that "since pain is still present, I am not really improving." By looking at the sequential analog markings *made by the patient,* the value of treatment can be observed. (Note: This is an adjunctive evaluation tool to complement more familiar evaluation techniques.)

Of course, there are instances where the subjective analog suggests that the patient is *not* responding favorably to the therapy. When evaluation of both the objective and subjective responses suggests this to be the case, it gives cause to determine whether, in fact, the present treatment should be continued, altered, or discontinued.

This subjective analog monitoring process has been helpful in determining when a patient may be primarily motivated by secondary gains to stay in the current treatment program. This has often been observed to be the case when a patient does not present closely clustered responses on the analog, as illustrated previously, but responses tend to move randomly from one extreme end to the other on the horizontal line. This response pattern is illustrated in Figure 7-1, D. When this random, highly variable response pattern is noted, it is our practice to alert the attending physician and other appropriate parties in order to determine rather early the presence or absence of secondary gain factors.

How long the relief persists after T.E.N.S. therapy has been discontinued can be evaluated by simply having the patient measure and record the time interval from discontinuation of T.E.N.S. therapy until the pain returns. Establishing the duration of relief becomes an integral part of determining how often T.E.N.S. therapy should be repeated. The exact method of determining this, and its significance, will be presented later in this chapter.

3. Should the T.E.N.S. therapy be provided only in the clinical setting?

Based on the responses we have obtained from several hundred clinicians throughout the United States, T.E.N.S. therapy has been used primarily as a short-duration modality within the clinical setting. A pattern of success has been established with this protocol. However, it is our opinion that the usefulness of T.E.N.S. can often be profoundly extended if T.E.N.S. is not restricted to use only while the patient is in the clinical setting.

As a new patient initially presents himself or herself to the practitioner, the clinician's past experiences allow for an early judgment as to whether the clinical problem displayed by the patient appears to be rather mild and probably self-limiting within a narrow time frame or whether the symptoms indicate the problem may persist for a rather prolonged period of time. In the former instance, the use of the T.E.N.S. therapy as an adjunctive treatment restricted initially to the clinical setting would probably be appropriate. However, if the patient continues to display significant symptomatology after two or three treatments or days at the clinical setting, it is our opinion that the patient probably would benefit from a more extended use of the T.E.N.S. therapy while in the hospital room or at home. In the latter instance, T.E.N.S. therapy should be used adjunctively within the clinical setting and continued in some form of hospital or home treatment program beginning with the initial clinical visits.

The basis for this premise can be observed by comparing the use of T.E.N.S. therapy for analgesia with the use of analgesic drugs, as might be prescribed by a physician. Seldom would a physician prescribe one single analgesic dose daily to adequately control the painful symptoms throughout a 24-hour period. In similar fashion, it is our opinion that to provide T.E.N.S. therapy to a patient once or even twice a day is as self-limiting as would be the analgesic medication provided once daily. Since T.E.N.S. therapy is noninvasive and nonaddictive and the T.E.N.S. generators are small, portable, and very safe to use, it is very easy to incorporate the T.E.N.S. therapy into a program to be extended beyond the clinical setting. Furthermore, to effectively manage the pain cycle, it is highly beneficial to offer the patient a treatment modality that has the characteristics of T.E.N.S. therapy.

The suggestion that an improved clinical protocol would use T.E.N.S. as an extension of the clinical treatment involves other considerations that will be addressed in the following program design, which is based on the next four question areas.

As previously stated, T.E.N.S. therapy is noninvasive and nonaddictive. Although this is true, consideration should be given to the factor of possible "dependence" on the part of the patient for any treatment form administered. The following program design was established to prevent overdependence on the part of patients just beginning T.E.N.S. therapy and to offer an alternative to reduce and ultimately abate overdependence demonstrated by patients who may have already developed a dependence.

4. How often should the T.E.N.S. therapy be repeated?

5. How long should each stimulation period be?

T.E.N.S. therapy should be provided as often as is required to maintain the patient in a reduced-pain state or pain-free state, and it should be provided for long enough periods so that the analgesia after stimulation will persist for a significant period of time. More simply stated, it should be provided on a prn basis. This program design is intended for the use of T.E.N.S. therapy as an extension of the clinical setting. (*Note:* An often-repeated reason for not using T.E.N.S. has been that the clinician does not have time to provide this service.) It will be noted that *instead of adding a time burden to the clinician, T.E.N.S. relieves the burden while having the added characteristic of overall improvement in the patient's response pattern.* Having established initially that the patient would benefit from T.E.N.S. therapy, the program will be enhanced if the patient is instructed by the clinician (after proper procedural instructions have been provided) to self-apply the T.E.N.S. electrodes and the T.E.N.S. generator. First, this frees the clinician from this time obligation. Second, this ensures that the patient is capable of understanding and applying the T.E.N.S. system accurately and successfully and provides the clinician an opportunity to correct any deficiencies while the patient is in the clinical setting. The patient is instructed that the electrodes may remain in place on the body within the time constraints dictated by the electrode system chosen. It is recommended that an electrode system be chosen that may remain on the patient for a minimum of 24 hours. During this initial experience, the patient should be directed to be concerned only with how rapidly a reduced-pain or a pain-free state may be achieved. We have chosen to call this the *effective time of onset* (ETO). With all output parameters (except amplitude) preset as per the directions of the clinician, the patient should be directed to turn the unit on and increase the amplitude to a moderate or strong sensory input level. The patient should be further directed to time the interval from the onset of stimulation until pain relief is obtained and then record that interval on the appropriate record sheets; by so doing, the initial indication of the ETO is established. As soon as the pain relief is obtained, the patient should turn the unit off with the understanding that if and when the pain returns, the process of measuring the ETO should be repeated. In most instances, the patient will experience an ETO of 30 minutes or less. The fact that the patient is instructed to discontinue stimulation in this initial phase as soon as pain relief is obtained and then to repeat the process if pain is re-experienced pointedly allows the *patient to experience and exercise control over the pain* many times throughout a 24-

hour period. This has a very sound psychologic benefit since patients in pain frequently feel that they are completely controlled by the pain and that their activities of daily living are dictated by the pain.

There will be instances where the patient will return for the next clinical visit and state that the T.E.N.S. unit has not been turned off because pain relief has not been achieved. This should alert the clinician that the electrode sites should be re-evaluated or perhaps the settings of output parameters need to be readjusted. Occasionally, failure to obtain analgesia even with the alternate electrode placement sites or with modified output parameters may indicate that a different T.E.N.S. generator be provided to evaluate the patient's response to another waveform. If exploring all of these alternatives continues to provide no significant benefit for the patient within five to seven clinical visits, the patient is usually considered a poor candidate for T.E.N.S. therapy.

Although complete pain relief may not be obtained in the initial phase, it may be established that the patient has partial relief of the painful symptoms. At that point, it is the obligation of the clinician to help the patient establish whether the level of relief, although not complete, is adequate to suggest continued evaluation and/or treatment with T.E.N.S. therapy. In some instances, the degree of relief, even partial, may be better than the amount of relief the patient has been able to accomplish with previous forms of treatment.

In the most common patient example wherein the ETO is achieved in a reasonable period of time, it is usually noted that the analgesia does not persist for longer than 30 minutes to 1 hour after stimulation. This phase we call *positive carry over* (PCO). Focus on the PCO will usually begin at the second or third visit, depending on when the ETO has been established. When the phase of determining the PCO is initiated, the sequence of directions to the patient should be:

1. Turn the unit on and continue to measure the effective time of onset (ETO).

2. When relief has occurred, then stimulation may be continued for *up to 1 hour.* This recommendation is made to the patient because by extending the treatment period up to 1 hour in the pain-reduced or pain-free state, the patient will experience an improved PCO after stimulation has been terminated. Also, it provides a definite temporal limit when the stimulation must be terminated. This, we feel, is a strong intervention designed to reduce dependency on the T.E.N.S. therapy. Further, this protocol improves factors such as skin condition in response to stimulation and enhances the battery life of the T.E.N.S. generator. The instruction should be explicit that the patient may stimulate *up to 1 hour* in the pain-free state. This is so designed that if the patient has the desire for a period of stimulation less than 1 hour as dictated by activities of daily living, he or she will have "permission" to use the device for a lesser period of time, while still having an upper limit imposed wherein the stimulation must be discontinued.

3. In the same way that the patient measured the time interval to establish the ETO, the interval from the time the unit is turned *off* until pain returns should be measured. This establishes the time interval called the positive carry over (PCO). Now, the patient has experienced that:

   a. he or she can control the pain.
   b. the pain can be diminished or abated in probably 30 minutes or less.
   c. the pain will probably be improved for a period of one hour or greater after stimulation has been discontinued.

4. Having established both the ETO and the PCO, the patient is instructed to continue use of the T.E.N.S. device in this manner. It provides the patient with rapid onset of pain relief, a regulated period of stimulation, and a reasonable time of positive carry over. When

pain is re-experienced, the process from ETO to PCO is repeated. It is our feeling that this allows the patient to use the device on a prn basis and to *let experience and clinical need dictate how often the stimulation should be repeated* in order to effectively manage the pain cycle. As stated previously, the regulated period regarding *how long* (1 hour maximum) each stimulation period can persist tends to prevent dependency on the part of the patient. Further, it allows the patient to grow into a life style of less pain and greater activity, more toward a normal existence and life style.

We have observed that with this protocol, the PCO is often spontaneously extended to approach nearly 2 hours in even the worst patient circumstances. We have not established a rigid protocol for treatment, for example, a set number of treatments for a set number of hours each day. Instead, the patient is permitted to use the T.E.N.S. as required for symptomatic relief and to meet the needs of his or her altering painful experiences. Conversely, the patient is encouraged to use the T.E.N.S. no more than is required, thus reducing dependence.

5. With the ETO in the range of 30 minutes and the PCO having extended to the 2-hour level, another phase of instruction begins that we call the *divorce process.* At this time, the patient is instructed to remove the unit and the electrodes from his or her person and to extend out from what has been his or her normal, confined environment and do something more "normal." This may be as simple as going shopping or taking a child to a swimming meet. Whatever the choice, the two essentials at this point are:

a. The unit and electrodes are removed.
b. The patient is doing something to alter his or her previous environment.

With some patients, anxiety resulting from the prospect of separation from the T.E.N.S. unit will be noted. This is understandable, but it may be overcome by reminding the patient that he or she may return home to reapply the T.E.N.S. system and effectively manage the pain in a reasonably short time. Usually, this explanation permits the divorce process to proceed as described. However, there have been instances where a modification has been required in this procedure because the heightened anxiety of the patient could jeopardize the progressive response to treatment. In this case, we suggest that the system be removed from the patient, but it be taken along in the carrying case to be applied immediately if necessary.

In most patients, the divorce process is carried out rather successfully. However, there have been patients who approached the 2 hours of PCO but do not experience benefits beyond that level. For these patients, the divorce process was modified further. Since removing and reapplying the T.E.N.S. system every 2 hours is an excessive demand, these patients are permitted to leave the electrodes and T.E.N.S. unit in place within the limits dictated by the electrode type. However, stimulation on a continuous basis is not permitted. Instead, the patient is instructed to follow the procedure as described up to but excluding the divorce process. This includes measuring and recording each ETO and PCO interval so a sequential record of response will be maintained.

There is no deviation from this intermittent pattern (except in T.E.N.S. therapy for postoperative pain) because it is believed to have many advantages for all of the patients. Perhaps most importantly, *a period where no stimulation is experienced is demanded so that the patient can be monitored with regard to progress or the absence of same.* Constant stimulation may mask the pain sufficiently and without interruption so that the patient's underlying condition and responses could not adequately be evaluated by the medical team. As previously stated, this intermittent pattern of stimulation reduces the possibility of adverse reactions of the skin and improves the battery life of the T.E.N.S. generator.

6. How many days, weeks, months, or years will this therapy be required?

When T.E.N.S. therapy has been used for the control of postoperative pain, the literature has recommended that it be continued for 3 to 7 days. Our initial experiences demonstrated that it was very difficult to decide, even with these guidelines, precisely which day therapy should be discontinued. Such a decision was frequently based on random, educated guesses. Currently, our patients maintain constant stimulation for the first 24 to 48 hours after surgery. Thereafter, the patient changes to a prn basis as described. Thereby, the clinical condition, not a random guess, indicates when therapy should be discontinued. By utilizing the unit prn, it is inevitable that at one of the daily visits by the clinician, the patient will simply report that the use of the T.E.N.S. is no longer required because the pain has not returned since the generator was last turned off.

A similar response is noted in patients who receive T.E.N.S. therapy for management of pain associated with the acute response to trauma. There too, by using the prn protocol, the patient will simply report when T.E.N.S. therapy can be discontinued based on the clinical response.

For the patient with chronic pain who is successfully using T.E.N.S., the duration of treatment is obviously extended weeks or months instead of days. Although many such patients will "outgrow the daily need for T.E.N.S. therapy," many will not. We feel that some provision for intermittent, prn stimulation is essential for allowing the patient to adopt a protocol that permits a balance between adequate periods of stimulation and overdependence.

These variable patient experiences have generated another question that clinicians are often pressed to answer.

7. Should the patient rent or buy a unit?

It has been our categoric policy that no patient should purchase a T.E.N.S. unit before the completion of a successful trial period of 30 to 60 days. Within this policy, patients who are successfully using T.E.N.S. for the management of pain in the acute phase will obviously be limited to renting the system.

To facilitate the use of T.E.N.S. devices on a rental and/or purchase basis as an extension of the clinical facility, a well-developed relationship with one or more dealers should be established and maintained. By developing a relationship, both the dealer(s) and clinician recognize and respect the needs of the other. Such a program usually can be carried out with a clinical facility owning or otherwise possessing approximately five units that are used to initially assess the patient's responses to T.E.N.S. therapy, while having the inventory of the dealer available for rental or purchase as required to meet the needs of a large number of patients. Many dealers and manufacturers have a combination of rental agreements that allow clinicians to work within the constraints of a fixed budget and still retain an adequate number of T.E.N.S. systems to meet the multiple needs of the patient populations.

THIRD-PARTY REIMBURSEMENT

An important consideration for each patient and clinician is the extent of third-party reimbursement for T.E.N.S. systems. Nearly all third-party providers, in our experience, have reimbursed the patient up to 80 percent of the cost of the rental during the "trial" or initial treatment regimen. (In the United States in 1981, the average rental charge was $90.00 a month or $3.00 a day.) It has been our experience where T.E.N.S. therapy has been beneficial after a minimum of 30 days, but the intractable painful condition will probably persist for an indefinite period, the third-party payors will reimburse the patient approximately 80 percent of the purchase price. A prescription for a purchase of a T.E.N.S. device must contain the following indicators of need:

1. The pain is otherwise intractable.
2. The condition will probably exist for an indefinite period of time.
3. A successful evaluation period of at least 30 days has preceded the request for purchase.

Since T.E.N.S. is available only upon the prescription of a physician, a request for purchase must have the prescribing physician's signature attesting to the conditions as described on the prescription.

The medical policy for reimbursement set forth by Medicare, through 1981, is provided below.

Assessing Patient's Suitability for Electrical Nerve Stimulation Therapy

Electrical nerve stimulation is an accepted modality for assessing a patient's suitability for ongoing treatment with a transcutaneous or an implanted nerve stimulator. Accordingly, program reimbursement may be made for the following techniques when used to determine the potential therapeutic usefulness of an electrical nerve stimulator:

A. *Transcutaneous Electrical Nerve Stimulation (T.E.N.S.).* This technique involves attachment of a transcutaneous nerve stimulator to the surface of the skin over the peripheral nerve to be stimulated. It is *used by the patient* on a trial basis and its effectiveness in modulating pain is monitored by the physician or physical therapist. Generally, the physician or physical therapist should be able to determine whether the patient is likely to derive a significant therapeutic benefit from continued use of a transcutaneous stimulator within a trial period of 1 month. In a few cases, this determination may take longer to make. The medical necessity for such services which are furnished beyond the first month must be documented. If T.E.N.S. significantly alleviates pain, it may be considered as primary treatment. If it produces no relief or greater discomfort than the original pain, electrical nerve stimulation therapy is ruled out. However, where T.E.N.S. produces incomplete relief, further evaluation with percutaneous electrical nerve stimulation (described below) may be considered to determine whether an implanted peripheral nerve stimulator would provide significant relief from pain.

   Usually, the physician or physical therapist providing the services will furnish the equipment necessary for assessment. Where the physician or physical therapist advises the patient to rent the T.E.N.S. from a supplier during the trial period rather than supplying it himself, program payment may be made for rental of the T.E.N.S. as well as for the services of the physician or physical therapist who is evaluating its use. However, the combined program payment which is made for the physician's or physical therapist's services and the rental of the stimulator from a supplier should not exceed the amount which would be payable for the total service, including the stimulator, furnished by the physician or physical therapist alone.

B. *Percutaneous Electrical Nerve Stimulation (P.E.N.S.).* This diagnostic procedure, which involves stimulation of peripheral nerves by a needle electrode inserted through the skin, is performed only in a physician's office, clinic, or hospital outpatient department. Therefore, it is covered only when performed by a physician or incident of physician's service. If pain is effectively controlled by percutaneous stimulation, implantation of electrodes is warranted. As in the case of T.E.N.S. (described above), the physician should generally be able to determine whether the patient is likely to derive a significant therapeutic benefit from continuing use of an implanted nerve stimulator within a trial period of 1 month. In a few cases, this determination may take longer to make. The medical necessity for such diagnostic services which are furnished beyond the first month must be documented.

Note: Electrical nerve stimulators do not prevent pain, but only alleviate pain as it occurs. A patient can be taught how to employ the stimulator and once this is done, can use it safely and effectively without direct physician supervision. Consequently, it is inappropriate for a patient to visit his physician, physical therapist, or an outpatient clinic on a continuing basis for treatment of pain with electrical nerve stimulation. Once it is determined that electrical nerve stimulation should be continued as therapy and the patient has been trained to use the stimulator, it is expected that a stimulator will be implanted or the patient will employ the T.E.N.S. on a continual basis in his home. Electrical nerve stimulation treatments furnished by a physician in his office, by a physical therapist, or outpatient clinic are excluded from coverage by section 1862 (a) (1) of the law.

Within the considerations of renting and/or purchasing a unit is another question that clinicians must answer in order to facilitate the daily utilization of the T.E.N.S. therapy.

8. How much should the patient be charged?

When the *patient is being evaluated* to establish if T.E.N.S. therapy would be appropriate, most departments have a "patient evaluation" unit charge already designated within the cost center. When the patient evaluation is performed to assess the benefits from T.E.N.S. therapy, it is recommended that associated fees be assigned the same unit value as that assigned to more traditional forms of neuromuscular evaluation. It is further recommended that the reimbursement request be for "patient evaluation."

Fees for ongoing T.E.N.S. therapy, when performed by the clinician, should be integrated into the reimbursement request just as T.E.N.S. is integrated into therapeutic treatment as a whole. Such fees should probably reflect the existing formula used to set fees for therapeutic neuromuscular stimulation sessions.

9. What evaluation procedures other than those already used might be useful in charting the patient's progress?

In addition to the subjective analog previously discussed, a very simple chart for recording activities of daily living (Fig. 7-2) is useful. We suggest using a simple three-column form, labeled reclining, sitting, and standing, with 31 lines to accommodate a 31-day month. At the end of each day, the patient records on the appropriate line what percentage of the day was spent reclining, sitting, and standing. Only daytime hours are logged. For patients with a great deal of discomfort, comparison of the amount of time reclining compared with standing will usually reveal that more time is spent in bed. It is generally noted that as the patient improves symptomatically, this proportion tends to even out. As the patient approaches normal, the percentage of time standing is more than that reclining. In our experience, the sitting column does not seem to be a valuable comparative indicator. It appears that the amount of time that the patient records as sitting time is directly proportional to the amount of time watching television. It depends further on whether the television is in the bedroom and watched while reclining or is in a sitting room. However, as a general indicator, the sitting time seems to vary by inverse proportion to wellness and to standing as the patient improves.

Patients are also requested to maintain a daily log of medications, including dosage and frequency.

Obviously, it would be expected that as the patient improves, the amount of medication taken would diminish, the subjective analog profile would improve, the activities of daily living profile would improve, and all other methods of clinical evaluation for objective assessment would improve. Conversely, if there is no improvement in pain status, the profiles would remain essentially unchanged or perhaps even worsen. There are instances

RECORD FORM
ACTIVITIES OF DAILY LIVING

	RECLINING	SITTING	STANDING
1			
2	% of each day's		
3	Activities of Daily	% of ADL	% of ADL
4	Living (ADL)		
5			
6			
7			
8			
9			
10			
11			
12			
13			
14	This column usually reflects relatively high percentages during the most severe pain periods, and decreases with an improved pain status.	This column appears to indicate the relative interest an individual has in television. Also, it often reflects whether the T.V. is in the bedroom for reclined viewing or a family room for seated viewing.	Discomfort may initally restrict standing activities, but the percentage of ADLs for standing posture often increases with an improved pain status.
15			
16			
17			
18			
19			
20			
21			
22			
23			
24			
25			
26			
27			
28			
29			
30			
31			

INSTRUCTIONS: Each day before retiring for your night of sleep, reflect on your activities during that day and record in the spaces provided for each day the percentage or amount of the day for the activities listed. The three columns should each have a percentage listed in the appropriate spaces. The percentages for all three columns added together should equal 100%.

FIGURE 7-2. Wellness assessment form: reflected by Activities of Daily Living Indicators.

where a patient will indicate improvement on the subjective profile and perhaps even on the activities of daily living profile, but remain unchanged in the record of medications taken and other objective indicators. One reason for this might be that the patient maintains the treatment program to retain access to the medication. However, a general pattern of improvement should be indicated simultaneously by *all* of the methods of evaluation. If inconsistencies begin to present themselves relative to the various scales and methods of evaluation, in general, it should alert the clinicians involved in the patient's care to assess why the mixed, contradictory response patterns exist.

10. What should be the protocol for follow-up observation and supervision?

When the patient uses the T.E.N.S. therapy for a prolonged period of time and in an environment that does not provide for frequent clinical visits for rechecks, we recommend the patient return for evaluation after *1, 3, and 6 months* to ensure the continued effective use of the therapy and the continued safety of the patient. The reason for this recommendation can be illustrated by the following example.

> A patient who was successfully using T.E.N.S. for "self-treatment under supervision" for lumbar spine region pain with radiating symptoms into one of his lower extremities was to return for a follow-up visit. At the time of his scheduled appointment, the patient called the clinician and asked if he knew of another patient who would like to buy the T.E.N.S. stimulator that he had used successfully and felt was no longer required because the pain symptoms had abated. The clinician directed the patient to present himself to the office to discuss the matter. Upon the patient's arrival at the office, it was noted that he displayed a gait abnormality—foot drop. The initial condition of nerve root irritation had progressed to nerve root compression with motor paralysis of the dorsiflexor muscles. Although the patient thought he had gotten progressively better because his painful symptoms had abated, he had, in fact, become worse.

If the clinician had not had the policy of continued follow-up for observation, re-evaluation, and supervision, this condition may have gone unnoted or at least its identification would have been delayed. A good follow-up policy also lets the patient know that the clinician is concerned for his continued well-being far beyond the last treatment provided in the clinical setting. This should also serve as an example that T.E.N.S. is only a symptomatic modality and should be adjunctive to an ongoing, comprehensive treatment program geared to correcting the cause of pain as well as controlling the symptom.

HOME INSTRUCTIONS

It is our practice to provide each patient with a set of home instructions (Appendix 1). These instructions are used adjunctively with the product literature and the patient instruction manual that are provided by the manufacturer of the T.E.N.S. unit acquired by the patient. They are also used as a mechanism for patient follow-up.

The illustrations of the body (frontal, posterior, and lateral views) in the home instructions are primarily guides for electrode placement. However, we frequently use these figures for evaluation of the patient's perception of pain. The patient is first instructed to relax. He or she is then instructed to imagine within the body the painful condition that he or she is experiencing, paying particular attention to the location and the characteristics of the image formed relative to size, structure, and color and whether or not the painful condition is static or moving. When the patient has completed this imaging exercise, he or she is asked to draw the pain as imaged in the appropriate location or locations of the body, utilizing the appropriate colors. Colored pencils should be provided. Inform the patient that artistic skill is not important and that there is no right or wrong way to perform the exercise.

This gives the clinician added insight into the patient's perception of the pain, and it gives a further basis for the process of guided imagery if the clinician chooses to incorporate this form of treatment at a later date. It is not within the scope of this text to deal extensively with the process of the cognitive strategy called guided imagery, but it is our opinion that clinicians may find this to be a valuable adjunctive treatment. It has been our experience that obtaining this symbolic information, which is otherwise unobtainable, and using it for guided imagery processes to assist the patient in cognitively managing the discomfort by processes of symptom substitution, mind-controlled analgesia, and/or creation of an inner advisor have provided a valuable added dimension to management of patients with painful symptoms. Guidance for establishing such a program in the therapeutic setting may be obtained by becoming familiar with the work done by David Bresler at the Pain Control Unit, Department of Anesthesiology, Franz Hall, UCLA; and by O. Carl Simonton and Stephanie Simonton of the Cancer Counseling Center of Fort Worth, Texas. (Refer to bibliography in Chapter 1.)

FOLLOW-UP T.E.N.S. QUESTIONNAIRE

When the patient has been dismissed from formal clinical treatment in our facilities, a follow-up T.E.N.S. questionnaire is forwarded to the patient for completion so that information may be obtained for long-term follow-up. The questionnaire thus becomes an adjunctive measure in providing continued monitoring of the patient's response to T.E.N.S therapy. A sample of the questionnaire is shown in Appendix 2.

SUMMARY

The effective integrated use of T.E.N.S. begins with understanding and respecting the complexities of the persons who experience pain. For continued effectiveness, evaluations and instructions regarding the painful experience are necessary. Scheduled follow-up of the patients, even beyond the period of formal therapy, is an important program element. All of this will be facilitated if the aim of the patient-clinician partnership is directed toward getting well.

APPENDIX 1. T.E.N.S. HOME INSTRUCTION FORM

PATIENT NAME _____

DATE _____

MANUFACTURER _____

SERIAL NUMBER _____

THERAPIST'S NAME _____

#1. READ the manufacturer's instruction manual carefully and completely.

#2. READ these instructions completely.

For Your Information. . . . .

T.E.N.S. (Transcutaneous Electrical Nerve Stimulation) is a nonmedicinal, noninvasive modality for the relief of pain. Its use has been suggested by your physician and physical therapist as a means of treating your pain at home. If you have any questions, do not hesitate to call your therapist for the answer.

WARNINGS

a. Do *not* use your T.E.N.S. unit for any undiagnosed problem or in any area for which T.E.N.S. has not been prescribed.

b. Do *not* use your T.E.N.S. unit in any of the following areas unless specifically indicated by your therapist:
   —front or sides of the neck or throat
   —eyelids
   —on dry, scaly skin
   —on open wounds or burns

GENERAL GUIDELINES

1. T.E.N.S. may be used as often as necessary to relieve your pain. There is no limit to the frequency of treatment in one day; however, do not leave the unit turned on for longer than 1 hour (60 min) at a time. Turn the unit off for at least 5 minutes to reassess the pain.

2. If pain is present intermittently throughout the day or relatively constant, keep the electrodes in place all the time so that the unit can be activated whenever pain occurs.

3. You may use placement sites in one area until pain subsides and then move the electrodes to an alternate site as long as you have been so instructed by your therapist.

4. Various types of parameter modulation or use of the burst mode may be activated during the treatment period. Please consult your therapist for specific instructions regarding use and stimulator adjustment for your unit if it contains modulation features.

5. Regardless of the stimulation mode, if the desired sensation gets weaker or disappears, readjust the amplitude and/or pulse width until it is restored. However, if weak or subthreshold stimulation provides for sufficient relief, it is also acceptable.

STIMULATION MODE ADJUSTMENT

Unless your unit has an ON-OFF switch, either one of the two amplitude controls will activate the stimulator. Your therapist may provide you with specific guidelines for the adjustment and operation of your stimulator or instruct you to follow one of the following methods:

A. Acupuncture-like

STEP 1. *Pulse Rate:* Preset to the lowest adjustable level (1–4 cycle-per-second range).

STEP 2. *Pulse Width:* Preset to the highest adjustable level.

STEP 3. *Amplitude:* Turn the unit on and increase one channel at a time to the strongest tolerable level. You should see and feel strong rhythmic muscle contractions. Treatment time should be at least 30 minutes but not longer than 1 hour.

B. Brief, Intense

STEP 1. *Pulse Rate:* Preset to the highest adjustable level.

STEP 2. *Pulse Width:* Preset to the highest adjustable level.

STEP 3. *Amplitude:* Turn the unit on and increase one channel at a time to the strongest tolerable sensation. Dependent upon area of pain and electrode placement, the sensation will consist of a constant tingling (pins and needles) with either nonrhythmic (fasciculation) muscular contractions or a constant (tetanic) muscular contraction. Treatment time should be brief (5–15 minutes) unless one or more forms of modulation is added.

STEP 4. Independent readjustment of the pulse width and/or amplitude controls can be performed to obtain optimal current flow and sensation. Modulation can also be activated as directed by your therapist.

C. Conventional

STEP 1. *Pulse Rate:* Preset either to the highest adjustable level or within the 50–100 cycle-per-second range.

STEP 2. *Pulse Width:* Preset either to the lowest adjustable setting or within the 30–75 microsecond range.

STEP 3. *Amplitude:* Turn the unit on and increase one channel at a time until a comfortable tingling (pins and needles) sensation (without muscle contraction) is perceived throughout the distribution of pain. Independent readjustment of pulse width and/or amplitude controls can be performed to maintain and achieve optimal current flow and sensation. Treatment time will vary depending upon the severity of pain. An average time of 20 minutes is sufficient, but this can vary from 5–60 minutes. If it is necessary to stimulate for 1 hour, turn the unit off for at least 5 minutes to reassess if it is still needed. If discomfort returns immediately or has not subsided sufficiently, the unit can be turned on again. Modulation can also be activated as long as it does not produce strong muscle contraction.

D. Pulse-train or Burst

NOTE: Depending upon the manufacturer, activation of the burst mode may be controlled by the pulse rate dial or a separate switch. When a burst mode switch is present along with a separate pulse rate dial, variations in the number of pulses per burst can be performed.

STEP 1. *Pulse Rate:* Preset to within the 50–100 cycle-per-second range or to the burst mode indicator (B) if present on the rate dial.

STEP 2. *Pulse Width:* Preset to mid range level 75–150 microseconds.

STEP 3. *Burst Switch:* If present, turn to the on position.

STEP 4. *Amplitude:* Turn the unit on and increase one channel at a time to a comfortable level or to tolerance if strong muscle contractions are desired. A tingling (pins and needles) sensation as well as rhythmic pulses or muscle contractions should be perceived. Treatment should be at least 20 minutes in length but not longer than 1 hour at a time. Independent readjustment of pulse width and/or amplitude can be performed to maintain and achieve optimal current flow and sensation.

E. Simultaneous Bimodal Stimulation

Units that have complete channel separation (independent amplitude, rate, and width controls for each channel) allow for simultaneous stimulation with two different modes (one for each channel). Follow the guidelines for modes A through D for each channel as directed by your therapist.

SPECIAL SITUATIONS

Depending upon the severity, quality, duration or distribution of pain, your therapist may provide specific directions for use of the stimulator. Examples of such situations would be as follows:

A. Severe pain that is not sufficiently relieved by the mild conventional mode may require stronger stimulation. However, you may not tolerate strong stimulation initially when pain is severe, even when applied at an area remote from the most intense region. An acceptable treatment procedure could thus begin with 10–20 minutes of stimulation via the conventional mode followed by a gradual change in stimulation parameters to the acupuncture-like or pulse train (burst) mode.

B. Pain is not always present at the same intensity and distribution but varies during the day as well as each day of the week. Optimal pain control with T.E.N.S. may therefore require the utilization of one mode of T.E.N.S. during the day (conventional) as well as the acupuncture-like or pulse train (burst) mode on awakening and prior to bedtime. Amplitude and pulse width settings will thus need to be varied dependent upon changes in pain characteristics.

C. If stimulation on the head is necessary, this is best accomplished with a very high frequency (8–15 K cycles per second) at a low intensity and narrow pulse width. This allows for perception of a flashing-light sensation without feeling electrical stimulation, which is frequently uncomfortable on the head. Your therapist will instruct you in the specific utilization of this stimulation mode if required.

PRIMARY ELECTRODE PLACEMENT SITES
AND CHANNEL ARRANGEMENTS

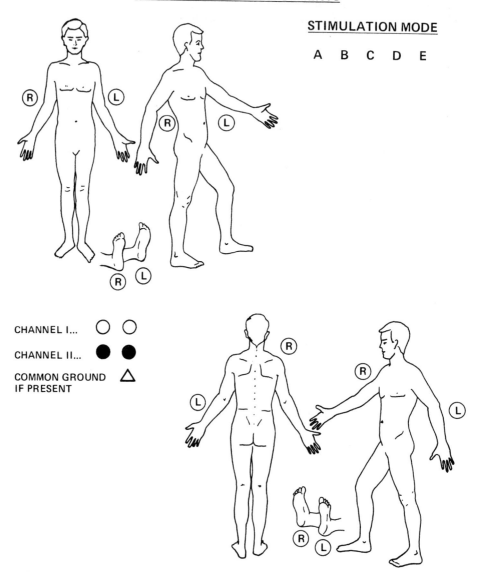

STIMULATION MODE

A   B   C   D   E

CHANNEL I... ○ ○

CHANNEL II... ● ●

COMMON GROUND △
IF PRESENT

The above diagrams represent the electrode placement sites that have been determined for your use by your physical therapist. Electrode placement sites and channel arrangements will vary according to the specific stimulation mode. Be sure to follow channel designations when you apply your electrodes. Variations from these arrays can be performed. Many times you may find that repositioning of one or more electrodes will provide better pain control. Electrode placement may be recommended by your therapist using the acupuncture-like or pulse-train (burst) mode.

CLINICAL T.E.N.S.

ALTERNATE PLACEMENT SITES
AND CHANNEL ARRANGEMENTS

STIMULATION MODE

A   B   C   D   E

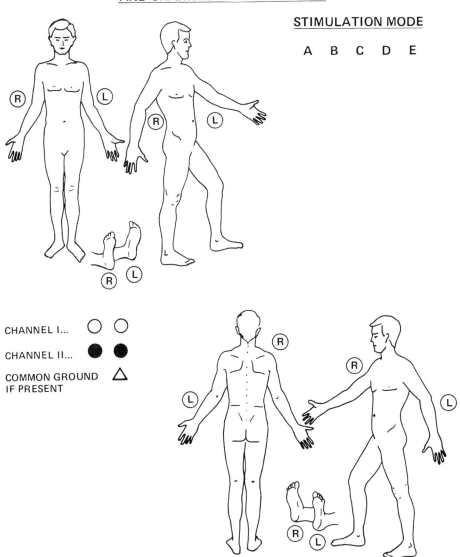

CHANNEL I...   ○ ○
CHANNEL II...   ● ●
COMMON GROUND   △
IF PRESENT

REMINDERS

1. When terminating a T.E.N.S. treatment, be sure that the unit is turned off. This means that both amplitude controls should be turned down as low as they can go and "click" into the "off" position (or "O" if "OFF" is not written on the control). The light-emitting diode (LED), which is usually red, should be off.

2. Do not remove electrodes by pulling on the lead wires; this will shorten the life of your electrodes and could possibly damage the lead wires. Remove by slowly lifting from one of the corners.

3. Karaya and synthetic polymer electrodes should be moistened with warm water on the sticky surface prior to their application. After use, they should be returned, sticky side down, to the paper (shiny side) or plastic they came on; otherwise they will dry out. They should be stored in a cool, damp place.

4. There should be no metal or rubber showing through the sticky side of your electrodes; if so, *do not* use them and call the distributor of the T.E.N.S. unit (the phone number is located on the front of the case that your unit came in) to order more electrodes.

5. If prolonged treatment is needed, turn the unit off at the end of each hour to assess the degree of persistent discomfort. If pain continues and relief can be obtained only by continual stimulation, the unit can again be activated.

6. The degree of relief as well as the duration varies with your posture (standing, sitting, lying) as well as activities of daily living at home, work or play. *DO NOT USE YOUR STIMULATOR TO CONTROL THE PAIN THAT MAY BE BROUGHT ON BY IMPROPER POSTURE OR ACTIVITIES.* This will only serve to worsen or prolong your pain. Your therapist should instruct you in proper posture, therapeutic exercises, and activities that you can or should not do pertaining to your problem.

7. The indicator (LED) light or audio feature may have additional meanings depending upon the manufacturer. It can indicate pulse rate changes, poor electrode connections, high skin resistance, or a low battery. Consult the manual supplied with your unit for specific information.

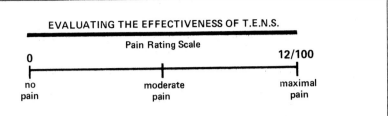

EVALUATING THE EFFECTIVENESS OF T.E.N.S.

Pain Rating Scale

0		12/100
no pain	moderate pain	maximal pain

Date, Time	Pain rating Pre T.E.N.S.	Treatment time	Pain rating Post T.E.N.S.	Time before pain returned	Comments/ Stimulation mode

APPENDIX 2. FOLLOW-UP T.E.N.S. QUESTIONNAIRE

The purpose of this questionnaire is to obtain information from patients who are presently renting or have purchased a transcutaneous electrical nerve stimulator (T.E.N.S.) from a distributor. The information obtained from your completion of this form will ultimately be of benefit to you and other patients who may be in need of similar devices for the control of acute pain while actual treatment is in progress to eliminate the cause of discomfort. In addition, patients with chronic pain who have been through unsuccessful rehabilitation programs may benefit from the use of T.E.N.S. in lieu of medication or surgery.

Your answers to the following questions will help me to determine if you are having any problems with the unit or if pain control is no longer satisfactory. Appropriate action will be taken if necessary to correct any difficulties with the unit or to enhance the degree of pain control if it has decreased. Please return the completed questionnaire as soon as possible.

*1. When did you receive your T.E.N.S. unit? _____

    Have you returned the unit to the distributor? _____

    *If you have returned the unit to the distributor, there is no need to complete the questionnaire, but please return it to us with the date on which the unit was returned.

2. Is the unit continuing to provide effective pain relief?

3. Have you been satisfied with the unit?

4. How often do you now use the unit? _____ times per day. How long is the unit left on until effective relief is obtained? _____ minutes. How long does pain relief last when the unit is turned off? _____ hours.

5. How do your answers to the above compare with those at the time when you first obtained the unit (the first few months)?

6. What degree of relief does the unit provide?
    Initially   *Present*

                      Complete   (100%)
                      Good   (75%)
                      Fair   (50%)
                      Poor   (25%)
                      Zero   (0%)

7. Are you having any problems with the electrodes? If yes, please specify below:
    Skin reaction _____
    Tape irritation _____
    Time consuming to apply _____
    Electrodes wear out too fast _____

8. Have you been able to progressively decrease your use of the unit?

9. Do you find that the pain relief which you obtain from the unit is better than that derived from any pain medication that you were or have been taking?

10. Have you noticed any overall decrease in your normal level of pain that makes you feel as though your condition is improving since obtaining the unit? If yes, please explain.

11. Have you been able to decrease or eliminate any pain medication that you may have been taking since obtaining the unit?

12. Have you noticed any overall increase in your normal level of pain or any increasing weakness in any of your arm or leg muscles? If yes, please explain.

13. Have you been able to progressively increase your everyday level of activity since obtaining the unit?

14. Have you been able to resume your normal employment since obtaining the unit?

15. Were you satisfied with the way in which the evaluation of the unit was conducted to determine its effectiveness and the optimal electrode placement sites?

16. Were you adequately instructed in how to operate the unit?

17. Do you have any questions in regard to this questionnaire or any suggestions that may be helpful?

18. If you are approaching the end of your initial month's rental, a decision needs to be made regarding continued use of the stimulator. The distributor will credit only the initial month's rental charge toward purchase of the unit. If you feel that you will need the unit for an extended period of time and it is providing satisfactory benefit, then the unit should be purchased. If this is your decision, please contact your physician in order to obtain a prescription for purchase and inform us as well.

The unit can, of course, continue to be rented from the distributor. If you feel that you may need it for only another few weeks or one more month, please contact us and your physician for such approval and return this form indicating ongoing benefit.

If your unit is presently not performing to your satisfaction, please let me know. Many times this can easily be corrected by minor adjustments in the way in which the unit is being used or by changes in electrode placement.

Thank you very much for your promptness in completing and returning this questionnaire.

Please Sign Name: _____

CHAPTER 8

ELECTRODE PLACEMENT SITES AND THEIR RELATIONSHIP

JEFFREY S. MANNHEIMER M.A, R.P.T., AND GERALD N. LAMPE, B.S., R.P.T.

As previously stated, noninvasive pain modulation with electrical stimulation can be performed easily by the patient. Other techniques such as acupuncture, nerve blocks, percutaneous electrical stimulation (P.E.S.), epidural stimulation, dorsal column stimulation (D.C.S.), and deep brain stimulation (D.B.S.) are invasive and thus require a clinician to perform the technique.

Irrespective of the method of stimulation employed to modulate pain, the resultant neural mechanisms that occur require that the stimulus be directed into the central nervous system (CNS). Transcutaneous stimulation that can result in the propagation of an impulse into the CNS is best accomplished at the spinal column, at superficial aspects of peripheral nerves (mixed, cutaneous, and cranial), and at acupuncture, motor, and trigger points.

SPINAL COLUMN

A brief review of the structural components and anatomic distribution of a spinal cord segment and the spinal nerve that originates from it is necessary to fully establish their value in electrode placement and various pain syndromes. Only the anatomic arrangements that are truly relative to electrode placement will be discussed. For more detailed information, consult the cited references and the extensive bibliography at the end of this chapter.[1-3]

The spinal cord is a segmental structure linking the spinal nerves and their peripheral processes to the brain. The segmentation of the spinal cord originates in the developing embryo. Mesodermal somites, composed of mesenchymal tissue, representing primitive segments or metameres, constitute the origin of the segmental innervation of the body. Cells from the ventromedial and dorsolateral region of the somite represent the early sclerotomal and dermomyotomal distribution, respectively. The sclerotome consists of the axial skeleton, ribs, and sacrum. The mesial region of each sclerotome surrounds the developing spinal cord (notochord) and develops into the vertebral bodies and the majority of the intervetebral disk. The vertebral body, its neural arch, and corresponding spinous and transverse processes have an intersegmental position, with the myotome overlying the intervertebral joints.[4] Further proliferation provides for separate delineation of the dermatome and myotome.[1,2] An inner layer, known as the endoderm, is the precursor of the visceral organs and constitutes the segmental autonomic innervation of the viscera or enterotome.[5]

As embryologic development progresses, each spinal cord segment establishes nerve innervation with skin, muscle, bone, body tissues, and visceral structures that are derived from it. This segmental relationship basically maintains itself throughout life, although only the thoracic region is the true example. The high degree of overlap among segmental innervations complicates the picture.[1,2]

Thirty-one pairs of spinal nerves exit from the vertebral column segmentally at the intervertebral foramen.[1-3] The intervertebral foramen is formed anteriorly by the intervertebral disks, posterior longitudinal ligament, and adjacent portions of the vertebral bodies (inferior and superior pedicles). The posterior boundary consists of the articular process of the facet joints and their capsules. The lateral edge of the ligamentum flavum overlies the joint capsule and also contributes to the posterior border of the foramen (Fig. 8-1).[6,7]

A typical spinal nerve contains motor, sensory, and sympathetic components. Nerve fibers from the dorsal (posterior) and ventral (anterior) horns of the spinal cord form the sensory (afferent) and motor (efferent) roots, respectively. Thus the spinal nerve is connected to the spinal cord by the ventral and dorsal roots.[1] Dorsal roots of adjacent segments are connected via threadlike oblique bundles of nerve fibers that are most frequently seen in the cervical and lumbosacral regions.[1]

The dorsal and ventral roots converge and exit the foramen as the mixed spinal nerve. Each spinal nerve passing through the intervertebral foramen travels with an artery, vein, and connective tissue, all including the fat content adding protective cushioning.[1,7-9]

The dorsal root contains the spinal ganglion, which is primarily within the intervertebral foramen just lateral to the region where the dura mater is perforated by the nerve root. However, the spinal ganglia of C1 and C2 lie on the vertebral arch of the atlas and axis. The ganglia of the sacral and coccygeal nerves are located outside of the foramen and within the dura mater, respectively.[1]

The dura mater is a tough, fibrous connective tissue attached to the interior of the cranial cavity surrounding the skull. At the foramen magnum, it extends into the spinal column as a tubular sheath surrounding the spinal cord. Cranial nerves pass through the foramina at the base of the skull within dural sleeves or sheaths of the meningeal layer of the cerebral dura mater. Spinal nerves pass through similar sleeves that are continuous with the epineurium of the nerves.[1,8-9] The spinal dura mater runs uninterrupted from the circumference of the foramen magnum, posterior surfaces of the bodies of C2 and C3, and fibrous connections from the posterior longitudinal ligament to the periosteum of the coccyx. Innervation of the cerebral dura mater is via the trigeminal nerve and branches from C1 to C3 along with the cervical sympathetic trunk. Branches may also come from the vagus, hypoglossal, facial, and glossopharyngeal nerves. The sinuvertebral nerve innervates the spinal dura mater only on its anterior aspect.[1]

Transcutaneous electrodes overlying the region of the intervertebral foramen will provide for stimulation of the posterior primary ramus (PPR). Innervation of the skin (dermatome), muscle (myotome), and bone plus fibrous septa (sclerotome) of the scalp, neck, and trunk is provided by the PPR through its medial and lateral branches. The anterior primary ramus (APR) innervates the dermatome, myotome, and sclerotome of the

INTERVERTEBRAL FORAMEN

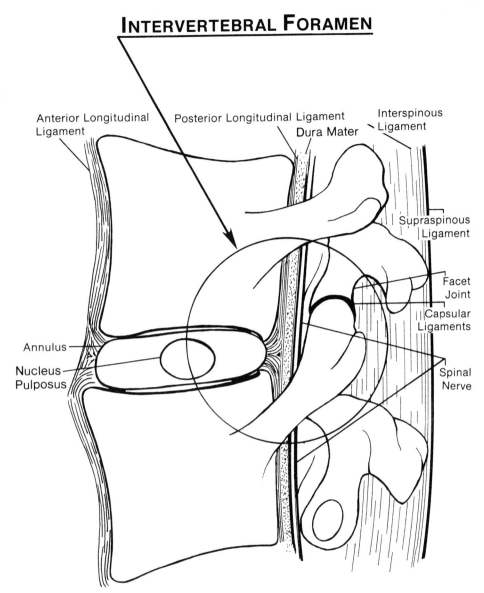

FIGURE 8-1. The intervertebral foramen (lateral view).

extremities, anterolateral trunk, and neck through its lateral and anterior branches. The cervical, brachial, lumbar, and sacral plexuses are formed by the APR.[1–3,7,8,10,11]

At this point, we are primarily concerned with the PPR, which originates from the spinal nerve just lateral to the foramen and divides into medial and lateral branches 5 mm from its origin.[14] Lateral branches innervate ligaments and muscles lateral to the facet joints and run caudally in an oblique and lateral manner across the back of the transverse processes.[1,10–13]

Medial branches of the PPR descend through a groove or notch formed by the inferior border of the transverse process and the anterior-inferior border of the superior articular facet at its corresponding level. The PPR traverses this area as part of a neurovascular bundle covered by an intertransverse ligament and fascia.[1,10-13]

Innervation of the posterior facet joints and capsule is provided by the medial branch of the PPR at its corresponding level. Innervation to the superior part of the next caudal facet and capsule is via a continuing branch that anastomoses with similar medial branches from adjacent levels (see Fig. 5-23). Local muscles (multifidus, interspinales, and erector spinae) are also innervated by the medial branch of the PPR.[1,10-13]

The medial branches of PPR may have a varied distribution depending on their origin from the cervical, thoracic, or lumbar spine. A general consensus is that a single facet joint receives innervation from two adjacent segmental levels (see Fig. 5-23).[1,7,10]

A relatively small and somewhat unknown branch arises just beyond the spinal ganglion from the anterior aspect of the spinal nerve. This branch is termed the sinuvertebral, or recurrent meningeal, nerve, which courses medially for 2 to 3 mm and receives a sympathetic component from either a gray ramus communicans or directly from a thoracic sympathetic ganglion.[1,11] At this point, the sinuvertebral nerve re-enters the intervertebral foramen and spinal cord, ventral to the dorsal root ganglion, where it divides into two to six filaments.

The main filament ascends around the base of the pedicle toward the posterior longitudinal ligament, which it innervates. At this point, it divides again into ascending, descending, and transverse components to innervate the vertebral body and lamina, outer annular fibers of the intervertebral disk primarily in the dorsolateral region, dura mater, and epidural blood vessel walls.[1] An anterior branch of the sinuvertebral nerve even innervates the anterior longitudinal ligament and outer annular fibers of the disk in the cervical region.[19,20] As with the medial branch of the PPR, there again is no true consensus concerning the levels of innervation via the sinuvertebral nerve. Variations may occur according to the section of the spine, but a general agreement is that branches of the sinuvertebral nerve on one side anastomose with those of the corresponding contralateral level as well as with levels above and below.[1,10-13,15-22] Thus, those structures innervated by the sinuvertebral nerve receive innervation from at least two or more spinal cord segments, as does the facet joint, except that the sinuvertebral nerve also anastomoses contralaterally.

A consensus concerning innervation of the outer annular fibers of the intervertebral disk has not been attained. However, it is agreed that the nucleus pulposus is devoid of sensory innervation.[1,10-13,15-22] An intervertebral disk that has degenerated may have nerve fibers running deeper into the annulus, along with granulation or scar tissue. Furthermore, Cloward infers that the sinuvertebral nerve may in fact innervate the posterior and anterior periphery of the disk.[19,20] It is interesting to note that of three articles published in an issue of a journal devoted entirely to low back pain, two stated that the outer annulus fibrosus was not innervated and one stated it was.[23-25]

The paraspinal placement of electrodes directly over or between the nonpalpable underlying transverse processes thus represents the first area where pain modulation of numerous structures innervated by a spinal nerve and its component branches can occur.

AUTONOMIC COMPONENTS

Anatomically, the sympathetic chain of ganglia extends from the base of the skull to the coccyx, primarily on the anterolateral aspect of the spinal column. The exact anatomic location of the sympathetic chain varies with the segmental level of the spinal cord. Sympathetic ganglia are situated in front of the vertebral transverse processes, anterior to the heads of the ribs, on the side of the vertebral bodies, and anterior to the sacrum in the cervical, thoracic, lumbar, and sacral spinal cord levels, respectively.[1,3] The ganglion impar is significant in that it represents the convergence of the right and left sympathetic chain into one ganglion in front of the coccyx. A similar merging is thought to occur in the cephalic region at the ganglion of Ribes.[1,26]

The sympathetic and parasympathetic components of the autonomic nervous system (ANS) are known as the thoracolumbar and craniosacral divisions according to their segmental origin. Vasomotor, pilomotor, glandular, and visceral innervation is provided by the ANS. The connection between the ANS and CNS is through the rami communicantes. Preganglionic cell bodies located between the dorsal and ventral horns in the thoracic and upper lumbar spinal cord (intermediolateral cell or secondary visceral gray column) give rise to the myelinated fibers of the sympathetic division.[1,3,27,28] Preganglionic fibers course from the anterior primary ramus to the sympathetic chain via the white rami communicantes (WRC). Postganglionic (unmyelinated) fibers course back to the anterior primary ramus (APR) from the sympathetic chain via the gray rami communicantes (GRC). This arrangement exists primarily from T1 to L2 and occasionally to L3.[1,3,27,28]

The spinal nerves all receive visceral afferent fibers from the chain ganglia via the GRC. These fibers have cell bodies in the dorsal root ganglia, not the chain ganglia. WRC merge with spinal nerves only from the intermediolateral cell column (ICC). Thus, in the cervical, low lumbar, and sacral regions, sympathetic ganglia send fibers to the APR of a spinal nerve via the GRC without receiving input from WRC.[1,3,27,28]

Input via descending pathways from the hypothalamus, the ANS regulator, synapse with preganglionic sympathetic fibers from APR in the ICC. The hypothalamus provides for facilitatory or inhibitory stimuli to all autonomic structures.[1,3,27,28]

The part of the sympathetic trunk or chain that ascends above T2 consists of three additional ganglia. These are the superior, middle, and inferior (cerviocothoracic) ganglia.[1,26,28] This region connects with the cranial nerves, significantly the trigeminal, vagus, and glossopharyngeal, and with the cardiac nerves. In addition, the cervical portion of the sympathetic chain innervates the walls of the internal and external carotid arteries, the dura mater, and the cervical spinal nerves.[1,26,28]

Afferent pain fibers, known as general visceral afferents, can be myelinated or unmyelinated. They are found in preganglionic and postganglionic fibers of both divisions of the ANS. General visceral afferents parallel some of the cranial nerves, particularly the vagus and glossopharyngeal, and a large number of sympathetic nerves conveying noxious input from the viscera and blood vessels to the ICC. Visceral pain fibers from distal portions of the rectum, bladder, and colon enter the spinal cord via the sacral parasympathetic nerves. Afferent input from the lower esophagus and diaphragm carried by the phrenic nerve (C3 to C5) should not be overlooked as a means of referred pain to the shoulder.[1,3,27,28]

There is also a segmental relationship of visceral innervation. Visceral afferents enter the spinal cord and synapse in the same segment as the preganglionic fibers of the efferent distribution. The mechanism of referred pain and associated reflexes due to visceral and somatic convergence in the spinal cord are discussed in Chapter 5. Lamina 5 in the dorsal horn has been shown to receive visceral, somatic, and cutaneous afferent input that may form the basis for this convergence.[29–36]

A knowledge of the segmental innervation of the viscera will enable the clinician to determine the distribution of referred pain and appropriate electrode placement sites (Table 8-1).[1] Innervation to the pericardium, pleura, and parietal peritoneum is provided by penetrating spinal nerves overlying the abdomen or thorax. This would account for dual innervation from both visceral and spinal nerves.[1,27,28,32] Such an occurrence results in a localized

TABLE 8-1. Segmental Innervation of Viscera[1]

Viscera	Segment
Head and neck	T1–T5
Upper limb	T2–T5
Lower limb	T10–L2
Heart	T1–T5
Bronchi and lung	T2–T4
Esophagus (caudal part)	T5–T6
Stomach	T6–T10
Small intestine	T9–T10
Large intestine as far as splenic flexure	T11–L1
Splenic flexure to sigmoid colon and rectum	L1–L2
Liver and Gallbladder	T7–T9
Spleen	T6–T10
Pancreas	T6–T10
Kidney	T10–L1
Ureter	T11–L2
Suprarenal	T8–L1
Testes and ovary	T10–T11
Epididymis, ductus deferens, and seminal vesicles	T11–T12
Urinary bladder	T11–L2
Prostate and prostatic urethra	T11–L1
Uterus	T12–L1
Uterine tube	T10–L1
Diaphragm	T7–T8

pain to the cutaneous area overlying the involved structure as well as referred pain throughout the dermatomal segments related to the embryologic development of the structure. This is well illustrated in appendicitis with initial discomfort in the right T10–T12 dermatomal region referred by visceral afferents. Inflammation of the overlying parietal peritoneum later produces pain in the right iliac fossa via somatic afferents and may also give rise to muscle guarding.[32]

The anatomic connections between the ANS and CNS may account for the reports of the effectiveness of T.E.N.S. in the modulation of visceral pain, circulation, and skin temperature.[37–46] In one study, no significant ANS changes could be observed.[42] However, experimental evidence has been presented for the modulation of the ANS by cutaneous stimulation.[33–36] We have observed ANS effects such as circulatory changes, sweating, nausea, and headaches with T.E.N.S. (see Chapter 9).

SPINAL CORD SEGMENT

A spinal cord segment giving rise to a spinal nerve root provides an excellent site for pain modulation to any structure that it innervates. It has already been stated that T.E.N.S. at the spinal column is best accomplished by electrode placement parallel (paraspinal) to the palpable spinous processes. To be more exact, consideration must be given to the nonpalpable transverse processes that actually form the superior and inferior borders of the stimulation site where the cutaneous branches of the dorsal rami become superficial.

The anatomic relationship at each level of the spinal column among the vertebral body, spinous process, intervertebral foramen, spinal cord segment, and nerve root is nonuniform and changes at each section of the spine. Spinal cord segments vary in size, and two distinct enlargements of the spinal cord exist between the C3–T2 and T9–T12 segments for the upper and lower extremity nerves, respectively.[1] Furthermore, the spinal cord and the vertebral column do not grow at the same rate, resulting in an upward displacement of spinal cord segments in relation to their corresponding vertebrae. This nonuniform relationship becomes more pronounced at lower levels of the spinal cord. Therefore, the lumbar and sacral nerve roots have a larger distance to traverse from their segmental origin to foraminal emergence (Fig. 8-2). The location of a specific spinous process, such as that of the fifth cervical vertebra, does not ensure that an electrode placed directly adjacent will provide for stimulation of the C5 root. In actuality, stimulation will be of the C6 and/or C7 root depending on the size of the electrode. Most commonly employed T.E.N.S. electrodes are large enough to stimulate at least two adjacent roots when placed paraspinally.

In the cervical region, spinal segments give rise to roots that emerge through intervertebral foramina above their corresponding vertebral bodies. There are eight cervical roots but only seven vertebral bodies and hence seven spinous processes (actually six since the atlas does not have a palpable spinous process). The first cervical root exits between the occiput and atlas and the eighth between the seventh cervical and first thoracic vertebrae. The thoracic, lumbar, and sacral roots exit the intervertebral foramina below the corresponding vertebral body. The cervical spinous processes correspond with the spinal cord segment one greater than itself. The spinous process of C5 thus provides the landmark for the sixth cervical segment, which gives rise to the C6 root exiting from the foramen at C5–C6. The spinous process of C7 is level with spinal cord segment C8 giving rise to the C8 root that exits the foramen of C7–T1.

In the upper thoracic region to about T10, each spinous process corresponds to the spinal cord segment two greater than itself because of the increased angulation of the spinous processes. Therefore, the spinous process of T9 is level with the 12th thoracic segment, giving rise to the T12 root exiting the T12–L1 intervertebral foramen. The spinal cord ends at the region of the lower border of L1 or upper border of L2.[1–3] Thus, the spinous processes from T11 to L1 lie anatomically over the first lumbar to first sacral spinal cord segments. The nerve roots originating from these segments travel distally through the spinal canal and exit below the bodies of their respective vertebrae. Therefore, an electrode placed paraspinally between the spinous processes of L5 and S1 will most likely stimulate the L5 root. The sacral foramen on the posterior aspect of the sacrum provides excellent sites for stimulation of the sacral nerves.

The angle at which the spinous processes are directed posteriorly also changes. If spinous processes are to be used as landmarks, accuracy can be enhanced by having the patient stand with the arms in the anatomic position and palpating for specific landmarks.[47,48] In this position, palpation from the occiput down reveals that the first spinous process palpated is that of C2. The spinous process of C7 is the next most prominent, but it is sometimes difficult to delineate it from that of C6 or T1. If the head is bent backward, the spinous process of C6 becomes less prominent so that the one below is that of C7. When performing this simple test, the clinician should place the index finger on what is thought to be the spinous process of C7 and the middle finger on the one above (C6). If backward bending does not produce the aforementioned change, palpation is at C7 and T1 or below. Bending the head forward while palpating down from C2 will assist in location of the individual spinous processes. The spinous process will usually correspond to that of the inferior articular process of the facet joint of the same vertebral body unless a malalignment is present.

The spinous processes of T3, T7, and T11 correspond to the level of the spine of the scapula, its inferior angle, and the last rib, respectively. The iliac crest is usually at the level of L4. Passive mobility testing by backward bending of the superior leg while the patient is side lying will allow for palpation on movement of the L5 spinous process above the fused sacrum. The posterior-superior iliac spines correspond with the level of the spinous process of S2.

DERMATOME, MYOTOME, SCLEROTOME

A knowledge of the innervation of the structures of the body by spinal cord segments and peripheral nerves is essential for the successful clinical use of T.E.N.S. Numerous studies have been conducted to delineate the segmental innervation of skin, muscle and

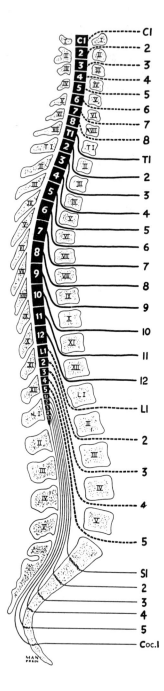

FIGURE 8-2. The anatomic relationship between spinal cord segments, vertebral body, spinous process, intervertebral foramen, and nerve root. (From Haymaker and Woodhall,[2] with permission.)

TABLE 8-2. Anatomic and Clinical Factors Behind the Development of the Dermatomes

Electrode placement should *not* be based solely on dermatomal distribution.

1. There are no anatomic landmarks delineating each dermatome
2. High degree of overlap
3. Boundaries dependent on degree of afferent input entering a spinal cord segment at any given time
4. The dermatome does not always correspond with the myotome and sclerotome (head, pectoral, scapula, and intrathoracic regions, buttock, scrotum, and posterolateral thigh are regions where this is true).
5. EMG studies demonstrate nonuniform innervation of skin and underlying musculature
   Thoracic—anterior myotome differs by 2 segments from dermatome
   Cervical and lumbar—difference may equal 6 segments
6. Dermatome charts are all different
7. Experimental methods of mapping dermatomes vary:
   a. Blocking or cutting nerve root above and below one segment
   b. Saline injection into spinal or paraspinal structures
   c. Faradic stimulation of a single nerve root
   d. Herpes zoster mapping
   e. Point of spinal nerve severance
      —Distal to dorsal root ganglia = 2x area of innervation in remaining intermediate and intact nerve root
      —Proximal to dorsal root ganglia (within dura) = decrease in area of remaining sensibility
8. Theories of limb bud and subsequent extremity dermatomes differ
9. Tests on animals, patients, and normal medical student volunteers yield different dermatomal maps

---

soft tissue, and bone plus fibrous septa relating to the dermatome, myotome, and sclerotome, respectively. A segmental arrangement has also been applied to the cutaneous distribution of sympathetic nerves as related to a specific spinal cord segment (sympathetic dermatome).[33] Dermatomal distinction is by far the most common and familiar means of segmentation.

A dermatome is considered to be the cutaneous region that is innervated by one spinal nerve through both of its rami.[1] This accounts for the existence of anterior and posterior dermatomes innervated by the same spinal nerve or segment. Dermatomes, however, are not as segmental nor easily delineated as they appear to be on commonly used charts. Dermatome charts frequently available from T.E.N.S. manufacturers have distinct differences, which can lead to confusion if they are used as the sole means of evaluation or electrode placement (Table 8-2).

Dermatomes do not possess distinct anatomic boundaries outlining their location, partly because of the high degree of overlap.[1,2] Dermatomal boundaries may also vary depending on the degree of afferent input entering a spinal cord segment at any given time.[48,51,53] Noxious and non-noxious stimuli entering the dorsal horn from superficial and deep structures can converge on or summate with internuncial neurons, resulting in facilitation, inhibition, or projection of sensation to and from adjacent dorsal horns.[54,55] The spread of afferent stimuli extrasegmentally via Sherrington's reflex principles, Lissauer's tract in the marginal layer of dorsal horn, and the sympathetic chain may account for dermatomal variables.[1,33–36,48–52] The resultant afferent activity can influence the perception of pain both ipsilaterally and contralaterally. (This process is discussed in more detail in Chapter 5.)

Experimental methods used in the study and subsequent mapping of dermatomes vary, thus leading to obvious differences. Commonly used methods consisted of blocking or severing nerve roots above and below a particular root, injection of saline solution into various spinal or paraspinal structures, and faradic stimulation of a single nerve root to determine the area of vasodilation.[33,56–67] These experiments were performed on animals, patients, and normal medical student volunteers. Further delineation among patients in these studies consisted of nerve root involvement via the nucleus pulposus and by herpes zoster.

Furthermore, the point at which spinal nerves are severed to determine the area of remaining sensitivity in one nerve can result in an increase or decrease in the size of the cutaneous field. Sherrington sectioned spinal nerves distal to their dorsal root ganglia.[56,57] This produced an area of innervation in the remaining intermediate and intact nerve root that was almost double that which existed prior to the experiment. When these same dorsal roots were resectioned within the dura, there was a decrease in the area of remaining sensitivity 3 to 4 days later, which was equal to that of the classic dermatomes. Kirk and Denny-Brown obtained similar findings in their experiments on the Macaque monkey.[67]

Consideration must also be given to the theories concerning the development of the limb buds and subsequent extremity dermatomes along dorsal and ventral axial lines (Figs. 8-3, 8-4).[65]

Figures 8-5 through 8-8 illustrate the dermatomal mapping of earlier investigators. The mapping of Foerster compares favorably with those dermatomes seen clinically by Grieve[48] and Cyriax.[68]

The next area of consideration is the relationship among the dermatome, myotome, and sclerotome. Generally, there is a fairly uniform segmental relationship among the three. However, only the myotome and sclerotome distinctly correspond. According to Hilton's law, the nerve supply of the myotome acting on a joint provides for the innervation of that

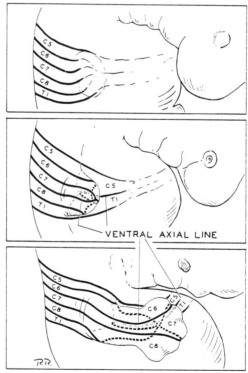

FIGURE 8-3. Keegan and Garrett's conception of dermatomal development in the limb bud. (From Keegan, JJ and Garrett, FD: *The segmental distribution of the cutaneous nerves in the limbs of man.* Anat Rec 102:409, 1948, with permission.)

CLINICAL T.E.N.S.

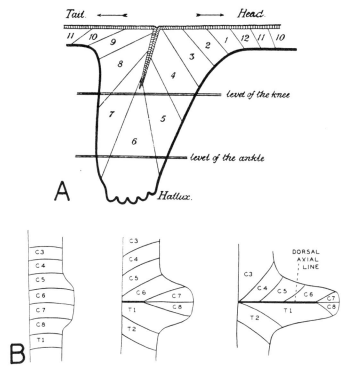

FIGURE 8-4. *A,* Sherrington's (1893) scheme of the sensory skin fields of the hind limb of Macacus rhesus. *B,* Bolk's (1898) conception of the migration of the extremity dermatomes in limb bud development. (From Keegan, JJ and Garrett, FD: *The segmental distribution of the cutaneous nerves in the limbs of man.* Anat Rec 102:409, 1948, with permission.)

joint as well as its overlying cutaneous region.[69,70] This is not apparent at the head, pectoral region, scapula, intrathoracic structures, hand, buttock, and scrotum.[68]

The nonuniform innervation of skin and its underlying musculature has been demonstrated by electromyography of the erector spinae. Results showed that the innervation of an anterior myotome differs by two segments from that of the corresponding dermatome. The difference is more pronounced with cervical and lumbar posterior myotomes, sometimes approaching six segments. Cloward, in his studies with cervical diskography, delineated the difference between the pain referred from the cervical spine to the region innervated by the T2–T7 dermatomes.[19,20] Various studies on referred pain from muscular, ligamental, diskal, and skeletal structures show a similar pattern, which differs from that of the dermatome.[59–61,63,64,66] The use of dermatomes as the sole means of determining electrode placement sites is thus a nonspecific method.

An accurate diagnosis of the structural cause of the pain cannot be made solely on the basis of where the patient states it hurts. The perceived reference of pain will vary depending on whether or not it is arising from a superficial, deep somatic, or visceral structure. It therefore becomes necessary to know the myotomal, sclerotomal, and dermatomal segmental arrangements. The clinician who initially conducts a thorough evaluation to determine the nature, distribution, and structural source of pain, followed by localization of segmentally related stimulated sites, will achieve better results with T.E.N.S.

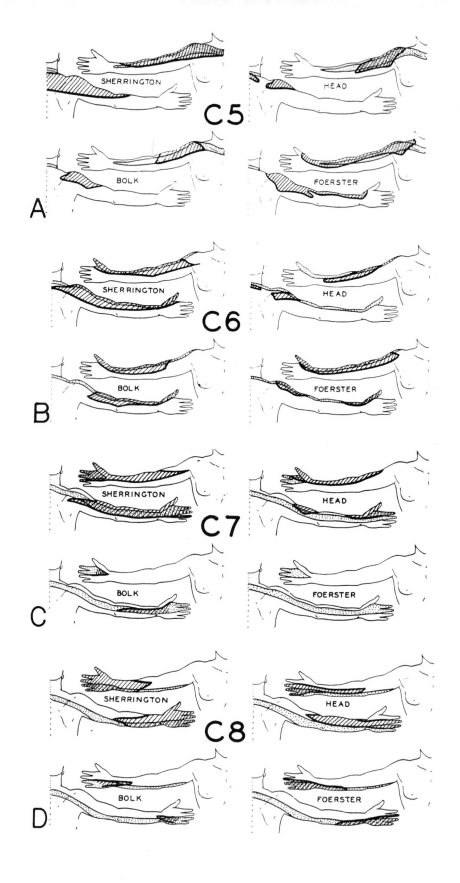

SHERRINGTON HEAD **C5**
BOLK FOERSTER **A**

SHERRINGTON HEAD **C6**
BOLK FOERSTER **B**

SHERRINGTON HEAD **C7**
BOLK FOERSTER **C**

SHERRINGTON HEAD **C8**
BOLK FOERSTER **D**

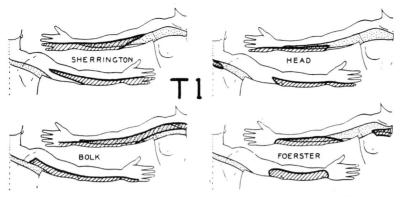

FIGURE 8-6. First thoracic dermatomal mappings and comparison of Sherrington, Bolk, Head, and Foerster. (From Keegan, JJ and Garrett, FD: *The segmental distribution of the cutaneous nerves in the limbs of man.* Anat Rec 102:409, 1948, with permission.)

PERIPHERAL NERVES

The peripheral nervous system (PNS) is comprised of 12 pairs of cranial nerves and 31 pairs of spinal nerves. The sympathetic trunks may also be included in this system. The origin of the PNS is from limb plexus formed by ventral rami of spinal nerves. The exception is in the thoracic region where ventral rami are fairly segmental in their distribution and do not unite into a plexus formation. The ventral rami of spinal nerves in the cervical, lumbar, and sacral regions come together near their origin to form a plexus. Peripheral nerves that emerge from a plexus are thus supplied by fibers from two or more spinal cord segments. This provides for a more extensive connection to the spinal cord, resulting in overlap of innervation to cutaneous and motor fields.[1-3] Overlap of innervation is more extensive in the extremities than in the trunk and accounts for the difference between the peripheral nerve field and that of the dermatome. When a peripheral nerve is stimulated, at least two or more dermatomal regions will also be stimulated. This relationship is important to the clinician when he or she must distinguish the objective and subjective signs of a peripheral nerve injury from those seen in nerve root involvement.

Peripheral nerves usually have one or more regions where they are superficial and easily accessible to stimulation by surface electrodes. The most well-known region is the ulnar nerve within the olecranon groove. Motor and sensory nerve conduction velocity testing is performed at these superficial regions.[71-74]

In addition to the superficial regions of the major peripheral nerves, numerous cutaneous branches exist that are relatively unknown or unfamiliar to many clinicians. These cutaneous nerves have distinct anatomic pathways. A knowledge of the anatomy of these cutaneous distributions provides an important adjunct to successful electrode placement with T.E.N.S. (see the figures at the end of this chapter).

FIGURE 8-5. Dermatomal mappings and comparison of Sherrington, Bolk, Head, and Foerster. *A,* Fifth cervical dermatome. *B,* Sixth cervical dermatome. *C,* Seventh cervical dermatome. *D,* Eighth cervical dermatome. (From Keegan, JJ and Garrett, FD: *The segmental distribution of the cutaneous nerves in the limbs of man.* Anat Rec 102:409, 1948, with permission.)

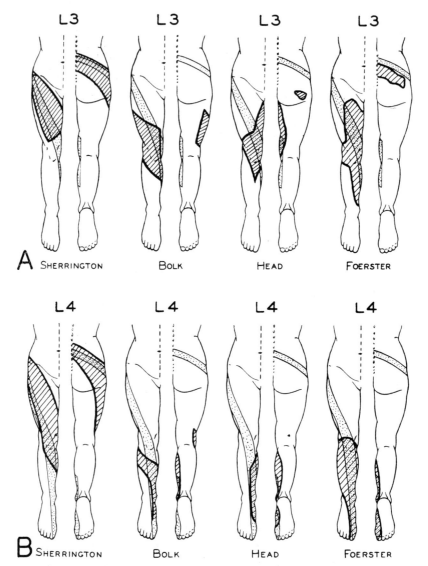

FIGURE 8-7. Dermatomal mappings and comparison of Sherrington, Bolk, Head, and Foerster. *A,* Third lumbar dermatome. *B,* Fourth lumbar dermatome.

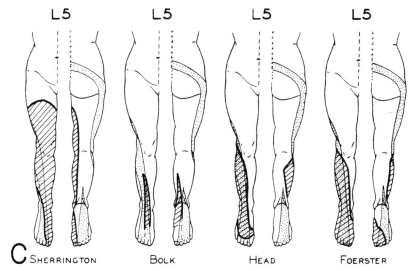

L5   L5   L5   L5

C SHERRINGTON   BOLK   HEAD   FOERSTER

FIGURE 8-7 (continued). *C*, Fifth lumbar dermatome. (From Keegan, JJ and Garrett, FD: *The segmental distribution of the cutaneous nerves in the limbs of man.* Anat Rec 102:409, 1948, with permission.)

Cranial nerves, primarily the trigeminal, also have superficial branches that can be stimulated by surface electrodes. A knowledge of the anatomic distribution and numerous superficial branches of the trigeminal nerve is important for the determination of electrode placements in the management of headaches, toothaches, trigeminal neuralgia, and other facial pain syndromes. An impulse propagated along the trigeminal nerve must enter its semilunar ganglion and nucleus caudalis. The caudal nucleus contains a substantia gelatinosa region (see Chapter 3) similar in structure and function as well as continuous with that of the spinal cord dorsal horn.[1,75-83] The spinal tract of the trigeminal nerve descends into the upper cervical spinal cord to the level of C2 and perhaps as far as C4.[75-83,273] There are synaptic connections between the trigeminal nerve and upper cervical spinal cord. The implication of these anatomic relationships should allow for electrode placement at the upper cervical spine for facial and head pain as well as at the superficial trigeminal nerve branches for upper cervical pain.

MOTOR POINTS

Muscles innervated by fibers from motor branches of peripheral nerves are optimally stimulated at sites known as the motor point, which is characterized by an area of high electrical conductance and low skin resistance. Coers, through muscle biopsy, established that the motor point is a distinct anatomic entity at which muscle is excitable at a low threshold of electricity compared with the surrounding area.[72,73] The neurovascular hilus of muscle is the anatomic region at which nerve fibers and blood vessels pierce the deep surface of muscle to provide afferent and efferent linkages to muscle fibers, spindles, Golgi tendon organs, free nerve endings (nociceptive), and circulatory components. The greatest density of sensory end organs exists at the neurovascular hilus, making it a region susceptible to palpable tenderness.[84-90] The neurovascular hilus is a relatively minute, elongated,

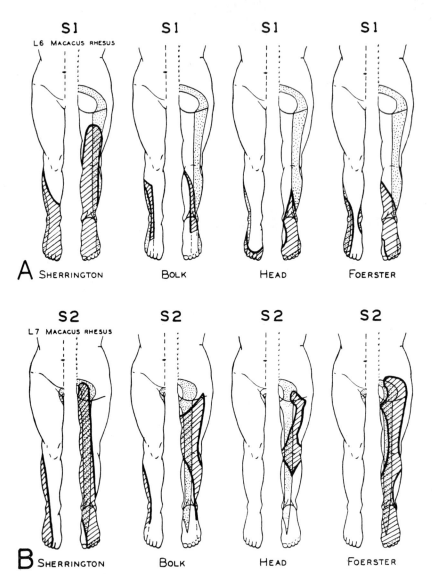

FIGURE 8-8. Dermatomal mappings and comparison of Sherrington, Bolk, Head, and Foerster. *A,* First sacral dermatome. *B,* Second sacral dermatome. (From Keegan, JJ and Garrett, FD: *The segmental distribution of the cutaneous nerves in the limbs of man.* Anat Rec 102:409, 1948, with permission.)

and oval-shaped area. In line with and running through the muscle to its superficial region is a zone of innervation known as the transverse motor band. Nerve endings are concentrated within the transverse motor band. The skin that overlies the motor band is the actual motor point.

The motor point should not be confused with what is called the motor line.[88] A motor line (½ to 1 inch long) is present at a region where the main nerve trunk is superficial. Low amplitude current at the motor line can excite all distal musculature innervated by that nerve. The motor line also corresponds to areas where motor conduction velocity tests are performed. Acupuncture points are also located at all of these regions.

Gunn and Milbrandt present clinical findings that strongly support their contention that motor points in segmentally related muscle or myotomes exhibit tenderness to palpation that becomes more pronounced with the extent of the pathology.[68,84,86–91,93] The segmental localization of the lesion may in part be determined by the tenderness existing in muscles that are innervated by both the anterior and posterior rami of a single nerve root. Palpation at the paravertebral motor points approximately 2.5 cm lateral to the midline (spinous processes) may serve to confirm the localization of the lesion segmentally.[91–94] Glover has noted the existence of small paraspinal tender spots with a surround hyperesthesia ½ inch to 2 inches lateral to the midline as well as over the sacroiliac joints.[95] These sensitive spots can be located by manual pressure and are not considered to be due to nerve root irritation. These tender areas correspond to the bladder meridian points, new paraspinal points, motor points of the erector spinae, and paraspinal trigger points.[96]

Motor points thus provide the clinician with a specific anatomic site at which to place surface electrodes to stimulate the CNS.

TRIGGER POINTS

Trigger points are considered to be hypersensitive regions primarily found in muscles but also in connective tissue, ligaments, tendons, joint capsules, and skin. They are characterized by tenderness, increased resistance to palpation, a surround hyperesthesia, and the production of referred pain. The location of common trigger points and their respective pain distribution patterns are predictable and well documented in the literature.[97–101]

The trigger point as an existing concept is generally accepted, but controversy lies in whether or not its histologic makeup constitutes an actual anatomic entity. Numerous explanations have been provided in an effort to explain the development of trigger points as a result of histologic changes. Simons indicates an increase in fibrous connective tissue, edema, alterations of muscle viscosity, ground substance or fatty infiltration, muscle fiber contraction, and vascular engorgement as possible predisposing factors behind palpable hardness.[101]

Others have related trigger points to fibrositic nodules, waxy degeneration of muscle fibers, fatty infiltration of muscle, and a regional increase in muscle fiber nuclei.[97–100] Travell has noted that trigger points may not be distinguished by pathologic changes.[102,103] Mac-Donald states that an increased excitability of alpha motor neurons as determined electromyographically leads to palpable muscle tension.[104]

Simons and Travell have presented a most descriptive hypothesis relating to the development of trigger points.[105] They mention the fact that many muscles that contain trigger points show electrical silence at rest and that some of the resting motor unit activity observed electromyographically may develop from a muscle within the area of referred pain. They hypothesized that a stressor may disrupt the sarcoplasmic reticulum, resulting in a release of calcium ions. In the presence of adenosine triphosphate, the free calcium could then activate the actin-myosin contractile mechanism of the sarcomeres. If this mechanism took place in a contiguous group of muscle fibers, it could result in a palpable tense fibrous band. If such a process occurs, then treatment consisting of deep pressure massage would serve to stretch the shortened sarcomeres to a degree sufficient to separate the overlap of the actin-myosin elements, restore normal function, and stop the pain-spasm-pain cycle. Needling of active trigger points would also serve to disrupt the pain cycle. A release of intracellular K^+ as a result of needle insertion and a blockage of pain and reflex pathways from the injected anesthetic would take place. Simons and Travell further infer that calcium ions and tissue metabolites that excite sensory nerve endings could be washed out by the injected agent, thus decreasing a prime source of nerve irritability and ongoing sarcomere shortening.[105]

Mennell and Zohn are of the opinion that a muscle trigger point may be a hyperactive or irritable muscle spindle. They suggest, but with some reservation, that a trigger point in a tendon or joint capsule may possibly represent an irritable Golgi tendon organ or Ruffini ending, respectively.[106,107] Simons states that a trigger point may be a well-innervated structure occupying a small area of muscle.[101] This would definitely lend some support to the existence of a trigger point as an anatomic entity. The concept of a hyperactive muscle spindle and Golgi tendon organ is supported by Tarsy.[108] He also produces evidence for and against the existence of fibrositic nodules, and that muscle biopsies do not consistently yield histologic changes at tender points.

Cyriax presents a different and interesting interpretation of a trigger point. He considered this localized tender spot in muscle to result from pressure on the dura mater. The dura mater is highly innervated on its anterior aspect by the sinuvertebral nerve and gives rise to extrasegmental referred pain. Pressure on the dura mater is the result of a small intervertebral disk herniation pushing the posterior longitudinal ligament against it.[64] Trigger points are frequently mentioned as producing extrasegmental referred pain; however, they may also produce a segmental pain referral.[84] Cyriax does not consider the trigger point to be an actual anatomic entity since it can shift in location and disappear as a result of traction and manipulation. We agree with this and have seen it clinically. However, this represents only one etiologic factor in trigger point production, namely, nerve root or spinal complex irritation. The trigger point may still be considered an anatomic entity that becomes tender when nerve fibers innervating it are irritated. The tenderness disappears when the irritation is relieved. If irritation shifts to another segment, a different trigger point becomes tender and may in fact be the motor point or other sensory end organ of a segmentally related soft-tissue structure.

Thus far, there is no consensus on the phenomenon of trigger points. However, they exist clinically and represent excellent stimulation sites, possibly due to a dense CNS input from sensory end organs.[109] Table 8-3 outlines the specific anatomic relationships of motor and trigger points. A discussion concerning the nature, mechanism, and treatment of trigger points was presented in Chapter 5.

TABLE 8-3. Specific Anatomic Relationships of Motor and Trigger Points

Motor Point	Trigger Point
Point at which nerve enters muscle	Primarily at insertion or periphery of muscle
Nerve endings near skin surface	Also deep in muscle tissue at neurovascular hilus
Motor end plate	TP and MP ≈ to each other as well as to AP (Gunn
Myoneural junction	and Milbrandt)
Large compact disks	TP related to cardiac disease ≈ to MP in same area
Clusters of chains	Maximal tender areas—regions where superficial
Motor line—point or ½ to 1 inch long skin	nerves and blood vessels are near skin surface
projection of motor nerves. Location dependent on	TP between or at muscle periphery and loose fascial
pattern of muscle fiber insertion into tendon	structures where nerve trunks are generally found
Scattered zones = increased number of MPs	Hyperactive or irritable muscle spindle, GTO, or
Overlies NV hilus and zone of innervation (↑	Ruffini ending (Zohn and Mennell)
number of motor end plates)	

MP = motor point; TP = trigger point; AP = acupuncture point; NV = neurovascular; GTO = Golgi tendon organ

ACUPUNCTURE POINTS

The stimulation of acupuncture points for pain relief has long been performed by various means (heat, pressure, needling, electricity, injection).[109-120] Research has shown that acupuncture is effective only when there is an intact nervous system.[100,106-110] The physiologic effects of acupuncture, therefore, require stimulation of the CNS. What is an acupuncture point? Mann has termed acupuncture points "tender areas at certain points on the surface of the body which disappear when the related illness is cured."[117] He states that a stimulus anywhere within the appropriate or related dermatome may be effective, but the response can be enhanced by stimulation of an area within a region that exhibits the greatest degree of tenderness and possesses either a hard, tense, or indurated area as well as a fibrositic component or nodule. Such areas of tenderness and fibrositis maintain a fairly constant position and are seen in different pathologies.[117] It is interesting to note that any area of the body can become tender at certain times; thus, according to Mann, there can be an infinite number of acupuncture points. In fact, new or extra points as well as meridians are constantly being developed. However, in spite of the number of acupuncture points in the low thousands, only about 50 to 100 are commonly used.[115-117] Some of these points always seem to be tender to palpation, such as GB 21, within the upper trapezius muscle. In appendicitis, reflex tenderness and referred pain occur at McBurney's point where acupuncture point ST 26 is located.

To date, no one has stated that an acupuncture point represents an entity anatomically distinct from that of known neural and circulatory structures as well as sensory end organs.

The Korean researcher Kim Bong Han did describe a system of ducts and corpuscles that corresponded to the distribution of acupuncture meridians.[117,120-123] The Bong Han corpuscle is considered structurally different from all other known corpuscles. Bong Han claims to have found these corpuscles in deep tissue around internal organs, blood vessels, and lymphatic vessels, all connected by ductlike systems (Bong Han duct). He reported four systems of ducts: internal, intra-external, external, and neural.[123] The internal duct system was considered to exist within the vascular and lymphatic vessels. The intra-external duct system existed on the surface of the visceral organs. The external (superficial) duct system was distributed along the outer surface of vascular and lymphatic vessel walls as well as the corium. The neural duct system obviously was distributed in the central and peripheral nervous systems.[123] Bong Han felt that all four systems were interlinked and the corpuscles corresponded to the acupuncture points.

Bong Han claims to have injected radioactive phosphorus into an acupuncture point and then traced its flow through the related meridian.[121-123] In actuality, this may simply represent the flow of the radioactive substance through the axon of the nerve via a process known as axoplasmic transport (see Chapter 12).[124] Axoplasmic transport is the mechanism of movement of proteins, neurotransmitters, and other vital nerve substances within the axon. Bong Han also noted the presence of a "duct liquor" containing various amino acids, corticosteroids, estrogen, epinephrine, deoxyribonucleic acid (DNA), and ribonucleic acid (RNA) that flowed in a unidirectional manner.[122,123] The flow of "duct liquor" may actually be the process of axoplasmic transport. The work of Bong Han has not yet been supported or duplicated.[120,122,126,130] Radioactive and nonradioactive substances have been employed to track the movement of proteins from their cell bodies to respective axon terminals when injected into the vicinity of a nerve.[124,125] Various subcellular structures such as the endoplasmic reticulum, neurofilaments, and microtubules have been found. These structures, frequently seen in neurons as well as myelinated and nonmyelinated axons, may take part in axoplasmic transport and could well represent the structures that Bong Han was describing.

However, there have been numerous reports correlating the location of acupuncture points with that of superficial nerve branches and sensory end organs. A general agreement is that most of the commonly used acupuncture points either overlie or are innervated or surrounded by superficial cutaneous nerves.[117,118,126–137] A consensus of four articles concerning acupuncture anesthesia was that stimulation of sensory nerve endings was the basis for the analgesic action. It did not matter whether the stimulated points were on the regional meridian as long as they were near the nerve supply of the involved region.[131–134] Matsumoto found that the most effective areas for needle acupuncture were at sites where somatic nerves were superficial.[120]

Dornette and Fleck strongly support the view that acupuncture has a neural basis and that many meridians follow peripheral nerve distributions. They also state that acupuncture points lie over concentrations of dermal and musculoskeletal sensory end organs such as muscle spindles, Ruffini's endings, Meissner's corpuscles, and free nerve endings.[138,139] The Chinese consider acupuncture points to be small and measured in millimeters.[117,162] Mann, however, states that the existence of small, specific acupuncture points is rare and does not agree that specific sensory end-organs are found at acupuncture points.[117] Mann does support the theory of nervous system transmission in acupuncture and discusses various intersegmental reflexes that may help explain the action of acupuncture.

If one studies acupuncture and compares the anatomic locations of the points and their respective meridians with the peripheral nervous system, an interesting relationship is seen (see figures at the end of this chapter). (A meridian consists of a line connecting acupuncture points that seem to be related to a particular organ or produce an effect on that organ.) Many acupuncture points lie directly over or near superficial aspects of peripheral nerves and their branches. The bladder meridian follows the spinal column, and the acupuncture points of this meridian are located between the transverse processes of respective vertebrae where stimulation of the dorsal ramus can be performed. These stimulation sites also correspond to the motor points of the erector spinae muscles. The spleen meridian follows the distribution of the great saphenous vein. Acupuncture point spleen 6 overlies the saphenous branch of the femoral nerve. The heart meridian follows the distribution of the ulnar nerve, and the acupuncture points along its course are the same as those used in conduction velocity tests. A relationship between other acupuncture points and surface stimulation sites for motor and sensory nerve conduction velocity testing are listed in the table entitled "Major Peripheral Nerve Trunks" at the end of this chapter.[84,71–73] A comparison between conventional nerve blocks and the location of acupuncture points at similar sites has been clearly illustrated by Matsumoto and Lyu.[140]

In light of the characteristics of acupuncture points, their use in electrode placement is excellent. The effectiveness of transcutaneous electrical stimulation of acupuncture points has been documented.[141–143] The Chinese obviously had an excellent knowledge of peripheral neuroanatomy. They coupled this knowledge with the extensive observation and documentation of somatic pain areas as reported by patients suffering from illness and pain syndromes to develop the elaborate system of acupuncture. Our intent here is not to discuss the efficacy of acupuncture but merely to support our view that acupuncture points are effective stimulation sites and basically represent peripheral nerve stimulation sites. Table 8-4 outlines the specific results of anatomic studies of acupuncture point locations.

SPECIFIC POINTS

A specific point represents a stimulation site that is either an acupuncture, motor, or trigger point. The term will be used to discuss the anatomic and clinical relationship of these points with the peripheral nervous system.

TABLE 8-4. The Results of Anatomic Studies of Acupuncture Points

Mann: Best performed at site of greatest tenderness, may have hard, tense or indurated areas
Bong Han: Ducts and corpuscles
Dornette and Fleck: AP overlies dermal plus MS sensory end organs; meridians follow peripheral nerve distribution
Matsumoto and Lyu: Superficial somatic nerves are best sites for acupuncture $\approx$ with nerve block sites. —$\approx$ with stimulation sites for motor and sensory conduction velocity testing. —$\approx$ with bladder meridian points, erector spinae motor points, and trigger points. —Surgery via electroacupuncture analgesia—best stimulation sites are in segmentally related areas at, near or adjacent to operative site
Melzack, Stillwell, and Fox: 71% anatomic plus clinical correlation of TP and AP
Liao: AP and TP $\approx$
Liu: AP and MP $\approx$ all MPs are acupuncture loci, but not all acupuncture loci are MPs
Gunn and Milbrandt: 4 classes of acupuncture points. All with a rich supply of cutaneous nerves; (1) MPs, (2) spine, (3) nerve plexus or superficial cutaneous nerves, (4) musculotendinous junction
Bossy: 201—dissections (5 mm), 58—superficial peripheral nerve, 69—venous structures, 74—NV hilus
Others: 324—170 → deep nerves, (macro) 149—superficial + deep nerves, (micro) dense groupings of nerve endings plus fibers
Plummer: Perforating, communicating or feeder veins (connect superficial plus deep veins at some APs), sympathetic fibers.
Nakatani and others: Skin resistance studies

MP = motor point; TP = trigger point; AP = acupuncture point; NV = neurovascular; MS = musculoskeletal

Our initial use of electrical stimulation was in the treatment of peripheral nerve injuries. Muscles were stimulated electrically for re-education, and electrodes were placed at motor points where the strongest contraction with the least amount of current could be obtained. As our awareness of the phenomenon of trigger points and their pain referral patterns grew, it was found that some trigger points and motor points were located at the same anatomical sites. We also noted that some of the most effective acupuncture points were located in the same areas. To determine if these specific points represent the same entity, the characteristics of the specific points, namely, tenderness, soft-tissue changes, skin resistance, anatomic structure, and location, must be compared (Table 8-5).

We have previously supported the characteristic of tenderness possessed by active acupuncture and trigger points. Related to this are small areas of skin that become hypersensitive and are thought to be related to an irritated or diseased visceral organ. Such areas have been termed reaction points, neural reflections, head zones, or cutaneovisceral reflex

TABLE 8-5. The Relationship of Specific Points

Characteristics	Acupuncture	Motor	Trigger
1. Tenderness to palpation in presence of segmentally related pathology	Yes	Yes	Yes
2. Decreased resistance to electricity	Yes	Yes	Yes
3. Increased resistance to pressure (hardness, firmness) (muscle guarding or spasm)	Yes	Yes	Yes
4. Anatomically situated at, near, or over superficial nerve fibers and blood vessels	Yes	Yes	Yes
5. Contain fibrositic components	Sometimes	Sometimes	Sometimes
6. Give rise to referred pain on pressure	Yes	Yes	Yes
7. Exist anatomically at similar locations	Yes	Yes	Yes
8. Represent or are located at dense groupings of sensory end organs, on or just below the skin surface	Yes	Yes	Yes

points.[5,54,115] They supposedly represent ANS junctions of corresponding organs and dermatome segments. A great deal of similarity in location exists among these neural reflections with trigger and acupuncture points. Various treatment techniques such as connective-tissue massage and Shiatsu concentrate therapy at these regions. The theories as to the neurophysiologic action of the aforementioned procedures, as well as those of acupuncture, trigger point therapy, and T.E.N.S., are remarkably similar. Neurolymphatic points also known as Chapman's reflexes are stimulation sites used in applied kinesiology and muscle energy techniques.[145-150] They are considered to be gangliform contractions of lymphoid tissue[145] and are palpable at specific areas in the fascia, usually at distal ends of spinal nerves. In acute conditions, Chapman's reflex points, or neurolymphatic points, represent small circumscribed areas or indurations that exhibit soreness or are tender to palpation. In chronic pathologic conditions, they supposedly are manifested as relatively nontender masses.

The locations of the most common neurolymphatic points are adjacent to the sternum within the intercostal spaces and posteriorly along the spine at the midpoint between the spinous processes.[145,149] Other neurolymphatic and/or neurovascular points are located about the skull on the temporosphenoidal line.

The fact that tenderness exists at acupuncture, trigger, and cutaneovisceral reflex points in regions segmentally related to a pathologic process has also been shown to occur with motor points. Cervical spine involvement can result in tenderness of motor points within myotomes segmentally related to the level of spinal pathology. Motor points have also been shown to become tender in the myotome corresponding to the spinal cord or root lesion level in low back pain.[91-94]

Acupuncture, trigger, and motor points possess a variable degree of tenderness depending on their location (over bony areas, and so forth) and ongoing related pathology. Such tenderness may at times be nonexistent and at other times highly sensitive.[84,86,87,89,90-94,97-100,106-108,117,144]

Soft-tissue changes as determined by histologic and microscopic studies have shown fibrositic components at some but not all acupuncture and trigger points. Such a process must take some time to become apparent. In addition, there have been reports of areas of discoloration, swelling, induration, and a tense or hard region within muscle, which supposedly are indicative of specific points.[96,145-150]

Another point of comparison concerns the electrical conductance as determined by the degree of skin resistance at the specific points. Trigger points frequently produce areas of decreased skin resistance[151] (see Chapter 5). Motor points manifest themselves in part by a skin resistance that is less than that of the area surrounding or directly adjacent to them. Acupuncture points also seem to possess a decreased skin resistance to electricity.[115,117,120,130,152-158] Mann, however, claims to have found thousands of skin areas that possess low resistance and do not all correspond to known acupuncture points.[117] Electrical resistance of the skin will vary according to physical and emotional tension, temperature, circulation, sweat gland activity, condition of the skin (surface moisture, dryness), and other factors.[159,160,161] Tension (physical and emotional) lowers skin resistance, and relaxation raises it.[159] The range of skin resistance in ohms varies from a million or more to only a few thousand when the skin is wet. Thus, all acupuncture points do not always exhibit the lowest degree of resistance. Skin conductance will also change according to the degree or extent of a related pathologic process. The more advanced the pathology, the greater the change in skin resistance. In fact, the degree and amount of pressure, rubbing, scratching, or rolling friction by a probe over an area being tested can lead to decreased skin resistance via the production of erythema, histamine reaction, or destruction of the stratum corneum.[146,147,162]

Low skin-resistance areas have been shown to correspond well to regions identified as producing pain and tenderness both clinically and experimentally.[33–36,55,160,163–166] Areas of decreased skin resistance were found in segmentally related dermatomes in conditions such as pancreatitis, duodenal ulcers, abnormal spinal mobility, vertebral segment pathology, and cardiac involvement and were able to be produced by sympathetic hyperactivity that stemmed from the resultant visceral or somatic dysfunction. According to Omura, a specific area of decreased skin impedance (resistance) generally is associated with hyperactivity of an internal organ corresponding segmentally to that cutaneous region. A hypoactive visceral organ generally produces a segmental increased impedance at its corresponding cutaneous region.[146,147] However, the results of skin-resistance testing as a means of verifying the existence of acupuncture points are still considered somewhat controversial.[162,167]

The basis for the location of acupuncture points by electrical testing of the skin was developed by Nakatani in 1950.[152] His conclusions were similar to those of Denslow, Korr, and others in that a pathologic process stimulates the sympathetic nervous system, resulting in dilation of the pores and a decrease in resistance at acupuncture points along the meridian related to the involved organ.[163,164,166]

The cellular structure of motor points and of some trigger points as determined by histologic and microscopic means has been previously discussed. Other than the work of Bong Han, acupuncture points representative of unknown neurovascular structures have not been found by such means, but they are present at or near superficial nerve branches, dense areas of sensory receptors, and the neurovascular hilus of muscles, structures found to exist microscopically.

In one specific region, the dorsal web space between the thumb and index finger, an acupuncture, a motor, and two trigger points can be found according to their respective anatomic locations (see the figure entitled "Posterolateral Shoulder & Dorsal Region of U.E." at the end of this chapter).[3,73,98,107,115–117] Electrical stimulation at this region with a standard-sized T.E.N.S. electrode conceivably should activate all of the aforementioned points simultaneously. The parameters of the stimulating current (amplitude, rate, and width) may secondarily determine which points and nerve fiber type are activated to an extent greater than another (see Chapter 12).

The anterior tibialis region also contains an acupuncture point (ST 36), the superior motor point of the anterior tibialis, and the trigger point of the same muscle. The deep peroneal and lateral sural cutaneous nerves innervate this region. The two acupuncture points classically called HO-KU (LI 4) and TSU-SAN-Li (ST 36) are the most frequently used acupuncture points on the upper and lower extremities, respectively. The high degree of innervation and dense concentration of sensory end organs at these regions may account for their frequent use.[161,168] Thus far, no one has been able to dissect and microscopically study a region such as this to locate three entities anatomically distinct from one another. The motor point of the first dorsal interosseus can be found. The trigger points of the adductor pollicis and first dorsal interosseus may be represented by a fibrositic component or hyperactive sensory end organs. The fourth point along the large intestine meridian (LI 4) is the acupuncture point at this region. LI 4 may merely represent an area that is highly innervated (superficial radial, musculocutaneous, and ulnar-motor) and exhibits a high degree of conductance in a region containing a dense grouping of sensory end organs, but does not depict an entity with a distinct anatomic difference. A dense grouping of neurovascular fibers, vessels, and sensory end organs at a distinct location may therefore represent the acupuncture point.[169]

The concept of a dense grouping of sensory end organs is supported in the literature.[170–172] Whether or not a single sensory end organ represents the anatomic entity known as a trigger point cannot be further documented. Specific end organs need not be present for the perception of each type of sensation. The human cornea contains only one type of nerve ending, but touch, pain, heat, and cold can all be perceived. Conversely, stimulation of the tooth pulp in man primarily produces only one sensation, pain,[54,173,174] but recent studies also mention the perception of heat, cold, and tingling.[272]

Studies of single skin spots show nerve fibers coming from all directions. There is a complex unit of fibers terminating in numerous endings that have been termed a subcutaneous plexus or sensory net.[175,176] It can therefore be stated that regardless of the mode of transcutaneous stimulation (heat, cold, pressure, electricity), the resultant nerve impulse arises from a combination of excited end organs via myelinated and nonmyelinated nerve fibers.[173–180]

Strong support is given for the location of acupuncture points at regions characterized by a high degree of neurovascular components. Plummer[136,137] and Reichmanis and Becker[153,155–157] cite the work of Bossy, who performed macroscopic dissections of 201 acupuncture points to a depth of 5 mm. He found a superficial peripheral nerve at 58 points, venous structures at 69, and a neurovascular hilus at 74. Further macroscopic dissection of 324 acupuncture points found deep nerves at 170 and a combination of superficial and deep nerves at 149 points. Dense groupings of nerve endings and fibers were found microscopically at the single points not represented by macroscopic neural structures.[136,137] Anatomic studies performed by Plummer confirm these findings as well as that of nearby peripheral nerves that run subcutaneously and pierce the dermis at some acupuncture loci.[137] Stimulation at points overlying superficial cutaneous nerves has been shown to be highly effective in producing pain modulation. Furthermore, Plummer has located veins (termed as perforating, communicating, or feeder veins) that connect superficial and large veins at some acupuncture points. The acupuncture point may thus be a minute hole or opening within which neurovascular and/or lymphatic elements are located.[136] Since sympathetic nerve fibers parallel vascular structures, the significance of such findings may point to the relationship of acupuncture to the ANS.[136]

Acupuncture, motor, and trigger points may in fact all represent the same anatomic entity. Further support for such a statement can be found in research that has compared the specific points according to anatomic location and clinical significance.

Melzack, Stillwell, and Fox correlated trigger and acupuncture points anatomically and clinically.[109] In comparing charts of these points, they found an overall correspondence of 71 percent. Anatomically, a corresponding acupuncture point was found for every trigger point depicted in the classic charts of Travell and Rinzler.[97] Trigger points other than those depicted by Travell and Ringler have been described.[99,266,267]

Kennard and Haugen investigated the relationship of subcutaneous sensitivity and referred pain from visceral disease.[181] They noted a similar pattern of trigger points related to cardiac involvement with motor points in the same location. The areas of maximal tenderness, which they called "trigger spots," were found at regions where superficial nerves and blood vessels are near the surface of the skin. In addition, they stated that the trigger spots always were between or at the muscular periphery and loose fascial structures where nerve trunks are generally found. Kennard and Haugen also state that these trigger spots were characterized by an increased resistance to pressure, but distinct nodules or fatty deposits were unable to be palpated. This is in line with the previously discussed controversy concerning the nature of the trigger point.

Liao also noted the correspondence of many acupuncture and trigger points and their relationship to cutaneovisceral reflex points (Head's zones).[203]

Liu and coworkers compared acupuncture and motor points. They found that some acupuncture points are located at the same anatomic region as motor points and hypothesized that "all motor points are acupuncture loci, but not all acupuncture loci are motor points." Thus, motor points represent one distinct class of acupuncture points.[129] Gunn and associates did similar work[128] with 70 frequently used acupuncture points and concluded that there are three distinct classifications of acupuncture points: 47 points were anatomically similar to motor points (Type I); 11 were found in the sagittal plane where superficial nerves from both sides of the body converge (Type II); and 12 were over nerve plexuses or superficial cutaneous nerves (Type III). Common to all three classes was a rich supply of superficial nerves. In a subsequent article, Gunn discussed a fourth type of acupuncture point at the musculotendinous junction where the Golgi tendon organ is located.[168] The musculotendinous junction of the supraspinatus is an example of a Type IV acupuncture point. We have found this point (LI 16) to be extremely effective with shoulder pain.

SEGMENTAL RELATIONSHIP

Now that we have established the anatomic and clinical relationship of the various stimulation sites that are most conducive to T.E.N.S., two additional factors must be considered. These factors are the choice of stimulation sites that are anatomically or physiologically related to the source of pain and an explanation of the effectiveness of stimulation sites that cannot be shown to have such a relationship.

A stimulation site that is related to the involved structure or source of pain is innervated by the same peripheral nerve or spinal cord segments. An example would be pain in the ulnar distribution of the hand from a peripheral nerve (ulnar) lesion. Segmentally related stimulation would best be accomplished at superficial aspects of the ulnar nerve (usually above the level of the lesion), specific points within the innervated area of the ulnar nerve, or paraspinally at C7–T1.

Numerous studies have demonstrated a greater degree of pain relief with stimulation via acupuncture, electroacupuncture, or T.E.N.S. when stimulation was directed to regions segmentally related to the area of pain as opposed to stimulation of unrelated areas.[89,131–134,182–202] With acupuncture anesthesia, the greatest effectiveness has been obtained by stimulation of points at or near the nerves innervating the operative regions.[133] Stimulation of segments adjacent to those innervating the painful region was also more effective than extrasegmental stimulation. In comparing the effectiveness of acupuncture and T.E.N.S. (surface electrode stimulation only), the degree of pain relief or increase of the pain threshold was greater with surface electrodes than with needles.[185,186,190,191,193,195,198] It is imperative, however, that such surface stimulation be at a low rate with strong, visible muscle contractions within the related myotome. In direct relationship to high-intensity, low-rate stimulation (1 to 4 Hz), pain relief could be reversed by naloxone, which seemed to indicate a neurohumoral or endorphin release.[195,196,198] Strong, low-rate or high-intensity, pulse-train (burst) T.E.N.S. may prove beneficial in more severe or chronic pain syndromes when conventional T.E.N.S. is not effective.

The pain-modulating action of T.E.N.S. at the segmental level via input from stimulation at corresponding levels is easily understood. However, the action of peripheral stimulation, regardless of the mode, at unrelated or distant sites is not. The literature provides a small degree of support, and obviously, there are numerous explanations if all the philosophic and anatomic relationships of the acupuncture points, meridians, and theories are considered. We will, however, discuss this based on existing anatomic arrangements within the ANS and CNS.

The cortical inhibitory surround theory is a possible explanation for the action of unrelated stimulation sites.[127,132,133,203-205] The arrangement of Penfield's somatomotor and somatosensory cortices forms the basis for this theory. It is proposed that acupuncture stimulation excites representative cells in the cortex. When such stimulation increases, an area of inhibition develops surrounding the excited region and decreases sensitivity in its representative body region. An example of this process may occur when the pain modulation obtained from stimulation of the first dorsal web space on the hand (LI 4) in headaches, trigeminal neuralgia, and other facial pain syndromes are considered. Observation of the somatosensory cortex shows the region indicative of the thumb and index finger to be situated adjacent to that of the head, neck, and face. Innervation of the LI 4 region is by the C5–T1 spinal cord segments and anatomically unrelated to the neck, face, and head.

A closely related explanation is Bull's theory relating to a phenomenon called the "busy cortex."[206] Bull states that a sufficient external stimulus may result in the area of the cortex surrounding a region of excitation, as in an epileptic episode, becoming refractory to additional stimulation. In addition, a rhythmic external stimulus at a rate of 1 to 25 Hz may cause large regions of the cortex to become "locked on" to such a frequency, thus disturbing their normal function. The stimulation rate commonly employed in strong, low-rate (acupuncture-like) T.E.N.S. is within this range (1 to 4 Hz).

An inhibitory surround mechanism has also been shown to occur in other areas of the CNS, termed feed-forward or lateral inhibition.[1,204] The thalamic neuron theory relates closely to that of the cortical inhibitory surround. Lee postulates the existence of a fetal homunculus in the thalamus.[269] A great deal of modulation of afferent input occurs at the thalamus, and it has been supported as a possible site to explain the action of extrasegmental stimulation.[126,182,207]

The spread of afferent stimuli extrasegmentally via Lissauer's tract, the propriospinal system, the sympathetic chain, and reflex principles of Sherrington should also be considered for the effectiveness of stimulation at segmentally unrelated sites.[27,28,49,50,52,54,117,174,208] Lissauer's tract is a prime example of a means by which afferent input may spread extrasegmentally. The tract consists of a fine fiber system located at the entrance of the posterior dorsal roots to the dorsal horn of the spinal cord. It is considered to be part of the marginal layer of the dorsal horn also known as lamina 1. Lissauer's tract extends the full length of the spinal cord and merges with the spinal tract of the trigeminal nerve at the first and second cervical segments. Cervical afferent fibers from at least as low as C4 and possibly C5 are found in the dorsal horn at the C2 level.[273] Myelinated and unmyelinated fibers run in this tract with synaptic connections from substantia gelatinosa (SG) neurons. These fibers usually run for two to three segments and possibly as many as six segments before re-entering the deeper layers of the dorsal horn to synapse in the SG and ultimately the brainstem and somatosensory cortex.[50,174,208-213] Thus, strong stimulation giving rise to an afferent input entering the dorsal horn at a given segment can conceivably have a modulating effect on pain that may exist as far as six segments away.

Voll and Schuldt's interpretation[214-217] of the mechanisms of acupuncture, specifically electroacupuncture according to Voll (EAV), is not based solely on a neuroanatomic concept, but is a process of bioenergetics to ultimately change the electrical potential of certain body points and restore equilibrium or homeostasis that has been altered by pathology. Voll considers the acupuncture point to be the area at which the exchange of energy between the external environment and the body occurs. Many of the measurement and stimulation sites employed by Voll are not classic acupuncture points, but points that have been discovered through his research.[214-223] He supposedly elucidated the relationship between individual teeth, paired organ systems, and various bodily structures such as joints, muscles, and sinuses.[148,218,219] The work of Voll has only recently been introduced into this country from Germany and is not well known. The concepts relating to EAV may revolutionize health care if they stand up to careful and thorough scrutiny and examination.[147] Omura has made some initial attempts to examine the techniques of applied kinesiology and EAV.[146,147] The significant diagnostic and therapeutic capabilities of EAV, which is performed transcutaneously, necessitate the consideration of this approach.[126,136,147,214–217] Voll considers the optimal therapeutic points to be at the beginning and end of the meridians (hands, feet, and head). This is similar to the Ryodoraku approach of Nakatani.[126,152]

The bioenergetic explanation of Voll seems to correspond in part to what is termed psychotronic or bioplasmic energy. Such energy is supposedly able to be recorded and photographed by a process known as Kirlian photography. Kirlian photography has been used to study the aura of living things.[121,123,224,225] The flares seen in Kirlian photographs of the body have been thought to be emitted from acupuncture points.[226] The primary research and development of this method of producing photographs from high-frequency current were performed in Russia.[121,123]

Bioplasmic energy is thought to be transported by the meridian system. The avenue by which this energy is exchanged between the body and the external environment is considered to be the acupuncture point. Such concepts of energy flow as related to life and the practice of medicine have also been conceived by other cultures. The Indians called this energy "Prana" or "Kundalini" and the Chinese, "Chi."[121,225] Directly related to the approach of Voll and Nakatani is that originated by Nogier of France, who developed the technique of auriculotherapy, which is based on the testing and treatment of ear points.[126] There is considered to be a representative point on the ear for each body part and organ mapped out on an inverted fetus. The clinical effectiveness of this technique in relieving pain and in diagnosis has recently been shown to be quite impressive.[227,228] The six major meridians all are seen to merge at the ear, which is highly innervated by cranial nerves as well as nerves from the superior cervical plexus.[229]

The work of Becker corresponds to many of the above theories.[230–234] Becker presents evidence of a primitive communication system that carries signals possibly related to pain and self-healing mechanisms. The perineural or Schwann cells on the myelin sheath supposedly transmit low-intensity direct current impulses along the path of least resistance, which are amplified at various points along the nerve. Becker theorized that these points of amplification are acupuncture loci since they coincide anatomically to well-known acupuncture points. Perhaps the corpuscles of Bong Han actually are the Schwann cells. Experimental evidence has shown that tissue regeneration and bone healing are delayed if nerve innervation to the damaged area is interrupted at the time of injury.[169] Becker has used extremely low-amperage currents to grow new bone. Transmission of impulses along this system can occur even though the internal axons are not intact, since conduction is mediated via the myelin sheath.[230–233]

It is imperative to state that the previous discussion of theoretical concepts has a distinct purpose and is not just an attempt to explain some of the actions of pain-modulating methodologies. Theories give rise to interest that results in questions leading to research and the ultimate development of scientifically proven techniques. Perhaps the clearest example of such a process occurred after the publication of Melzack and Wall's gate control theory of pain in 1965.[52]

In 1975, we witnessed the most recent scientific advance in the field of pain research, the isolation of endogenous morphine-like compounds—enkephalins and endorphins. The discovery of these natural pain-modulating peptides answered a number of questions pertaining to the effects of acupuncture and invasive and noninvasive electrical stimulation. Pain modulation that results from stimulation of segmentally unrelated areas may also be explained by a release of endorphins. The substantia gelatinosa region in the dorsal horn of the spinal cord, trigeminal nucleus, and the thalamus contain a high density of opiate receptor sites.[240,249] These three regions have been implicated as being gating or modulating areas for pain impulses. (See Chapters 3 and 12.) The fact that each spinal cord segment contains a substantia gelatinosa region could account for the binding of endorphins to opiate receptor sites at any segmental level. Presently, only strong, low-rate and high-intensity, pulse-train (burst) modes have resulted in actual endorphin release, as has invasive stimulation of brainstem regions.[186,195,196,198,250-252] Recent experiments with somatosensory evoked responses may yet provide the answers and neurophysiologic rationale for pain relief that occurs with stimulation of segmentally unrelated sites.[270,271]

THE FACILITATED SEGMENT

The basis behind the placement of electrodes on tender areas can also be supported by a concept known as the facilitated segment.[162,253-255] The facilitated segment is an excellent means of summarizing all the information previously discussed pertaining to the anatomic relationship between the autonomic and central nervous systems, referred pain mechanisms, specific point similarities, and viscerosomatic reflexes.

A facilitated segment is considered to be a segment with a decreased motor threshold

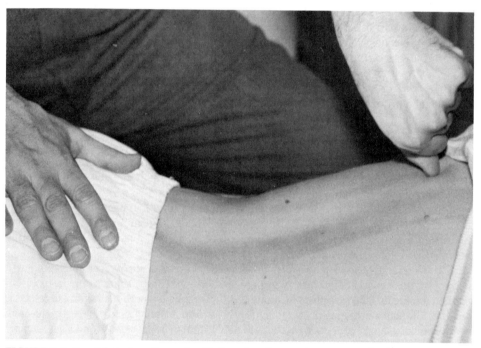

FIGURE 8-9. Scratch test performed with thumbnail over the paravertebral area. Normally, a solid line of erythema should develop within 30 seconds. An area of unilateral or bilateral skin blanching could be related to an underlying joint dysfunction resulting in vasomotor disturbances. Another means of assessment specifically to elicit areas of sweating is to lightly run the volar (distal phalanx) surfaces of the index and middle fingers parallel to the spine. If an area of moisture (sweating) is encountered, the finger will jump slightly as the smooth glide is interrupted. This may need to be repeated a few times and may be totally misleading on a hot or humid day.

CLINICAL T.E.N.S.

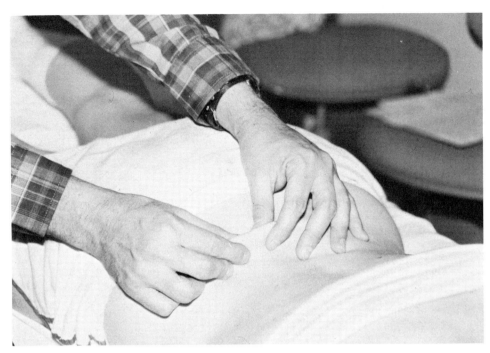

FIGURE 8-10. Skin rolling test optimally applied on each side of the spine as well as centrally over the spinous processes. The skin normally can be lifted and rolled painlessly. Skin rolling that is painful, is difficult to lift (boggy or fibrotic), or illustrates the peau d'orange effect may be indicative of trophic disturbances from chronic joint dysfunction.

due to sustained nociceptive afferent input.[162] Pathology, injury, or dysfunction involving cutaneous, visceral, musculotendinous, ligamental, arthrodial, circulatory, or neural structures is the precipitating factor that leads to such facilitation. Figures 8-9 to 8-16 illustrate manual tests the clinician can perform to evaluate skin, muscle, joint, and superficial peripheral nerve regions to determine anatomically related areas of tenderness or hyperalgesia occurring as a result of segmental facilitation.[90,92,93,256]

A facilitated segment can be created by experimental means. Denslow and Korr have used heel lifts to produce postural changes, resulting in facilitation of segments receiving increased afferent input as a result of paraspinal muscle tension.[163,164,257] The injection of hypertonic saline solution into the C5 segment has produced anginal spasm and characteristics similar to those that occur after a myocardial infarction.[253] Injection into the L1 segment resulted in signs synonymous with renal colic and elicited a cremasteric reflex.

The early work of Denslow and Korr led to usage of the term "facilitated segment."[163,164,166,254,255,257] This was equated with the work of MacKenzie, who coined the term "irritable focus." In addition, the features of an osteopathic lesion relate to that described as a facilitated segment.[162] An osteopathic lesion of an intervertebral joint and adjacent vertebrae exhibits hypomobility or hypermobility, positional faults, pain and tenderness, muscular tension, reflex changes in skin and muscle, and vasomotor and visceromotor changes.[162,166]

Physiologically abnormal (noxious) afferent inputs enter the dorsal horn of the spinal cord and synapse on neurons, creating what has been termed an irritable focus, increased central excitatory state, or area of excitation. Axons of neurons receiving afferent input can

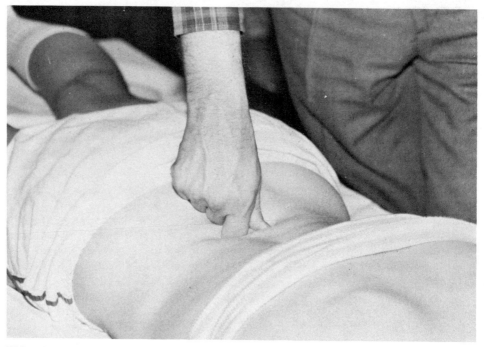

FIGURE 8-11. Spring test of individual vertebral segments. This is optimally perfomed via a short, quick thrust or oscillation (posterior-anterior glide) of the pisiform bone over the spinous process or between the flexed PIP joint of the index finger and the thumb. Vertebral springing is normally painless. Localized segmental discomfort may be indicative of simple joint dysfunction. Discomfort that results in pain referral could signify possible nerve root irritation as a result of intervertebral disk herniation.

synapse with efferent neurons of anterior horn cells, thus producing motor as well as sympathetic activity primarily in segmentally related peripheral nerves, blood vessels, sweat glands, and visceral organs.

In nonpathologic states, dorsal horn neurons do not receive sustained noxious input and thus exhibit a high reflex threshold. Segmentally related structures will then manifest normal palpable texture, no hyperalgesia, high skin resistance, and no prolonged discomfort as a result of minor trauma (percussion, oscillation, or springing of vertebral segments).[166] The existence of a facilitated segment results in a decrease in the threshold required to excite effector mechanisms. Thus non-noxious afferent input may result in discomfort. Korr believes that there is some subthreshold bombardment of motor neurons that contributes to their hyperresponsiveness and hyperirritability.[253] Denslow and Korr have demonstrated contraction of paraspinal musculature as a result of pressure on the spinous processes.[255] In normal individuals, 7 kg of pressure on the spinous processes was needed to cause paraspinal muscle contraction. However, in the presence of pathology, only 3 to 4 kg was required, and at times 1 to 2 kg initiated contraction. Facilitation also seemed to spread bilaterally more toward the cephalic region than the caudal region.

Along with motoneuron facilitation, the segmentally related cutaneous areas demonstrated hyperesthesia as well as a doughy and boggy texture or resiliency best seen with skin rolling.[253,255] Gunn has also demonstrated similar trophic changes and motor point tenderness.[89,90,256]

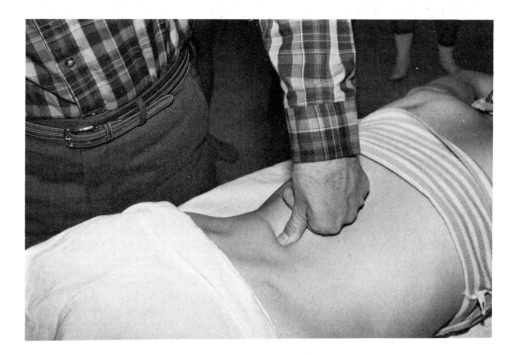

FIGURE 8-12. Deep palpation between the transverse processes. This test is used to determine tenderness of erector spinae motor points, which correspond exactly to the location of
bladder meridian acupuncture points and underlying trigger points of deeper paraspinal
musculature. Palpation should be performed bilaterally and rechecked at least twice to rule
out misinterpretation.

Korr and Coote state that segmental facilitation extends to cells of the intermediolateral column.[163,258] The sympathetic and cutaneous dermatomes do not always coincide,
which gives rise to segmental differences between low skin resistance areas and regions of
decreased motor reflex thresholds. The explanation for the production of low-resistance
areas (LRA) is related to sympathetic activity. Facilitation will also involve preganglionic
sympathetic neurons.[163,258] Koizumi and Korr state that somatic responses always produce
concomitant autonomic nervous system responses.[34,253] They call such a response a somatosympathetic reflex. The somatic component of this reflex is segmental, but a widespread
and generalized autonomic response can occur as a result of supraspinal action.

Koizumi[34] and Sota[36] have demonstrated somatosympathetic reflex responses in the
cat and rat. Cutaneous excitation was performed to evoke changes in blood pressure, heart
rate, bladder function, and gastric and duodenal motility. Noxious pinch of the abdominal
skin sufficient to excite the whole spectrum of afferent nerve fibers resulted in a segmental
activation of sympathetic preganglionic and postganglionic neurons. This resulted in an
inhibition of intestinal motility due to a dampening of sympathetic innervation. The supraspinal effect occurred as a result of stimulation of cutaneous areas of the neck, chest,
forelimb, and hindlimb, which are not segmentally related to the intestinal viscera. Stimulation was again noxious and resulted in ascending input to the higher centers. The result
of this supraspinal stimulation was an inhibition of sympathetic preganglionic neurons due
to a descending postganglionic sympathetic discharge producing an increase in intestinal
motility. Cutaneous areas of low skin resistance have been observed in patients with vis-

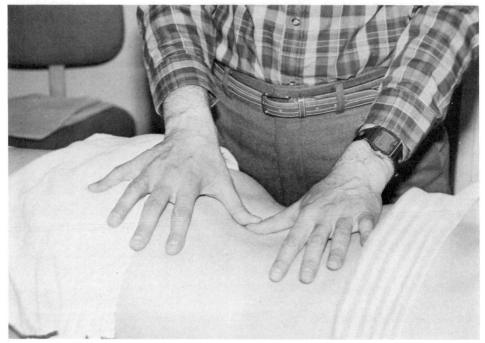

FIGURE 8-13. Transverse oscillation of vertebral segments. This test is performed by placing one thumb over the other, spreading the fingers apart. Pressure is applied lateral to the spinous process via an oscillatory pressure-relax technique. The test should be performed bilaterally and is helpful in determining not only the level of dysfunction but also, if apparent, its laterality. The gentle oscillation should normally be painless.

ceral disease. Selzer and Spencer have demonstrated experimentally the interaction between cutaneous and visceral stimuli.[30,31] These LRA were segmentally related to the involved organ and seem to be consistent in similar disease entities.[164,259] This fact may, in part, support the work of Voll. Patients who have had myocardial infarctions demonstrated LRA over two or more of the upper four thoracic vertebrae. LRA were found near the sternum (Chapman's reflexes) at corresponding rib levels as well as the vertebral borders of the scapula in the same dermatome. In one patient, such LRA were observed three weeks before the onset of the infarction.[165,184]

Similar development of LRA has also been observed in patients with duodenal ulcers. LRA in such visceral conditions coincided with points exhibiting the greatest degree of pain and tenderness to palpation. Improvement in the related pathology resulted in a concomitant increase in skin resistance.[165]

It is known that dendrites from lamina 5 neurons ascend into laminae 1 and 2 where they can synapse with neurons in the tract of Lissauer.[260] Neurons in the substantia gelatinosa also descend into lamina 5, whose cells send axons to higher centers, resulting in the appreciation and localization of pain.[258,261] Lissauer's tract can result in the spread of afferent input extrasegmentally. This proces could account for nonsegmental effects of the facilitated segment, as does sympathetic involvement. Travell, in her extensive work on trigger point referral mechanisms, has demonstrated that referred pain does not always follow a segmental distribution.[64]

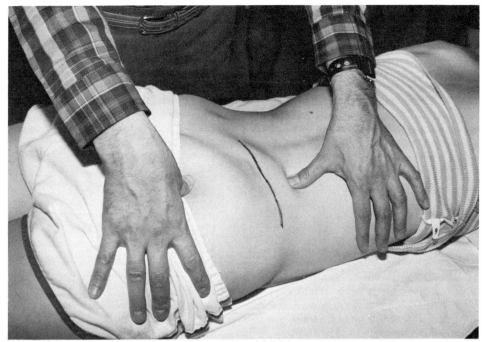

FIGURE 8-14. Palpation to determine tenderness of peripheral motor points. The black line delineates the iliac crest. Deep tenderness that exists above the iliac crest may signify dysfunction of the low thoracic or upper lumbar spine (quadratus lumborum, iliocostalis lumborum). Tenderness existing below the iliac crest may be indicative of low lumbar dysfunction (gluteals). This test can thus be used to correlate spinal dysfunction with tenderness in segmentally related (innervated) musculature.

The most reliable and consistent changes in skin impedance produced as a result of segmental facilitation occur along the spine.[162] Concomitant with decreased skin impedance is hyperesthesia. Glover noted this in a series of patients with low back pain.[95] Stoddard is of the opinion that a majority of adults eventually develop one or more facilitated segments in the spine that may persist for months or years, usually as a result of postural deformities. This is very evident in patients with dowager's humps due to a prolonged forward head and round shoulder posture. The resultant cervicothoracic kyphosis places a constant stretch upon the interspinous ligaments and produces joint dysfunction. Patients who manifest this abnormality demonstrate a decreased threshold to vertebral spring tests, skin rolling, palpation, and joint mobility.

Decreased skin impedance is considered to result from increased secretory activity due to sympathetic stimulation. Sweating (non-noxious stimuli) may serve to perpetuate segmental facilitation and maintain the decreased motor reflex threshold.[35] Studies of skin impedance changes as a means of evaluating pain and dysfunction can provide worthwhile information.[164-165]

Any prolonged or repetitive afferent stimulus may produce a facilitated segment. Regardless of the use of palpation, mobility testing, or evaluation of electrical skin resistance to locate acupuncture, motor, or trigger points, the clinician in reality is searching for the facilitated segment. The segmental location of the LRA or tender point provides valuable

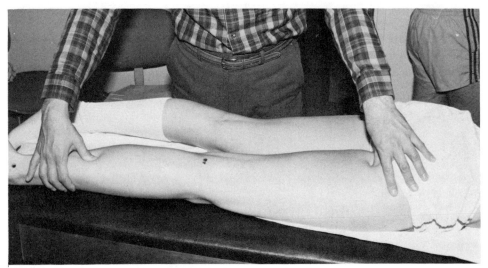

FIGURE 8-15. Palpation of superficial aspects of peripheral nerves. Pressure is being applied at superficial aspects of the sciatic nerve (BL 50) and sural nerve (BL 57). Location of the exact point exhibiting the greatest degree of tenderness within the pain distribution signifies the optimal electrode placement site. The black marker depicts the popliteal space, which is another area that should be palpated in the presence of referred sciatic pain.

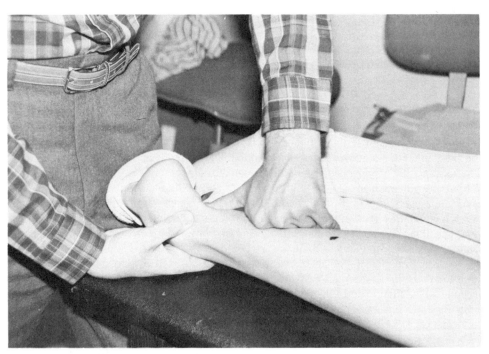

FIGURE 8-16. Palpation of superficial aspects of peripheral nerves. Pressure is being applied at superficial aspects of the sural and posterior tibial nerves, lateral malleolus and heelcord (B 60), and medial malleolus and heelcord (K 3), respectively. The black marker depicts the superior superficial aspect of the sural nerve.

CLINICAL T.E.N.S.

FACILITATED SEGMENT

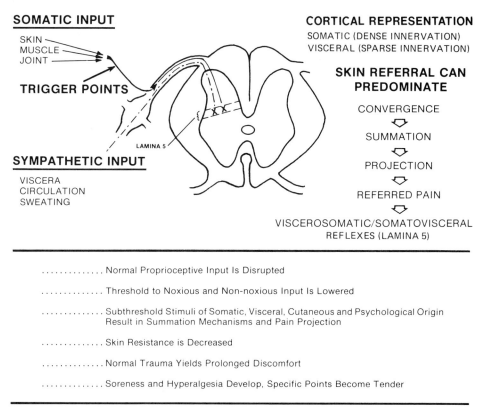

SOMATIC INPUT

SKIN
MUSCLE
JOINT

TRIGGER POINTS

LAMINA 5

SYMPATHETIC INPUT

VISCERA
CIRCULATION
SWEATING

CORTICAL REPRESENTATION
SOMATIC (DENSE INNERVATION)
VISCERAL (SPARSE INNERVATION)

SKIN REFERRAL CAN PREDOMINATE

CONVERGENCE
⇩
SUMMATION
⇩
PROJECTION
⇩
REFERRED PAIN
⇩
VISCEROSOMATIC/SOMATOVISCERAL
REFLEXES (LAMINA 5)

. . . . Normal Proprioceptive Input Is Disrupted

. . . . Threshold to Noxious and Non-noxious Input Is Lowered

. . . . Subthreshold Stimuli of Somatic, Visceral, Cutaneous and Psychological Origin
Result in Summation Mechanisms and Pain Projection

. . . . Skin Resistance is Decreased

. . . . Normal Trauma Yields Prolonged Discomfort

. . . . Soreness and Hyperalgesia Develop, Specific Points Become Tender

FIGURE 8-17. Disruption of the normal excitation threshold of a vertebral segment by abnormal physiologic input and the resultant objective and subjective changes that occur.

information as to the possible level of the spinal lesion or diseased viscus. This, however, should constitute only one part of a thorough clarifying evaluation of the patient. Voll, Nogier, and others feel that definitive diagnoses and treatment can be performed solely by the use of skin impedance scanners and concomitant electrical stimulation.

Figure 8-17 presents the factors relating to the production of the facilitated segment and resultant physiologic disturbances. A proper evaluation by the clinician should include procedures to localize the existence of one or more facilitated segments, which can provide objective means to determine proper electrode placement with T.E.N.S.

OPTIMAL STIMULATION SITES (OSS) FOR T.E.N.S. ELECTRODES: METHODS OF LOCATION

The decision as to which stimulation sites to use is dependent upon the actual pathology as well as the location and character of the pain, as described in Chapter 5. It is well known that the surface of the skin is densely innervated. This accounts for a fairly good degree of success when electrodes are merely placed at or around the painful region. However, stimulation at an area that is segmentally related to the involved structure or painful region should be more effective. The lack of success with T.E.N.S. can be dramatically improved by the selection of optimal stimulation sites (OSS).

The use of noninvasive as opposed to invasive stimulation limits the choice of electrode sites to the spinal column (paraspinally between the transverse processes), superficial aspects of peripheral nerves, and acupuncture, motor, or trigger points.

In order for an area of the body to be labeled as an OSS, the following criteria must be met:

1. A region where stimulation can be directed into the CNS.
2. A region easily accessible to a T.E.N.S. electrode. This eliminates most bony prominences and areas primarily covered with hair that may be only accessible to a needle or probe.
3. An area that is segmentally related to the source of pain.
4. An anatomic site that can distinctly be located. Further delineation as to an OSS requires that two or more of the five acceptable anatomic entities exist at the same location.

Figures of OSS at the end of the chapter consist of separate views of body regions showing anatomic landmarks, distribution of peripheral nerves, superficial cutaneous branches, acupuncture meridians, and motor, trigger and acupuncture points. The OSS are depicted by the following marks: triangle, acupuncture point; circle, motor point; and square, trigger point. An OSS at which all three points occur is depicted as a combination of the three marks. On some views, only a part of a meridian is shown because its remaining portion may not relate to the specific region. Tables at the end of the chapter list OSS for major joints, major peripheral nerves, and acupuncture meridians. The innervation of each OSS by spinal cord segments (C1–T1 and L1–S4) are presented in the last two tables. (All these figures and tables appear at the end of this chapter.)

Each OSS is characterized as overlying a superficial aspect or cutaneous branch of at least one peripheral nerve. In addition, one or more acupuncture points are situated at regions along the superficial distributions of the various peripheral nerves. The number of existing acupuncture points is much greater than the combined amount of motor and trigger points.[115–118] Thus, even though each OSS manifests itself as overlying a superficial nerve branch and also as an acupuncture point, motor and/or trigger points may also be found at some but not all of the selected locations. Since each OSS contains at least one acupuncture point, the internationally accepted classification and numbering system of acupuncture has been used.[115–118]

Dermatomes have not been included since the exact cutaneous innervation of each selected stimulation site by spinal segmental levels is given. If a specific stimulation site possesses a motor point, motor innervation via segmental levels is noted. It should also be noted that not all acupuncture meridians correspond to the dermatomal distributions of the respective parts of the body through which they course.[117]

The anterior trunk has not been included because of its almost pure segmental distribution.[1–3] However, intercostal regions that become tender to palpation in the presence of related pathology reflect the location of the intercostal nerves plus the anterior and lateral cutaneous branches of the thoracic nerves.[1–3,262] The stomach and kidney meridians course through this region, and related acupuncture points exist in the intercostal spaces approximately 1 and 2 inches lateral to the midline.[115–118] Acupuncture points on the anterior trunk and back correspond to the segmental reference of deep pain.[117] Intercostal and paraspinal placement at segmental levels above and below and/or medial and lateral to an area of discomfort from conditions, such as post-herpetic neuralgia, emphysema, rib fractures, or postoperatively, is extremely effective. Bilateral placement may provide even greater effectiveness.[263]

OSS at which motor points and/or a superficial aspect of a major mixed peripheral nerve exist may prove to be the best areas at which to stimulate when performing strong, low-rate or high-intensity pulse-train (burst) T.E.N.S. (see Chapters 9 and 12).[128,185,186,190,191,193–198,202,264] The strong, visible muscle contractions in segmentally related myotomes required with these stimulation modes may prove beneficial in more severe pain syndromes or when conventional T.E.N.S. is not effective. If these stronger variations of T.E.N.S. cannot be tolerated in the painful region, stimulation of nonpainful muscles within other remote but related myotomes may be beneficial. The choice of OSS, therefore, depends not only on the distribution of pain but also on the specific stimulation mode to be used. A change in the stimulation mode for a specific area of pain may also require use of different stimulation sites.

When using the conventional; low-intensity, pulse-train (burst); or brief, intense modes, the choice of OSS must ensure that perception of the electrical paresthesia is throughout the entire area of pain (see Chapters 9 and 12 for more details). Electrodes should be placed at the proximal and distal extents of the pain. If pain originates from the spine (referred pain), at least one electrode should be placed at the appropriate posterior primary ramus and the others at superficial aspects of the peripheral nerve innervating the painful region.

The use of brief, intense T.E.N.S. to allow for sufficient analgesia to perform skin debridement, suture removal, or transverse friction massage must use OSS that produce a tetanic contraction. These procedures will then be unhampered by movement of the involved body part. The OSS chosen should be motor points or should overlie superficial aspects of the mixed nerve innervating the area of pain. When joint mobilization or contract-relax stretching is to be performed with ongoing brief, intense T.E.N.S., OSS should be chosen that do not result in tetany but merely produce nonrhythmic fasciculations of the related musculature. Electrodes should then be placed on superficial aspects of cutaneous (sensory) nerves. OSS that are close to the area of pain are recommended.

The following guidelines are suggested as a means of locating those optimal stimulation sites that may be most beneficial for a particular pain distribution and stimulation mode.

Specific Guidelines To Optimal Stimulation Site Selection
1. Delineate the nature, location, and structural source of pain.
2. Determine the spinal cord and segmental levels that innervate the involved structure (joint, muscle, peripheral nerve, etc.) or region of pain.
3. Utilize the illustrations and related tables to initially locate optimal stimulation sites (OSS) that are anatomically and/or physiologically related to the involved structure or area of pain.
4. Palpate for tenderness or scan for increased electrical conductance (decreased skin resistance) those OSS that exist within, adjacent to, or which innervate the area of pain.
5. The choice of OSS and electrode placement arrangements depends upon the specific stimulation mode to be utilized as well as the pain distribution.
   a. When conventional, low-intensity pulse-train (burst) or brief, intense modes are utilized, electrode placement must ensure the perception of electrical paresthesia throughout the entire area of pain (use OSS at related spinal cord segments and over superficial aspects of the peripheral nerves that arise from them).
5. b. Strong, low-rate and high-intensity, pulse-train (burst) modes require muscle contraction of segmentally related myotomes, which may or may not be located away from the painful region (use OSS that are motor points and/or located over superficial aspects of mixed nerves innervating the painful region).
   c. It may be necessary to stimulate bilaterally in a criss-cross manner, contralaterally, or only proximal to the painful region in specific pain syndromes such as bilateral low back

pain, post-herpetic neuralgia, or peripheral nerve injury, respectively, in order to obtain greater benefit.

6. Electrodes of varying sizes and shapes may also need to be utilized.

The following are examples of how these guidelines should be used. The numbered statements following each example correspond to the numbered guideline.

Examples

A. Patient complaining of knee joint pain.
   1. Chronic pain secondary to rheumatoid arthritis exists anteriorly from the region of the vastus lateralis and medialis to the level of the fibular head.
   2. The knee joint is innervated by the spinal cord segments L 2, L 3, and L 4.
   3. OSS ST 33–36, extra 31, 32, and 34, SP 9–10, LIV 8, and K 10 are all present at the painful region and are segmentally related to the knee (L 2, L 3, and L 4).
   4. ST 34, SP 9, SP 10, and E 34 exhibit the greatest degree of tenderness to palpation.
   5a. ST 34 and SP 9 are coupled for one channel, and SP 10 plus E 34 are coupled for the second channel, providing for a criss-cross method over the knee using the conventional stimulation mode.
B. Patient with acute low back pain and lower extremity referral.
   1. Pain secondary to a left L5–S1 posterolateral disk herniation; patient has a sciatic scoliosis to the right. Pain exists primarily in the left lumbosacral region with a constant paresthesia down the posterior aspect of the left leg through the buttock to just above the lateral malleolus.
   2. Region is innervated by the spinal cord segments L4–S2.
   3. OSS B 25, B 26 (erector spinae motor points), B 27, B 48, B 49, B 50, B 53, B 54, B 57, and B 60 exist throughout the area of pain, proximal to distal, and are all segmentally related to the involved region as they are innervated by one or more distributions of the sciatic nerve (L4–S2).
   4. B 26, B 50, B 53–54, and B 60 exhibit the greatest degree of tenderness to palpation.
   5. B 26 and B 50 are coupled for one channel, and B 53–54 and B 60 constitute the second channel. Electrodes placed about 1 inch above or below the popliteal space can provide equal effectiveness. The OSS chosen in this case may not allow for perception of the electrical paresthesia with conventional T.E.N.S. between B 50 and the popliteal space. An alternate arrangement would be to cross-couple the channels (B 26 to the popliteal space and B 50 to B 60). This would, however, require an increase in amplitude and/or pulse-duration due to the increased interelectrode distance.
C. Patient with forearm pain.
   1. Pain is secondary to a fracture of the radius and is characterized as a constant burning sensation in the brachioradialis region to the thumb and index finger.
   2. Pain is distributed through the C6 dermatome and involves the spinal cord segments C5–T1.
   3. OSS LI 11, LI 10, LI 6, and LI 4 are present proximal to, within, and distal to the painful region and are segmentally related to the source of pain (C5–T1).
   4. LI 11 and LI 4 exhibit the greatest degree of tenderness to palpation.
   5. LI 11 and LI 4 are coupled for one channel, using the conventional stimulation mode. However, the patient does not perceive any electrical sensation under the

electrode at the LI 4 OSS unless amplitude or pulse duration is significantly increased, producing tetany.

6. Electrodes of unequal size are thus used, with the smaller placed at the LI 4 site, producing a greater current density with less energy, thus ensuring perception of paresthesia without muscle tetany.

D. Patient with cervical spine pain.

1. Pain is secondary to an auto accident resulting in a cervical strain. Constant muscular ache exists in the suboccipital region (splenius capitis muscles, C2–4), the upper trapezius bilaterally and distally to the upper thoracic spine.
2. Upper trapezius muscles are innervated by C3–4.
3. OSS GB 20, GB 21, B 10, SI 15, and SI 14 exist throughout the painful region and are all segmentally related to the involved structure.
4. All of the above OSS are extremely tender to palpation.
5. OSS B 20 and B 21 are coupled, using both a right and a left channel. This arrangement, however, may produce uncomfortable fasciculations of the upper trapezius muscles since the current of each channel is running throughout the muscle. An alternative approach would be to use the criss-cross method, B 20 on the right to SI 15 or SI 14 on the left, and a second channel in the opposite fashion. This method would allow for perception of the electrical paresthesia throughout the distribution of pain (conventional T.E.N.S.) and eliminate upper trapezius fasciculation.

E. Patient with chronic low back pain persisting after two surgical procedures.

1. Pain is described as a relatively constant deep ache present from the L4 to S2 (upper buttock) levels bilaterally.
2. The involved region is innervated by descending cutaneous fibers from the upper lumbar spine as well as L4 and S2 ventral rami.
3. OSS B 25–28, B 31–32, B 48, and B 49 exist within the area of pain and are segmentally related to the involved region.
4. All of the above sites except B 49 are equally tender to palpation.
5a. The conventional mode is used, employing a criss-cross channel arrangement from B 25 on the right to B 48 on the left and the opposite for the other channel. However, this does not provide the patient with sufficient pain relief or long-lasting benefit.
5b. The strong, low-rate mode is then used with the same electrode placement sites; however, this is not tolerated well by the patient due to discomfort from the ongoing muscle contraction. Electrodes are then placed at segmentally related OSS that are *not* within the pain distribution. B 53–54 and K 3 are used to provide for rhythmic muscle contractions of both gastrocnemius-soleus groups. These OSS ensure that stimulation is provided bilaterally to the posterior tibial nerves, which innervate the calf musculature. The posterior tibial nerve is a branch of the sciatic that originates from the L4–S2 spinal cord segments and is thus segmentally related to the painful region and allows for an ascending input to the dorsal horn of the L4–S2 segments via the sciatic nerve.

F. Patient with bilateral low back pain, secondary to an intervertebral disk herniation and unilateral sciatic pain.

1. Pain is described as an ache across the low back at the lumbosacral junction that is referred down the sciatic distribution of the right leg to the calf.
2. The involved region is innervated by the L4–S2 segments giving rise to the sciatic nerve.
3. OSS B 26–28, B 31, B 32, B 48–50, B 53–54, B 57, and B 60 exist proximal to, within, and distal to the distribution of the pain and are all segmentally related.

4. B 26 bilaterally, B 50, B 53–54, and B 57 exhibit the greatest degree of palpable tenderness.

5a. Electrodes are placed bilaterally at the B 26 site to form one channel, with a second channel consisting of B 50 and B 57 on the right leg. This provides for satisfactory paresthesia at both areas but does not produce long-lasting pain relief.

5b. Simultaneous multimodal stimulation is then provided with a T.E.N.S. unit capable of allowing for conventional T.E.N.S. at one channel and strong, low-rate T.E.N.S. at the other. Conventional T.E.N.S. is applied to the low back with the same arrangement described above. Strong, low-rate T.E.N.S. is tried simultaneously to the right leg with electrodes at the popliteal space and K 3. However, the patient is unable to tolerate prolonged rhythmic muscle contractions of the painful right calf. Strong, low-rate T.E.N.S. would then be given to the same sites on the contralateral extremity.

G. Patient with shoulder pain due to a subdeltoid bursitis that has led to adhesive capsulitis.

1. Pain is described as a low-grade ache that increases on active or passive movement of the glenohumeral and acromioclavicular joints. Pain exists primarily about the shoulder but is referred down the C5–6 dermomyotome when capsular and soft-tissue stretching occurs.

2. The involved region is innervated by the C3–6 spinal cord segments.

3. OSS LI 16, LI 15, LI 14, LI 11, LI 10, LI 6, LI 4, and TW 14 exist within the pain distribution.

4. Significant tenderness to palpation and decreased skin resistance are evident at all OSS but to a lesser degree at sites below the elbow.

5a. The goal is to obtain some degree of pain control during performance of gentle joint mobilization and contract-relax stretching to increase ROM using the brief, intense stimulation mode. When this mode is used, electrode placement as close as possible to the area of pain is recommended. In this instance, we do not want to cause muscle tetany, as that will prevent the desired procedures from being performed. Our choice of electrode placement sites and channel arrangements in this specific instance would consist of one electrode at LI 16 and the other of the same channel at LI 14. A second channel would consist of electrodes at the TW 15 and LI 15 sites. This dual-channel arrangement would allow for effective paresthesia throughout the shoulder complex without tetany since the chosen OSS do not overlie superficial aspects of a mixed peripheral nerve but only cutaneous (sensory) distributions. Analgesia could be enhanced in this example by stimulation with a noninvasive electroacupuncture device prior to the treatment procedure. To accomplish this, we would stimulate all the OSS listed in guideline 3, starting distally and progressing proximally. In addition, we would stimulate at related spinal cord segments paraspinally and possibly use appropriate auriculotherapy points as well. Each OSS would be stimulated for 30 to 60 seconds at a rate of 4 Hz with amplitude to tolerance. This is also known as brief, intense hyperstimulation analgesia and is discussed in Chapter 12.

Each segmental nerve is composed of motor, sensory, and autonomic fibers. Thus, electrode placement at OSS that also possess motor points will probably provide for stronger stimulation since the stimulus will be conducted through a greater number of nerve fibers entering the spinal cord at several segments (sensory plus motor innervation). The stronger and more widespread stimulation obtained with strong, low-rate and high-intensity, pulse-train (burst) T.E.N.S. may in part help to explain the liberation of endogenous opiates that has been shown to occur with these methods.[186,190,191,195,196,198]

Electrical probes and to some degree palpation are valuable but can be misleading. Continued pressure, rubbing, scratching, or rolling friction over the region being scanned can lead to erythema or histamine reaction.[167] This can have the net effect of producing areas of decreased electrical resistance or tenderness through the region being evaluated that may not actually be an OSS.[117,130] A recent investigation by McCarroll and Rowley determined that the stratum corneum layer of the epidermis primarily determines the degree of skin impedance.[167] Standard probes used for point location were found small enough to produce a sufficient force per square millimeter to alter the stratum corneum layer and dramatically decrease skin impedance.

The difference in impedance at acupuncture points has been reported as within one half to one twentieth of the impedance of the surrounding cutaneous region. A tear or penetration in the stratum corneum produced a decrease in skin impedance at the point by 94 percent. McCarroll and Rowley concluded that electrical location of acupuncture points was not an acceptable method because of the large fluctuation in impedance depending on how the probe was used. It is therefore imperative that the clinician have sufficient anatomic knowledge to delineate the area of search so that simple finger pressure or brief electrical scanning can detect an optimal stimulation site.[86,89] Exact placement of the electrode may be necessary when using needles or probes but is not so with T.E.N.S. The average T.E.N.S. electrode provides stimulation to a larger surface area, and current will flow to the region of least resistance under the electrode placed in the general location.

Specific formulas of stimulation sites for various pain syndromes have not been included since each patient or pain syndrome does not represent the exact same clinical picture continually. Pain syndromes frequently manifest themselves by varying degrees of severity that change the distribution of the pain and thus require varied electrode placements. Further substantiation for this can be justified by the low success rate with T.E.N.S. when performed by nonprofessionals who lack the required background in anatomy, physiology, and pathology. Professionals who attempt to treat without first performing a thorough clarifying evaluation and merely refer to a text containing recommended formulas for all patients with the same condition may also experience poor results.

The benefit from and successful use of T.E.N.S. require the clinician to be prepared to spend time with the patient and try various electrode placements and techniques. In many cases, after a thorough clarifying evaluation, immediate pain modulation can be obtained with T.E.N.S. merely by placing electrodes at, near, or within the painful region without having to resort to greater specificity.[263]

NONINVASIVE ELECTROACUPUNCTURE

Surface electrical stimulation can also be performed by using hand-held electrical probes. Electrical stimulators that incorporate this treatment approach usually are designated "point finders." The unit is capable of locating the precise low-resistance stimulation sites and, when they are found, activates a light or sound. Stimulation is then performed through the probe, noninvasively, without attaching a T.E.N.S. electrode or using transmission gel.

Our experience with this means of pain modulation has been very positive. The units usually have adjustable frequency and amplitude controls to vary the stimulation mode. The extremely small-diameter probe allows for the use of microamperes of current (greater current density under electrode) as opposed to milliamperes with the common portable T.E.N.S. units. We have found that a rate of 4 Hz for a 60-second stimulation period is tolerated best at various stimulation sites to provide the longest lasting and most profound degree of analgesia. We usually stimulate about 12 sites (peripheral and spinal) unilaterally or bilaterally depending on the location and area of pain. Pain relief can be quite rapid, sometimes occurring after stimulation of the third site, or relief may not occur until 30 to 60 minutes after stimulation. The best results occur with the amplitude to patient tolerance, which is somewhat uncomfortable. We therefore stimulate OSS distal to the source of pain prior to stimulation of the painful region. The patient develops an initial tolerance to the noxious sensation at a nonpainful but frequently segmentally related site, which may also decrease discomfort in the involved region and promote patient relaxation. These devices also allow for stimulation of sites that are not conducive to the application of T.E.N.S. electrodes, such as the head, near or at bony prominences, and around the eye.

Our primary use of noninvasive electroacupuncture devices is to obtain pain control before or after a specific therapeutic procedure designed to correct the cause of the pain. Such procedures may be painful or not well tolerated due to hyperesthesia. Relief from discomfort and tolerance to the procedure are frequently obtained with T.E.N.S. or noninvasive electroacupuncture. When ongoing pain control is necessary, stimulation is given via surface electrodes during the procedure.

After treatment that may cause irritation, the frequent quick relief from pain with noninvasive electroacupuncture is justified so the patient can leave the clinic feeling comfortable. A few patients, however, are unable to tolerate the discomfort of noninvasive electroacupuncture therapy, and thus conventional T.E.N.S. is used.

SUMMARY

A neuroanatomic review was presented prior to an analysis of the relationship of optimal stimulation sites for T.E.N.S. electrodes. Explanations based on extensive anatomic and physiologic research have illustrated the connections and segmental relationship of the central to peripheral nervous system and subsequent innervation of skin, muscle, bone, and viscera.

Acupuncture, motor, and trigger points, along with superficial aspects of peripheral nerves and the intervertebral foramen, were shown to be excellent sites for placement of T.E.N.S. electrodes. An acupuncture point may merely be a term applied to a highly innervated (neural and circulatory) region that frequently overlies peripheral nerves at their superficial aspects and not a mystical point. Thus, stimulation of acupuncture points with T.E.N.S. electrodes is synonymous with transcutaneous peripheral nerve stimulation.

The method by which the clinician should determine electrode placement sites on a patient-to-patient basis is outlined and differs demonstrably from a cookbook approach. Pain quality and distribution differ from patient to patient, as well as during changes in the pathologic process, which necessitates adjustment of electrode placement sites and a change of stimulation modes.

The important role that manual techniques play in the performance of a comprehensive evaluation has been discussed in Chapter 5. Some of these same techniques must constitute a significant part of the evaluation to determine the location of optimal stimulation sites for T.E.N.S. The specific guidelines to optimal stimulation site (OSS) selection require the clinician to initially determine the nature, location, and structural source of pain. Furthermore, another important guideline is to evaluate by palpation or via electrical point finders those OSS that exhibit the greatest degree of tenderness or sensitivity. Such a definitive evaluation is not always required to determine the best stimulation sites, but when success is not initially apparent, this approach could make the difference. It is of prime importance to state that only the overall findings resulting from these manual tests should be used. The determination of an optimal stimulation site should not be made by a positive response of only one test. Many other tests can be used, and the clinician should rely on the whole emerging picture from a comprehensive evaluation, not the results of a single test.

REFERENCES

1. WARWICK, R AND WILLIAMS, PL: *Gray's Anatomy*, ed 35. WB Saunders, Philadelphia, 1973.
2. HAYMAKER, W AND WOODHALL, B: *Peripheral Nerve Injuries*, ed 2. WB Saunders, Philadelphia, 1953, p 1.
3. CHUSID, JG: *Correlative Neuroanatomy and Functional Neurology*, ed 16. Lange Medical Publications, Los Altos, Calif, 1976.
4. FARFAN, HF: *Mechanical Disorders of the Low Back*. Lea & Febiger, Philadelphia, 1973, p 2.
5. DICKE, E, SCHLIACK, H, AND WOLFF, A: *A Manual of Reflexive Therapy of the Connective Tissue*. Sidney S Simon, Scarsdale, NY, 1978, p 11.
6. KAPANDJI, IA: *The Physiology of the Joints*, Vol 3. Churchill Livingstone, London, 1974, p 120.
7. SUNDERLAND, S: *Anatomical perivertebral influences on the intervertebral foramen*. In GOLDSTEIN, M (ED): *The Research Status of Spinal Manipulative Therapy*. DHEW Publication No. (NIH) 76-998, Bethesda, Md, 1975, p 129.
8. SUNDERLAND, S: *Traumatized nerves, roots, and ganglia: Musculoskeletal factors and neuropathological consequences*. In KORR, IM (ED): *The Neurobiologic Mechanisms in Manipulative Therapy*. Plenum Press, New York, 1978, p 137.
9. SCHAUMBERG, HH AND SPENCER, PS: *Pathology of spinal root compression*. In GOLDSTEIN, M (ED): *The Research Status of Spinal Manipulative Therapy*. DHEW Publication No. (NIH) 76-998, Bethesda, Md, 1975, p 141.
10. BRADLEY, KC: *The anatomy of backache*. Aust NZ J Surg 44:227, 1974.
11. EDGAR, MA AND GHADIALLY, JA: *Innervation of the lumbar spine*. Clin Orthop 115:35, 1976.
12. MOONEY, V AND ROBERTSON, J: *The facet syndrome*. Clin Orthop 115:149, 1976.
13. PEDERSEN, HE, BLUNCK, CFJ, AND GARDNER, E: *The anatomy of lumbosacral posterior rami and meningeal branches of spinal nerves (sinuvertebral nerves)*. J Bone Joint Surg [Am] 38:377, 1956.
14. HICKEY, RFJ AND TREGONNING, GD: *Denervation of spinal facet joints for treatment of chronic low back pain*. NZ Med J 85:96, 1977.
15. CULBERSON, JL: *Origins of low back pain: The intervertebral foramen*. In KENT, B (ED): *Third International Seminar on Manual Therapy: Proceedings of the International Federation of Orthopaedic Manipulative Therapists*. International Federation of Orthopaedic Manipulative Therapists, Hayward, Calif, 1977, p 21.
16. MAIGNE, R: *Orthopedic Medicine: A New Approach to Vertebral Manipulations*. Charles C Thomas, Springfield, Ill, 1972, p 5.
17. FISK, JW: *The Painful Neck and Back*. Charles C Thomas, Springfield, Ill, 1977, p 15.
18. WHITE, AA AND PANJABI, MM: *Clinical Biomechanics of the Spine*. JB Lippincott, Philadelphia, 1978, p 277.
19. CLOWARD, RB: *Cervical diskography: A contribution to the etiology and mechanism of neck, shoulder and arm pain*. Ann Surg 150:1952, 1959.
20. CLOWARD, RB: *The clinical significance of the sinu-vertebral nerve of the cervical spine in relation to the cervical disc syndrome*. J Neurol Neurosurg Psychiatry 23:321, 1960.
21. WYKE, BD: *The neurological basis of thoracic spine pain*. Rheumatol Phys Med 10:356, 1967.
22. WYKE, BD: *Neurological aspects of back pain*. In JAYSON, M (ED): *The Lumbar Spine and Back Pain*. Grune & Stratton, New York, 1976.
23. BURKART, SL AND BERESFORD, WA: *The aging intervertebral disc*. Phys Ther 59:969, 1979.
24. LAMB, DW: *The neurology of spinal pain*. Phys Ther 59:971, 1979.
25. KESSLER, RM: *Acute symptomatic disc prolapse, clinical manifestations and therapeutic considerations*. Phys Ther 59:978, 1979.

26. PICK, TP AND HOWDEN, R: *Gray's Anatomy: The Classic Collector's Edition.* Bounty Books, New York, 1977, p 801.

27. GILLILAN, LA: *Clinical Aspects of the Autonomic Nervous System.* Little, Brown & Co, Boston, 1954.

28. EVERETT, NB: *Functional Neuroanatomy.* Lea & Febiger, Philadelphia, 1965, p 249.

29. POMERANZ, B, WALL, PD, AND WEBER, WV: *Cord cells responding to fine myelinated afferents from viscera, muscle and skin.* J Physiol (Lond) 199:511, 1968.

30. SELZER, M AND SPENCER, WA: *Convergence of visceral and cutaneous afferent pathways in the lumbar spinal cord.* Brain Res 14:331, 1969.

31. SELZER, M AND SPENCER, WA: *Interactions between visceral and cutaneous afferents in the spinal cord: Reciprocal primary afferent fiber depolarization.* Brain Res 14:349, 1969.

32. HANNINGTON-KIFF, JG: *Pain Relief.* JB Lippincott, Philadelphia, 1974, p 58.

33. APPENZELLER, O: *Somatoautonomic reflexology: Normal and abnormal.* In KORR, IM (ED): *The Neurobiologic Mechanisms in Manipulative Therapy.* Plenum Press, New York, 1978, p 179.

34. KOIZUMI, K: *Autonomic system reactions caused by excitation of somatic afferents: Study of cutaneo-intestinal reflex.* In KORR, IM (ED): *The Neurobiologic Mechanisms in Manipulative Therapy.* Plenum Press, New York, 1978, p 219.

35. KORR, IM: *Sustained sympathicotonia as a factor in disease.* In KORR, IM (ED): *The Neurobiologic Mechanisms in Manipulative Therapy.* Plenum Press, New York, 1978, p 229.

36. SATO, A: *The somatosympathetic reflexes: Their physiological and clinical significance.* In GOLDSTEIN, M (ED): *The Research Status of Spinal Manipulative Therapy.* DHEW Publication No. (NIH) 76-998, Bethesda, Md, 1975, pp 163–172.

37. DOOLEY, DM AND KASPRAK, M: *Modification of blood flow to the extremities by electrical stimulation of the nervous system.* South Med J 69:1309, 1976.

38. ABRAM, SE: *Increased sympathetic tone associated with transcutaneous electrical stimulation.* Anesthesiology 45:575, 1976.

39. ABRAM, SE, ASIDDAO, CB, AND REYNOLDS, AC: *Increased skin temperature during transcutaneous electrical stimulation.* Anesth Analg (Cleve) 59:22, 1980.

40. ROWLINGSON, J, CARRON, H, AND GOLDNER, R: *The effect of transcutaneous nerve stimulation on blood flow in normal extremities.* In *Pain Abstracts,* Vol 1. Second World Congress on Pain, International Association for the Study of Pain, Seattle, 1978, p 155.

41. IGNELZI, RJ, STERNBACH, RA, AND CALLAGHAN, M: *Somatosensory changes during transcutaneous electrical analgesia.* In BONICA, JJ AND ALBE-FESSARD, D (EDS): *Advances in Pain Research and Therapy,* Vol 1. Raven Press, New York, 1976, p 421.

42. EBERSOLD, MJ, LAWS, ER, AND ALBERS, JW: *Measurements of autonomic function before, during and after transcutaneous stimulation in patients with chronic pain and in control subjects.* Mayo Clin Proc 52:228, 1977.

43. ROBERTS, HJ: *Transcutaneous electrical nerve stimulation in the management of pancreatitis pain.* South Med J 71:396, 1978.

44. ROBERTS, HJ: *Transcutaneous electrical nerve stimulation in the symptomatic management of thrombophlebitis.* Angiology 30:249, 1979.

45. OSTROWSKI, MJ AND DODD, VA: *Transcutaneous nerve stimulation for relief of pain in advanced malignant disease.* Nursing Times, August 11, 1977, p 1233.

46. OSTROWSKI, MJ: *Pain control in advanced malignant disease using transcutaneous nerve stimulation.* Br J Clin Pract 33:157, 1979.

47. FINNESON, BE: *Diagnosis and Management of Pain Syndromes.* WB Saunders, Philadelphia, 1969, p 185.

48. GRIEVE, G: *Mobilization of the Spine.* Churchill Livingstone, Edinburgh, 1979.

49. SHERRINGTON, CS: *The Integrative Action of the Nervous System.* Yale University Press, New Haven, 1947.

50. KERR, FWL: *Pain: A central inhibitory balance theory.* Mayo Clin Proc 50:685, 1975.

51. WALL, PD AND DUBNER, R: *Somatosensory pathways.* Annu Rev Physiol 34:315, 1972.

52. MELZACK, R: *The Puzzle of Pain.* Basic Books, New York, 1973.

53. STERLING, P: *Referred cutaneous sensation.* Exp Neurol 41:451, 1973.

54. LIVINGSTON, WK: *Pain Mechanisms: A Physiologic Interpretation of Causalgia and its Related States.* Plenum Press, New York, 1976.

55. ROPPEL, RM AND MITCHELL, F; *Skin points of anomalously low electrical resistance: Current voltage characteristics and relationship to peripheral stimulation therapies.* JAOA 74:877, 1975.

56. SHERRINGTON, CS: *Experiments in examination of the peripheral distribution of the fibers of the posterior roots of some spinal nerves. I.* Philos Trans R Soc London [Biol] 184:641, 1893.

57. SHERRINGTON, CS: *Experiments in examination of the peripheral distribution of the fibers of the posterior roots of some spinal nerves. II.* Philos Trans R Soc London [Biol] 190:45, 1898.

58. FOERSTER, O: *The dermatomes in man.* Brain 56:1, 1933.

59. KELLGREN, JH: *Observations on referred pain arising from muscle.* Clin Sci 3:175, 1938.

60. KELLGREN, JH: *On the distribution of pain arising from deep somatic structures with charts of segmental pain areas.* Clin Sci 4:35, 1939.

61. LEWIS, T AND KELLGREN, JH: *Observations relating to referred pain, visceromotor reflexes and other associated phenomena.* Clin Sci 4:47, 1939.

62. RAY, BS, HINSEY, JC, AND GEOHEGAN, WA: *Observations on the distribution of the sympathetic nerves to the p and upper extremity as determined by stimulation of the anterior roots in man.* Ann Surg 118:647, 1943.

63. INMAN, VT AND SAUNDERS, JBM: *Referred pain from skeletal structures.* J Nerv Ment Dis 99:660, 1944.

64. TRAVELL, J AND BIGELOW, NH: *Referred somatic pain does not follow a simple segmental pattern.* Fed Proc 5:106, 1946.

65. KEEGAN, JJ AND GARRETT, FD: *The segmental distribution of the cutaneous nerves in the limbs of man.* Anat Rec 102:409, 1948.

66. FEINSTEIN, B, LANGTON, JNK, AND JAMESON, RM: *Experiments on pain referred from deep somatic tissues.* J Bone Joint Surg [Am] 36:981, 1954.

67. KIRK, EJ AND DENNY-BROWN, D: *Functional variation in dermatomes in the macaque monkey following dorsal root lesions.* J Comp Neurol 139:307, 1970.

68. CYRIAX, J: *Textbook of Orthopaedic Medicine.* Vol 1, ed 6. Williams & Wilkins, Baltimore, 1975, p 32.

69. WYKE, B: *The neurology of joints.* Ann R Coll Surg Eng 41:25, 1967.

70. NEUFELD, I: *Pathogenic concepts of fibrositis.* Arch Phys Med June 1952, p 363.

71. GOODGOLD, J: *Anatomical Correlates of Clinical Electromyography.* Williams & Wilkins, Baltimore, 1974.

72. GOODGOLD, J AND EBERSTEIN, A: *Electrodiagnosis of Neuromuscular Diseases,* ed 2. Williams & Wilkins, Baltimore, 1978.

73. WALTHARD, KM AND TCHICALOFF, M: *Motor points.* In LICHT, S (ED): *ElectroDiagnosis and Electromyography.* Elizabeth Licht, Publisher, New Haven, Conn, 1961, p 153.

74. LIVESON, JA AND SPIELHOLZ, NI: *Peripheral Neurology: Case Studies in Electrodiagnosis.* FA Davis, Philadelphia, 1979.

75. HASSLER, R AND WALKER, AE: *Trigeminal Neuralgia.* WB Saunders, Philadelphia, 1970, p 50.

76. APPENZELLER, O: *Pathogenesis and Treatment of Headache.* Spectrum Publications, New York, 1976.

77. LANCE, JW: *Headache.* Charles Scribner's Sons, New York, 1975, p 16.

78. EDMEADS, J: *Headaches and head pains associated with diseases of the cervical spine.* Med Clin North Am 62:533, 1978.

79. ELVIDGE, AR AND LI, CL: *Central protrusion of cervical intervertebral disc involving descending trigeminal tract.* Archives of Neurology and Psychiatry 63:455, 1950.

80. BRODAL, A: *The Cranial Nerves: Anatomy and Anatomico-Clinical Correlations.* Blackwell Scientific Publications, Oxford, 1965, p 79.

81. DUBNER, R, GOBEL, S, AND PRICE, DD: *Peripheral and central trigeminal pain pathways.* In BONICA, JJ AND ALBE-FESSARD, D (EDS): *Advances in Pain Research and Therapy.* Raven Press, New York, 1976, p 137.

82. GOBEL, S: *Principles of organization in the substantia gelatinosa layer of the spinal trigeminal nucleus.* In BONICA, JJ AND ALBE-FESSARD, D (EDS): *Advances in Pain Research and Therapy.*

Raven Press, New York, 1976, p 165.

83. SESSLE, BJ AND GREENWOOD, LF: *Role of trigeminal nucleus caudalis in the modulation of trigeminal sensory and motor neuronal activities.* In BONICA, JJ AND ALBE-FESSARD, D (EDS): *Advances in Pain Research and Therapy.* Raven Press, New York, 1976, p 185.

84. GUNN, CC AND MILBRANDT, WE: *Utilizing trigger points.* The Osteopathic Physician 44:29, 1977.

85. GUNN, CC AND MILBRANDT, WE: *The neurological mechanism of needle-grasp in acupuncture.* American Journal of Acupuncture 5:115, 1977.

86. GUNN, CC AND MILBRANDT, WE: *Shoulder pain, cervical spondylosis and acupuncture.* American Journal of Acupuncture 5:121, 1977.

87. GUNN, CC, MILBRANDT, WE, AND LITTLE, A: *Peripheral nerve injuries mimicking lumbar disc herniations.* British Columbia Med J 19:350, 1977.

88. GUNN, CC: *Motor points and motor lines.* American Journal of Acupuncture 6:55, 1978.

89. GUNN, CC, ET AL: *Dry needling of muscle motor points for chronic low-back pain.* Spine 5:279, 1980.

90. GUNN, CC: *"Prespondylosis" and some pain syndromes following denervation supersensitivity.* Spine 5:185, 1980.

91. GUNN, CC AND MILBRANDT, WE: *Tennis elbow and the cervical spine.* Can Med Assoc J 114:803, 1976.

92. GUNN, CC AND MILBRANDT, WE: *Tenderness at motor points: A diagnostic and prognostic aid for lowback injury.* J Bone Joint Surg [Am] 58:815, 1976.

93. GUNN, CC AND MILBRANDT, WE: *Early and subtle signs in low-back sprain.* Spine 3:267, 1978.

94. GUNN, CC AND MILBRANDT, WE: *Tenderness at motor points: An aid in the diagnosis of pain in the shoulder referred from the cervical spine.* JAOA 77:196, 1977.

95. GLOVER, JR: *Back pain and hyperaesthesia.* Lancet:1165, May 28, 1960.

96. HAO-HUI, C: *The new para-spine acupuncture points.* American Journal of Acupuncture 8:157, 1980.

97. TRAVELL, J AND RINZLER, SH: *The myofascial genesis of pain.* Postgrad Med 11:425, 1952.

98. BONICA, JJ: *Management of myofascial pain syndromes in general practice.* JAMA 164:732, 1957.

99. KRAUS, H: *Clinical Treatment of Back and Neck Pain.* McGraw-Hill, New York, 1970, p 92.

100. WYANT, GM: *Chronic pain syndromes and their treatment. II: Trigger Points.* J Can Anaesth Soc 26:216, 1979.

101. SIMONS, DG: *Special review: Muscle pain syndromes, Part II.* Am J Phys Med 55:15, 1976.

102. TRAVELL, J: *Pain mechanisms in connective tissue.* In RAGAN C (ED): *Connective Tissues: Transactions of the Second Conference.* Josiah Macy Jr. Foundation, New York, 1952, p 86.

103. TRAVELL, J: *Temporomandibular joint dysfunction: Temporomandibular joint pain referred from the head and neck.* J Prosthet Dent 10:745, 1960.

104. MACDONALD, AJR: *Abnormally tender muscle regions and associated painful movements.* Pain 8:197, 1980.

105. SIMONS, DG AND TRAVELL, J: *Myofascial trigger points, a possible explanation.* Pain 10:106, 1981.

106. MENNELL, JM: *The therapeutic use of cold.* JAOA 74:1146, 1975.

107. ZOHN, DA AND MENNELL, JM: *Musculoskeletal Pain.* Little, Brown & Co, Boston, 1976, p 190.

108. TARSY, JM: *Pain Syndromes and their Treatment.* Charles C Thomas, Springfield, Ill, 1953, p 274.

109. MELZACK, R, STILLWELL, DM, AND FOX, EJ: *Trigger points and acupuncture points for pain: Correlations and implications.* Pain 3:3, 1977.

110. STILLINGS, D: *A survey of the history of electrical stimulation for pain to 1900.* Med Instrum 9:255, 1975.

111. KANE, K AND TAUB, A: *A history of local electrical analgesia.* Pain 1:125, 1975.

112. SADOVE, MS, NAKAMURA, N, AND OKAZAKI, K: *Acupuncture in the treatment of chronic pain.* In VORIS, HC AND WHISLER, WW (EDS): *Treatment of Pain.* Charles C Thomas, Springfield, Ill, 1975, p 48.

113. KHOE, WH: *The many modalities of modern acupuncture.* American Journal of Acupuncture 2:199, 1974.

114. ROSSMAN, ML, WEXLER, J, AND OYLE, I: *The use of sonopuncture in some common clinical syndromes.* Am J Chin Med 2:199, 1974.

115. AUSTIN, M: *Acupuncture Therapy.* ASI Publishers, New York, 1972.

116. THE ACADEMY OF TRADITIONAL CHINESE MEDICINE: *An Outline of Chinese Acupuncture.* Foreign Languages Press, Peking, 1975.

117. MANN, F: *Acupuncture: The Ancient Chinese Art of Healing and How it Works Scientifically.* Vintage Books, New York, 1973.

118. MATSUMOTO, T: *Acupuncture for Physicians.* Charles C Thomas, Springfield Ill, 1974.

119. MURPHY, TM AND BONICA, JJ: *Acupuncture analgesia and anesthesia.* Arch Surg 112:896, 1977.

120. MATSUMOTO, T: *Acupuncture for Physicians.* Charles C Thomas, Springfield, Ill, 1974.

121. OSTRANDER, S AND SCHROEDER, L: *Handbook of Psychic Discoveries.* Berkeley Publishing, New York, 1974, p 72.

122. LEVINE, D: *Acupuncture in review: A mechanistic perspective.* American Journal of Acupuncture 8:5, 1980.

123. KRIPPNER, S AND RUBIN, D: *The Kirlian Aura.* Anchor Press, Garden City, NY, 1974.

124. SAMSON, F: *Axonal transport: The mechanisms and their susceptibility to derangement; anterograde transport.* In KORR, IM (ED): *The Neurobiologic Mechanisms in Manipulative Therapy.* Plenum Press, New York, 1978, p 291.

125. THOENEN, H, SCHWAB, M, AND BARDE, YA: *Transfer of information from effector organs to innervating neurons by retrograde axonal transport of macromolecules.* In KORR, IM (ED): *The Neurobiologic Mechanisms in Manipulative Therapy.* Plenum Press, New York, 1978, p 311.

126. WEI, LY: *Scientific advance in acupuncture.* Am J Chin Med 7:53, 1979.

127. BRESLER, DE AND FROENING, RJ: *Three essential factors in effective acupuncture therapy.* Am J Chin Med 4:81, 1976.

128. GUNN, CC ET AL: Acupuncture loci: A proposal for their classification according to their relationship to known neural structures. Am J Chin Med 4:183, 1976.

129. LIU, YK, VARELA, M, AND OSWALD, R: *The correspondence between some motor points and acupuncture loci.* Am J Chin Med 3:347, 1975.

130. REICHMANIS, M AND BECKER, RO: *Physiological effects of stimulation at acupuncture loci: A review.* Comp Med East and West 6:67, 1978.

131. CH'I, H: *Why surgical operations are possible under acupuncture anesthesia.* Am J Chin Med 1:159, 1973.

132. CH'I, H: *Some insights concerning the principles of acupuncture anesthesia.* Am J Chin Med 1:167, 1973.

133. CH'I, H: *An inquiry into the analgesic principles of acupuncture anesthesia.* Am J Chin Med 1:167, 1973.

134. CH'I, H: *Loci position, meridians and anastomoses, and the principles of acupuncture anesthesia.* Am J Chin Med 1:177, 1973.

135. CHEN, GS; *Enkephalin, drug addiction and acupuncture.* Am J Chin Med 5:25, 1977.

136. PLUMMER, JP: *Anatomical findings at acupuncture loci.* Am J Chin Med 8:170, 1980.

137. PLUMMER, JP: *Acupuncture points and cutaneous nerves.* Experientia 35:1534, 1979.

138. DORNETTE, WHL: *The anatomy of acupuncture.* Bull NY Acad Med 51:895, 1975.

139. FLECK, H: *Acupuncture and neurophysiology.* Bull NY Acad Med 51:903, 1975.

140. MATSUMOTO, T AND LYU, BS: *Anatomical comparison between acupuncture and nerve block.* Am Surg, January 1975, p 11.

141. GUNN, CC AND MILBRANDT, WE: *Review of 100 patients with "low back sprain" treated by surface electrode stimulation of acupuncture points.* American Journal of Acupuncture 3:224, 1975.

142. FOX, EJ AND MELZACK, R: *Transcutaneous electrical stimulation and acupuncture: Comparison of treatment for low back pain.* Pain 2:141, 1976.

143. LAITINEN, J: *Acupuncture and transcutaneous electric stimulation in the treatment of chronic sacrolumbalgia and ischalgia.* Am J Chin Med 4:169, 1976.

144. GUNN, CC AND MILBRANDT, WE: *Tennis elbow and acupuncture.* Am J Acupuncture 5:61, 1977.

145. MITCHELL, FL, MORAN, PS, AND PRUZZO, NA: *An Evaluation and Treatment Manual of Osteopathic Muscle Energy Procedures.* FL Mitchell, PS Moran, and NA Pruzzo, Valley Park, Mo, 1979, p 47.

146. OMURA, Y: *Applied kinesiology using the acupuncture meridian concept: Critical evaluation of its potential as the simplest non-invasive means of diagnosis, and compatibility test of food and drugs—Part I.* Acupunct Electrother Res 4:165, 1979.

147. OMURA, Y: *Acupuncture (with possible roles of serotonin and melatonin) and related unorthodox methods of diagnosis and treatment: Non-invasive spheno-palatine ganglionic block, abrasion of naso-pharyngeal mucosa, and applied kinesiology.* Acupunct Electrother Res 4:69, 1979.

148. EVERSAUL, G: *Dental Kinesiology.* G Eversaul, Las Vegas, 1977.

149. DIAMOND, J: *Behavioral Kinesiology.* Harper & Row, New York, 1979.

150. SOPLER, D: *Unpublished material, 1980.*

151. SOLA, AE AND WILLIAMS, RL: *Myofascial pain syndromes.* Neurology 6:91, 1956.

152. NAKATANI, Y: *A Guide for Application of Ryodoraku Autonomous Nerve Regulatory Therapy.* Japanese Society of Ryodoraku Autonomic Nervous System, Tokyo, 1972.

153. REICHMANIS, M, MARINO, AA, AND BECKER, RO: *Electrical correlates of acupuncture points.* IEEE Trans Biomed Eng 22:533, 1975.

154. BERGSMANN, O AND WOOLEY HART, A: *Differences in electrical skin conductivity between acupuncture points and adjacent skin areas.* American Journal of Acupuncture 1:27, 1973.

155. REICHMANIS, M, MARINO, AA, AND BECKER, RO: *DC skin conductance variation at acupuncture loci.* Am J Chin Med 4:69, 1976.

156. BECKER, RO, ET AL: *Electrophysiological correlates of acupuncture points and meridians.* Psychoenergetic Systems 1:105, 1976.

157. REICHMANIS, M, MARINO, AA, AND BECKER, RO: *Laplace plane analysis of impedance between acupuncture points H-3 and H-4.* Comp Med East and West 5:289, 1977.

158. BROWN, ML, ULETT, GA, AND STERN, JA: *Acupuncture loci: Techniques for location.* Am J Chin Med 2:67, 1974.

159. SHEALY, CN: *Ninety Days to Self-Health.* Dial Press, New York, 1977.

160. RILEY, LH AND RICHTER, CP: *Uses of the electrical skin resistance method in the study of patients with neck and upper extremity pain.* Johns Hopkins Med J 137:69, 1975.

161. GUNN, CC: *Transcutaneous neural stimulation, needle acupuncture and "Teh Ch'i phenomenon."* American Journal of Acupuncture 4:317, 1976.

162. STODDARD, A: *Manual of Osteopathic Practice.* Harper & Row, New York, 1969.

163. KORR, IM: *Experimental alterations in segmental sympathetic (sweat gland) activity through myofascial and postural disturbances.* Fed Proc 7:67, 1948.

164. KORR, IM: *Skin resistance patterns associated with visceral disease.* Fed Proc 8:87, 1949.

165. YAMAGATA, S, ET AL: *A diagnostic re-evaluation of electric skin resistance, skin temperature and deeper tenderness in patients with abdominal pain.* Tohoku J Exp Med 118 (Suppl):183, 1976.

166. DENSLOW, JS: *Pathophysiologic evidence for the osteopathic lesion. Data on what is known, what is not known, and what is controversial.* In GOLDSTEIN, M (ED): *The Research Status of Spinal Manipulative Therapy.* DHEW Publication No. (NIH) 76-998, Bethesda, Md, 1975, p 227.

167. DUNCAN MCCARROLL, G AND ROWLEY, BA: *An investigation of the existence of electrically located acupuncture points.* IEEE Trans Biomed Eng 24:177, 1977.

168. GUNN, CC: *Type IV acupuncture points.* American Journal of Acupuncture 5:51, 1977.

169. KENYON, JM: *Bioelectric potentials and their relation to acupuncture.* Acupunct Electrother Res 4:37, 1979.

170. IGGO, A: *Pain receptors.* In BONICA, JJ, PROCACCI, P, AND PAGNI, CA (EDS): *Recent Advances on Pain: Pathophysiology and Clinical Aspects.* Charles C Thomas, Springfield, Ill, 1974, p 3.

171. GRANIT, R: *Receptors and Sensory Perception.* Yale University Press, New Haven, 1955.

172. CRUE, BL, KENTON, B, AND CARREGAL, EJA: *Review article—Neurophysiology of pain—Periph-*

eral aspects: Speculation concerning the possibility of a unitary peripheral cutaneous input system for pressure, hot, cold and tissue damage. In CRUE, BL (ED): Chronic Pain: Further Reflections from City of Hope Medical Center. SP Medical and Scientific Books, New York, 1979, p 59.

173. WILSON, ME: The neurological mechanisms of pain. Anesthesia 29:407, 1974.
174. NATHAN, PW: The gate-control theory of pain: A critical review. Brain 99:123, 1976.
175. WEDDELL, G: The pattern of cutaneous innervation in relation to cutaneous sensibility. J Anat (Lond) 75:346, 1941.
176. WEDDELL, G: The multiple innervation of sensory spots in the skin. J Anat (London) 75:441, 1941.
177. MUMFORD, JM AND BOWSHER, D: Pain and protopathic sensibility: A review with particular reference to the teeth. Pain 2:223, 1976.
178. BLOEDEL, JR AND McCREERY, DB: Organization of peripheral and central pain pathways. Surg Neurol 4:65, 1975.
179. CASEY, KL: The neurophysiological basis of pain. Postgrad Med 53:58, 1973.
180. IGGO, A: Peripheral and spinal pain mechanisms and their modulation. In BONICA, JJ AND ALBE-FESSARD, D (EDS): Advances in Pain Research and Therapy, Vol 1. Raven Press, New York, 1976, p 381.
181. KENNARD, MA AND HAUGEN, FP: The relation of subcutaneous focal sensitivity to referred pain of cardiac origin. Anesthesiology 16:297, 1955.
182. TUNG, CH: Integrative action of thalamus in the process of acupuncture for analgesia. Am J Chin Med 2:1, 1974.
183. BURGESS, PR: The physiology of pain. Am J Chin Med 2:122, 1974.
184. ANDERSON, SA AND HOLMGREN, E: On acupuncture analgesia and the mechanism of pain. Am J Chin Med 3:311, 1975.
185. HOLMGREN, E: Increase of pain threshold as a function of conditioning electrical stimulation: An experimental study with application to electro-acupuncture for pain suppression. Am J Chin Med 3:133, 1975.
186. ERIKSSON, M AND SJOLUND, B: Acupuncturelike electroanalgesia in TNS-resistant chronic pain. In ZOTTERMAN, Y (ED): Sensory Functions of the Skin. Pergamon Press, Oxford, 1976, p 575.
187. CHAPMAN, CR, WILSON, ME, AND GEHRIG, JD: Comparative effects of acupuncture and transcutaneous stimulation of the perception of painful dental stimuli. Pain 2:265, 1976.
188. CHAPMAN, CR, CHEN, AC, AND BONICA, JJ: Effects of intrasegmental electrical acupuncture on dental pain: Evaluation by threshold estimation and sensory decision theory. Pain 3:213, 1977.
189. DEBRECENI, L: On the possible role of acupuncture loci in therapeutics. Comp Med East and West 5:177, 1977.
190. ANDERSSON, SA, HOLMGREN, E, AND ROOS, A: Analgesic effects of peripheral conditioning stimulation parameters. Acupunct Electrother Res 2:237, 1977.
191. ANDERSSON, SA, AND HOLMGREN, E: Analgesic effects of peripheral conditioning stimulation. III. Effect of high frequency stimulation; segmental mechanisms interacting with pain. Acupunct Electrother Res 3:23, 1978.
192. MANN, F, ET AL: Treatment of intractable pain by acupuncture. Lancet 2:57, 1973.
193. ANDERSSON, SA, ET AL: Evaluation of the pain suppressive effect of different frequencies of peripheral electrical stimulation in chronic pain conditions. Acta Orthop Scand 47:149, 1976.
194. ANDERSSON, SA AND HOLMGREN, E: Pain threshold effects of peripheral conditioning stimulation. In BONICA, JJ AND ALBE-FESSARD, D (EDS): Advances in Pain Research and Therapy, Vol 1. Raven Press, New York, 1976, p 761.
195. SJOLUND, B, TERENIUS, L, AND ERIKSSON, M: Increased cerebrospinal fluid levels of endorphins after electro-acupuncture. Acta Physiol Scand 100:382, 1977.
196. ERIKSSON, MBE, SJOLUND, BH, AND NIELZEN, S: Long term results of peripheral conditioning stimulation as an analgesic measure in chronic pain. Pain 6:335, 1979.
197. WONG, CC, WONG, PC, AND JENKINS, LC: Management of post-traumatic neuralgia by electro-acupuncture and transcutaneous electrical stimulation of acupuncture points. In Pain Ab-

stracts, Vol 1. Second World Congress on Pain of the International Association for the Study of Pain, Seattle, 1978, p 157.

198. Sjölund, BH and Eriksson, MBE: *Electro-acupuncture and endogenous morphines.* Lancet 2:1085, 1976.

199. Anderson, SA, et al: *Electroacupuncture: Effect on pain threshold measured with electrical stimulation of teeth.* Brain Res 63:393, 1973.

200. Handwerker, HO, Iggo, A, and Zimmerman, M: *Segmental and supraspinal actions on dorsal horn neurons responding to noxious and non-noxious skin stimuli.* Pain 1:147, 1975.

201. Shanghai Acupuncture Anesthesia Coordinating Group: *Acupuncture anesthesia: An anesthetic method combining traditional Chinese and western medicine.* Comp Med East and West 5:301, 1977.

202. Gunn, CC: *Transcutaneous neural stimulation: Acupuncture and the current of injury.* American Journal of Acupuncture 6:191, 1978.

203. Liao, SJ: *Recent advances in the understanding of acupuncture.* Yale J Biol Med 51:55, 1978.

204. Li, C: *Neurological basis of pain and its possible relationship to acupuncture anesthesia.* Am J Chin Med 1:61, 1973.

205. Tien, HC: *Neurogenic interference theory of acupuncture anesthesia.* Am J Chin Med 1:105, 1973.

206. Bull, GM: *Acupuncture anesthesia.* Lancet 2:417, 1973.

207. Wancura, I and Konig, G: *On the neurophysiological explanation of acupuncture analgesia.* Am J Chin Med 2:193, 1974.

208. Wagman, IH, Dong, WK, and McMillan, JA: *Possible physiological bases for acupuncture analgesia.* Am J Chin Med 4:313, 1976.

209. Pawl, RP: *Chronic Pain Primer.* Year Book Medical Publishers, Chicago, 1979, p 34.

210. Kerr, FW: *Segmental circuitry and spinal cord nociceptive mechanisms.* In Bonica, JJ and Albe-Fessard, D (eds): *Advances in Pain Therapy,* Vol 1. Raven Press, New York, 1976, p 75.

211. Lu Motte, C: *Distribution of the tract of Lissauer and the dorsal root fibers in the primate spinal cord.* J Comp Neurol 172:529, 1977.

212. Szentagothai, J: *Propriospinal pathways and their synapses.* Prog Brain Res 11:155, 1964.

213. Bishop, B: *Pain: Its physiology and rationale for management: Part I. Neuroanatomical substrate for pain.* Phys Ther 60:13, 1980.

214. Voll, R: *Twenty years of electroacupuncture diagnosis in Germany: A progress report.* American Journal of Acupuncture 3:7, 1975.

215. Voll, R: *Twenty years of electroacupuncture therapy using low-frequency current pulses.* American Journal of Acupuncture 3:291, 1975.

216. Voll, R: *Verification of acupuncture by means of electroacupuncture according to Voll.* American Journal of Acupuncture 6:5, 1978.

217. Schuldt, H: *Bioenergetics in acupuncture and electroacupuncture according to Voll.* American Journal of Acupuncture 6:17, 1978.

218. Madill, PV: *First, doctor to the whole body: Electroacupuncture according to Voll and the cause of holistic dentistry.* American Journal of Acupuncture 8:299, 1980.

219. Voll, R: *Energetic reactions between organ pairs and paranasal sinuses, odontons, and tonsils in electroacupuncture according to Voll.* American Journal of Acupuncture 5:101, 1977.

220. Voll, R: *Foci and fields of disturbance as reasons for short term or insufficient therapeutic success in classical acupuncture.* American Journal of Acupuncture 6:97, 1978.

221. Voll, R: *New electroacupuncture measurement points for the various eye structures.* American Journal of Acupuncture 7:5, 1979.

222. Voll, R: *Acupuncture points for the ear, nose and throat specialist.* American Journal of Acupuncture 7:191, 1979.

223. Thomsen, J: *The frequent involvement of "vital teeth" in focal disturbances.* American Journal of Acupuncture 8:25, 1980.

224. Oyle, I: *The Healing Mind.* Celestial Arts, Millbrae, Calif, 1975, p 65.

225. Samuels, M and Samuels, N: *Seeing with the Minds Eye.* Random House, New York, 1975, p 227.

226. WORSLEY, JR: *Chinese acupuncture and Kirlian photography.* In KRIPPNER, S AND RUBIN, D (EDS): *The Kirlian Aura.* Anchor Press, Garden City, NY, 1974, p 141.

227. LEUNG, CY AND SPOEREL, WE: *Effect of auriculotherapy on pain.* Am J Chin Med 2:247, 1974.

228. OLESON, TD, KROENING, RJ, AND BRESLER, DE: *An experimental evolution of auricular diagnosis: The somatotopic mapping of musculoskeletal pain at ear acupuncture points.* Pain 8:217, 1980.

229. BOSSY, J, ET AL: *Innervation and vascularization of the auricle correlated with the loci of auriculotherapy.* Acupunct Electrother Res 2:247, 1977.

230. BECKER, RO: *Longitudinal direct current gradients of spinal nerves.* Nature 196:675, 1962.

231. BECKER, RO: *The basic biological data transmission and control system influenced by electrical forces.* Ann NY Acad Sci 238:236, 1974.

232. CROMIE, WJ: *Electric basis is reported in acupuncture.* The Philadelphia Inquirer, April 25, 1976.

233. BECKER, RO: *The significance of bioelectric potentials.* Bioelectrochem Bioenergetics 1:187, 1974.

234. SCHIEFELBEIN, S: *The miracle of regeneration: Can human limbs grow back?* Saturday Review, July 8, 1978, p 8.

235. HUGHES, J, ET AL: *Identification of two related pentapeptides from the brain with potent opiate agonist activity.* Nature 258:577, 1975.

236. MARX, JL: *Neurobiology: Researchers high on endogenous opiates.* Science 193:1227, 1976.

237. FREDERICKSON, RC AND NORRIS, FH: *Enkephalin induced depression of single neuron in brain areas with opiate receptors—antagonism by naloxone.* Science 194:440, 1976.

238. MAYER, DJ AND PRICE, DD: *Central nervous system mechanisms of analgesia.* Pain 2: 379, 1976.

239. KOSTERLITZ, HW AND HUGHES, J: *Possible physiological significance of enkephalin on endogenous ligand of opiate receptors.* In BONICA, JJ AND ALBE-FESSARD, D (EDS): *Advances in Pain Research and Therapy.* Raven Press, New York, 1976, p 641.

240. SNYDER, SH: *Opiate receptors and internal opiates.* Sci Am 236:44, 1977.

241. POMERANZ, B: *Brain's opiates at work in acupuncture?* New Scientist, January 6, 1977, p 12.

242. VILLET, B: *Opiates of the mind.* Atlantic Monthly 241:82, 1978.

243. POMERANZ, B: *Do endorphins mediate acupuncture analgesia?* In COSTA, E AND TRABUCCHI, M (EDS): *Advances in Biochemical Psychopharmacology,* Vol 18. Raven Press, New York, 1978, p 351.

244. TERENIUS, L: *Significance of endorphins in endogenous antinociception.* In COSTA, E AND TRABUCCHI, M (EDS): *Advances in Biochemical Psychopharmacology,* Vol 18. Raven Press, New York, 1978, p 31.

245. NEALE, JH AND BARKER, JL: *Enkephalin-containing neurons visualized in spinal cord cell cultures.* Science 201:467, 1978.

246. GIESLER, GL ET AL: *Long ascending projections from substantia gelatinosa rolandi and the subjacent dorsal horn in the rat.* Science 202:984, 1978.

247. KOSTERLITZ, HW: *Editorial: Endogenous opioid peptides and the control of pain.* Psychol Med 9:1, 1979.

248. MILLER, RJ AND DEYO, SN: *Pain psychology, opiate receptors and endorphins.* In *The Use of Analgesics in the Management of Mild to Moderate Pain.* Postgraduate Medicine Communications, Riker Labs Inc, Northridge, Calif, 1980, p 5.

249. BISHOP, B: *Pain: Its physiology and rationale for management. Part II. Analgesic systems of the CNS.* Phys Ther 60:21, 1980.

250. ADAMS, JE: *Naloxone reversal of analgesia produced by brain stimulation in the human.* Pain 2:161, 1976.

251. HOSOBUCHI, Y, ADAMS, J, AND LINCHITZ, R: *Pain relief by electrical stimulation of the central grey matter in humans and its reversal by naloxone.* Science 197:183, 1977.

252. RAY, CD: *New electrical stimulation methods for therapy and rehabilitation.* Ortho Review 4:29, 1977.

253. KORR, IM: *The facilitated segment.* In KENT, B (ED): *Proceedings of the International Federation*

of Orthopaedic Manipulative Therapists. International Federation of Orthopaedic Manipulative Therapists, Hayward, Calif, 1977, p 81.

254. KORR, IM, THOMAS, PE, AND WRIGHT, HM: *Symposium on the functional implications of segmental facilitation.* JAOA 54:265, 1955.

255. DENSLOW, JS, KORR, IM, AND KREMS, AD: *Quantitative studies of chronic facilitation in human motoneuron pools.* Am J Physiol 150:229, 1947.

256. GUNN, CC: *Causalgia and denervation supersensitivity.* American Journal of Acupuncture 7:317, 1979.

257. DENSLOW, JS AND HASSETT, CC: *The central excitatory state associated with postural abnormalities.* J Neurophysiol 5:393, 1944.

258. COOTE, JW: *Somatic sources of afferent input as factors in aberrant autonomic, sensory and motor function.* In KORR, IM (ED): *The Neurobiologic Mechanisms in Manipulative Therapy.* Plenum Press, New York, 1978, p 91.

259. DORAN, FSA: *The sites to which pain is referred from the common bile duct in man and its implication for the theory of referred pain.* Br J Surg 54:599, 1967.

260. KERR, FWL AND FUKUSHIMA, T: *New observations on the nociceptive pathways in the central nervous system.* In BONICA, JJ (ED): *Pain. Research Publication of the Association for Research in Nervous and Mental Disease* 58:47, 1980.

261. WALL, PD: *The role of substantia gelatinosa as a gate control.* In BONICA, JJ (ED): *Pain. Research Publication of the Assocation for Research in Nervous and Mental Disease* 58:205, 1980.

262. GRANT, JCB: *Grant's Atlas of Anatomy,* ed 5. Williams & Wilkins, Baltimore, 1962.

263. MANNHEIMER, JS: *Electrode placements for transcutaneous electrical nerve stimulation.* Phys Ther 59:1455, 1978.

264. MELZACK, R: *Prolonged relief of pain by brief, intense transcutaneous electrical stimulation.* Pain 1:357, 1975.

265. HOVELACQUE, A: *Anatomie des nerfs rachidiens et due systeme grand sympathique.* Doin, Paris, 1927. In MAIGNE, R: *Orthopaedic Medicine.* Charles C Thomas, Springfield, Ill, 1972, p 262.

266. MARKOVICH, SE: *Pain in the head: A neurological appraisal.* In GELB, H (ED): *Clinical Management of Head, Neck and TMJ Pain and Dysfunction.* WB Saunders, Philadelphia, 1977, p 125.

267. SOLA, AE, RODENBERGER, ML, AND GETTYS, BB: *Incidence of hypersensitive areas in posterior shoulder muscles.* Am J Phys Med 34:585, 1955.

268. BROWN, BR: *Diagnosis and therapy of common myofascial syndromes.* JAMA 239:646, 1978.

269. LEE, TN: *Thalamic neuron theory: A hypothesis concerning pain and acupuncture.* In *Abstracts of Management of Pain—A Holistic and Multidisciplinary Approach.* Sponsored by Pacific Medical Center and Academy of Pain Research, San Francisco, 1978, p 25.

270. CARMON, A: *Considerations of the cerebral response to painful stimulation: Stimulus transduction versus perceptual event.* Bull NY Acad Med 55:313, 1979.

271. STOWELL, H: *Event related brain potentials from somatosensory nociceptive stimulation.* In CRUE, BL (ED): *Chronic Pain: Further Observations from City of Hope National Medical Center.* SP Medical and Scientific Books, New York, 1979, p 105.

272. MUMFORD, JM AND STANLEY, SJ: *Sensations on stimulating the pulps of human teeth, thresholds and tolerance ratio.* Pain 10:391, 1981.

273. KERR, FWL: *Mechanisms, diagnosis and management of some cranial and facial pain syndromes.* Surg Clin North Am 43:951, 1963.

Key to Illustrations and Tables on Following Pages

▼   Acupuncture point   K. or k. . . .   kidney meridian
○   Motor point   LI. or li. . . .   large intestine
□   Trigger point   LU. or lu. . . .   lung
○   Cutaneous nerve   LV. or lv. . . .   liver
○   Peripheral nerve   P. or p. . . .   pericardium
                                                    SI. or si. . . .   small intestine

BL. or bl. . . .   bladder meridian   SP. or sp. . . .   spleen
GB. or gb. . . . gallbladder meridian   ST. or st. . . .   stomach
H. or h. . . .   heart meridian   TW. or tw. . . . triple warmer

Researched and developed by Jeffrey S. Mannheimer, M.A., R.P.T.,
and Barbara J. Behrens, A.A.S.P.T.A. © 1980.

Face

Supraorbital n.

Supratrochlear n.

Auriculotemporal n.

Zygomaticotemporal n.

Infratrochlear n.
Lacrimal n.

Zygomaticofacial n.
Infraorbital n.
External nasal n.

Buccal n.
Great auricular n.

Mental n.

Transverse cervical n.
ant. cut. n. of neck

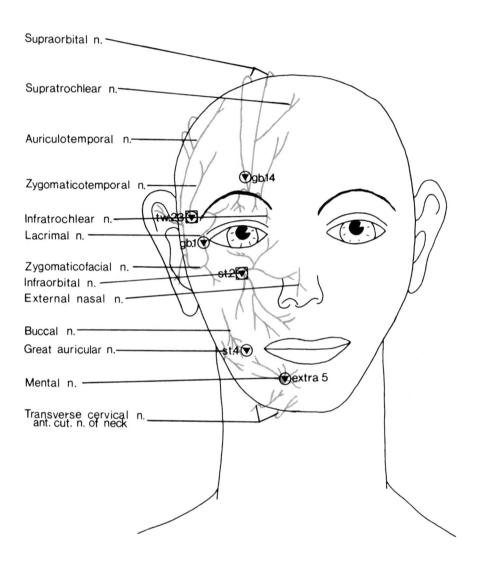

gb.14

tw.23

gb.1

st.2

st.4

extra 5

Optimal Stimulation Sites
for TENS Electrodes

Face

Location	Superficial Nerve Branch	Acupuncture Point	Motor Point	Trigger Point	Segmental Level
½″ above midpoint of eyebrow, directly above supraorbital foramen	Supraorbital connections with greater and lesser occipital	GB14	Frontalis (facial nerve)		Cranial C2–3
In depression at lateral end of eyebrow	Zygomatico-temporal nerve, branch of trigeminal	TW 23	Temporalis (trigeminal)	Temporalis in general vicinity	Cranial C2–3
In depression at lateral angle of eye	Zygomatico-facial and lacrimal branch of trigeminal	GB 1	Orbicularis oculi (facial nerve)		Cranial C2–3
Infraorbital foramen	Infraorbital nerve, branch of trigeminal	ST 2	Caninus (facial nerve)	Frequent trigeminal nerve trigger area	Cranial C2–3
½″ lateral to corner of mouth	Lower buccal nerve, branch of trigeminal	ST 4	Orbicularis oris (facial nerve) mandibular branch		Cranial C2–3
½″ lateral to mental labial groove	Mental nerve branch of trigeminal	Extra 5	Triangularis (facial nerve) mandibular and buccal branches		Cranial C2–3

Lateral Head & Neck

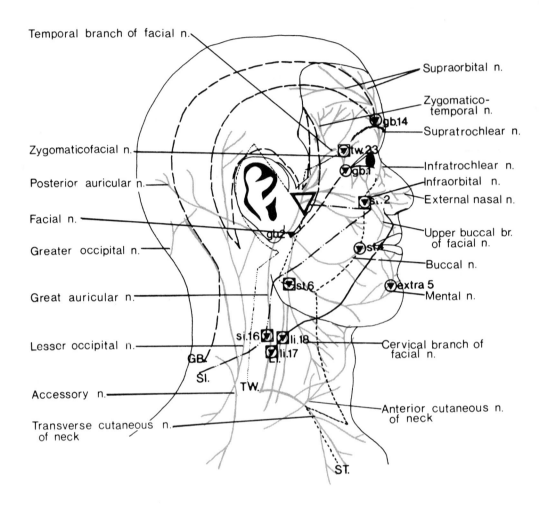

Temporal branch of facial n.

Supraorbital n.

Zygomatico-temporal n.

Supratrochlear n.

Zygomaticofacial n.

Posterior auricular n.

Infratrochlear n.

Infraorbital n.

External nasal n.

Facial n.

Greater occipital n.

Upper buccal br. of facial n.

Buccal n.

Great auricular n.

Mental n.

Lesser occipital n.

Cervical branch of facial n.

Accessory n.

Anterior cutaneous n. of neck

Transverse cutaneous n. of neck

gb.14

tw.23

gb.1

si.2

gb.2

st.4

st.6

extra 5

si.16 li.18

li.17

GB.

SI.

TW.

ST.

▽ REPRESENTS TW.21, GB.3, SI.19, ST.7
WHICH ARE ALL ACUPUNCTURE POINTS

Optimal Stimulation Sites
for TENS Electrodes

Lateral Neck and Head

Location	Superficial Nerve Branch	Acupuncture Point	Motor Point	Trigger Point	Segmental level
Mouth open stylomastoid foramen	Facial and communications with great auricular, vagus, glossopharyngeal and auriculo-temporal nerves	GB 2			Cranial C2–3
Anterior and superior to angle of jaw. Prominence of masseter with mouth tightly closed	Facial nerve in communication with trigeminal	ST 6	Masseter (anterior and posterior deep temporal nerves) mandibular portion of trigeminal	Masseter	Cranial C2–3
Midpoint of sternocleido-mastoid (SCM) on posterior border	Transverse cutaneous nerve of neck, great auricular nerve and spinal accessory	SI 16 LI 17–18	SCM (accessory) spinal portion (C2–3)	SCM	Cranial plus C3–4 communi-cation
Temporo-mandibular joint	Zygomatic and auriculo-temporal branches of facial nerve plus branch from trigeminal	TW 21 GB 3 SI 19 ST 7			Cranial C2–3

Explanation of optimal stimulation sites GB 14, TW 23, GB 1, ST 2, ST 4, and Extra 5 can be found on the facial view.

Spine & Occiput

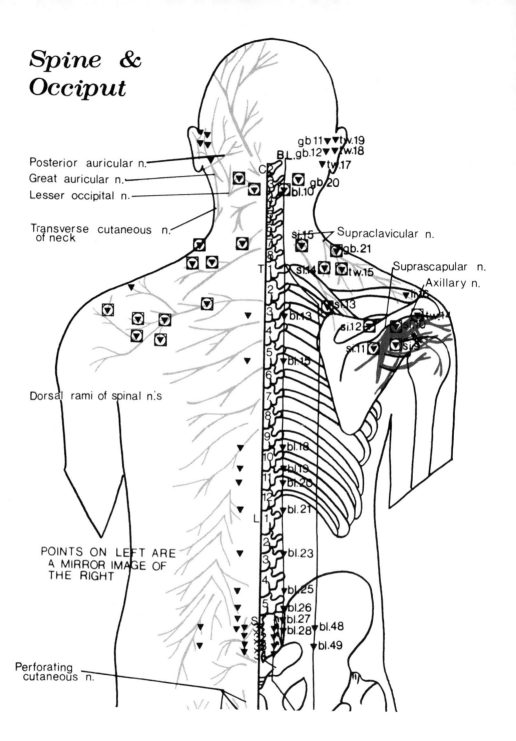

Posterior auricular n.
Great auricular n.
Lesser occipital n.

Transverse cutaneous n. of neck

gb 11 ▼ ▼ tw.19
BL.gb.12 ▼ ▼ tw.18
▼ tw.17
gb.20
bl.10

si.15 — Supraclavicular n.
gb.21

si.14 ▼ tw.15 — Suprascapular n.
Axillary n.
li.16

bl.13
si.13
si.12
si.10
si.11
si.9

Dorsal rami of spinal n.'s

bl.15

bl.18
bl.19
bl.20
bl.21

bl.23

POINTS ON LEFT ARE A MIRROR IMAGE OF THE RIGHT

bl.25
bl.26
bl.27
bl.28 ▼ bl.48
bl.49

Perforating cutaneous n.

Optimal Stimulation Sites
for TENS Electrodes

Occiput

Location	Superficial Nerve Branch	Acupuncture Point	Motor Point	Trigger Point	Segmental Level
Posterior ear upper third (TW 19) same level but slightly more medial on occiput (GB 11)	Great auricular, posterior branch communicates with lesser occipital, auricular branch of vagus, posterior auricular branch of facial. Transverse cutaneous nerve of neck	TW 19 GB 11 is just medial			Cranial C2–4
Posterior ear middle third (TW 18) same level but slightly more medial on occiput (GB 12)	Same as above	TW 18 GB 12 is just medial			Cranial C2–4
Behind ear in depression between angle of mandible and mastoid process	Great auricular, posterior branch and lesser occipital	TW 17			C2–4
Suboccipital depression, between sternocleido-mastoid (SCM) and upper trapezius	Greater and lesser occipital nerves	GB 20 B 10 is nearby, slightly medial and inferior	Splenius capitis (branches from C2–4) semispin-alis capitis	Splenius capitis Semispin-alis capitis	C2–3

The explanation of optimal stimulation sites for the shoulder girdle as seen on this view can be found on the view of posterolateral shoulder and dorsal region of the upper extremity.

Optimal Stimulation Sites
for TENS Electrodes

The Spine

Location	Superficial Nerve Branch	Acupuncture Point	Motor Point	Trigger Point	Segmental Level
In depression between medial border of posterior superior iliac spine (PSIS) and 1st sacral spinous process	Dorsal ramus of L2	B 27			L2
2″ lateral to spinous process of S2	Dorsal ramus of L2	B 48	Gluteus maximus (upper motor pt) (inferior gluteal L5–S2)	Gluteus maximus	L2 L5–S2
2″ lateral to spinous process of S4	Dorsal rami of L2–3	B 49	Gluteus maximus (lower motor pt) (piriformis directly below) (inferior gluteal) (L5–S2)	Gluteus maximus (piriformis directly below)	L2–3 L5–S2
Directly over 1st sacral foramen	Dorsal ramus of S1	B 31			S1
Directly over 2nd sacral foramen	Dorsal ramus of S2	B 32			S2
Directly over 3rd sacral foramen	Dorsal ramus of S3	B 33			S3
Directly over 4th sacral foramen	Dorsal ramus of S4	B 34			S4

The twelve cutaneous branches of thoracic posterior primary rami become superficial adjacent to the spinous processes. They each have multiple cutaneous twigs. Havelacque considers the dorsal ramus of T2 to be the largest and most diffuse.[265]

The cutaneous distribution of the dorsal ramus of T2 reaches up to the posterior aspect of the acromion, covering the mid-back (to the region of T5 6) and laterally to the superior region of the posterior axillary fold. A number of optimal stimulation sites are depicted as overlying this nerve.

Cutaneous branches of the dorsal rami of L1–3 descend as far as the posterior part of the iliac crest, skin of the buttock and almost to the greater trochanter of the femur (see lower extremity, lateral and posterior views).[1(p1033),93]

Antero-medial Shoulder & Volar Region of U.E.

Supraclavicular n.

Intercosto-brachial n.

Musculocutaneous n.

Cutaneous branches of axillary n.

Median n.

Lower lateral cutaneous n. of arm

Posterior cutaneous n. of forearm

Radial n.

Lateral cutaneous n. of forearm

Superficial branch of radial n.

Palmar cutaneous br.'s of radial and musculocutaneous n.'s

LU.

li.15

lu.1

sp.20

sp.19

P.

h.1

p2

lu.3

lu.4

Medial cutaneous n. of arm

h.2

Ulnar n.

lu.5

p.3

h.3

Medial cutaneous n. of forearm

p.5

p.6

lu.7

lu.8

p.7

h.4

lu.9

h.5

h.6

lu.10

h.7

Dorsal branch of ulnar n.

Palmar cutaneous branch of ulnar n.

Palmar cutaneous branch of median n.

Optimal Stimulation Sites
for TENS Electrodes

Anteromedial Shoulder and
Volar Region of Upper Extremity

Location	Superficial Nerve Branch	Acupuncture Point	Motor Point	Trigger Point	Segemen-tal Level
Between first and second ribs, about 4" lateral to sternum, medial to coracoid process	Musculocu-taneous nerve	LU 1	Coraco-brachialis is nearby (musculo-cutaneous) (C6)		C5–7
Radial side of biceps brachii 2" below anterior axillary fold. 3" below anterior axillary fold	Musculocu-taneous nerve and its lower lateral cutaneous branch	LU 3 LU 4	Biceps brachii (musculo-cutaneous) C5–6		C5–7
In antecubital fossa on crease at radial side of biceps tendon	Lateral cutaneous nerve of arm	LU 5	Brachialis (musculo-cutaneous) (C5–6)		C5–7
Just lateral to radial artery from 1st volar crease to just above radial styloid	Lateral cutaneous nerve of forearm communicating with superficial radial nerve	LU 7–9			C5–7 C6–8
Volar surface of hand at midpoint of 1st metacarpal	Superficial branch of radial nerve and palmar cutaneous of median	LU 10	Abductor pollicis brevis (median) (C8–T1)		C6–8 C5–T1

Optimal Stimulation Sites
for TENS Electrodes

Anteromedial Shoulder and
Volar Region of Upper Extremity

Location	Superficial Nerve Branch	Acupuncture Point	Motor Point	Trigger Point	Segmental Level
Between heads of biceps brachii 2″ below anterior axillary fold	Musculo-cutaneous and intercostal brachial nerves, may communicate with medial cutaneous nerve of forearm	P 2			C5–7 T2 C8–T1
Just medial to biceps tendon in antecubital fossa	Median nerve and anterior branch of medial cutaneous nerve of forearm	P 3	Pronator teres (median) (C 6)		C5–T1 C8–T1
Between tendons of flexor carpi radialis (FCR) and palmaris longus (PL) 2″ and 1½″ above volar crease respectively	Median and anterior branch of medial cutaneous nerve of forearm	P 5 P 6 is 1″ below			C5–T1 C8–T1
Between tendons of FCR and PL at midpoint of transverse volar wrist crease	Median and anterior branch of medial cutaneous nerve of forearm and palmar cutaneous branch of median	P 7			C5–T1 C8–T1
Between ribs 2–3 and 3–4, midway between anterior axillary fold and sternum	Medial and intermedial supraclavicular nerves to 2nd rib, lateral cutaneous nerves of thorax (2–4), the 2nd nerve is the intercostal brachial nerve	SP 19–20	Pectoralis major (medial and lateral anterior thoracic nerves)	Pectoralis major	C3–4 T2–4

Optimal Stimulation Sites
for TENS Electrodes

Anteromedial Shoulder and
Volar Region of Upper Extremity

Location	Superficial Nerve Branch	Acupuncture Point	Motor Point	Trigger Point	Segmental Level
Medial to brachial artery in axilla	Ulnar nerve, intercosto-brachial, medial cutaneous nerve of arm and median nerve which is just lateral to artery	H 1			C7–T1 T2 C9–T1 C5–T1
In groove medial to lower ⅓ of biceps brachii medial to brachial artery	Median and medial cutaneous nerve of arm	H 2			C5–T1 C8–T1
Just superior to cubital tunnel by medial epicondyle	Medial cutaneous nerve of forearm	H 3			C8–T1
Ulnar aspect of wrist lateral to flexor carpi ulnaris (FCU) tendon from 1½″ above 1st volar wrist crease to pisiform bone	Ulnar nerve and its palmar cutaneous branch	H4–7			C7–T1
In depression anterior and inferior to acromion	Upper lateral cutaneous nerve branch of axillary	LI 15	Anterior deltoid (axillary) (C5–6)		C5–6

Postero-lateral Shoulder & Dorsal Region of U.E.

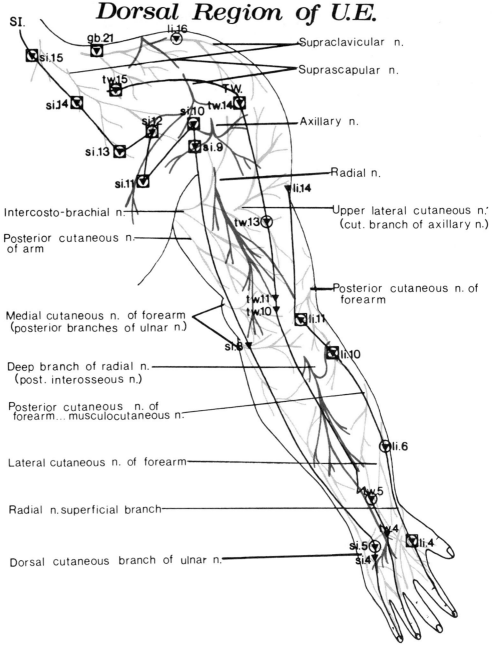

SI.

si.15

gb.21

li.16 — Supraclavicular n.

Suprascapular n.

tw.15

si.14

T.W.

si.12

si.10

tw.14

Axillary n.

si.13

si.9

Radial n.

si.11

li.14

Intercosto-brachial n. — Upper lateral cutaneous n.
(cut. branch of axillary n.)

Posterior cutaneous n. of arm

tw.13

Posterior cutaneous n. of forearm

Medial cutaneous n. of forearm
(posterior branches of ulnar n.)

tw.11
tw.10
li.11

si.8

li.10

Deep branch of radial n.
(post. interosseous n.)

Posterior cutaneous n. of
forearm... musculocutaneous n.

li.6

Lateral cutaneous n. of forearm

tw.5

Radial n. superficial branch

tw.4

si.5
li.4

Dorsal cutaneous branch of ulnar n.

si.4

314

Optimal Stimulation Sites
for TENS Electrodes

Posterolateral Shoulder and Dorsal
Region of Upper Extremity

Location	Superficial Nerve Branch	Acupuncture Point	Motor Point	Trigger Point	Segmental Level
1½″ lateral to spinous process of C7	Medial branch of supraclavicular	SI 15	Levator scapulae (spinal accessory and dorsal scapular (C3–4)	Levator scapulae	Cranial C3–4
1½″ above superior angle of scapula at the level of the spinous process of T1	Lateral (posterior) branch of supraclavicular	SI 14 TW 15 is just lateral	Middle trapezius (spinal accessory (C3–4)	Middle trapezius	Cranial C3–4
Suprascapular fossa (medial end) 3″ lateral to spinous process of T2	Lateral (posterior) branch of supraclavicular and dorsal ramus of T2	SI 13	Middle trapezius (spinal accessory) (C3–4)	Middle trapezius	Cranial C3–4 T2
At midpoint of suprascapular fossa	Dorsal ramus of T2	SI 12	Supra-spinatus (supra-scapular) (C5–6)	Supra-spinatus	C5–6 T2
At midpoint of infrascapular fossa	Dorsal ramus of T2	SI 11	Infra-spinatus (supra-scapular) (C5–6)	Infra-spinatus	C5–6 T2
Directly above posterior axillary fold. Just below spine of scapula	Dorsal ramus of T2 and axillary (posterior branch), which continues as the upper lateral cutaneous nerve of the arm	SI 10	Posterior deltoid (axillary) (C5–6)	Posterior deltoid	C5–6 T2
Directly below SI 10. Just superior to posterior axillary fold	Axillary and dorsal ramus of T2	SI 9	Teres major (subscapu-lar) (C5–6)	Teres major	C5–6 T2
In groove between olecranon and medial epicondyle of humerus	Ulnar nerve and its medial cutaneous branches	SI 8			C7–T1

Posterolateral Shoulder and Dorsal
Region of Upper Extremity

Location	Superficial Nerve Branch	Acupuncture Point	Motor Point	Trigger Point	Segmental Level
In depression between pisiform bone and ulnar styloid	Dorsal and palmar cutaneous branches of ulnar nerve	SI 5			C7–T1
In depression between fifth metacarpal and triquetral	Dorsal and palmar cutaneous branches of ulnar nerve	SI 4	Palmaris brevis (median) (C8–T1)		C7–T1
On cephalad surface of upper trapezius directly above superior angle of scapula	Supraclavicular	GB 21	Upper trapezius (spinal accessory)	Upper trapezius	Cranial C3–4
In depression posterior and inferior to acromion and above greater tubercle of humerus with arm in anatomical position	Intercostal brachial, upper lateral cutaneous nerve—branch of axillary, and dorsal ramus of T2	TW 14	Posterior deltoid (axillary) (C5–6)		C5–6 T2
Just below deltoid insertion by lateral head of triceps	Upper lateral cutaneous nerve branch of axillary	TW 13	Lateral head of triceps (radial) (C7–8)		C5–6
In depression 1″ above olecranon with the elbow flexed to 90°	Posterior cutaneous of arm (radial) medial cutaneous of forearm (ulnar posterior branches) posterior cutaneous nerve of forearm	TW 10, TW 11 is just above			C5–8 C8–T1 C5–8
Between radius and ulna on dorsal surface about 2″ proximal to transverse wrist crease	Posterior cutaneous nerve of forearm, branch of radial communications with lateral cutaneous nerve of forearm, branch of musculocutaneous	TW 5	Extensor indicis proprius (radial) (C7)		C5–8 C5–6

Optimal Stimulation Sites
for TENS Electrodes

Posterolateral Shoulder and Dorsal
Region of Upper Extremity

Location	Superficial Nerve Branch	Acupuncture Point	Motor Point	Trigger Point	Segmental Level
In depression on dorsum of hand between tendons of extensor digitorum communis (EDC) and extensor indicis proprius (EIP) just distal to transverse crease of wrist	Posterior cutaneous nerve of forearm (radial, superficial radial and dorsal cutaneous branch of ulnar nerve)	TW 4			C5–8 C6–8 C8–T1
In depression between acromioclavicular (AC) joint and spine of scapula	Posterolateral branch of supraclavicular nerve	LI 16	Musculo-tendinous junction of supra-spinatus		C3–4
In depression anterior and inferior to acromion	Upper lateral cutaneous nerve branch of axillary	LI 15	Anterior deltoid (axillary) (C5–6)		C5–6
Lateral arm at deltoid insertion	Upper lateral cutaneous	LI 14			C5–6
Lateral end of cubital crease in depression with elbow flexed.	Posterior cutaneous nerve of forearm (medial), communicates with intercostal brachial nerve	LI 11	Brachiora-dialis (radial) (C5–6)	Brachiora-dialis	C5–8
Just below lateral epicondyle of humerus with forearm pronated	Superficial radial nerve superior to posterior interosseus nerve	LI 10	Extensor carpi radialis longus, supinator nearby (radial) (C6)	Extensor carpi radialis longus, supinator nearby	C6–8
8–10 cm above radial styloid with arm in anatomical position	Superficial radial and lateral cutaneous nerve of forearm	LI 6	Extensor pollicis brevis (radial) (C7)		C6–8 C5–6
Midpoint of radial aspect of second metacarpal	Superficial radial in communication with distal branches of musculocu-taneous	LI 4	First dorsal interosseus (ulnar nerve) (C8–T1)	First dorsal interosseus & adductor pollicis	C6–8 C5–7 C7–T1

Lower Extremity Anterior View

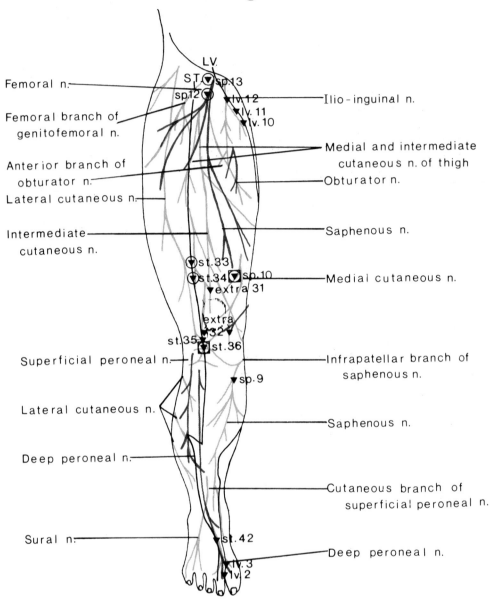

Femoral n.

Femoral branch of genitofemoral n.

Anterior branch of obturator n.

Lateral cutaneous n.

Intermediate cutaneous n.

Superficial peroneal n.

Lateral cutaneous n.

Deep peroneal n.

Sural n.

LV.
ST. sp.13
sp.12
lv.12
lv.11
lv.10

st.33
st.34 sp.10
extra 31
extra 32
st.35 st.36
sp.9
st.42
lv.3
lv.2

Ilio-inguinal n.

Medial and intermediate cutaneous n. of thigh

Obturator n.

Saphenous n.

Medial cutaneous n.

Infrapatellar branch of saphenous n.

Saphenous n.

Cutaneous branch of superficial peroneal n.

Deep peroneal n.

Optimal Stimulation Sites
for TENS Electrodes

Lower Extremity,
Anterior View

Location	Superficial Nerve Branch	Acupuncture Point	Motor Point	Trigger Point	Segmental Level
2″ lateral to superior border of symphysis pubis	Anterior cutaneous branches of iliohypogastric, ilioinguinal and genitofemoral	LIV 10–12	Pectineus (femoral) (L2–4)		L1 L1 L1–2
Between 1st and 2nd metatarsals just above web space junction on dorsum of foot	Deep peroneal nerve via its medial terminal and interosseous branches	LIV 2–3	1st dorsal interosseus (lateral plantar) (S1–2)		L4–5 S1–2
From inguinal ligament to femoral triangle lateral to femoral artery	Anterior branch of obturator communicating with medial cutaneous. Forms subsartorial plexus.	SP 12 SP 13	Iliopsoas (femoral) (L2–4)		L2–4 L2–4
2″ above medial aspect of patellar base	Medial cutaneous nerve of thigh and saphenous nerve (infrapatellar branch)	SP 10	Vastus medialis (femoral) (L2–4)	Vastus medialis	L2–4 L2–3
Just below medial condyle of tibia, level with tibial tuberosity between sartorius and gracilis	Saphenous nerve	SP 9			L3–4
Just superior to midpoint of patellar base	Intermediate cutaneous nerve of the thigh	Extra 31			L2–3
Medial to patellar tendon	Medial cutaneous nerve of thigh	Extra 32 (medial)			L2–3
In depression just below patella, lateral to tendon with knee flexed	Medial and lateral cutaneous nerve of thigh and infrapatellar branch of saphenous which form a patellar plexus	ST 35 Extra 32 (lateral)			L2–3 L3–4
2–3″ above lateral aspect of patellar base	Intermediate and lateral cutaneous nerve of thigh	ST 33–34	Vastus lateralis (femoral) (L2–4)		L2–4
In depression just below patella, lateral to tendon with knee flexed	Medial and lateral cutaneous nerve of thigh and infrapatellar branch of saphenous which form a patellar plexus	ST 35 Extra 32 (lateral)			L2–3 L3–4
2″ below inferior angle of patella, lateral to tibial crest.	Infrapatellar branch of saphenous	ST 36	Superior motor point of anterior tibialis (deep peroneal) (L4–5, S1)	Anterior tibialis	L3–4
Below malleoli at center of dorsum of foot, lateral to anterior tibialis tendon	Superficial peroneal	ST 42			L4–S2

Lower Extremity Medial View

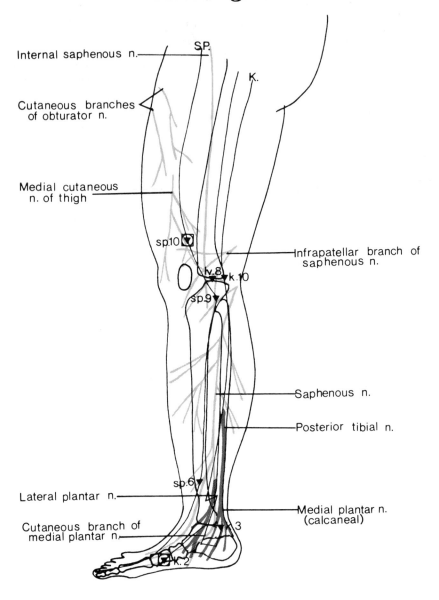

Internal saphenous n.

S.P.

K.

Cutaneous branches of obturator n.

Medial cutaneous n. of thigh

sp.10

Infrapatellar branch of saphenous n.

lv.8 k.10

sp.9

Saphenous n.

Posterior tibial n.

sp.6

Lateral plantar n.

Medial plantar n. (calcaneal)

Cutaneous branch of medial plantar n.

3

k.2

Optimal Stimulation Sites
for TENS Electrodes

Lower Extremity,
Medial View

Location	Superficial Nerve Branch	Acupuncture Point	Motor Point	Trigger Point	Segmental Level
2″ above medial aspect of patellar base	Medial cutaneous nerve of thigh (posterior branch) and infrapatellar branch of saphenous (subsartorial plexus)	SP 10	Vastus medialis (femoral) (L2–4)	Vastus medialis	L2–4 L2–3
Just below medial condyle of tibia level with tibial tuberosity between sartorius and gracilis	Saphenous nerve (infrapatellar branch)	SP 9			L3–4
3″ above medial malleolus just behind tibia	Saphenous	SP 6	Flexor digitorum longus (posterior tibial nerve) (L5–S1)		L3–4
Between tendons of semitendinosus and semi-membranosus at medial end of popliteal crease	Medial cutaneous nerve of thigh. Communicates with infrapatellar branch of saphenous	K 10 LIV 8 is just anterior			L2–4 L2–3
Between medial malleolus and heelcord	Saphenous and posterior tibial nerves	K 3			L3–4 L4–S3
Below navicular on medial aspect of foot	Cutaneous branches of medial plantar nerves	K 2	Abductor hallucis (medial plantar from tibial S1–2)	Abductor hallucis	S1–2

Lower Extremity Lateral View

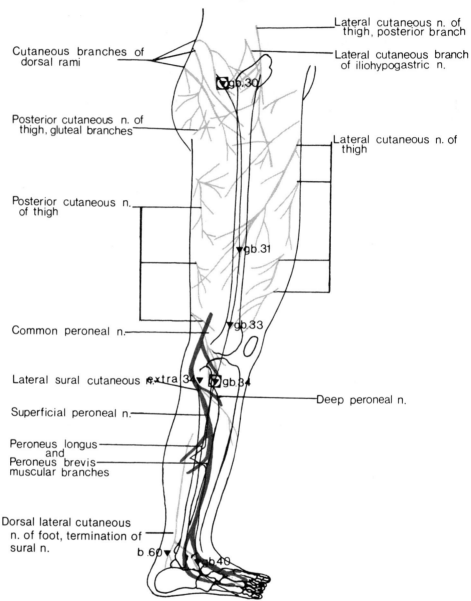

Cutaneous branches of dorsal rami

Lateral cutaneous n. of thigh, posterior branch

Lateral cutaneous branch of iliohypogastric n.

gb.30

Posterior cutaneous n. of thigh, gluteal branches

Lateral cutaneous n. of thigh

Posterior cutaneous n. of thigh

gb.31

gb.33

Common peroneal n.

Lateral sural cutaneous n.

extra 3

gb.34

Deep peroneal n.

Superficial peroneal n.

Peroneus longus and Peroneus brevis muscular branches

Dorsal lateral cutaneous n. of foot, termination of sural n.

b.60

gb.40

Optimal Stimulation Sites
for TENS Electrodes

Lower Extremity,
Lateral View

Location	Superficial Nerve Branch	Acupuncture Point	Motor Point	Trigger Point	Segmental Level
⅓ the distance from the greater trochanter to last sacral foramen. Locate in sidelying position	Posterior branch of lateral cutaneous nerve of thigh, cutaneous branches of dorsal rami, and lateral cutaneous branch of iliohypogastric	GB 30	Gluteus maximus (middle motor pt) (inferior gluteal L5–S2)	Gluteus maximus	L2–3 S1–3 L1
Lateral thigh between vastus lateralis and biceps femoris about 6½″ above lateral aspect of popliteal crease	Lateral cutaneous nerve of thigh	GB 31			L2–3
In depression just above lateral epicondyle of femur	Lateral cutaneous nerve of thigh (anterior branch) which communicates with femoral nerve (cutaneous branches of anterior division) and infrapatellar branch of saphenous forming the patellar plexus	GB 33			L2–3 L3–4
Anterior and inferior to fibular head	Sural communicating branch of common peroneal nerve	GB 34			L4–S2
In depression anterior and inferior to lateral malleolus	Lateral cutaneous branch of superficial peroneal. Communicates with sural nerve	GB 40	Extensor digitorum brevis is just superior (deep peroneal) (L5–S1)		L4–S2
Posterior and inferior to fibular head	Superficial peroneal	E 34			L4–S2
Between lateral malleolus and heelcord	Dorsal lateral cutaneous nerve-end of sural	B 60			L4–S2

Lower Extremity Posterior View

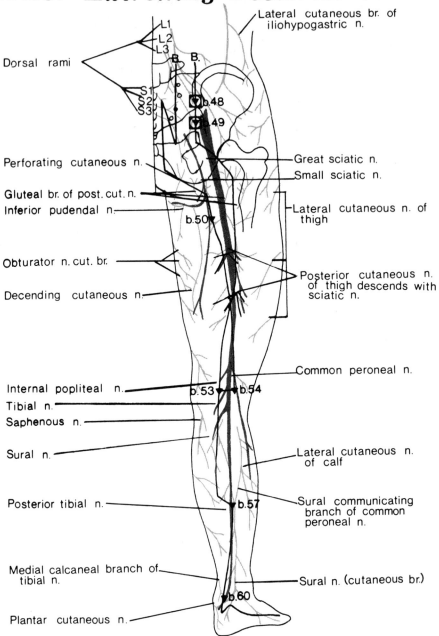

Lateral cutaneous br. of iliohypogastric n.

L1
L2
L3

Dorsal rami

B. B.

S1
S2
S3

b.48

b.49

Perforating cutaneous n.

Great sciatic n.

Small sciatic n.

Gluteal br. of post. cut. n.

Inferior pudendal n.

b.50

Lateral cutaneous n. of thigh

Obturator n. cut. br.

Decending cutaneous n.

Posterior cutaneous n. of thigh descends with sciatic n.

Common peroneal n.

Internal popliteal n.

b.53 b.54

Tibial n.

Saphenous n.

Sural n.

Lateral cutaneous n. of calf

Posterior tibial n.

b.57

Sural communicating branch of common peroneal n.

Medial calcaneal branch of tibial n.

Sural n. (cutaneous br.)

b.60

Plantar cutaneous n.

Optimal Stimulation Sites
for TENS Electrodes

Lower Extremity,
Posterior View

Location	Superficial Nerve Branch	Acupuncture Point	Motor Point	Trigger Point	Segmental Level
2″ lateral to spinous process of S2	Dorsal ramus L2	B 48	Gluteus maximus (upper motor pt) (inferior gluteal L5–S2)	Gluteus maximus	L2 L5–S2
2″ lateral to spinous process of S4	Dorsal rami L2–3	B 49	Gluteus maximus (lower motor pt) (piriformis directly below) (inferior gluteal L5–S2)	Gluteus maximus (piriformis directly below)	L2–3 L5–S2
At midpoint of junction between buttock and posterior thigh	Posterior cutaneous nerve of thigh, medial and lateral branches	B 50			S1–3
Popliteal fossa between biceps femoris and semitendinosus tendons	Posterior cutaneous nerve of thigh, medial and lateral branches	*B 54/40 *B 53/39 (lateral aspect of popliteal fossa medial to biceps femoris tendon)			S1–3
Midline of leg below heads of gastrocsoleus at junction of upper ⅔ and lower ⅓ of leg	Sural, communicating branch of lateral cutaneous nerve of calf (common peroneal)	B 57	Soleus (tibial nerve) S1–2	Soleus	L5–S2 L4–S2
Between lateral malleolus and heelcord	Dorsal lateral cutaneous nerve-end of sural	B 60			L4–S2

*Numerical systems differ according to texts.

B 53 & 54 Acupuncture Therapy[115]
B 39 & 40 An Outline of Chinese Acupuncture[116]

Optimal Stimulation Sites
for TENS Electrodes

Major Joints

TMJ	TW 17–19, 21 GB 2, 3, 11, 12	SI 19 ST 6, 7	
Shoulder	LI 14–16 TW 13, 14 SI 9–15 SP 19, 20	LU 1, 3, 4 P 2 H1	GB 21
Elbow	SI 8 TW 10, 11	LI 10, 11 LU 5	P 3 H 3
Wrist	LU 7–10 P 5–7 H 4–7	LI 4, 6 TW 4, 5 SI 4, 5	
Hip	LIV 10–12 SP 12–13 GB 30	B 48–50	
Knee	B 53, 54 K 10 LIV 8	SP 9, 10 GB 33, 34 Extra 31, 32, 34	ST 33–36
Ankle	ST 42 B 57, 60 GB 40	SP 6 K 3	

The above stimulation sites should be used in combinations either parallel to the joint, above and below the joint, or in a criss-cross fashion. These points are recommended when pain is confined solely to the joint itself. When referred pain is present, further assessment is necessary, and stimulation sites should be utilized that are within or encompass the extent of the pain pattern. A common example would be shoulder pain from a subdeltoid bursitis that is referred down the C5–6 dermatomes. An electrode placed at LI 4 would be recommended as the distal site. When joint pain is due to spinal involvement, electrode placement at the segmentally related spinal levels should be employed in addition to stimulation at the joint. Most major nerves that course anywhere near a joint usually send a twig to innervate the joint. Each joint has a dual pattern of innervation via specific articular nerves that branch from adjacent peripheral nerves as well as nonspecific branches arising from muscles acting upon or attached to the joint.[69]

Since it has been established that the optimal stimulation sites all overlie superficial nerve branches, the anatomic and physiologic principle of electrode placement applies. When pain modulation is desired for the hand or foot, utilize optimal stimulation sites that pick up major nerves at the wrist and ankle, respectively.

Optimal Stimulation Sites
for TENS Electrodes

Major Peripheral Nerve Trunks

Facial	GB 2, 3 TW 17, 21 ST 7 SI 19
Occipital	GB 20
Axillary	SI 9, 10 TW 14 LI 14
Musculocutaneous	LI 1, 5
Median	P 3, 7 H 1
Ulnar	SI 8, H 1–7
Radial	H 1, LI 6
Obturator	SP 12, 13
Femoral	LIV 10–12
Saphenous	K 3, 10
Lateral Cutaneous of Thigh	GB 31, 33

Sciatic
  A. Posterior tibial
  B. Peroneal
  C. Sural
	B 50, 53, 54
	B 53, 54, K 3
	GB 34, ST 42, E 34
	B 57, 60

Most of the optimal stimulation sites listed above represent primarily the same sites utilized in motor and sensory conduction velocity testing.[132,292] It should be pointed out that there are acupuncture points at all these regions. All other optimal stimulation sites listed in these tables overlie cutaneous branches of peripheral nerves.

C1–T1 Spinal Segments

Meridian	C1	C2	C3	C4	C5	C6	C7	C8	T1
Bladder		10	10						
Gallbladder		1–3, 11, 12, 14, 20	1–3, 11, 12, 14, 20, 21	11, 12, 21					
Heart					1, 2	1,2	1, 2, 4–7	1–7	1–7
Kidney									
Large Intestine			16–18	16–18	4, 6, 11, 14, 15	4, 6, 10, 11, 14, 15	4, 6, 10, 11	4, 6, 10, 11	4
Liver									
Lung					1, 3–5, 7, 9, 10	1, 3–5, 7, 9, 10	1, 3–5, 7, 9, 10	7–10	10
Pericardium					2, 3, 5–7	2, 3, 5–7	2, 3, 5–7	2, 3, 5–7	2, 3, 5–7
Small Intestine*		19	13–16, 19	13–16	9–12	9–12	4, 5, 8	4, 5, 8	4, 5, 8
Spleen			19, 20	19, 20					
Stomach		2, 4, 6, 7	2, 4, 6, 7						
Triple Warmer*		17–19, 21, 23	17–19, 21, 23	17–19	4, 5, 10, 11	4, 5, 10, 11	4, 5, 10, 11	4, 5, 10, 11	4, 10, 11
Extra Points		5	5						

*Points SI 9–13 and TW 13 overlie the cutaneous branch of the dorsal ramus of T2.

Optimal Stimulation Sites
for TENS Electrodes

L1–S4 Spinal Segments

Meridian	L1	L2	L3	L4	L5	S1	S2	S3	S4
Bladder	21	23, 27, 48, 49	23, 49	25, 57, 60	25, 60	31, 50, 53, 54, 57, 60	28, 32, 50, 53, 54, 57, 60	28, 33, 50, 53, 54	34, 39
Gallbladder	30	30, 31, 33, 34	30, 31, 33, 34	33, 34, 40	34, 40	30, 34, 40	30, 34, 40	30	
Heart									
Kidney		10	3, 10	3, 10	3	2, 3	2, 3	3	
Large Intestine									
Liver	10–12	8, 10–12	8	2, 3	2, 3	2, 3	2, 3		
Lung									
Pericardium									
Small Intestine									
Spleen		10, 12, 13	6, 9, 10, 12, 13	6, 9, 10, 12, 13					
Stomach		33–35	33–36	33–36, 42	36, 42	36, 42	36, 42		
Triple Warmer									
Extra Points		31, 32	31, 32	32, 34	34	34	34		

CHAPTER 9

ELECTRODE PLACEMENT TECHNIQUES

JEFFREY S. MANNHEIMER, M.A., R.P.T., AND
GERALD N. LAMPE, B.S., R.P.T.

One of the most critical determinants of success with T.E.N.S. is electrode placement. Electrode placement techniques must be adapted to the pain referral pattern and based on anatomic and physiologic factors. Therefore, the clinician must be prepared to try electrode placement techniques at the site of pain or at regions quite removed from the site of pain. The use of the same electrode placement technique for different patients with similar pain syndromes is not always effective, and implies a cookbook approach to pain syndromes regardless of their varying degrees of severity and referral patterns.

An analysis of electrode placement sites based on the innervation of the human body was presented in Chapter 8. This chapter will present the general, specific, and alternative methods of arranging electrodes with regard to specific patients with varied pain syndromes.

Suggestions as to alternative electrode placement and mode of T.E.N.S. will be provided relative to each case study. Specific case studies will include the comprehensive evaluation of the patient, the full treatment program, reasons behind the choice of electrode placement, mode of T.E.N.S., outcome, and follow-up information.

A discussion of the total treatment program will include a general explanation of the modalities and/or specific manual techniques that were used to rehabilitate the patient. In practically every complete case study, T.E.N.S. was employed primarily in an adjunctive capacity, and additional therapy was designed to treat the cause of the pain and prevent its return.

T.E.N.S. is a pain-modulating modality, and its effectiveness must be evaluated when the patient is in pain. Therefore, patients taking pain medication are requested to refrain from doing so at least 4 to 6 hours prior to their clinic visit. When an inpatient is to be evaluated, the physician should be contacted to write a hold order for pain medication. It is important to evaluate a specific electrode arrangement in the position or during the activity that results in pain. Obviously, if an improper or pathologic position is responsible for the patient's discomfort, it is expected that the professional will correct this, if possible, which may in turn negate the need for T.E.N.S. In direct relationship, if an activity that can be avoided is detrimental to the patient's welfare or causes excessive stress, torsion, or strain on a body part, T.E.N.S. should not be used and appropriate retraining should be instituted.

Regardless of the many electrode placement arrangements that will be discussed, more than one should be able to be evaluated during an average patient visit. However, this cannot be done when the physical therapist is restricted by hospital procedures to a 20- to 30-minute treatment period per patient. The various modes of T.E.N.S. (conventional; brief, intense; acupuncture-like; and pulse-train) require different induction periods necessary to optimally evaluate their effectiveness. The effectiveness of conventional T.E.N.S. may sometimes be determined within a few minutes, whereas that of acupuncture-like T.E.N.S. requires a minimum of 20 to 30 minutes of stimulation to evaluate its benefit.

When T.E.N.S. was first introduced in the early 1970s as a new method of pain modulation, instruction in its use was empirical. The practitioner was merely told to place the electrode within the appropriate dermatome or area of pain. Few if any alternatives were suggested, and thus the success rate was low. In our early seminars on T.E.N.S., we frequently were informed that T.E.N.S. did not work. Many physical therapists stated, "I tried it a few times without success so I stopped using it." Subsequent questioning revealed that only one electrode placement technique was employed using one channel.

At that time, the literature pertaining to T.E.N.S. was sparse. Most available stimulators contained only one channel of two electrodes, and instruction in the operation of the unit was not based on specific physiologic data relative to the nerve fibers that were to be stimulated (see Chapter 8). Conventional T.E.N.S. was the only stimulation mode used, and all those who used T.E.N.S. were told to keep the current below the level that caused muscle contraction. Many other factors contributed to the low initial success rate with T.E.N.S. as outlined in Table 9-1.

Perhaps the major cause of failure has been due to a poor approach to the patient when introducing T.E.N.S. and evaluating its effectiveness. Chapters 6 and 7 present the approach to the patient in a manner conducive to obtaining optimal success with T.E.N.S.

The patients discussed in this chapter were referred to Delaware Valley Physical Therapy Associates (DVPTA) for rehabilitation or pain management as outpatients. In practically every case, a comprehensive approach was taken toward the rehabilitation of the patient. The description, history, and treatment were taken in whole or in part from the actual patient's records, plus evaluation and progress notes that were forwarded to the referring physicians. We, of course, were unable to adequately treat behavioral or psychologic components that existed in the patients with chronic pain (appropriate referral was made when necessary), but every effort was made to prevent these from occurring in

TABLE 9-1. Factors Contributing to a Low Success Rate With T.E.N.S.

1. Improper patient evaluation prior to use of T.E.N.S.
2. Patient under the influence of pain medication at the time of evaluation
3. Poor approach to the patient
4. Evaluation of only one electrode channel
5. Utilization of only one mode of T.E.N.S.
6. Evaluation of stimulation sites with time-consuming and irritative rubber electrodes, tape, and gel
7. Spending too much time evaluating one electrode arrangement, resulting in negative feeling on the part of the patient
8. Forcing the patient to rent or purchase the unit prior to determining its efficiency
9. Employed as a last-resort modality

patients with acute pain. It is beyond the scope of this book to discuss all the physical modalities and techniques used in the development of a comprehensive treatment program. Therefore, the following material from the DVPTA clinic flyer supplies a short but basic explanation of the procedures that will be mentioned or alluded to throughout the case presentations.

Clinical Objectives

1. Treat the cause rather than the symptom early in the acute phase to prevent the development of chronic pain and/or disability.
2. The restoration of the involved tissues to their normal state.
3. Increase in neuromusculoskeletal function through a comprehensive rehabilitation program.
4. Pain management during rehabilitation for the acute patient.
5. Decrease the incidence of re-injury.

Services Provided: Evaluation

Evaluation consists of biomechanical analysis, joint mobility, neuromuscular function, and pain assessment. We place emphasis on conducting a thorough evaluation of each patient in conjunction with the referring physician. A combined effort is thus made to determine the nature and location of the pain or dysfunction as well as the structure from which it is arising. When this has been accomplished, our clinical objectives can be achieved by directing specific techniques to the involved structure or source of pain. Traditional physical therapy modalities serve as an adjunct to new treatment techniques that aim to relieve pain, irritation and edema, restore joint mobility and increase strength and endurance. The addition of specific home exercise programs along with instruction in proper body mechanics serve to prevent recurrence and form the basis of a comprehensive rehabilitation program. The following therapeutic techniques constitute the backbone of our clinical approach.

Joint Mobilization

Joint mobilization is the performance of passive tractional and gliding movements of joint surfaces to increase ROM in the stiff extremity and spinal joints. This is safe, painless, and efficient when compared with forcing gross passive ROM on a stiff joint, which can be traumatic, or by using only active ROM, which is slow and inefficient. One can restore ROM of the joint with these maneuvers, which selectively stretch the joint capsule in all directions, thereby allowing a pain-free increase in ROM to occur.

Isokinetics (Orthotron)

Isokinetic exercise represents the most recent advance in exercise and conditioning. Unlike weight-lifting (progressive resistance exercises) in which there is a fixed weight and the speed of movement is varied by the individual, the orthotron moves at fixed speeds and matches the amount of force of the muscular contraction. This is called accommodating resistance, which allows a muscle to work maximally throughout the entire joint ROM. Isokinetics is a safe method of strengthening even in most postsurgical conditions. Isokinetic exercise units also employ immediate readout of torque, which can be used to assess the status of injury as well as progress.

Cyriax Traction

Cyriax traction is a unique form of static mechanical traction developed by an orthopedic physician. Traction is slowly increased, held for a period of 20 minutes, and then slowly decreased to prevent a relapse of back pain, which is common with intermittent mechanical traction. An extremely effective means of reduction for intervertebral disk herniation with or without neurologic signs.

Transverse Friction Massage

Transverse friction massage (TFM) is performed for muscle, tendon, and ligament injury or strain. The most common indication is tendinitis. TFM results in a longer-lasting localized hyperemia and the breakup of adherent scar tissue. Proper position of the involved tendon is imperative.

Cryotherapy

Ice is a much more effective counterirritant and analgesic than heat. Fluorimethane is a safe, nonvolatile vapocoolant spray that chills the skin and not the muscle. It is effective in the relief and gradual stretching (restoration of normal rest length) of muscle guarding due to irritable trigger points or acute stretch injuries.

Transcutaneous Electrical Nerve Stimulation (T.E.N.S.)

T.E.N.S. uses various intensities of current to selectively stimulate either large (proprioceptive) or small (pain) afferent nerve fibers via surface electrodes. Depending upon actual stimulation parameters, T.E.N.S. may modulate pain by blocking small afferent fiber input at the dorsal horn, interfering with the ability of the brain to recognize pain input patterns or resulting in a liberation of endogenous opiates (natural pain-relieving peptides). Frequently compared with acupuncture in terms of effectiveness and physiologic action, T.E.N.S. can provide a safe, nonmedicinal, noninvasive, and nonaddictive means of pain control. A T.E.N.S. device is small, portable, battery-operated and can be used by the acute patient for pain control at home while clinical treatment aimed at correcting the cause of the pain is being performed. Patients with chronic pain who have been through unsuccessful rehabilitation courses may also be able to obtain pain control in lieu of narcotics and frequently addictive medication. T.E.N.S. can be used postoperatively for immediate pain control and to decrease the incidence of ileus and atelectasis.

Biofeedback

Biofeedback provides a means of immediately feeding information back to the patient by devices that amplify minute muscle action potentials, skin temperature, galvanic skin resistance, and so forth. Visual and auditory feedback indicative of muscle function and peripheral vasodilation and constriction is helpful in teaching the patient to gain voluntary self-regulation of abnormal physiologic states that may persist in maintaining many painful musculoskeletal syndromes. Electromyographic feedback may be utilized in the patient with muscle guarding or muscle contraction (tension) headaches and as a means of re-education after peripheral nerve, spinal cord, or cerebral vascular injuries. Temperature biofeedback training has been shown to be effective in migraine headaches and peripheral vascular conditions such as Raynaud's phenomenon. Relaxation training with the aid of autogenic tapes may constitute an essential ingredient in a biofeedback training program.

High-Voltage Galvanic Stimulation

High-voltage, low-amperage direct current has a variety of beneficial uses. This comfortable form of electrical stimulation is an excellent adjunctive means of reducing synovitis, edema, pain, and muscle guarding as well as to increase granulation of open wounds. It can also aid in the softening of scar tissue and adhesions, which can help to increase range of motion. In cases of severe edema from acute musculoskeletal injury or after fracture, intermittent gradient pressure can also be utilized via a Jobst Compression unit.

Specific Exercise Program

Each patient does not experience an increase or decrease in pain and function from the same postures or activities. Thus, exercise programs must be developed on an individual basis. A common example is the patient with low back pain. Most mechanical low back injuries occur in a forward-bent position with resultant loss of the normal lordotic curve. There is thus little value in Williams flexion exercise for these patients. Instead, graded *passive* backward-bending exercises performed by the patient in the standing or prone position have been shown to be very beneficial in relieving pain, restoring full active ROM and the lordotic curve of the lumbar spine. Continued periodic use of such an exercise program as well as instruction in proper body mechanics can help prevent recurrence.

The discussion of electrode placements will be based in large part on the information presented in Chapters 5 and 8; thus an understanding of this information is essential. A detailed analysis of anatomic relationships will not be reiterated in this section. Refer to the charts and tables in Chapter 8 for musculoskeletal landmarks and segmental relationships of electrode placement sites.

The main objective is to determine the optimal electrode sites and arrangement that provide the best and most prolonged degree of pain relief with the shortest period of stimulation. A thorough evaluation of the pain pattern is mandatory. It is also imperative that electrode placement allow for the perception of the current throughout the area of pain.[1-4] This is beneficial primarily when performing conventional; low-intensity, pulse-train (burst); and brief, intense T.E.N.S. but not so with the other modes of stimulation.

The use of self-adhering electrodes substantially decreases the time required to switch electrodes to different sites (Fig. 9-1, A and B). Karaya and other self-adhering (synthetic polymer) electrodes require only water for activation. These electrodes are used for patient evaluation and are recommended for the patient who is using a unit at home. They can be used on a number of patients undergoing clinical evaluation provided no open wound or infectious skin lesions are present. Depending on the frequency of use, one set of four electrodes may last 1 to 2 months in the clinic. A recently produced synthetic polymer electrode is Neuro-Aid (Medtronic).

Sponge electrodes using water as a transmission medium may be employed as a means of evaluating different electrode sites without the hindrance of tape and gel. Instructions to make a set of sponge electrodes at little or no cost are outlined in Figure 9-1, C.

Gel pads (3M Corp.) and premoistened pads (Parker Laboratories) can also be used to avoid having to apply a gel (see Appendix).

Electrode placement arrangements and the size and number of electrodes may differ according to not only the pain syndrome but the particular area of the body to be treated. In addition, the quality and depth of the pain may necessitate using different modes of stimulation for optimal success. Depending on the stimulation mode, the placement as well as the channel arrangement of electrodes differs according to the stimulation parameters.

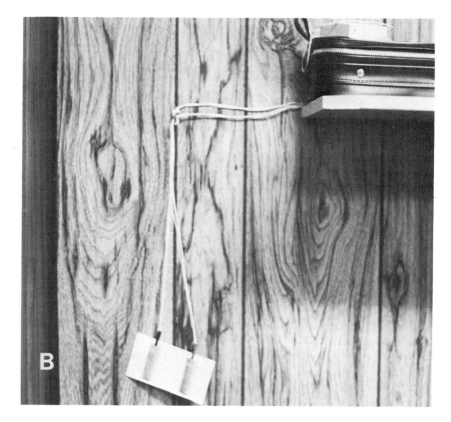

No Cost Spotting Electrodes

These spotting electrodes are extremely helpful in obtaining the optimal placement of TENS electrodes. The benefit for the patient would be the difference between partial and total relief of symptoms. They could also provide a way for home bound patients to realign electrodes.

To make your own set of electrodes -
1. Obtain two childproof medicine caps about 1" to 1½" in diameter.
2. Pop the plastic insert out.
3. Drill a hole in the side large enough to insert the plastic part of a pin electrode.
4. Place a small electrode on the exposed pin electrode inside the cap. A suggestion is to use one half of the carbon strip from a disposable Tenzcare™ reusable electrode.
5. Insert a wet sponge or ¼" thick felt cut to fit the medicine cap.
6. Mark tender points on patient.
7. Move electrodes over optimal stimulation sites.
8. Optimal placement is determined by those sites which provide for the most significant paresthesia throughout the pain distribution.

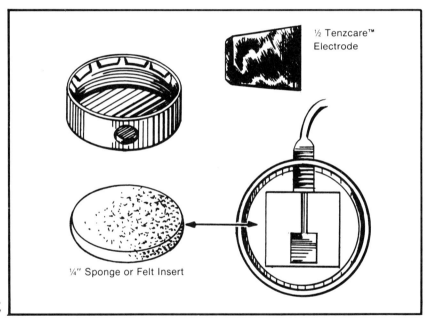

½ Tenzcare™ Electrode

¼" Sponge or Felt Insert

C

FIGURE 9-1. *A,* **Four karaya electrodes (Dermaforms, Stim-tech Inc.) hanging from lead wires connected to T.E.N.S. unit on shelf. A piece of cellophane is between the electrodes. *B,* Self-adhering synthetic polymer electrodes (Tenzcare Reusable, 3M Inc.). *C,* Instructions for making spotting electrodes. (Reproduced with permission of K. Lamm.[202])**

There is virtually no limit to the number of electrodes and methods of arrangement that can be employed with T.E.N.S.[5] Many practitioners decide on stimulation sites for specific pain syndromes by referral to texts on acupuncture and related methodologies. The rules, laws, and principles of acupuncture can become quite specific regarding the exact points to stimulate and the precise order in which to do so. However, there is a distinct difference between applications when T.E.N.S. is compared with electroacupuncture.

T.E.N.S. was basically designed to be able to be used by the patient. Stimulators have become quite simplified and can be operated by practically every patient with ease. T.E.N.S. electrodes are quite large when compared with acupuncture needles or electrical probes, and placement on specific regions of the body does not require precision accuracy.

The only acupunctural technique that can be performed by the patient is acupressure. Here again, the means of stimulation is large, one fingertip, in comparison with that of a needle or probe. The small contact point between a needle and the skin may necessitate exact placement, which is not the case with T.E.N.S.

A literature review relative to the establishment of stimulation characteristics and electrical parameters follows. Clinical and experimental findings pertaining to the conventional; strong, low-rate (acupuncture-like); pulse-train or burst; and brief, intense stimulation modes are presented. Optimal stimulation parameters based on the literature review and our clinical experience for initial settings of the various modes are presented in Table 9-2. When stimulation modes are listed for each case study, parameter adjustment is in line with these settings. Variability of pulse duration and amplitude settings, however, change with pain quality and intensity.

SPECIFIC STIMULATION MODES: A LITERATURE REVIEW

Note: When reading this section and succeeding sections in Chapter 12, specific references to the pulse width or duration of the stimulating current may be given in microseconds (μsec) or milliseconds (msec). There does not seem to be any international standardization, and this can lead to confusion for the reader.

The majority of publications pertaining to T.E.N.S. in the United States denote pulse

TABLE 9-2. T.E.N.S. Modes: Optimal Initial Stimulation Parameter Settings

	Conventional	Strong, Low-Rate (Acupuncture-like)	High-intensity, Pulse-Train (Burst)*	Brief, Intense
Frequency	50–100 Hz	1–4 Hz	Trains of high-frequency (70–100 Hz) pulses modulated at a rate of 2 Hz	100–150 Hz
Pulse Duration	40–75 μsec	150–250 μsec	100–200 μsec	150–250 μsec
Amplitude	Perceptible, paresthesia up to but not causing significant muscle contraction or fasciculation	To tolerance, giving rise to strong, rhythmic muscle contractions	To tolerance; strong, rhythmic contractions plus a background paresthesia	To tolerance, will cause either a tetanic contraction or non-rhythmic fasciculations
	10–30 mA	30–80 mA	30–60 mA	30–80 mA

Note: Pulse duration and amplitude ranges are quite variable and depend a great deal on the quality and distribution of pain, interelectrode distance, number of electrodes utilized, and patient tolerance.

*Pulse-train (burst) parameters can also be delivered at low intensity similar to the conventional mode. When used in this manner, amplitude and pulse width will be in the range of the conventional mode, and the sensation will consist of mild paresthesia plus a rhythmic background pulsing.

width in microseconds. However, foreign publications utilize milliseconds. The reader should, therefore, be aware of this and convert milliseconds to microseconds as follows:

$$0.02 \text{ msec} = 20 \text{ } \mu\text{sec}$$
$$0.3 \text{ msec} = 300 \text{ } \mu\text{sec}$$
$$70 \text{ msec} = 70,000 \text{ } \mu\text{sec}$$

There are a few studies that report using a 70- to 80-msec pulse width. This seems unusually high, and there may be a reporting error. Those studies that report using a 70- to 80-msec pulse duration were performed with the pulse-train mode. A 70- to 80-µsec pulse duration would be within our acceptable range, although at the low end.

CONVENTIONAL T.E.N.S.

The most common T.E.N.S. mode is one that uses a high rate, narrow pulse width, and moderate intensity. This is the conventional mode, designed to selectively activate the large myelinated afferent fibers.[6,7] Muscle contraction or fasciculation should not be apparent with conventional T.E.N.S. If effective, this mode of T.E.N.S. results in a fast onset of relief but has a relatively short aftereffect, generally not exceeding the length of stimulation.[7–13] There are, however, reports attesting to a prolonged aftereffect of hours and occasionally a day or more with conventional T.E.N.S.[8–14] We frequently are able to obtain 1 to 3 hours of pain relief and occasionally even a longer-lasting aftereffect with this mode of stimulation. Conventional T.E.N.S. produces the sensation of a mild to moderate, comfortable paresthesia that is most effective when perceived throughout the area of pain.[7,8,15,16]

When utilizing conventional T.E.N.S., parameter adjustment begins by presetting the rate high (approximately 50 to 100 Hz) and the width low (approximately 40 to 75 µsec), and then raising the intensity to a level of comfort with a deep perception of paresthesia throughout the area of pain. Slight increases in the pulse width are occasionally required if the current is not felt throughout the area of pain. Rapid accommodation to the current necessitates periodic increases in the intensity (amplitude or pulse width) by the patient.

Campbell and Taub employed percutaneous electrical stimulation (PES) of the digital nerves in the median distribution in humans.[17] A 100-Hz, 1-msec current of variable intensity, 10 to 12 V, 22 V, and 50 V, was used. Stimulation was increased over a 5- to 20-minute period. The lowest voltage (10 to 12 V) raised the threshold to touch but not pain at the tip of the stimulated finger; 22 V raised the threshold to both touch and pain. Continuous stimulation at 50 V with a duration of 0.5 msec resulted in no perception of stimuli via a needle to the skin and only a brief jabbing sensation with piercing of the skin.

Andersson and associates obtained marked pain relief in 7 of 12 patients with chronic back and/or leg pain with high-frequency T.E.N.S.[12] Stimulation parameters were a rate of 50 to 100 Hz, 0.2-msec duration, and an intensity just below patient tolerance for 15 minutes (brief, intense T.E.N.S.). Only 1 of the 12 patients obtained partial pain relief with low-frequency T.E.N.S. at 2 Hz. Low-frequency T.E.N.S. produced strong, beating muscle contractions that were not tolerated either at a high enough intensity or for a long enough time by these patients. The aftereffect of the high-rate T.E.N.S. was short, lasting only about 30 minutes, with a range of a few minutes to 1 hour. Relief lasted for several hours in one patient. Onset of pain relief was within a few minutes after the start of stimulation. Stimulation at rates of 10 and 25 Hz was not as effective as stimulation at rates of 50 to 100 Hz.

Walmsley and Flexman studied the effects of low-intensity T.E.N.S. using variable frequencies in a group of 10 patients with chronic low back pain.[18] The intensity used was just above the level of sensation, and stimulation rates were 25, 100, and 300 Hz. There was no mention of the pulse duration settings during any of the treatment sessions. Results showed an overall mean decrease in pain of 64 percent for the 10 patients, and the length of relief varied from 1 hour to 4 days, with a mean of 19 hours. The most prolonged aftereffect was achieved with a 100-Hz frequency. Mean durations of pain relief were 34.5, 19.6, and 16 hours with frequencies of 100, 25, and 300 Hz, respectively. In retrospect, this study compared the effect of variable rates of stimulation using an intensity compatible with that of conventional T.E.N.S. Any comparison to true strong, low-rate (acupuncture-like) T.E.N.S. is unjustified since a rate of 1 to 4 Hz with a wide pulse width and strong intensity to muscle contraction level should be employed. In addition, stimulation was provided only for a period of 20 minutes. True acupuncture-like T.E.N.S. may require 30 minutes to achieve a supraspinal endorphin liberation, which should promote a longer period of pain relief.

Jancko and associates stimulated the sensory fibers of the median nerve with variable frequencies and waveforms.[19] The same type of stimulation occurred with variable pulse shapes, but high-frequency stimulation (50 to 100 Hz) produced a profound loss of both tactile and pain sensation after a few minutes, distal to the stimulating electrodes. An associated reflex vasoconstriction also was observed.

Reports dealing with experimental pain on normal subjects show similar patterns. Wolf used a 100-Hz, 0.25-msec stimulus at an intensity that was sufficient to cause definite paresthesia but was not unpleasant.[20] It was determined that a noxious level of T.E.N.S. was required to modify thermal or mechanical experimental pain.

In a study comparing the effects of 3-, 50-, 100-, 300-, 500-, and 1000-Hz stimulation percutaneously, it was found that frequencies of 50 and 100 Hz were most effective in producing analgesia to radiant heat pain.[21] Paresthesia was necessary for the effective modulation of pain. Frequencies of 3, 500, and 1000 Hz were not successful, and at the highest rates paresthesia decreased to a sensation of only slight pressure. Omura, however, has noted an almost immediate decrease in pain with very high frequencies of 10 kHz and 500 kHz.[203]

Nyquist and Ignelzi experimented with individual fibers of the sciatic nerve of the toad.[22] Stimulation percutaneously via a cuff electrode for 5 to 10 minutes at a threshold high enough to activate the fibers was performed. Variable frequencies between 12.5 and 180 Hz produced a reversible increase in the electrical threshold and, therefore, a decrease in excitability of 90 percent of the fibers immediately after the stimulation period. Below-threshold intensities produced no change in excitability.

Mannheimer and Carlsson evaluated the effectiveness of different frequencies utilizing 70 Hz, 3 Hz, and pulse trains of 3 Hz with an internal rate of 70 Hz on patients with rheumatoid arthritis.[23] The greatest effectiveness with the most prolonged period of pain relief was obtained with a rate of 70 Hz (mean of 18 hours), the least with 3 Hz (mean of 4 hours), and a mean of 15 hours with pulse-train stimulation. Stimulation time was 10 minutes with the amplitude increased to just below the painful level (brief, intense mode). Pulse duration was set at 80 msec. Electrodes in all cases were placed just proximal to the wrist on the volar and dorsal surfaces (see Case Study 25).

Johansson and associates evaluated the effectiveness of a high-rate (conventional) T.E.N.S. on a group of 72 patients with chronic pain.[24] All patients had received unsuccessful treatment and/or surgery prior to the study and had had chronic pain for at least 6 months. None of the participants had taken narcotic medication or was misusing alcohol or tranquilizers. Each patient was classified into one of three groups: neurogenic, somatogenic, and psychogenic pain. A rate of 80 to 100 Hz was employed for three to six daily treatments over a consecutive 2- to 4-day period. Electrode placement was over painful regions or main afferent nerve trunks. There was no information provided concerning pulse duration or amplitude of the stimulation current. Results showed two thirds of the patients received 50 to 100 percent pain relief lasting more than 2 hours after stimulation. The remaining one third obtained 20 to 50 percent pain relief lasting 30 minutes to 2 hours after stimulation. Patients with neurogenic pain confined to the extremities as opposed to the midline obtained the greatest degree of success.

Andersson and Holmgren determined that high-rate T.E.N.S. produced a faster increase in pain threshold but also a short aftereffect with ongoing stimulation.[10,13] Transient increases in pain threshold were produced by further increases in intensity.

The effect of T.E.N.S. on the flexor withdrawal response of the tail of the rat was recently reported.[25] Reaction time was prolonged following 30 minutes of stimulation at a rate of 100 Hz and pulse duration of 0.2 msec at an intensity high enough to cause slight fibrillation of the tail but no escape behavior due to pain. A similar degree of reaction time delay was produced by 7.5 mg/kg of morphine.

Experimental and clinical results present certain factors relating to conventional T.E.N.S. It is apparent that a frequency between 50 to 100 Hz is most effective. No significant benefit has been shown with frequencies in the 100- to 1000-Hz range, but ultra-high frequency (above 1000 Hz) needs further study. Gammon and Starr, in a study of counterirritation techniques for pain relief, found that a frequency of 50 to 60 Hz was optimal.[16] They studied frequencies within the 1- to 300-Hz range. Stimulation was most beneficial when paresthesia was perceived throughout the area of pain. Stimulation below perceptible sensation was not as effective, and the stronger the paresthesia, as long as muscle contraction was not significant, the better the analgesia. Onset of relief was relatively quick if paresthesia was perceived throughout the area of pain. Length of relief generally equaled the time of stimulation, but this is dependent on numerous variables and related factors (discussed in Chapter 12). It is quite common in our clinical experience to obtain 1 to 2 hours of pain relief with this stimulation mode.

STRONG, LOW-RATE (ACUPUNCTURE-LIKE) T.E.N.S.

Electrical parameters adjusted to provide a low rate (1 to 4 Hz), wide pulse width (150 to 250 μsec), and high intensity are known as strong, low-rate (acupuncture-like) T.E.N.S. To be effective, this mode of T.E.N.S. requires an induction period of at least 20 to 30 minutes and must produce strong, visible muscle contractions in segmentally related myotomes.[4,9–13,26,27–34] In those experiments comparing the effects of needle or surface stimulation (percutaneous versus transcutaneous), similar results were obtained and in many cases they were somewhat better with surface stimulation.[28,35–36]

This mode of stimulation provides a definite prolonged aftereffect of pain relief, which seems to be related to the long onset.

One distinct problem with this is that in many cases it is not well tolerated by the patient in the area of pain. Strong muscle contractions of the already painful area do not facilitate tolerance long enough for pain relief to ensue.[12,37]

The most informative work on strong, low-rate (acupuncture-like) T.E.N.S. comes from experimental studies with dental students. Studies from Sweden have compared the changes in the pain threshold of teeth with a 2-Hz frequency and different levels of intensity.[13,35] Six intensity levels were employed:

1. Subliminal, causing no sensation or muscle contractions.
2. Slightly supraliminal, perceived as a weak tapping sensation.

3. A weak but clear beating sensation with minor muscle contractions.
4. A strong beating sensation with distinct muscle contractions.
5. Maximal tolerable intensity for up to 60 minutes, producing intense muscle contractions.
6. Very intense stimulation, which was tolerated with difficulty for 20 minutes and distinctly painful.

The intensity at all six levels was kept constant for 20 minutes. Level 4 produced a slight increase in pain threshold; level 5, an increase 2.7 times that of the control level; and level 6, an increase 3.8 times that of the control level. A stimulation intensity of at least 19 mA was required to only slightly increase the tooth pain threshold. In the study by Holmgren, stimulation was for 1 hour, after which pain threshold was increased two and one half to three times above the control level.[35] Intense stimulation also gave the best result.

Chapman, Chen, and Bonica confirmed the findings of the Swedish investigators in an experiment on induced dental pain.[27] They employed a frequency of 2 Hz for 80 minutes with a strong throbbing sensation. Tooth pain threshold increased by 187 percent after 20 minutes of stimulation at the cheek. The threshold remained constant for the remaining stimulation period. In an earlier study, Chapman, Wilson, and Gehrig used electroacupuncture and T.E.N.S. only at bilateral "hoku" (LI 4) dorsal web space points.[26] They demonstrated a small but significant analgesia that was compared with that of 33 percent nitrous oxide. This seems to relate to the findings obtained with ice massage.[38]

Eriksson and Sjölund compared the effects of conventional and acupuncture-like T.E.N.S. in 30 patients with trigeminal neuralgia.[39] There was no mention of specific current parameters in the abstract cited, but it is assumed that they were compatible with the previous given ranges. Of these 30 patients, 22 had previously undergone surgical procedures with good but transient pain relief in 60 percent of cases. Conventional T.E.N.S. was successful in only 4 of the 22, and 8 others obtained success with acupuncture-like T.E.N.S.[39]

Takakura and associates analyzed different electrical parameters and determined by patient preference an optimal frequency of an irregular 1-Hz current.[40] Four of five patients with intractable pain who were unable to obtain relief by regular T.E.N.S. obtained pain relief with the 1-Hz fluctuating current. The abstract did not present other stimulating parameters but did report a longer aftereffect with irregular as opposed to regular (unchanging) 1-Hz stimulation.

As previously mentioned, stimulation parameters that provide optimal pain relief with the noninvasive electroacupuncture units are equivalent to the acupuncture-like mode. One distinct difference, however, is that the onset of pain relief may occur in a shorter period of time with noninvasive electroacupuncture than the 20 to 30 minutes needed with acupuncture-like T.E.N.S. However, the aftereffect (length of poststimulation pain relief) is sometimes longer.

Experimental and clinical results show that the stimulation characteristics of strong, low-rate (acupuncture-like) T.E.N.S. differ distinctly from those of the conventional mode. A frequency between 1 and 4 Hz is the desired range, and 2 to 3 Hz may be optimal. The intensity of stimulation must produce visible muscle contractions, optimally in segmentally related myotomes, and the stronger the contraction the better the analgesia. Stimulation must be given for at least 20 to 30 minutes before pain relief ensues, and the duration of poststimulation pain relief seems to be longer lasting than with the conventional mode. When the term acupuncture-like is used to refer to the strong, low-rate mode, this does not mean that acupuncture points must be stimulated. Electroacupuncture via needle electrodes is employed at a rate of 1 to 4 Hz, and manual twirling of acupuncture needles also occurs at a similar frequency. The same rate is used with the strong, low-rate mode, and thus it is also referred to as acupuncture-like T.E.N.S. Acupuncture-like T.E.N.S. is com-

TABLE 9-3. Conventional and Acupuncture-like T.E.N.S.: A Physiologic Comparison

Conventional	Strong, Low-Rate (Acupuncture-like)
1. Primarily large (proprioceptive) afferent fiber stimulation (narrow pulse width and high pulse rate)	1. Primarily small (pain) afferent and (motor) efferent fiber stimulation (wide pulse width and low pulse rate)
2. Produces a comfortable mild paresthesia without muscle contraction (not as effective below perception level).	2. Produces a strong muscle contraction that may be uncomfortable. Effectiveness increased by highest tolerable muscle contractions
3. Fast onset (accommodation occurs, necessitating amplitude or pulse width readjustment)	3. Slow onset (Little or no accommodation. May activate summation mechanisms)
4. Relatively short aftereffect	4. Relatively long aftereffect
5. No endogenous opiate liberation	5. Endogenous opiate liberation
6. No reversal by naloxone	6. Reversal by naloxone
7. Primarily local CNS effects (segmental)	7. Primarily higher CNS effects (supraspinal)
8. Stimulation by surface electrodes in segmentally related regions is most effective	8. Stimulation by surface electrodes in segmentally related myotomes is more effective

monly employed via surface electrodes overlying superficial aspects of mixed peripheral nerves as well as motor points. As discussed in Chapter 8, acupuncture points also exist at these locations. Table 9-3 depicts the physiologic differences between acupuncture-like and conventional T.E.N.S.

PULSE-TRAIN (BURST) STIMULATION

Pulse-train (or burst) stimulation employs current parameters of a wide pulse width, high intensity, and combination train of pulses providing high-frequency bursts with each low-rate pulse. There is a low repetition rate, yet a high internal frequency. Pulse trains may require only one half to two thirds of the current needed for strong, low-rate (acupuncture-like) T.E.N.S. with comparable results and appears to be better tolerated by the patient.[14,30] Pulse-train (burst) T.E.N.S. may also be delivered at low intensity levels equal to or slightly greater than those of the conventional mode. When T.E.N.S. is used in this manner, muscle contractions do not occur, but the perception of paresthesia plus mild rhythmic pulsing is present. We have found low-intensity, pulse-train (burst) T.E.N.S. to be clinically similar to conventional T.E.N.S. but to be preferred by some patients for reasons of comfort. Thus, use of the low-intensity, pulse-train (burst) mode is an effective means of modulating conventional T.E.N.S.

Good results in modulating the pain of rheumatoid arthritis were obtained with pulse trains using a repetition rate of 3 Hz and internal frequency of 70 Hz. Current intensity was just below that which would cause pain.[23,41] Segmentally related electrode placement was required.

Eriksson and Sjolund, in a study of 50 patients with chronic pain, obtained satisfactory electroanalgesia with a conventional mode of T.E.N.S. in 20 patients.[14] The 30 patients who did not obtain relief were treated with pulse trains at 2-Hz repetition rate with internal frequency of 100 Hz, and 70-msec duration, which reduced the total required current. An induction period of 30 minutes was necessary, and segmentally related muscle contractions visible throughout the treatment period. Ten of the remaining 30 patients were able to obtain satisfactory electroanalgesia with the pulse-train (burst) mode.

Fox and Melzack compared the effects of acupuncture with pulse-trains at a 3-Hz repetition rate and internal frequency of a 60-Hz sine wave for the treatment of low back pain.[42] Stimulation in all cases was at the same acupuncture points. One minute of needle acupuncture with strong manual rotation was performed at three sites in succession, and T.E.N.S. was given for 10 minutes at each of the same sites. Both means of stimulation were painful but not unbearable. Results showed no significant superiority of one stimulation type over the other, both appearing to be beneficial in a majority of patients, 75 percent via acupuncture and 66 percent via T.E.N.S. The aftereffect, however, showed a mean duration of 4 hours in the acupuncture group and 23 hours in the T.E.N.S. group.

Another study using dental students to test tooth pain threshold was conducted with stimulation parameters of a 2-Hz pulse train with 100-Hz internal frequency.[43] The difference in this experiment was that the intensity level was well tolerated and kept below that which would cause strong muscle contractions for a period of 30 minutes. Four different electrode placement arrangements were employed, with the most effective being bilateral infraorbital stimulation. Stimulation was solely transcutaneous in each group. At the 30-minute stimulation mark, pain threshold showed the highest increase, 48 percent for the upper jaw and 50 percent for the lower jaw. Pain threshold decreased to the prestimulation level within 30 minutes after stimulation had ceased. Obviously, elevation of the tooth pain threshold was not as great as in the previously cited experiments and may be explained by the low current intensity, which did not produce muscle contraction.

In a study by Eriksson, Sjolund, and Nielzen, 123 patients were treated with surface electrode stimulation via conventional or pulse-train parameters.[14] High-frequency conventional usage varied between 10 and 100 Hz, and pulse trains had a repetition rate of 1 to 4 Hz with an internal frequency of 100 Hz and pulse duration of 70 msec. The stimulation levels employed were two and one-half to three times and three to five times the perception threshold in conventional and pulse-train modes, respectively. It was found that by utilizing both stimulation modes, the percentage of patients who benefited from T.E.N.S. was 30 percent greater than if only conventional T.E.N.S. was used.

BRIEF, INTENSE T.E.N.S.

Melzack initially reported on a mode of T.E.N.S. that he called "brief-intense."[44] He used a rate of 3 or 10 Hz to modulate a 60-Hz sine wave train for a period of 20 minutes. Pulse width was not mentioned in the report, and intensity, which was adjustable to a maximum of 35 V, was increased until it became painful and then slightly decreased to a level at which it could be tolerated for the 20-minute stimulation period. This intensity level was maintained by minor periodic increases or decreases in amplitude. Electrodes were applied to painful trigger points in patients with chronic pain who had not achieved pain relief with other modalities.

In our opinion, this type of brief, intense T.E.N.S. more closely approximates that of the pulse-train (burst) mode. Our method of brief, intense T.E.N.S. differs from that reported by Melzack. We use a stimulation mode consisting of a high rate, wide pulse width, and high intensity for periods of 5 to 15 minutes. Parameter adjustment specifically consists of presetting the rate high (approximately 100 to 150 Hz) and the pulse width high (approximately 150 to 250 μsec), and then raising the amplitude to the highest tolerable level. This high-rate, high-intensity stimulation produces nonrhythmic muscle contractions that are either fasciculatory or tetanic in nature. If electrode placement is directly over the major peripheral nerve innervating the stimulated area, then a tetanic contraction of the related musculature will occur. The placement of electrodes on superficial aspects of purely cutaneous nerves that are not directly stimulating the motor or mixed nerve or in a crisscross manner over the painful region produces fasciculatory contractions of the corresponding musculature. The obtained fasciculations will not hinder the performance of gentle manual therapeutic techniques; whereas repetitive strong, low-rate (acupuncture-like) T.E.N.S. producing strong, rhythmic contractions will interfere with such techniques. Electrode placement over the digital nerves (fingers and toes) usually will not produce fasciculatory or tetanic contractions.

There have been only a few reports in the literature documenting clinical usage of this particular mode of T.E.N.S.[4,10,12,13,23,45] Stimulation at a rate of 70 Hz for 10 minutes at an intensity just below that which caused pain was found to be very effective in modulating wrist pain in patients with rheumatoid arthritis.[23] Pulse trains of 70-Hz internal frequency with a repetition rate of 3 Hz and 80-msec duration were also effective.

Cheng and Pomeranz performed electroacupuncture via needles to the first dorsal interosseous muscle (corresponds to acupuncture point LI 4) of both forepaws in mice to test analgesia to a hot-lamp stimulus at the nose.[4] Electrical stimulation at an intensity above that needed for muscle contraction but less than that which evoked pain was used. Frequency varied at 0.2, 4, and 200 Hz at a pulse duration of 0.1 msec. Results showed that the best electroanalgesia occurred with a 200-Hz stimulus, less at 4 Hz, and none at 0.2 Hz after 20, 40, and 90 minutes of stimulation, respectively. There was some analgesia after 90 minutes with a rate of 0.2 Hz, but it was much less at its peak than with higher frequencies.

With brief, intense T.E.N.S., the most effective electrode placements are those close to the painful regions (proximal or surrounding).[23] Electroanalgesia can be achieved relatively quickly (1 to 15 minutes) with this mode but diminishes rapidly once the stimulator is turned off. Placing one electrode on the volar aspect of the fifth finger just proximal to the distal phalanx and the second on the volar aspect of the wrist (flexor carpi ulnaris tendon, H 4–7, ulnar nerve) will produce rapid analgesia with the brief, intense mode. The degree of analgesia will increase with continued stimulation so that suture removal, skin debridement, and possibly even minor surgical procedures can be performed to the distal phalanx of the fifth finger with pain control solely by T.E.N.S.[10,13,45] Using a second channel above and below the olecranon groove (ulnar nerve) can further enhance the electroanalgesia effect. Strassburg, Krainick, and Thoden have performed stimulation with electrodes placed proximal to the site of minor surgical procedures or surrounding the operative area to produce adequate analgesia for muscle biopsies and median nerve decompression.[45]

PRINCIPAL CHARACTERISTICS OF DIFFERENT STIMULATION MODES

Electrode placement techniques must take into account the type of pain, its distribution, and the stimulation mode employed. We have been unable to specifically delineate different pain syndromes or qualities of pain as responding best to one distinct stimulation mode. However, conventional T.E.N.S. is always the first mode to be evaluated. Table 9-4 lists the critical procedures for the T.E.N.S. evaluation.

Conventional T.E.N.S. is the most comfortable mode and is tolerated the best by most patients. Success with this mode is dependent on arranging the electrodes and channel distribution so that perception of the paresthesia (electrical) is perceived throughout the area of pain without any significant muscle fasciculation. We recommend using optimal stimulation sites (OSS) that overlie superficial aspects of peripheral nerves that innervate the painful region (see Chapter 8). At least one electrode should be placed at the distal extent of the pain to ensure current flow throughout the entire pain distribution. Electrodes

TABLE 9-4. The T.E.N.S. Evaluation: Critical Procedures

Pain:	Patient should be in pain and therefore not under the influence of pain medication.
Time:	Appointment must be provided at time of day when pain is usually intense.
Position:	Evaluation should be performed in the position in which pain is present (lying, sitting, standing, etc.), providing that the specific posture or activity is consistent with proper body mechanics.
Evaluate:	Delineate nature, location, chronology, and structural source of pain. Select optimal stimulation sites (see guidelines in Chapter 8).
Familiarize:	Stimulate a nonpainful (normal) body region initially.
Electrode Placement:	Arrange electrodes according to pain distribution and stimulate with the conventional mode. Perception of electrical paresthesia must be throughout area of pain and present during the stimulation period. Accommodation can be decreased by modulation of stimulus parameters or use of the low-intensity, pulse-train (burst) mode.
Re-arrange:	If all above factors have been followed and a significant degree of pain relief has not occurred within 10 to 20 minutes, rearrange the electrodes.
Switch Modes:	If effectiveness cannot be obtained with conventional T.E.N.S., switch to other stimulation modes: strong, low-rate (acupuncture-like) or high-intensity, pulse-train (burst). At least 30 minutes of stimulation must be allowed prior to assessing benefit from these modes. Occasionally, 60 minutes should be allotted. Visible muscle contractions are essential in segmentally related myotomes which may be located at or away from the painful region.
Modulation:	Modulation of stimulation parameters will allow for increased tolerance to the stronger stimulation modes.
Followup:	Re-evaluate and follow up at specific intervals after unit is obtained.

WHEN THE ABOVE FAILS

1. Try brief, intense T.E.N.S. Strong stimulation proximal to, crisscrossing, or surrounding painful region.
2. Tolerance may be obtained by modulation.
3. Stimulate at unrelated remote or contralateral areas with the stronger modes.
4. Simultaneous bimodal stimulation may be necessary at different sites.
5. Check list of factors that hinder effectiveness* (see Chapter 12).
6. Different modes may work best at different times of the day.

*ADL, posture, body mechanics are probably the most significant factors that hinder success.

can also be placed at related spinal cord segments that give rise to peripheral nerves innervating the area of pain.

Electrodes can be arranged in many ways and are based on each patient's needs.[5] A patient with pain in one joint may do well with a single channel of two electrodes placed medial and lateral to the joint; others may require a crisscross arrangment.[5] Someone with pain in both lower extremities will require a dual (bilateral) channel arrangement (one channel per extremity). If necessary, additional electrodes (beyond two) can be added to each channel via the use of a "Y" cable adapter or piggyback array. Table 9-5 lists the primary and secondary electrode placement techniques for each stimulation mode.

An advantage of using conventional T.E.N.S. as the initial stimulation mode is that it provides a fast onset of pain relief, providing that the patient is in pain at the time, not malingering, and electrode placement along with adjustment of the unit is consistent with the previous guidelines. Relief may be instantaneous in hyperesthesia, causalgia, and superficial and acute pain. We recommend turning the unit off and rearranging the electrodes (stimulation sites and/or channel arrangement) if significant pain relief with the conventional mode is not apparent within 10 minutes and at the most 20 minutes.

Depending on the area of pain, it may be necessary to use electrodes of unequal size to ensure perception of the current throughout the painful region (see Chapter 12). The smaller the electrode, the greater the current density. This may make the difference between no sensation and perception of the current at a particular placement site. Accommodation is a common occurrence with conventional T.E.N.S., which may necessitate periodic readjustment (elevation) of the amplitude and/or pulse duration parameters to regain adequate

TABLE 9-5. Principal Characteristics of the Stimulation Modes

Characteristic	Conventional	Strong, Low-rate (acupuncture-like)	Pulse-train (burst)	Brief, Intense	Modulation
Sensation	Tingling (paresthesia) without muscle contraction	Visible muscle contractions (rhythmic)	Rhythmic contractions or pulsing plus background paresthesia (tingling)	Nonrhythmic muscle fasciculation or muscle tetany	Fluctuation in pulse rate and pulse width (massage effect)
Strength	Comfortable	Strong to level of tolerance	Variable, ranging from mild to strong	Strong to level of tolerance	Variable, dependent upon mode to be modulated
Optimal area of perception	Throughout complete distribution of pain	Within segmentally related myotomes at or remote from area of pain	Throughout complete distribution of pain or at segmentally related but remote sites	Proximal, surrounding or crisscross over area of pain	Throughout area of pain or at related but remote sites
Electrode placement methods	*Primary:* single- or dual-channel unilateral/bilateral linear pathway crisscross V-shape with 3 electrodes *Secondary:* contralateral, upper cervical or transcranial	*Primary:* single- or dual-channel unilateral/bilateral linear pathway *Secondary:* contralateral unrelated areas	*Primary:* single- or dual-channel unilateral/bilateral linear pathway crisscross V-shape with 3 electrodes *Secondary:* contralateral unrelated areas	*Primary:* single- or dual-channel bilateral/unilateral linear pathway crisscross *Secondary:* contralateral unrelated areas	Can be used with any of the primary and secondary methods
Onset of relief	Fast—instantaneous—20 min	Slow—20–30 min or up to 1 hour	Moderate	Fast, instantaneous—10–15 min	Depends on mode that is being modulated
Duration of relief	20–30 minutes—2 hours is most common; totally dependent upon ADL, posture, and pain level	Usually 2–6 hr totally dependent upon ADL, posture, and pain level	Somewhere between that of conventional and SLR T.E.N.S. but also totally dependent upon ADL, posture, and pain level	Short, usually lasting only as long as stimulation persists	Variable, depends on degree of modulation and primary stimulation mode
Accommodation	Common	Uncommon, summation mechanisms occur	Uncommon, summation mechanisms occur—a means of modulating the conventional mode at low intensity.	Common only in that tolerance to stronger stimulation occurs	Uncommon—the prime means of decreasing accommodation and promoting tolerance to stronger stimulation
Helpful hints	Place electrodes at proximal and distal limits of pain. May need to use electrodes of unequal size placed on optimal stimulation sites or superficial aspects of peripheral nerve innervating painful area	Place electrodes on motor points of segmentally related myotomes or superficial aspects of motor nerves. More effective with larger muscle groups.	Mild stimulation: electrode placement as for conventional mode. Strong stimulation: electrode placement as for SLR mode.	(Depends upon Rx) Electrodes should be placed on optimal stimulation sites overlying superficial aspects of cutaneous or mixed peripheral nerves innervating area of pain	Depends upon primary stimulation mode

SLR = strong, low-rate.
Developed by JS Mannheimer for Book I of Biostim *Clinical Manual.* Reproduced with permission of Biostim Inc.

perception of the paresthesia. The use of low-intensity, pulse-train (burst) stimulation with conventional T.E.N.S. parameters can decrease accommodation and also increase comfort. T.E.N.S. units that incorporate automatic parameter modulation features can substantially decrease the incidence of accommodation. (See Chapter 12 for a discussion of accommodation and the means to inhibit it.)

When success cannot be achieved with conventional T.E.N.S., either the strong, low-rate (acupuncture-like) or pulse-train (burst) mode should be tried. Generally, these modes are more effective in patients with chronic pain and pain of deep and achy quality. These stimulation modes may require different electrode placement sites and arrangements. The objective is to obtain strong, rhythmic muscle contraction in segmentally related myotomes. Based on clinical experience, the stronger the muscle contraction and the more fibers contracting, the greater the pain-relieving effect will be. Therefore, the aim is to obtain muscle contractions of the largest muscle groups available. A short but bulky muscle is preferred over a long and thin muscle. For example, in a patient with lumbosacral pain who cannot tolerate these strong modes on the painful low back, the electrodes should be arranged so that the gastrocsoleus muscle group is stimulated. The calf musculature represents a segmentally related myotome since it is innervated by a peripheral nerve arising from the L4–S2 spinal cord segments, namely the posterior tibial, a branch of the sciatic (L4–S2).

With these stimulation modes, the choice of OSS would be motor points of the related musculature or superficial aspects of the mixed or motor peripheral nerve innervating the muscles. Placing one electrode proximal and the other distal to the muscle is recommended.

Use of strong, low-rate or pulse-train (burst) modes at areas that are unrelated to the source of pain has proven successful. This represents a secondary choice. Secondary techniques for the conventional mode would be to stimulate contralateral to the area of pain at the same peripheral nerve or place electrodes at the upper cervical spine or transcranially.[5] Secondary techniques for the brief, intense mode would also be contralateral and at unrelated regions remote from the painful area.

When using the strong, low-rate or pulse-train (burst) mode, it is necessary to stimulate for at least 20 and preferably 30 minutes (occasionally up to 1 hour) before any significant pain relief will become apparent. Accommodation is rare; therefore, parameter readjustment will be minimal.

Electrode placement with the brief, intense mode necessitates perception of the paresthesia proximal to, surrounding, or crisscrossing over the area of pain. Relief should occur within 5 to 15 minutes and at times even sooner depending on the area of pain. When this stimulation mode is being employed to modulate pain during the performance of specific therapeutic procedures such as joint mobilization, muscle tetany is not desired, as it will hinder joint movement. OSS then should be utilized that are not also motor points or that overlie superficial aspects of mixed or motor nerves innervating the muscles that act upon that joint. OSS that overlie superficial aspects of related cutaneous (sensory) nerves are recommended. There is little accommodation to this mode, but tolerance may gradually increase, allowing for the use of stronger stimulation to obtain even more analgesia. Table 9-5 summarizes the characteristics of the different stimulation modes.

FACTORS THAT INFLUENCE ELECTRODE PLACEMENT TECHNIQUES

Other than being knowledgeable about the distribution and superficial aspects of peripheral nerves, the location of optimal stimulation sites, and the segmental innervation of the body (as discussed in Chapter 8), success with T.E.N.S. depends on an awareness of current flow and stimulation channel arrangements.

POLARITY

The literature pertaining to clinical studies with T.E.N.S. does not contain information pertaining to the stimulation effects of the positive and negative poles, which may influence efficacy. It is known that in the external circuit electrically charged ions conventionally flow from the positive pole (anode) to the negative pole (cathode). Current flow within a battery is, however, negative to positive. If the lead wires on T.E.N.S. units delineate polarity by color coding (red = anode, black or white = cathode), the polarity of each electrode and therefore the direction of current flow (proximal-distal) can be determined. If the polarity is not noted, determination of the positive electrode can be made by immersion of the lead wires into a beaker of a weak saline solution. After approximately 5 minutes of stimulation at the maximum amplitude and pulse width with lowest pulse rate, a greater number of hydrogen bubbles should form at the cathode.[175]

Most T.E.N.S. units have symmetric or asymmetric biphasic waveforms, producing a zero net DC potential. This is accomplished by having the total energy of the positive and negative deflections relatively equal. Production of a zero net DC potential thus minimizes the possibility of skin irritation, which can occur from anodal or cathodal galvanism. Kahn, however, reports that biphasic waveforms may not have a true zero net DC potential, and therefore one electrode may be stronger than the other.[175] The positive pole is considered to hyperpolarize the underlying peripheral nerve membrane and thus produce a decrease in nerve excitability (anodal block) known as anelectrotronus.[206] The negative pole depolarizes the nerve, which results in an increase in excitability (catelectrotonus) and initiation of the wave of depolarization as discussed in Chapter 6.

IMPEDANCE

The impedance under each electrode is easily changed by the type of transmission medium. Transmission gel under a standard carbon-silicone electrode offers the least impedance. Karaya and synthetic polymer electrodes have increased impedance. An electrode with high impedance interferes with conduction of the T.E.N.S. stimulus. For deep-seated pains that usually require higher pulse energy levels (amplitude plus pulse width), the electrode impedance may represent the critical factor between success and failure.

We therefore recommend trying different electrode media when strong electrical paresthesia or muscle contractions cannot be accomplished with various units at peak output.

ELECTRODE SIZE AND CONFIGURATION

The size and shape of the electrode can also influence effectiveness. Current density under an electrode is in part determined by the size of the electrode. With two electrodes of one channel of equal surface area, the sensation under either electrode can be changed by making one smaller and the other larger. When perception needs to be increased or decreased at a particular site that cannot be adequately adjusted by use of the pulse width control, use of electrodes of unequal size per channel may be helpful to increase efficacy. The smaller the electrode, the greater the current density and increased sensation.

In certain body regions, smaller electrodes may adhere better than larger ones. The placement of a large electrode suboccipitally on a patient with a small neck may not allow for full adherence of the electrode to the stimulation site. This can, in effect, decrease the surface area (increasing density) under the electrode and result in a "hot spot" or uncomfortable sensation, thus decreasing efficacy. On the other hand, a patient with a large suboccipital fossa would do better with a large electrode to cover greater surface area so that density under the electrode is decreased. We recommend use of small electrodes on the face when necessary, to decrease current spread to the eye.

The effects of each pole may be modified by the depth of the peripheral nerve to be stimulated, placement of each electrode, and the distance between the electrodes of one channel. The specific effect of either pole will be further minimized by a greater depth of the peripheral nerve in the tissue underlying the electrodes. Increased conductance occurs in tissues that have a high water content, thus decreasing impedance as the following comparison illustrates:

> High Conductance and Low Impedance
> > Muscle
> > Brain
> > Fat
> > Peripheral Nerve
> > Skin
> > Bone
> Low Conductance and High Impedance

Muscle has the lowest impedance and highest conductance, whereas bone has the lowest conductance and highest impedance. Most peripheral nerves are surrounded by fat and a fibrous sheath, which are poor conductors. Thus the closer the nerve to the skin surface, the less the impedance. The arrangement of muscle fibers is also important. Conduction is four times better with a longitudinal arrangement of muscle fibers than in a muscle with fibers arranged transversely.[206]

DEPTH OF PERIPHERAL NERVE

These factors provide further support for electrode placement at superficial aspects of peripheral nerves as discussed in Chapter 8. Therefore, it may make no difference whether or not deeply situated peripheral nerves are stimulated with the positive (+) or negative (−) electrode. Current density increases between closely spaced electrodes as well as smaller electrodes, but depth of penetration decreases. Conversely, depth of penetration is greater but current density less with a large interelectrode distance. The strength of the stimulus perceived under each electrode depends greatly not only on the impedance of the underlying skin and tissue (dry, scaly skin significantly increases impedance) but also on the density of nerve innervation at the electrode site. A highly innervated site such as the dorsal web space is very sensitive to stimulation. When the direction or polarity of current (ionic flow) is known, efficacy may be increased by proximal or distal placement of the anode. This is purely speculative, as we obtain good results in most cases without paying much attention to polarity. Electrode arrangements that provide for a crisscross current pathway basically negate the polarity effects. Exact replication of the work of others cannot be done if polarity is not known. However, we have not noticed any specific benefits from polarity changes affecting the direction of the T.E.N.S. current, and it is known that once a nerve is depolarized, the impulse is propagated in both directions. A definitive physiologic study relative to the direction of current flow with T.E.N.S. is necessary to decide if efficacy can be enhanced in certain situations by polarity changes.

ELECTRODE PLACEMENT ARRANGEMENTS

The final remaining factor now pertains to the arrangement of the electrodes per channel. There are numerous methods of arranging electrodes, and variations in such arrangements can also affect efficacy, as does the choice of stimulation sites as discussed in Chapter 8.

The following electrode placement techniques are used with the case studies and alternative suggestions presented in this chapter:

1. *Unilateral:* The placement of electrodes on one side of a peripheral joint, the spine, face, head, or one extremity. Can be performed with a single- or dual-channel unit.
2. *V-Shape:* An arrangement of three electrodes with a dual-channel unit in which the anode is at the apex and the negative electrodes of channels 1 and 2 are at the base. Conduction from the anode to both electrodes produces a V-shaped pathway in which each negative electrode essentially uses one half of the positive. This arrangement is valuable for spinal and intrinsic peripheral joint pain.
3. *Bilateral:* Can be performed by placing each electrode of a single channel on both sides of the spine, face, head, or peripheral joint. When employed with a dual-channel unit, two electrodes of a single channel can be placed on opposite sides or can be used to stimulate the same peripheral nerve on opposite extremities. *Note:* A dual-channel unit can be used to stimulate two related or unrelated pain sites simultaneously.
4. *Proximal:* An arrangement whereby the electrodes of one or two channels are all placed above the level of a lesion. Beneficial in peripheral nerve injuries, spinal cord lesions, or phantom pain.
5. *Distal:* Involves the placement of at least one electrode at the periphery of referred pain to ensure the perception of paresthesia throughout the whole distribution.
6. *Linear Pathway:* Involves proximal and distal electrode placement as well as at sites along the distribution of a trigger point or nerve root referral pattern.
7. *Overlapping:* It is sometimes beneficial when using the linear pathway technique to overlap channels to ensure complete perception of the electrical paresthesia throughout the pain distribution.
8. *Crisscross:* Also known as interferential. Occurs when the pathways of a dual-channel unit intersect the area of pain, thus concentrating perception of current at a painful site.
9. *Segmentally Related Myotome:* When the strong, low-rate or high-intensity, pulse-train (burst) mode cannot be tolerated at the locus of pain, benefit may be obtained by stimulation of muscle groups innervated by nerves from the involved spinal levels. Segmentally related myotomes can be located at, near, or remote from the painful area.
10. *Remote:* Electrodes with one or two channels at sites that are segmentally related or unrelated to the painful region. A remote site can be located proximal, distal, or contralateral to the area of pain. Generally, the stronger stimulation modes are employed at remote sites.
11. *Contralateral:* When stimulation of the involved extremity or side of the body cannot be performed (usually in the presence of burns or hyperesthesia from shingles), stimulation of the same nerve contralaterally can be beneficial. When contralateral stimulation is performed, it should be noted that relief will not be as demonstrative, long-lasting, or quick to occur as seen with ipsilateral stimulation.
12. *Unrelated Sites:* When the above techniques are not beneficial, efficacy may be obtained

by stimulation of superficial aspects of the median, ulnar, or sciatic nerves; the top and bottom of the spine; the upper cervical or transcranial regions.

13. *Upper Cervical Spine:* Stimulation anterolaterally of the highest cervical region can be accomplished with a single channel of two electrodes placed behind the ear and just below the mastoid process.

14. *Transcranial:* Stimulation via one channel of two electrodes placed on either side of the temporal fossa. Generally recommended to be used by Pain Suppression Labs. The exact site is 1 inch anterior and superior to the ear.

15. *Simultaneous Bimodal:* Can be employed only with a dual-channel stimulator that offers independent adjustment of stimulation parameters per channel. Adjustment of the unit allows for the delivery of a different mode per channel at the same time. This can be performed at two related or unrelated sites.

ELECTRODE PLACEMENT TECHNIQUES RELATIVE TO SPECIFIC PAIN SYNDROMES AND ANATOMIC AREAS

HEAD AND FACE

Pain syndromes of the head and face commonly include headaches, toothaches, trigeminal neuralgia, and temporomandibular joint (TMJ) syndrome. Electrode placement on the head is in part hindered by the hair unless sponge electrodes with water as the transmission medium are used. Shealy has introduced a unique application of T.E.N.S. to the head known as transcranial stimulation.[46] He used a T.E.N.S. device known as the Pain Suppressor* (see Appendix), which is a low-amperage unit (4 mA maximum), to deliver stimulation on both sides of the skull. An electrode was placed on each temporal region of the head, above and slightly anterior to the ear. Stimulation at this region for 12 minutes, five to eight times a day produced changes in the metabolite of serotonin (5-HIAA). Shealy noted that some patients had mood changes after such stimulation, indicative of a reduction in psychologic depression. The study was performed with 27 patients with chronic pain. Patients whose prestimulation 5-HIAA levels were normal did not respond well to T.E.N.S., but those patients with high or low baseline 5-HIAA levels obtained satisfactory improvement with T.E.N.S. (50 to 100 percent improvement) and a 12-day chronic pain treatment program.

We have employed the Pain Suppressor steadily for a 20-minute period. Efficacy, however, may be enhanced by intermittent application throughout the day as Shealy has done. When either a perceptible flashing or flickering sensation at the eye was attained, the intensity was turned down slowly until this sensation disappeared. (This is consistent with the manufacturer's operating directions.) If the sensation, which has been considered to be either stimulation of the retina or phosphene action, returned, the intensity was again reduced. Pain Suppression Labs recommends that when its device is used transcranially, polarity should be reversed after 10 minutes. It reports that some patients experience an increase in headache with this application due to cerebral vasodilation, and a polarity change may negate this occurrence.

The Pain Suppressor is quite different from most conventional T.E.N.S. units in that its output is quite low, making its use on the head or face tolerable. Amplitude or intensity is the only adjustable parameter. The unit generates a combination of direct and alternating

---

*Pain Suppression Labs, Inc., 559 River Drive, Elmwood Park, NJ 07407.

current with a burst frequency of 15 times per second and a carrier frequency of 15,000 cycles per second.

TMJ Syndrome and Dental Application

We have used transcranial stimulation with the pain suppressor in patients with headaches and TMJ syndrome. Figure 9-2 illustrates electrode placement. Because of its low intensity, it is a frequent choice for headaches, but only as an adjunctive modality.[47-50] Definitive treatment should include physical therapy to the cervical spine and TMJ, which usually consists of joint mobilization, manual cervical traction, spray and stretch techniques, noninvasive electroacupuncture stimulation or deep pressure massage, postural and/or corrective exercises, and relaxation training with biofeedback. Many TMJ syndrome patients need to be referred to a dentist for an orthopedic mandibular appliance. Case Study 1 describes such a patient.

Case Study 1

Clarifying Evaluation: A 35-year-old female referred for treatment of headaches on 3/21/80. History dates back a few years to when she developed emotional problems after her child had an accident.

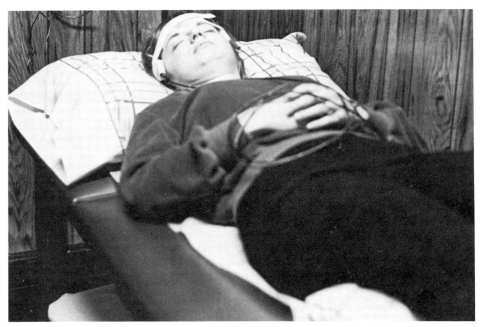

FIGURE 9-2. *Dx:* **Temporomandibular joint syndrome and tension headaches.** *Electrode placement technique:* **Transcranial.** *Electrode placement sites:* **Single channel of two electrodes placed 1 inch superior and slightly anterior to each ear.** *Anatomic characteristics:* **Primarily overlies trigeminal nerve branches.** *Electrodes:* **Sponge, with water as transmission medium, in plastic cup held in place by Velcro headband.** *T.E.N.S. mode:* **Subthreshold conventional.** *T.E.N.S. unit:* **Pain suppressor.** *Rationale:* **Possible serotonin liberation.**

She developed daily headaches that persisted for a few months. During the past year, headaches continued, initially characterized as the tension/muscle-contraction variety and then intensifying into a migraine.

At the time of the initial evaluation, the patient complained of constant bilateral upper trapezius and suboccipital pain giving rise to tension headaches. Tension headaches were aggravated by prolonged sitting and forward bending of the cervical spine and eased by lying supine. There was also some interscapular discomfort as well as facial pain. Migraines were reported as being unilateral, usually on the right. She related a description of prodromal symptoms consisting of blurred vision, gastrointestinal discomfort, nasal stuffiness, and occasional tearing of the eyes. The headaches were characterized as throbbing and/or a tight band around her head that persisted at peak intensity for 15 to 45 minutes. The headache was aggravated by sound, cold, exertion, straining, emotional stress, alcohol, and menstruation. She was able to sleep well at night, usually arising in a relaxed state but occasionally with the sensation of an impending migraine.

Other complaints were occasional numbness of the hands (unilateral or bilateral without a distinctive pattern) and mild bilateral lumbosacral pain. The patient had recently discontinued use of all pain medication except aspirin.

Structurally, the patient exhibited a forward head posture and alar scapulae. Active ROM of the cervical spine was grossly within normal limits (WNL) except for a slight limitation of 15 percent in rotation bilaterally and backward bending. Strength of the C1–T1 myotomes was normal bilaterally and upper extremity reflexes hyperactive. The patient was noted as having difficulty relaxing. She had been under the care of a psychiatrist for emotional problems and depression. Evaluation of the temporomandibular joints revealed a decreased oral aperture and deviation of the jaw to the right upon closure. There was tenderness to palpation at both joints and the temporalis muscle, more on the right than the left.

Resting frontalis EMG level was 20 to 40 microvolts. The patient had difficulty relaxing, which caused large fluctuations in the EMG meter. Resting temperature of the index fingers was 79°F on the right and 80°F on the left. She reported that her hands and feet were always cold.

Goals: Decrease, control, and, if possible, eliminate pain.

Treatment Plan: Treatments were initiated, consisting first of transcranial T.E.N.S. to decrease pain and promote relaxation training with the aid of EMG biofeedback and autogenic tapes (Fig. 9-3). As progression occurred, temperature biofeedback training was added. The "Quieting Response" series of eight tapes by Dr. Charles Stroebel* was used. In addition, treatment to the TMJ joint (Fig. 9-4) and the cervical spine consisted of mobilization, fluorimethane spray and stretch, and manual cervical traction. The patient was instructed in proper body mechanics, a home program of corrective postural and stretching exercises, and acupressure massage for headache pain, and was encouraged to practice relaxation training and autogenic exercises with the aid of tapes. Treatments were given once or twice a week.

Transcranial T.E.N.S. was effective in decreasing headache pain, generally by about 50 percent. This was employed only when the patient arrived for treatment and complained of an existing headache. Occasionally, transcranial T.E.N.S. was more effective, usually when the headache had just begun. When the headache was present for a considerable period of time, transcranial T.E.N.S. was either not effective or of minimal value.

The patient was discharged on 5/8/80 after receiving 10 treatments since it was felt that maximum progress had been reached. She completed the biofeedback/relaxation training program, obtained a set of cassette tapes for practice at home to maintain carryover, and contacted her dentist on our advice for further TMJ treatment. At the time of discharge, she still complained of periods of discomfort due either to emotional tension or TMJ dysfunction, or a combination of the two. The patient was contacted by telephone on 2/6/81, at which time she reported feeling considerably better after obtaining an orthopedic mandibular appliance from her dentist.

---

*Biomonitoring Applications Inc.

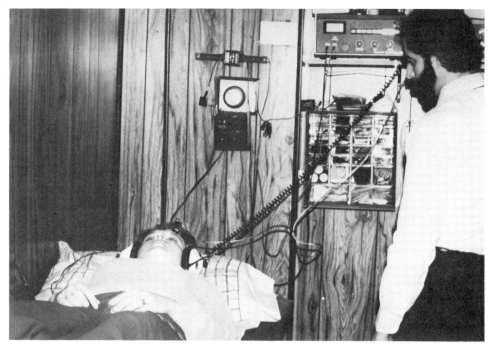

FIGURE 9-3. *Dx:* Temporomandibular joint syndrome and tension headaches. Relaxation training with the aid of EMG biofeedback and autogenic tapes. Biofeedback sensors in place on frontalis muscle. Therapist adjusting biofeedback unit. Tape player located against wall on side of patient. Biofeedback sensors were also placed on suboccipital and upper trapezius musculature to make the patient aware of muscle tension from improper head position.

Patients with TMJ syndrome may need to use T.E.N.S. temporarily until a dental appliance is obtained. A recent article by Melzack reported on the use of ice massage to the hand ipsilateral to the involved side for relief of dental pain.[38] Ice massage was performed to the "Hoku" point (LI 4) until the dorsal web space became numb or 7 minutes had elapsed. A majority of the dental patients performing this technique obtained 50 percent or more pain relief.

Picaza and associates concluded from one study that subliminal stimulation may suppress pain and that the perception of tingling within the painful area was not essential for pain relief to occur.[8] A small percentage of the patients tested obtained pain relief with subliminal stimulation.

We have used the "Hoku" point as one of the electrode placement sites in patients with TMJ pain (Case Study 2).

Case Study 2

Clarifying Evaluation: A 10-year-old female referred for physical therapy on 1/22/81 for pain control as a result of TMJ syndrome. The patient had a history of chronic inner ear infections, and had recently sustained trauma to the left side of her face and mandible after being hit by a locker door at

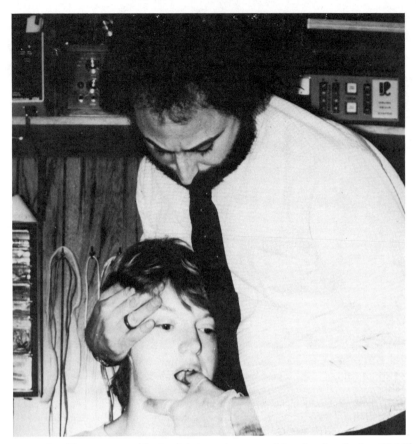

FIGURE 9-4. *Dx:* **Temporomandibular joint syndrome and tension headache. Mobilization of TMJ; therapist wearing sterile glove.**

school. During the few days prior to referral, the patient had severe left ear pain that was worse at night, interfering with sleep. This recent episode was equated with another ear infection, but when medication failed to relieve the pain, evaluation by an ear, nose, and throat specialist revealed the presence of TMJ syndrome.

At the time of the initial visit, there was a functional but painful mandibular opening with deviation to the left. The left masseter, temporalis, digastric, and medial pterygoid were painful to palpation, as was the left temporomandibular joint. The resting vertical dimension was diminished. Pain was described by the patient as inside and around the left ear. There was a palpable click at the left TMJ with movement, and bruxism was evident at night according to the parents.

Goals: Decrease and/or control discomfort until orthopedic mandibular appliance could be fabricated.

Treatment Plan: Pain relief of 50 to 75 percent was achieved after 20 minutes with T.E.N.S. Figure 9-5 illustrates the electrode placement with the conventional stimulation mode. This was followed by fluorimethane spray and stretch for the masseters bilaterally, which resulted in 95 percent pain relief (Fig. 9-6).

Three treatments were given with pain control maintained at home with T.E.N.S. and ice massage to the dorsal web space. After obtaining the dental appliance (Fig. 9-7), the patient has been pain-free and was under the care of a dentist specializing in TMJ syndromes. However, subsequent orthodontic work triggered a temporary return of pain that became bilateral and necessitated the change in electrode placement, which was highly effective (Fig. 9-8).

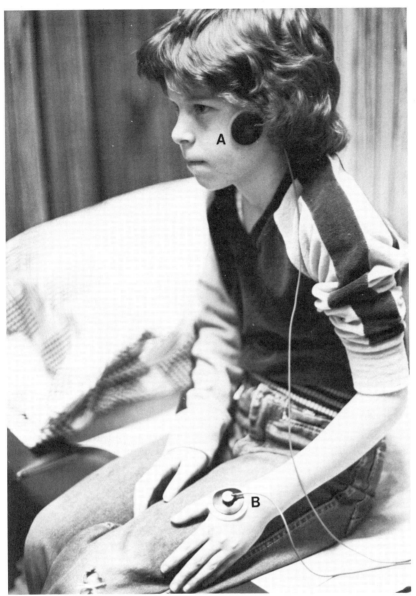

FIGURE 9-5. *Dx:* Temporomandibular joint syndrome. *Electrode placement technique:* Single-channel/unilateral. *Electrode placement sites:* A, Directly over TMJ (superior electrode). B, In dorsal web space (inferior electrode). *Anatomic characteristics:* A, Auriculotemporal, masseteric, deep temporal, and lateral pterygoid nerves; cutaneous branches of trigeminal, motor branches of facial, and autonomic fibers from otic ganlion. Corresponds with four acupuncture points: TW 21, GB 3, SI 19, and ST 7. B, Motor/trigger point of first dorsal interosseus and adductor pollicis. Corresponds to acupuncture point LI 4. *Nerve innervation:* A, As above. B, Superficial radial and musculocutaneous (sensory); ulnar (motor). *T.E.N.S. mode:* Conventional, producing electrical paresthesia and analgesia at TMJ. *T.E.N.S. unit:* Stim-tech Stimpulse. *Electrodes:* Medgeneral circular with karaya pads and snap leads (carbon-silicone). *Rationale:* Cortical inhibitory surround theory (see Chapter 8).

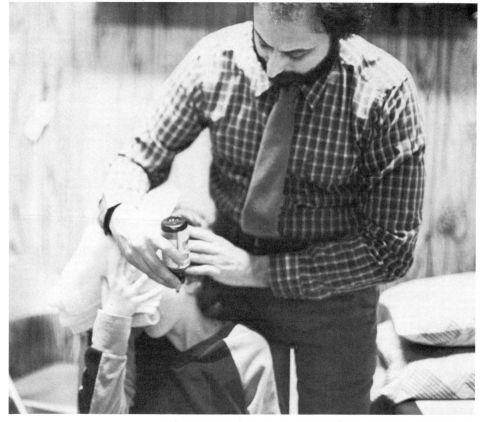

FIGURE 9-6. *Dx:* Temporomandibular joint syndrome. Spray and stretch of masseter being performed with fluorimethane. The patient is holding a towel over the side of her face to keep spray from eyes. Cardboard cover of spray bottle is covered with napkin and held in patient's mouth between teeth to provide stretch.

The electrode placement arrangement depicted in Figure 9-5 can be used with the Pain Suppressor. If conventional T.E.N.S. cannot be tolerated or sometimes causes irritation of the ipsilateral eye (probably due to stimulation of infraorbital and supraorbital branches of trigeminal nerve by electrode placement near the TMJ), use of the Pain Suppressor may be helpful and definitely more tolerable.

This electrode placement (see Fig. 9-5) can also be used with an intensity level between the conventional and brief, intense modes. A sensation comparable to receiving a procaine hydrochloride (Novocain) injection should result within about 5 minutes. When using stronger stimulation, it is suggested that an alternative placement on the masseter instead of directly over the joint be employed to again avoid eye irritation (Fig. 9-9). Stimulation of ST 6 (masseter motor trigger point) and LI 4 (dorsal web space) optimal stimulation sites with the brief, intense mode was used for pain control during periodontal work. Sponge electrodes on ST 6 were used (due to beard) and held in place by a dental assistant from behind, and dorsal web space electrodes (LI 4) were taped in place. The T.E.N.S. unit was controlled by hand, adjusting amplitude as needed. Only pressure, no sharp pain, was perceived, and no other means of pain control was necessary.

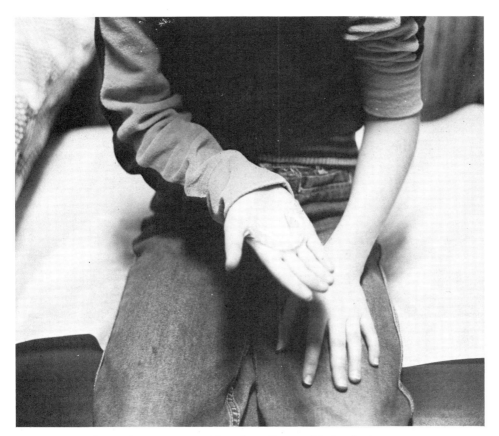
FIGURE 9-7. TMJ syndrome patient with orthopedic mandibular device.

A great deal of recent research with T.E.N.S. has consisted of experiments to test the tooth pulp pain threshold. Innervation of the tooth was previously considered to consist solely of A-delta and C fibers, thereby providing a definitive mechanism for pain sensations.[26] Recent reports show that stimulation of human tooth pulp also produces sensations of heat, cold, and tingling.[51] Early reports relating to T.E.N.S. and dentistry outlined the use of a drill that delivered a minute electrical impulse (0.6 V) to the tooth during drilling. The current was subliminal but considered effective in decreasing pain.[52–55] Electrical desensitization of hypersensitive teeth has also been performed, but resultant tissue damage from intraoral stimulation seems to have halted this procedure.[53] Andersson and associates demonstrated that drilling of teeth could be performed without pain sensation if strong T.E.N.S. was given to the cheeks (ST 2 bilaterally, infraorbital nerve.)[13] The pain threshold needed to be increased at least three to four times beyond normal using the acupuncture-like mode (2 Hz). An intensity producing strong, visible muscle contractions for 15 to 30 minutes was needed. In order for the tooth pain threshold to be increased even slightly, an amplitude of 19 mA was required.[13,35]

Strassburg, Krainick, and Thoden reported on the use of T.E.N.S. to produce electroanalgesia sufficient to allow for tooth extraction as well as for minor surgical procedures.[45] Twenty-nine of 30 dental patients obtained adequate pain control with one electrode at the mandible and another at the main trigeminal nerve trunk.

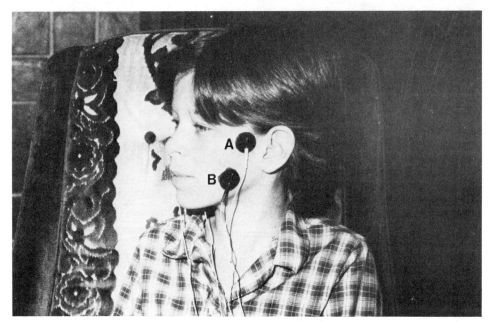

FIGURE 9-8. *Dx:* Temporomandibular joint syndrome. *Electrode placement technique:* Dual-channel, bilateral. *Electrode placement sites:* A, Directly over TMJ (superior electrode). B, On masseter muscle (inferior electrode). Same for each channel. *Anatomic characteristics:* A, Auriculotemporal, masseteric, deep temporal, and lateral pterygoid nerves; cutaneous branches of trigeminal; motor branches of facial; and autonomic fibers from otic ganglion. Corresponds with four acupuncture points: TW 21, GB 3, SI 19, and ST 7. B, Motor/trigger points of masseter. Corresponds to acupuncture point ST 6. *Nerve innervation:* A, As above. B, Facial and trigeminal nerve branches. *T.E.N.S. mode:* Conventional, producing electrical paresthesia and analgesia throughout painful region. *T.E.N.S. unit:* Dynex. *Electrodes:* Small Medtronic carbon-silicone electrodes with karaya pads. *Rationale:* Both electrode sites have innervation via facial and trigeminal nerve branches.

A composite of the research related to tooth pain points to the fact that strong stimulation was needed to elevate the pain threshold to a level sufficient to allow for drilling and other dental procedures.[11,13,26,35,43] The segmental effects of stimulation were quite interesting. Stimulation of the dorsal web space (LI 4) plus the infraorbital region provided results equal to those of bilateral cheek stimulation.[11,13] Stimulation of the dorsal web space bilaterally did not change the tooth pain threshold but did seem to prolong the aftereffect if employed after stimulation of the cheeks.[11,13] Chapman, Wilson, and Gehrig used electroacupuncture and T.E.N.S. only at bilateral "Hoku" points (LI 4).[26] They demonstrated a small but significant analgesia, which was compared to that of 33 percent nitrous oxide, and findings similar to those of Melzack, Guite, and Gonshor, who reported that 7 minutes of ice massage solely at the dorsal web space, ipsilateral to the side of pain, decreased discomfort by at least 50 percent in patients with acute dental pain.[38] Ottoson, Ekblom, and Hansson experimented with vibration at 100 Hz as a form of modulating dental pain.[56] They determined that the best stimulation sites were ipsilateral to the side of pain or in the midline and generally within the region innervated by trigeminal nerve branches.

Andersson and Holmgren were unable to duplicate the pain threshold elevation effects using high-rate (100 Hz) stimulation applied solely to the infraorbital region.[10] They

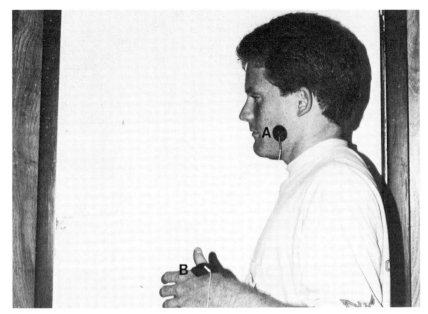

FIGURE 9-9. *Dx:* Alternate electrode array for pain of TMJ or dental origin. *Electrode placement technique:* Single-channel, unilateral. *Electrode placement sites:* A, Small electrode on masseter muscle. B, Large electrode in ipsilateral dorsal web space. *Anatomic characteristics:* A, Motor/trigger points of masseter. B, Motor/trigger point of first dorsal interosseus and adductor pollicis corresponding to acupuncture point LI 4. *Nerve innervation:* A, Facial and trigeminal nerve branches. B, Superficial radial and musculocutaneous (sensory); ulnar (motor). *T.E.N.S. mode:* Conventional, producing electrical paresthesia and analgesia at cheek and TMJ. *Rationale:* Cortical inhibitory surround theory (see Chapter 8).

attributed this to the small amount of musculature present in this area, which hindered the production of strong muscle contractions.

Ihalainen and Perkki experimented with T.E.N.S. as a means of pain control after extraction of a lower-jaw wisdom tooth.[57] They used a 100-Hz current for 30 minutes ipsilateral to the side of the extraction immediately after the procedure. Optimal results were obtained with stimulation at the mental foramen and angle of the mandible. Bilateral infraorbital stimulation was not as effective. Pain intensity was decreased for 2 hours posttreatment but then approached the level of the control group. The authors concluded that the use of T.E.N.S. at home postoperatively would be difficult but would be the only way to eliminate postoperative pain. For such patients, we strongly endorse the use of T.E.N.S. at home, which is easily performed and very successful.

Omura has used the electrode placement technique shown in Figure 9-8 with the acupuncture-like mode. He constructed reusable electrodes of folded aluminum foil, adhesive tape, transmission gel, and a thumbtack (flat side against skin and nail side for alligator clip connection).[58] These electrodes were larger, and placement was on the TMJ and upper masseter bilaterally (one channel on each side of the face). A rate of 1 Hz for 20 minutes, producing visible but not painful muscle contractions, was performed. Full opening of the mouth was able to be accomplished. This was not possible prior to stimulation because of TMJ dysfunction. Similar results have also been obtained by use of the Myo-Monitor.

A neuromuscular stimulator known as a Myo-Monitor was developed in 1969 to obtain a muscularly oriented maxillomandibular registration, occlusal adjustment, impressions for the construction of dentures, treatment of TMJ syndromes, and reduction of postsurgical edema and pain.[59,60] The Myo-Monitor is used by dentists to obtain relaxation of the masticatory muscles, primarily the masseter and pterygoids. The Myo-Monitor has a fixed frequency of one pulse every 15 seconds (40/min) and fixed pulse width of 500 μsec. The amplitude is adjustable to 25 mA. Transcutaneous stimulation using three electrodes performed with one active electrode over each temporomandibular joint, or slightly inferior, to also cover the upper part of the masseter and a ground electrode at the midline suboccipitally is the desired method of placement (Fig. 9-10, B and C). [56,61] An alternative placement using one channel of two electrodes is depicted in Figure 9-10, A. The Myo-Monitor is adjusted to an intensity producing mild but visible contractions of the facial musculature, lips, or mandibular movement and performed for 45 to 60 minutes. Once relaxation of the masticatory muscles has been obtained, the dentist is able to determine the patient's resting vertical dimension and neuromuscular occlusal positions of the maxillary and mandibular teeth.[48,59,62] These determinations and measurements are then followed by the placement of an acrylic putty over the teeth to obtain tooth contact sufficient to make an impression for the manufacture of an orthopedic mandibular appliance. A slight increase in amplitude of the stimulator may be required at this time to allow for adequate registration on the putty.

T.E.N.S. units that incorporate lower-frequency parameters can also be used like the Myo-Monitor. Medical Devices Inc., a T.E.N.S. manufacturer, provides material specifically related to the use of one of its units for dental procedures.* Biostim manufactures a unit that utilizes a three-electrode lead cable by which the exact electrode placement used with the Myo-Monitor can be performed.† Synchronous firing of each channel is required.

The use of T.E.N.S. in dentistry is gaining momentum. The Myo-Monitor functioned as a T.E.N.S. unit prior to the advent of stimulators designed specifically for pain control. The value of T.E.N.S. as a means of pain control for TMJ syndrome, toothache, and after procedures such as tooth extraction has been established. Experimentation is proceeding to determine whether or not T.E.N.S. has a viable role as a means of electroanalgesia during specific dental procedures such as drilling and tooth extraction. The use of strong, low-rate (acupuncture-like) T.E.N.S. during such procedures would seem to hinder the work of the dentist, since muscular contraction would hamper intraoral work. This is specifically mentioned in light of the research that shows that placement on the cheeks is more effective than remote stimulation.

Electrodes placed on the medial and lateral aspects of the gums may be necessary for pain control in some dental procedures.[49,63] Toothpaste can be used in place of transmission gel, but electrode configurations need to be altered. Perhaps the use of very small electrodes with a stimulator in the microampere range would be ideal. Mumford recommends placing one electrode over the painful area and the other on an area that is not involved in the pain process.[64]

Our experience has shown that conventional T.E.N.S. with one electrode on the masseter and the other on the ipsilateral dorsal web space provides effective pain modulation after dental surgery. Brief, intense T.E.N.S. used with the same electrode array can provide for almost immediate analgesia during superficial dental procedures without producing rhythmic muscle contractions. A long induction period is not needed as in the strong, low-rate (acupuncture-like) mode. Therefore, in procedures such as periodontal

---

*Medical Devices Inc., 833 Third Street SW, St. Paul, Minn 55112.
†Biostim, Inc., P.O. Box 3138, Clarksville Rd. and Everett Drive, Princeton, NJ 08540.

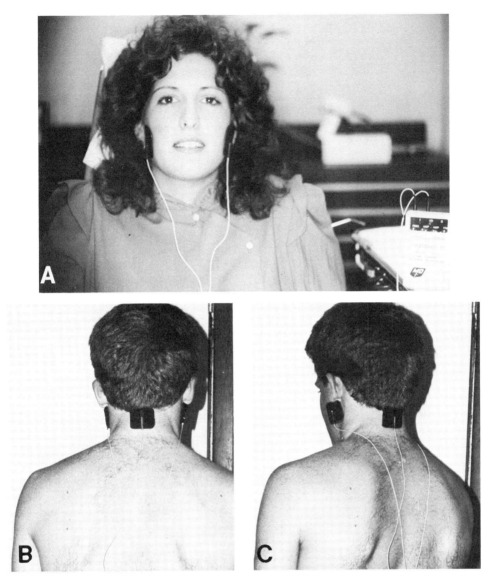

FIGURE 9-10. *A,* T.E.N.S. electrodes in place over each TMJ and upper region of masseter. Stimulation is being performed to achieve normal resting vertical dimension and neuromuscular occlusal positon prior to registration with acrylic putty. Acrylic impression will be used to manufacture an orthopedic mandibular appliance for TMJ syndrome. *Electrode placement technique:* Single-channel, bilateral. *T.E.N.S. mode:* Low rate of moderate intensity, 40 pulses per minute to produce comfortable, rhythmic muscle contractions. (Courtesy of Dr. David I. Schor, Lawrenceville, N.J.) *B,* Posterior view and *C,* lateral view of electrode placement to obtain normal resting vertical dimension and neuromuscular occlusal position for fabrication of orthopedic mandibular appliance. *Electrode placement technique:* Dual-channel, bilateral, with three-lead cable (see Fig. 9-11, C, for explanation). *Electrode placement sites:* Positive electrode at midline just below occiput. Negative electrodes placed inferior to mastoid process to region overlying masseter and inferior aspect of TMJ. *T.E.N.S. mode:* Low rate of moderate intensity at 40 pulses per minute to produce comfortable, rhythmic muscle contractions.

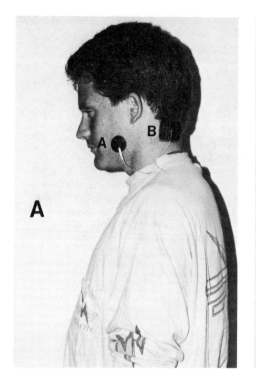

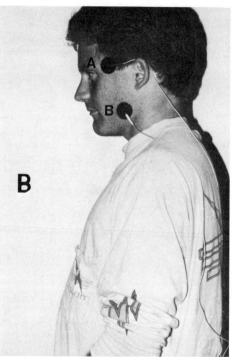

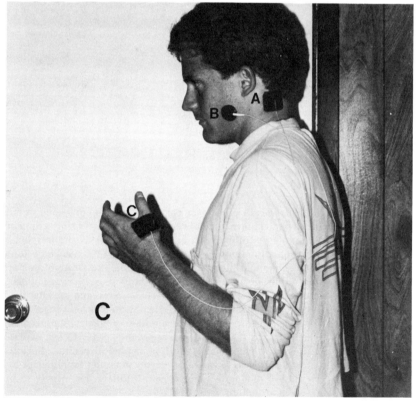

CLINICAL T.E.N.S.

work and minor surgery, brief, intense T.E.N.S. may have a role. Following the procedure, pain can be managed by conventional T.E.N.S.

Based on experience, it is recommended that electrodes of unequal size be utilized when placement at the dorsal web space (LI 4) and masseter (ST 6) is employed. Frequently, an arrangement with equal sized electrodes produces perception of current at the LI 4 site only or a spread of current to the eyes that is irritating. We suggest placing a smaller electrode at the facial site, thus producing a greater current density to allow for successful facial paresthesia. Alternate electrode placement sites depicted in Figure 9-11, A through C, work best with a small electrode. We have found that placement of one electrode behind the ear overlying the great auricular and lesser occipital nerves (TW 17) and another at the masseter motor point (ST 6) is also a highly effective alternative arrangement for TMJ pain. When TMJ syndrome produces concomitant cervical spine and/or upper extremity pain referral, electrode placement techniques illustrated in subsequent sections dealing with the

◀ ───

FIGURE 9-11. *Dx:* Alternate electrode arrays for pain of TMJ or dental origin.

Figure A. *Electrode placement technique:* Single-channel, unilateral. *Electrode placement sites:* A, Small electrode on masseter muscle. B, Large electrode in ipsilateral suboccipital fossa. *Anatomic characteristics:* A, Motor/trigger point of masseter corresponding to acupuncture point ST 6. B, Motor/trigger point of splenius and semispinalis capitis corresponds to acupuncture point GB 20. *Nerve innervation:* A, Facial and trigeminal nerve branches. B, Greater and lesser occipital nerves. *T.E.N.S. mode:* Conventional, producing electrical paresthesia and electroanalgesia at cheek and TMJ. *Electrodes:* Small circular Medtronic carbon-silicone and rectangular Biostim Bioform electrodes, both with Lec-Tec karaya pads. *Rationale:* Occipital nerves originate from the C2–3 segmental levels. The spinal tract of the trigeminal nerve synapses in the upper cervical spine between C2 and C4 (see Chapter 8).

Figure B. *Electrode placement technique:* Single-channel, unilateral. *Electrode placement sites:* A, Superior small electrode in temporal fossa lateral to eyebrow. B, Inferior small electrode on masseter muscle. *Anatomic characteristics:* A, Motor/trigger point of temporalis muscle. Corresponds to acupuncture point TW 23. B, Motor trigger point of masseter muscle. Corresponds to acupuncture point ST 6. *Nerve innervation:* A, Zygomatico-temporal branch of trigeminal. B, Facial and trigeminal nerve branches. *T.E.N.S. mode:* Conventional, producing electrical paresthesia and analgesia throughout area of pain. *Electrodes:* Small Medtronic carbon-silicone with Lec-Tec karaya pads. *Rationale:* Both muscles have similar cranial nerve innervation.

Figure C. *Electrode placement technique:* Dual-channel/unilateral using three-lead cable. *Electrode placement sites:* A, Large (+) electrode at suboccipital fossa. B, Small (−) electrode on masseter muscle. C, Large (−) electrode in dorsal web space. *Anatomic characteristics:* A, Motor/trigger point of splenius and semispinalis capitis corresponds to acupuncture point GB 20. B, Motor/trigger point of masseter muscle corresponds to acupuncture point ST 6. C, Motor/trigger point of first dorsal interosseus and adductor pollicis corresponds to acupuncture point LI 4. *Nerve innervation:* A, Greater and lesser occipital nerves. B, Facial and trigeminal nerve branches. C, Superficial radial and musculocutaneous (sensory), ulnar (motor). *T.E.N.S. mode:* Conventional, combining the techniques illustrated in Figures 9-9 and 9-11, A. *T.E.N.S. unit:* Biostim System 10. *Electrodes:* Small circular Medtronic and rectangular Biostim (Bioform) electrodes with Lec-Tec karaya pads. *Rationale:* Combines segmental relationship of occipital nerves to spinal tract of the trigeminal with philosophy of the cortical inhibitory surround theory. *Note:* With this T.E.N.S. unit and three-lead cable system, one lead wire is positive (red) and the other two negative (white, channel 1, and black, channel 2). The total energy (pulse width and amplitude) of the single electrodes of channels 1 and 2 can be controlled independently. Therefore, the circuitry of both channels includes the positive electrode, each essentially using one half of its power.

cervical spine should be employed. Table 9-6 summarizes suggested techniques for TMJ and dental pain.

Headaches

Our experience in employing T.E.N.S. solely for headaches has been minimal for the reasons previously discussed. The Pain Suppressor may be the initial choice if placement on superficial periosteum is required. The transcranial method is most commonly used (see Fig. 9-2). Additional electrodes can be added to the Pain Suppressor by the piggyback method to stimulate suboccipitally or on other areas simultaneously with the transcranial placement.[50] On a few occasions, we have even used the Pain Suppressor transcranially while conventional T.E.N.S. was applied suboccipitally and at the dorsal web space simultaneously with a different unit when one method was unsuccessful. Results with this approach have not been overwhelming but at times beneficial with long-standing headaches. When cranial stimulation is not necessary, other arrangements can be employed. Figure 9-12 illustrates the electrode arrangement for a patient with a bilateral frontal headache as a result of cervical strain. The patient stated she had had the headache for at least 3 hours prior to the appointment. In consideration of the time that the headache was present, it was decided to try high-intensity T.E.N.S. using the pulse-train mode. Since this was unable to be tolerated on the head, electrodes were arranged suboccipitally and at the dorsal web space, constituting both a right and a left channel. This was extremely beneficial in relieving the entire headache after a 20-minute stimulation period.

Omura has reported on the use of T.E.N.S. in the treatment of headaches that he classifies as cephalic hypertension or hypotension.[58] He used a bilateral suboccipital (GB 20) or upper trapezius (GB 21) trigger point placement for 20 minutes at a rate of 1 or 2 Hz

TABLE 9-6. Suggested Electrode Placement Techniques for TMJ and Dental Pain

Technique	Placement Sites	Mode	Illustration
1. Single channel (unilateral)	Masseter and dorsal web space	Subthreshold, conventional, or brief, intense	9-9, A
2. Single channel (unilateral)	TMJ and dorsal web space	Subthreshold or conventional	9-5
3. Single channel (unilateral)	Temporalis to masseter	Subthreshold or conventional	9-11, B
4. Single channel (unilateral)	Suboccipital to masseter	Subthreshold or conventional	9-11, A
5. Single channel (unilateral)	Below mastoid to masseter	Subthreshold or conventional	Not illustrated
6. Single channel (bilateral)	Masseter bilaterally	Conventional or low-rate	9-10, B
7. Single channel (bilateral)	Dorsal web space bilaterally	Strong, low-rate or high-intensity, pulse-train (burst)	9-13
8. Dual channel (3-lead system)	Suboccipital, masseter, and dorsal web space	Conventional	9-11, C
9. Dual channel (unilateral/bilateral)	Masseter and suboccipital (channel 1); dorsal web space bilateral (channel 2)	Conventional or low-intensity, pulse-train (channel 1); strong, low-rate or high-intensity, pulse-train (channel 2)	Not illustrated

HELPFUL HINTS

A. Use small electrode on facial sites.
B. If subthreshold or conventional modes are not effective, the brief-intense mode may be beneficial.

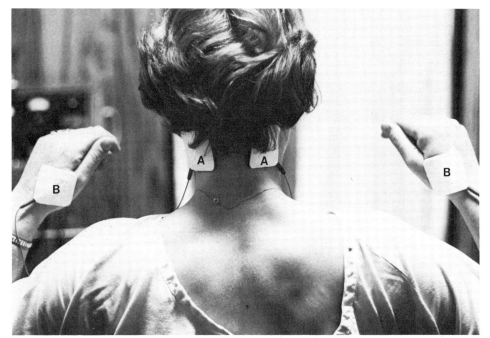

FIGURE 9-12. *Dx:* Bilateral frontal headache as a result of cervical strain. *Electrode place-ment technique:* Dual-channel, bilateral. *Electrode placement sites:* Suboccipital (A) and dorsal web space (B) constitute right and left channels. *Anatomic characteristics:* A, Motor/trigger points of splenius and semispinalis capitis correspond to acupuncture point GB 20. B, Motor/trigger points of first dorsal interosseus and adductor pollicis correspond to acu-puncture point LI 4. *Nerve innervation:* A, Greater and lesser occipital nerves. B, Superfi-cial radial and musculocutaneous (sensory); ulnar (motor). *T.E.N.S. mode:* Pulse-train (burst). Electrodes: Stim-tech Dermaforms. *T.E.N.S. unit:* Medtronic Comfort Burst. *Ratio-nale:* Possible neuropeptide release, cortical inhibitory surround theory, or interference with spike-interval pain pattern in thalamus. Electrical paresthesia perceived suboccipitally with propagation to supraorbital nerves from occipitals.

(strong, low-rate [acupuncture-like] mode) and reported a significant improvement in brain microcirculation. He has also placed electrodes at the frontalis motor point (GB 14) and TMJ region bilaterally in the treatment of intractable cephalic hypotension and TMJ syn-drome.[58] When cervical and upper thoracic pain is also present, Omura recommends another pair of electrodes at the upper trapezius trigger points bilaterally. Pain Suppression Labs reports that use of its unit can produce a decrease in blood pressure of 10 to 30 points (systolic and diastolic) with transcranial applications in hypertensive patients. It, therefore, recommends monitoring blood pressure changes in the hypotensive patient with transcra-nial applications greater than 5 minutes.

Reports in the literature pertaining specifically to the use of T.E.N.S. in headaches are sparse. A brief mention of clinical use and results is given without sufficient information relative to stimulation parameters, electrode placements, or treatment protocols. Shealy, however, recommends placement over the occipital nerves with an intensity of stimulation high enough to produce paresthesia from occiput to vertex. If this is not successful, stimu-lation over the eyebrows (forehead) or temples is recommended, and, at times, bilateral stimulation over the carotid sinuses may be beneficial. He cautions that the patient should be observed closely during this method since respiratory problems may ensue. Shealy's final recommendation is to use the dorsal web space (LI 4). Recently, we have been using a bilateral (single-channel) LI 4 (dorsal web space) arrangement with the strong, low-rate (acupuncture-like) or high-intensity, pulse-train mode for severe headaches or when stimulation cannot be tolerated at the head or occiput. This has been initially quite beneficial not only for headaches but for cervical spine pain when stimulation on the head or neck cannot be tolerated (Fig. 9-13).

The effectiveness of T.E.N.S. in the relief of headaches is entirely dependent on how long the headache has existed. Our best results have taken place when stimulation is initiated at or close to the onset of the headache. This is in agreement with the findings of Shealy.[49,63]

Alternative electrode placement arrangements for patients with headaches depend on the actual location of the pain (occipital, temporal, vertex, or frontal). Figures 9-14 to 9-18

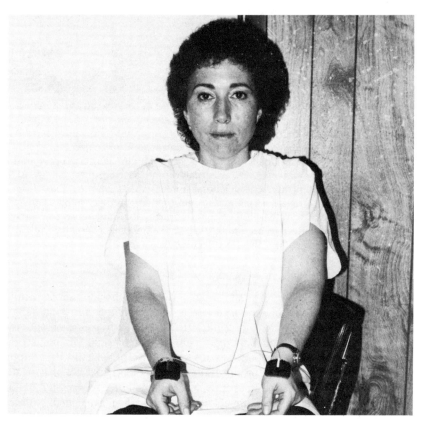

FIGURE 9-13. Alternate electrode array for headaches and cervical spine pain. *Electrode placement technique:* **Single-channel, bilateral at remote sites.** *Electrode placement sites:* **Dorsal web space.** *Anatomic characteristics:* **Motor/trigger points of first dorsal interosseus and adductor pollicis correspond to acupuncture point LI 4.** *Nerve innervation:* **Superficial radial and musculocutaneous (sensory); ulnar (motor).** *T.E.N.S. mode:* **Strong, low-rate (acupuncture-like) or high-intensity, pulse-train (burst).** *Rationale:* **Possible neuropeptide release. Cortical inhibitory surround mechanism.**

illustrate examples of alternate electrode placement arrangements for headaches. Although T.E.N.S. is not recommended as the treatment of choice for headaches, electrode placement can be determined by the guidelines discussed in Chapter 8.

Atypical Facial Pain

The following case study illustrates the benefit of T.E.N.S. in a patient with atypical facial pain.

Case Study #3

Clarifying Evaluation: Patient was a 67-year-old female referred on 10/7/80 who was involved in a severe auto accident on 7/6/63. She sustained multiple fractures of the right maxillofacial region that required surgical repair. Postoperatively, she developed severe discomfort in the right infraorbital and temporal region and had double vision of the right eye.

There was normal voluntary control of all facial musculature. Sensation was present but characterized by an intense hyperesthesia and background ache. This was most intense at the right side of the nose, infraorbital region, and cheek. The patient characterized the pain as a "hot poker," and at times pain became unbearable. Pain was aggravated by damp weather and emotional tension. Patient was unable to take medication due to allergies and a kidney condition. The patient received a series of acupuncture treatments from a physician, which provided about 9 months of relief prior to referral.

Figure 9-19 illustrates the right eye deeply set in the socket (enophthalmos). Evaluation to determine optimal stimulation sites was performed with the aid of sponge electrodes that could be easily held in place and moved by the patient. Figure 9-20 depicts the first electrode placement arrangement, consisting of supraorbital and infraorbital stimulation. This provided some immediate

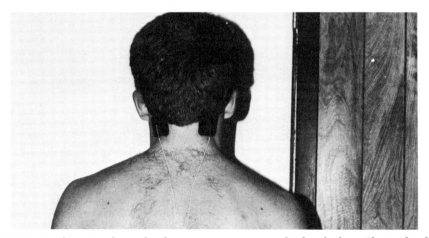

FIGURE 9-14. **Alternate electrode placement arrangement for headaches.** *Electrode placement technique:* **Single-channel, bilateral.** *Electrode placement sites:* **Suboccipital.** *Anatomic characteristics:* **Motor/trigger point of splenius and semispinalis capitis. Corresponds to acupuncture point GB 20.** *Nerve innervation:* **Greater and lesser occipital nerves.** *T.E.N.S. mode:* **Conventional.** *Rationale:* **Spinal tract of the trigeminal nerve connects with upper cervical spine between C2–4. Occipital-supraorbital anastomosis at vertex of head.**

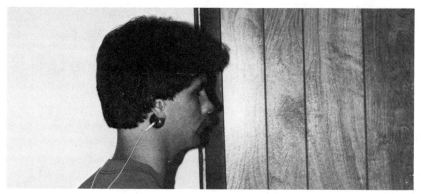

FIGURE 9-15. Alternate electrode placement arrangement for headaches. *Electrode placement technique:* Single-channel, bilateral (upper cervical). *Electrode placement sites:* Behind ear, in depression between mandible and mastoid. *Anatomic characteristics:* At C1–2 level. Corresponds to acupuncture points GB 2 and TW 17. *Nerve innervation:* Facial, communicating with great auricular, vagus, glossopharyngeal, and auriculotemporal nerves. *Electrodes:* Small circular carbon-silicone with karaya pad. *T.E.N.S. mode:* Conventional or low-intensity, pulse-train (burst). *Rationale:* Possible excitation of lateral cervical nucleus.

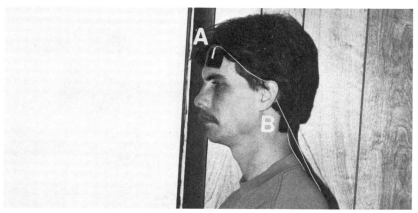

FIGURE 9-16. Alternate electrode placement arrangement for frontal headaches. *Electrode placement technique:* Single-channel, unilateral. *Electrode placement sites:* A, Supraorbital. B, Suboccipital. *Anatomic characteristics:* A, Motor point of frontalis muscle corresponds to acupuncture point GB 14. B, Motor/trigger point of splenius and semispinalis capitis muscles corresponds to acupuncture point GB 20. *Nerve innervation:* A, Supraorbital nerve (sensory); facial nerve (motor). B, Greater and lesser occipital nerves. *T.E.N.S. mode:* Conventional or subthreshold (Pain Suppressor). *Rationale:* Spinal tract of trigeminal connection with upper cervical spine. Occipital-supraorbital anastomosis at vertex of head.

CLINICAL T.E.N.S.

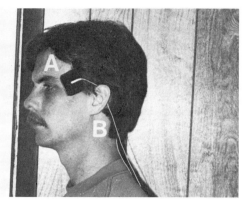

FIGURE 9-17. Alternate electrode placement arrangement for temporal headaches. *Electrode placement technique:* Single-channel, unilateral. *Electrode placement sites:* A, Temporal fossa, lateral to eyebrow. B, Suboccipital. *Anatomic characteristics:* A, Motor point of temporalis muscle. Corresponds to acupuncture point TW 23. B, Motor/trigger point of splenius and semispinalis capitis. Corresponds to acupuncture point GB 20. *Nerve innervation:* A, Zygomatico-temporal (branch of trigeminal). B, Greater and lesser occipital. *T.E.N.S. mode:* Conventional or subthreshold (Pain Suppressor). *Rationale:* Spinal tract of trigeminal connection with upper cervical spine. *Note:* Another arrangement with one electrode on the upper trapezius trigger point instead of suboccipital is a viable alternative. This approach would follow the pathway of pain referral from an upper trapezius trigger point and therefore involve a linear pathway technique.

pain relief. The supraorbital electrode was then moved to the temporal region, as shown in Figure 9-21. This arrangement was also helpful but not significantly better than the first. Optimal benefit was provided with the arrangement of the electrodes shown in Figure 9-22. The patient was extremely satisfied and desired to obtain the stimulator immediately. She was given her choice of units, and an order was placed with the distributor to obtain one on a rental basis.

Second Visit: Patient instructed in operation of T.E.N.S. and given home evaluation form. She was instructed to call after 1 week and report on efficiency. A return visit was necessary only if she developed difficulty. Figure 9-23 illustrates the final electrode arrangement.

Follow-Up: After the first week, the patient called and stated that she was obtaining 12 hours of pain relief with a 10-minute stimulation period. She was using the unit once in the morning and again prior to bedtime. After the rental period, the patient purchased the unit from the distributor. At the time of this report, the patient had been using the unit for 2 months with excellent success. Pain relief was at least 75 percent and entirely satisfactory to the patient. The stimulation mode employed was conventional.

The patient was also instructed to try strong, low-rate (acupuncture-like) stimulation but to date it has been unnecessary. The patient sent follow-up letters stating that she required the stimulator less and less. A letter dated 1/15/81 reported use of the stimulator for 20 minutes every 2 weeks. When occassional flare-ups of pain occur, they are controlled by use of the stimulator four to six times per day.

Head and Face Pain: Implications for T.E.N.S.

The literature contains little information and few reports pertaining to the effectiveness of T.E.N.S. in patients with atypical facial pain and headache. An excellent report by Bates and Nathan outlining their results with T.E.N.S. over a 7-year period stated that

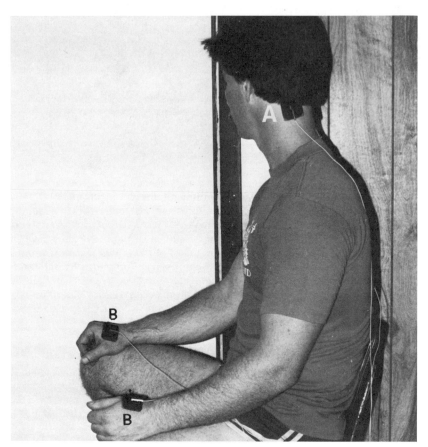

FIGURE 9-18. Alternate electrode placement arrangement for headaches or cervical spine pain. *Electrode placement technique:* Dual-channel, bimodal simultaneous. *Electrode placement sites:* A, Channel 1—bilateral suboccipital. B, Channel 2—bilateral dorsal web space. *Anatomic characteristics:* A, Motor/trigger point of splenius and semispinalis capitis muscles. Corresponds to acupuncture point GB 20. B, Motor/trigger points of first dorsal interosseus and adductor pollicis. Correspond to acupuncture point LI 4. *Nerve innervation:* A, Greater and lesser occipital nerves. B, Superficial radial and musculocutaneous (sensory); ulnar (motor). *T.E.N.S. mode:* A, Channel 1—conventional or low-intensity, pulse-train (burst). B, Channel 2—strong, low-rate (acupuncture-like) or high-intensity, pulse-train (burst). *T.E.N.S. unit:* Medical Devices Ultra II offers complete channel isolation and independent adjustment of all three parameters per channel but does not offer pulse-train (burst) mode. Capable of performing conventional mode on one channel and strong, low-rate on the other channel simultaneously. Biostim Biomod offers complete channel isolation and independent adjustment of amplitude and pulse width per channel but has single rate control. Capable of performing low-intensity, pulse-train mode on one channel and high-intensity, pulse-train on the other channel simultaneously. *Rationale:* Use when only low-intensity stimulation can be tolerated suboccipitally but does not provide adequate benefit. Simultaneous use of stronger mode at dorsal web space may increase efficacy.

FIGURE 9-19. Patient with severe hyperesthesia and constant ache of right infraorbital and cheek regions. Note enophthalmos of right eye.

patients with facial pain were not helped by T.E.N.S.[67] There are, however, reports by others of benefit with T.E.N.S. for patients with trigeminal neuralgia and facial pain.[8,68–71]

Eriksson and Sjolund specifically reported on 30 patients, 18 of whom had typical and 12 atypical trigeminal neuralgia.[39] Many of these patients had previously undergone destructive surgical procedures and had used medication. Sixty percent of the patients reported good relief of pain with T.E.N.S. through an 8-month average follow-up period. When relief was not obtained with conventional T.E.N.S., strong, low-rate (acupuncture-like) T.E.N.S. was tried. Eight patients obtained success only when using acupuncture-like T.E.N.S., which was not employed by Bates and Nathan.

Picaza found that suboccipital placement was more effective and better tolerated than supraorbital, infraorbital, or facial nerve stimulation for patients with head and neck pain.[8] Subcutaneous wire implantation (percutaneous T.E.N.S.) was used in 21 of 25 patients for pain control after eye surgery.[72] Four patients received similar stimulation transcutaneously. Electrodes or wires were placed near the supraorbital and infraorbital nerves and stimulation began after surgery, continuing for 1 to 3 days. The patients reported a pleasant sensation, with 9 obtaining complete pain relief and 13 having diminished pain.

Pain Suppression Labs reports that transcranial prophylactic use of its unit seems to help extend the time interval between migraine attacks. Results obtained by temperature

FIGURE 9-20. *Dx.* Atypical facial pain. *Electrode placement technique:* Single-channel, proximal and distal. *Electrode placement sites:* A, Supraorbital. B, Infraorbital. *Anatomic characteristics:* A, Motor point of frontalis muscle. Corresponds to acupuncture point GB 14. B, Motor point of caninus muscle. Corresponds to acupuncture point ST 2. *Nerve innervation:* A, Supraorbital (sensory); facial (motor). B, Infraorbital (sensory); facial (motor). *Electrodes:* Stim-tech sponge with water as transmission medium. *T.E.N.S. mode:* Conventional. *T.E.N.S. unit:* Stim-tech EPC #6011. *Rationale:* Both electrode placement sites innervated by trigeminal nerve branches. Arrangement allows for stimulation of nerves at superficial branches and perception of electrical paresthesia throughout area of pain.

biofeedback, relaxation, and autogenic training were discussed in Chapter 5. Obviously, T.E.N.S. is not needed if the same result can be obtained by volitional mechanisms. However, for patients who do not achieve such results, the use of T.E.N.S. may prove helpful. This method may be beneficial to patients who cannot tolerate T.E.N.S. on the head or face. T.E.N.S. can also be used to augment the action of volitional techniques early in a training program.

We also obtain good results with the use of noninvasive electroacupuncture stimulation. The recommended procedure for patients with cervical, head, or facial pain would begin with stimulation of OSS at the hand and wrist (LI 4, P 7, and H 4–7), representing the superficial radial and musculocutaneous, median, and ulnar nerves, respectively (Fig. 9-24). Proximal progression would then be performed at OSS within the distribution of any referred pain and finally at the specific region (neck, head, or face) if tolerated. This type of

FIGURE 9-21. *Dx:* Atypical facial pain. *Electrode placement technique:* Single-channel, unilateral. *Electrode placement sites:* A, Temporal depression lateral to eyebrow. B, Infraorbital. *Anatomic characteristics:* A, Temporalis motor point. B, Caninus motor point. *Nerve innervation:* A, Zygomatico-temporal. B, Infraorbital (sensory); facial (motor). *Electrodes:* Stim-tech sponge with water as transmission medium. *T.E.N.S. mode:* Conventional. *T.E.N.S. unit:* Stim-tech EPC #6011. *Rationale:* Both electrode placement sites innervated by trigeminal nerve branches. Arrangement allows for stimulation of nerves at superficial aspects and perception of electrical paresthesia throughout area of pain.

T.E.N.S., provided in the clinic by a blunt-end small-diameter probe, is given at a rate of 4 Hz with the intensity to patient tolerance (Fig. 9-25). None of our patients has been able to initially tolerate this at the area of pain, but initial distal and contralateral site stimulation provides some significant pain relief so that stimulation can subsequently be given to the appropriate area of pain.

A recommended protocol for stimulation of the face or head should therefore begin with placement at the suboccipital and/or dorsal web space sites first, since this will be more tolerable than stimulation on the face or head. When stimulation on the face or head is tried initially, the Pain Suppressor should be used. Periosteum is highly innervated and sensitive, especially when there is not much soft tissue between it and the skin. If necessary, we suggest using only one electrode on the face or head. A bilateral suboccipital arrangement would, of course, be the initial choice so that stimulation is not being applied to the face. Other techniques involve the strong, low-rate (acupuncture-like) or high-intensity,

FIGURE 9-22. *Dx:* **Atypical facial pain.** *Electrode placement technique:* **Single-channel, unilateral.** *Electrode placement sites:* **A, Infraorbital. B, Dorsal web space.** *Anatomic characteristics:* **A, Motor point of caninus muscle. Corresponds to acupuncture point ST 2. B, Motor/trigger points of first dorsal interosseus and adductor pollicis. Corresponds to acupuncture point LI 4.** *Nerve innervation:* **A, Infraorbital (sensory); facial (motor). B, Superficial radial and musculocutaneous (sensory); ulnar (motor).** *Electrodes:* **Stim-tech sponge with water as transmission medium. Electrode on dorsal web space held in place by 3M foam tape patch.** *T.E.N.S. mode:* **Conventional.** *T.E.N.S. unit:* **Stim-tech EPC #6011.** *Rationale:* **Cortical inhibitory surround theory, relationship between dorsal web space and face.**

pulse-train (burst) mode. The anatomic relationship of the spinal tract of the trigeminal nerve to the upper cervical spine and the arrangement of the somatosensory cortex (cortical inhibitory surround), as discussed in Chapter 8, is of prime importance in electrode placement for head and face pain. Table 9-7 lists suggested arrangements for headaches and facial pain.

Chapter 5 contains information relative to the phenomenon that mild stimuli may bring on pain. Conventional T.E.N.S. should be the first choice in sensory deprivation syndromes, such as trigeminal neuralgia, but brief, intense or strong, low-rate (acupuncture-like) T.E.N.S., as used by Ericksson and Sjolund, may be more effective if tolerated by the patient.[39] Contralateral electrode placement may be necessary if pain is triggered by ipsilateral stimulation.

Stimulation of similar or related areas contralateral to the painful side has been demonstrated.[8,55,70,73,74] Superficial aspects of peripheral nerves innervating the painful area,

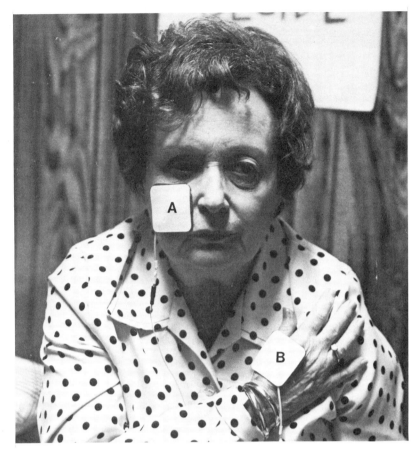

FIGURE 9-23. *Dx:* Atypical facial pain. *Electrode placement technique:* Single-channel, unilateral. *Electrode placement sites:* A, Infraorbital. B, Dorsal web space. *Anatomic characteristics:* A, Motor point of caninus muscle. Corresponds to acupuncture point ST 2. B, Motor/trigger points of first dorsal interosseus and adductor pollicis. Corresponds to acupuncture point LI 14. *Nerve innervation:* A, Infraorbital (sensory); facial (motor). B, Superficial radial and musculocutaneous (sensory); ulnar (motor). *Electrodes:* Stim-tech Dermaforms (karaya). *T.E.N.S. mode:* Conventional. *T.E.N.S. unit:* Dynex.

segmentally related optimal stimulation sites, or paraspinal placement is recommended. If a right trigeminal nerve branch is involved and stimulation at its superficial branches cannot be tolerated, contralateral stimulation of the same nerve should be tried. Stimulation contralateral to the pain may need to be more prolonged, and obtained relief will not last as long and will be of less benefit than ipsilateral stimulation.[8] A recent study has demonstrated that T.E.N.S. performed ipsilateral to the pain was of significantly greater benefit than contralateral stimulation.[75] However, Laitinen demonstrated that T.E.N.S. performed on the uninvolved side of the body may provide better long-term effectiveness than stimulation of the painful region.[73] After 9 months of T.E.N.S., there was a 46 to 47 percent decrease in the subjective intensity and frequency of pain and the need for medication in phantom limb, herpes zoster, and thalamic pain syndromes.[73] A local anesthetic block of the sympathetic ganglia on the affected side produced ipsilateral and contralateral changes such as the disappearance of trigger points and less pain contralaterally for up to 4 hours.[74]

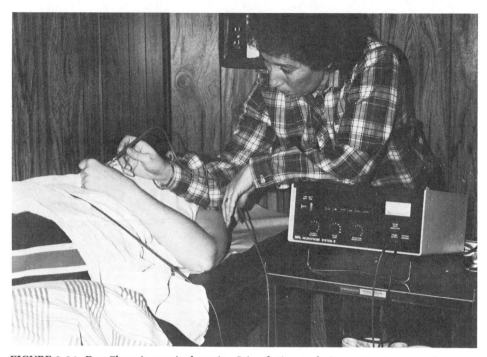

FIGURE 9-24. *Dx:* Chronic cervical strain. *Stimulation technique:* Noninvasive electroac-upuncture. *Electrode sites:* Dorsal web space. *Anatomic characteristics:* Motor/trigger points of first dorsal interosseus and adductor pollicis. Corresponds to acupuncture point LI 4. *Nerve innervation:* Superficial radial and musculocutaneous (sensory); ulnar (motor). *T.E.N.S. mode:* Strong, low-rate (acupuncture-like). *Electrodes:* Ground electrode is standard car-bon-silicone T.E.N.S. electrode held in contralateral hand. Blunt-end stimulating probe is active electrode. *T.E.N.S. unit:* MRL Neuroprobe System II. *Rationale:* Stimulation given for 30 to 60 seconds to tender or low-resistance optimal stimulation sites within pain distri-bution. Distal stimulation sites LI 4 (radial, musculocutaneous, and ulnar nerves), P 7 (me-dian nerve), H 4–7 (ulnar nerve), and LI 11 (radial nerve) are treated in succession. Stimu-lation then progresses from distal to proximal sites. At least a 50 percent reduction in pain to allow for tolerance of gentle soft-tissue and joint mobilization techniques is achieved prior to treatment. *Note:* Treatment being performed by physical therapy student Regina Rosen-thal.

The physiologic mechanism of cross stimulation may be explained by spinal cord reflexes. Supraspinal crossover may take place through long reflex loops in the corpus collosum between the cerebral hemispheres.[8,76,77]

CERVICAL SPINE

Unlike T.E.N.S. performed on the face or head, stimulation of the cervical spine is usually well tolerated. We have used T.E.N.S. adjunctively for pain control in syndromes such as occipital neuralgia, cervical strains, and radiculopathy. One of the most frequently treated acute pain situations is cervical strain (whiplash). T.E.N.S. is commonly used by the patient at home as a means of pain control while outpatient treatment directed toward the cause of the pain is being performed.

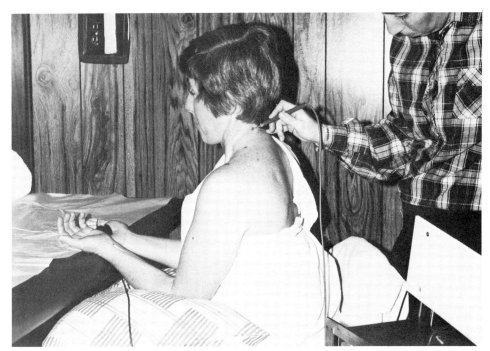

FIGURE 9-25. *Dx:* Chronic cervical strain. *Stimulation technique:* Noninvasive electroacupuncture. Proximal stimulation sites are delineated by black dots at deltoid insertion, musculotendinous junction of supraspinatus, upper trapezius trigger point, and posterior primary ramus of C5.

The placement of electrodes for cervical spine pain is paraspinal between the transverse processes overlying the intervertebral foramen. The optimal stimulation sites (OSS) of the spine are located at this region. The dorsal ramus of the spinal nerve, bladder meridian acupuncture points, erector spinae motor points, and muscle trigger points are also represented at this region.

Case Study 4 describes a post–auto accident patient with a severe cervical strain. Normally, a patient such as this would be lying down feeling the impact of constant nociceptive small-fiber input. Conventional T.E.N.S. is usually the only mode of stimulation tolerated in acute cervical strains. The resultant large-fiber input of conventional T.E.N.S. can provide a balancing effect to the constant small-fiber (pain) input. Pain relief would allow the patient to move about, try mild active ROM, and participate in the recovery process. There are occasions when it may be difficult to avoid muscle fasciculation of the upper trapezius with the electrode array shown in Figure 9-26 because current flow runs directly within the upper trapezius. However, mild fasciculations may not be bothersome to every patient. An alternative electrode arrangement to modulate cervical spine pain is shown in Figure 9-27. Electrodes may be placed paraspinally or on the OSS of the levator scapulae. Channel arrangements producing horizontal or longitudinal directions of current flow are not as effective. We have found through experience that the crisscross method (suboccipital to cervicothoracic junction or middle trapezius OSS) is generally the best tolerated and most effective method.

TABLE 9-7. Suggested Electrode Placement Techniques for Headaches and Facial Pain

Technique	Placement Sites	Mode	Illustration
1. Single channel (bilateral)	Suboccipital	Conventional or low-intensity, pulse-train (burst)	9-14
2. Single channel (bilateral)	Transcranial	Subthreshold or conventional	9-2
3. Single channel (bilateral)	Dorsal web space	Strong, low-rate or high-intensity, pulse-train (burst)	9-13
4. Single channel (bilateral)	Upper cervical Below mastoid process	Conventional or low-intensity, pulse-train (burst)	9-15
5. Single channel (unilateral)	Supraorbital and suboccipital	Subthreshold or conventional	9-16
6. Single channel (unilateral)	Suboccipital and temporal fossa	Subthreshold or conventional	9-17
7. Dual channel (bilateral)	Suboccipital to dorsal web space	Conventional or pulse-train (burst)	9-12
8. Dual channel (bilateral) (bimodal)	Suboccipital bilateral Dorsal web space bilateral	Conventional or low-intensity, pulse-train (burst); strong, low-rate, or high-intensity, pulse-train (burst)	9-18
9. Single (unilateral) or dual channel (bilateral)	Upper trapezius trigger point to temporal fossa	Conventional	Not illustrated

HELPFUL HINTS

A. Stimulation on the face or head should initially be tried with the Pain Suppressor.

B. In the presence of trigeminal neuralgia, contralateral stimulation may be effective if ipsilateral or remote sites are not.

C. Effectiveness is enhanced by stimulation as close as possible to onset of headache.

Case Study 4

Clarifying Evaluation: A 19-year-old male referred for rehabilitation on 8/7/79 following a severe cervical strain sustained as a result of an auto accident on 7/31/79. At the time of referral, the patient was wearing a soft cervical collar and held his head extremely rigid. He complained of constant pain described as an ache, which would become sharp with any active movement of the head or neck. Pain was eased only by lying supine on the floor. Pain existed throughout the cervical and upper thoracic region with myotomal referral to the right scapula plus periodic occipitofrontal headaches on the right.

Active ROM of the cervical spine was severely limited, with only about 10 percent of range in each direction. Constant muscle guarding was evident on attempted passive ROM. The entire region of discomfort was hypersensitive to even gentle touch. Neither further palpation nor vertebral segmental glides could be performed. Strength of the C1–T1 myotomes was WNL but could not be adequately tested through the full ROM due to pain.

Goals: Eliminate pain and muscle guarding, restore normal function

Treatment Plan: Because of pain, muscle guarding, and hypersensitivity to touch, it was initially impossible to perform any definitive treatment beyond a symptomatic approach. The patient was evaluated with a T.E.N.S. unit for pain control. Electrodes were placed at the most tender sites (see Fig. 9-26). A dual-channel arrangement was found to be most effective, with the electrodes of each channel placed in the suboccipital fossa and at the trigger point of the upper trapezius. The conventional mode was tolerated best. A prescription for rental of the unit from the distributor was obtained from the referring physician.

The patient was instructed to wear the electrodes constantly during the day and turn the unit on and off for 20- to 60-minute periods, keeping track of effectiveness on the home instruction form. When pain relief occurred, he was to attempt active ROM exercises. Until the rental unit was delivered, the patient was instructed to use ice packs for pain relief. The patient was also instructed

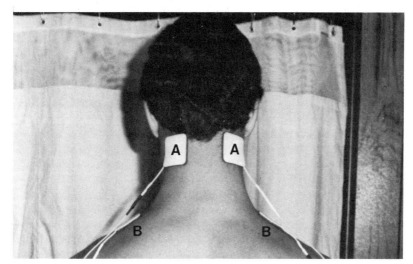

FIGURE 9-26. *Dx:* Severe, acute cervical strain. *Electrode placement technique:* Dual-channel, bilateral. *Electrode placement sites:* A, Superior electrodes in suboccipital fossa. B, Inferior electrodes at upper trapezius. Each channel consists of a suboccipital and upper trapezius electrode. *Anatomic characteristics:* A, Motor/trigger points of splenius and semispinalis capitis muscles. Corresponds to acupuncture point GB 20. B, Motor/trigger point of upper trapezius. Corresponds to acupuncture point GB 21. *Nerve innervation:* A, Greater and lesser occipital nerves. B, Supraclavicular (sensory) and spinal accessory. *T.E.N.S. mode:* Conventional. *Electrodes:* Stim-tech Dermaforms. *T.E.N.S. unit:* Stim-tech Stimpulse. *Rationale:* Electrode placement on segmentally related stimulation sites. Electrical paresthesia throughout area of pain.

in proper cervical spine mechanics. At times, the patient also complained of discomfort solely throughout the right scapula. Figure 9-28 illustrates the electrode arrangement used for this area.

At the time of the patient's first therapy session after obtaining the stimulator, he reported that he could not be comfortable without it. He was using it throughout the day for 20- to 40-minute periods and obtaining anywhere from 30 minutes to 1½ hours of 75 percent relief. The patient was then instructed to begin weaning himself from the cervical collar. Treatment consisting of gentle grade I articulatory techniques was now able to be initiated, along with manual suboccipital traction and additional active ROM exercises to begin stretching the tight suboccipital musculature, scalenes, levator scapulae, and upper trapezius. Fluorimethane spray and stretch was added later in the rehabilitation program along with high-voltage galvanic stimulation, advanced joint mobilization techniques, and stronger manual cervical traction. The treatment program was thus geared to decrease pain, increase joint mobility, and restore normal muscle rest length and function. The patient was treated on a three-times-a-week basis.

The progress note of 8/31/79 revealed a significant decrease in pain and active muscle guarding. Active ROM had improved to 75 percent of forward and backward bending and 60 percent of both side bending and rotation bilaterally.

Treatments continued for the following month and were decreased to twice a week. Progress note of 10/4/79 stated that cervical and right scapular pain was no longer present except when the patient attempted activities requiring lifting. A home exercise program for the upper extremities was initiated, and the patient was discharged on 10/11/79, at which time he also returned the T.E.N.S. unit to the distributor.

The use of T.E.N.S. in this case was adjunctive to the comprehensive treatment program. If this patient had been referred weeks or months after the accident, rehabilitation

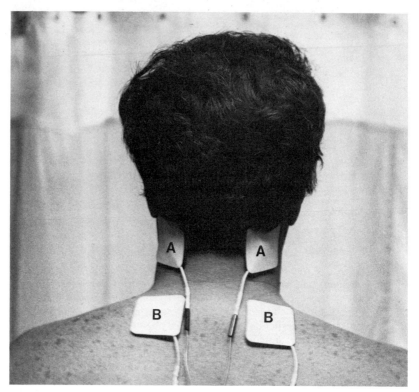

FIGURE 9-27. *Dx:* Chronic cervical syndrome. *Electrode placement technique:* Crisscross. *Electrode placement sites:* A, Superior electrodes in suboccipital fossa. B, Inferior electrodes at cervicothoracic junction paravertebrally. Each channel consists of a suboccipital and C-T junction electrode from opposite sides of the spine. *Anatomic characteristics:* A, Motor/trigger points of splenius and semispinalis capitis muscles. Corresponds to acupuncture point GB 20. B, Motor/trigger point of levator scapulae. Corresponds to acupuncture point SI 15. *Nerve innervation:* A, Greater and lesser occipital nerve. B, Medial branch of supraclavicular and segmental posterior primary rami. *T.E.N.S. mode:* Conventional. *Electrodes:* Stim-tech Dermaforms. *T.E.N.S. unit:* Medical Devices Ultra II. *Rationale:* Electrical paresthesia perceived throughout the cervical region and concentrated at the cervical spine. Placement of the distal electrodes just above the superior medial (vertebral) angle of the scapula is recommended when pain extends distally to the shoulder blade. This distal site is over the motor/trigger points of the middle trapezius muscle, which correspond to acupuncture point SI 13. The region is innervated superficially by the large dorsal ramus of T2.

would have been much longer and costlier. Patients with severe ROM limitations that persist develop muscle atrophy, weakness, tightness, and joint hypomobility. They are unable to tolerate any manual techniques and develop behavioral patterns indicative of chronic pain. Patients with cervical strains who are referred early and do not have initial severe active ROM limitations or other complications such as TMJ syndrome can usually be rehabilitated within 2 to 4 weeks.

An alternative arrangement for the cervical spine using three electrodes is illustrated in Figure 9-29. This patient was able to tolerate joint mobilization techniques only with T.E.N.S. This electrode placement technique allowed gentle manual glides and oscillations

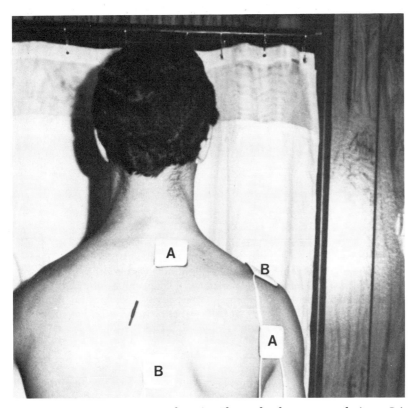

FIGURE 9-28. *Dx:* Severe, acute cervical strain. *Electrode placement technique:* Crisscross, dual-channel. *Electrode placement sites:* A, Channel 1—posterior axillary fold and cervicothoracic junction. B, Channel 2—musculotendinous junction of supraspinatus and paraspinal at T6–7. Stimulation is thus in a crisscross pattern. *Anatomic characteristics:* A, Motor/trigger point of posterior deltoid and levator scapulae. Corresponds to acupuncture points SI 10 and SI 15, respectively. B, Musculotendinous junction of supraspinatus. Corresponds to acupuncture point LI 16. Paraspinal electrode overlies segmental posterior primary rami. *Nerve innervation:* A, Dorsal ramus of T2 (sensory) and posterior branch of axillary nerve (motor) for SI 10 site. Medial branch of supraclavicular (sensory) and dorsal scapular nerve (motor) for SI 15 site. B, Posterolateral branch of supraclavicular nerve (sensory) and suprascapular nerve (motor) for LI 16 site. Segmental posterior primary rami for paraspinal site. *T.E.N.S. mode:* Conventional. *Electrodes:* Stim-tech Dermaforms. *T.E.N.S. unit:* Stim-tech Stimpulse. *Rationale:* Arrangement allows for the perception of electrical paresthesia over the entire region of discomfort.

of the cervical vertebrae with ongoing conventional stimulation parameters. The patient is currently using the T.E.N.S. unit in this manner at home while treatment continues.

Case Study 5

Clarifying Evaluation: A 45-year-old female referred for rehabilitation on 8/23/79. An extensive history of chronic pain complaints dates to 1958 when she had a lumbar laminectomy after having 1½ years of back strain. Pain persisted for 6 months postoperatively, then subsided. The patient was relatively

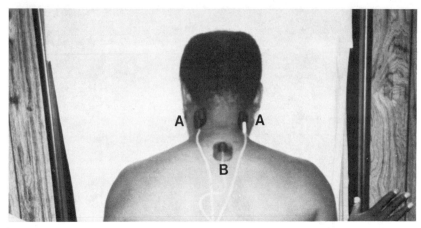

FIGURE 9-29. *Dx:* Chronic cervical strain. *Electrode placement technique:* Dual-channel, bilateral, forming a V-shaped pathway with a three-lead cable. *Electrode placement sites:* A, Right and left suboccipital electrodes. B, On midline over cervicothoracic junction. *Anatomic characteristics:* A, Motor/trigger points of splenius and semispinalis capitis muscles. Corresponds to acupuncture point GB 20. B, Over posterior primary rami of C7–T1. *Nerve innervation:* A, Greater and lesser occipital nerves. B, Posterior primary rami of C7–T1. *T.E.N.S. mode:* Conventional. *Electrodes:* Unipatch carbon-silicone with Lec-Tec karaya pad. *T.E.N.S. unit:* Biostim System 10. *Rationale:* Provides for perception of electrical paresthesia over all cervical posterior primary rami bilaterally. *Note:* With this T.E.N.S. unit and three-lead cable system, one lead wire is positive (red) and the other two negative (white, channel 1 and black, channel 2). There are separate pulse width and amplitude controls for each channel to allow for independent control of total energy. The circuitry of both channels includes the positive electrode (cervicothoracic junction), which directs current flow to each negative suboccipital electrode (channels 1 and 2). Therefore, each channel essentially uses one half of the power of the positive electrode.

pain-free until 1965, when she again developed periodic episodes of low back pain that eventually decreased.

In 1973, she stated that she developed a "stiff neck," right upper extremity pain, and weakness. She was hospitalized, received only 5 to 6 days of physical therapy without improvement, then underwent an anterior cervical fusion. She did well postoperatively. In 1974, a similar problem occurred, but this time with the left arm. A second anterior cervical fusion was performed. It was unclear as to the levels that were fused, but x-ray reports indicated the C6–7 and C7–T1 levels.

She remained relatively pain-free after the second cervical procedure until she was involved in an auto accident in 1975. As a result, she developed bilateral cervical and upper extremity pain, worse on the right, with referral to the first, fourth, and fifth fingers. Pain referral on the left was within the C5–C6 dermomyotome.

She underwent a myelogram at this time, which indicated degenerative joint disease of the cervical and lumbar spine and was subsequently hospitalized on bed rest and medication. This was followed by 2 weeks of acupuncture treatments without pain relief.

She was involved in a second auto accident in 1976 and since then has missed a great deal of work. She went to a pain clinic once a week for 1 month, which was not beneficial. She became depressed, complained of constant pain, was not eating, and took an overdose of medication. She was then placed under the care of a psychiatrist, who referred her for physical therapy.

At the time of the initial evaluation, the patient was complaining of bilateral upper trapezius, cervical spine, and scapula pain present for the past 3 weeks. Pain was increased by laughing, coughing, and deep breathing and was eased by moist heat but only during the application period. She awakened at night with every turn and sometimes had immediate pain on awakening in the morning. Pain was described as a tight, stabbing pain constantly present and aggravated by work or active movement.

Active ROM of the cervical spine was limited by 50 percent in all directions. Pain occurred with all movements of the C1–T1 myotomes, which made strength assessment unreliable. However, there seemed to be some triceps weakness bilaterally. Upper extremity reflexes were slightly hyperactive. Springing of the vertebral segments (midthoracic-cervical) produced discomfort only at T7 and T4. Skin rolling paravertebrally was painful only on the left. There were active left upper trapezius, levator scapulae, and right middle trapezius trigger points. Gentle manual cervical compression did not change the pain, but manual cervical traction decreased pain.

Goals: Decrease pain and teach prophylaxis.

Treatment Plan: The patient reported significant pain relief for 1½ days following manual cervical traction performed during the evaluation. The referring physician was contacted and approval obtained to initiate a program of high-voltage galvanic stimulation followed by joint mobilization to the mid to upper cervical spine, fluorimethane spray and stretch, and manual cervical traction performed in the neutral position. T.E.N.S. was considered at this time but not employed due to pain relief with good carryover from treatment.

On 9/19/79, the patient reported feeling 150 percent better. Treatments were thus reduced to once a week. On 10/18/79, the patient began complaining of severe low back pain. A note was sent to the referring physician concerning approval to provide treatment to the lumbar spine and a suggestion that the patient also be seen by a local orthopedist. Approval was obtained, and evaluation of the lumbar spine on 11/15/79 showed a significant loss of the lumbar lordosis with the patient unable to stand upright, being deviated toward the left in slight forward bending. Pain was centered at the right lumbosacral spine. Active ROM was severely limited due to pain in all directions except for left side bending. There was a complete loss of active backward bending. Strength of the L1–S2 myotomes was normal.

Treatment was initiated, consisting of McKenzie's lateral shift maneuver followed by small-arc active backward bending exercise once the upright position was obtained.[204] This was followed by high-voltage galvanic stimulation and joint mobilization to increase backward bending and promote maintenance of the lumbar lordosis. A back-support cushion was obtained for use at work, at home, and while driving to maintain the lumbar lordosis. She was evaluated with T.E.N.S., was extremely pleased by the pain relief, and rented then purchased a unit from the distributor. T.E.N.S. now provides her with a means of nonmedicinal pain control whenever needed, especially when there are acute flare-ups and she is unable to come for treatment.

She now comes for treatment only when acute discomfort occurs. Due to the nature of her condition (multiple spinal surgical procedures), she probably will have periodic episodes of pain, causing temporary incapacitation. However, she is an excellent patient, continues to work, and has been able to virtually eliminate all pain medication. She has been instructed in proper cervical and lumbar spine mechanics as well as specific therapeutic exercises such as axial extension, suboccipital stretching, and McKenzie lumbar backward bending.

Returned questionnaire on 6/15/80 reflected patient's satisfaction with the T.E.N.S. unit. She was subsequently instructed to increase the pulse width of each channel, which increased a carryover of pain relief after the unit was turned off. Previously, mild conventional T.E.N.S. provided about 75 percent pain control only when the stimulator was on.

Figures 9-30 and 9-31 illustrate the electrode arrangements that provided the best degree of relief. The electrode placement depicted in Figure 9-31 was used when pain was referred to the scapula myotomes innervated by the cervical spine. Placement was over the most tender sites. This arrangement was devised by the patient.

CERVICAL RADICULOPATHY

Pain is commonly referred from the cervical spine to the upper extremity. This can occur in acute or chronic conditions. When pain is referred to an extremity, T.E.N.S. will be most effective if at least one electrode is placed at the distal extent of the pain.[78] This is

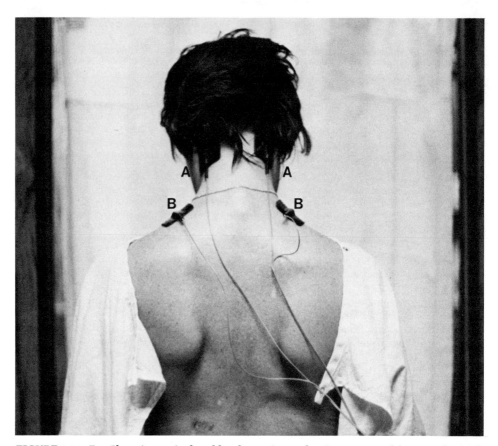

FIGURE 9-30. *Dx:* Chronic cervical and lumbar pain postlaminectomy and fusion. *Electrode placement technique:* Dual-channel, bilateral. *Electrode placement sites:* A, Superior electrodes in suboccipital fossa. B, Inferior electrodes at upper trapezius. Each channel consists of a suboccipital and upper trapezius electrode unilaterally. *Anatomic characteristics:* A, Motor/trigger points of splenius and semispinalis capitis muscles. Correspnds to acupuncture point GB 20. B, Motor/trigger point of upper trapezius. Corresponds to acupuncture point GB 21. *Nerve innervation:* A, Greater and lesser occipital nerves. B, Supraclavicular (sensory) and spinal accessory. *T.E.N.S. mode:* Conventional. *Electrodes:* Stim-tech perforated carbon-silicone with karaya pad. *T.E.N.S. unit:* Medical Devices Ultra II. *Rationale:* Arrangement allows for the perception of paresthesia throughout the entire region of discomfort.

always suggested unless pain is due to a peripheral nerve injury, which usually necessitates placement above the level of the lesion, therefore not hindering T.E.N.S. transmission.[79-81]

Pain referral stemming from a radiculopathy may follow a specific dermatomal distribution, peripheral nerve course, acupuncture meridian, or trigger point pain pattern. Lampe has noted this and coined the term linear pathway of pain.[82] Evaluation of the patient using the guidelines to optimal stimulation site selection is therefore necessary to determine the pain pattern and resultant electrode placements. Case Study 6 illustrates this approach.

The electrode arrangement depicted in Figure 9-32 is enhanced by overlapping channels. This technique will allow for the perception of current flow in a continuous pattern

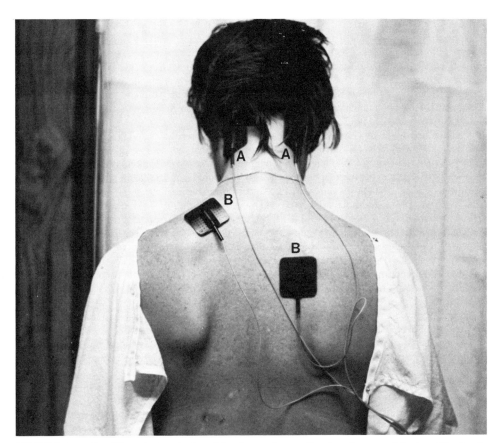

FIGURE 9-31. *Dx:* Chronic cervical and lumbar pain postlaminectomy and fusion. *Electrode placement technique:* Dual-channel, bilateral. *Electrode placement sites:* A, Superior electrodes at suboccipital fossa. B, Inferior electrode on the right just below spine of scapula on vertebral border. Inferior electrode on the left just inferior to upper trapezius motor/trigger point. Each suboccipital electrode was coupled to the distal electrode on its own side. *Anatomic characteristics:* A, Motor/trigger point of splenius and semispinalis capitis. Corresponds to acupuncture point GB 20. B, Upper trapezius motor/trigger point on right. Corresponds to acupuncture points GB 21 and TW 15. Middle trapezius motor/trigger point on left. Corresponds to acupuncture point SI 13. *Nerve innervation:* A, Greater and lesser occipital nerves. B, Posterior branch of supraclavicular. *T.E.N.S. mode:* Conventional. *Electrodes:* Stim-tech perforated carbon-silicone with karaya pad. *T.E.N.S. unit:* Medical Devices Ultra II. *Rationale:* Technique devised by patient that provided increased relief when tender myotomal trigger points were stimulated.

throughout the pain distribution. One channel overlaps the other, ensuring perception of the paresthesia throughout the pain referral area.

Case Study 6

Clarifying Evaluation: A 60-year-old female referred on 10/16/79 for multiple pain complaints. She previously underwent two lumbar laminectomies in 1966 and 1970 for what she stated were intervertebral disk problems. In 1974, she underwent a cervical laminectomy, also apparently for inter-vertebral disk problems. The patient was unaware of the exact levels of surgery. She was also a diabetic with neuropathies of both posterior tibial nerves.

Decreased active ROM of the cervical and lumbar spinal regions existed. Strength of the ankle dorsiflexors were graded as fair. The patient complained of the worst pain in both feet "as though there are stones under my heels," a toothache pain of the left upper extremity to the elbow, and low back pain. The patient ambulates with bilateral plastic orthoses for dorsiflexion assistance.

Goals: Pain modulation with T.E.N.S.

Treatment Plan: Initial application of electrodes to the sural nerve (B 57) and posterior tibial nerve (K 3) bilaterally proved to be effective in controlling discomfort of the feet (see Fig. 9-67). This arrange-ment was able to be used while ambulating with the orthoses (see Fig. 9-68). Optimal stimulation sites B 57 and K 3 were the most tender to palpation. It should be noted that the tibial nerve bifurcates into the medial and lateral plantar nerves between the medial malleolus and heelcord (K 3). The sural nerve was stimulated at the midline of the lower leg two thirds of the distance from the popliteal space to the insertion of heelcord (B 57). Both of these sites were thus anatomically and physiologi-cally related to the area of pain. See Figure 9-69 for an alternative arrangement for calf pain.

A different electrode array was arrived at for the cervical and left upper arm pain. The most tender palpable sites were the paravertebral region from C3–C5, the trigger point of the upper trape-zius (GB 21) and optimal stimulation sites TW 14 and TW 10 on the posterior aspect of the shoulder and arm, respectively (Fig. 9-32).

Low back pain was satisfactorily controlled with a crisscross (interferential-type) arrangement from the most proximal level of pain to the most distal. This arrangement is shown in Figure 9-54. Conventional T.E.N.S. was used as the stimulating mode for all three arrangements.

The patient primarily used the T.E.N.S. unit on the legs, as this was her most irritating and constant area of discomfort. She reported at the end of the rental period that she was obtaining about 4 hours of satisfactory pain relief (50 to 75 percent) after a stimulation period of 20 to 30 minutes for cervical, lumbar, and lower extremity pain. She used the stimulator for the left arm and the low back when discomfort occurred at these regions, which was only occasionally.

The patient thus purchased the unit from the distributor after the initial month's rental period. Five visits were required to complete the T.E.N.S. evaluation process. She was fully instructed in the use of the unit and given written home instructions. Follow-up by mail questionnaire could not be accomplished as the patient had moved out of the state and a forwarding address could not be obtained.

Case Study 7 demonstrates the benefit of changing electrode placement and stimula-tion mode to obtain optimal success. This patient ultimately required stimulation bilaterally followed by the dual-channel/linear pathway arrangement for the right forearm.

Case Study 7

Clarifying Evaluation: A 44-year-old male injured in an automobile accident on January 29, 1981, referred for T.E.N.S. evaluation on March 22, 1982. The patient sustained head lacerations, fracture of the right wrist, and fracture of C4 and 5, which were surgically fused. The patient had not worked since the accident and was receiving physical therapy at another facility. The patient developed a right carpal tunnel syndrome, which was surgically decompressed. Since cervical surgery, he com-plained of a constant toothache-like pain at the C6–T1 region with "neck spasms" three or four times per day. He also complained of bilateral paresthesia to the fourth and fifth fingers (ulnar distribution). Active ROM of the cervical spine was severely limited in all directions. Strength of the C1–T1 myotomes was WNL bilaterally.

Goals: Obtain pain control with T.E.N.S.

Treatment Plan: Evaluation with T.E.N.S. revealed that the conventional mode using a crisscross placement at the cervical spine (suboccipital to cervicothoracic junction) provided only relief of neck pain. The electrodes were rearranged at the cervicothoracic junction and ulnar nerve H 4–7 at the

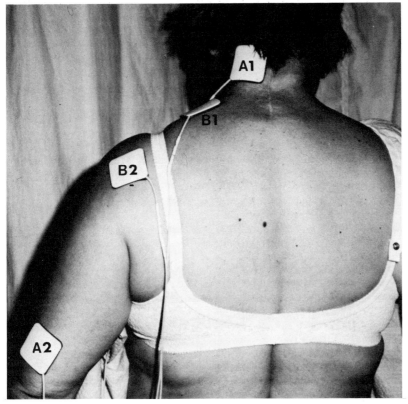

FIGURE 9-32. *Dx:* Chronic cervical spine pain, postlaminectomy. *Electrode placement technique:* Linear pathway, dual-channel. *Electrode placement sites:* A1, Paravertebral at C3–5. A2, Posterior aspect of arm just above elbow (channel II). B1, Upper trapezius. B2, In depression below posterior aspect of acromion (channel I). *Anatomic characteristics:* A1, Overlies posterior primary rami of C3–5. A2, Corresponds to acupuncture point TW 10–11. B1, Motor/trigger point of upper trapezius. Corresponds to acupuncture point GB 21. B2, Motor/trigger point of posterior deltoid. Corresponds to acupuncture point TW 14. *Nerve innervation:* A1, Posterior primary rami of C3–5. A2, Upper lateral cutaneous nerve, branch of axillary and dorsal ramus of T2. B1, Supraclavicular. B2, Posterior cutaneous of arm (radial), medial cutaneous of forearm (ulnar, posterior branches), and posterior cutaneous nerve of forearm. *T.E.N.S. mode:* Conventional. *Electrodes:* Stim-tech Dermaforms (karaya). *T.E.N.S. unit:* Stim-tech Stimpulse. *Rationale:* Overlapping linear pathway technique provided for perception of electrical paresthesia throughout entire pain distribution.

wrist, bilaterally, and the strong, low-rate (acupuncture-like) mode employed. (Fig. 9-33). This electrode arrangement provided for muscle contraction of ulnar innervated myotomes and was well tolerated. The patient reported 50 percent pain relief after a 30-minute treatment, providing him with what he felt was satisfactory pain relief. He desired to obtain a unit, and one was ordered from the distributor. He was subsequently instructed in the use of the stimulator (told to increase treatment time to 1 hour) and was given written home instructions and evaluation forms to complete.

Re-evaluation on April 15, 1982, revealed that the patient was obtaining complete relief of pain in the LUE and left cervical region. This was obtained with 1 hour of strong, low-rate T.E.N.S., after which he was pain-free an average of 6 to 7 hours and at times up to a full day. This method, however,

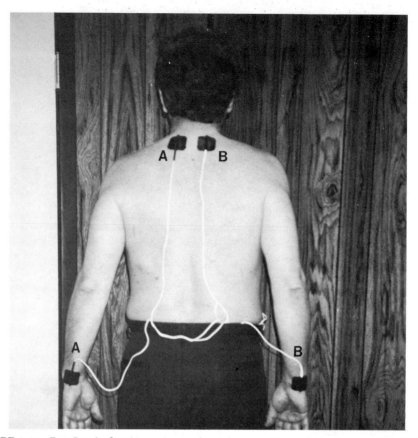

FIGURE 9-33. *Dx:* Cervical spine pain postlaminectomy. *Electrode placement technique:* Dual-channel, bilateral. *Electrode placement sites:* A, Cervicothoracic junction and overlying flexor carpi ulnaris (left-sided channel). B, Same, but on right side. *Nerve innervation:* Segmental posterior primary rami and ulnar nerve, which correspond to acupuncture points H 4–7. *T.E.N.S. mode:* Strong, low-rate (acupuncture-like). *Electrodes:* Medtronic Neuro-Aid (synthetic polymer). *T.E.N.S. unit:* Empi DC. *Rationale:* Conventional T.E.N.S. unable to provide adequate pain relief with a crisscross arrangement (suboccipital to cervicothoracic junctions bilaterally). The strong, low-rate mode thus was used. Consistent with recommended guidelines, electrode placement ensured rhythmic muscle contractions of segmentally related myotomes.

was of no benefit for the right side, but he also reported that his neck spasms had decreased in frequency to only five or six per week.

Electrodes were thus rearranged to provide for stimulation solely to the right cervicothoracic junction and upper extremity. Placement of one electrode at the cervicothoracic junction and another above the olecranon groove (ulnar nerve) constituted one channel. A second channel was composed of one electrode at the lower axilla (ulnar nerve) and the other at the ulnar aspect of the wrist (Fig. 9-34). Twenty to 30 minutes of conventional T.E.N.S. with a cycled (on 2 seconds and off 3 seconds) modulation provided full pain relief, but this did not persist beyond 1 hour. The patient at this time reported that pain in the RUE was also present in the dorsal forearm to the thumb and index finger. He stated that the dorsal forearm pain was not being relieved by T.E.N.S.

In light of this, another electrode arrangement was developed to provide for stimulation using the strong, low-rate mode to the radial and ulnar myotomes of the forearm (Fig. 9-35). This provided

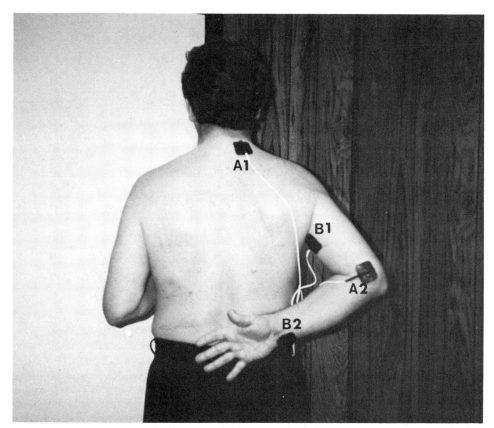

FIGURE 9-34. *Dx:* **Cervical spine pain postlaminectomy.** *Electrode placement technique:* **Linear pathway, dual-channel overlap.** *Electrode placement sites:* **A1, Cervicothoracic junction. A2, Above olecranon. B1, Lower axilla. B2, Ulnar border of wrist.** *Anatomic characteristics and nerve innervation:* **A1 and A2 as well as B1 and B2 constitute separate channels. A1, Overlies segmental posterior primary rami. A2, Overlies ulnar nerve. Corresponds to acupuncture point H 3. B1, Overlies ulnar nerve. Corresponds to acupuncture point H 1. B2, Overlies ulnar nerve. Corresponds to acupuncture point H 4–7.** *T.E.N.S. mode:* **Conventional.** *Electrodes:* **Medtronic Neuro-Aid, synthetic polymer.** *T.E.N.S. unit:* **Empi DC.** *Rationale:* **Provides for an overlapping perception of electrical paresthesia along the course of the ulnar nerve.**

excellent pain relief after 30 minutes of stimulation. The patient was told to continue utilizing the stimulation method depicted in Figure 9-33 and to follow, as needed, with the method shown in Figure 9-34 or 9-35.

A note was sent to the referring physician outlining the progress. In addition, the physician was informed that if he felt that the patient would need the unit beyond another month, he should consider purchase. Follow-up now is to be provided by a mail questionnaire.

Cervical Spine Pain: Implications for T.E.N.S.

Electrode placement arrangements for cervical spine pain used methods involving the upper cervical spine, spinal cord segment, linear pathways, bilateral stimulation, and dual-channel arrays. A more in-depth discussion of other electrode placements follows.

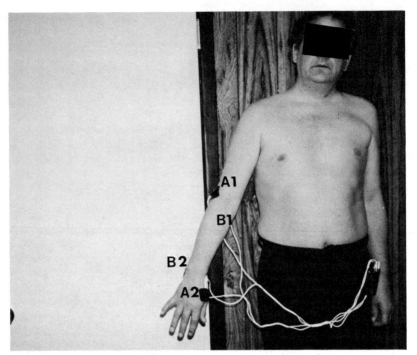

FIGURE 9-35. *Dx:* Cervical spine pain postlaminectomy. *Electrode placement technique:* Dual-channel, unilateral. *Electrode placement sites:* A1, In depression at end of lateral elbow crease with arm flexed to 90°. A2, Dorsal web space (channel 1). B1, Below olecranon groove. B2, At ulnar aspect of wrist just proximal to second volar crease (channel 2). *Anatomic characteristics:* A1, Motor/trigger point of brachioradialis. Corresponds to acupuncture point LI 11. A2, Motor/trigger point of first dorsal interosseus and adductor pollicis. Corresponds to acupuncture point LI 4. B1, Overlying superficial aspect of ulnar nerve. B2, Overlying flexor carpi ulnaris tendon. Corresponds to acupuncture point H 4–7. *Nerve innervation:* A1, Posterior cutaneous nerve of forearm and superficial radial. A2, Superficial radial and musculocutaneous (sensory); ulnar (motor). B1, Ulnar. B2, Ulnar. *T.E.N.S. mode:* Strong, low-rate (acupuncture-like). *Electrodes:* Medtronic Neuro-Aid (synthetic polymer). *T.E.N.S. unit:* Empi DC. *Rationale:* Electrode placement ensures rhythmic muscle contractions of segmentally related myotomes.

    Suboccipital stimulation bilaterally at OSS GB 20 is frequently the most proximal electrode placement site on the spine. Hindered only by hair, this stimulation site is extremely effective in the control of upper neck pain, occipital neuralgia, and many headaches (specifically occipital, vertex, and frontal). Pain relief in frontal headaches with suboccipital stimulation may be due to the relationship of the supraorbital nerves to the occipital nerves at the vertex of the head. Shealy considers paraspinal upper cervical stimulation to be effective occasionally in the control of pain existing in unrelated areas.[49,63]

    Closely related to suboccipital stimulation is electrode placement over the transverse processes of C2 below the mastoid process bilaterally (see Fig. 9-15). The initial reports on use of this stimulation site were by Crue and associates.[83–85] This technique was first performed with terminal cancer patients who initially obtained a 60 percent reduction in pain. Further study of 48 patients with chronic pain who had both malignant and benign syndromes treated with T.E.N.S. at the upper cervical spine showed that 31 percent (15 of

48 patients) had full or partial pain relief for only a few days to weeks. A 100-Hz, 0.2-msec square wave was used with intensity adjusted by the patient (range of 1 to 35 mA) to a level strong enough to produce painful contraction of the cervical musculature, including the upper trapezius. The amplitude was gradually increased as tolerance occurred. Stimulation was first provided for a few hours, then given for 24-, 48-, 72-, and 96-hour periods. Three patients obtained prolonged pain relief by this method, but benefit was short-lived for the majority of patients. Other than the close approximation of upper cervical spine stimulation to the brainstem possibly resulting in a liberation of endorphins, activation of descending pathways, or a placebo response, the lateral cervical nucleus may play a role. The lateral cervical nucleus located at the C1–2 level is considered to be involved in the relay of somatosensory impulses from the spinocervicothalamic tract to the contralateral thalamus and cortex. Although separate from the spinothalamic and medial lemniscal systems, the spinocervicothalamic tract may function with them in the mediation of noxious stimuli.[86–88]

A recent study strongly supports the use of T.E.N.S. for patients with acute cervical strains. Nordemar and Thorner found rapid improvement in pain and cervical mobility when conventional T.E.N.S. was added to conservative care.[89] Three groups of randomly selected patients all received treatment via a cervical collar and analgesics at home. One group received T.E.N.S. and another group manual therapy in the clinic, whereas the third group was treated solely by a cervical collar and pain medication. T.E.N.S. was given on a three-times-per-week basis for 15 minutes with a rate of 80 Hz, 0.2-msec pulse duration, and intensity of definite sensation below the pain threshold (conventional mode). All three groups improved rapidly, but the group that received T.E.N.S. exhibited a significantly more rapid restoration of cervical mobility. The patients who received manual therapy also improved rapidly, some even faster than those in the T.E.N.S. group. Pain reduction with T.E.N.S. persisted between 1 hour and 1 day. There was no significant difference in the amount of analgesics utilized among the groups.

The majority of the patients who participated in this study improved after 1 week. After 6 weeks, all patients had regained full cervical mobility. When unilateral cervical spine pain exists, the use of three electrodes can provide a triangular or V-shaped current pathway. Such an array produces electrical paresthesia through the distribution of pain (Fig. 9-36).

Unfortunately, patients with cervical strains are rarely referred in the acute stage. Patients present in the subacute or chronic stage usually weeks or months postinjury, which necessitates a considerably longer and costlier rehabilitation period. We thus recommend T.E.N.S. for the acute patient at home in conjunction with an exercise program and outpatient treatment consisting of postural and diaphragmatic breathing exercises, specific therapeutic procedures such as joint mobilization, contract-relax techniques, and fluorimethane spray and stretch to eliminate pain and restore normal function.

Table 9-8 summarizes electrode placement techniques for cervical spine pain.

SHOULDER PAIN

Shoulder pain may be intrinsic to the joint, its soft-tissue components, or contractile structures and can be referred distally through the C5–6 dermomyotome. Case Study 8 is indicative of the patient referred with adhesive capsulitis who either never received proper treatment in the acute phase or did not consult with a physician until the pain intensified and led to dysfunction.

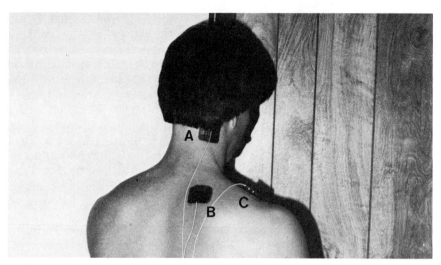

FIGURE 9-36. Alternative electrode arrangement for unilateral cervical spine pain. *Electrode placement technique:* Dual-channel, unilateral using three-lead cable system. *Electrode placement sites:* A, Suboccipital (positive electrode). B, Superior medial angle of scapula (negative electrode, channel 1). C, Just superior to acromion (negative electrode, channel 2). *Anatomic characteristics:* A, Motor/trigger point of splenius and semispinalis capitis. Corresponds to acupuncture point GB 20. B, Motor-trigger point of middle trapezius. Corresponds to acupuncture point SI 14. C, Musculotendinous junction of supraspinatus. *Nerve innervation:* A, Greater and lesser occipital nerves. B, Lateral branch of supraclavicular. C, Lateral branch of supraclavicular and dorsal rami of T2. *Suggested T.E.N.S. mode:* Conventional. *T.E.N.S. unit:* Biostim System 10 (see Figs. 9-11, C, and 9-29 for explanation). *Rationale:* Current flow can be directed so that electrical paresthesia is perceived across the whole lateral cervical to acromial region and scapular trigger point.

Case Study 8

Clarifying Evaluation: A 66-year-old male referred for rehabilitation on 11/7/79 as a result of adhesive capsulitis of the left shoulder. History dated to 2/79 when he began to develop left shoulder pain while working. His job required stressful functioning of the upper extremities, and previous episodes of shoulder pain had always dissipated. At the initial visit, he complained of constant pain in the left shoulder to the deltoid insertion that had decreased somewhat since a recent injection by the referring physician. Pain would increase with active ROM or when sleeping on the shoulder.

Active ROM measurements showed shoulder flexion 0 to 140 degrees, abduction 0 to 120 degrees, internal rotation 0 to 50 degrees, and external rotation 0 to 75 degrees. The patient complained of a clicking sensation and sharp pain at the suprahumeral joint space when he actively externally rotated. Resisted movement testing in internal and external rotation plus abduction were all painful.

Goals: Decrease pain and increase function.

Treatment Plan: The patient went through a treatment program of phonophoresis with hydrocortisone cream followed by transverse friction massage to the infraspinatus and supraspinatus tendons, joint mobilization, therapeutic exercise, and high-voltage galvanic stimulation twice a week.

Pain subsided and active ROM increased, but pain persisted at end-range, limited by only 10 to 15 degrees in all directions. Isokinetic strengthening was instituted on 12/27/79. Treatments were reduced to once a week as of 1/3/80 and discontinued on 2/27/80.

The patient was then referred for evaluation with T.E.N.S. on 3/20/80 as he reported that shoulder pain would flare up at times. Active ROM was unchanged from the above grades, being

TABLE 9-8. Suggested Electrode Placement Techniques for Cervical Spine Pain

Technique	Placement Sites	Mode	Illustration
1. Single-channel (bilateral)	Suboccipital	Conventional or low-intensity, pulse-train (burst)	9-14
2. Dual-channel (bilateral) V-shaped pathway	Suboccipital (bilateral) and cervicothoracic junction	Conventional or low-intensity, pulse-train (burst)	9-29
3. Dual-channel (bilateral)	Upper trapezius trigger point to suboccipital	Conventional	9-26
4. Dual-channel (crisscross)	Suboccipital to cervicothoracic junction or superior medial angle of scapula	Conventional	9-27
5. Dual-channel (bilateral)	Dorsal web space and suboccipital	*Strong, low-rate or high-intensity, pulse-train (burst)	9-13
6. Single-channel (bilateral)	Behind ear between mandible and mastoid process	Conventional or low-intensity, pulse-train	9-15
7. Dual-channel linear pathway	Superficial aspects of peripheral nerve	Conventional	9-32

HELPFUL HINTS

A. Proximal and distal placement is necessary for efficiency with referred pain.
B. Overlapping of channels with linear pathway technique is recommended. (see Fig. 9-34)
C. Bilateral paraspinal stimulation at appropriate levels should augment unilateral cervical and upper extremity referral.
D. Use three-lead cable system (see Fig. 9-37) for unilateral cervical spine pain.
E. Use of specific parameter modulation features can enhance comfort, tolerance, and efficiency.

*Alternative: low-intensity, pulse-train (burst) suboccipitally and high-intensity, pulse-train (burst) at dorsal web space.

limited only at end-range by 10 to 15 degrees. The patient had since retired and desired to obtain pain control. The most tender optimal stimulation sites were LI 16 (musculotendinous junction of the supraspinatus) and LI 14 (deltoid insertion). These sites were coupled for one channel, and a second channel arranged anterior and posterior to the acromion overlying the supraclavicular nerves (LI 15 and TW 14, respectively) was added for increased effectiveness (Fig. 9-37). This initial electrode arrangement provided 50 to 75 percent pain relief lasting for 2 to 6 hours with a 30- to 60-minute stimulation period. Conventional T.E.N.S. was used. Other electrode arrangements were also employed when pain occasionally was referred to the elbow or wrist (Figs. 9-38, 9-39).

The patient was instructed to continue his home exercise program, and on 4/7/80 reported that he felt increased mobility and function of the shoulder. Pain had decreased to the point where he only needed to use the unit once or twice a day. The patient desired to purchase the unit on 4/15/80, at which time he reported excellent pain relief and improved function.

Follow-up by telephone on 2/4/81 revealed that the patient was continuing to use the unit approximately once each day. He is able to sleep through the night without being awakened by pain. He has been able to resume landscaping around the house as well as carpentry. The patient's wife reported that prior to obtaining the T.E.N.S. unit her husband had been impossible to live with due to constant pain complaints.

Figure 9-40 illustrates an array with three electrodes that was very effective in controlling pain from rotator cuff surgery. A dual-channel array that is recommended for bicipital tendinitis or pain referral from the cervical spine to the biceps is depicted in Figure 9-41.

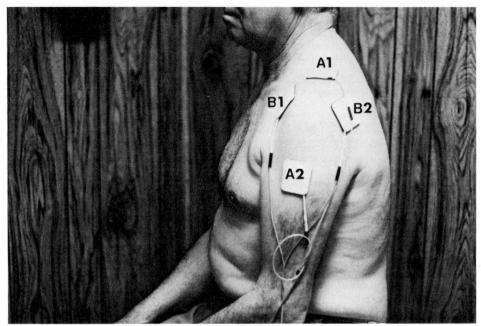

FIGURE 9-37. *Dx:* Chronic shoulder pain (adhesive capsulitis). *Electrode placement technique:* Dual-channel, unilateral (crisscross). *Electrode placement sites:* A1, In depression bordered by the acromion laterally, spine of the scapula posteriorly, and clavicle anteriorly. A2, Insertion of deltoid at lateral aspect of arm. B1, In depression below acromion anteriorly. B2, In depression below acromion posteriorly. A1 and A2, and B1 and B2 constitute separate channels. *Anatomic characteristics:* A1, Musculotendinous junction of supraspinatus. Corresponds to acupuncture point LI 16. A2, Insertion of deltoid. Corresponds to acupuncture point LI 16. B1, Motor point of anterior deltoid. Corresponds to acupuncture point LI 15. B2, Motor point of posterior deltoid. Corresponds to acupuncture point TW 14. *Nerve innervation:* A1, Posterolateral branch of supraclavicular nerve. A2, Upper lateral cutaneous nerve, branch of axillary. B1, Upper lateral cutaneous nerve, branch of axillary. B2, Intercostal brachial, upper lateral cutaneous, and dorsal ramus of T2. *T.E.N.S. mode:* Conventional. *Electrodes:* Stim-tech Dermaforms. *Rationale:* Arrangement allows for the perception of electrical paresthesia throughout the shoulder.

Shoulder Pain: Implications for T.E.N.S.

T.E.N.S. is extremely effective in the modulation of shoulder pain due to musculoskeletal dysfunction. The most common referrals are those due to tendinitis and bursitis. Excellent comprehensive treatment protocols can be initiated in the acute phase to prevent the development of chronic problems. T.E.N.S. can play an important role in such rehabilitation programs. Concomitant with symptomatic treatment, the initiation of outpatient treatment on a three-times-a-week basis, consisting of joint mobilization techniques to maintain laxity of the capsule and prevent loss of joint play and component motions, can serve to prevent the development of adhesive capsulitis. Electrode placement for a subdeltoid bursitis in the acute stage would be the same as that shown in Figure 9-37. However, after a few days, pain may be referred distally to the elbow or radial border of the wrist through the C5–6 dermomyotome. Removing the electrode from the musculotendinous junction of the supraspinatus (LI 16) to the LI 11 or 4 site should control the distal referred

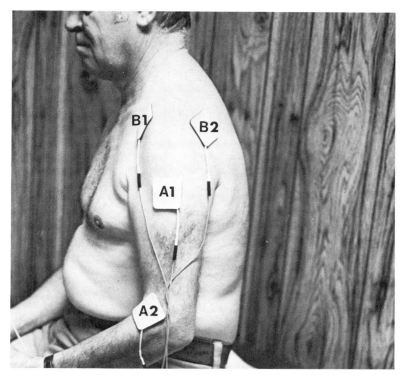

FIGURE 9-38. *Dx:* Chronic shoulder pain (adhesive capsulitis). *Electrode placement technique:* Dual-channel, unilateral. *Electrode placement sites:* A1, Insertion of deltoid at lateral aspect of arm. A2, In depression at end of lateral elbow crease with arm flexed to 90 degrees. B1, In depression below acromion anteriorly. B2, In depression below acromion posteriorly. A1 and A2, and B1 and B2 constitute separate channels. *Anatomic characteristics:* A1, Insertion of deltoid. Corresponds to acupuncture point LI 14. A2, Motor/trigger point of brachioradialis. Corresponds to acupuncture point LI 11. B1, Motor point of anterior deltoid. Corresponds to acupuncture point LI 15. B2, Motor point of posterior deltoid. Corresponds to acupuncture point TW 14. *Nerve innervation:* A1, Upper lateral cutaneous nerve, branch of axillary. A2, Posterior cutaneous nerve of forearm and superficial radial. B1, Upper lateral cutaneous nerve, branch of axillary. B2, Intercostal brachial, upper lateral cutaneous, and dorsal rami of T2. *T.E.N.S. mode:* Conventional. *Electrodes:* Stim-tech Dermaforms. *T.E.N.S. unit:* Medical Devices Ultra II. *Rationale:* Distal placement of one electrode to provide for continued perception of electrical paresthesia throughout entire area of local and referred pain. This modification of the array in Fig. 9-37 is necessary to control referred pain.

pain. Conventional T.E.N.S. is the stimulation mode. However, brief, intense T.E.N.S. may need to be used during treatment (discussed in this chapter).

Shoulder pain due to hemiplegia frequently occurs.[90] The therapeutic methods employed to facilitate the flaccid upper extremity involve sensory reintegration (vibrating, brushing, cooling, stretching, and tapping) techniques. The proprioceptive afferent fibers that are stimulated by these methods will also be activated by conventional or low-intensity, pulse-train (burst) T.E.N.S. Conceivably, conventional T.E.N.S., designed to selectively stimulate the large A fibers, may provide another means of facilitation. One advantage might be ongoing sensory input since T.E.N.S. could be used for long periods of time.

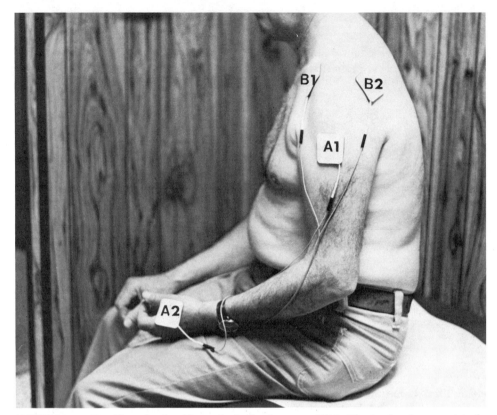

FIGURE 9-39. *Dx:* Chronic shoulder pain (adhesive capsulitis). *Electrode placement technique:* Dual-channel, unilateral. *Electrode placement sites:* A1, Insertion of deltoid at lateral aspect of arm. A2, Dorsal web space. Channel 1. B1, In depression below acromion anteriorly. B2, In depression below acromion posteriorly. Channel 2. *Anatomic characteristics:* A1, Corresponds to acupuncture point LI 14. A2, Motor/trigger points of first dorsal interosseus and adductor pollicis. Corresponds to acupuncture point LI 4. B1, Motor point of anterior deltoid. Corresponds to acupuncture point LI 15. B2, Motor point of posterior deltoid. Corresponds to acupuncture point TW 14. *Nerve innervation:* A1, Upper lateral cutaneous nerve, branch of axillary. A2, Superficial radial and musculocutaneous (sensory); ulnar (motor). B1, Upper lateral cutaneous nerve, branch of axillary. B2, Intercostal brachial, upper lateral cutaneous, and dorsal rami of T2. *T.E.N.S. mode:* Conventional. *Electrodes:* Stim-tech Dermaforms. *T.E.N.S. unit:* Medical Devices Ultra II. *Rationale:* Distal placement of one electrode to provide for perception of electrical paresthesia throughout entire area of local and referred pain. A modification of the array depicted in Figure 9-38.

Regardless of the flaccid upper extremity, many painful conditions can ensue as a result of disuse. Paralysis may give rise to spasticity, hypomobility, inflammation, and tendinitis. Pain resulting from these conditions may be relieved by T.E.N.S. Electrode placement would be similar to that in Case Study 8.

The use of T.E.N.S. as a means to enhance sensory reintegration may be supported by the results of studies by Callaghan and Ignelzi and their associates.[71,91] They observed changes in somatic sensitivity during T.E.N.S. in patients with peripheral radiculopathy or nerve injury who had received good to excellent pain relief with T.E.N.S. Electrical parameters were not given, but it was stated that settings that were customary for the patients

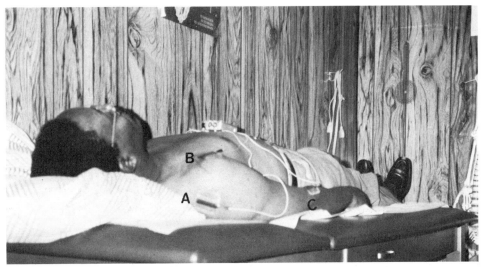

FIGURE 9-40. *Dx:* Persistent shoulder pain following rotator cuff surgery. *Electrode placement technique:* Dual-channel, unilateral, forming a V-shaped pathway with a three-lead cable. *Electrode placement sites:* A, In depression below acromion posteriorly (negative electrode of channel 1). B, In depression below acromion anteriorly (negative electrode of channel 2). C, In depression at end of lateral elbow crease with arm flexed at 90 degrees (positive electrode). *Anatomic characteristics:* A, Motor point of posterior deltoid. Corresponds to acupuncture point TW 14. B, Motor point of anterior deltoid. Corresponds to acupuncture point LI 15. C, Motor/trigger point of brachioradialis. Corresponds to acupuncture point LI 11. *Nerve innervation:* A, Intercostal brachial, upper lateral cutaneous branch of axillary, and dorsal ramus of T2. B, Upper lateral cutaneous nerve, branch of axillary. C, Posterior cutaneous nerve of forearm and superficial radial. *T.E.N.S. mode:* Mild to moderate pulse-train (burst). *Electrodes:* 3M Tenzcare. *T.E.N.S. unit:* Biostim System 10 (see Figs. 9-11, C, and 9-29 for explanation). *Rationale:* Arrangement allowed for the perception of electrical paresthesia throughout pain distribution.

were used, most probably the conventional mode. It was found that T.E.N.S. improved sensitivity to temperature, two-point discrimination, light touch, and position sense of the painful limb. There was no effect on the normal (contralateral) limb except an impairment of cool temperature sensitivity. It was concluded that T.E.N.S. applied to the painful extremity decreased or inhibited some of the small-fiber activity to a greater degree than it stimulated large-fiber activity. This would account for a decrease in clinical pain and enhancement of sensory perception. Conventional T.E.N.S. (selective large-fiber stimulation) seemed to impair sensation in the normal extremity.

Table 9-9 summarizes suggested techniques for shoulder pain.

ELBOW AND FOREARM PAIN

The successful use of T.E.N.S. to achieve pain relief or control of elbow pain adjunctive to specific treatment is again dependent upon a proper evaluation of the patient. Elbow fractures, lateral epicondylitis, and tendinitis are examples of intrinsic conditions that can give rise to pain. Pain in the elbow or forearm can be referred from the cervical spine

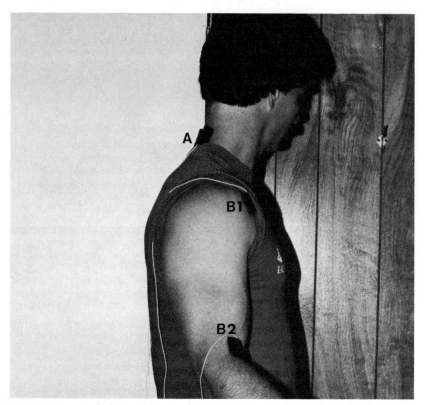

FIGURE 9-41. Suggested electrode array for bicipital tendinitis. *Electrode placement technique:* Dual-channel. *Electrode placement sites:* A, Spinal channel placed bilaterally at C5– 7. Superior surface of electrode at C4 spinous process, inferior surface at C7 spinous process. B1, Between first and second ribs just medial to coracoid process. B2, Lateral to biceps tendon in antecubital fossa. *Anatomic characteristics:* A, Posterior primary rami of C5–7. B1, Motor point of coracobrachialis. Corresponds to acupuncture point LU 1. B2, Motor point of brachialis. Corresponds to acupuncture point LU 5. *Nerve innervation:* A, Posterior primary rami of C5–7. B1, Musculocutaneous nerve. B2, Lateral cutaneous nerve of arm and musculocutaneous. *T.E.N.S. mode:* Conventional or low-intensity, pulse-train (burst). *Rationale:* Electrode channel placed at superficial proximal and distal aspects of peripheral nerve innervating painful muscle and tendon is augmented by a second channel at the related cervical segments.

distally or the wrist proximally. Case Study 9 illustrates the adjunctive role of T.E.N.S. in rehabilitation following an elbow fracture.

Case Study 9

Clarifying Evaluation: A 70-year-old female referred on 4/22/80 for rehabilitation and pain control following a fracture of the left olecranon and open reduction on 3/17/80. Related history was one of osteoarthritis, general joint pain, and ROM limitation. At the time of the initial visit, the patient complained of a "steady aching" in the left antecubital fossa and a "stiff-sharper" pain at the olecranon region. Pain was maximum in the morning and eased with movement throughout the day.

TABLE 9-9. Suggested Electrode Placement Techniques for Intrinsic Shoulder Pain

Technique	Placement Sites	Mode	Illustration
1. Dual-channel (unilateral)	Supraspinatus musculotendinous junction, deltoid insertion. In depression anterior and posterior to acromion.	Conventional	9-37
2. Dual-channel (unilateral), three-lead cable	In depression anterior and posterior to acromion. In depression at lateral end of elbow crease.	Conventional	9-40

HELPFUL HINTS

A. The deltoid insertion is a common referral site for intrinsic shoulder joint problems.
B. If pain is referred, at least one electrode should be placed at distal extent of pain (see Figs. 9-38, 9-39).
C. Augmentation of unilateral arm pain can occur via placement of second channel at appropriate spinal segments bilaterally (see Fig. 9-41).

Active ROM measurements showed limitations of 32 degrees in elbow extension, 28 degrees in flexion, and 10 degrees in forearm supination. The patient stated that ROM limitations were primarily the result of her arthritis. Strength of the elbow and forearm musculature was normal.

Goals: Decrease pain and attempt to restore further function.

Treatment Plan: Evaluation with T.E.N.S. in the conventional mode was performed, and 75 percent pain relief was obtained after a 20-minute stimulation period. The patient reported at the next visit that pain relief lasted for 3½ hours and that when discomfort returned it was not as intense as prior to the use of T.E.N.S. Gentle joint mobilization and therapeutic exercises were also performed and the patient instructed in a home exercise program.

A T.E.N.S. unit was obtained for the patient on a rental basis, and she was fully instructed in its use. At the time of the last treatment on 5/1/80, the patient reported good pain control with T.E.N.S. and showed increased active ROM, which patient stated was now equal to that which existed prior to her accident. Active ROM measurements now showed elbow flexion to 103 degrees (13-degree increase), extension to 158 degrees (10-degree increase), and normal forearm supination. Treatments of joint mobilization and therapeutic exercise were discontinued at this time, but the patient desired to continue use of the T.E.N.S. unit at home.

A follow-up questionnaire was sent to the patient and returned on 6/9/80. Reviewing the patient's answers showed that pain relief with conventional T.E.N.S. persisted for 3 to 4 hours initially and then increased to 7 hours after 20- to 30-minute treatment periods.

Figure 9-42 illustrates the electrode placement. These areas exhibited the greatest degree of palpable tenderness and represented stimulation of the radial, ulnar, and median nerves supplying innervation to the joint. The anatomic and physiologic principles of electrode placement were thus employed. The patient returned the T.E.N.S. unit to the distributor on 6/16/80 as it was no longer needed. The rental period was 7 weeks.

Elbow and Forearm Pain: Implications for T.E.N.S.

The close proximity of the major nerves of the upper extremity (median, ulnar, radial, and musculocutaneous) to the elbow provides the clinician with many effective stimulation sites. In cases of lateral epicondylitis, brief, intense stimulation to active trigger points via electrical probes or conventional T.E.N.S. units may provide pain relief sufficient to negate the need for a home unit. Ice massage may also provide satisfactory pain relief in lieu of T.E.N.S.

Figure 9-43 illustrates a suggested electrode placement technique using a three-electrode system for lateral epicondylitis. This array would be an alternative to a single channel

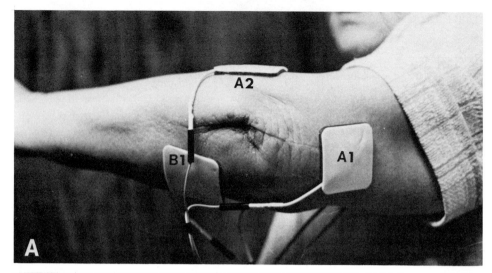

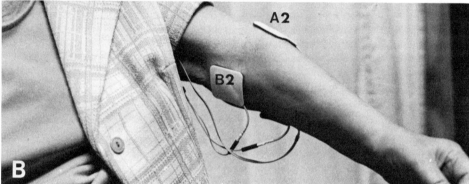

FIGURE 9-42. *Dx:* Fracture of left olecranon, open reduction

Figure A. *Electrode placement technique:* Dual-channel, bilateral to peripheral joint. *Electrode placement sites:* A1, In depression just above olecranon with elbow flexed to 90 degrees. A2, In lateral depression at end of elbow crease with elbow flexed to 90 degrees. B1, Just below groove between olecranon and medial epicondyle of humerus. B2, Just above medial epicondyle and antecubital fossa, medial to biceps tendon. A1–A2 and B1–B2 constitute separate channels. *Anatomic characteristics:* A1, Overlies superficial aspects of cutaneous nerve branches. Corresponds to acupuncture point TW 10. A2, Motor/trigger point of brachioradialis. Corresponds to acupuncture point LI 11. B1, Overlies superficial aspects of cutaneous nerve branches. Corresponds to acupuncture point SI 8. B2, Overlies superficial aspects of cutaneous nerve branches. Corresponds to acupuncture point H 3. *Nerve innervation:* A1, Posterior cutaneous of arm (radial), medial cutaneous of forearm (ulnar, posterior branches). A2, Posterior cutaneous nerve of forearm (medial) communicates with intercostal brachial and superficial radial. B1, Ulnar nerve and its medial cutaneous branches. B2, Medial cutaneous nerve of forearm. *T.E.N.S. mode:* Conventional. *Electrodes:* Stim-tech Dermaforms. *T.E.N.S. unit:* Medical Devices Ultra II. *Rationale:* Provides for the perception of electrical paresthesia across the lateral and medial epicondyle. Any nerve crossing near a joint sends a branch to innervate that joint.

Figure B. *Electrode placement technique:* Dual-channel (bilateral to peripheral joint). *Electrode placement sites:* Anterior view of Figure A, illustrating electrode placement site B2. The remaining electrode placement sites and related information are given in Figure A (posterior view).

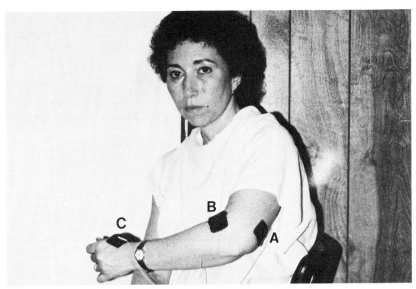

FIGURE 9-43. *Dx:* Lateral epicondylitis, suggested electrode array. *Electrode placement technique:* Dual-channel, unilateral, using a three-lead cable system. *Electrode placement sites:* A, In depression just above the olecranon with elbow flexed to 90 degrees (negative electrode, channel 2). B, In depression at end of lateral elbow crease with elbow flexed to 90 degrees (positive electrode). C, Dorsal web space (negative electrode, channel 1). *Anatomic characteristics:* A, Overlies superficial aspects of cutaneous nerve branches. Corresponds to acupuncture point TW 10. B, Motor/trigger point of brachioradialis muscle. Corresponds to acupuncture point LI 11. C, Motor/trigger point of first dorsal interosseus and adductor pollicis. Corresponds to acupuncture point LI 4. *Nerve innervation:* A, Posterior cutaneous of arm (radial), medial cutaneous of forearm (ulnar, posterior branches), and posterior cutaneous nerve of forearm. B, Posterior cutaneous nerve of forearm (medial) communicates with intercostal brachial and superficial radial. C, Superficial radial and musculocutaneous nerves (sensory); ulnar nerve (motor). *T.E.N.S. mode:* Conventional, with or without parameter modulation, or low-intensity, pulse-train (burst). *Rationale:* Provides for the perception of electrical paresthesia across the entire lateral epicondyle (anode to cathode) as well as down the anterolateral forearm (anode to cathode). The electrode B is part of both stimulating channels (see Figs. 9-11, C, and 9-29 for further explanation).

of two electrodes as it also provides for stimulation across the lateral epicondyle and down the forearm. Figure 9-44 depicts a recommended arrangement for pain control in De-Quervain's syndrome.

WRIST AND HAND PAIN

Pain in the hand, specifically the fingers, can easily be controlled provided proper nerve innervation is considered for electrode placement. Knowledge of the anatomic location of the superficial aspects of the major peripheral nerves is of utmost importance. Electrode placement at the volar surface of the wrist can effectively stimulate the median and/or ulnar nerves. Electrode placement at the dorsal web space and brachioradialis provides for stimulation of the radial nerves.

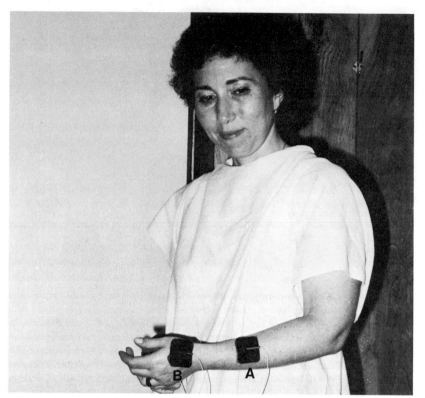

FIGURE 9-44. *Dx:* DeQuervain's syndrome, suggested electrode array. *Electrode placement technique:* Single-channel, unilateral. *Electrode placement sites:* A, 8 to 10 cm above radial styloid with arm in anatomic position. B, Dorsal web space. *Anatomic characteristics:* A, Motor point of extensor pollicis brevis. Corresponds to acupuncture point LI 6. B, Motor and trigger point of first dorsal interosseus and adductor pollicis. Corresponds to acupuncture point LI 4. *Nerve innervation:* A, Superficial radial and lateral cutaneous nerve of forearm. B, Superficial radial and musculocutaneous (sensory); ulnar (motor). *T.E.N.S. mode:* Conventional or low-intensity, pulse-train (burst). *Rationale:* Optimal stimulation sites were chosen that are proximal and distal to area of pain and segmentally related. Arrangement allows for perception of electrical paresthesia throughout painful region.

Figure 9-45 illustrates the finger of a 26-year-old male who sustained a vascular insult as a result of punching a wall. Referral for therapy to regain function of the finger prompted the use of T.E.N.S. to relieve pain and allow for manual therapeutic techniques (joint mobilization and ROM exercises) to be performed. Twenty minutes after application of T.E.N.S., it was noted that not only had pain substantially subsided but that temperature (measured with thermal biofeedback probe) had increased at the distal phalanx by 5°F. Low-intensity, pulse-train (burst) mode was used to produce pain-relieving paresthesia along with mild rhythmic muscle contraction for venous pumping. Figure 9-46 illustrates the electrode placement.

Specific case histories relating to the use of T.E.N.S. for pain in the forearm, wrist, and hand are presented later in this chapter.

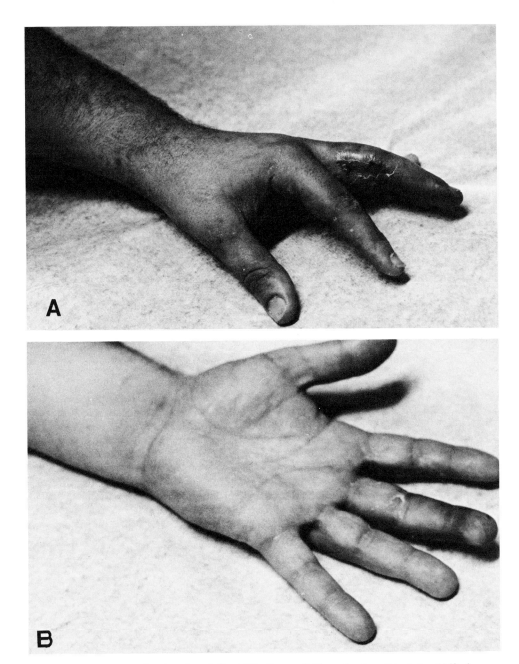

FIGURE 9-45. *A,* Vascular insult to left middle finger. *B,* Vascular insult to left middle finger. Note areas of blanching at volar surface of middle finger.

ELECTRODE PLACEMENT TECHNIQUES

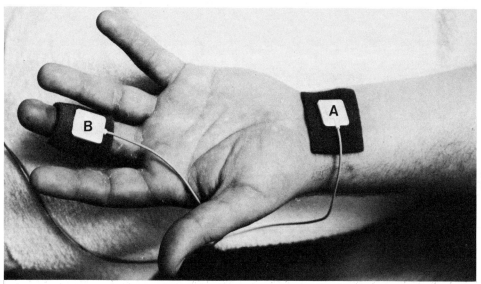

FIGURE 9-46. *Dx:* Vascular insult to third finger. *Electrode placement technique:* Single-channel, unilateral. *Electrode placement sites:* A, Volar aspect of wrist. B, Proximal to distal phalanx wrapped around volar surface of third finger. *Anatomic characteristics:* A, Corresponds to acupuncture point P 7. B, Overlies palmar cutaneous branches. *Nerve innervation:* A, Median, anterior branch of medial cutaneous nerve of forearm. B, Palmar cutaneous branch of median nerve. *T.E.N.S. mode:* Low-intensity, pulse-train (burst). *Electrodes:* Lec-Tec karaya, Velcro lead adapters. *T.E.N.S. unit:* Medtronic Comfort Burst. *Rationale:* Electrode array stimulates innervating peripheral nerve. Pulse-train (burst) mode used to provide reflex vasodilation as well as pain relief.

MULTIPLE JOINT PAIN

Shoulder-hand syndrome is a common complication from wrist fractures. Many of the patients referred for rehabilitation after removal of an upper extremity cast due to Colles' or other wrist fractures develop reflex sympathetic dystrophy (RSD). We have noted that in many cases of RSD, shoulder pain and resultant dysfunction are more difficult to treat than the fracture site itself.

Case Study 10 describes the rehabilitation course of a patient with RSD.

Case Study 10

Clarifying Evaluation: A 65-year-old female referred for rehabilitation on 3/6/79 as a result of a fracture of both the distal radius and ulna sustained in an auto accident on 1/17/79. Cast was just removed on 3/5/79, and the patient presented with severe edema of the hand and significant active ROM limitations in all joints of the right arm with constant pain. Active ROM measurements were as follows: shoulder flexion 0 to 59 degrees, abduction 0 to 58 degrees, internal rotation 0 to 45 degrees, external rotation 0 to 25 degrees, elbow flexion to 85 degrees and extension to 135 degrees, forearm pronation 0 to 45 degrees, no supination, wrist flexion 0 to 25 degrees, no visible extension beyond the neutral position, normal ulnar deviation, and radial deviation only to neutral.

Active ROM of the thumb at the MCP and DIP joints could be performed only through a range of 10 to 15 degrees. ROM measurements in flexion of the finger joints were as follows:

	MCP	PIP	DIP
2	35°	45°	15°
3	30°	50°	20°
4	25°	50°	15°
5	35°	50°	30°

Extension was normal at the MCP and DIP joints, but the PIP joints all lacked 35 degrees from full extension.

There was slight upper trapezius and cervical spine pain. All muscle motor points throughout the right arm including the splenius capitis and upper trapezius were very tender to palpation. The constant pain was described as a burning sensation with a background ache. The slightest touch in certain areas would cause immediate, intense discomfort. Active ROM of the cervical spine was limited by 50 percent in right rotation. Signs and symptoms certainly seemed consistent with that of a reflex sympathetic dystrophy (shoulder-hand syndrome).

Goals: Establish pain control, decrease edema, and increase function.

Treatment Plan: Treatments consisting of cool whirlpool with high-voltage galvanic stimulation were initiated. This was followed by gentle joint mobilization, which initially could be tolerated only with T.E.N.S., to all involved joints and therapeutic exercise three times a week.

The patient was evaluated with T.E.N.S. as a means of pain control at home, and it was determined that electrode arrangement was dependent on the region of pain.

Approximately 3 weeks after removal of the cast, the hand was still edematous and the fingers could not be fully extended (Fig. 9-47). Figure 9-48 illustrates the electrode placement when pain was present throughout the upper extremity. One channel of two large electrodes overlies the median and ulnar nerves at the axilla and volar aspect of the wrist. The second channel consists of two electrodes at the dorsal web space (LI 4) and posterolateral to the deltoid insertion (TW 13). This channel was designed to control lateral arm pain as well as stimulation of the superficial radial nerve.

The electrode arrangement in Figure 9-49 was used to provide simultaneous stimulation to the cervical spine and shoulder. This array used a total of six electrodes. Two electrodes anterior and posterior to the acromion were added to those stimulating the dorsal web space and deltoid insertion to provide for control of shoulder pain and referral within the C5–6 distribution. A second channel of two larger electrodes provided stimulation to the right cervical spine and supraspinous fossa of the scapula.

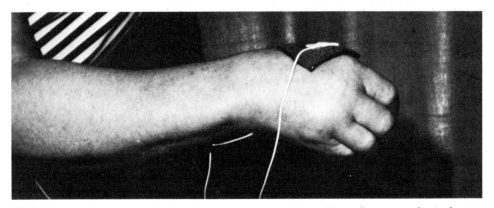

FIGURE 9-47. Fracture of distal radius and ulna complicated by reflex sympathetic dystrophy. Note the edema of the hand as well as fixation in ulnar deviation and finger flexion. Dorsal web space electrode in place.

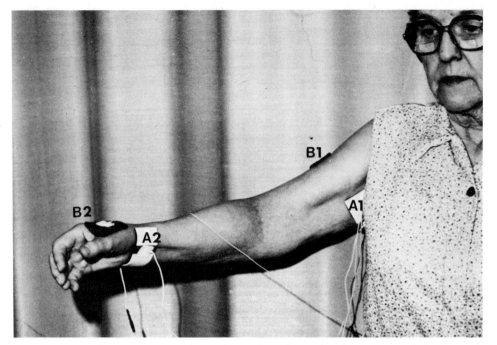

FIGURE 9-48. *Dx:* Reflex sympathetic dystrophy. *Electrode placement technique:* Dual-channel, unilateral. *Electrode placement sites:* A1, Lower axilla, medial to brachial artery. A2, Volar surface of wrist (channel 1). B1, Spiral groove of humerus, just posterolateral to deltoid insertion. B2, Dorsal web space (channel 2). *Anatomic characteristics:* A1, Corresponds to acupuncture point H 1. A2, Corresponds to acupuncture points LU 7–9, P 7, and H 4–7. B1, Motor point of lateral head of triceps. Corresponds to acupuncture point TW 13. B2, Motor/trigger points of first dorsal interosseus and adductor pollicis. Corresponds to acupuncture point LI 4. *Nerve innervation:* A1, Ulnar nerve, intercostal brachial, and median nerve. A2, Lateral cutaneous nerve of forearm, median and ulnar nerves. B1, Upper lateral cutaneous nerve (axillary branch) and radial. B2, Superficial radial and musculocutaneous (sensory); ulnar (motor). *T.E.N.S. mode:* Conventional. *Electrodes:* Lec-Tec karaya with Velcro lead wire adapter. *T.E.N.S. unit:* Dynex. *Rationale:* Electrode arrangement designed to provide stimulation to major upper extremity nerves for relief of arm, wrist, and hand pain.

The patient obtained a T.E.N.S. unit from the distributor, which was eventually purchased. She continued treatment as an outpatient, and active ROM improved steadily. She also obtained a finger splint to facilitate extension of the extremely rigid PIP joints. Suboccipital stretching, joint mobilization, and manual cervical traction were added to the treatment program.

She was no longer in need of the T.E.N.S. unit as of 8/25/79, at which time treatments were also discontinued. Active ROM of the shoulder, elbow, and forearm were then WNL; wrist flexion could be accomplished to 70 degrees and extension to 40 degrees. There remained an active extension lag of 25 to 45 degrees for the PIP joints.

The patient returned for re-evaluation 1 month after discharge, exhibiting increased cervical spine discomfort and a continued loss of active ROM solely at the PIP joints. Treatments to the neck and hand were re-instituted on a twice-a-week basis. The patient was finally discharged on 12/27/79. There was an improvement in active PIP joint extension to limitations of 20 to 35 degrees, passively 10 to 25 degrees. The hand was functional, and cervical spine discomfort was just about fully eliminated. The patient was re-instructed in a proper home exercise program to follow.

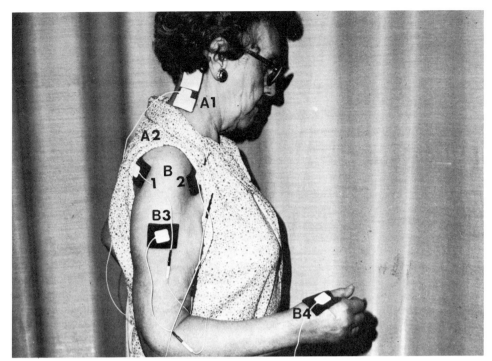

FIGURE 9-49. *Dx:* Reflex sympathetic dystrophy. *Electrode placement technique:* Dual-channel, unilateral. *Electrode placement sites:* A1, Lateral to cervical spine, suboccipital to C6. A2, Supraspinous fossa (not visible; channel 1). B1, In depression posterior to acromion. B2, In depression anterior to acromion. B3, Insertion of deltoid. B4, Dorsal web space (channel 2). *Anatomic characteristics:* A1, Overlies posterior primary rami from occiput to C6. A2, Motor/trigger points of middle trapezius. B1, Motor point of posterior deltoid. Corresponds to acupuncture point TW 14. B2, Motor point of anterior deltoid. Corresponds to acupuncture point LI 15. B3, Corresponds to acupuncture point LI 14. B4, Motor/trigger point of the first dorsal interosseus and adductor pollicis. Corresponds to acupuncture point LI 4. *Nerve innervation:* A1, Cervical posterior rami suboccipital to C7. A2, Overlies posterior branch of supraclavicular nerves. B1, Overlies dorsal rami of T2. B2, Upper lateral cutaneous nerve branch of axillary. B3, Upper lateral cutaneous nerve branch of axillary. B4, Superficial radial, musculocutaneous (sensory); ulnar (motor). *T.E.N.S. mode:* Conventional. *Electrodes:* Lec-Tec karaya. *T.E.N.S. unit:* Dynex (one two-lead and one four-lead cable). *Rationale:* Six electrodes were needed to control the cervical and arm pain.

Figure 9-50 illustrates an alternative technique for RSD. Stimulation of the volar and dorsal surfaces of the wrist with one channel of rectangular electrodes can provide the sensation of electrical paresthesia throughout the wrist and hand. Care must be taken to place the volar electrode at least as far lateral as the ulnar aspect to ensure stimulation of the ulnar nerve. The second channel can consist of two or four electrodes, depending on the painful region, placed on the most tender sites about the shoulder.

We have since treated at least six other patients who also developed reflex sympathetic dystrophy complications following wrist fracture. All these patients experienced neck, shoulder, and arm pain that frequently was more painful than the actual fracture site. Four of these six patients also required the use of a T.E.N.S. unit on a rental basis.

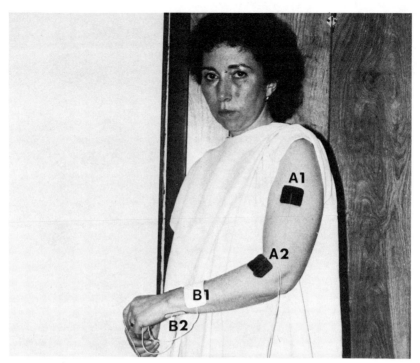

FIGURE 9-50. Suggested alternate technique for reflex sympathetic dystrophy. *Electrode placement technique:* Dual-channel, unilateral. *Electrode placement sites:* A1, Insertion of deltoid. A2, In depression at end of lateral elbow crease with elbow flexed to 90 degrees (channel 1). B1, Dorsal surface of forearm just superior to ulnar styloid. Rectangular electrodes. B2, Volar surface of forearm at second volar wrist crease (channel 2). *Anatomic characteristics:* A1, Corresponds to acupuncture point LI 14. A2, Motor/trigger point of brachioradialis. Corresponds to acupuncture point LI 11. B1, Corresponds to acupuncture point TW 5. B2, Corresponds to acupuncture points LU7–9, P 5–6, and H 4–7. *Nerve innervation:* A1, Overlies superficial aspect of upper lateral cutaneous nerve (branch of axillary). A2, Overlies superficial aspect of posterior cutaneous nerve of forearm and superficial radial. B1, Overlies posterior and lateral cutaneous branch of ulnar and superficial radial. B2, Overlies superficial aspects of median and ulnar nerves. *T.E.N.S. mode:* Conventional, with or without modulation, or low- to moderate-intensity, pulse-train (burst). *Rationale:* This arrangement allows for stimulation of major peripheral nerves of the arm (median, ulnar, and radial) to provide electrical paresthesia throughout the wrist, hand, and anterolateral arm. If pain is referred proximally in an ulnar, median, or musculocutaneous distribution, electrodes of channel 1 would be placed on superficial aspects of those nerves at and above the elbow.

Shoulder-Hand Syndrome: Implications for T.E.N.S.

The primary hindrance to rehabilitation of patients with reflex sympathetic dystrophy (RSD) is a causalgic pain.[94,97,98] Cauthen,[69] Stilz,[95] Owens,[96] and their associates noticed a return of hair growth in the lower extremity, consistent with the use of T.E.N.S., along with clinical recovery that was evident by thermographic testing.[69,95,96] Edema and hyperesthesia decreased; normalization of skin color and temperature also became apparent.

Conventional T.E.N.S. was the stimulation mode used in cases of RSD and causalgia. Meyer and Fields obtained almost immediate relief of pain after obtaining satisfactory paresthesia throughout the painful region. After 2 to 3 minutes, stimulation was discontinued and relief persisted for a minimum of 5 minutes to a maximum of 10 hours.[81] Patients were also able to undergo physical therapy after the use of T.E.N.S. Obviously, a longer stimulation period would have provided a greater aftereffect. Parry recommends using T.E.N.S. for up to several hours per day in the presence of causalgia. Satisfactory relief was attained in 38 of 70 patients followed for 1 to 3 years or more.[98] Unsuccessful results were thought to be due to late referrals. However, Parry believes that a significant amount of patients with causalgia do not benefit from any type of treatment.[98] Early intervention in the form of sympathetic blocks and T.E.N.S. is recommended.

Parry states that optimal benefit from T.E.N.S. occurs with a longer stimulation period; however, the stimulation mode was not specified. Treatment for 2 hours two to three times a day is suggested, and this can be increased to 6 to 8 hours. Parry believes that a cumulative effect occurs since complete pain relief may develop after 5 days' usage. Sixty-five percent of patients with peripheral nerve pain obtain significant relief, which may range to permanent relief.[98]

Our clinical findings with similar patients confirms that conventional T.E.N.S. is the mode of choice in this pain entity. Brief, intense stimulation has been employed in order to accomplish specific manual techniques. Electrode placement should primarily be proximal to the lesion and ipsilateral to the side of involvement. Bilateral stimulation may enhance the effect of T.E.N.S. Contralateral treatment may need to be performed before tolerance to ipsilateral stimulation can be achieved.

Optimal stimulation sites of choice are those overlying superficial aspects of the involved peripheral nerves proximal to the lesion. Tender points within the pain distribution as well as paraspinal stimulation at segments giving rise to innervation of the painful region should also be employed.

Table 9-10 summarizes important suggestions for upper extremity pain control with T.E.N.S.

CHEST PAIN

T.E.N.S. has been used to control postoperative chest pain. Chapters 10 and 11 cover the use of postoperative T.E.N.S., relating its ability not only to control pain but also to decrease the incidence of ileus and atelectasis. Case Study 11 discusses the adjunctive use of T.E.N.S. in a patient with asthma and emphysema in which eight electrodes were required to obtain optimal benefit. The electrode placement used was a multiple-electrode technique. The unit that was chosen allowed for four electrodes to be attached to the channel lead wires without the need for adapters.* Piggyback electrode systems or the use of "Y" adapter cables can be obtained from other manufacturers to allow for the use of more than two electrodes per channel at one time.

The easiest and most frequently employed method of electrode placement is to arrange the electrodes so stimulation is provided within or around the area of pain. Such an approach is similar to that used postoperatively, in which electrodes are placed above and below and/or medial and lateral to the operative site. The novice practitioner of T.E.N.S. and/or one without sufficient background in neuromusculoskeletal anatomy is advised to

---

*Dynex, La Jolla Technology Inc.

TABLE 9-10. Helpful Hints for Intrinsic Joint Pain of the Upper Extremity

1. Any nerve coursing adjacent to a joint sends a nerve to innervate that joint. Therefore, use sites overlying superficial aspects of peripheral nerves.
2. Electrode arrangement should encompass the joint (crisscross for shoulder), longitudinal over lateral epicondyle, rectangular volar and dorsal electrodes for wrist.
3. The dorsal web space can be an effective stimulation site for pain in the fourth and fifth fingers when local stimulation cannot be provided. The ulnar nerve innervates the first dorsal interosseous muscle. Conventional stimulation at the dorsal web space can produce the perception of electrical paresthesia at the fifth finger. Th·s can also be demonstrated by acupressure at the dorsal web space.
4. Rectangular electrodes on volar and dorsal surfaces of the wrist is an effective technique to produce electrical paresthesia into all fingers of the hand as well as around the wrist. This allows for utilization of a second channel for pain control at more proximal joints.
5. Contralateral stimulation can be tried when ipsilateral techniques cannot be tolerated.
6. Stimulation of appropriate cervical segments (bilaterally or unilaterally) can serve to augment upper extremity pain of reflex sympathetic dystrophy.
7. The use of modulation features (see Chapter 12) can enhance comfort, tolerance, and effectiveness to the conventional stimulation mode.

initially use this method. The more experienced clinician will be able to obtain a more thorough evaluation of electrode placement sites.

Directly related to chest pain syndromes is the discomfort resulting from rib fractures. Myers and associates used T.E.N.S. to control the acute pain resulting from fractured ribs in a group of 39 patients.[99] Ninety percent of the patients obtained some pain relief, and 62 percent felt that the relief was considerable or complete. Also noted were side benefits of increased mobility, easier breathing, and less painful coughs. Electrodes were placed paravertebrally or above and below the fracture site on the chest wall. Increased benefit may have been achieved if more than two electrodes had been used. Information pertaining to specific electrical parameters was not included, but it was stated that intensity was increased to a slightly uncomfortable level and then decreased to one of comfort. Treatment time was 3 to 4 hours for 2 to 3 days.

The use of a dual-channel stimulator with one channel of two electrodes arranged above and below the fracture in a parallel fashion and a second channel at the related paraspinal segments plus the most anterior region of pain would have increased the success rate as well as the degree of relief. Placement on the rib cage should be at the intercostal spaces to provide for stimulation of the intercostal nerves. The use of rectangular electrodes to increase the stimulation area should serve to enhance success (see Fig. 9-52). Case Study 12 concerns a patient with lateral rib cage pain who obtained excellent benefit with a similar approach.

Case Study 11

Clarifying Evaluation: 7/11/79. A 55-year-old female with asthma and emphysema producing chronic chest wall pain. Patient has had a T.E.N.S. unit since January obtained from a different facility. She now reports that its effectiveness has diminished and desires to be re-evaluated. She has been hospitalized on and off for a total of 40 days due to respiratory problems and has been on high doses of medication for pain. She recently took herself off medication and went through a withdrawal stage. She has since resumed taking some medication.

Pain medication has decreased her pain by about 70 percent, but relief lasts only for 2 hours and she is then in pain until she can take the next dose. Pain is described as being present 24 hours a day and exists from T5–T12 circumferentially around the chest. Substernal pain is also a factor.

She presently has a dual-channel T.E.N.S. unit. Electrodes were placed posteriorly at about T5 (paraspinal) and anteriorly on both sides of the upper end of the sternum. This placement would relieve upper chest pain, but electrodes would then need to be moved distally to modulate lower chest pain. This process, along with the problem of tape and gel, was quite annoying to the patient. In addition, relief has not been as good as that previously obtained and may be due to the fact that the lead wires are loose and the unit itself surges up and down as it is turned, indicating a loose connection.

Goals: Obtain pain control with T.E.N.S.

Treatment Plan: The use of different electrodes with her T.E.N.S. unit was unsuccessful due to the aforementioned problems. A stimulator able to accommodate four electrodes per channel obtained a result satisfactory to the patient. Electrodes were placed bilaterally parallel to the spine at T5 and T12 posteriorly and at similar levels anteriorly close to the sternum (one channel anteriorly and one posteriorly) (Fig. 9-51, A and B). The patient reported acceptable relief after 15 minutes with this approach while also not under the influence of any pain medication. Self-adhering karaya gum electrodes were used. These do not require any tape or gel and eliminate all problems that she previously had with the carbon-silicone electrodes. The patient desired to obtain this unit with a supply of karaya electrodes. A prescription for purchase from the distributor was obtained. In addition, the patient was advised not to use the unit continuously for 24 hours as she had been doing. She was instructed to keep the electrodes in place but to turn the unit on for 30- to 60-minute periods or until comfort was achieved, then turn the unit off. The mode of stimulation employed was conventional, but the pulse width and amplitude were raised due to the extensive stimulation area and number of electrodes. Thus, the mode was more in line with the recommended parameters of brief, intense stimulation although not raised to the highest tolerable level and not left on for only brief periods.

It was felt that the patient would benefit from a more comprehensive approach to the management of her pain. The referring physician was contacted and a comprehensive program approved. This included training in diaphragmatic breathing exercises, joint mobilization to the thoracic spine and rib cage to increase mobility, and relaxation training in conjunction with EMG biofeedback to achieve a decrease in accessory (respiratory) muscle tension. T.E.N.S. was merely an adjunctive technique to manage the symptom, namely pain. The above techniques helped to teach her how to prevent part of the pain from developing, which in turn required either medication or T.E.N.S. for relief.

Follow-Up: 10/8/79. The patient was doing very well with the T.E.N.S. unit, and karaya electrodes that work best for her were ordered. The patient had gone through a program of EMG biofeedback training for relaxation and control of muscle tension and continued to practice the techniques at home. In addition, she was instructed in diaphragmatic breathing exercises to strengthen the diaphragm and take stress away from the accessory (upper chest) muscles of respiration. Joint mobilization to the costovertebral joints and ribs was also performed. The T.E.N.S. unit was working satisfactorily, and the patient stated that she was feeling better. She still had occasional episodes of severe chest pain but seemed to be more in control of the situation at this time. She was informed to keep in touch to let us know how she was doing. Treatments were discontinued on 11/1/79.

Follow-up mail questionnaires were not returned, but a telephone conversation with the patient on 1/20/81 revealed continued satisfaction with the unit. She wears the electrodes constantly, turning the unit on and off throughout the day. Due to her irreversible condition, she must now keep the stimulator on for 2 hours constantly and is then able to turn it off for 1 hour during the day. Pain relief at this time varies between 30 to 50 percent. She also reported that she is unable to sleep at night without having the stimulator on constantly.

Case Study 12

Clarifying Evaluation: A 61-year-old female with 12-year history of right lower rib cage pain referred for evaluation with T.E.N.S. on 4/1/82. Etiology and diagnosis unknown and all tests (x-ray, CAT and bone scan) were negative. Intercostal neuralgia was a possible diagnosis. The patient complained of a constant pulling sensation within the right T8–12 lateral rib cage. There were associated hyperalgesia and tenderness to touch. Pain was present constantly when in the standing position and when sitting

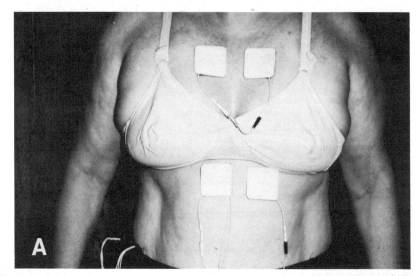

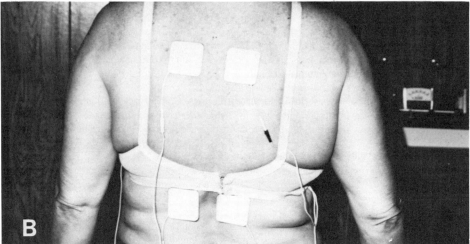

FIGURE 9-51. *A, Dx:* Substernal chest pain due to emphysema. *Electrode placement technique:* Dual-channel, anterior and posterior with multiple electrodes. *Electrode placement sites:* Four electrodes of channel 1 arranged on right and left aspects of proximal and distal sternum. *Nerve innervation:* Segmental intercostal nerves. *T.E.N.S. mode:* Conventional (increased amplitude and pulse width needed with multiple electrodes). *Electrodes:* Stim-tech Dermaforms. *T.E.N.S. unit:* Dynex, with four-lead electrode cable per channel. *Rationale:* Segmental electrode arrangement provides for electrical paresthesia throughout sternal region. *Note:* The use of two rectangular (postoperative) electrodes placed medial and lateral to the sternum is a suggested alternative. Posterior array is illustrated in *B. B, Dx:* Posterior chest pain due to emphysema. *Electrode placement technique:* Dual-channel, anterior and posterior with multiple electrodes. *Electrode placement sites:* Four electrodes of channel 2 arranged on right and left sides at proximal and distal aspects of pain (T5–T12). *Nerve innervation:* Segmental posterior primary rami and intercostal nerves. *T.E.N.S. mode:* Conventional (increased amplitude and pulse width needed with multiple electrodes). *Electrodes:* Stim-tech Dermaforms. *T.E.N.S. unit:* Dynex with four-lead cable per channel. *Rationale:* Segmental electrode arrangement provides for electrical paresthesia throughout posterior rib cage and thoracic spine.

with her back against a chair but not when lying down. She had no difficulty sleeping, awakening pain-free with the onset of pain on standing. Pain intensity did not change, and the distribution remained constant each day.

Evaluation revealed no significant structural abnormalities and normal active ROM of the thoracic and lumbar spine. Strength of related musculature was normal. Palpation revealed tenderness at the T8–12 levels paraspinally as well as within the right T8–12 intercostal region. There was significant discomfort to stretching of the involved ribs but only slight discomfort to vertebral provocation (springing and lateral oscillations).

Goals: Obtain pain control with T.E.N.S.

Treatment Plan: T.E.N.S. was explained to the patient. Evaluation revealed almost complete pain relief with the conventional mode using cycled modulation (2-sec on time; 3-sec off time). Initial electrode placement arrangement was very successful (Fig. 9-52). The same degree of relief was able to be obtained with smaller electrodes using a crisscross arrangement (Fig. 9-53). Pain relief was obtained almost instantaneously.

The patient continued to have excellent pain control with the unit during the rental period. She stated that she was now able to put her back against a chair without pain. Toward the end of the

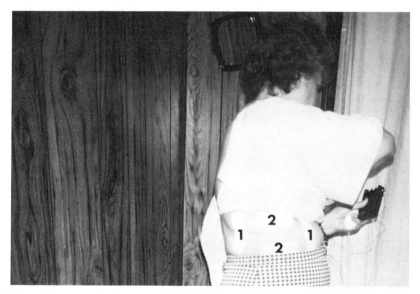

FIGURE 9-52. *Dx:* **Lateral rib cage pain, possible intercostal neuralgia.** *Electrode placement technique:* **Dual-channel, crisscross.** *Electrode placement sites:* **Channel 1, Paraspinal to T8–T12 and at anterior extent of pain. Channel 2, Inferior and superior to pain.** *Nerve innervation:* **Segmental posterior primary rami and intercostal nerves.** *T.E.N.S. mode:* **Conventional with cycled modulation.** *Electrodes:* **Rectangular Mentor postoperative reusable karaya.** *T.E.N.S. unit:* **EMPI DC.** *Rationale:* **Electrical paresthesia is obtained throughout painful region by this method. Placement at posterior-anterior and superior-inferior aspects of pain distribution is needed. Concentration of stimulation is at intersection of both channels.**

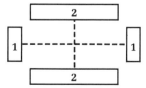

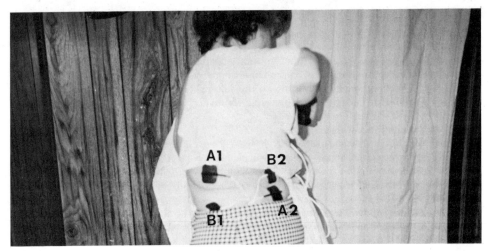

FIGURE 9-53. *Dx:* Lateral rib cage pain, possible intercostal neuralgia. *Electrode placement technique:* Dual-channel, crisscross. *Electrode placement sites:* A1, Superior and posterior to pain distribution. A2, Inferior and anterior to pain distribution (channel 1). B1, Inferior and anterior to pain distribution. B2, Superior and anterior to pain distribution (channel 2). *Nerve innervation:* Segmental posterior primary rami and intercostal nerves. *T.E.N.S. mode:* Conventional with cycled modulation. *Electrodes:* Medtronic Neuroaid. *T.E.N.S. unit:* EMPI DC. *Rationale:* Provides a similar distribution of electrical paresthesia as obtained with the arrangement illustrated in Figure 9-52. Concentration of stimulation occurs at intersection of both channels.

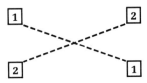

rental period, the patient was in need of the unit for only one 30-minute period twice a day. Pain was no longer steady. The patient needed the unit for only 1 month. At the end of the rental period, she no longer had any significant pain and decided to return the unit. Follow-up 1 month later revealed that pain had not returned.

Chest Pain: Implications for T.E.N.S.

The effectiveness of T.E.N.S. in the prevention and reversibility of ileus and atelectasis after surgery and acute spinal cord injuries has been well documented.[100,101] One report concerning the effectiveness of T.E.N.S. in patients with asthma concluded that any acute branchodilation was probably psychogenic or placebo response.[102] Twenty asthmatic patients were initially given placebo stimulation (no current) for 15 minutes at the upper sternum and back. This was followed by 15 minutes of T.E.N.S. at a frequency of 50 Hz, 0.8-msec pulse duration, and amplitude to 15 percent less than the level of discomfort. Results showed that peak expiratory flow (PEF) increased significantly (21.5 percent) after placebo stimulation in 11 patients, but that T.E.N.S. did not have any significant effect on PEF in any subject.

Results with T.E.N.S. in postoperative patients and patients with acute spinal cord injury showing a reduction in ileus and atelectasis were obtained with 1 to 5 days of stimulation, as opposed to a one-time 15-minute application.[100,101] Other comprehensive studies are needed to determine the value of T.E.N.S. in patients with asthma, emphysema, and related pulmonary syndromes.

LOW PACK PAIN

Patients with low back syndromes constitute the largest group of pain patients that obtain benefit from T.E.N.S.[103] Patients with cervical pain syndromes are second. Case Studies 13 to 21 illustrate the value of T.E.N.S. in low back pain. The optimal success with T.E.N.S. in low back pain necessitates a thorough evaluation on the part of the clinician to distinctly delineate the region of pain and the distal extent of any referral.

The greatest benefit occurs when T.E.N.S. is instituted in the acute phase as an adjunctive technique. This should allow for patient participation and promote increased mobility and the performance of corrective postural exercises. Early in the acute phase, when the patient is in severe muscle guarding and unable to be thoroughly examined or begin specific treatment, the use of T.E.N.S. at home for 1 to 3 days along with proper instruction in body mechanics may serve to decrease pain sufficiently to allow for the completion of the evaluation and initiation of treatment.

Sacroiliac joint dysfunction can lead to low back and/or sciatic pain. This condition is usually not taken into consideration as part of a thorough clarifying evaluation of the low back. Case Study 15 discusses the history and comprehensive treatment performed with a patient with pain arising from the sacroiliac joint.

The patient with chronic low back pain persisting after one or more operative procedures may find that T.E.N.S. provides the only means of ongoing effective pain control in lieu of medication. Case Study 16 concerns a patient that had been through extensive rehabilitation postoperatively and received benefit only after referral to the Pain and Health Rehabilitation Center in LaCrosse, Wisconsin. Rehabilitation at the pain clinic consisted in part of the use of T.E.N.S.

Chronic low back pain may also cause continuous or periodic pain in one or both lower extremities. Case Studies 17, 18, and 19 reflect lower extremity referral through varying distributions, thus necessitating specific electrode placements and different modes of stimulation for optimal success. A crisscross electrode array is highly effective for low back pain without lower extremity referral. Case Study 20 discusses the use of simultaneous bimodal stimulation. This technique is beneficial when two different (related or unrelated) areas of pain must be treated simultaneously. Such a technique can be performed with only certain stimulators that provide complete channel adjustment and independence.

Case Study 13

Clarifying Evaluation: A 36-year-old male referred for physical therapy on 9/26/80 after auto accident on 9/4/80. He developed severe low back pain within 2 days. The patient complained of constant pain in the lumbosacral region bilaterally, described as a deep ache that became sharp upon movement. Pain was increasing since the accident and aggravated by coughing, forward bending, sitting, and driving. Pain was eased only by sitting upright. He was unable to sleep comfortably at night, and pain intensified in the morning as movement increased.

Structurally, there was a complete loss of the normal lumbar lordosis, but pelvic levels were symmetric. Active ROM of the lumbar spine was severely limited in all directions, except side bending, by 75 percent. Pain occurred with movement in each direction, the most painful being forward bending. Forward bending of the head in the standing position increased lumbar pain. Strength of the L1–S2 myotomes was unable to be tested adequately due to severe pain from all movements. Lower extremity reflexes and sensation were normal. The patient was unable to fully extend the knees in the sitting position, the left being limited by 50 degrees and the right by 35 degrees. SLR of each leg produced almost immediate lumbosacral pain below 30 degrees, which was intensified by passive dorsiflexion of the ankle or forward bending of the head. Gentle palpation of the paravertebral region revealed extreme tenderness throughout the whole lumbosacral area. Signs and symptoms seemed consistent with those of a central posterior disk herniation.

Goals: Eliminate pain, increase function.

Treatment Plan: The initial treatment plan consisted of high-voltage galvanic stimulation followed by Cyriax traction, gentle joint mobilization (grade I posterior/anterior glides), instruction in proper lumbar mechanics, and a home exercise program to regain the lumbar lordosis and progressive prone lying.

A prescription for a T.E.N.S. unit to be used on rental was obtained. Figure 9-54 illustrates the electrode placement arrangement that was most beneficial. The patient was instructed to wear the unit during the day, turning it on and off as needed. The patient reported 50 to 75 percent pain control using the conventional mode. Treatments designed to eliminate the cause of the pain were initiated three times a week.

Cyriax traction needed to be added to the treatment program in an attempt to achieve reduction of the herniation before prone lying could be adequately tolerated. McKenzie's mobilization techniques were also performed, which together with the traction helped restore the lumbar lordosis, and the patient gradually achieved full backward bending in the prone position and increased SLR. Treatments continued three times a week following McKenzie's progression, and treatments were discontinued on 12/18/80 with the patient having regained full active ROM in all directions except for forward bending, which was limited by 40 percent. Complete forward bending was not possible prior to the accident. The T.E.N.S. unit was returned to the distributor, as the patient was totally pain-free except at end-range forward bending. He was instructed to continue following a home exercise program to attempt to gain further increases in forward bending.

Case Study 14

Clarifying Evaluation: A 30-year-old male seen initially on 8/17/78 for rehabilitation of chronic low back and left sciatic pain. History of back problems dates to 8/31/73 when he fell from a scaffold at work. Patient has not had surgery but has been permanently disabled for at least 2 years. At the time of the initial T.E.N.S. evaluation, pain existed in the left lumbar region and was referred along the sciatic nerve to the lateral malleolus. Prior to use of T.E.N.S., the patient received eight treatments consisting of pelvic traction, joint mobilization, backward bending exercises (McKenzie's extension principle), and instruction in proper body mechanics designed to regain the lumbar lordosis and prevent further recurrence. Constant pain became periodic and was able to be relieved by T.E.N.S.

Goals: Eliminate pain, prevent recurrence.

Treatment Plan: Using the guidelines for optimal stimulation site selection, it was determined that the most tender segmentally related sites within the pain referral pattern were paraspinal at L5–S1 (dorsal rami), the sciatic hiatus (B 50), just above the popliteal space (sciatic bifurcation), at the sural nerve, and depression between the lateral malleolus and heelcord (B 60) (Fig. 9-55). The two proximal sites were coupled to constitute one channel, and the two distal sites were connected to the second channel.

This arrangement using the conventional stimulation mode provided 2 to 4 hours of almost complete pain relief after a 30-minute treatment period. The patient purchased the stimulator from the distributor after the 1 month's evaluation period. The patient was instructed at the time of the last visit to contact the referring physician if there was a return of severe discomfort or lower extremity weakness.

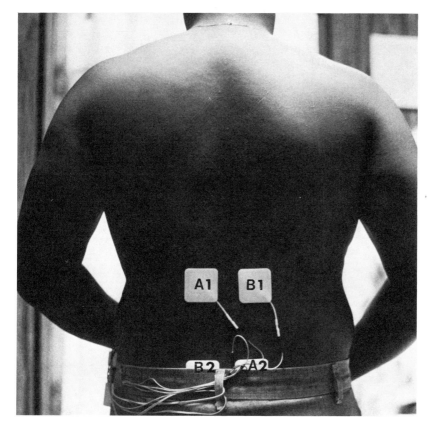

FIGURE 9-54. *Dx:* Possible central posterior lumbar intervertebral disk herniation. *Electrode placement technique:* Dual-channel, crisscross. *Electrode placement sites:* A1, Paraspinal on left at L3 level. A2, Paraspinal on right at S2 level (channel 1). B1, Paraspinal on right at L3 level. B2, Paraspinal on left at S2 level (channel 2). *Anatomic characteristics:* Motor point of erector spinae. A1 and B1, Corresponding to segmental bladder meridian acupuncture points. A2 and B2, Corresponding to segmental bladder acupuncture points. *Nerve innervation:* A1 and B1, Overlie segmental posterior primary rami. A2 and B2, Overlie dorsal ramus of S2 and descending cutaneous nerves from upper lumbar (L1–3) spine. *T.E.N.S. mode:* Conventional. *Electrodes:* Stim-tech Dermaforms. *T.E.N.S. unit:* Medical Devices Ultra II. *Rationale:* Electrical paresthesia concentrates on spine at involved segments and includes proximal and distal extent of pain. *Note:* Lead wires are placed within belt loops. This is helpful when the electrode sites are a short distance from the stimulator.

Follow-up questionnaire has not been returned, but the last follow-up visit to the referring physician 2 years postdischarge revealed continued satisfaction with the T.E.N.S. unit. The patient subsequently moved back to Puerto Rico and has not been able to be contacted since.

Case Study 15

Clarifying Evaluation: A 30-year-old female referred on 5/12/78 with low back pain. History dates to 3/14/77 when she was involved in an auto accident. She was hospitalized for tests, which included x-rays and a myelogram. Prior to the accident, she complained of a burning pain in the left posterior

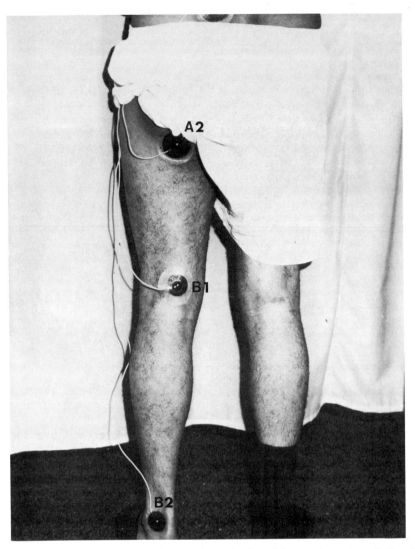

FIGURE 9-55. *Dx:* Posterolateral lumbar intervertebral disk herniation with sciatica. *Electrode placement technique:* Dual-channel, linear pathway. *Electrode placement sites:* A1, Paraspinal at L5–S1 level. A2, Sciatic hiatus at midjoint between ischial tuberosity and greater trochanter at level where buttock meets posterior upper thigh (channel 1). B1, Just above popliteal crease at midline. B2, In depression between lateral malleolus and heelcord (channel 2). *Anatomic characteristics:* A1, Segmental erector spinae motor point. Corresponds to local bladder meridian acupuncture point. A2, Corresponds to acupuncture point B 50. B1, Corresponds to acupuncture points B 53 and B 54. B2, Corresponds to acupuncture point B 60. *Nerve innervation:* A1, Overlies segmental dorsal rami. A2, Overlies posterior cutaneous nerve of thigh (sciatic). B1, Overlies posterior cutaneous nerve of thigh (sciatic). B2, Dorsal lateral cutaneous (distal portion of sural nerve) *T.E.N.S. mode:* Conventional. *Electrodes:* MedGeneral carbon-silicone with transmission gel and hypoallergenic tape patch. *T.E.N.S. unit:* MedGeneral Miniceptor II. *Rationale:* Electrodes placed on superficial aspects of sciatic nerve branches to provide electrical paresthesia throughout pain distribution. Electrodes placed at proximal and distal extent of pain. An overlap of channels could be performed, A1–B1 and A2–B2, as an alternative.

rib cage. Structurally, it was noted that there was a slight loss of the lumbar lordosis, the left PSIS was higher than its counterpart, and the left ASIS was lower than that on the right (Fig. 9-56).

Active ROM of the lumbar spine showed a limitation of 50 percent in forward bending and 25 percent in backward bending with a slight shift to the right upon movement. The left PSIS moved superiorly before the right on forward bending of the lumbar spine. There was tenderness to palpation at the left PSIS, buttock, midthoracic and lumbosacral paraspinal regions, and the left groin. The patient was most comfortable when lying supine with the hips and knees flexed. Left side lying was the most uncomfortable position. SLR was negative, producing hamstring pain only at 70 degrees.

Strength of the L1–S2 myotomes was normal, as were reflexes. Sacroiliac torsion tests produced pain on anterior torsion of left ilium on sacrum, and there was a positive long sitting test indicative of leg length differential due to movement of the acetabulum (see Chapter 5). The patient had been on contraceptive pills for 6 years.

Goals: Decrease pain, prevent recurrence.

Treatment Plan: Anterior torsion of the left ilium on the sacrum was reduced with a contract-relax mobilization technique. There was almost 75 percent pain relief and equalization of PSIS levels plus leg length after mobilization procedure. The patient was instructed in a corrective exercise to maintain reduction as well as proper body mechanics. However, she continued to exhibit the same findings over a period of 2 weeks, the reduction lasting for a day or two. She was then advised to obtain a sacroiliac belt (Fig. 9-57), and elimination of the birth control pills was suggested.

A T.E.N.S. unit was obtained for the patient to use until the belt was fabricated and during periods of pain when she was unable to come for treatment. The sacroiliac ligaments were obviously lax, and the joint had become hypermobile. She would not wear the belt all the time during working hours and periodically would experience discomfort. She came to the clinic one day wearing both

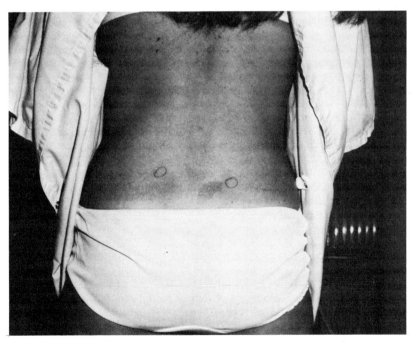

FIGURE 9-56. *Dx:* **Sacroiliac joint dysfunction (recurrent hypermobility). Note asymmetric levels of posterior-superior iliac spines (PSIS). Left PSIS is higher than right PSIS. Left anterior-superior iliac spine (ASIS) was lower than right ASIS. Findings consistent with anterior torsion of left ilium on sacrum. Circles delineate PSIS levels.**

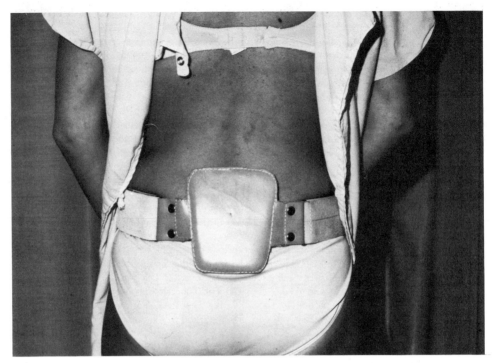

FIGURE 9-57. *Dx:* Sacroiliac joint dysfunction (recurrent hypermobility). Sacroiliac belt in place between iliac crests and greater trochanters of femur to minimize torsion (hypermobility).

the sacroiliac belt and the T.E.N.S. unit (Fig. 9-58). She was again in anterior torsion on the left, and the stimulator was relieving the discomfort but the belt was merely maintaining the abnormal torsion.

Prior evaluation with T.E.N.S. determined optional electrode placements to be L5–S1 paraspinally and B 50 (sciatic hiatus) at junction of buttock and posterior upper thigh (Fig. 9-58). An additional channel was employed for the thoracic pain, which seemed to be postural in origin. She exhibited alar scapulae and round shoulders and was taught corrective exercises.

The patient desired to continue using the T.E.N.S. unit as needed and eventually purchased it. The patient has had subsequent treatment consisting primarily of reduction of the sacroiliac joint on an as-needed basis. The patient was last treated on 6/5/80, at which time she reported continued use of the unit when pain developed before she could come into the office.

Case Study 16

Clarifying Evaluation: A 57-year-old female referred on 1/21/80 for outpatient therapy, consisting of massage, moist heat, ultrasound, and electrical stimulation three times a week. Patient reported a history of back pain dating back 15 years when she slipped and fell on ice. Initial low back pain slowly subsided but returned 2 years later in the neck, low back, and legs. In 1967 she underwent a lumbar laminectomy and fusion at L4–5. She continued to experience discomfort and in 1975 underwent a cordotomy, which apparently was unsuccessful and even increased her discomfort.

She subsequently was hospitalized for intense biofeedback training, which was not successful in decreasing her pain or her coping ability. Following this, she was admitted to a chronic pain clinic as an inpatient, which also was unsuccessful. She then became addicted to narcotic pain medication.

CLINICAL T.E.N.S.

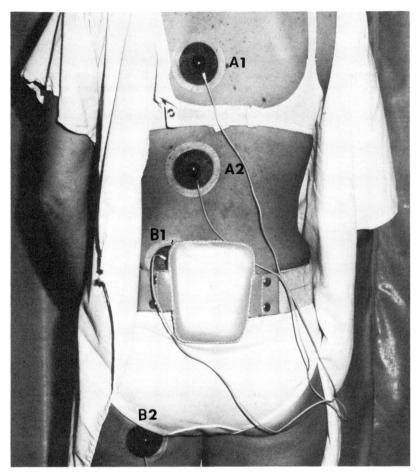

FIGURE 9-58. *Dx:* Sacroiliac joint dysfunction (recurrent hypermobility). *Electrode placement technique:* Dual-channel, unilateral isolated pain sites. *Electrode placement sites:* A1, Paraspinal at T7 level. A2, Paraspinal at T12 level (channel 1). B1, Paraspinal at L5–S1 level. B2, Sciatic hiatus at midpoint between ischial tuberosity and greater trochanter at level where buttock meets posterior upper thigh (channel 2). *Anatomic characteristics:* A1, Segmental erector spinae motor point corresponds with local bladder meridian acupuncture point (between transverse processes). A2, Segmental erector spinae motor point corresponds with local bladder meridian acupuncture point. B1, Segmental erector spinae motor point corresponds with local bladder meridian acupuncture point. B2, Corresponds to acupuncture point B 50. *Nerve innervation:* A1, Overlies segmental dorsal rami. A2, Overlies segmental dorsal rami. B1, Overlies segmental dorsal rami. B2, Overlies posterior dorsal rami, posterior cutaneous nerve of thigh (sciatic). *T.E.N.S. mode:* Conventional. *Electrodes:* Carbon-silicone with transmission gel and hypoallergenic tape patches. *T.E.N.S. unit:* Med-General Microceptor II. *Rationale:* Segmentally related electrode placement sites provide electrical paresthesia to areas of pain.

Finally in the early 1970s, she was referred to Dr. C. Norman Shealy's Pain and Health Rehabilitation Center in LaCrosse, Wisconsin. She was weaned from her medication and was able to establish satisfactory pain control by the use of biogenics (relaxation, autogenics, and biofeedback) and T.E.N.S. On discharge she continued to practice her home techniques of biogenics with cassette tapes and used the T.E.N.S. unit daily.

The patient reported that a few years later the T.E.N.S. unit was not functioning properly and pain was intensified. She was then referred to a local hospital for outpatient physical therapy consisting of moist heat, ultrasound, and massage for 1 month, which did not decrease her discomfort.

At the time of this referral, the patient was complaining of a constant burning and tingling pain at the right ilium (donor site), buttock, and lumbar spine throughout the length of the surgical incision. Pain was aggravated by lying supine and eased by ice for up to 30 minutes or by lying prone.

Active ROM of the lumbar spine was significantly limited in forward and backward bending. Left side bending bilaterally was normal but produced right buttock and ilium pain. The normal lumbar lordosis was lost, the entire lumbar region being flat. SLR was negative bilaterally. Strength and reflexes of the lower extremities were normal.

Goals: Reduction and/or control of pain.

Treatment Plan: The referring physician was contacted regarding the patient to suggest a change in the prescribed treatment plan. In view of the extensive history and previous treatment, it was stated that this patient would benefit primarily from pain control with a T.E.N.S. unit and instruction in proper body mechanics. The previous unit that she obtained had only one channel and the patient reported that the two electrodes could not adequately control her pain. She had been placing them paravertebrally at the low lumbar spine and thus was not obtaining pain relief in the other areas of discomfort. It was determined that a stronger mode of T.E.N.S. and a second channel were needed. The original unit could not be adapted satisfactorily for this and was also in need of repair.

Satisfactory pain control was able to be obtained at the third visit by the use of an EMPI dual-channel unit with modulation. This unit can be made to function in a mode where the current will be on for 3 seconds and off for 2 seconds. This can be accomplished at any rate within the adjustable range. Evaluation with different stimulation modes determined that the brief, intense method was the best, but the patient could not tolerate this constantly. However, with the EMPI DC unit, she was able to tolerate brief, intense T.E.N.S. and obtain the best degree of relief. When brief, intense stimulation is required for ongoing usage, we suggest that a stimulator with modulation capabilities be utilized. At present, manufacturers that offer units with modulation features include EMPI (Epix), Biostim (Biomod), Agar Electronics (Neurogar), Intermedics (Orion), and Dynex.

The electrodes shown in Figure 9-59 were used during the evaluation process. The patient continued to use the Dermaforms on the spine, but carbon-silicone electrodes with tape and gel or Con-Med* pregelled adhesive electrodes are used in place of the Stim-tech S-20s due to cost factors.

The patient obtained satisfactory pain relief. A prescription for rental of the unit was subsequently obtained. The patient was fully instructed in the use of the unit and given written home instructions on delivery of the rental unit. She was seen on follow-up prior to the end of the rental period on 2/20/80, reported continued satisfactory pain control, and desired to purchase the stimulator. A prescription for purchase was obtained from the referring physician.

Follow-up continued by mail questionnaire and telephone call on 1/16/81, at which time the patient reported she was unable to get out of bed unless she used the stimulator. She used it all day long and obtained at least 50 percent pain relief after a treatment of 30 minutes, but there was little carryover of pain relief. Strong, low-rate (acupuncture-like) T.E.N.S. on lumbosacral myotomes of the lower extremities did not provide satisfactory relief.

Review of the returned questionnaire revealed the patient's satisfaction with the T.E.N.S. unit but dissatisfaction with the various electrodes.

The electrodes presently available are the weakest part of the T.E.N.S. system. The self-adhering electrodes are better but substantially increase the cost factor. Pregelled pads must

---

*Consolidated Medical Equipment, Inc., 10 Hopper St., Utica, NY 13501.

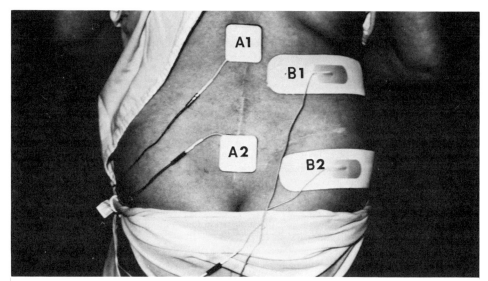

FIGURE 9-59. *Dx:* Chronic low back pain, postlaminectomy and fusion. *Electrode placement technique:* Dual-channel, isolated pain sites. *Electrode placement sites:* A1, On midline of spine at proximal end of surgical scar. A2, On midline of spine at distal end of surgical scar (channel 1). B1, Superior to donor site scar. B2, Inferior to donor site scar (channel 2). *Nerve innervation:* A1–A2, Overlie segmental posterior primary rami. B1, Overlies lower intercostal nerves. B2, Overlies cutaneous branches from L1–3. *T.E.N.S. mode:* Brief, intense with modulation. *Electrodes:* Stim-tech Dermaforms and S-20 postoperative electrodes. *T.E.N.S. unit:* EMPI DC. *Rationale:* Conventional T.E.N.S. did not provide good benefit. Brief, intense stimulation worked well, but this could not be tolerated for a prolonged period. Therefore, cycled (on-off) modulation was used. The placement of electrodes on the spine was enhanced by removal of the spinous processes by the fusion. *Note:* There should be no problem with electrode placement on the spine. This is, of course, performed invasively with dorsal column stimulation.

be inspected for expiration date. Such dates should be checked prior to use since gel may have dried out, increasing the chance of skin irritation.

Case Study 17

Clarifying Evaluation: A 32-year-old female referred on 11/16/78 for evaluation with T.E.N.S. for pain control. History dates back to November 1975 when she fell at work, injuring her low back. She was diagnosed as having a lumbosacral strain and concussion. After hospitalization, she wore a neck and back brace and began to deteriorate. She was referred for outpatient physical therapy at a local hospital and failed to improve after 20 treatments, which were primarily of a symptomatic nature. A neurosurgeon was consulted, and a myelogram was done. At that time, the patient was complaining of low back and left sciatic pain, weakness of the left leg, and severe headaches. A lumbar laminectomy was performed in 1976, and the patient stated that she did well up until 1 year ago, when intermittent pain began to return.

The patient had been working after recovery from surgery but was now complaining of low back and left lower extremity pain at times to the popliteal space and/or to the toes. She stated that there are days when she is relatively pain-free but always develops discomfort toward the end of each working day. Associated neck and headache pain persist periodically. Active ROM of the cervical spine was WNL except for backward bending, which was limited by 50 percent. Active ROM of the lumbar spine was limited by 25 percent in forward and backward bending. There was a decreased left heelcord reflex and sensory deficit throughout the left L4–S1 dermatomes. Posture was good, no pelvic asymmetry noted. Strength of the left L1–S2 myotomes revealed good quadriceps and ankle dorsiflexors compared with normal on the right.

Goal: Control pain with T.E.N.S.

Treatment Plan: The patient was evaluated with T.E.N.S. It was found that there was significant tenderness to palpation within the main distribution pattern, bilaterally at the L5–S1 level paravertebrally as well as the sciatic notch (B 50) and at the distal superficial aspect of the tibial nerve between the medial malleolus and heelcord (K 3). One channel was then arranged for the low back and another on the left leg (Fig. 9-60). The channel on the left leg required a higher amplitude than the one on the low back due to the larger interelectrode distance. The patient was given a written home instruction and evaluation form to complete upon obtaining the rental unit from the dealer.

After the rental period, it was determined that the patient was able to obtain an average of 4 hours of almost complete pain relief with a 20- to 30-minute stimulation period using conventional T.E.N.S. At the time, the patient was using the unit two to four times a day and desired to purchase the stimulator from the distributor.

The patient was seen for a total of three visits. At the last visit, she was instructed to keep track of strength, function, and sensation of the left leg and to contact the referring physician if any increased weakness was noted or a cessation of pain replaced by numbness. She was also instructed in proper cervical and lumbar spine body mechanics and a home exercise program.

Follow-up questionnaires were not returned, but the patient was contacted by telephone on 1/20/81. She stated at that time that she was still using the stimulator but needed it only a few times each week and occasionally only once a week, mainly during worktime. She was obtaining 75 to 80 percent pain relief after a 30- to 45-minute stimulation period. Pain relief would last for hours and occasionally days.

I informed her of the availability of new electrodes that can be used without tape or gel and she was to call for an appointment to evaluate them.

Case Study 18

Clarifying Evaluation: A 31-year old female initially referred for conservative physical therapy on 4/3/79 as a result of low back pain. History dates back to 1964 when she underwent a spinal fusion (T3–L4) due to severe developmental scoliosis. On 6/25/77 she was involved in an auto accident, subsequently followed by hospitalization on three occasions for therapy to the low back and cervical spine, consisting of cervical traction, whirlpool, moist heat, and ultrasound. She obtained symptomatic relief but no carryover. In December 1978 the patient mentioned that she was unable to bear weight on her legs or sit without a great deal of discomfort.

Prior to her referral, she had just been discharged from her most recent hospitalization and was not working. Her pain complaints were at the lumbosacral region, more on the right, with referral to the right lower extremity and occasionally the left. Pain was intermittent, most intense in the evening, and aggravated by prolonged sitting, standing, coughing, and sneezing. Lying supine provided pain relief. There was no cervical discomfort.

Structurally, pelvic levels were normal, but a thoracic scoliosis was still evident. Active ROM of the lumbar spine was obviously limited by the fusion. SLR was negative; strength of the L1–S2 myotomes was normal. Palpation revealed generalized tenderness and sensitivity to touch throughout the lumbosacral region and right lower extremity.

Goals: Decrease pain and establish means of control.

Treatment Plan: The prescription from the referring physician called for moist heat, ultrasound, and whirlpool three times a week for 6 weeks. Clearly, this approach of "heat-heat-heat" provided only symptomatic relief without carryover. The physician was contacted to obtain a change in the treatment approach. Since a year of similar conservative therapy had already been provided and the patient continued to request treatment, being unable to function without it, evaluation with T.E.N.S.

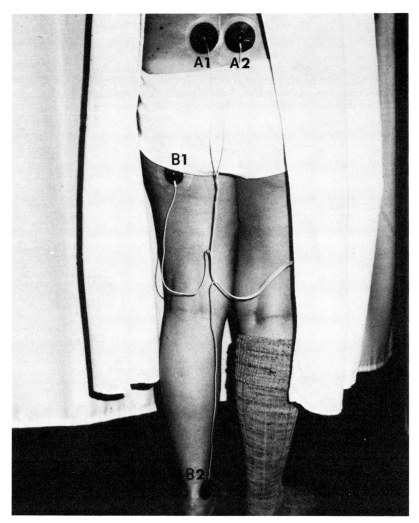

FIGURE 9-60. *Dx:* Chronic low back and sciatic pain, post–lumbar laminectomy. *Electrode placement technique:* Dual-channel, bilateral and linear pathway. *Electrode placement sites:* A1, At L5–S1 level on left. A2, At L5–S1 level on right (channel 1). B1, Sciatic hiatus at junction of buttock and posterior upper thigh. B2, In depression between heelcord and medial malleolus. *Anatomic characteristics:* A1–A2, Segmental erector spinae motor point corresponds to local bladder meridian acupuncture point. B1, Corresponds to acupuncture point B 50. B2, Corresponds to acupuncture point K 3. *Nerve innervation:* A1–A2, Overlie segmental dorsal rami. B1, Overlies posterior cutaneous nerve of thigh (sciatic). B2, Overlies superficial aspect of saphenous and posterior tibial nerves. *T.E.N.S. mode:* Conventional. *Electrodes:* MedGeneral carbon-silicone with transmission gel and hypoallergenic tape patches. *T.E.N.S. unit:* MedGeneral Microceptor II. *Rationale:* Segmentally related stimulation sites at structural source of pain as well as proximal and distal aspects of referral. Provides for electrical paresthesia throughout the pain distribution. Channel 2 required increased amplitude due to greater interelectrode distance.

was suggested and agreed to by the physician. The idea was that T.E.N.S. should be able to provide a similar means of symptomatic relief with the added benefit that the patient could treat herself as needed, would not need to come in for continuous therapy, and cost would be considerably less. The cost of the physician's prescription over a 6-week period would equal the cost of purchasing a T.E.N.S. unit.

Due to previous fusion, the only definitive treatment, other than symptomatic, was instruction in proper body mechanics, which was carried out.

The patient was thus evaluated with T.E.N.S. and obtained satisfactory pain control with the unit. At the end of the 1-month rental period, the unit was purchased from the distributor. The patient was fully instructed in the use of the unit. Follow-up questionnaires were not returned, but the patient was seen again on 12/22/80 to obtain another stimulator.

She reported the unit had been stolen and she was in acute discomfort, not having a means of treatment. A verbal prescription was obtained from her physician and re-evaluation performed. The patient was complaining of constant pain in the lumbosacral region, worse on the right with referral to the right posterolateral thigh and popliteal space. Palpation within the painful region revealed extreme tenderness paraspinally at the L4–5 level, optimal stimulation sites B 48 and GB 30 (motor/trigger points of buttock), and just superior to the popliteal space. Electrodes were arranged as illustrated in Figure 9-61. Conventional T.E.N.S. provided 80 percent pain relief after a 30-minute

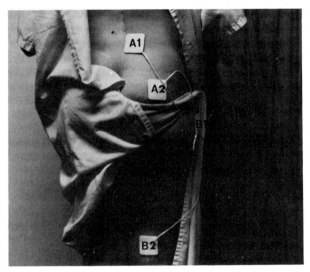

FIGURE 9-61. *Dx:* Chronic low back pain. Spinal fusion for scoliosis from T3 to L4. *Electrode placement technique:* Dual-channel, linear pathway. *Electrode placement sites:* A1, Paraspinal at L5–S1 level. A2, Tender site on right buttock (channel 1). B1, Behind greater trochanter of femur. B2, Just superior to popliteal crease (channel 2). *Anatomic characteristics:* A1, Segmental erector spinae motor point. Corresponds to local bladder meridian acupuncture point. A2, Upper motor/trigger point of gluteus maximus. Corresponds to acupuncture point B 48. B1, Middle motor/trigger point of gluteus maximus. Corresponds to acupuncture piont GB 30. B2, Corresponds to acupuncture points B 53 and B 54. *Nerve innervation:* A1, Overlies segmental dorsal rami. A2, Overlies dorsal ramus of L2 and inferior gluteal nerve. B1, Overlies posterior branch of lateral cutaneous nerve of thigh, cutaneous branches of dorsal rami, and lateral cutaneous branch of iliohypogastric. B2, Overlies posterior cutaneous nerve of thigh, medial and lateral branches. *T.E.N.S. mode:* Conventional. *Electrodes:* Stim-tech Dermaforms. *T.E.N.S. unit:* Stim-tech Stimpulse. *Rationale:* Stimulation of segmentally related sites to provide electrical paresthesia throughout distribution of pain.

treatment period. The unit was loaned to the patient until one was delivered by the distributor. The patient subsequently reported she was obtaining 1½ to 2 hours of almost complete pain relief with treatments of 30 minutes.

Case Study 19

Clarifying Evaluation: A 28-year-old male referred on 8/20/80 for rehabilitation due to continued discomfort and decreased function as a result of chronic low back pain. He was unable to work at this time. History dates back to 1969 when he hurt his back in high school after falling on his buttock and fracturing the coccyx. Subsequently, he underwent spinal surgery for the removal of the L4–5 intervertebral disk. On 1/12/79 when lifting a cabinet, he again injured his back and developed bilateral lumbosacral pain and left lower extremity sciatic pain referral to the lateral malleolus.

The patient underwent a second lumbar laminectomy on 12/10/79 for removal of entrapping scar tissue and bone spurs, which brought about pain relief and a restoration of function. In July 1980, while tacking down carpeting, he became fixed in a forward-bent position and was unable to straighten up. This brought on bilateral low back pain (left > right) referral to the L5–S1 dermatomes, numbness of the left fifth toe and lateral border of the foot. Pain was described as being intermittent and aggravated by activity, forward bending, prolonged sitting, standing, coughing, and sneezing. Pain was eased only by rest.

Structurally, there was a loss of the normal lumbar lordosis. Active ROM of the lumbar spine was limited by 75 percent in forward bending. There was a slight limitation of right side bending, which produced left lumbar pain. Backward bending was limited by 25 percent and gave rise to left posterior thigh pain. Side bending to the left was WNL and painless.

SLR on the left was limited by hamstring pain at 50 degrees. There were no obvious signs of muscle weakness. The L3, L4, and L5 segments were painful to gentle springing.

Goals: Decrease pain, increase function, and prevent recurrence.

Treatment Plan: The patient was started on a program of Cyriax traction, high-voltage galvanic stimulation, joint mobilization, and therapeutic exercise. Joint mobilization and exercise were designed to restore the normal lumbar lordosis, maintain it, and prevent recurrence of low back pain. The McKenzie techniques were used.

The patient was evaluated for pain control at home via T.E.N.S. Initially, the conventional mode with stimulation solely of the lumbosacral spine was used, but this did not provide acceptable relief for lower extremity pain. The guidelines to the selection of optimal stimulation sites were then followed, and the most tender points within the pain distribution pattern were used with the high-intensity, pulse-train mode. Figure 9-62 illustrates the electrode placement.

The patient initially reported pain relief of 80 percent after a 30-minute treatment period, lasting maximally up to 5 to 6 hours depending on his activity level and the weather. When the patient was working and pain was severe, relief was only 40 to 80 percent and persisted for 1 to 2 hours. The patient subsequently purchased the T.E.N.S. unit. He returned to work October 1980 and has been working full-time ever since. Follow up on 2/3/81 revealed the T.E.N.S. unit was being used at least twice a day, primarily after work and prior to bedtime. In the morning, pain is at the lowest point. Up to 90 percent pain relief of the achy pain in the back and left leg with treatments of 20 to 30 minutes is obtained. The high-intensity, pulse-train mode is used and pain relief persists for at least 1 hour and frequently up to 5 hours depending on the weather and pain level prior to treatment. When pain is severe, the conventional mode is initially used on the lumbosacral spine for 5 to 10 minutes. This is then followed by high-intensity, pulse-train stimulation for 30 minutes.

Case Study 20

Clarifying Evaluation: A 28-year-old male referred for T.E.N.S. evaluation on 12/15/80. History of low back pain began when he fell from a scaffold at work 3 months prior to referral. He developed severe low back pain and was hospitalized for evaluation and treatment. A myelogram proved negative, and the patient was discharged to the care of a psychiatrist.

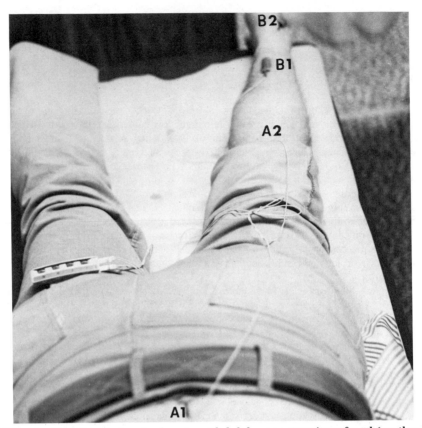

FIGURE 9-62. *Dx:* Chronic low back pain with left lower extremity referral (postlaminectomy). *Electrode placement technique:* Dual-channel, linear pathway. *Electrode placement sites:* A1, Paraspinal at L5–S1 level. A2, Just superior to popliteal crease (channel 1). B1, At junction of upper two thirds and lower one third of lower leg at midline. B2, In depression between lateral malleolus and heelcord (channel 2). *Anatomic characteristics:* A1, Erector spinae motor point. Corresponds to local bladder meridian acupuncture point. A2, Corresponds to acupuncture points B 53 and B 54. B1, Corresponds to acupuncture point B 57. B2, Corresponds to acupuncture point B 60. *Nerve innervation:* A1, Segmental dorsal rami. A2, Overlies posterior cutaneous nerve of thigh (sciatic). B1, Overlies superficial aspect of sural nerve and lateral cutaneous nerve of calf. B2, Overlies superficial aspect of dorsal lateral cutaneous nerve (end of sural). *T.E.N.S. mode:* High-intensity, pulse-train (burst). *Electrodes:* 3M Tenzcare (synthetic polymer). *T.E.N.S. unit:* 3M Tenzcare. *Rationale:* Rhythmic muscle contraction and background paresthesia at segmentally related stimulation sites to provide possible neuropeptide release for prolonged carryover.

At the time of the initial clinic visit, the patient complained of a throbbing pain in the lumbosacral region unchanged since hospital discharge. Pain was aggravated by coughing, sneezing, forward bending in the sitting or standing position, and lying prone. Pain was eased by lying supine with knees flexed or sitting upright. Structurally, there was a significant loss of the lumbar lordosis. Pelvic levels were symmetric.

Active ROM of the lumbar spine was severely limited in all directions by 75 percent. Backward bending was almost fully blocked. Pain increased upon forward and backward bending. SLR was positive bilaterally at 30 to 35 degrees and low back pain was increased by passive dorsiflexion of the ankle and active forward bending of the head. Strength of the L1–S2 myotomes was WNL. Palpation revealed tenderness and muscle guarding throughout the lumbar spine. Attempted passive mobility testing was met with muscle guarding. In light of the findings, it was determined that this patient might benefit from therapeutic procedures designed to reduce pain and increase lumbar mobility so that function could be improved. T.E.N.S. would merely be used adjunctively for pain modulation. The referring physician was contacted and approval obtained.

Goals: Initially control discomfort, increase function, restore normal lumbar lordosis, eliminate pain, and prevent recurrence.

Treatment Plan: T.E.N.S. for pain control at home and treatment consisting of Cyriax traction, followed by joint mobilization, therapeutic exercise, and instruction in proper body mechanics.

The unit was rented from the distributor for home use and the patient given written home instructions. Treatment began on 1/5/81 with Cyriax traction and progressed after 2 weeks to McKenzie's low back program, and mobilization techniques. The crisscross lumbosacral arrangement using conventional T.E.N.S. proved effective during the day (Fig. 9-63). The patient would use the unit 5 to 10 times for periods ranging from 10 to 20 minutes each and obtain satisfactory (described as good) pain relief for up to 1 hour after the stimulation was discontinued. However, in the morning and evening, pain was more intense and this technique was not as helpful. A trial of strong, low-rate (acupuncture-like) T.E.N.S. was performed solely to the lower extremities, but its effect on low back pain was not fast enough to suit the patient. Simultaneous bimodal stimulation was then employed, using conventional T.E.N.S. on the low back along with strong, low-rate (acupuncture-like) stimulation on the lower extremities. This technique employing eight electrodes provided optimal benefit for this patient with a treatment time of 30 to 40 minutes. Carryover of pain relief increased to 1 to 3 hours if ambulation was not attempted.

Figure 9-63 illustrates simultaneous stimulation on the back and legs with different modes. Conventional T.E.N.S. is used for the lumbosacral array with a single channel. Strong, low-rate (acupuncture-like) T.E.N.S. is used on the lower extremities with the second channel. With complete channel separation (independent amplitude, rate, and width controls) for each channel, one T.E.N.S. unit* can be used.

Case Study 21

Clarifying Evaluation: A 48-year-old male referred on 4/1/82 who had already received a T.E.N.S. unit on rental at another facility but was referred because of unsatisfactory pain relief. The patient was being treated at the other facility for low back pain sustained when he fell out of a truck while at work on 7/29/81 (diagnosis not provided). After hospitalization with traction, he returned to work and was doing well until September 1981 when low back and LLE pain returned while unloading a truck. In October 1981, he underwent a lumbar laminectomy but has continued to experience low back and LLE pain.

The patient complained of bilateral lumbosacral pain with occasional referral to the left posterior upper thigh. Structurally, there was partial loss of the normal lumbar lordosis. Active ROM of the lumbar spine was severely restricted, demonstrating a loss of 65 percent of forward bending (with a shift to the right) and 85 percent of backward bending. Side bending was limited to 50 percent to the right and 60 percent to the left.

Goals: Obtain satisfactory pain control with T.E.N.S.

Treatment Plan: He had previously been instructed to use the T.E.N.S. unit in the conventional mode with a crisscross lumbosacral electrode arrangement. He reported obtaining initial relief with this technique, but this was short-lived as perception of the electrical paresthesia dissipated and pain returned (accommodation). Frequency (rate) modulation was used to decrease the apparent accommodation. In addition, the patient was instructed in use of the strong, low-rate (acupuncture-like)

---

*Medical Devices Ultra II.

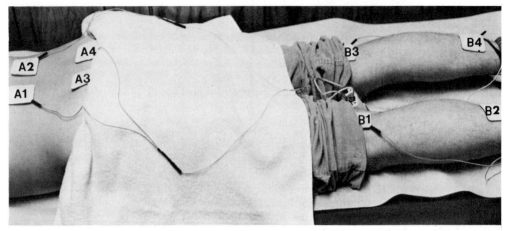

FIGURE 9-63. *Dx:* Chronic low back pain. *Electrode placement technique:* Dual-channel, simultaneous bimodal. *Electrode placement sites:* A1–A4, Paraspinal from upper to lower distribution of low back pain (channel 1). B1, Just below popliteal crease. B2, At midline two-thirds the distance from the popliteal space to the heelcord insertion. B3, Just below popliteal crease. B4, At midline two-thirds the distance from the popliteal space to heelcord insertion (channel 2). *Anatomic characteristics:* A1–A4, Motor points of local erector spinae. Correspond to local bladder meridian acupuncture points. B1 and B3, Correspond to acupuncture points B 53 and B 54. B2 and B4, Correspond to acupuncture point B 57. *Nerve innervation:* A1–A4, Dorsal rami from T12 to L5. B1 and B3, Overlie superficial aspect of posterior cutaneous nerve of thigh (sciatic). B2 and B4, Overlie superficial aspect of sural and lateral cutaneous nerve of calf. *T.E.N.S. mode:* Channel 1, conventional; channel 2, strong, low-rate (acupuncture-like). *Electrodes:* Stim-tech Dermaforms. *T.E.N.S. unit:* Medical Devices Ultra II, offering complete channel separation and independent adjustment of all parameters per channel. *Rationale:* Simultaneous bimodal stimulation to provide for pain relief for the painful low back and increased carryover. Cable adapters were added to allow for eight electrodes per channel.

mode. Placement consisted of one electrode at the popliteal space and the second between the medial malleolus and heelcord bilaterally (tibial nerve) (Fig. 9-64). This technique can be employed to obtain muscle contraction of the gastrocsoleus group. Complete evaluation with this method was unable to be performed due to lack of time on the part of the patient. He was, however, fully instructed in how to proceed at home. The patient was also instructed to call in one week to report his progress.

He called on 4/8/82 and stated that he was doing well obtaining 1 to 2 hours of relief with a 30-minute application of strong, low-rate T.E.N.S. on the lower extremities. Six weeks later he was continuing to experience satisfactory benefit.

Case Study 22

Clarifying Evaluation: A 47-year-old male referred on 8/5/82 for treatment of long-standing neck and back pain dating back 20 years from a work injury and cervical spine pain when he hit his head, resulting in hypomobility and double vision. On 6/27/82, he slipped at work, twisted, and landed on his back and right side. The next day, he had significant discomfort at the neck and back. He has been able to continue work as a supervisor.

Presently he complains of periodic sharp pain and stiffness in the cervical and lumbar spine. Pain in each area is aggravated by prolonged sitting, forward bending, lifting, and coughing/sneezing. He states that there is no position that provides prolonged comfort. He complains of an achy discom-

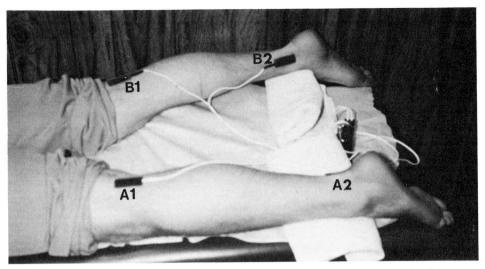

FIGURE 9-64. *Dx:* Chronic low back pain, post–lumbar laminectomy. *Electrode placement technique:* Dual-channel, bilateral. *Electrode placement sites:* A1, At or just below popliteal space. A2, In depression between medial malleolus and heelcord (channel 1). B1, At or just below popliteal space. B2, In depression between medial malleolus and heelcord (channel 2). *Anatomic characteristics:* A1, Corresponds to acupuncture points B 53 and B 54. A2, Corresponds to acupuncture point K 3. B1, Corresponds to acupuncture points B 53 and B 54. B2, Corresponds to acupuncture point K 3. *Nerve innervation:* A1, Posterior cutaneous nerve of thigh. A2, Overlies saphenous and posterior tibial nerves. B1, Posterior cutaneous nerve of thigh (sciatic). B2, Overlies saphenous and posterior tibial nerves. *T.E.N.S. mode:* Strong, low-rate (acupuncture-like). *Electrodes:* Tenzcare (3M). *T.E.N.S. unit:* EMPI. *Rationale:* When conventional T.E.N.S. is not beneficial, the strong, low-rate or high-intensity, pulse-train (burst) mode may be helpful. Electrodes are placed on segmentally related but remote sites to produce strong, rhythmic contractions.

fort and stiffness in the morning. Cervical spine pain is most apparent on the right with associated C5–6 paresthesia.

Structurally, he is overweight and exhibits a forward head posture with significant extension of occiput on C1–2. There is a thoracic kyphosis, and the iliac crest on the right is slightly lower than the left. The LLE is about one-fourth to one-half inch longer than the right. Bilateral clicks were apparent at both TMJs, but there was good vertical dimension and no facial pain or headaches.

Active ROM of the cervical spine is severely limited as follows: 65 percent in backward bending, 50 percent in rotation bilaterally, and 75 percent in side bending bilaterally. Active ROM of the lumbar spine is even more restricted by 80 percent in forward bending, 90 percent in backward bending, and 80 percent in side bending bilaterally. Active ROM of the shoulders is grossly WNL.

Strength of all cervical and lumbar myotomes is WNL. He was unable to fully extend both knees in the sitting position (– 30 to 40 degrees). SLR was positive on the left at 45 degrees and right at 35 degrees, both producing bilateral lumbosacral pain. Both hip joints exhibited severely restricted ROM in all directions. Palpation revealed tenderness throughout the cervical, upper thoracic, and lumbar spine.

He was unable to lie supine without two pillows under his head because of the thoracic kyphosis/forward head posture. He had great difficulty turning from supine to prone and getting up off the plinth.

Goals: Decrease pain, increase function, and prevent recurrence.

Treatment Plan: High-voltage galvanic stimulation followed by joint mobilization, postural corrective exercises, and instruction in proper body mechanics.

Progress Note 8/13/82: Patient states that he feels increased mobility now and a decrease in pain of 40 to 50 percent after four treatments. Active ROM of the cervical spine is now limited by 60 percent in backward bending, 25 percent in left rotation and 35 percent in right rotation, and 60 percent in side bending bilaterally. Active ROM of the lumbar spine has increased to where forward bending is limited by 65 percent, backward bending by 60 percent, and side bending bilaterally by 60 percent.

The previously noted severe postural deformities remain, and it is doubtful that this can be reduced. I feel that this patient could benefit from the use of a T.E.N.S. unit. Physician approval obtained.

Evaluation revealed that bilateral cervicothoracic electrode placement provided the best relief of cervical spine pain. A bilateral lumbosacral placement was also most effective for the low back. The patient also stated that pain occurred frequently in the thoracic area as well but not as severe as the neck and low back pain.

Utilization of separate channels at the neck and back would not help thoracic pain, and a longitudinal arrangement of the channels on each side of the spine necessitated a significant inter-electrode distance. The use of five electrodes functioning in essentially the same circuitry might enhance benefit (Fig. 9-65). A Biostim System 10 unit with a three-lead cable system in which one electrode acts as a common positive for the two negatives of channels 1 and 2 was tried. Two Y adapters were added to the channel 1 and 2 lead wires to allow for two electrodes per channel. Placement of the positive electrode between the cervical and lumbar electrodes provided for current flow in a V-shaped pathway to both the cervical and lumbar electrodes. The patient reported that this arrangement worked well.

Discharge Note 9/9/82: Patient states that he feels he now has much more mobility in the cervical spine than he has had for a long time. The areas of greatest functional limitation remain side bending bilaterally and backward bending. Active ROM of the lumbar spine remains about the same as that outlined in the previous note, and I do not feel that any further increases can be obtained due to the long-standing hypomobility.

Pain has decreased but still persists relatively constant. He continues to use the T.E.N.S. unit five to six times a day for 20 to 25 minutes at a time, and it provides about 75 percent relief. He desires to continue using the T.E.N.S. unit, and as a result I would suggest initiating purchase of the unit at this time.

Treatments were discontinued at this time.

Low Back Pain: Implications for T.E.N.S.

The electrode placement depicted in Figure 9-62 worked well for that particular patient. If he had not been able to tolerate high-intensity, pulse-train stimulation on the involved side, contralateral stimulation would be the next choice. Distal optimal stimulation sites that exhibited the greatest degree of tenderness to palpation for this patient were along the course of the sural nerve. The patient preferred this electrode arrangement since it was more tolerable. We would, however, recommend using superficial aspects of the posterior tibial nerve instead (see Fig. 9-64), as these should allow for better muscle contraction of segmentally related myotomes. The posterior tibial nerve provides for muscle innervation (gastrocsoleus group), while the sural nerve is purely cutaneous (sensory innervation). Muscle contraction, however, does occur with stimulation of the sural nerve due to its being a branch of the sciatic.

When employing the strong, low-rate (acupuncture-like); high-intensity, pulse-train, or burst mode, electrode placement sites that allow for strong contraction of the largest segmentally related muscle group are preferred. With the low back, we recommend the gastrocsoleus group over the anterior tibial, since the former exhibits greater bulk over a shorter distance as opposed to the latter being long and relatively thin. We have not used the gluteals because this muscle group is in close proximity to the low back, and placement at the L5–S1 region paraspinally would be required for the proximal electrode. The ham-

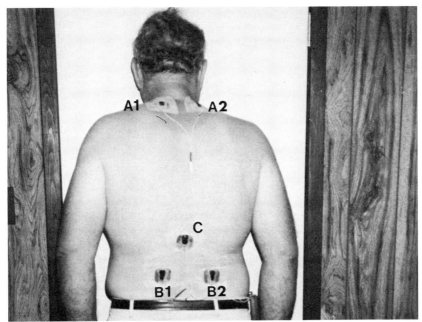

FIGURE 9-65. *Dx:* Degenerative arthritis of the cervical, thoracic, and lumbar spine. *Electrode placement technique:* Dual-channel, proximal and distal V-shaped pathways using a three-lead cable system. *Electrode placement sites:* A1–A2, Paraspinal at cervicothoracic junction (negative electrodes of channel 1). C, On midline at level of T12–L1 (positive electrode). B1–B2, Paraspinal at lumbosacral junction (negative electrodes of channel 2). *Anatomic characteristics:* A1–A2, Motor points of segmental erector spinae. Correspond to local bladder meridian acupuncture points (between transverse processes). C, Segmental posterior primary rami. B1–B2, Motor points of segmental erector spinae. Correspond to local bladder meridian acupuncture points. *Nerve innervation:* A1–A2, Overlie segmental posterior primary rami. C, Segmental posterior primary rami. B1–B2, Overlie segmental posterior primary rami. *T.E.N.S. mode:* Conventional. *Electrodes:* Unipatch carbon-silicone with transmission gel and hypoallergenic tape patches. *T.E.N.S. unit:* Biostim System 10. *Rationale:* When pain control is required throughout a large distance (neck-back), longitudinal placement of electrodes is necessary (one channel on right and one on left). The resultant large interelectrode distance requires a great deal of energy to provide appropriate perception of electrical paresthesia throughout the entire painful region. A suggested alternative as used with this patient consisted of placement of the positive electrode on the midline (closer to the low back since this was the more painful region). The electrodes of channels 1 and 2 each use one half of the power of the positive electrode, which directs energy flow (electrical paresthesia) to the two electrodes of channels 1 and 2 in V-shaped pathways (see Fig. 9-11, C, for explanation).

strings are not recommended, as this group of long thin muscles would require high intensity to obtain strong, rhythmic muscle contractions as compared with the short but bulky calf musculature.

Stimulation of the anterior tibial compartment (anterior tibialis and peroneals) would be the choice for pain referred in a more lateral rather than posterior distribution or if adequate muscle contraction could not be tolerated at the gastrocsoleus group. Bilateral lower extremity stimulation with T.E.N.S. modes requiring strong muscle contractions is preferred. This has proven to be much more effective than unilateral stimulation and seems to produce a faster and more profound pain relief.

We have not encountered any patients who were able to tolerate high-intensity rhythmic muscle contraction, acupuncture-like, pulse-train, or burst stimulation solely on the painful low back. However, most patients are able to tolerate strong muscle contractions when stimulation is solely on the lower extremities. All of the suggested lower extremity muscle groups are segmentally related to the lumbosacral spine. The use of simultaneous bimodal stimulation is another alternative. Conventional T.E.N.S. can be used on the low back while simultaneous stimulation in the form of the strong, low-rate (acupuncture-like) mode is used on one or both lower extremities. This provides some immediate relief of low back pain (conventional T.E.N.S.) and is enhanced and prolonged by the simultaneous use of acupuncture-like T.E.N.S. on the lower extremities. The patient will not have to turn the unit off and change electrodes or stimulus parameters.

In order to obtain simultaneous stimulation with two different modes at separate body regions, a unit that provides complete channel separation (independent adjustment of rate, width, and amplitude parameters) is required. One channel could provide a high rate and low pulse width and amplitude (conventional T.E.N.S.), while the other generates a low rate and high pulse width and amplitude (strong, low-rate [acupuncture-like] T.E.N.S.).

The use of noninvasive electroacupuncture stimulation given to distal sites at the ankle (K 3 and B 60), representing superficial aspects of the posterior tibial and sural nerves, respectively, can result in a rapid decrease in low back pain. Stimulation can then be given in a proximal progression at OSS within the area of referred pain or areas that manifest a high degree of conductance (low skin resistance). Noninvasive electroacupuncture can provide pain reduction in the clinic prior to or after treatment geared to correcting the cause of pain and/or increase in function. T.E.N.S. can then be used by the patient at home during the rehabilitation course.

Reports in the literature pertaining specifically to the use of T.E.N.S. in the management of the patient with low back pain support its efficacy.[18,42,104–107] T.E.N.S. should not become a treatment in itself to be used solely in the clinic, but adjunctive to a comprehensive approach. The case studies pertaining to low back pain support this philosophy. However, if T.E.N.S. is equated with modalities such as ultrasound or diathermy, its role in the management of chronic low back pain is nil.[108]

Table 9-11 summarizes the electrode placement techniques for low back pain.

KNEE PAIN

Pain that is solely confined to one joint is easily modulated with T.E.N.S. Optimal stimulation sites representative of nerve innervation to the respective joint should be used. Case Study 23 reflects the use of T.E.N.S. on a patient with bilateral osteoarthritis and synovitis of the knees. There are a number of reports of clinical success with T.E.N.S. in arthritic or specific joint pain.[41,63,70,103,109,110] The placement of electrodes close to the site of pain is supported by the literature.[41,63,110]

A recent study of 10 patients with osteoarthritis of the knee reported statistically significant pain relief with T.E.N.S.[110] Parameters consistent with those of conventional T.E.N.S. were used for 30-minute periods. Electrode placement was on the anterior, posterior, medial, and lateral sides of the knee. However, the arrangement of the stimulator channels was not provided, so it is not known whether the current flowed in a longitudinal, vertical, or crisscross manner. Taylor and colleagues reported that in some patients pain relief persisted for several hours after stimulation, while others reported relief only with

TABLE 9-11. Suggested Electrode Placement Techniques for Low Back Pain

Technique	Placement Sites	Mode	Illustration
1. Dual-channel (bilateral/crisscross)	Upper and lowest painful sites paraspinally	Conventional	9-54
2. Dual-channel (linear pathway unilateral)	Superficial aspects of sciatic nerve	Conventional or low-intensity, pulse-train (burst)	9-55
3. Dual-channel (bilateral paraspinal and unilateral leg)	Bilaterally at appropriate spinal levels and superficial aspects of sciatic nerve proximal and distal	Conventional or low-intensity, pulse-train (burst)	9-60
4. Dual-channel (unilateral)	Superficial aspects of peripheral nerves	Strong, low-rate or high-intensity, pulse-train (burst)	9-62
5. Dual-channel (bimodal)	Paraspinal or crisscross on back; longitudinal on leg	Conventional (back) and strong, low-rate (leg)	9-63
6. Dual-channel (bilateral/remote)	Segmentally related myotomes (motor points or peripheral nerve)	Strong, low-rate or high-intensity, pulse-train (burst)	9-64
7. Dual-channel stimulation of neck and back (five electrodes)	Paraspinal at cervical and lumbar with electrode on midline in thoracic area	Conventional	9-65

HELPFUL HINTS

A. If strong stimulation cannot be tolerated at the painful low back and mild stimulation modes are not effective, stimulate remote but segmentally related myotomes with the strong, low-rate or high-intensity, pulse-train (burst) modes.

B. Multiple electrodes may be needed to obtain optimal efficiency when pain exists in the neck or legs besides the low back.

C. If the strong muscle contraction modes cannot be tolerated on the involved leg, stimulation of the non-painful extremity may be beneficial.

D. Benefit may also be obtained by paraspinal electrode placement 2–3 segments proximal to the involved root level.[209] This may be due to stimulation of fibers crossing in Lissauer's tract (see Chapters 5 and 8).

stimulation. Only two patients continued to use T.E.N.S. beyond 1 month. There was no mention of any attempt to restore effectiveness when patients reported that the stimulator did not continue to be beneficial.

Figure 9-66 illustrates a common and most effective electrode arrangement for knee pain. Stimulation of the lateral cutaneous nerve of the thigh (GB 33) and the saphenous nerve (medially) (LIV 8 and K 10) is obtained in this manner. Figure 9-71 depicts an alternative arrangement using a crisscross array for intrinsic knee pain such as due to chrondromalacia.

Case Study 23

Clarifying Evaluation: A 56-year-old female referred on 1/22/81 for rehabilitation. History dates to 9/19/80 when she fell, landing on the anterior aspect of both knees and then onto her abdomen. She sustained contusions and developed pain and effusion of both knees. She complained of her knees "giving way," and pain on standing, walking, and on steps. Pain was more intense at the left knee (medial and lateral) and only at the lateral aspect of the right knee. Edema was present at both knees.

Active ROM showed right knee flexion to 110 degrees and left to 90 degrees; extension was complete. Resisted testing in both flexion and extension was painful. Pain also hindered the performance of ligamental and meniscal tests.

Goals: Decrease pain and edema, increase strength and function.

Treatment Plan: A program of high-voltage galvanic stimulation followed by ultrasound and active ROM exercises was initiated. Isokinetic strengthening to be started when feasible.

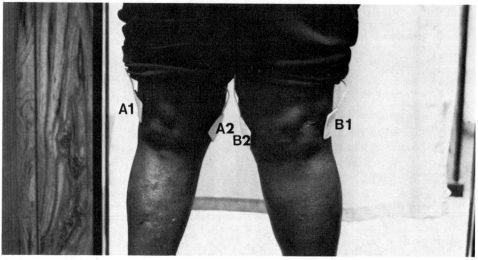

FIGURE 9-66. *Dx:* Degenerative arthritis and synovitis of both knees. *Electrode placement technique:* Dual-channel, bilateral. *Electrode placement sites:* A1, Just superior to lateral joint line in depression above femoral condyle. A2, Medial joint line between tendons of semitendinosus and semimembranosus (channel 1). B1, Just superior to lateral joint line in depression above femoral condyle. B2, Medial joint line between tendons of semitendinosus and semimembranosus (channel 2). *Anatomic characteristics:* A1 and B1, Correspond to acupuncture point GB 33. A2 and B2, Correspond to acupuncture points LIV 8 and K 10. *Nerve innervation:* A1 and B1, Superficial aspect of lateral cutaneous nerve of thigh. A2 and B2, Infrapatellar branch of saphenous nerve and medial cutaneous nerve of thigh. *T.E.N.S. mode:* Conventional. *Electrodes:* Stim-tech Dermaforms (karaya). *T.E.N.S. unit:* Stim-tech Stimpulse. *Rationale:* Any nerve that courses alongside or adjacent to a joint sends a branch to innervate that joint. Electrodes are thus placed at superficial aspects of cutaneous nerves innervating the knee. Electrical paresthesia is thus perceived across the knee.

The patient received two treatments but complained of a return of pain at home after leaving the clinic. She was thus evaluated with T.E.N.S. and obtained almost complete pain relief after a 20-minute stimulation period (Fig. 9-66). A prescription for a rental unit was obtained.

At the time of this report, the patient was in the third week of treatment and progressing, now being able to exercise on the orthotron (isokinetic exercise). She was continuing to use the T.E.N.S. unit at home.

Although we have not yet used T.E.N.S. for any patients with knee pain due to rheumatoid arthritis, we would recommend strict guidelines with such patients. Instruction concerning the amount of increased ADL while using T.E.N.S. should be given. Patients should periodically check the knees for increased edema or temperature (inflammation) when ambulating with a functioning T.E.N.S. unit. T.E.N.S. may control the pain sufficiently to allow for increased ambulatory endurance. The therapist should instruct the patient in a graduated and periodic increase in ADL as a preventive measure.

FOOT AND ANKLE PAIN (DIABETIC NEUROPATHY)

Pain in the ankle and foot can be referred from the lumbar spine and peripheral neuropathies, or exist due to instrinsic dysfunction. Case Study 6 concerned the use of

T.E.N.S. for pain modulation of a patient with a multitude of complaints. The primary problem was one of foot pain as a result of diabetic neuropathies of the tibial and/or sural nerves bilaterally. Figures 9-67 and 9-68 illustrate the electrode technique found to be most beneficial at the time. Figure 9-69 illustrates a suggested alternative arrangement.

Gersh, Wolf, and Rao have presented the case history of a similar patient who obtained complete pain relief with T.E.N.S. while the stimulator was on. Two to 3 hours after the unit was turned off, pain would return if the patient remained ambulatory.[111] A single channel consisting of one electrode on OSS K 3 (posterior tibial nerve) bilaterally was found to provide the best effect. The posterior tibial nerve bifurcates at the medial malleolus,

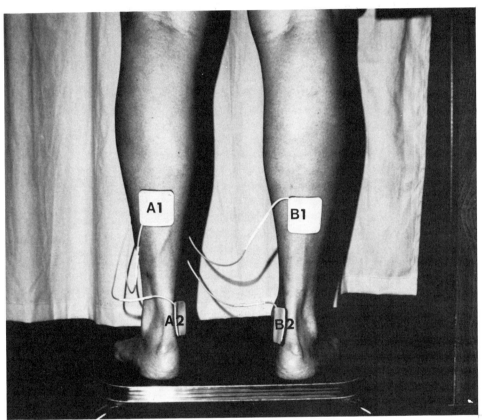

FIGURE 9-67. *Dx:* Bilateral diabetic neuropathy of both feet. *Electrode placement technique:* Dual-channel, bilateral. *Electrode placement sites:* A1, At two-thirds the distance between the popliteal crease and heelcord insertion (midline). A2, In depression between the medial malleolus and heelcord (channel 1 on left). B1–B2, Same as A1 and A2, but on right (channel 2). *Anatomic characteristics:* A1 and B1, Motor/trigger point of soleus muscle. Corresponds to acupuncture point B 57. A2 and B2, Correspond to acupuncture point K 3. *Nerve innervation:* A1 and B1, Sural nerve (cutaneous branch of sciatic) and lateral cutaneous nerve of calf (common peroneal). A2 and B2, Saphenous and posterior tibial nerves. *T.E.N.S. mode:* Conventional. *Electrodes:* Stim-tech Dermaforms (karaya). *T.E.N.S. unit:* Stim-tech Stimpulse. *Rationale:* Stimulation of both the sural and posterior tibial nerves allows the perception of pain-relieving paresthesia throughout the heel and plantar surface of foot.

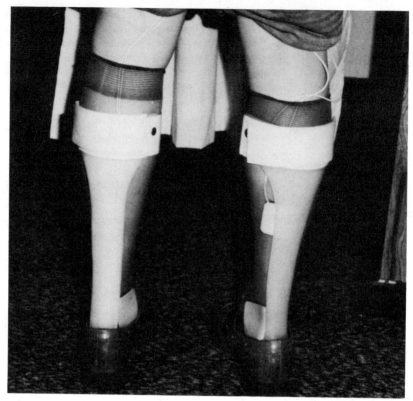

FIGURE 9-68. *Dx:* **Bilateral diabetic neuropathy of both feet. Electrodes in place, under stockings, as shown in Figure 9-67 with the addition of the overlying posterior plastic orthoses.**

giving rise to the medial and lateral plantar nerves innervating the sole of the foot. T.E.N.S. has now been used successfully by podiatrists for the modulation of postoperative foot pain.[112] Of 175 patients, 74 percent reported 75 to 100 percent relief and 20 percent reported 50 to 75 percent relief of postoperative podiatric pain.

FRACTURE OR SPRAIN

Pain in the ankle or foot can be effectively managed by the use of a single channel of two postoperative-size electrodes—one 4- to 6-inch electrode placed posteriorly inferior to the malleoli and another placed anteriorly or posteriorly superior to the malleoli (Fig. 9-70). This is also a recommended podiatric arrangement for pain in the foot, but electrode placement depends upon whether or not pain exists in the lateral or medial toes. In either instance, the proximal electrode is placed posteriorly around the ankle just above or below the malleoli, providing for stimulation of the posterior tibial and sural nerves simultaneously (Figs. 9-71, 9-72). The distal electrode is placed around the instep of the foot superior to the painful region. If pain involves the medial toes, the distal electrode should be placed over the dorsal and plantar surfaces of the medial side of the foot. A reversal of this electrode will allow for electrical paresthesia to become more evident at the lateral aspect

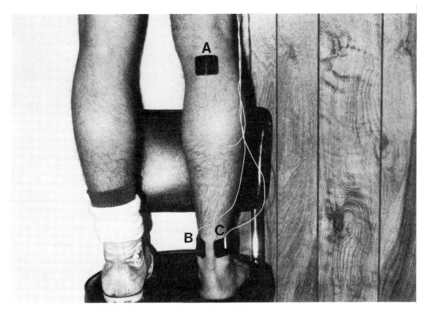

FIGURE 9-69. *Dx:* Suggested alternate array for diabetic neuropathy of calf or foot. *Electrode placement technique:* Dual-channel, unilateral with three-lead cable (V-shaped pathway). *Electrode placement sites:* A, Positive electrode just below popliteal crease. B, Negative electrode of channel 2 in depression between medial malleolus and heelcord. C, Negative electrode of channel 1 in depression between lateral malleolus and heelcord. *Anatomic characteristics:* A, Corresponds to acupuncture points B 53 and B 54. B, Corresponds to acupuncture point K 3. C, Corresponds to acupuncture point B 60. *Nerve innervation:* A, Posterior cutaneous nerve of thigh (sciatic). B, Saphenous and posterior tibial nerves. C, Dorsal lateral cutaneous nerve, end of sural. *T.E.N.S. mode:* Conventional or low-intensity, pulse-train (burst). *T.E.N.S. unit:* Biostim System 10, using three-lead cable. *Rationale:* This arrangement allows for the perception of pain-relieving electrical paresthesia throughout the calf and sole of the foot. The single electrodes of channels 1 and 2 both use one half of the positive electrode. Current flow is thus from the proximal positive electrode across the medial and lateral aspects of the calf to the ankle in an inverted V-shaped pathway.

of the foot when pain exists at the lateral toes (see Figs. 9-71, 9-72). Figure 9-73 illustrates an alternative technique utilizing four electrodes in a bilateral or crisscross arrangement.

POST-HERPETIC NEURALGIA

Post-herpetic neuralgia frequently involves the trigeminal nerve as well as the intercostals and major extremity peripheral nerves. We have treated only two patients with post-herpetic neuralgia. The first patient was seen 3 years ago on only two occasions during the initial onset of pain. He had involvement of the sciatic, obturator, and femoral nerves. Minimal relief was able to be obtained, but because of the extensive area of involvement, benefit was not satisfactory.

Case Study 24 concerns a patient with post-herpetic neuralgia of the left sciatic nerve. Electrodes were placed on the side of involvement at optimal stimulation sites that did not contain skin lesions (Fig. 9-76). Contralateral placement of electrodes was not attempted

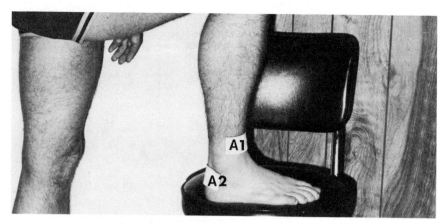

FIGURE 9-70. *Dx:* Suggested array for intrinsic ankle pain. *Electrode placement technique:* Single-channel, proximal and distal. *Electrode placement sites:* A1, Superior to malleoli on dorsum of leg. A2, Inferior to malleoli on posterior aspect of ankle. *Nerve innervation:* A1, Cutaneous branch of superficial and deep peroneal as well as saphenous nerves. A2, Saphenous and posterior tibial nerves (medial); sural nerve (lateral). Corresponds to acupuncture points K 3 and B 60. *T.E.N.S. mode:* Conventional or low-intensity, pulse-train (burst). *Electrodes:* Inmedco (Minnetonka, Minn) rectangular karaya postoperative (cut to desired size). *Rationale:* Large electrodes and placement sites assure the perception of electrical paresthesia throughout the ankle. *Note:* If pain is present only at the posterolateral and medial aspects of the ankle, the anterior electrode should be positioned above both malleoli on the posterior aspect of the leg. When pain is primarily at the lateral or medial aspects, electrodes should be placed proximal and distal to the appropriate malleolus.

since ipsilateral stimulation provided satisfactory relief. Laitinen has reported success with contralateral stimulation in post-herpetic neuralgia.[73] Conventional T.E.N.S. was the stimulation mode employed, and success has been obtained in this manner by others with similar patients.

Wolf, Gersh, and Rao obtained 60 percent relief of post-herpetic neuralgia pain in 7 of 10 patients using conventional T.E.N.S.[113] Nathan and Wall obtained maximal relief with their patients when paresthesia from T.E.N.S. was perceived.[114] Some of their patients used the stimulator for a few minutes and others for up to 12 hours for relief of pain and hyperesthesia. Other reports of success with T.E.N.S. in the management of post-herpetic pain are noted.[8,67,68,70,80,109,115,116]

Bates and Nathan reported results with T.E.N.S. over a 7-year period in which the largest specific pain entity were patients with post-herpetic neuralgia.[67] Electrode placement consisted of ipsilateral stimulation outside of the scarred area proximal and distal to the painful region or over a peripheral nerve. The most commonly used parameters consisted of an intensity producing paresthesia below pain threshold with a rate between 20 and 70 Hz. Pulse duration settings were not given, but the description seems consistent with those of the conventional mode. These authors did not find any one specific stimulation parameter that provided consistently better results. Seventy-four of the 161 patients had post-herpetic neuralgia. Thirty of the patients returned the stimulator after the first week, stating that it was of no benefit. Pain was increased in three patients. Of the 44 who had kept the units, eight returned the units after 1 month, stating that the stimulation relieved their pain but it intensified after the stimulator was turned off (see Chapter 12 for a discussion of increased pain after T.E.N.S.), and eight others returned the units within 2

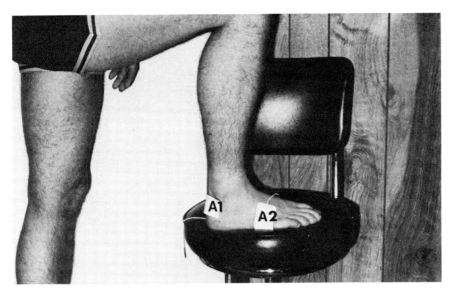

FIGURE 9-71. *Dx:* Suggested array for post–podiatric surgery involving the lateral toes. *Electrode placement technique:* Single-channel, unilateral. *Electrode placement sites:* A1, inferior to malleoli on posterior aspect of ankle. A2, Proximal to the fourth and fifth metatarsals on dorsal and plantar surface. *Nerve innervation:* A1, Saphenous and posterior tibial nerves (medial); sural nerve (lateral). Corresponds to acupuncture points K 3 and B 60. A2, Dorsal lateral cutaneous nerve of foot (branch of sural) and lateral plantar nerve (branch of tibial). *T.E.N.S. mode:* Conventional or low-intensity, pulse-train (burst). *Electrodes:* Inmedco rectangular karaya postoperative (cut to desired size). *Rationale:* Large electrodes and placement sites assure the perception of electrical paresthesia to all surfaces of the fourth and fifth toes. Placement of the distal electrode medially is recommended for pain control following surgery to the first and second toes.

months, stating that T.E.N.S. did not help or that its benefit did not outweigh the problems or difficulty in using the stimulators. One third of the remaining patients used the unit for a full year and one quarter for 2 years or more. All of these patients reported using the stimulator periodically as needed instead of daily as was initially suggested (2 to 8 hours or longer during the first few days). Fourteen of the 44 patients obtained almost immediate improvement. This was similar to the results of Nathan and Wall.[114]

Bates and Nathan noted that if the patients with thalamic syndrome, facial, and scar pain were excluded from the 7-year study, 50 percent of the chronic pain patients obtained relief from T.E.N.S. for a period of 1 to 3 weeks, and 25 percent of the patients obtained continuous relief that was better than any other modality. They also inferred that the use of stimulation modes other than conventional T.E.N.S. may have increased their success rate. These statistics are in line with other reports concerning the effectiveness of T.E.N.S. in patients with chronic pain. Results are significantly higher, in the 80 percent range, for the acute pain patient, especially those who have not had other medical interventions. Long has reported that about 33 percent of patients with chronic pain admitted to a comprehensive pain rehabilitation center obtained benefit solely from T.E.N.S. and did not require other direct therapy.[117]

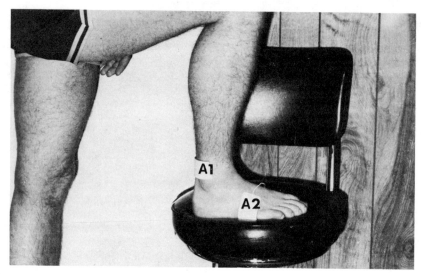

FIGURE 9-72. *Dx:* Suggested array for post–podiatric surgery involving the lateral toes. *Electrode placement technique:* Single-channel, unilateral. *Electrode placement sites:* A1, Superior to malleoli on posterior aspect of ankle. A2, Proximal to the fourth and fifth metatarsals on the dorsal and plantar surface. *Note:* All other factors involving this array are the same as those in Figure 9-71. Placement of the proximal electrode above instead of below the malleoli may produce greater efficacy.

Case Study 24

Clarifying Evaluation: A 77-year-old female with a prior history of multiple myeloma (now controlled according to the patient) and subsequent left hip fracture. Patient had a hip prosthesis and 6 months ago developed herpes zoster involving the left sciatic nerve. Patient ambulated with a straight cane but was unable to do so extensively due to pain. She spent most of the day in bed, which was most comfortable.

Pain was described as being like "biting ants and a burning sensation," primarily from the left lumbosacral junction to the buttock and posterior thigh to popliteal space. Post-herpes skin lesions were clearly visible throughout the area. Minor areas of discomfort not represented by skin lesions existed at the anteromedial groin and sole of the left foot. Pain was present with sitting and walking. Patient would sit on right buttock due to tenderness of sciatic nerve at junction of buttock and posterior upper thigh. Patient already had a T.E.N.S. unit that she was not able to use successfully. She was of the opinion that the use of the unit was going to "cure" her pain. I informed her that it would only symptomatically control the pain.

Goals: Control pain with T.E.N.S.

Treatment Plan: The patient was instructed in the proper use of the unit, including parameter adjustment and electrode placement. One electrode was placed at the left L5–S1 region paraverte-brally and the other at a tender motor point of the gluteus maximus (channel 1). The second channel consisted of one electrode at the junction of the buttock and posterior upper thigh (sciatic hiatus) and another just above the popliteal space (Fig. 9-74). Karaya electrodes were used to avoid skin irritation from tape and gel.

The use of stimulation parameters for conventional T.E.N.S. (high rate, low pulse width, and comfortable amplitude with perceptible tingling) was employed. The patient was able to ambulate pain-free and stand pain-free for at least 30 minutes. Pain was not controlled while sitting, which was expected due to the distinct pressure on the sciatic nerve which had a decreased excitation threshold as a result of the demyelination of A fibers from the shingles.

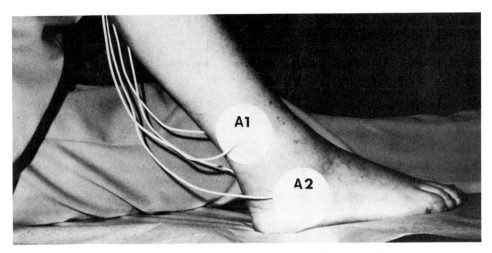

FIGURE 9-73. *Dx:* Alternate electrode array for medial and lateral ankle pain. *Electrode placement technique:* Dual-channel, bilateral. *Electrode placement sites:* A1, Between lateral malleolus and heelcord at superior aspect of malleolus. A2, Just below lateral malleolus (channel 1). B1, Between medial malleolus and heelcord at superior aspect of malleolus. B2, Just below medial malleolus (channel 2). *Nerve innervation:* A1 and A2, Overlie superficial aspect of dorsal lateral cutaneous nerve (end of sural). B1 and B2, Overlie superficial aspect of saphenous and posterior tibial nerves. *T.E.N.S. mode:* Conventional or low-intensity, pulse-train (burst). *Electrodes:* Ins-Tens by Stim-tech with snap leads. *Rationale:* This arrangement provides for the perception of electrical paresthesia throughout the lateral and medial malleoli. *Note:* Electrodes may also be arranged via channels to provide for a crisscross technique. In such an arrangement, electrodes A1–B2 and A2–B1 would constitute separate channels. B1 and B2 are on medial side and are not visible.

The patient was given a written home instruction form and because of her distant location was told to contact the clinic if any difficulties ensued. Follow-up was to be done by mail.

The patient was previously using the unit only at night and while in bed when she did not have much pain. She now was instructed to place the electrodes on in the morning and turn the unit on only when pain began to occur. The unit would then be turned off when pain was decreased but not kept on continuously for more than 1 hour at a time. If after 1 hour pain still existed, she would turn the unit off for at least 5 to 15 minutes to reassess the discomfort. The unit could then be turned on as often as necessary when pain began to occur since the electrodes would remain on all day. She did not need to use the unit while in bed.

On 6/25/80, patient returned for a checkup. She was doing well and was satisfied with the pain relief. Further follow-up by mail questionnaire went unanswered, and the patient was contacted by telephone on 2/2/81. She stated that she continued to use the T.E.N.S. unit for a few months after her last visit. Pain continued to exist primarily when she was out of bed. The patient mentioned that she had had a return of the hip pain, which existed prior to the shingles, and was again undergoing chemotherapy for multiple myeloma. She has, therefore, been primarily confined to bed and therefore returned the T.E.N.S. unit.

The conventional stimulation mode is the suggested method in the presence of post-herpetic neuralgia. The affinity of the herpes zoster virus for the myelin sheath destroys proprioceptive input. The conventional mode most closely simulates non-noxious proprioceptive input and can, therefore, serve to balance noxious or small-fiber input that predominates in this sensory deprivation pain syndrome.

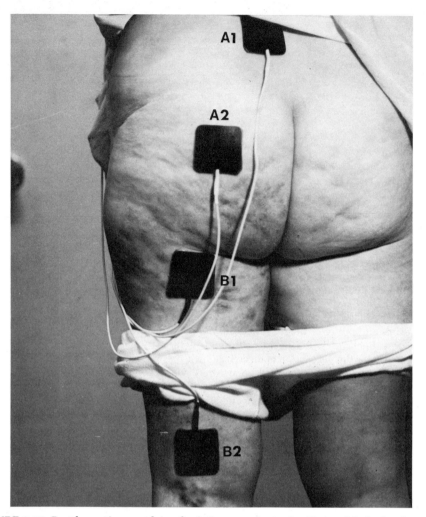

FIGURE 9-74. Post-herpetic neuralgia of sciatic nerve (note significant skin lesion in popliteal fossa). *Electrode placement technique:* Dual-channel, linear pathway. *Electrode placement sites:* A1, Paravertebrally at L5–S1 level. A2, On tender buttock motor point (channel 1). B1, At midpoint between ischial tuberosity and greater trochanter at level of buttock and posterior upper thigh. B2, Just superior to popliteal crease (channel 2). *Anatomic characteristics:* A1, Segmental erector spinae motor point. Corresponds to local bladder meridian acupuncture point. A2, Upper motor/trigger point of gluteus maximus. Corresponds to acupuncture point B 48. B1, Corresponds to acupuncture point B 50. B2, Corresponds to acupuncture points B 53 and B 54. *Nerve innervation:* A1, Posterior primary ramus of L5 and descending cutaneous branches of L1–3 dorsal rami. A2, Cutaneous branch of L2 and inferior gluteal nerve. B1, Posterior cutaneous nerve of thigh (sciatic). B2, Posterior cutaneous nerve of thigh at region of sciatic bifurcation. *T.E.N.S. mode:* Conventional. *Electrodes:* Stim-tech perforated carbon-silicone with karaya pad. *T.E.N.S. unit:* Stim-tech Stimpulse. *Rationale:* Electrodes placed on segmentally related stimulation sites between skin lesions. Electrical paresthesia perceived throughout pain distribution. If ipsilateral stimulation could not be tolerated, contralateral stimulation at similar sites would be the next choice. Overlapping of channels A1–B1 and A2–B2 may enhance efficacy.

Electrical stimulation of peripheral nerves can be performed percutaneously and transcutaneously. Electrode placement should be proximal to the level of the lesion.[80,81,118,119] After surgical decompression or repair, placement proximal and distal to the lesion can be performed. Walmsley and Flexman reported that paravertebral stimulation proximal to the painful region provided more pain relief than distal placement.[18] Others have found that stimulation on superficial aspects of peripheral nerves related to the painful region provide the best results.[49,63,69,113,120,121] Parry states that 65 percent of patients with peripheral nerve pain obtain significant relief with T.E.N.S.[98] Parry also has found that T.E.N.S. following peripheral nerve lesions can increase the ability of the patient with hyperesthesia to recognize objects and texture differences, and to localize a stimulus.[98] Conventional T.E.N.S. was the stimulation mode employed. Figures 9-75 and 9-76 illustrate electrode placement techniques used after surgical decompression of superficial radial and median nerves respectively.

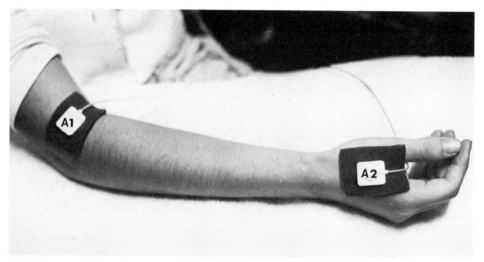

FIGURE 9-75. *Dx:* **Post–surgical decompression of superficial radial nerve (panniculitis).** *Electrode placement technique:* **Single-channel, unilateral (proximal-distal).** *Electrode placement sites:* **A1, In depression at lateral end of elbow crease with elbow flexed to 90 degrees. A2, Dorsal web space.** *Anatomic characteristics:* **A1, Motor/trigger point of brachioradialis. Corresponds to acupuncture point LI 11. A2, Motor/trigger point of first dorsal interosseus and adductor pollicis. Corresponds to acupuncture point LI 4.** *Nerve innervation:* **A1, Posterior cutaneous nerve of forearm communicates with intercostal brachial and superficial radial nerve. A2, Superficial radial and musculocutaneous (sensory); ulnar (motor).** *T.E.N.S. mode:* **Conventional.** *Electrodes:* **Lec-Tec karaya pads (Velcro backing). Velcro adapter added to lead wires.** *T.E.N.S. unit:* **Medical Devices Ultra II.** *Rationale:* **Use of the dorsal web space, the best optimal stimulation site below the lesion (surgical scar), was able to be used postsurgery. Proximal and distal electrode sites provided for the perception of pain-relieving electrical paresthesia throughout distribution of pain. Augmentation of this arrangement can be performed by use of a second channel paraspinally.**

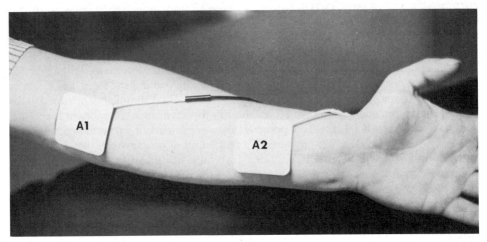

FIGURE 9-76. *Dx:* **Post–surgical decompression of median nerve (carpal tunnel syndrome).** *Electrode placement technique:* **Single-channel, unilateral (proximal).** *Electrode placement sites:* **A1, In antecubital fossa lateral to biceps tendon. A2, At proximal end of surgical scar of forearm.** *Anatomic characteristics:* **A1, Motor point of brachialis. Corresponds to acupuncture point LU 5. A2, Overlies tendons of flexor carpi radialis and palmaris longus. Corresponds to acupuncture point P 7.** *Nerve innervation:* **A1, Lateral cutaneous nerve of arm (median). A2, Median nerve and its medial cutaneous branch.** *T.E.N.S. mode:* **Conventional.** *Electrodes:* **Stim-tech Dermaforms.** *T.E.N.S. unit:* **Mentor 100.** *Rationale:* **Optimal stimulation sites proximal to the lesion (surgical scar) were used. Postsurgical discomfort was all above the wrist. Augmentation of this arrangement can be performed by use of a second channel paraspinally.**

ROOT AND PLEXUS AVULSION INJURIES

Parry reported that patients with root and plexus avulsion injuries complain of a continuous burning, crushing pain in the forearm and hand as well as periodic paroxysmal pain lasting for a few seconds with a variable frequency.[98] The quality of the pain in this instance is similar to that of causalgia and other sensory deprivation pain syndromes.

Albe-Fessard and Lombard used T.E.N.S. contralateral to the side of the lesion.[122] Stimulation consisted of an 80-Hz frequency for 30 minutes at an amplitude producing light muscular twitching. This would be in line with the parameters of conventional T.E.N.S. Unilateral lesions of the C5 to T1 dorsal roots were performed on animals. The animals (species not mentioned) usually exhibit behavior consisting of scratching the side of the lesion, producing open wounds, or chewing the ipsilateral forelimb, causing self-amputation. T.E.N.S. performed contralateral to the involved side for 21 days commencing the day after the lesion delayed the onset and/or extent of the scratching. Self-amputation was not stopped, but its extent was reduced. All the results were reported as being statistically significant. When T.E.N.S. was discontinued, behavior returned to the same level as the control group that underwent similar lesions but did not receive T.E.N.S.

A thorough knowledge of the course of the major peripheral nerves, their segmental origin, superficial aspects, and the muscles that they innervate is imperative to the successful use of T.E.N.S. Pain that exists in a muscle innervated by a nerve that has only one nearby superficial aspect can be managed with one electrode on a tender motor point of the muscle and the other on the peripheral nerve.[5]

Parry reported on the use of T.E.N.S. in the management of pain in 37 patients with avulsion injuries of the brachial plexus.[98,124,125] T.E.N.S. was found to be highly effective in 19 patients, provided some relief for 6 others, and was not of benefit to 12. The most effective electrode placement sites were centrally at the C5–7 levels and just proximal to the site of pain where afferent input still existed. With this arrangement, most patients decreased their pain by 50 percent with 30 minutes to several hours of stimulation. The 12 patients in whom T.E.N.S. was not beneficial had total lesions of the plexus, which may have negated proper conduction of the current. Parry states that T.E.N.S. should be used for at least 2 hours at a time, two to three times a day and sometimes for up to 6 to 8 hours due to a cumulative effect He states further that some patients who have used T.E.N.S. for 5 subsequent days obtain complete relief for the sixth day. A return of pain is usually evident in the seventh day, but relief can again be obtained by reinitiation of T.E.N.S. Table 9-12 summarizes the important guidelines for success with T.E.N.S. in the presence of sensory deprivation pain syndromes and peripheral nerve injuries.

LEPROSY

T.E.N.S. has also been used successfully to obtain relief from leprous neuritis.[123] A recent study of 40 leprosy patients who were treated with T.E.N.S. showed that the majority of patients obtained total pain relief with one treatment of a few hours' duration.

STIMULATION OF SITES UNRELATED TO THE LESION

There are reports in the literature pertaining to stimulation of areas unrelated to the source of pain.[6,8,49,63,77,109] The unrelated regions most commonly mentioned are ulnar and median nerves, upper cervical spine, and the top and bottom of the spine. Picaza and associates found in their study that those patients who obtained good results with stimulation of nerves that directly innervated the painful region usually had similar results when nerves remote to the painful area were stimulated.[8] Patients not benefiting from stimulation of related areas also did not benefit from remote stimulation. Pain was suppressed, although weakly, in 42 of 280 tests using stimulation of areas unrelated and remote from the painful region. Upper cervical (see Fig. 9-15) and transcranial placements (see Fig. 9-2) are also recommended as unrelated stimulation sites.

TABLE 9-12. Suggested Electrode Placement Guidelines for Sensory Deprivation Pain Syndromes and Peripheral Nerve Injuries

1. Electrode placement should be proximal to the level of the lesion.
2. If surgical decompression has been performed, stimulation proximal and distal to the lesion can be performed.
3. Electrode placement at superficial aspects of peripheral nerves is recommended.
4. If ipsilateral stimulation cannot be tolerated, electrode placement at appropriate spinal levels or on superficial aspects of the same nerve contralaterally should be tried.
5. A longer evaluation time is necessary when performing contralateral stimulation. If successful, relief will take longer to occur, may not be as demonstrative nor as long lasting.
6. The conventional mode is usually the most successful.
7. Benefit may be enhanced by the use of pulse-train (burst) stimulation or parameter modulation features.
8. Prolonged stimulation (hours) may be needed to obtain significant benefit.

ITCH

Carlsson and associates found that general body itching could be relieved by T.E.N.S. with stimulation solely at the midthoracic region.[126] Seventeen patients were treated for 1 to 2 minutes with a 60-Hz, 0.2-msec current with the amplitude just below pain threshold. Itch disappeared during the stimulation in all patients except three, and relief persisted for a few hours to 1 week after treatment. Carlsson inferred that there may have been a supraspinal mechanism involved with the strong stimulation, but some patients achieved relief with stimulation at subliminal levels. The transmission of itch seems to be via the same pathways as pain.[127] Krisch, Lewis, and Simon reported on the successful use of T.E.N.S. in a patient with intractable itching (polycythemia vera) in which long-term relief was established with T.E.N.S.[68]

GUILLAIN-BARRÉ SYNDROME

McCarthy and Zigenfus presented a case study of a patient with Guillain-Barré syndrome who developed intense burning of the feet as well as low back, hip, thigh, and calf pain.[128] T.E.N.S. was placed paravertebrally to the spinous processes of L4–S2 and at the midpoint between the femoral greater trochanter and ischial tuberosity (B 50). Stimulation from 30 minutes to 3½ hours one to four times a day provided approximately 75 to 80 percent pain relief and allowed physical therapy treatment to continue. Information relative to specific stimulation parameters was not given.

PREGNANCY

The literature and most T.E.N.S. manufacturers list stimulation over the pregnant uterus as either a contraindication or precaution. This is due to the fact that it has not been determined if any harm will come to the fetus or if labor/abortion will be induced. Of course, this type of study would not be performed.

We have used T.E.N.S. paraspinally for two patients in the last trimester of pregnancy, both of whom sustained cervical and lumbosacral strains as a result of car accidents. The pregnancy contraindicated most common physical therapy modalities as well as medication for pain relief. Conventional T.E.N.S. applied with a paraspinal arrangement on the cervical spine and lumbosacral region provided excellent pain relief with absolutely no ill effects. Both patients obtained rental units, used T.E.N.S. up to the time of delivery, and gave birth to normal infants.

In keeping with the important concept of a comprehensive approach, each patient was also instructed in proper cervical and lumbar body mechanics as well as postural corrective exercises to minimize pain. T.E.N.S. applied paraspinally in the conventional mode is actually no different than a gentle superficial massage to the area. We would definitely advise against using the stronger stimulation modes in this case.

LABOR AND DELIVERY

T.E.N.S. has been used successfully to control pain during labor and delivery. The recommended electrode placement has been to stimulate with rectangular electrodes paraspinally. One channel at T10–L1 for the first stage of labor and the second channel at S2–

S4 for the second stage.[129] First-stage labor pain is described as an ache and probably mediated by C fibers. Second-stage pain can be more easily localized and is sharper and correlated more with A delta fiber transmission.[129] The iliohypogastric and pudendal nerves are stimulated by this method. No complications were reported. One study reported by Augustinsson and associates was performed with 147 patients: 44 percent obtained good to very good pain control, 44 percent obtained moderate relief, and 17 percent had no benefit.[129] Shealy and Maurer reported excellent relief of back pain during parturition in most patients studied, but only 3 of 50 obtained satisfactory relief of anterior pain.[130] Anterior pain can be relieved by placement of electrodes on the abdomen or groin. Such an arrangement should be tried and at this stage probably would not harm the fetus.

Stimulation of low amplitude (conventional mode) was performed continuously during the first stage, and intensity increased during uterine contractions. A rate of 60 to 80 Hz was used. Augustinsson also states that others in Sweden have used a rate of 2 Hz on the back and legs in 27 patients. Good to very good pain relief was reported in 48 percent and some relief in 37 percent of the patients. Bundsen has successfully used pulse-train stimulation.[208]

Studies performed in Germany with T.E.N.S. during labor and delivery have shown significantly good results without complications or side effects on the fetus or mother.[131,132,207] Of 102 women, 57 (55.9 percent) obtained good to very good pain relief, 24 (23.5 percent) received some relief, and 21 (20.6 percent) had no pain relief with the use of T.E.N.S. One possible precaution might be interference with the fetal monitor by the T.E.N.S. current. This problem, however, can be overcome by prior testing and adaptations (T.E.N.S. interference filter) if necessary by the manufacturer of the specific T.E.N.S. unit or the hospital biomedical engineer.[208]

Bundsen and associates have conducted the most definitive work with T.E.N.S. during labor and delivery. They have found no harmful effects to mother or fetus with stimulation on the low back.[207,208] Lumbosacral pain has been controlled well but not suprapubic pain. Bundsen has, therefore, recommended that suprapubic electrode placement be studied.[208] After the first stage of labor, the T10–L1 electrode channel can be removed and placed in the suprapubic region. It may be easier to place a suprapubic channel prior to labor and just connect the lead wires when the second stage commences. Suprapubic stimulation has been successfully performed on patients with bladder pain.[133] Bundsen has initially found no adverse effect on the mother or fetus with suprapubic stimulation.[208]

BLADDER PAIN

A recent paper reports substantial benefit with T.E.N.S. in patients with bladder pain and frequent micturition.[133] The study was conducted on 14 patients who had previously been treated unsuccessfully by conservative means. Nine patients used T.E.N.S. suprapubically with the electrodes 10 to 15 cm apart. Four patients used intravaginal stimulation with flexible electrodes secured by inflatable means. Stimulation was for 15 minutes to 2 hours per day at the maximum tolerated level. All patients showed slight increases in bladder volume (12 percent mean and doubling in two patients) after the first application of T.E.N.S. Voiding frequency decreased and pain was reduced in four patients to less than one third of the prestimulation level. Bladder lesions also significantly decreased over a 6-month period.

Intravaginal stimulation was to the level of perception at a rate of 10 Hz and pulse width of 2 msec. Electrodes were worn all day and removed in the evening. Voiding was not hindered by the electrodes or the stimulation. Suprapubic stimulation was at a rate of

50 Hz and pulse width of 0.2 msec. The authors concluded that no other conservative treatment provided better results with these patients.

Leyson and associates investigated the effects of T.E.N.S. on bladder and sphincter function in a group of 17 acute and chronic spinal cord–injured patients.[134] T.E.N.S. was initially employed due to drug-resistant pain that existed primarily in the C4–6, T10, L5, and S2 dermatomes. Specific electrical parameters were not given, although conventional stimulation seemed to be the desired mode. Treatments were given for 20 to 30 minutes daily for at least 30 days and if satisfactory pain relief occurred treatments were continued.

Urodynamic function was not periodically measured but was found to be demonstrably affected by T.E.N.S. in acute patients (sitting or supine) or when stimulation was given in the L5 and S2 dermatomes. It was concluded that in order to influence vesicourethral function, direct spinal cord, pudendal nerve, or transrectal pelvic stimulation is needed. Stimulation at segments above the T10 level, which correspond more closely to the sympathetic ganglia and their CNS connections, resulted in an increase of residual urine volumes.

The possibility that the effect of T.E.N.S. in chronic spinal cord–injured patients may be blocked by new nerve fibers growing across the site of the lesion was presented. In addition, indirect stimulation of the proximal pudendal nerve roots may occur in acute paraplegia, which could facilitate detrusor-urethral dyssynergia and impair voiding. Leyson and associates concluded that ongoing urodynamic observation be conducted whenever T.E.N.S. is used with spinal cord–injured patients.[134]

MULTIPLE SCLEROSIS

T.E.N.S. has increased function impaired by multiple sclerosis (MS) not only by relieving pain and allowing for the performance of treatment, but also as a means of augmenting sensory reintegration or the normalization of physiologic transmission. Winter has reported on the use of T.E.N.S. with six MS patients.[135] Electrodes were placed paraspinally between the spinal cord and pathologic region. When paraplegia or paresis was evident, electrodes were placed paravertebrally at the sacrum. Placement at the posterior aspect of the ipsilateral trapezius and deltoid was utilized when upper extremity involvement existed. Stimulation parameters consisted of 100 Hz with amplitude to the level of just tolerable discomfort. Pulse width and treatment time were not given. Results indicated a decrease of spasticity and increased mobility. A 2-year follow-up of 135 cases showed a general overall improvement with only two regressions.

Dooley and associates used dorsal column stimulation with 42 MS patients.[136] They reported a significant decrease in dysfunction of sensory modalities, voluntary as well as involuntary, in 21 patients.

SPINAL CORD INJURY

Patients with partial and complete spinal cord lesions can perceive pain below the level of lesion. The first report on the use of T.E.N.S. for pain after spinal cord lesions appeared in 1974.[137] Banerjee reported on five patients, two of whom had phantom pain below the lesion. Of particular interest was the fact that T.E.N.S. was applied below the level of the lesion over the related peripheral nerve, producing almost complete relief for 8 to 10 hours despite the presence of a supposedly complete lesion. Stimulation at muscle contraction intensity was needed for pain relief.[137]

Davis and Lentini utilized T.E.N.S. on 31 spinal cord–injured patients.[138] All had previously required narcotic medication for pain relief. The patients had lesions at different levels, from C3 to L5. No benefit was reported in the four patients who had cervical lesions. Pain relief was successful in 11 of the other 27 patients. Patients with localized spinal column pain, as opposed to radiating nerve root and referred spinal cord pain, responded better. There was no information concerning electrode placement or stimulation parameters, although conventional units were used.

Hachen reported on 39 patients with intractable pain present for 6 to 35 months.[139] These patients previously underwent treatment with narcotic medication, dorsal column stimulation, and cordotomy. Low-intensity stimulation daily for 6 hours was used during the first week of study. Complete or almost complete relief was obtained in 49 percent of the patients. Slight relief was obtained in 41 percent. A 3-month follow-up revealed persistent complete relief in 28 percent and slight relief in 49 perent of the patients. Again, there was no information provided concerning stimulation parameters or electrode placement; only the adjustable range of the units was given.

Heilporn used T.E.N.S. with three spinal cord–injured patients who had completed their rehabilitation but had true spinal root pain.[140] Electrodes were placed at the level of the painful region paraspinally. Two patients obtained temporary modification of their pain, but there was no carryover of relief. The other patient did not obtain any benefit even with high-intensity stimulation. No information regarding stimulation parameters, electrode placement, and length of treatment was given.

Richardson and associates reported significant benefit from T.E.N.S. when used on patients with acute spinal cord injuries.[100,101] Forty-four patients with complete traumatic spinal cord lesions were treated within 48 hours postonset. They had made no neurologic recovery below the lesion. Electrodes were placed on each side of the abdomen on the lower quadrants, and stimulation was performed constantly for 3 days or until bowel movement, diarrhea, flatus, or good bowel sounds became apparent. None of the patients developed ileus, gastrointestinal hemorrhage, or obstruction as a result of T.E.N.S. used postinjury. Seven patients in the control group who developed complications were then treated with T.E.N.S. for 3 to 5 days until the ileus resolved. There was no information given as to stimulation parameters, but it is assumed that they were similar to those used with postoperative T.E.N.S. The authors attribute this excellent result to possible direct stimulation of the parasympathetic plexi and ganglia. They infer that the T.E.N.S. current may cause afferent input to a reflex arc, causing parasympathetic efferent outflow to the abdominal viscera.

The second study reported on by Richardson and colleagues concerned the use of T.E.N.S. with 20 spinal cord–injured patients with associated acute postinjury or traumatic pain.[101] T.E.N.S. was employed paravertebrally at the site of injury immediately in the emergency room or on the hospital floor within 24 hours postinjury. T.E.N.S. was used constantly until the patient was virtually pain-free. Initial significant relief of 50 to 100 percent of their pain was achieved in 18 of the 20 patients. Regular medication was not required but was given as needed. Three days after injury, 15 of the 20 patients still had 50 percent or more pain relief without ileus and with increased peripheral circulation.

The two previous studies provide excellent data concerning the value of T.E.N.S. when employed in the acute phase. In comparison to use after chronic pain and dysfunction have set in, the difference is quite dramatic. Reports have been published concerning the value of T.E.N.S. as an adjunctive technique in the acute stage to be used in the emergency room, recovery room, athletic field, and physician's office. Shealy discusses the use of T.E.N.S., ice, biofeedback, and a calm and reassuring attitude on the part of the physician or allied health team member. These techniques when used in the acute stage can significantly decrease narcotic use, and prevent chronic pain and secondary complications such as ileus and atelectasis.

Ersek reported on the value of T.E.N.S. as used in the emergency room of Dover Air Force Base.[145] T.E.N.S. was employed as the initial treatment during a 6-month trial period. Thirty-four of 35 patients with musculoskeletal injuries all obtained satisfactory pain relief with T.E.N.S.

The only problem with the use of T.E.N.S. in the acute stage is that it does not take the place of a thorough evaluation and comprehensive treatment if needed. This is well illustrated in sports medicine where its use should be confined to injuries that will not progress if the player returns to activity after pain has been relieved. T.E.N.S. will not prevent breakthrough pain as medication may do; thus, the value of pain as a danger sign may in part be preserved.

VISCERAL PAIN

Visceral pain must be distinguished from pain of somatic origin. Often each is mistaken for the other, treatment does not help, and the condition progresses.

Pancreatitis

Roberts used T.E.N.S. to manage pancreatitis pain in five patients.[150] Electrodes were placed on the upper abdomen or epigastrium. Stimulation was performed two to six times for 30 to 60 minutes at intervals of 1 to 3 days. Conventional T.E.N.S. was used, but brief, intense stimulation was occasionally employed to initially break through persistent pain. All five patients had prompt and lasting pain relief of upper abdominal pain after two treatments. Subsequent painful episodes were able to be managed with T.E.N.S., and hospitalization was not required.

Thrombophlebitis

Roberts also used T.E.N.S. to manage the pain of thrombophlebitis in 39 patients.[151] Electrodes were placed over the painful venous segment and its peripheral nerve. Treatments were performed bilaterally if extremities were involved. Stimulation was performed three to four times for 30 to 60 minutes over a period of 1 to 3 days. Conventional T.E.N.S. was used but, as with the pancreatitis patients, brief, intense stimulation occasionally was needed to break through severe pain. Good relief was obtained in 32 patients; 3 obtained fair relief; and 4 had no relief. The patients were cautioned not to stand and/or ambulate immediately after pain relief but to gradually increase or resume their normal activities.

Eriksson and Mannheimer employed T.E.N.S. with 11 patients who had severe arterial insufficiency of the lower extremities.[152] Five of the patients had skin ulcerations. T.E.N.S. was performed for 5 minutes at 80 Hz with an intensity that produced slight vibrations radiating down the calf to the foot. Patients were tested prior to T.E.N.S. by ambulating until pain became severe. Pre-T.E.N.S. treadmill rate of 0.5 m/sec was maintained for 9 minutes. Post-T.E.N.S., they were able to ambulate for 45 minutes at the same speed. All patients were able to increase their ambulatory distance after T.E.N.S. Seven of the patients who complained of severe aching while ambulating noted that this disappeared after T.E.N.S.

Schuster has noted vasodilation, increased circulation and ROM, and a decrease in edema and numbness after the use of T.E.N.S. in patients with neurovascular conditions.[153] Dooley and Kasprak noted that electrical stimulation applied via T.E.N.S. or implanted stimulators can produce arterial dilation.[154] Electrical stimulation of the spinal cord or dorsal roots produced arterial dilation in one or more extremities. The exact stimulation parameters were not given, but stimulation was provided for only 5 minutes. Cook has reported that antidromic electrostimulation of C fibers augments peripheral circulation.[155]

Abram has noted changes in sympathetic tone with T.E.N.S.[156] He reports on one case but fails to provide the exact stimulation parameters. Increases as well as decreases in skin temperature have been seen. Ebersold and associates noted no significant differences in autonomic function with T.E.N.S.[157] A recent study conducted by Owens and associates used thermography to determine changes in sympathetic tone with T.E.N.S.[96] Seven normal subjects received stimulation for 1 minute at the ulnar groove and ulnar aspect of the wrist at the region of maximal arterial pulsation. A modulated frequency of 75 ± 25 Hz, 100-μsec pulse duration, with an amplitude of definite current sensation but without discomfort or overt muscular fasciculations was utilized. T.E.N.S. was performed primarily ipsilateral to the tested side; two subjects were later evaluated with contralateral stimulation. Results of the study showed that all seven subjects obtained an average skin temperature increase of 1.0° distal to the electrodes (hand) which returned to the pretested temperature 5 to 10 minutes after stimulation. There was no measurable increase in skin temperature contralateral to the side of stimulation. However, hand temperature in both the thenar and hypothenar regions increased. It was concluded that the immediate increase in distal cutaneous temperature is possibly indicative of cutaneous vasodilation and decreased sympathetic tone. The value of continuous T.E.N.S. in the presence of causalgia and reflex sympathetic dystrophy was elucidated due to the results of this study.

Our findings based solely on clinical observation seem to show that vasoconstriction and concomitant decreased skin temperature will occur with high-rate, high-amplitude T.E.N.S. This has been demonstrated experimentally by Janko and Trontelj.[19] They used parameters of 50 to 100 Hz at the threshold of discomfort for 10 minutes on one finger. A progressive numbness occurred, with sensitivity to light touch and pinprick decreasing within 10 minutes. The subjects also noted a cooling sensation, the skin became pale, and temperature decreased. The tetanic contraction as a result of this mode of stimulation will cause impairment of circulation distal to the site of stimulation. Strong, low-rate and high-intensity, pulse-train (burst) T.E.N.S. primarily at comfortable levels producing a muscle pumping effect should promote increased circulation, vasodilation, and a concomitant rise in cutaneous temperature. Low-intensity electrical stimulation has been used to promote granulation and increased circulation in the treatment of skin ulcerations.[158]

The results from contralateral stimulation depend on the length of treatment. As shown in the study by Owens, 1 minute of stimulation produced no visible change on the opposite side.[96] Contralateral stimulation for a longer period may show changes in skin temperature. Evaluation of the results of these studies is difficult because they were performed differently and not all stimulation parameters were provided.

Raynaud's Phenomenon

Kaada has demonstrated excellent benefit from T.E.N.S. in four patients with Raynaud's disease.[205] Stimulation at remote sites (dorsal web space, superficial aspects of ulnar, and sciatic and peroneal nerves) with the pulse-train mode for 30 to 45 minutes produced a dramatic increase in peripheral vasodilation in the cold extremities with a 7 to 10°C increase in skin temperature that persisted for a least 4 to 8 hours. There was an associated relief of the ischemic pain as well.

The best results occurred in all four limbs with stimulation of the LI 4 point at the dorsal web space. Contralateral effects were quite common. Stimulation with parameters consistent with the conventional mode was also effective but not as great as that obtained with pulse-train stimulation. Specific parameters consisted of 0.2-msec pulse duration at a 2 to 5 Hz rate or a burst rate of 2 Hz (five pulses per burst with an interval frequency of 100 Hz). Intensity was increased to 20 to 30 mA, producing nonpainful muscle contractions.

One significant side effect reported by three female patients with Raynaud's phenomenon was the development of migraine-type headaches with concomitant extremity vasodilation. These patients had no previous history of migraine. One of the four patients now uses the stimulator at home for 30 minutes every second or third day to keep the feet warm and pain-free. The other three benefit from continued stimulation at home only when sitting or reclining.

Visceral Pain: Implications for T.E.N.S.

The clinical reports of Roberts include the fact that strong stimulation (brief, intense) was occasionally needed to break through visceral pain. This is supported by previous research in animals relating to visceral and cutaneous interactions. Pomeranz, Wall, and Weber, along with Selzer and Spencer, studied the response of lamina 5 cells that receive fine myelinated (A-delta) input from viscera, muscle, or skin.[163–165] They found that supramaximal cutaneous stimuli could suppress visceral pain.

Common interneurons in lamina 5 receive convergent visceral and cutaneous input, which give rise to the mechanism of referred pain (see Chapter 5). Therefore, common interneurons can be activated by either cutaneous or visceral afferent input.[164] Furthermore, a reciprocal inhibitory action has been demonstrated between visceral and cutaneous pathways in the dorsal horn.[165] A-delta cutaneous fibers seem to mediate such inhibition by depolarizing visceral A-delta fibers. Inhibition can be enhanced by a gradual increase in the intensity needed to activate all afferent fibers. A brief train of impulses was shown to be more effective than single shocks.[165] Cutaneous afferent input was in fact facilitated by single shock stimuli to visceral afferents, possibly relating to the mechanism behind referred hyperalgesia of visceral origin.

CANCER PAIN

T.E.N.S. has been utilized to relieve cancer pain.[70,159] Ostrowski and Dodd presented three case histories in which T.E.N.S. was used to decrease pain due to malignancy.[159] Clinical studies have documented the successful use of T.E.N.S. in cancer pain.[8,37,68,83,116,160] Ventafridda and associates used T.E.N.S. in 37 patients with intractable pain due to cancer.[160] Initially (10 days), T.E.N.S. was successful in markedly reducing pain in 96 percent of the patients, but this declined dramatically after 30 days. Only four patients (11 percent) continued to obtain pain relief. The use of analgesia, however, was reduced in 54 percent of the patients after 1 month of T.E.N.S. Specific electrical parameters were not given, but it was stated that the whole range of tolerable outputs was investigated to obtain optimal success with each patient. A wide variety of electrode placement sites was also utilized. There was little information given regarding precise stimulation parameters.

Barr, a physical therapist who works exclusively with oncology patients, also stated that pain relief with T.E.N.S. declined after initial success.[161] However, effectiveness was frequently restored by rearranging electrode placements and/or using different stimulation modes. Changes in the location and perception of pain due to a progression of pathology necessitate re-evaluation of optimal stimulation sites. Barr reported that effectiveness is also enhanced by using the strong, low-rate (acupuncture-like) mode when conventional T.E.N.S. is not beneficial.

ANGINA PECTORIS

Gordon and associates have reported a significant decrease in the frequency and severity of angina pectoris in five patients with intractable angina who used T.E.N.S. for 1 year.[162] Treadmill tests, however, showed no increase in exercise tolerance via the use of T.E.N.S. in three patients.

CENTRAL PAIN STATES

Patients suffering from diffuse body pain as a result of lesions in the thalamus do not respond well to T.E.N.S. Treatment of thalamic pain syndromes with T.E.N.S. has been unsuccessful.[34,67,68,80,116,166] This failure is possibly due to location of the lesion itself, in an area of the CNS concerned with integration and modulation of afferent input, including T.E.N.S. All afferent input may no longer be properly processed, and facilitation and inhibition of pain via T.E.N.S. and other means of counterirritation become mixed up, thus decreasing effectiveness.

BURNS

We are not aware of any specific published reports relating to the effectiveness of T.E.N.S. in the management of pain due to burns. We have not had experience with this type of patient, although we feel T.E.N.S. would be effective. Electrodes would be best applied above the level of the burn, preferably at superficial aspects of major peripheral nerves innervating the region of the burn. Conventional or low-intensity, pulse-train (burst) modes are recommended. It has been suggested that a sterile gauze pad could be applied within the burned area and a standard carbon-silicone electrode placed over it to provide for stimulation with conventional T.E.N.S.[167] Alternative suggestions include electrode placement at uninvolved but related spinal segments, stimulation of the contralateral extremity, and remote or unrelated site stimulation with stronger modes.

PEDIATRICS

There are few reports pertaining to the use of T.E.N.S. for pain modulation with children. Epstein and Harris stated that 60 percent of the patients in the pediatric pain treatment center at John Hopkins required no other treatment for pain than T.E.N.S.[168] It appears that the implications for T.E.N.S. in the adolescent or adult patient would also apply to the child. The benefit of T.E.N.S. in children with reflex sympathetic dystrophy has previously been presented.[95,97,192]

GRANULATION

There are reports of low-intensity direct current (LIDC) being successfully used to promote healing of ulcerated skin lesions.[158] T.E.N.S. may, therefore, provide a similar effect since it can be performed at a low intensity with a rate conducive to promoting vasodilation. Direct current (monophasic) T.E.N.S. units are available. T.E.N.S. was used in one specific case to promote granulation, but the result was no different than that seen with the use of LIDC or other means of stimulating healing, such as ultraviolet light or high-voltage galvanic electrical stimulation. Healing was apparently stimulated but no faster than with the other methods.

DYSMENORRHEA

T.E.N.S. can be used to decrease the discomfort of painful menstruation known as dysmenorrhea. A recent experiment was conducted to compare the effects of conventional and strong, low-rate (acupuncture-like) T.E.N.S. in a group of college students.[171] Twenty-seven subjects (nine per group), with a history of menstrual pain and not on oral contraceptives, were randomly assigned to one of three groups: control, conventional T.E.N.S., and acupuncture-like T.E.N.S. Each group received similar instructions, used the same T.E.N.S. units and electrodes, and completed a post-treatment questionnaire. Treatment time was kept constant at 30 minutes whenever pain occurred for each group. Electrode placement was the same for the control group (who used dead batteries) and conventional group, but different for the acupuncture-like group. Figures 9-77 and 9-78 illustrate the electrode arrangements.

Preliminary results showed a mean decrease in pain of 72.2 percent, 51.8 percent, and 26.1 percent for the conventional; strong, low-rate (acupuncture-like); and control groups, respectively. An analysis of variance (ANOVA) and multiple comparison (Tukey test) revealed that the mean decrease in pain between the conventional and control group was statistically significant but that other group comparisons were not. Seventy percent of the subjects in the conventional T.E.N.S. group desired to continue its use if it were available. Only 44 percent of the strong, low-rate (acupuncture-like) group wished to continue its use.

The mean duration of pain relief was 4.2 hours in the conventional group and 2.5 hours in the strong, low-rate (acupuncture-like) group. The reverse was expected. Participants in the conventional group were able to pursue their usual activities during stimulation. Those in the strong, low-rate (acupuncture-like) group found ambulation difficult due to ongoing rhythmic muscle contractions and needed to sit or lie down during stimulation. The electrode placements used with the strong, low-rate (acupuncture-like) mode (SP 6 and 10) were recommended acupuncture stimulation sites.[169,170] Other electrode placement arrangements need to be explored for this pain syndrome, and the complete results of the study are not yet available. The study has been submitted for publication.[171] The value of T.E.N.S. for control of menstrual pain is limited by cost factors, that is, the short-term need for a T.E.N.S. unit may not be worth the expense. However, participants in the conventional group stated that they would use T.E.N.S. for dysmenorrhea if it was available at a low cost and was cosmetic so that it could be concealed. Figure 9-79 illustrates a very small, thin, and lightweight T.E.N.S. unit specifically developed for dysmenorrhea based on the results of this study. The use of the pulse-train (burst) mode and parameter modulation are worthwhile alternatives. Another electrode array to try would consist of bilateral stimulation at SP 10 and the suprapubic region.

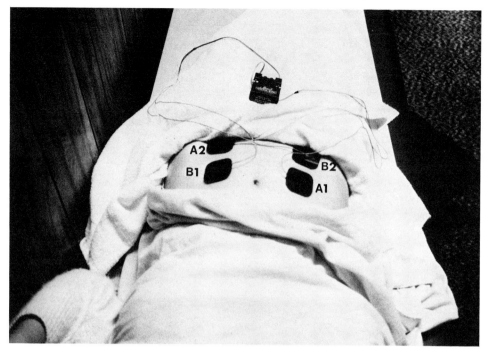

FIGURE 9-77. *Dx:* Dysmenorrhea. *Electrode placement technique:* Dual-channel, crisscross. *Electrode placement sites:* **A1, On abdomen at most anterolateral area of pain below umbilicus on right. A2, On abdomen at most anterolateral area of pain above anterior-superior iliac spine (ASIS) on left (channel 1). B1, Same as A1, but on left. B2, Same as A2, but on right.** *Nerve innervation:* **Anterior primary rami and cutaneous branches of iliophypogastric and ilioinguinal nerves.** *T.E.N.S. mode:* **Conventional.** *Electrodes:* **Carbon-silicone with karaya pad.** *T.E.N.S. unit:* **Medical Devices Ultra II.** *Rationale:* **Arrangement provides for the perception of pain-relieving electrical paresthesia to concentrate at most intense region of pain below umbilicus.** *Note:* **One or more types of parameter modulation may enhance results.**

BONE HEALING

Considering the recent publications concerning the benefit of electrical stimulation in fracture healing, the role of T.E.N.S. should be investigated.[172–174] Microcurrents used subcutaneously, transcutaneously, and invasively have been shown to be effective. Electrode placement should be arranged so current flow is across the fracture site. Kahn recommends the use of a mild current at the fracture site, obtained by a large interelectrode distance.[175] The use of a monophasic waveform is suggested with parameters at the lowest frequency, widest pulse width, and lowest amplitude. When performed for 1 hour, four times a day in the presence of nonhealing fractures, x-ray evidence of new callous formation was demonstrated after 1 month when there was no prior healing during a 5-month period.[175]

PSYCHOGENIC PAIN

Patients with psychogenic pain generally do not respond well to T.E.N.S. Many patients who lack an organic basis to their pain complaints may in fact report an increase of

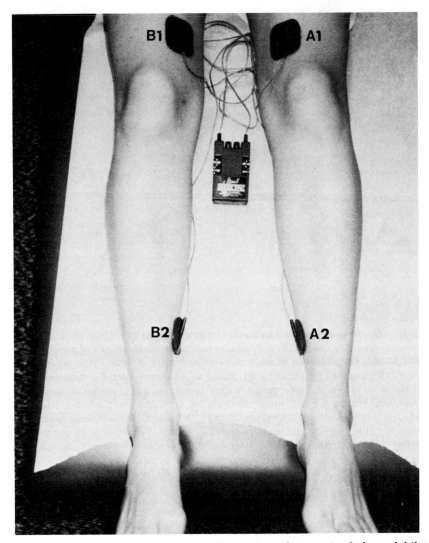

FIGURE 9-78. *Dx:* Dysmenorrhea. *Electrode placement technique:* Dual-channel, bilateral. *Electrode placement sites:* A1, Two inches above the medial aspect of patellar base. A2, Three inches above medial malleolus just behind tibia (channel 1). B1 and B2, Same as above, but placement is on opposite extremity (channel 2). *Anatomic characteristics:* A1 and B1, Motor/trigger point of vastus medialis. Corresponds to acupuncture point SP 10. A2 and B2, Motor point of flexor digitorum longus. Corresponds to acupuncture point SP 6. *Nerve innervation:* A1 and B1, Medial cutaneous nerve of thigh and infrapatellar branch of saphenous nerve (cutaneous); femoral (motor). A2 and B2, Saphenous nerve (cutaneous); tibial nerve (motor). *T.E.N.S. mode:* Strong, low-rate (acupuncture-like). *Electrodes:* Carbon-silicone with karaya pad. *T.E.N.S. unit:* Medical Devices Ultra II. *Rationale:* Recommended acupuncture points for dysmenorrhea. Both stimulation sites are also motor points and thus optimal for excitation of rhythmic muscle contractions. *Note:* The high-intensity, pulse-train (burst) mode can also be used.

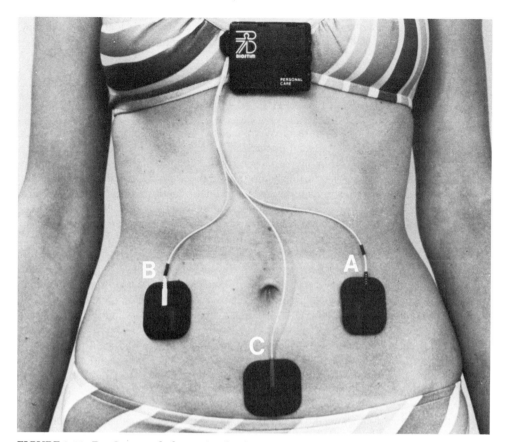

FIGURE 9-79. *Dx:* Suggested alternative for dysmenorrhea. *Electrode placement technique:* Dual-channel, V-shaped pathway, using three-lead cable system. *Electrode placement sites:* A, Uppermost painful anterolateral aspect of abdomen, below umbilicus on left (negative electrode of channel 1). B, Uppermost painful anterolateral aspect of abdomen, below umbilicus on right (negative electrode of channel 2). C, Most intense area of pain at midline below umbilicus. (positive electrode). *Nerve innervation:* Anterior primary rami and cutaneous branches of iliohypogastric and ilioinguinal nerves. *T.E.N.S. mode:* Conventional or low-intensity, pulse-train (burst). *Electrodes:* Carbon-silicone with karaya pad. *T.E.N.S. unit:* Biostim Personal Care with three-lead cable. *Rationale:* Each proximal negative electrode uses one half of the energy of the midline positive electrode. The perception of pain-relieving electrical paresthesia is thus in a V-shaped pathway from the positive to both negative electrodes across the abdomen.

pain with T.E.N.S.[80,116,117] We have used T.E.N.S. via conventional surface electrodes as well as with blunt-end probes in part to weed out the malingerer from the legitimate patient population. The use of probes with point locators that beep on completion of a circuit through low skin resistance regions is particularly effective. If patients are not told in advance that the audible tone does not result in the generation of a stimulating current, they frequently complain of discomfort upon hearing the tone or beep. Other patients will report that the stimulation is too strong when in fact no actual current is being emitted from the T.E.N.S. unit or probe. A patient who consistently demonstrates this response pattern when coupled with unusual objective findings or discrepancies from evaluative testing may confirm the clinician's feeling of malingering or of a psychogenic mechanism.

THE USE OF T.E.N.S.
DURING SPECIFIC THERAPEUTIC PROCEDURES

T.E.N.S. has primarily been used as a means of pain control for the patient with chronic pain who has been through an unsuccessful rehabilitation program and/or surgery. In our practice, T.E.N.S. is commonly employed early in the acute phase when discomfort is severe enough and cannot be diminished or eliminated within a few days. Specifically, patients with acute cervical strains (whiplash), shoulder bursitis, tendinitis, and low back pain syndromes constitute such a group. These patients benefit quite well from the use of T.E.N.S. at home for ongoing pain modulation while specific clinical treatment geared to the source of pain is performed on an outpatient basis.

The use of T.E.N.S. adjunctively early in the acute phase allows the patient to perform activities of daily living that could not ordinarily be accomplished. This is extremely helpful in speeding up the recovery, preventing chronicity, and decreasing the cost of health care. Furthermore, it makes the patient participate in his or her own rehabilitation process, eliminates the need for medication and resultant side effects, increases large-fiber afferent input via movement (since the patient need not sit and contemplate the pain), and prevents the onset of negative mental thoughts or images that may compound the pain process.

T.E.N.S. is now being used to decrease pain that prevents the execution of various therapeutic procedures that are necessary to ultimately eliminate the cause of pain and restore normal mobility and function to the involved structure. Such therapeutic procedures may be employed as part of the comprehensive rehabilitation of the acute pain patient as well as those with chronic pain and/or dysfunction who have been unable to progress with rehabilitation due to pain.

In physical therapy, our concern is primarily with the restoration of function and elimination of pain due to neuromusculoskeletal disorders. Specific manual therapeutic procedures such as joint mobilization, transverse friction massage, and contract-relax stretching are extremely effective in restoring normal joint mobility, breaking up scar tissue, and stretching soft-tissue restriction or adhesions, respectively. Pain may hinder or totally negate the utilization of these manual techniques. In sensory deprivation pain syndromes, causalgia and hyperesthesia may hinder simple gentle touch necessary for active-assistive range of motion, grade I joint mobilization, and the placement of biofeedback electrodes. These techniques are totally painless when performed on normal skin or joints. In comparison, transverse friction massage and contract-relax stretching usually are painful on the normal subject, let alone the individual with pathology. The employment of T.E.N.S. prior to and during the actual technique can sufficiently decrease pain to allow the therapist to perform the treatment. Different modes of T.E.N.S. may be required for optimal results with different qualities of pain.

JOINT MOBILIZATION AND BIOFEEDBACK

The conventional mode was in most cases the only one tolerated by patients with acute cervical strains. Electrodes were arranged to provide perception of the T.E.N.S. current throughout the area of discomfort. This was either a crisscross or longitudinal paraspinal arrangement.[5] Parameters were adjusted based on the physiologic characteristics of the nerve fibers to be stimulated.[34,176] Muscle contractions, as necessary with strong, low-rate (acupuncture-like) and high-intensity, pulse-train T.E.N.S., were not only not tolerated by these patients but were found to interfere with the performance of the desired manual technique. Patients with chronic cervical involvement, however, may tolerate moderate pulse-train stimulation.

Following a cervical strain, patients are frequently referred to physical therapy for treatment. Initial findings usually consist of decreased cervical spine active motion, deep achy pain that may be referred, and associated muscle guarding. A cervical collar is usually apparent and regardless of its benefit may compound the joint hypomobility in the cervical and upper thoracic spine if worn continuously for a period exceeding 2 weeks.

Patients with cervical strains are usually seen in our clinic within 1 to 4 weeks postonset. Those patients previously reported on represented both early and late referrals. Referrals resulted from unsatisfactory pain relief with conservative care, such as rest, medication, and immobilization via a cervical collar for at least 1 month, as well as extended treatment consisting solely of heat modalities (moist heat, ultrasound, diathermy) and occasionally intermittent cervical traction.

Regardless of the patient's state on initial evaluation, whenever joint dysfunction (usually hypomobility) exists with associated cutaneous hyperesthesia and deep tenderness, joint mobilization techniques are employed. These techniques are essential to restore full and painless joint mobility.

The terms manipulation and mobilization are commonly used interchangeably but represent two distinctly different techniques. *Manipulation* is a sudden low-amplitude thrust that takes a joint beyond its restricted range of movement. The quickness of the technique makes it impossible for the patient to prevent it from occurring.[93,177–184] *Mobilization* implies gentle pressures or oscillations directed to a joint within the available range of movement. The patient can prevent this movement from occurring since it is slow and continuous.[93,177–184] Maitland divides mobilization into two types: *passive oscillatory* movements and *sustained stretching*.[177,178] Passive oscillatory movements are usually given at a rate of two to three per second. The amplitude will vary depending on the state of the joint and can be given anywhere within the joint range of movement. Sustained stretching is performed at end-range with the addition of tiny amplitude oscillations. Both mobilization techniques can be applied to peripheral and spinal joints via accessory and component motions such as gliding (translatoric), rolling (angular), spinning (rotation), and traction, which vary according to the joint.[93,182,183,185–188] Gross physiologic motions (flexion, abduction, etc.) are not used. Oscillations can be applied by a direct pressure-release pattern that is tolerated best by the patient when rhythmic.[179] When performed on the spinal joints, vertical or central pressures are applied to the spinous or transverse processes, producing slight anterior-posterior movement, as well as transverse to the spinous process, producing a rotational component. Total time spent at each segment is usually 15 to 30 seconds and may be repeated two to three times depending on the feedback (objective and subjective) from the patient.

The safety of such procedures is best exemplified by delineating such movements into four distinct grades.[177,178,184] Grade I consists of small-amplitude movements performed at the beginning of the range. Grade II employs a large-amplitude movement within the range but not to its limit. Grade III is a large-amplitude movement performed up to the limit of the range. Grade IV is a small-amplitude movement performed at end-range. The direction of movement is controversial and may be given toward the stiff and painful direction or away from restriction in the direction of no pain.[177–179,181]

When T.E.N.S. is used concomitantly with joint mobilization of the spine, only grades I and II oscillations are performed. Invariably, after a few days of treatment, pain is significantly decreased so more involved mobilization can be employed without the need for ongoing pain control with T.E.N.S. We have needed to increase the strength of the stimulation for a few patients by increasing either amplitude or pulse width parameters. However, when used paraspinally, muscle contractions were kept to a minimum with only occasional mild visible fasciculations.

T.E.N.S. is applied for 10 to 20 minutes prior to mobilization and left on while mobilization is performed. According to Wyke, these gentle manual techniques stimulate the joint mechanoreceptors giving rise to large myelinated fiber afferent input generally considered to have an ability to inhibit small-fiber or nociceptive input.[189] This is consistent with the interpretation of the gate control theory.[190,191] Conventional T.E.N.S. is designed to selectively activate the large myelinated A fibers as well. It is, therefore, conceivable that the combination of these two forms of large-fiber input may have a more profound effect on pain at the segmental level.

This treatment protocol serves to restore joint mobility, reduce pain, and allow for the performance of more involved joint mobilization techniques, fluorimethane spray and stretch of suboccipital and cervical musculature, as well as manual cervical traction.

Conventional T.E.N.S. has also proven to be quite effective in modulating the pain of causalgia and reflex sympathetic dystrophy following fractures, trauma, and peripheral nerve injury.[81,94,95,129,193] We have had excellent success with this mode of T.E.N.S. in patients with causalgia and hyperesthesia of the superficial radial, ulnar, and median nerves as well as reflex sympathetic dystrophy following Colles' fracture and a severe wrist sprain. In all of these cases, the constant pain and sensitivity to touch made treatment almost impossible. Patients were unable to perform active exercise due to pain exacerbation; manual mobilization and muscle re-education techniques (biofeedback and muscle stimulation) could not be tolerated. Case Study 25 highlights the role of T.E.N.S. in the rehabilitation of a patient who sustained a severe wrist sprain. The use of T.E.N.S. in conjunction with EMG biofeedback is discussed in Case Study 26.

Case Study 25

Clarifying Evaluation: A 70-year-old female who fell at home in the bathtub and sprained the right wrist 6 weeks prior to referral for physical therapy on 1/2/80. Patient complained of a constant, deep toothache type of pain that was aggravated by lifting objects, turning faucets and knobs, and so forth. Pain was present throughout the wrist and hand with intermittent referral proximally to the elbow and shoulder. Edema was evident throughout the hand and there was a great deal of morning stiffness. Active ROM testing of the shoulder, elbow, and forearm was normal, but wrist flexion was limited to 30 degrees, extension 35 degrees, and radial deviation to 15 degrees. Finger flexion was sufficient for an adequate fist and equal to that on the left. Limitations gradually developed due to arthritis according to the patient. Left wrist flexion measured 55 degrees and extension 45 degrees.
Treatment Goals: Decrease pain and edema, increase function.
Treatment Plan: High-voltage galvanic stimulation to the wrist and hand followed by joint mobilization and therapeutic exercise. Jobst intermittent compression treatments were to be added if edema did not subside after a few treatments. Patient to be instructed in a home exercise program.

After the first two treatments, it became evident that the patient was unable to tolerate mild grade I articulatory techniques and therapeutic exercise due to pain. T.E.N.S. was instituted. The electrode placement arrangement was designed to obtain stimulation of the radial, median, and ulnar nerves (Fig. 9-80). Pain control was sufficient to allow for the performance of the therapeutic techniques. The patient desired to obtain a rental unit for pain control at home.

After using the unit at home for the first 3 days, the patient reported complete pain relief lasting for at least 2 to 3 hours after a 15- to 20-minute period of stimulation, a substantial decrease in edema,

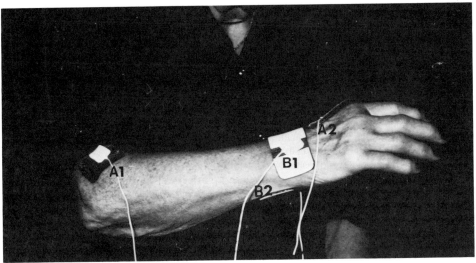

FIGURE 9-80. *Dx:* Wrist sprain with possible reflex sympathetic dystrophy. *Electrode placement technique:* Dual-channel, unilateral. *Electrode placement sites:* A1, In depression at lateral end of elbow flexed to 90 degrees. A2, Dorsal web space (channel 1). B1, On dorsum of wrist just proximal to distal crease. B2, On volar surface of wrist just proximal to edge of dorsal electrode (channel 2). *Anatomic characteristics:* A1, Motor/trigger point of brachioradialis. Corresponds to acupuncture point LI 11. A2, Motor/trigger points of first dorsal interosseus and adductor pollicis. Corresponds to acupuncture point LI 4. B1, Corresponds to acupuncture points TW 4 and SI 5. B2, Corresponds to acupuncture points LU 7–9, H 4–7, and P 5–6. *Nerve innervation:* A1, Posterior cutaneous nerve of forearm communicating with intercostal brachial nerve. Superficial radial. A2, Superficial radial and musculocutaneous (sensory); ulnar (motor). B1, Posterior cutaneous nerve of forearm, superficial radial and dorsal cutaneous branch of ulnar. B2, Lateral and medial cutaneous nerves of forearm, superficial radial, and palmar cutaneous branch of ulnar nerve. *T.E.N.S. mode:* Conventional. *Electrodes:* A1 and A2, Lec-Tec karaya electrodes with Velcro backing. Velcro adapters used for electrical connection. B1 and B2, Rectangular Lec-Tec karaya electrodes with Velcro backing and adapters. *Rationale:* This array provides for the perception of pain-relieving electrical paresthesia throughout the pain distribution and major nerves of the upper extremity. Electrical paresthesia perceived in all fingers of the hand.

and sleeping better at night. The progress note of 1/17/80 reflected this information, along with an improvement in wrist flexion to 40 degrees and extension to 45 degrees.

The patient was discharged on 2/1/80, and it was reported that edema was no longer evident and active ROM had improved to ranges consistent with those of the noninvolved left side but pain was still present periodically. The patient desired to rent the T.E.N.S. unit for another month. T.E.N.S. at this time was providing relief for longer periods of time (sometimes a full day) with a stimulation time of 30 to 60 minutes. The patient was instructed to continue the home program of active ROM exercises. The T.E.N.S. unit was returned to the distributor at the end of the second month's rental period, at which time pain was virtually nonexistent.

Case Study 26

Clarifying Evaluation: A 41-year-old male referred for rehabilitation on 9/7/78. History dated to 9/77 when he initially underwent surgery for an inguinal hernia. The patient reported postoperative complications and the development of intractable pain. An exploratory operation for possible nerve entrapment was not successful, and the patient then underwent a cordotomy for pain relief. The patient developed either a partial lesion of the left ulnar nerve or nerve irritation as a result of the cordotomy performed at the upper thoracic spine. Pressure on the ulnar nerve at the olecranon groove may also have contributed to this. He was unable to recall exactly when this took place. Diagnostic electromyography was not performed.

At the time of the initial visit, the patient was ambulating independently with the aid of a cane. There was total sensory loss of the entire left trunk (below T5) and lower extremity. He thus was unaware of positioning of the left leg due to lack of proprioceptive feedback. He had difficulty ascending and descending stairs. Strength and active ROM of the entire right half of the body were normal, as were the left shoulder and elbow.

There were extreme hypersensitivity to touch at the ulnar distribution of the left hand (palmar surface) and paresthesia of the fourth and fifth fingers plus a background ache. The fourth and fifth fingers were kept in flexion at midrange. There was atrophy of the left dorsal web space (first dorsal interosseus) and abductor digiti quinti. Strength of the ulnar innervated musculature was as follows: flexor carpi ulnaris (F), interossei (P), abductor digiti quinti (P−). Passive ROM testing of the left hand was unable to be adequately performed due to causalgia-like hypersensitivity (hyperesthesia) to touch. The left lower extremity exhibited fair to good strength throughout except for the hip flexors, which were graded as P−. The patient was unable to perform active ROM satisfactorily unless he observed the leg moving (visual feedback).

Goals: Improve ambulatory ability, function of left hand, and control hyperesthesia.

Treatment Plan: The patient was unable to tolerate active-assistive ROM exercises to the hand or even the placement of biofeedback electrodes because of painful hyperesthesia. T.E.N.S. was used successfully to control discomfort, which allowed for the initiation of electrical stimulation and EMG biofeedback for muscle re-education followed by exercise (Figs. 9-81 to 9-83). EMG biofeedback training, strengthening, and gait training were initiated for the left lower extremity.

The patient obtained 1 to 2 hours of complete relief of hyperesthesia and pain after a 30-minute stimulation period of T.E.N.S. The patient thus desired to obtain a T.E.N.S. unit, and a prescription was obtained for rental.

The patient improved considerably with treatments. On 11/14/78 he reported a 35 percent decrease in overall discomfort of the hand without the use of T.E.N.S. and was continuing to use the T.E.N.S. unit for relief four times a day. A ¼-inch shoe lift was obtained on the right to allow for easier movement of the left leg due to weakness of the hip flexors. Prism glasses were suggested as an additional aid since the patient cannot ambulate sufficiently without observing the left leg. Strength of the left hand musculature increased to within the good range and was now functional.

The patient desired to purchase the unit. Follow-up questionnaires were not returned, but a telephone conversation with the patient on 2/2/81 revealed continued satisfaction with the unit. He was at the time using it whenever discomfort increased, such as during damp and humid weather. A 30-minute stimulation period continued to provide very good pain relief for 2- to 3-hour periods.

Case Study 27 discusses the need for the use of adjunctive T.E.N.S. to allow for the performance of gentle Grade I and Grade II oscillating techniques to the cervical spine. Due to the extreme long-standing discomfort, this patient was unable to tolerate attempts at increasing severe cervical hypomobility unless T.E.N.S. was used during the procedure (Fig. 9-84).

Case Study 27

Clarifying Evaluation: A 35-year-old male referred on 6/27/79. The patient was hit on the left side of his forehead by a cable hoist and thrown against a steel wall on 2/23/78. He was hospitalized until 3/3/78 for bed rest and was heavily medicated. X-rays were negative. Patient complained of headaches (frontal, temporal, and occipital) associated with an apparent postconcussion syndrome.

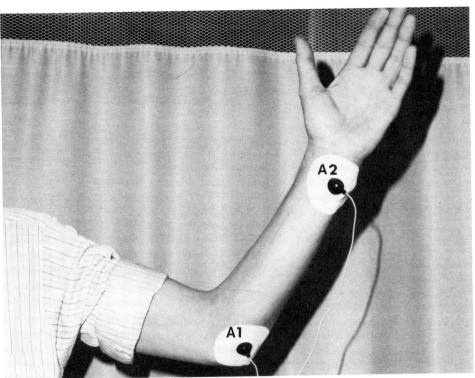

FIGURE 9-81. *Dx:* Ulnar nerve lesion with hyperesthesia. *Electrode placement technique:* Single-channel, unilateral. *Electrode placement sites:* A1, Just below groove between medial epicondyle and olecranon. A2, Ulnar aspect of wrist, superior to tendon of flexor carpi ulnaris. *Anatomic characteristics:* A1, Corresponds to acupuncture point SI 8. A2, Corresponds to acupuncture points H 4–7. *Nerve innervation:* A1, Ulnar nerve and its medial cutaneous branches. A2, Ulnar nerve and its palmar cutaneous branches. *T.E.N.S. mode:* Conventional. *Electrodes:* MedGeneral circular carbon-silicone with transmission gel and 3M foam pad tape patches. *T.E.N.S. unit:* MedGeneral Microceptor. *Rationale:* Electrode placement above the level of the sensitive region, fourth and fifth fingers, provided the perception of electrical paresthesia to the fourth and fifth fingers to allow for relief of hyperesthesia. The large proprioceptive fiber stimulation via conventional T.E.N.S. presumably balanced the nociceptive small-fiber input at the dorsal horn.

In July 1978, he was weaned from the heavy medication he had been taking since hospitalization and began to complain of severe neck pain and increasingly worse headaches. He returned to work on light and restricted duty, had to stop for a while, and then returned to work in late August. Pain went away "somewhat" at that time but returned as he continued working until he could no longer stand the neck and head pain. He was able to work until March 1979 and had been receiving physical therapy three times a week in the form of moist heat, ultrasound, massage, and mechanical traction but without benefit. He was only able to tolerate 12 lb of mechanical intermittent traction.

Presently, patient complains of right sided suboccipital pain and frontal, temporal, vertex, and occipital headaches. Pain is described as a constant ache that increases with any manual work. He gets severe headaches only three to four times every month but has a constant low-grade headache. There is no referral of pain into the upper extremities.

Active ROM of the cervical spine shows limitations by 50 percent in right rotation and 75 percent in backward bending. A bilateral 25 percent limitation exists in side bending. Pain was

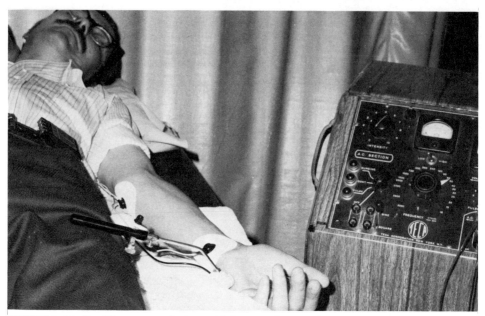

FIGURE 9-82. *Dx:* Ulnar nerve lesion with hyperesthesia. The use of T.E.N.S. to allow for muscle re-education. *Electrode placement technique:* Single-channel, unilateral. *T.E.N.S. mode:* Conventional. *Rationale:* Characteristics of stimulation sites explained in Figure 9-81. Patient was initially unable to tolerate electrical stimulation to abductor digiti quinti unless T.E.N.S. was used during the procedure. The large proprioceptive fiber stimulation via conventional T.E.N.S. presumably balanced the nociceptive small-fiber input at the dorsal horn.

increased with right rotation or backward bending actively or passively. Testing of the C1–T1 myotomes revealed weakness due only to pain within the right-sided musculature. Upper extremity reflexes were WNL, and sensation was intact. A great deal of tenderness even to mild palpation existed in the suboccipital and upper cervical region bilaterally but was greater on the right. There were no upper trapezius trigger points but splenius capitis trigger points were evident, which on pressure resulted in vertex and frontal headaches.

Gentle manual compression of the cervical spine increased pain, while gentle manual traction and suboccipital stretching decreased pain. Vertebral artery test was negative.

Goals: Eliminate pain and return active ROM of cervical spine to normal.

Treatment Plan: This patient has already had an extensive course of therapy at another facility, which was ineffective.

It is noted that manipulation was prescribed but cannot be attempted due to severe muscle guarding and tenderness to even gentle palpation. A safer method was tried to gently mobilize the facet joints at occiput-atlas, atlas-axis, axis-C3 primarily (as well as the rest of the cervical spine) initially into the less painful range and gradually work into the area of limitation. Muscle guarding prior to mobilization can be decreased by electrical stimulation to the cervical spine. The area is much too tender to tolerate massage, but gentle manual traction directed to the suboccipital region was tolerated and would be beneficial. The long-standing nature of the patient's problem and his low pain threshold in the suboccipital areas necessitate a slow, easy approach.

With the physician's approval, treatment as outlined above began on a 3-days-a-week basis. Progress notes were forwarded periodically.

Progress Note 7/27/79: Patient is progressing very well. The use of T.E.N.S. during mobilization controls pain sufficiently to allow for performance of the technique. He reports the headaches that

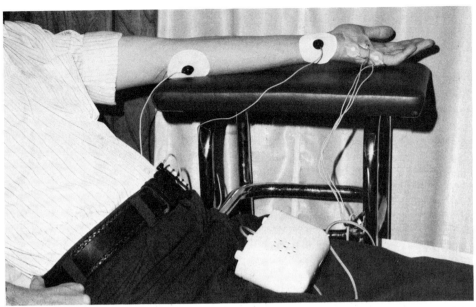

FIGURE 9-83. *Dx:* Ulnar nerve lesion with hyperesthesia. The use of T.E.N.S. to allow for biofeedback training. *Electrode placement technique:* Single-channel, unilateral. *T.E.N.S. mode:* Conventional. *Rationale:* Characteristics of stimulation sites explained in Figure 9-81. Patient was initially unable to tolerate the placement of biofeedback sensors on the abductor digiti quinti unless T.E.N.S. was used during the procedure. There was no interference by T.E.N.S. with the EMG biofeedback (Cyborg J 33). The larger proprioceptive fiber stimulation via conventional T.E.N.S. presumably balanced the nociceptive small-fiber input at the dorsal horn.

were constant prior to the initiation of treatment now occur only twice a week. He states that he feels relatively normal the majority of the time. He is able to sleep through the night now without awakening in pain.

Active ROM of the cervical spine is now within normal range in all directions. Some residual stiffness still causes pain in right rotation and backward bending, but he is able to complete the ROM in those directions. Previously he was limited by 50 percent in right rotation, 25 percent in side bending bilaterally, and 75 percent in backward bending. Suboccipital and upper cervical tenderness has decreased.

The patient has a better outlook now and is talking about gainful employment.

Periods of nausea and headaches that initially occurred immediately after treatment and persisted for 1 to 2 days now either do not occur or last only for a short time. Patient is now able to perform a home exercise program and has increased his daily activities.

Discharge Note 8/16/79: Treatments have been discontinued as of today. Patient now demonstrates totally normal active ROM of the cervical spine in all directions. He no longer complains of any cervical spine pain, and suboccipital tenderness has been eliminated. Headaches that previously were decreased to twice a week no longer occur except when he participates in strenuous physical work for a prolonged period of time.

The patient is presently on a PRN maintenance schedule. He calls for treatments when needed. When pain intensifies, he notices a loss of about 25 percent in right rotation and backward bending, which is relieved by joint mobilization and traction.

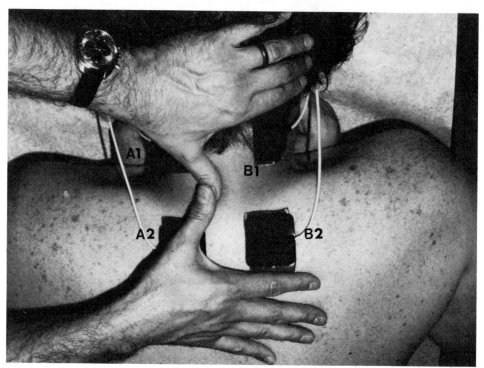

FIGURE 9-84. *Dx:* Chronic cervical strain. The use of T.E.N.S. during gentle articulation techniques to the cervical spine. *Electrode placement technique:* Dual-channel, longitudinal. *Electrode placement sites:* A1, Suboccipital depression. A2, Cervical-thoracic junction paraspinally (channel 1). B1 and B2, Same arrangement but on opposite side of spine (channel 2). *Anatomic characteristics:* A1 and B1, Motor/trigger point of splenius and semispinalis capitis. Corresponds to acupuncture point GB 20. A2 and B2, Segmental erector spinae motor point and local bladder meridian acupuncture point. *Nerve innervation:* A1 and B1, Greater and lesser occipital nerves. A2 and B2, Segmental posterior primary rami. *T.E.N.S. mode:* Conventional. *Electrodes:* Carbon-silicone with karaya pad. *T.E.N.S. unit:* Mentor 100. *Rationale:* Electrode arrangement provided for the perception of electrical paresthesia throughout the area of involvement to control pain during the rehabilitation process. Grades I and II mobilization techniques (lateral and central oscillations) being performed. Pain relief obtained by ongoing conventional T.E.N.S. and gentle joint mobilization to increase large-fiber proprioceptive input to cervical spine.

TRANSVERSE FRICTION MASSAGE AND CONTRACT-RELAX STRETCHING

Treatment consisting of transverse friction massage or contract-relax stretching and peripheral joint mobilization requires strong pain modulation since these techniques are frequently irritating and may compound the already existing discomfort. Modulation with brief, intense T.E.N.S. is a most effective stimulation mode in the performance of these techniques. Transverse friction massage is a manual technique employing deep friction over ligaments, tendons, and musculotendinous junctions.[93,180] It is performed in a direction transverse to the course of the involved tissue. The transverse friction serves to separate adhesions, break up scar tissue, smooth roughened surface, enlarge tendon sheaths, and cause a significant localized hyperemia.[93] Circulation is increased, mobility of soft tissue made easier, and pain decreased.

The parameters relative to brief, intense T.E.N.S.—high rate, wide width, and intensity to maximal tolerable level—are most effective in modulating the discomfort that occurs with transverse friction massage. A strong mode of stimulation is required and can be obtained by brief, intense T.E.N.S. using a high rate to avoid interference via rhythmic muscle contractions from low-rate stimulation. In some patients, this mode of T.E.N.S. can provide almost complete analgesia to the area between or distal to the stimulating electrodes, thus making transverse friction massage tolerable. Case Study 28 illustrates the use of T.E.N.S. to modulate pain during the performance of transverse friction massage.

Stimulation is instituted for at least 5 to 15 minutes prior to the procedure. Stimulation continues during the treatment, with electrodes placed above and below, medial and lateral, or crisscrossing over the specific aspect of the tendon or musculotendinous junction. Stimulation to the peripheral nerves innervating the involved tendon has also been successful. At the conclusion of the treatment, T.E.N.S. is usually continued for a few minutes in the conventional mode to relieve any discomfort that may persist. Patients with tendinitis receiving this technique may obtain a rental unit for home use if pain persists.

Case Study 28

Clarifying Evaluation: A 54-year-old woman initially seen 4/30/79 after an injury at work on 4/10/79. She uses heavy tongs and has hurt her wrist before in a similar manner. Her present complaint was of constant pain at the volar aspect of the wrist on the ulnar side, extending primarily to midforearm with mild paresthesia of the fourth and fifth fingers. Pain was aggravated by resistive wrist flexion, ulnar deviation, and passive stretching into extreme radial deviation. Discomfort of less intensity occurred with pronation and supination.

Active ROM revealed the following limitations: pronation 0 to 70 degrees, supination 0 to 45 degrees, wrist flexion 0 to 15 degrees, extension 0 to 45 degrees. Radial and ulnar deviation were not limited. There was a forward head and dowager's hump at the cervicothoracic junction, and active cervical ROM was limited by 25 percent in all directions except forward bending. Further testing of the cervical spine did not increase or decrease the wrist pain.

Goals: Eliminate pain and restore normal function.

Treatment Plan: Whirlpool with high-voltage galvanic stimulation followed by ultrasound and transverse friction massage to the tendon of the flexor carpi ulnaris. Gentle joint mobilization to be added as pain subsided.

Progress Note 5/9/79: The patient made excellent progress. She initially was unable to tolerate the transverse friction massage. We therefore used T.E.N.S. in a brief, intense mode for 10 minutes prior to as well as during the massage. This allowed for enough pain modulation so treatment could be effectively performed (Fig. 9-85).

Progress Note 5/16/79: Active ROM is WNL with only minimal pain at end-range. Paresthesia of the fourth and fifth fingers is just about gone, and only a slight ache remains at the flexor carpi ulnaris tendon. The use of brief, intense T.E.N.S. is no longer needed. The patient was discharged on 5/30/79 after having been pain-free for the prior week and returned to work but in a different capacity to avoid a recurrence of the tendinitis.

This method of brief, intense T.E.N.S. can also be beneficial in patients with acute subdeltoid bursitis. An excellent comprehensive treatment protocol with T.E.N.S. would include use of T.E.N.S. at home and outpatient physical therapy consisting of joint mobilization to maintain laxity of the capsule and mobility of the joint. The prevention of adhesive capsulitis, frequently seen after subdeltoid bursitis, and a faster and less costly rehabilitation process can be achieved with this protocol. When the bursitis has been resolved, T.E.N.S.

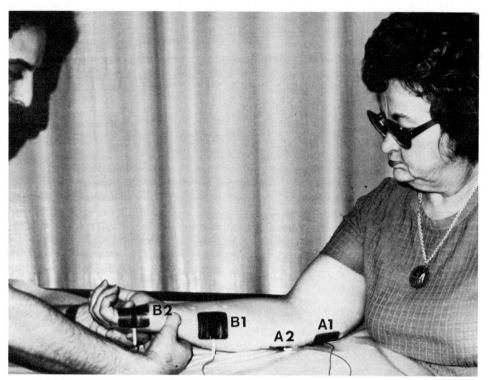

FIGURE 9-85. *Dx:* Tendinitis of flexor carpi ulnaris. *Electrode placement technique:* Dual-channel, unilateral (proximal and distal). *Electrode placement sites:* A1, Just above olecranon groove. A2, Just below olecranon groove (channel 1). B1, On volar surface of distal forearm about 2 inches proximal to second volar wrist crease overlying flexor carpi ulnaris tendon. B2, Ulnar aspect of hand (channel 2). *Anatomic characteristics:* A1, Corresponds to acupuncture point H 3. A2, Corresponds to acupuncture point SI 8. B1, Corresponds to acupuncture point H 4. B2, Motor point of abductor digiti quinti. *Nerve innervation:* A1, Superficial aspect of ulnar nerve proximal to olecranon groove. B1, Ulnar nerve. B2, Ulnar nerve and its palmar cutaneous branch. *T.E.N.S. mode:* Brief, intense. *Electrodes:* Silicone-carbon, transmission gel, and tape patch. *T.E.N.S. unit:* Mentor 100. *Rationale:* Electrode placement and stimulation mode produced significant electroanalgesia to allow for tolerance of therapeutic procedure (transverse friction massage to flexor carpi ulnaris tendon).

is no longer necessary, and the therapist can complete the rehabilitation program with the addition of therapeutic exercise.

Brief, intense T.E.N.S. has also been effective in modulating the pain that occurs during the treatment program for profound adhesive capsulitis. Such patients usually have shoulder bursitis, tendinitis, or trauma and either have not seen their physician early enough or received improper treatment. These patients are able to tolerate preliminary gentle joint mobilization techniques, but cannot tolerate contract-relax stretching, which may be necessary to regain full function. Intense pain occurs, usually related to the soft tissue lying in the direction of the stretching, hindering progress or completely negating it.

Complete pain control is unable to be achieved, but by brief, intense stimulation prior to and during the therapy enough discomfort can be modulated to allow continual progress on a treatment to treatment basis. Obviously, breakthrough pain will occur with T.E.N.S., making it totally safe to use as long as the following guidelines are adhered to:

1. Thoroughly evaluate the patient prior to using T.E.N.S.
2. Always grade active and passive range of motion (ROM) prior to T.E.N.S. at each treatment session.
3. Always reassess quality and distribution of pain at present end-range prior to T.E.N.S. at each treatment session.
4. Do not increase passive ROM beyond the pretested range by more than 10 to 20 degrees during any treatment session with T.E.N.S. for peripheral joints.
5. Do not perform mobilization of the spinal joints beyond Grade I and II oscillations with the use of T.E.N.S.

Adherence to these guidelines should avoid the possibility of tearing or damaging soft-tissue structures beyond that of adhesions.

Peripheral joint hypomobility and soft-tissue restriction following surgery, fractures, or soft-tissue trauma may necessitate brief, intense T.E.N.S. to obtain effective rehabilitation. We have successfully used this mode of T.E.N.S. to perform joint mobilization and contract-relax stretching in such patients. Case Study 29 describes the successful use of T.E.N.S. in the rehabilitation of a patient with chronic bilateral adhesive capsulitis. The prescription from the referring physician called for "vigorous passive ROM, three times a week for 1 month." The patient stated that she was told by the referring physician that manipulation of the shoulders under anesthesia would be performed if significant progress was not apparent after the month of therapy. In light of that statement, it was decided to perform joint mobilization and contract-relax stretching with pain control via T.E.N.S. The brief, intense mode was used, and tolerance to strong stimulation was gradually increased over the first few treatment sessions. The patient was unable to adequately perform joint mobilization and contract-relax stretching techniques without ongoing T.E.N.S.

The assessment of this patient's pain showed that at initial end-range, stretch pain was not present in the shoulder, but primarily in the bicipital and lateral arm regions. Two T.E.N.S. units were used (one stimulator per extremity).

Case Study 29

Clarifying Evaluation: A 37-year-old female with bilateral adhesive capsulitis of shoulders referred on 10/9/78. Etiology was possibly related to medication that she was taking for epilepsy. The patient was taking clonazepam (Clonopin), and side effects of this drug are muscle weakness and pain.[194] This may have certainly played a contributory role in the patient's bilateral shoulder dysfunction. The medication was subsequently changed. She also fell and landed on the left shoulder on 12/25/77. She was previously treated as an outpatient in a hospital physical therapy department with moist heat, ultrasound, and therapeutic exercise. Little progress was made. Active ROM as tested in the supine position showed the following:

	RIGHT	LEFT
Flexion	0–100°	0–120°
Abduction	0–85°	0–90°
Internal rotation	0–20°	0–15°
External rotation	0–15°	0–20°

Pain was present primarily not in the shoulder region but in the anterolateral aspect of the arms from the shoulder to the elbow. Active ROM of the cervical spine was WNL and pain-free. Neither gentle manual traction nor compression of the cervical spine had any effect on the upper extremity pain. Weakness due to pain existed primarily in abduction and rotation bilaterally. Other motions were within the good range.

Goals: Increase ROM to allow for normal functional usage of upper extremities.

Treatment Plan: Joint mobilization techniques to the glenohumeral, scapulothoracic, and acromioclavicular joints followed by gentle contract-relax stretching and therapeutic exercise. In an effort to reduce the pain during therapy, brief, intense T.E.N.S. was used adjunctively (Fig. 9-86). Prior to using T.E.N.S., the active and passive ranges were tested at each treatment session, and mobilization was not performed more than 10 to 20 degrees beyond that range while T.E.N.S. was being used to

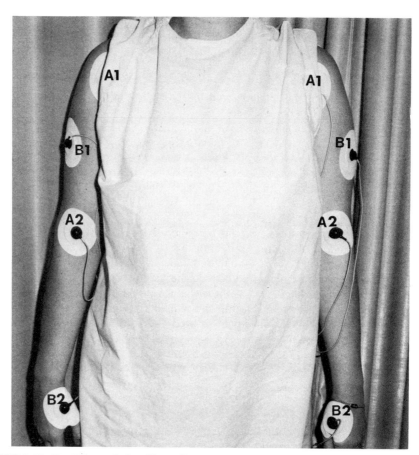

FIGURE 9-86. *Dx:* Bilateral shoulder adhesive capsulitis. *Electrode placement technique:* Dual-channel, unilateral linear pathway. *Electrode placement sites:* A1, Between first and second ribs just medial to coracoid process. A2, In antecubital fossa on radial side of biceps tendon (channel 1). B1, Lateral arm at deltoid insertion. B2, Dorsal web space (channel 2). *Note:* A second T.E.N.S. unit was used on the contralateral arm simultaneously with the same electrode array. *Anatomic characteristics:* A1, Motor point of coracobrachialis. Corresponds to acupuncture point LU 1. A2, Motor point of brachialis. Corresponds to acupuncture point LU 5. B1, Corresponds to acupuncture point LI 14. B2, Motor/trigger points of first dorsal interosseus and adductor pollicis. Corresponds to acupuncture point LI 4. *T.E.N.S. mode:* Brief, intense. *Electrodes:* MedGeneral circular carbon-silicone electrodes, with transmission gel and 3M foam adhesive patches. *T.E.N.S. unit:* Two MedGeneral Microceptors. *Rationale:* Two T.E.N.S. units (one per arm) were used as this was a bilateral problem necessitating two channels per arm. Electrode placement produced the perception of significant electrical paresthesia throughout pain distribution to decrease pain, thus increasing tolerance to the therapeutic procedures.

decrease discomfort. This prevented any possibility of damage to soft-tissue structures. T.E.N.S. will not mask breakthrough pain and is a safe adjunctive modality in such cases. The patient was also instructed in a home program of daily therapeutic exercises. Treatments were given three times a week.

Follow-up: The patient made substantial improvements in active ROM of both shoulders at the end of the first month, thereby negating the need for manipulation under anesthesia.

RIGHT SHOULDER	INITIAL	FOLLOW-UP
Flexion	0–100°	0–140°
Abduction	0–85°	0–120°
Internal rotation	0–20°	0–40°
External rotation	0–15°	0–25°
LEFT SHOULDER	INITIAL	FOLLOW-UP
Flexion	0–120°	0–155°
Abduction	0–90°	0–140°
Internal rotation	0–15°	0–45°
External rotation	0–20°	0–50°

The left upper extremity consistently was better than the right upper extremity. The right shoulder girdle was also limited in horizontal adduction, which was normal on the left. Improvements continued at a consistent rate, and we were able to discontinue the use of T.E.N.S. for pain control during treatment after the first month. This was extremely beneficial initially to allow for relaxation on the part of the patient and corresponding mobilization. Pain no longer represented a strong limiting factor in progress. Treatments continued three times a week, and the patient continued to follow a vigorous home exercise program.

Follow-up (5 weeks later): The patient continued to make excellent progress. The left shoulder was now totally normal in *active* ROM in every direction. The right shoulder showed substantial improvement and gains continued to occur. Treatments continued three times a week, consisting of joint mobilization techniques designed to provide increased capsular mobility as well as joint play and component motions. This was followed by gentle contract-relax stretching and strengthening exercises. *Passively*, the following ranges were obtained on the right: flexion to 170 degrees, normal abduction (180 degrees), internal rotation to 80 degrees, and external rotation to 70 degrees.

Discharge Note: Treatments were discontinued on 12/28/78. The patient displayed completely normal active ROM of both shoulders in all directions. Strength was also normal, and there was no residual pain. She could do everything, including sleeping on her side, which she had been unable to do for quite some time. The patient was advised to continue to perform her home exercise program at least once a day for the next month.

Case Study 30 discusses the role of T.E.N.S. in the rehabilitation of a patient with adhesive capsulitis and tendinitis.

Case Study 30

Clarifying Evaluation: A 56-year-old male referred for rehabilitation on 6/10/80. History began in September 1979 when he injured the left shoulder from a fall. X-rays were negative. The patient was referred with a diagnosis of adhesive capsulitis of left shoulder. He complained of periodic sharp pain at the shoulder with movement. Active ROM of the cervical spine was pain-free and WNL.

Active ROM of the left shoulder revealed a painful arc at 90 to 110 degrees of abduction. Range of motion measurements showed flexion 125 degrees, abduction 90 degrees, external rotation 25 degrees, and normal internal rotation. Pain was the primary limiting factor. Isometric resistive testing revealed increased pain upon abduction and external rotation. All other motions were painless. Strength of the left shoulder was graded as good within the active range as compared with normal on the right.

Goals: Decrease pain, increase ROM and function.

Treatment Plan: Ultrasound followed by transverse friction massage to the infraspinatus and supraspinatus tendons. This was followed by coldpack to the shoulder for 10 minutes, joint mobilization, and therapeutic exercise three times a week. The patient was also instructed in a home exercise program.

Active ROM improved, but there remained a limitation in abduction due to pain, which hampered progress. T.E.N.S. was thus started adjunctively to control pain sufficiently to allow for gentle contract-relax stretching and therapeutic exercises to be employed. The brief, intense mode was used and electrodes arranged to provide for stimulation throughout the pain distribution (Fig. 9-87). A supraspinatus tendinitis frequently produces pain at the musculotendinous junction through the deltoid insertion and occasionally within the distal extent of the C5-6 dermomyotome.

T.E.N.S. provided enough pain control so that the patient could abduct through the full range after a few treatments of T.E.N.S. plus eccentric abduction exercises. The arm was initially passively abducted (painful region [90 to 110 degrees] avoided by downward distraction of the humerus) to end-range and a series of eccentric then concentric exercises performed in ever-increasing arcs. This was able to be performed only with simultaneous use of T.E.N.S.

The patient was discharged on 7/31/80, at which time he demonstrated normal active ROM of the left shoulder in all directions. He did not need to use the T.E.N.S. at home, and therefore it was purely an adjunctive modality during office treatment. The patient was seen a few months later when he came in to visit the clinic and reported that he was doing fine.

We have successfully used the brief, intense mode for other patients with adhesive capsulitis who required T.E.N.S. to control pain sufficiently to allow for the performance of rehabilitating manual techniques. Figures 9-88 and 9-89 illustrate an electrode arrangement using five electrodes to control diffuse, intense pain. This patient is presently undergoing treatment. Initially, no progress was able to be obtained to increase range of motion. Pain was too intense at end-range. The addition of T.E.N.S. before and during joint mobilization and contract-relax stretching was able to take the intolerable edge off the pain to allow for increases in range of motion. Once active range of motion was able to be increased by 50 percent from the initial levels, T.E.N.S. was no longer needed.

The use of T.E.N.S. in this manner does not allow for complete pain control when joint mobilization or contract-relax stretching techniques are employed. However, if T.E.N.S. is successful in decreasing 25 percent of the discomfort, then 25 percent more progress can be achieved. It is necessary that stimulation is ongoing during, as well as prior to, the manual techniques because pain is most intense when the procedures are performed. The patient can control the intensity of stimulation as needed.

Case Study 31 deals with a patient who underwent corrective surgery following recurrent patellar subluxation.

Case Study 31

Clarifying Evaluation: A 32-year-old female who was referred for rehabilitation following surgery for recurrent subluxations of the right patella. Surgery was performed on 6/21/80. The patient was referred on 7/10/80, at which time she ambulated with the knee in full extension. Active flexion could be obtained only to 15 degrees, and gentle passive ROM could not be tolerated due to pain around the knee but worse on the medial aspect. She was also unable to voluntarily contract the quadriceps.
Goals: Control pain to allow for rehabilitative techniques to increase strength and function.
Treatment Plan: T.E.N.S. was added to the treatment program, which consisted of high-voltage galvanic stimulation, ultrasound, joint mobilization, therapeutic exercise, and EMG biofeedback training for muscle re-education. The patient was unable to tolerate gentle grade I and II articulatory techniques, let alone contract-relax stretching to increase ROM. T.E.N.S. was introduced to control pain sufficiently to allow for patient tolerance of rehabilitative techniques.

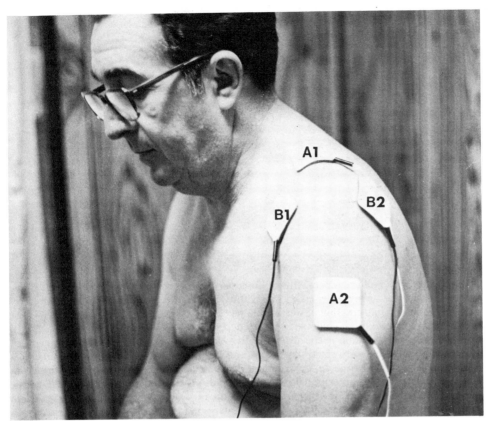

FIGURE 9-87. *Dx:* **Supraspinatus tendinitis and adhesive capsulitis.** *Electrode placement technique:* **Dual-channel, unilateral crisscross.** *Electrode placement sites:* **A1, In depression bordered by the acromion laterally, spine of scapula posteriorly, and clavicle anteriorly. A2, Insertion of deltoid at lateral aspect of arm (channel 1). B1, In depression below acromion anteriorly. B2, In depression below acromion posteriorly (channel 2).** *Anatomic characteristics:* **A1, Musculotendinous junction of supraspinatus. Corresponds to acupuncture point LI 16. A2, Corresponds to acupuncture point LI 14. B1, Motor point of anterior deltoid. Corresponds to acupuncture point LI 15. B2, Motor point of posterior deltoid. Corresponds to acupuncture point TW 14.** *Nerve innervation:* **A1, Posterolateral branch of supraclavicular nerve. A2, Upper lateral cutaneous nerve (axillary). B1, Upper lateral cutaneous nerve branch of axillary. B2, Intercostal brachial, upper lateral cutaneous nerve, and dorsal ramus of T2.** *T.E.N.S. mode:* **Brief, intense.** *Electrodes:* **Stim-tech Dermaforms (karaya).** *T.E.N.S. unit:* **Empi.** *Rationale:* **Significant electrical paresthesia perceived throughout pain distribution to allow for tolerance to therapeutic exercise techniques.**

Conventional T.E.N.S. was tried initially, but this mode could not provide enough ongoing pain control. Brief, intense stimulation was then applied for 10 to 15 minutes prior to treatment and during the manual therapy. Electrode placement was arranged to provide for current flow across the knee in a crisscross fashion. Electrodes were applied over optimal stimulation sites, providing for stimulation of nerves innervating the knee (Figs. 9-90, 9-91).

Progress in knee flexion was then able to be obtained up to a maximum of 80 degrees. When this point was reached, a plateau occurred, after which further increases could not be obtained and the patient would lose range between treatment sessions. She was able to exercise at home with the

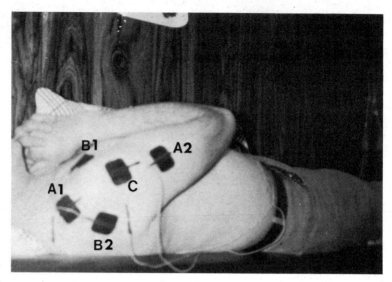

FIGURE 9-88. *Dx:* **Adhesive capsulitis of shoulder.** *Electrode placement technique:* **Dual-channel, unilateral, using three-lead cable with two Y adapters.** *Electrode placement sites:* **A1, Musculotendinous junction of supraspinatus. A2, Insertion of deltoid at lateral aspect of arm (negative electrodes of channel 1). B1, In depression below acromion anteriorly. B2, In depression below acromion posteriorly (negative electrodes of channel 2). C, Lateral aspect of arm at midpoint between electrodes A1 and A2 (positive electrode).** *Anatomic characteristics:* **A1, Corresponds to acupuncture point LI 16. A2, Corresponds to acupuncture point LI 14. B1, Motor point of anterior deltoid. Corresponds to acupuncture point LI 15. B2, Motor point of posterior deltoid. Corresponds to acupuncture point TW 14. C, Motor point of middle deltoid.** *Nerve innervation:* **A1, Posterolateral branch of supraclavicular nerve. A2, Upper lateral cutaneous nerve (axillary). B1, Upper lateral cutaneous nerve (axillary). B2, Intercostal brachial, upper lateral cutaneous nerve, and dorsal ramus of T2. C, Posterolateral branch of supraclavicular.** *T.E.N.S. Mode:* **Brief, intense.** *Electrodes:* **Medtronic Neuro-Aid (synthetic polymer).** *T.E.N.S. unit:* **Biostim System 10 (three-lead cable and two Y adapters).** *Rationale:* **This electrode array produces electrical transmission from the central positive electrode to all four negative electrodes. Stimulation is perceived at the most painful area (location of positive electrode) and to the periphery of pain in all directions (four negative electrodes). Strong stimulation (brief, intense) was needed with five electrodes.**

aid of the T.E.N.S. unit but felt her knee tighten up between exercise sessions. The referring physician was contacted and the patient re-admitted to the hospital. Subsequent exploratory surgery revealed the presence of a neuroma, which was removed. The patient did well after this, without needing the stimulator. The initial treatment program plus biofeedback training was re-instituted, and good functional mobility was obtained.

PHANTOM LIMB PAIN AND HYPERESTHESIA

Conventional and brief, intense T.E.N.S. have been used successfully to control phantom limb pain.[79,80,83,98,109] Electrodes have been placed on painful trigger points and related superficial peripheral nerve aspects and spinal cord segments giving rise to innervation of the painful region. In some cases, contralateral stimulation has been helpful as well as electrodes placed within a prosthesis.[195,196] Noordenbos states that hyperesthesia will dis-

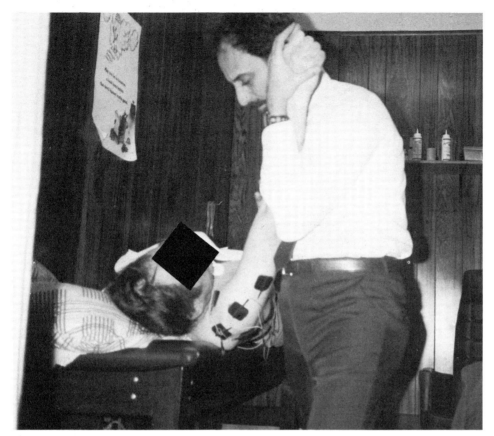

FIGURE 9-89. *Dx:* **Adhesive capsulitis. Contract-relax stretching performed with ongoing brief, intense T.E.N.S.** *Note:* **See Figure 9-88 for information regarding electrode placement technique.**

appear if T.E.N.S. electrodes are placed above the level of the lesion and paresthesia is produced in the hyperesthetic area.[197] This is consistent with our recommendation of stimulation proximal to the level of a peripheral nerve lesion.

Gyory and Caine reported on a specific case involving a patient with a below-elbow amputation.[195] Initial use of T.E.N.S. for phantom pain produced 20 minutes of pain relief after a 20- to 30-minute treatment period. The length of relief (aftereffect) increased over 10 days until the patient was virtually pain-free when the prosthesis was not worn but for only 20 minutes when wearing the prosthesis. Electrodes were then incorporated within the prosthetic socket, and stimulation given for 15 to 20 minutes at 25 percent of full amplitude with a frequency of 100 Hz, which produced 2¼ to 4 hours of pain relief. Pulse width was not given, but it is assumed that it was in line with conventional T.E.N.S. parameters.

Gunn has reported on the experiments of Lomo concerning denervation supersensitivity in animal muscle.[198–200] Hyperesthesia (hypersensitivity) was effectively diminished with electrical stimulation of 100 Hz at low amplitude.

Gessler and Struppler have presented another alternative to electrode placement for phantom limb pain.[201] They used T.E.N.S. with 10 patients suffering from chronic, cramp-

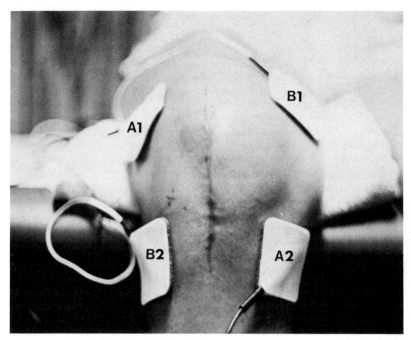

FIGURE 9-90. *Dx: Post–surgical repair of recurrent patellar subluxations. Electrode placement technique:* Dual-channel, crisscross. *Electrode placement sites:* A1, Two inches above lateral aspect of patellar base. A2, Just below medial condyle of tibia at level of tibial tuberosity (channel 1). B1, Two inches above medial aspect of patellar base. B2, Anterior and inferior to fibular head (channel 2). *Anatomic characteristics:* A1, Motor point of vastus lateralis. Corresponds to acupuncture point ST 33–34. A2, Corresponds to acupuncture point SP 9. B1, Motor/trigger point of vastus medialis. Corresponds to acupuncture point GB 34. B2, Common peroneal nerve. *T.E.N.S. mode:* Brief, intense (cycled), on 2 seconds, off 3 seconds. *Electrodes:* Stim-tech Dermaforms (karaya). *T.E.N.S. unit:* Empi DC. *Rationale:* Electrode arrangement provides for a concentration of current flow (electrical paresthesia) at the patella. The cycled mode with brief, intense stimulation allowed for contraction to occur during the on phase and relaxation plus stretching during the off phase.

like (flexion) phantom pain. They applied T.E.N.S. to the nerve supplying the corresponding extensor muscles and reported pain relief in all patients. The patients stated that they felt an opening of the cramp-like flexion. Best results were obtained with a 100-Hz, 0.2-msec pulse duration at an intensity of 5 to 20 mA. Stimulation of the nerve to the flexor muscle increased the phantom pain.

We have treated one patient who had a complete upper extremity disarticulation due to osteogenic sarcoma. At the time of referral she had been having phantom pain throughout the whole arm for more than 1 year described as constant elbow, hand, and finger flexion. This was preceded by 2 years of pain prior to the amputation. Extensive electrode placements ipsilaterally, contralaterally, cervical spine, transcranial, and varied combinations thereof were not helpful. The method of Gessler and Struppler could not be tried as there was no peripheral nerve or stump available. Stimulation at the pain-free surgical site at the region containing axillary hair also proved negative. Stimulation of the contralateral radial nerve and distal acupuncture points ipsilaterally and contralaterally were also not effective nor were different stimulation modes. It was determined that the long-standing

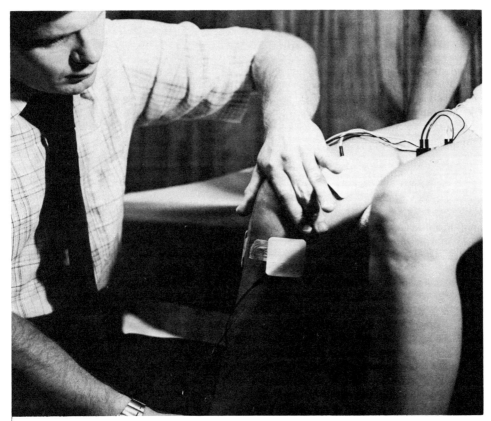

FIGURE 9-91. *Dx:* **Post–surgical repair of recurrent patellar subluxations: performance of contract-relax stretching. Electrode placement characteristics explained in Figure 9-90. Thomas E. Shaw, R.P.T. (partner in Delaware Valley Physical Therapy Associates) performing contract-relax stretching with brief, intense T.E.N.S. in cycled mode. Joint mobilization to increase capsular laxity performed prior to contract-relax stretching.**

pain, lack of any stump, and use of oxycodone hydrochloride (Percodan) for at least a year negated any benefit. It was suggested to the referring physician that a stellate ganglion block, weaning from narcotic medication, and use of tryptophan be tried prior to any surgical intervention. T.E.N.S. could also be attempted at a later date. However, Parry has had success with patients who have had total amputations of the upper limb.[98]

Case Study 32 describes the use of T.E.N.S. to control phantom finger pain after a traumatic amputation of the distal phalanx of the index finger. T.E.N.S. was also employed to allow for the performance of joint mobilization and therapeutic exercise (Figs. 9-92 to 9-94).

Case Study 32

Clarifying Evaluation: A 30-year-old policeman who sustained a traumatic amputation of the distal phalanx of the right index finger on 8/21/80. Patient was referred for therapy to increase active ROM

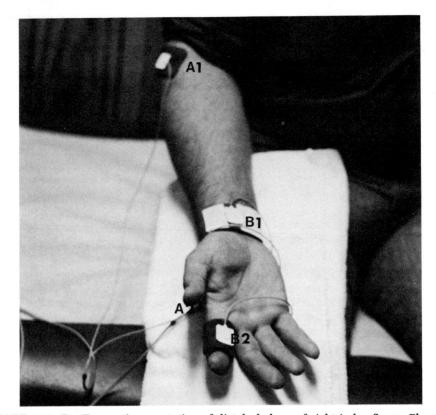

FIGURE 9-92. *Dx:* Traumatic amputation of distal phalanx of right index finger. Phantom finger pain and hyperesthesia. *Electrode placement technique:* Dual-channel, unilateral. *Electrode placement sites:* A1, In depression at lateral aspect of elbow crease with elbow flexed to 90 degrees. A2, Dorsal web space (channel 1). B1, On volar surface of wrist just proximal to distal crease. B2, On volar surface of index finger just proximal to PIP joint. *Anatomic characteristics:* A1, Motor/trigger point of brachioradialis. Corresponds to acupuncture point LI 11. A2, Motor/trigger point of first dorsal interosseus and adductor pollicis. Corresponds to acupuncture point LI 4. B1, Corresponds to acupuncture points LU 7–9, H 4–7, and P 5–6. B2, Overlies palmar cutaneous branches of radial and musculocutaneous nerves. *Nerve innervation:* A1, Posterior cutaneous nerve of forearm; intercostal, brachial, and superficial radial nerves. A2, Superficial radial and musculocutaneous (sensory); ulnar (motor). B1, Lower lateral cutaneous branch of musculocutaneous, superficial radial, ulnar nerve (palmar cutaneous branch), median nerve, and medial cutaneous nerve of forearm. B2, Palmar cutaneous branches of median and radial plus musculocutaneous nerves. *T.E.N.S. mode:* Conventional. *Electrodes:* Lec-Tec karaya electrodes with Velcro backing. Adapter for Velcro connection employed. *T.E.N.S. unit:* Medical Devices Ultra II. *Rationale:* Electrode array provides for the perception of electrical paresthesia throughout all surfaces of the index finger.

of the PIP joint. Active ROM measurements showed full extension, but flexion of 0 to 75 degrees and only 0 to 30 degrees existed at the MCP and PIP joints, respectively.

The patient complained of constant discomfort primarily at the distal end and volar surface of the finger. There was hyperesthesia to touch and a feeling of "cold" at all times. Periodically, the finger would throb and shake. Associated phantom sensations were also present.

Goals: Decrease pain, increase function.

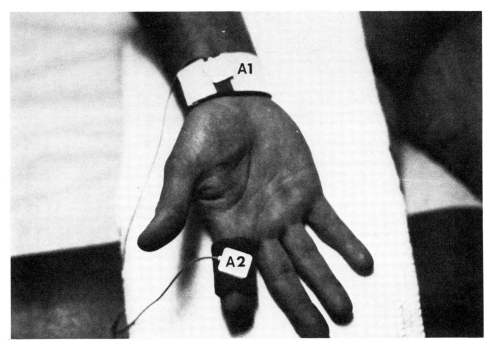

FIGURE 9-93. *Dx:* Traumatic amputation of distal phalanx of right index finger. Phantom finger pain and hyperesthesia. *Electrode placement technique:* Single-channel, unilateral. *Electrode placement sites:* A1, On volar surface of wrist just proximal to distal crease. A2, On volar surface of index finger just proximal to PIP joint. *Nerve innervation:* A1, Lower lateral cutaneous branch of musculocutaneous, superficial radial, ulnar nerve (palmar cutaneous branch), median nerve, and medial cutaneous nerve of forearm. A2, Palmar cutaneous branches of median and radial plus musculocutaneous nerves. *T.E.N.S. mode:* Conventional. *Electrodes:* Lec-Tec karaya with Velcro adapters. *T.E.N.S. unit:* Single-channel Stimpulse (Stim-tech). *Rationale:* This single-channel technique provided benefit equal to that obtained with the dual-channel array in Figure 9-92. Therefore, a single-channel stimulator was ordered for patient use at home.

Treatment Plan: A treatment program of whirlpool with high-voltage galvanic stimulation, followed by ultrasound to the PIP joint, joint mobilization (Fig. 9-94), and therapeutic exercise was initiated. The patient, however, was unable to tolerate gentle Grade I mobilization or contract-relax stretching due to pain and hyperesthesia. Therefore, T.E.N.S. was sucessfully used to control pain during these techniques. In this particular case, the first electrode placement array was designed to stimulate the radial, median, and ulnar nerves (Fig. 9-92). This method turned out to be successful. However, a single-channel setup was then used after the patient reported that pain was solely on the volar surface of the index finger (Fig. 9-93).

The patient borrowed a T.E.N.S. unit for a few days and obtained just about complete pain relief lasting for 2 to 6 hours after a 20- to 30-minute stimulation period. The patient subsequently obtained a T.E.N.S. unit on rental and has continued to use it at home as part of the home exercise program. As of the date of this writing, 2/2/81, the patient continues to use the unit as reported by the referring physician but has not returned the follow-up questionnaire.

As of September 1980, we had used T.E.N.S. prior to and during specific therapeutic procedures on a total of 23 patients. The results of this treatment method are summarized in Table 9-13. The grading of results as A, B, or C were based upon the following criteria:

TABLE 9-13. Pain Modulation with T.E.N.S. During Specific Therapeutic Procedures

Patient	Dx	Rx	T.E.N.S. Mode	Results
M.C.	Bilateral adhesive capsulitis shoulders	Joint mobilization, contract-relax stretch	Brief, intense	A
R.T.	Ankle sprain (left)	Joint mobilization, contract-relax stretch	Brief, intense	B
G.M°	Postop patella subluxation	Joint mobilization, contract-relax stretch	Brief, intense	B
E.M.	Open reduction left elbow fx	Joint mobilization, contract-relax stretch	Brief, intense	A
M.S.	Vascular insult left long finger	Joint mobilization, contract-relax stretch, ther. ex.	Pulse-train	B
J.F.	Fx olecranon	Joint mobilization, contract-relax stretch	Conventional	B
C.G.	Adhesive capsulitis right shoulder	Joint mobilization, contract-relax stretch	Brief, intense	B
G.F.	Subscapularis and bicipital tendinitis	Transverse friction massage, contract-relax stretch	Brief, intense	A
M.W.	Supraspinatus tendinitis, adhesive capsulitis (chronic)	Transverse friction massage, joint mobilization, contract-relax stretch	Brief, intense	B
M.N.	Colles' fx right, sympathetic reflex dystrophy	Joint mobilization, contract relax stretch	Conventional; brief, intense	B
C.S.	Adhesive capsulitis, left shoulder	Joint mobilization, contract relax stretch	Brief, intense	B
C.M.	Left supraspinatus tendinitis, adhesive capsulitis	Joint mobilization, contract relax stretch	Brief, intense	A
E.A.	Right flexor carpi radialis tendinitis	Transverse friction massage	Brief, intense	A
H.G.	Sprain right wrist	Joint mobilization	Conventional	B
R.R.	Post-carpal tunnel syndrome causalgia	Ther. ex.	Conventional	A
W.N.	Postcordotomy ulnar n. lesion causalgia of left hand	Biofeedback, muscle stim, re-education	Conventional	A
G.N.	Cervical strain A/A	Joint mobilization, grade I	Conventional	A
P.M°	Cervical strain	Joint mobilization, grade I	Conventional	A
A.G.	Cervical strain A/A	Joint mobilization, grade I	Conventional	C
C.B.	Cervical strain A/A	Joint mobilization, grade I	Conventional	A
A.C.	Chronic LBP postlaminectomy	Joint mobilization, grade I	Pulse-train	B
L.C.	Emphysema	Diaphragmatic breathing ex.	Conventional; brief, intense	B
D.W.	Cervical strain chronic	Joint mobilization, grade I	Pulse-train	B

A. Complete return of active ROM and function that could not be accomplished without the adjunctive use of T.E.N.S.

B. Partial increase in active ROM and function beyond that able to be accomplished without T.E.N.S. This had to be considered as yielding acceptable functional use of the involved region.

C. No significant change in active ROM or function beyond that which could be obtained without the use of T.E.N.S.

The addition of T.E.N.S. to the treatment program allowed for specific manual techniques to be performed, which provided for the full rehabilitation of 10 of the 23 patients. An additional 12 patients were able to obtain more increased function than achieved without the use of T.E.N.S. but did not have complete return. Only one patient showed no

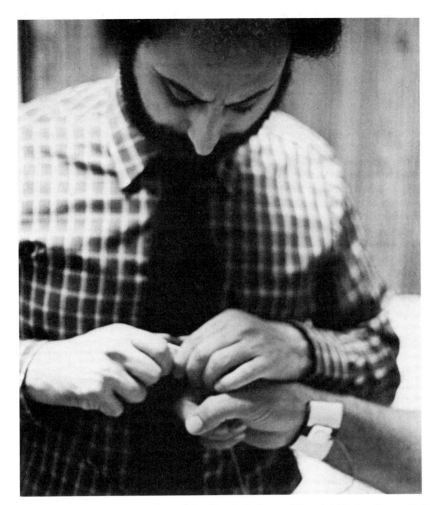

FIGURE 9-94. Traumatic amputation of the distal phalanx of the right index finger. Patient is being treated with joint mobilization to the PIP joint (anterior-posterior glides) while ongoing stimulation with conventional T.E.N.S. is applied. This specific therapeutic treatment could not be tolerated without use of conventional T.E.N.S. (See Fig. 9-93 for stimulation site characteristics.)

significant improvement. We have subsequently continued to use this therapeutic approach, when indicated, with other patients. Results continue to be quite favorable. Figures 9-95 and 9-96 illustrate the use of T.E.N.S. to allow for tolerance to rehabilitating manual techniques. Different electrodes were employed with this patient due to the presence of edema. Various electrodes can be adapted to increase efficacy with T.E.N.S.

Pain threshold and tolerance can also be increased prior to and during specific therapeutic techniques by cryotherapy and surface stimulation via electrical point stimulators. However when the results of these procedures are either short-lived or not effective enough, we resort to the use of T.E.N.S. as previously described to provide ongoing pain control during the performance of the procedure.

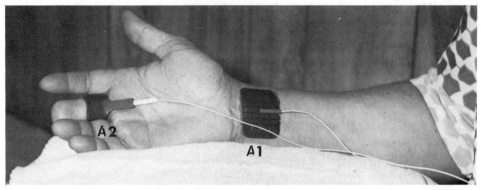

FIGURE 9-95. *Dx:* Traumatic amputation of distal phalanx of middle finger. Hyperesthesia, phantom pain, and edema. *Electrode placement technique:* Single-channel, unilateral. *Electrode placement sites:* A1, On volar surface of wrist (midline) just proximal to second volar crease. A2, On volar surface of middle finger between MCP and PIP joints. *Nerve innervation:* A1, Lower lateral cutaneous branch of musculocutaneous, median nerve, and medial cutaneous of forearm. A2, Plamar cutaneous branches of ulnar, median, and musculocutaneous nerves. *T.E.N.S. mode:* Conventional. *Electrodes:* A1, Carbon-silicone (Biostim-Bioform) electrode with karaya pad. A2, Standard carbon-silicone electrode with karaya pad cut in half. *T.E.N.S. unit:* Biostim Biomod. *Rationale:* Electrode arrangement provided for perception of electrical paresthesia throughout middle finger.

SUMMARY

The clinical application of T.E.N.S. for patients with specific pain syndromes or areas of pain has been presented via a literature review, case studies, and suggestions relative to choice of electrode arrangements and stimulation parameters. We have been unable to correlate specific stimulation modes to actual pain syndromes but have implied what seems to work best based on experience and the reports of others.

Our approach to the patient always begins with conventional T.E.N.S., the most mild and comfortable sensation. Modulation of the conventional mode to decrease accommodation and increase comfort can be obtained by low-intensity, pulse-train (burst) stimulation or by activation of pulse rate and/or pulse energy modulation features, as discussed in Chapter 12. If this mode does not prove helpful, the next choice is strong, low-rate (acupuncture-like) or high-intensity, pulse-train (burst) stimulation. Brief, intense T.E.N.S. is used as the last resort, but if required on an ongoing basis, modulation of the parameters should be added. We feel secure, however, in stating that acute injuries and superficial quality of pain including paresthesia, causalgia, hyperesthesia, and phantom sensations respond very well to conventional T.E.N.S. Patients with deep achy and long-standing discomfort may respond better to strong, low-rate (acupuncture-like) or high-intensity, pulse-train (burst) stimulation if the conventional mode is unsuccessful. Pulse energy modulation can increase tolerance to these strong modes.

The decision as to which stimulation sites to use and how to arrange the channels is also based upon the guidelines presented in Chapter 8 along with consideration of the chosen stimulation mode. Changes in distribution of pain will necessitate changes in stimulation sites and parameters.

A knowledge of the factors that inhibit, enhance, and restore the effectiveness of T.E.N.S. as presented in Chapter 12 is extremely important. Each patient should be thor-

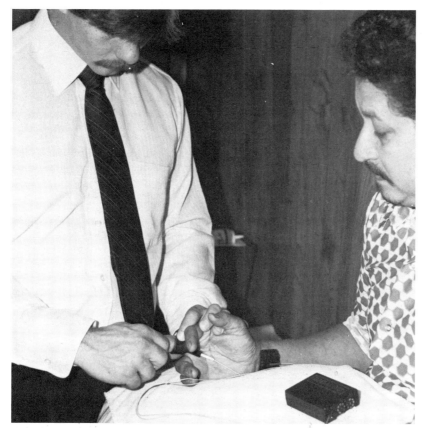

FIGURE 9-96. *Dx:* Traumatic amputation of distal phalanx of middle finger. Joint mobilization being performed with ongoing conventional T.E.N.S. See Figure 9-95 for characteristics of electrode sites. Physical therapy student Kevin Koob performing gentle joint mobilization techniques tolerable only with ongoing conventional T.E.N.S.

oughly screened to determine if he or she is using drugs that may hamper the action of T.E.N.S. Instruction in proper body mechanics and postural corrective exercise is a necessary adjunct to the use of T.E.N.S. and can enhance the degree as well as the duration of pain relief. The degree of success with T.E.N.S. is directly proportional to the amount of time spent with the patient.

REFERENCES

1. SHEALY, CN: *Dorsal column electrohypalgesia.* Headache 9:99, 1969.
2. NASHOLD, BS AND FRIEDMAN, H: *Dorsal column stimulation for control of pain.* J Neurosurg 36:590, 1972.
3. TUNG, CH: *Integrative action of the thalamus in the process of acupuncture for analgesia.* Am J Chin Med 2:1, 1974.
4. CHENG, RSS AND POMERANZ, B: *Electroacupuncture analgesia could be mediated by at least two pain relieving mechanisms: Endorphin and non-endorphin systems.* Life Sci 26:631, 1980.

5. MANNHEIMER, JS: *Electrode placement for transcutaneous electrical nerve stimulation.* Phys Ther 58:1455, 1978.

6. LINZER, M AND LONG, DM: *Transcutaneous neural stimulation for relief of pain.* IEEE Trans Biomed Eng 23:341, 1976.

7. BURTON, C AND MAURER, DD: *Pain suppression by transcutaneous electrical stimulation.* IEEE Trans Biomed Eng 21:81, 1974.

8. PICAZA, JA, ET AL: *Pain suppression by peripheral nerve stimulation: Part I. Observation with transcutaneous stimuli.* Surg Neurol 4:105, 1975.

9. REICHMANIS, M AND BECKER, RD: *Relief of experimentally induced pain by stimulation at acupuncture loci: A review.* Comp Med East and West 5:281, 1977.

10. ANDERSSON, DA AND HOLMGREN, E: *Analgesic effects of peripheral conditioning stimulation III. Effect of high frequency stimulation; segmental mechanisms interacting with pain.* Acupunct Electrother Res 3:23, 1978.

11. ANDERSSON, SA AND HOLMGREN, E: *On acupuncture analgesia and the mechanisms of pain.* Am J Chin Med 3:311, 1975.

12. ANDERSSON, SA, ET AL: *Evaluation of the pain suppression effect of different frequencies of peripheral electrical stimulation in chronic pain conditions.* Acta Orthop Scand 47:149, 1976.

13. ANDERSSON, SA, HOLMGREN, E, AND ROOS, A: *Analgesic effects of peripheral conditioning stimulation II. Importance of certain stimulation parameters.* Acupunct Electrother Res 2:237, 1977.

14. ERIKSSON, MBE, SJOLUND, BH, AND NEILZEN, S: *Long term results of peripheral conditioning stimulation as analgesic measure in chronic pain.* Pain 6:335, 1979.

15. EBERSOLD, MJ, ET AL: *Transcutaneous electrical stimulation for treatment of chronic pain: A preliminary report.* Surg Neurol 4:96, 1975.

16. GAMMON, GD AND STARR, I: *Studies on the relief of pain by counterirritation.* J Clin Invest 20:13, 1941.

17. CAMPBELL, JN AND TAUB, A: *Local analgesia from percutaneous electrical stimulation.* Arch Neurol 28:347, 1953.

18. WALMSLEY, RP AND FLEXMAN, NE: *Transcutaneous nerve stimulation for chronic low back pain: A pilot study.* Physiotherapy Canada 31:245, 1979.

19. JANCKO, M AND TRONTELJ, JU: *Transcutaneous electrical nerve stimulation: A micro-neurographic and perceptual study.* Pain 9:219, 1980.

20. WOLF, CJ: *Transcutaneous electrical nerve stimulation and the reaction to experimental pain in human subjects.* Pain 7:115, 1979.

21. HIEDL, P, STRUFFLER, A, AND GESSLER, M: *Local analgesia by percutaneous stimulation of sensory nerves.* Pain 7:129, 1979.

22. NYQUIST, JK AND IGNELZI, RJ: *The electrophysiological behavior of single peripheral nerve fibers of amphibian sciatic nerve in response to various frequencies of repetitive electrical stimulation: Implications for electroanalgesia.* In Scientific Program Abstracts. First Annual Meeting of American Pain Society, San Diego, 1979, p 60.

23. MANNHEIMER, C AND CARLSSON, CA: *The analgesic effect of transcutaneous electrical nerve stimulation (TNS) in patients with rheumatoid arthritis. A comparative study of different pulse patterns.* Pain 6:329, 1979.

24. JOHANSSON, F, ET AL: *Predictors for the outcome of treatment with high frequency transcutaneous electrical nerve stimulation in patients with chronic pain.* Pain 9:55, 1980.

25. WOLF, CJ, MITCHELL, D, AND BARRETT, D: *Antinociceptive effect of peripheral segmental electrical stimulation in the rat.* Pain 8:237, 1980.

26. CHAPMAN, CR, WILSON, ME, AND GEHRIG, JD: *Comparative effects of acupuncture and transcutaneous stimulation on the perception of painful dental stimuli.* Pain 2:265, 1976.

27. CHAPMAN, CR, CHEN, AC, AND BONICA, JJ: *Effects of intrasegmental electrical acupuncture on dental pain: Evaluation of threshold estimation and sensory decision theory.* Pain 3:213, 1977.

28. ANDERSSON, SA, ET AL: *Electroacupuncture: Effect on pain threshold measured with electrical stimulation of teeth.* Brain Res 63:393, 1973.

29. SJOLUND, BH, TERENIUS, L, AND ERIKSSON, MBE: *Increased cerebrospinal fluid levels of endorphin after electro-acupuncture.* Acta Physiol Scand 100:382, 1977.

30. ERIKSSON, MBE AND SJOLUND, BH: *Acupuncturelike electro-analgesia in TNS resistant chronic pain.* In ZOTTERMAN, Y (ED): *Sensory Functions of the Skin.* Pergamon Press, Oxford, 1976, p 575.

31. SJOLUND, BH AND ERIKSSON, MBE: *Electro-acupuncture and endogenous morphines.* Lancet 2:1085, 1976.

32. SJOLUND, BH AND ERIKSSON, MBE: *Endorphins and analgesia produced by peripheral conditioning stimulation.* In *Pain Abstracts.* Second World Congress on Pain. IASP, Montreal, 1978, p 15.

33. ANDERSSON, SA: *Pain control by sensory stimulation.* In *Pain Abstracts.* Second World Congress on Pain, IASP, Montreal, 1978, p 97.

34. SJOLUND, BH AND ERIKSSON, MBE: *Stimulation techniques in the management of pain.* In KOSTERLITZ, HW AND TERENIUS, LY (EDS): *Pain and Society.* Life Sciences Report #17, Weinheim, Deerfield Beach, Fla, 1980, p 415.

35. HOLMGREN, E: *Increase of pain threshold as a function of conditioning electrical stimulation: An experimental study with application to electroacupuncture for pain suppression.* Am J Chin Med 3:133, 1975.

36. ANDERSSON, SA AND HOLMGREN, E: *Pain threshold effects of peripheral conditioning stimulation.* In BONICA, JJ AND ALBE-FESSARD, D (EDS): *Advances in Pain Research and Therapy, Vol 6.* Raven Press, New York, 1976, p 761.

37. MCDONNELL, DE: *TENS in treating chronic pain.* AORN J 32:401, 1980.

38. MELZACK, R, GUITE, S, AND GONSHOR, A: *Relief of dental pain by ice massage of the hand.* Can Med Assoc J 122:189, 1980.

39. ERIKSSON, MBE AND SJOLUND, BH: *Pain relief from conventional versus acupuncturelike-TNS in patients with chronic facial pain.* In *Pain Abstracts.* Second World Congress on Pain, IASP, Montreal, 1978, p 128.

40. TAKAKURA, K, ET AL: *Pain control by transcutaneous electrical nerve stimulation using irregular pulse of 1 Hz fluctuation.* Appl Neurophysiol 42:314, 1979.

41. MANNHEIMER, C, LUND, S, AND CARLSSON, CA: *The effect of transcutaneous electrical nerve stimulation (TNS) on joint pain in patients with rheumatoid arthritis.* Scand J Rheumatol 7:13, 1978.

42. FOX, EJ AND MELZACK, R: *Transcutaneous electrical stimulation and acupuncture: Comparison of treatment for low back pain.* Pain 2:141, 1976.

43. IHALAINEN, V, PERKKI, K, AND OIKARINEN, VJ: *The effect of transcutaneous nerve stimulation on the tooth pain threshold.* Proc Finn Dent Soc 73:212, 1977.

44. MELZACK, R: *Prolonged relief of pain by brief, intense transcutaneous somatic stimulation.* Pain 1:357, 1975.

45. STRASSBURG, HM, KRAINICK, JV, AND THODEN, V: *Influence of transcutaneous nerve stimulation (TNS) on acute pain.* J Neurol 217:1, 1977.

46. SHEALY, CN, KWAKO, JL, AND HUGHES, S: *Effects of transcranial neurostimulation upon mood and serotonin production: A preliminary report.* Il Dolore 1:13, 1979.

47. MARKOVICH, SE: *Pain in the head: A neurological appraisal.* In GELB, H (ED): *Clinical Management of Head, Neck and TMJ Pain and Dysfunction.* WB Saunders, Philadelphia, 1977, p 125.

48. GELB, H: *Effective management and treatment of the craniomandibular syndrome.* In GELB, H (ED): *Clinical Management of Head, Neck and TMJ Pain and Dysfunction.* WB Saunders, Philadelphia, 1977, p 288.

49. SHEALY, CN: *The Pain Game.* Celestial Arts, Millbrae, Calif, 1976, p 80.

50. MCKELVY, P: *Clinical report on the use of specific T.E.N.S. units.* Phys Ther 58:1474, 1978.

51. MUMFORD, JM AND STANLEY, SJ: *Sensations on stimulating the pulps of human teeth, thresholds and tolerance ratio.* Pain 10:391, 1981.

52. BROOKS, B, REISS, R, AND UMANS, R: *Local electroanalgesia in dentistry.* J Dent Res 49:298, 1970.

53. FIELDS, RW, SAVARA, BS, AND TOCKE, R: *Regional electroanalgesia and its potentialities in control of orofacial pain.* Oral Surg 34:694, 1972.

54. BRADLEY, JF, BROOKS, B, AND UMANS, R: *Electroanalgesia in restorative dentistry.* J Prosthet Dent 32:171, 1974.

55. MUMFORD, JM AND NEWTON, AV: *Trigeminal convergence from human teeth: Influence of contralateral stimulation and stimulus frequency on the pain perception threshold.* Arch Oral Biol 19:145, 1974.

56. OTTOSON, D, EKBLOM, A AND HANSSON, P: *Vibratory stimulation for the relief of pain of dental origin.* Pain 10:37, 1981.

57. IHALAINEN, V AND PERKKI, K: *The preventive effect of transcutaneous nerve stimulation (TNS) on acute post-operative pain.* Acupunct Electrother Res 5:313, 1980.

58. OMURA, Y: *Simple custom made disposable surface electrode system for non-invasive "electro-acupuncture" or TNS and its clinical applications including treatment of cephalic-hypertension and hypotension syndromes as well as temporomandibular joint problems, tinnitus, shoulder and lower back pain, etc.* Acupunct Electrother Res 6:109, 1981.

59. JANKELSON, B: *Maxillo-mandibular Registration for Fixed and Removable Prosthesis.* Myo-Tronics Research, Seattle, 1974.

60. JANKELSON, B, ET AL: *Neural conduction of the myo-monitor stimulus: A quantitative analysis.* J Prosthet Dent 34:245, 1975.

61. JACH, ET: *Relief of myo-facial pain: Treatment of 5 patients.* Dental Survey June 1975, p 44.

62. JANKELSON, B AND RADKE, JC: *The myo-monitor: Its use and abuse II.* Quintessence Int 3:7, 1978.

63. SHEALY, CN: *Electrical control of the nervous system.* Med Prog Technol 2:71, 1974.

64. MUMFORD, JM: *Relief of orofacial pain by transcutaneous neural stimulation.* Journal of British Endodontic Society 9:71, 1976.

65. APPENZELLER, O AND ATKINSON, R: *Transcutaneous nerve stimulation in the treatment of hemicrania and other forms of headache.* Minerva Med 67:2023, 1976.

66. APPENZELLER, O AND ATKINSON, R: *Transcutaneous nerve stimulation for the treatment of migraine and other head pain.* Munch Med Wochenschr 117:1953, 1975.

67. BATES, JAV AND NATHAN, PW: *Transcutaneous electrical nerve stimulation for chronic pain.* Anesthesia 35:817, 1980.

68. KIRSCH, WM, LEWIS, JA, AND SIMON, RH: *Experiences with electrical stimulation devices for the control of chronic pain.* Med Instrum 9:217, 1975.

69. CAUTHEN, JC AND RENNER, EJ: *Transcutaneous and peripheral nerve stimulation for chronic pain states.* Surg Neurol 4:102, 1975.

70. LOESER, JD, BLACK, RG, AND CHRISTMAN, A: *Relief of pain by transcutaneous stimulation.* J Neurosurg 42:308, 1975.

71. IGNELZI, RJ, STERNBACH, RA, AND CALLAGHAN, M: *Somatosensory changes during transcutaneous electrical analgesia.* In BONICA, JJ AND ALBE-FESSARD, D (EDS): *Advances in Pain Research and Therapy,* Vol I. Raven Press, New York, 1979, p 509.

72. TICHOU-OLSHWANG, D AND MAGORA, F: *Relief of pain by subcutaneous electrical nerve stimulation after ocular surgery.* Am J Ophthalmol 89:803, 1980.

73. LAITINEN, L: *Placement of electrodes in transcutaneous stimulation for chronic pain.* Neuro-Chirurgie 22:517, 1976.

74. PROCACCI, P, ET AL: *Cutaneous pain threshold changes after sympathetic block in reflex dystrophies.* Pain 1:167, 1975.

75. MALOW, RM AND DOUGHER, MJ: *A signal detection analysis of the effects of transcutaneous stimulation on pain.* Psychosom Med 4:101, 1979.

76. SHERRINGTON, C: *The Integrative Action of the Nervous System.* Yale University Press, New Haven, 1947.

77. TIEN, HC: *Neurogenic interference theory of acupuncture anesthesia.* Am J Chin Med 1:108, 1972.

78. MATSUMOTO, T: *Acupuncture for Physicians.* Charles C Thomas, Springfield, Ill, 1974, p 171.

79. LONG, DM: *Electrical stimulation for relief of pain from chronic nerve injury.* J Neurosurg 39:718, 1973.

80. LONG, DM AND HAGFORS, N: *Electrical stimulation of the nervous system: The current status of electrical stimulation of the nervous system for relief of pain.* Pain 1:109, 1975.

81. MEYER, GA AND FIELDS, HC: *Causalgia treated by selective large fiber stimulation of peripheral nerve.* Brain 95:163, 1972.

82. LAMPE, GN: *A Clinical Approach to Transcutaneous Electrical Nerve Stimulation in the Treatment of Acute and Chronic Pain.* Medgeneral, Minneapolis, 1977, p 31.

83. CRUE, BL JR AND FELSOORY, A: *Transcutaneous high cervical "electrical cordotomy."* Minn Med J 57:204, 1974.

84. CRUE, BL JR, ET AL: *Preliminary report on cervical transcutaneous electrical cordotomy.* In CRUE, BL JR (ED): *Pain Research and Treatment.* Academic Press, New York, 1975, p 263.

85. YARTON, P, PINSKY, JJ, AND CRUE, BL JR: *The present status of the transcutaneous electrical stimulation program at City of Hope.* In CRUE, BL JR (ED): *Chronic Pain, Further Observations from City of Hope National Medical Center.* SP Medical and Scientific Books, New York, 1979, p 499.

86. MORIN, F: *A new spinal pathway for cutaneous impulses.* Am J Physiol 182:245, 1955.

87. HA, H AND LIU, C: *Organization of the spinocervico-thalamic system.* J Comp Neurol 127:445, 1966.

88. DENNIS, SG AND MELZACK, R: *Pain-signalling systems in the dorsal and ventral spinal cord.* Pain 4:97, 1977.

89. NORDEMAR, R AND THORNER, C: *Treatment of acute cervical pain—a comparative study group.* Pain 10:93, 1981.

90. CAILLIET, R *The Shoulder in Hemiplegia.* FA Davis, Philadelphia, 1980.

91. CALLAGHAN, M, ET AL: *Changes in somatic sensitivity during transcutaneous electrical analgesia.* Pain 5:115, 1978.

92. ZOHN, DA AND MENNELL, JM: *Musculo-skeletal Pain.* Little, Brown & Co, Boston, 1976.

93. CYRIAX, J: *Textbook of Orthopaedic Medicine,* ed 6. Williams & Wilkins, Baltimore, 1975.

94. STERNSCHEIN, MJ, ET AL: *Causalgia.* Arch Phys Med Rehabil 56:58, 1975.

95. STILZ, RJ, CARRON, H, AND SANDERS, DB: *Case history number 96: Reflex sympathetic dystrophy in a 6 year old: Successful treatment by transcutaneous nerve stimulation.* Anesth Analg 56:438, 1977.

96. OWENS, S, ATKINSON, ER, AND LEES, DE: *Thermographic evidence of residual sympathetic tone with TENS.* Anesthesiology 50:62, 1970.

97. RICHLIN, DM, CARRON, H AND ROWLINGSON, JC: *Reflex sympathetic dystrophy: Successful treatment by TENS.* J Pediatr 93:84, 1978.

98. PARRY, CBW: *Rehabilitation of the Hand,* ed 4. Butterworths, London, 1981, p 129.

99. MYERS, RMA, WOLF, CJ, AND MITCHELL, D: *Management of acute traumatic pain by peripheral transcutaneous electrical stimulation.* SA Med J 52:309, 1977.

100. RICHARDSON, RR, MEYER, PR, AND RAIMONDI, AJ: *Transabdominal neurostimulation in acute spinal cord injuries.* Spine 4:47, 1979.

101. RICHARDSON, RR, MEYER, PR, AND CERULLO, LJ: *Transcutaneous electrical neurostimulation in musculoskeletal pain of acute spinal cord injuries.* Spine 5:42, 1980.

102. SOVIJARVI, ARA AND POPPIUS, H: *Acute bronchodilating effect of TENS in asthma: A peripheral reflex or psychogenic response.* Scand J Resp Dis 58:164, 1977.

103. PAXTON, SL: *Clinical uses of T.E.N.S.: A survey of physical therapists.* Phys Ther 60:38, 1980.

104. ERSEK, RA: *Low back pain: Prompt relief with transcutaneous neurostimulation.* Orthop Rev 5:27, 1976.

105. GUNN, CC AND MILBRANDT, WE: *Review of 100 patients with low back sprain treated by surface electrode stimulation of acupuncture points.* Am J Acupuncture 3:224, 1975.

106. LAITINEN, J: *Acupuncture and transcutaneous electric nerve stimulation in the treatment of chronic sacrolumbalgia and ischalgia.* Am J Chin Med 4:169, 1976.

107. SERES, JL AND NEWMAN, RI: *Results of treatment of chronic low back pain at the Portland Pain Center.* J Neurosurg 45:32, 1976.

108. MOONEY, V AND CAIRNS, D: *Management of the patient with chronic low back pain.* Orthop Clin North Am 9:543, 1978.

109. INDECK, W AND PRINTY, A: *Skin application of electrical impulses for relief of pain in chronic orthopaedic conditions.* Minn Med 58:305, 1975.

110. TAYLOR, P, HALLETT, M, AND FLAHERTY, L: *Treatment of osteoarthritis of the knee with transcutaneous electrical stimulation.* Pain 11:233, 1981.

111. GERSH, MR, WOLF, SL, AND RAO, VR: *Evaluation of TENS for pain relief in peripheral neuropathy.* Phys Ther 60:48, 1960.

112. OLM, WA, GOLD, ML, AND WEIL, LS: *Evaluation of transcutaneous electrical nerve stimulation (TENS) in podiatric surgery.* J Am Podiatry Assoc 69:537, 1979.

113. WOLF, SL, GERSH, MR, AND RAO, VR: *Examination of electrode placement and stimulating parameters in treating chronic pain with conventional electrical nerve stimulation (TENS).* Pain 11:37, 1981.

114. NATHAN, PW AND WALL, PD: *Treatment of post-herpetic neuralgia by prolonged electrical stimulation.* Br Med J 3:645, 1974.

115. SHEALY, CN: *Electrical stimulation: The primary method of choice in pain relief.* Comp Ther 1:41, 1975.

116. LONG, DM: *Cutaneous afferent stimulation for the relief of pain.* Prog Neurol Surg 7:35, 1976.

117. LONG, DM: *The comparative efficacy of drugs vs. electrical modulation in the management of chronic pain.* In LE ROY, PL (ED): *Current Concepts in the Management of Chronic Pain.* Symposia Specialists, Miami, 1977, p 53.

118. GOLDNER, JL AND HENDRIX, PC: *Use of transcutaneous electrical stimulation in the management of chronic pain syndromes.* In LE ROY, PL (ED): *Current Concepts in the Management of Chronic Pain.* Symposia Specialists, Miami, 1977, p 111.

119. LAW, JD, SWETT, J, AND KIRSCH, WM: *Retrospective analysis of 22 patients with chronic pain treated by peripheral nerve stimulation.* J Neurosurg 52:482, 1980.

120. THORSTEINSSON, G, ET AL: *Transcutaneous electrical stimulation: A double-blind trial of its efficacy for pain.* Arch Phys Med Rehabil 58:8, 1977.

121. LONG, DM: *Electrical stimulation for the control of pain.* Arch Surg 112:884, 1977.

122. ALBE-FESSARD, D AND LOMBARD, MC: *Animal models for pain due to central deafferentation. Methods of protection against this sydrome.* Pain [Suppl I]:80, 1981.

123. MEHTA, JM, NIMBALKAR, ST, AND THALAYAN, K: *A new approach in the relief of pain of leprous neuritis.* Lepr India 51:459, 1979.

124. PARRY, CBW: *Pain in avulsion lesions of the brachial plexus.* Pain 9:41, 1980.

125. PARRY, CBW: *Therapies of pain due to spinal root avulsion.* Pain [Suppl I]:84, 1981.

126. CARLSSON, CA, ET AL: *Electrical transcutaneous nerve stimulation for relief of itch.* Experientia 15:191, 1975.

127. Editorial: *Itch.* Lancet 2:568, 1980.

128. McCARTHY, JA AND ZIGENFUS, RW: *TENS; an adjunct in the pain management of Guillain Barre syndrome.* Physical Therapy 58(1):23–24, 1978.

129. AUGUSTINSSON, LE, ET AL: *Pain relief during delivery by transcutaneous electrical nerve stimulation.* Pain 4:59, 1977.

130. SHEALY, CN AND MAURER, D: *Transcutaneous nerve stimulation for control of pain: A preliminary technical note.* Surg Neurol 2:45, 1974.

131. NEUMARK, J, PAUSER, G, AND SCHIRZER, W: *Pain relief in childbirth: An analysis of the analgesic effects of transcutaneous nerve stimulation (TNS), pethidine and placebos.* Prakt Anaesth 13:13, 1978.

132. KUBISTA, E, KUCERA, H, AND RISS, P: *The effect of transcutaneous nerve stimulation on labor pain.* Geburthshilfe Frauenheilkd 38:1079, 1978.

133. FALL, M, CARLSSON, CA, AND ERLANDSON, BE: *Electrical stimulation in interstitial cystitis.* J Urol 123:192, 1980.

134. LEYSON, JFJ, STEFANIWSKY, L, AND MARTIN, BF: *Effects of transcutaneous nerve stimulation on the vesicourethral function in spinal cord injury patients.* J Urol 121:635, 1979.

135. WINTER, A: *The use of transcutaneous electrical stimulation (TNS) in the treatment of multiple sclerosis.* J Neurosurg Nurs 8:125, 1976.

136. DOOLEY, DM, KASPRAK, M, AND STIBITZ, M.: *Electrical stimulation of the spinal cord in patients with demyelinating and degenerative diseases of the central nervous system.* J Fla Med Assoc 63:906, 1976.

137. BANERJEE, T: *Transcutaneous nerve stimulation for pain after spinal injury.* N Engl J Med 29:296, 1974.

138. DAVIS, R AND LENTINI, R: *Transcutaneous nerve stimulation for treatment of pain in spinal cord injured patients.* Surg Neurol 4:100, 1975.

139. HACHEN, HJ: *Psychological neuro-physiological and therapeutic aspects of chronic pain: Preliminary results with transcutaneous electrical stimulation.* Paraplegia 15:353, 1977–78.

140. HEILPORN, A: *Two therapeutic experiments on stubborn pain in spinal cord lesions: Coupling melitracen-flupenthixol and transcutaneous nerve stimulation.* Paraplegia 15:368, 1977–78.

141. RICHARDSON, RR, MEYER, PR, AND CERULLO, LJ: *Neurostimulation in the modulation of intractable paraplegic and traumatic neuroma pains.* Pain 8:75, 1980.

142. SHEALY, CN: *Management of acute pain in trauma.* Compr Ther 5:15, 1979.

143. SHEALY, CN: *The viability of external electrical stimulation as a therapeutic modality.* Med Instrum 9:211, 1975.

144. SHEALY, CN: *Biofeedback training in the physician's office: Transfer of pain clinic advances to primary care.* Wis Med J 77:541, 1978.

145. ERSEK, RA: *Relief of acute musculo-skeletal pain using transcutaneous electrical neurostimulation.* JACEP 6:300, 1977.

146. GARL, TC AND COOPER, RF: *Transcutaneous nerve stimulation: Treating pain in athletes.* J Miss State Med Assoc 20:253, 1979.

147. HAWKINS, RJ AND KENNEDY, JC: *Impingement syndrome in athletes.* Am J Sports Med 8:151, 1980.

148. ROESER, WM, ET AL: *The use of transcutaneous nerve stimulation for pain control in athletic medicine. A preliminary report.* Sports Med 4:210, 1976.

149. SCHULTZ, P: *TNS—The new current in sportsmedicine.* The Physician and Sports Medicine 7:116, 1979.

150. ROBERTS, HJ: *Transcutaneous electrical nerve stimulation in the management of pancreatitis pain.* South Med J 71:396, 1978.

151. ROBERTS, HJ: *TENS in the symptomatic management of thrombophlebitis.* Angiology 30:249, 1979.

152. ERIKSSON, H AND MANNHEIMER, C: *The effect of transcutaneous electric nerve stimulation on ischemic pain in the lower extremities.* AKT Gerontal 10:33, 1980.

153. SCHUSTER, GD: *The use of TENS for peripheral neurovascular diseases.* Journal of Neurological and Orthopaedic Surgery 1:219, 1980.

154. DOOLEY, DM AND KASPRAK, M: *Modification of blood flow to the extremities by electrical stimulation of the nervous system.* South Med J 69:1309, 1976.

155. COOK, AW: *Vascular disease of the extremities.* NY State Med J 76:366, 1976.

156. ABRAM, SE: *Increased sympathetic tone associated with transcutaneous electrical stimulation.* Anesthesiology 45:575, 1976.

157. EBERSOLD, MJ, LAWS, ER, AND ALBERS, JW: *Measurements of autonomic function before, during and after transcutaneous stimulation in patients with chronic pain and in control subjects.* Mayo Clin Proc 52:228, 1977.

158. GAULT, WR AND GATENS, PF: *Use of low intensity direct current in management of ischemic skin ulcers.* Phys Ther 56:265, 1976.

159. OSTROWSKI, MJ AND DODD, VA: *Transcutaneous nerve stimulation for relief of pain in advanced malignant disease.* Nursing Times Aug 11, 1977, p 1233.

160. VENTAFRIDDA, V, ET AL: *Transcutaneous nerve stimulation in cancer pain.* In BONICA, JJ AND VENTAFRIDDA, V (EDS): *Advances in Pain Research and Therapy,* Vol 2. Raven Press, New York, 1979, p 509.

161. BARR, S: Personal communication, 1981.

162. GORDON, MJ, ET AL: *Transcutaneous electrical nerve stimulation for the treatment of angina pectoris.* Circulation Abstracts 53&54[Suppl II]:126, 1976.

163. POMERANZ, B, WALL, PD, AND WEBER, WV: *Cord cells responding to fine myelinated afferents from viscera, muscle and skin.* J Physiol 199:511, 1968.

164. SELZER, M AND SPENCER, WA: *Convergence of visceral and cutaneous afferent pathways in the lumbar spinal cord.* Brain Res 14:331, 1969.

165. SELZER, M AND SPENCER, WA: *Interactions between visceral and cutaneous afferents in the spinal cord: Reciprocal primary afferent fiber depolarization.* Brain Res 14:349, 1969.

166. Gyory, AN: *Transcutaneous electric nerve stimulation (TENS) analgesia.* Med J Aust 1980.

167. Parras, T: Personal communication, 1979.

168. Epstein, MH and Harris, J: *Children with chronic pain, can they be helped?* Pediatric Nursing 4, 1978.

169. Austin, M: *Acupuncture Therapy.* ASI Publishers, New York, 1972.

170. The Academy of Traditional Chinese Medicine: *An Outline of Chinese Acupuncture.* Foreign Languages Press, Peking, 1975.

171. Mannheimer, JS and Whalen, E: *Transcutaneous electrical nerve stimulation for dysmenorrhea.* (Submitted for publication.)

172. Bassett, CAL, Mitchell, SN, and Gaston, SR: *Treatment of ununited tibial diaphyseal fractures with pulsing electromagnetic fields.* J Bone Joint Surg [Am] 63:511, 1981.

173. Sharrard, WJW, et al: *The treatment of fibrous non-union of fractures by pulsing electromagnetic stimulation.* J Bone Joint Surg [Br] 64:189, 1982.

174. Batten, GB and Lichtman, DM: *Electricity and bone healing: Historical development and review of the literature.* Ortho Survey 5:262, 1982.

175. Kahn, J: *Low Volt Technique Supplement.* J Kahn, Syosset, NY, 1981, p 44.

176. Lampe, GN: *Introduction to the use of transcutaneous electrical nerve stimulation devices.* Phys Ther 58:1450, 1978.

177. Maitland, GD: *Vertebral Manipulation,* ed 3. Butterworths, London, 1973.

178. Maitland, GD: *Peripheral Manipulation,* ed 2. Butterworths, London, 1977.

179. Nwuga, VC: *Manipulation of the Spine.* Williams & Wilkins, Baltimore, 1976.

180. Stoddard, A: *Manual of Osteopathic Technique.* Hutchinson, London, 1959.

181. Maigne, R: *Orthopaedic Medicine: New Approach to Vertebral Manipulations.* Charles C Thomas, Springfield, 1972.

182. Mennell, JM: *Joint Pain.* Little, Brown & Co, Boston, 1964.

183. Mennell, JM: *Back Pain.* Little, Brown & Co, Boston, 1960.

184. Grieve, GP: *Mobilisation of the Spine.* Churchill Livingstone, Edinburgh, 1979.

185. Warwick, R and Williams, PL: *Gray's Anatomy.* WB Saunders, Philadelphia, 1973, p 388.

186. Kapandji, IA: *The Physiology of the Joints. Vol I Upper Limb.* Churchill Livingstone, Edinburgh, 1970.

187. Kapandji, IA: *The Physiology of the Joints. Vol II Lower Limb.* Churchill Livingstone, Edinburgh, 1970.

188. Kapandji, IA: *The Physiology of the Joints. Vol II The Trunk and Vertebral Column.* Churchill Livingstone, Edinburgh, 1974.

189. Wyke, B: *The neurology of joints.* Ann R Coll Surg Eng 41:25, 1967.

190. Melzack, R and Wall, PD: *Pain mechanisms. A new theory.* Science 150:971, 1965.

191. Melzack, R: *The Puzzle of Pain.* Basic Books, New York, 1973.

192. Carron, H and McCue, F: *Reflex sympathetic dystrophy in a ten-year old.* South Med J 65:631, 1972.

193. Cooney, WP, Dobyns, JH, and Linshield, RL: *Complications of Colles' fractures.* J Bone Joint Surg [Am] 62:613, 1980.

194. Litton Industries Inc: *Physician's Desk Reference,* ed 33. Medical Economics, Oradell, NJ, 1979, p 1431.

195. Gyory, AN and Caine, DC: *Electric pain control (EPC) of a painful forearm amputation stump.* Med J Aust 2:156, 1977.

196. Miles, J and Lipton, S: *Phantom limb pain treated by electrical stimulation.* Pain 5:373, 1978.

197. Noordenbos, W: *Sensory findings in painful traumatic nerve lesions.* In *Pain Abstracts,* Vol I. International Association for the Study of Pain, Second World Congress on Pain, Montreal, 1978, p 7.

198. Gunn, CC: *Transcutaneous neural stimulation, acupuncture and the current of injury.* Am J Acupuncture 6:191, 1978.

199. Gunn, CC: *Causalgia and denervation supersensitivity.* Am J Acupuncture 7:317, 1979.

200. Gunn, CC: *"Prespondylosis" and some pain syndromes following denervation supersensitivity.* Spine 5:185, 1980.

201. GESSLER, M AND STRUPPLER, A: *Relief of phantom pain by stimulation of the nerve supplying the corresponding extensor muscles.* Pain [Suppl I]: 257, 1981.

202. LAMM, K: *No cost spotting electrodes.* Aptan 5:4, 1982.

203. OMURA, Y: *Electro-acupuncture: Its electro-physiological basis and criteria for effectiveness and safety—Part 1.* Acupunct Electrother Res 1:157, 1975.

204. McKENZIE, RA: *The Lumbar Spine.* Spinal Publications, Waikanae, New Zealand, 1981.

205. KAADA, B: *Vasodilation induced by transcutaneous nerve stimulation in peripheral ischemia (Raynaud's phenomenon and diabetic polyneuropathy).* Eur Heart J 3:303, 1982.

206. SHRIBER, WJ: *A Manual of Electrotherapy,* ed 4. Lea & Febiger, Philadelphia, 1977.

207. BUNDSEN, P, ET AL: *Pain relief during delivery by transcutaneous electrical nerve stimulation.* Prakt Anaesth 13:20, 1978.

208. BUNDSEN, P AND ERICSON, K: *Pain relief in labor by transcutaneous electrical nerve stimulation: Safety aspects.* Acta Obstet Gynecol Scand 61:1, 1982.

209. CAMPBELL, JN: *Examination of possible mechanisms by which stimulation of the spinal cord in man relieves pain.* Appl Neurophysiol 44:181, 1981.

CHAPTER 10

THE THERAPEUTIC VALUE OF POSTOPERATIVE T.E.N.S. (CASE STUDY)

ALAN HYMES, M.D.

Since both chronic pain and acute pain are apparently mediated in the same manner within the peripheral and central nervous systems, it seemed logical to apply T.E.N.S. for treating postoperative patients and those patients suffering trauma. Our preliminary study suggested that T.E.N.S. reduced pain and postoperative pulmonary complications and prevented ileus.[10,11]

The present study was designed as a forward randomized investigation to test the validity of those observations. This report deals with a total of 774 postoperative patients who were evaluated as to the efficiency of T.E.N.S. (Table 10-1).

MATERIALS AND METHODS

A forward randomized study was done involving 426 postsurgical patients whose operations fell into one of six categories: gastrectomy, cholecystectomy, colectomy, abdominal aortic repair, bilateral nephrectomy and splenectomy, and thoractomy. Of these patients, 221 were treated with T.E.N.S., and 205 served as controls.

An additional nonrandomized group of 155 patients underwent a variety of abdominal surgical procedures not in the above categories. All were treated with T.E.N.S. postop-

TABLE 10-1. Postoperative Patients Treated With T.E.N.S. (Total in Study: 774)

	Treated	Control
Abdominal surgery	179	162
Gastrectomy	26	17
Cholecystectomy	60	59
Colectomy	30	20
Abdominal aorta	38	33
Bilateral nephrectomy and splenectomy	25	33
Miscellaneous abdominal group	155	–
Thoracotomy	42	43
Nonrandomized thoracotomy	100	–
Postoperative ileus treated with T.E.N.S.	93	–
TOTAL	569	205

eratively. One hundred nonrandomized thoracotomy patients were treated with T.E.N.S., and a special group of 93 patients was referred by other surgeons for T.E.N.S. treatment of persistent postoperative ileus.

In each category, patients were selected for treatment or control by random selection prior to the time of the electrode placement. The attending nurses and physicians making the observations did not know which patients were treated with T.E.N.S.

All electrodes were connected to a T.E.N.S. unit. In control patients, the batteries were reversed. There was no preoperative patient education, thereby minimizing the placebo effect.

PARAMETERS EVALUATED

The incidence of atelectasis and postoperative ileus was evaluated. In this study, atelectasis was a clinical diagnosis based on postoperative fever, tachycardia, and rales and was confirmed by chest x-ray. No attempt was made to do analyses of subtle arteriovenous shunting nor were arterial blood gases determined in all individuals.

Ileus was defined as abdominal distention with the absence of bowel sounds by auscultation beyond the third postoperative day in a patient with continuous nasogastric suction.

Semiquantitative cough efforts were also noted by either the attending nurses or physicians before and after T.E.N.S. treatment.

Observations were made on the subjective reduction of pain, but no attempt was made to quantify this observation.

In many thoracotomy patients, the angle of the humerus to the chest wall was measured when the arm was raised maximally before and after therapy. All patients were compared within the subgroups of a particular surgical procedure. Patients who had severe complications of other organ systems were removed from the study so that the comparison curves would not be skewed. The results with the patients not randomized but treated were evaluated separately, except for the nephrectomy and splenectomy group.

All statistical analysis was done by Dr. Jacob Bearman, Professor of Biometrics, University of Minnesota.

METHODS OF STIMULATION

STIMULATORS

There are presently approximately 50 companies manufacturing T.E.N.S. units. Fundamentally, to be effective, these units must generate an adequate amount of electrical energy. Figure 10-1 denotes a modified square wave signal. The energy is the area under the square wave. As one can readily see, the total power of the signal is a combination of the amperage and the duration of the pulse. Some manufacturers may vary this signal by increasing the amperage and narrowing the pulse width. Clinical studies have shown that increased amperage with a pulse width of 150 μsec can be effective. A spiked wave form with a very narrow pulse width significantly decreases power output (Fig. 10-2). It has been our experience that low frequencies and/or narrow pulse width did not subjectively reduce pain well. Generally, the greater pulse width associated with a tolerable amperage resulted in the best pain reduction. The unit amperage output should be turned up to a point of comfortable tolerance and not to a point of causing pain.

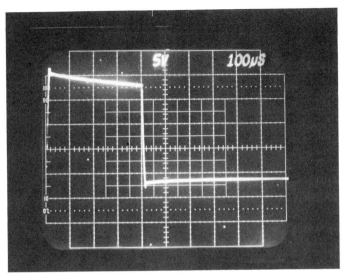

FIGURE 10-1. A modified rectangular pulse with a net DC component. This wave has a pulse width of 400 μsec and an amplitude of 40 mA. It is the preferred form and delivers an effective quantity of energy as noted by the area in the rectangle.

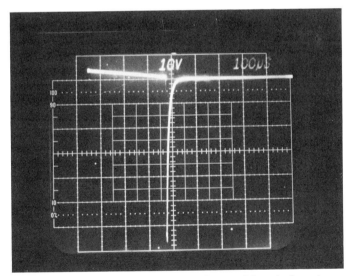

FIGURE 10-2. A symmetric biphasic "spike" wave form. Although there is an amplitude of 70 mA, the pulse width is only about 25 μsec. The area between the downward and upward deflection is minimal, indicating very little electrical energy. This wave form has been found to be rather inefficient in achieving postoperative T.E.N.S. therapy.

T.E.N.S. can be self-anesthetizing so that after a time of stimulation the patient can tolerate greater amperage. Reference has been made to this phenomenon as an accommodative wave form. Pulse width should be set before the unit is turned on because increasing pulse afterward may cause discomfort.

Further, the amperage should be turned down if it causes muscle stimulation since muscle contraction may aggravate pain.

Most manufacturers have built variable amperage, pulse width, and frequency into their units. In my opinion, any of these units that has enough electrical power with any combination of these variables should be adequate for successful analgesia from T.E.N.S. Also, in my opinion, units that have limited pulse width, thus limiting effective electrical power, should not be used in conjunction with surgery.

ELECTRODES

Since the area of analgesia from surgical T.E.N.S. was under the electrode, it seemed reasonable to use a large surface area of stimulation. To accomplish this end, two electrodes with dimensions of 2 × 8 inches were used. Initially, aluminum foil electrodes were used with a great quantity of gel on their surface and were held in place with a paper porous tape (3M) and changed every 24 to 48 hours. The incidence of minor skin irritation was about 50 percent. Because of the nonuniform spread of the gel, current density was increased in areas, causing skin reactions. Further, the adhesiveness of the tape was also irritating to some patients and contributed significantly to the 50 percent skin problem.

In the latter two thirds of this study, a formulated karaya gum electrode (2 × 8 inches) was designed to obviate the use of gel. This gum electrode molded to the skin and was self-adhering. However, the sides were covered with narrow paper tape if it was used in a dependent position. The incidence of minor skin irritations with the gum electrode was about 12 percent. With care, these gum electrodes could be moved from site to site and lasted up to 4 days, if necessary.

Since most T.E.N.S. units have some DC component, there is an ion electrophoretic effect carrying some of the prep solution into the skin, thus causing an irritation. Therefore, it is very important to completely remove all traces of the prep solution or soap from the skin with water or saline solution before applying the electrodes.

SITE OF THE ELECTRODES

Most of the pain from the surgical incision is not at the incision itself but from trauma to tissue and muscle secondary to surgical retraction. Therefore, the electrodes were placed 2 to 3 inches away from the surgical incision but parallel to it.

When nonsterile electrodes were used, a narrow dressing was applied with a nonsterile paper tape. The tape was applied parallel to the dressing rather than across it. If gum electrodes were used, the skin was first moistened with water or saline solution (Figs. 10-3, 10-4, and 10-5). The electrodes were then connected to a T.E.N.S. unit. The pulse width and frequency were present to 350 to 450 μsec and 100 to 150 cycles per second, respectively. The unit was turned on and the amperage increased slowly to a point of tolerance. If muscle stimulation occurred, even though the stimulation was comfortable, the amperage was reduced. This muscle stimulation was not uncommon with karaya electrodes because, generally, the skin stimulation was smooth without sharp, prickly sensations.

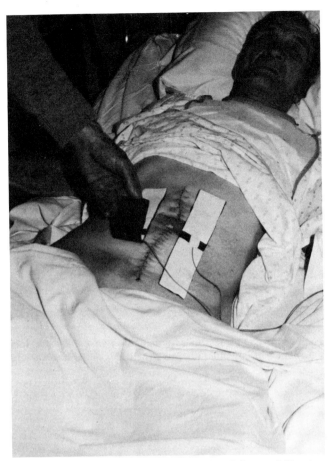

FIGURE 10-3. Karaya gum electrodes in position on the abdomen following surgery for an abdominal aortic aneurysm.

T.E.N.S. was started soon after the cessation of anesthesia in some patients and within 10 to 12 hours from the time of surgery in all patients. The first postoperative day, most patients were instructed in the use of T.E.N.S. The frequency and pulse width dials were taped, and the only dial the patients could turn was the amperage output. Patients were told to keep the level of stimulation comfortable and if muscle twitching was felt, the output was to be reduced. If the patient wished to deep breathe or cough, the output was increased prior to the cough to increase stimulus-produced analgesia and thereby reduce protective splinting. The ability to cough was improved significantly in all groups.

The power source was changed at least every 12 to 24 hours, and if two channels were used with four large electrodes, such as on a thoracotomy incision, the power source was changed every 4 to 6 hours.

RESULTS

In the 341 patients who underwent abdominal surgery, only 9 percent of the 179 treated patients developed postoperative atelectasis, compared with 18 percent of the 162

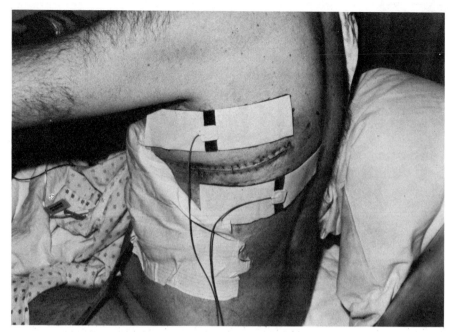

FIGURE 10-4. Position of electrodes on a patient following posterior lateral thoractomy. T.E.N.S. therapy for thoracotomy often utilizes two T.E.N.S. channels with four electrodes.

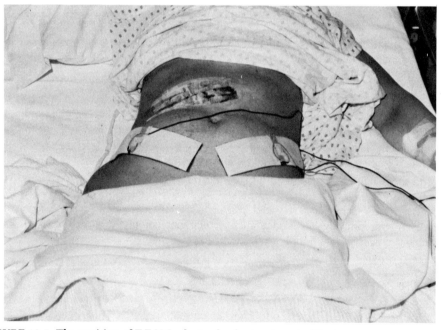

FIGURE 10-5. The position of T.E.N.S. electrodes for treatment of ileus.

control group (Fig. 10-6). The difference is significant (P = .005). Only 3 percent of patients treated with T.E.N.S. had postoperative ileus, compared with 9 percent in the control group (Fig. 10-7). Again, the difference is significant (P = .015). The ability to cough was improved significantly in all groups (Fig. 10-8).

ABDOMINAL AORTIC REPAIR

This category consisted of patients who underwent abdominal aortic aneurysmectomy with graft replacement and other revascularization processes such as aortofemoral bypass and/or endarterectomy or renal artery revascularization. A total of 71 patients were studied: 38 were treated with T.E.N.S. and 33 were controls. The age and sex distribution were equal. Atelectasis developed in 27 percent of the control group and only 13 percent of the treated group (P = .10). Although prolonged ileus is commonly associated with these types of operations, no treated patient developed postoperative ileus, whereas it occurred in six control patients (P = .006). In the treated patients, the nasogastric tube was removed on the average of 2.9 days following the surgery, compared with 3.4 days in control patients (P = .055). Approximately 70 percent of the treated patients improved their cough in the immediate postoperative period, while none of the control patients improved (P = .003).

GASTRECTOMY

Forty-three patients were studied: 26 treated, 17 control. In general, patients with gastric ulcers had partial gastrectomies. Bilateral truncal vagotomy and antrectomy was the standard procedure for patients who had chronic duodenal ulcer disease. Age and sex

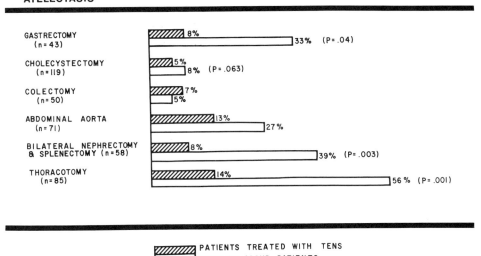

ATELECTASIS

FIGURE 10-6. The incidence of postoperative atelectasis in categories of abdominal surgery and thoracotomy. In the colectomy and abdominal aortic groups, the P values are 0.5 and 0.1, respectively.

ILEUS

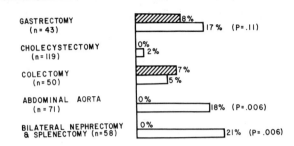

PATENTS TREATED WITH TENS
CONTROL GROUP PATIENTS

FIGURE 10-7. The postoperative incidence of ileus in the subgroups of abdominal surgery. There is a significant difference between the treated and control groups and the abdominal aorta and bilateral nephrectomy and splenectomy groups. The other groups showed no significant difference. However, in the gastrectomy group, there was a trend toward a lesser incidence of ileus in the treated group.

distribution were the same in both groups, as was the distribution of vagotomy and antrectomy. Likewise, patients with carcinoma of the stomach were equally distributed in both groups and underwent extensive gastrectomy depending on the location of the tumor.

Two of the treated patients developed postoperative atelectasis, compared with six in the control group (P = .05). Also, two treated patients developed postoperative ileus,

IMPROVED COUGH

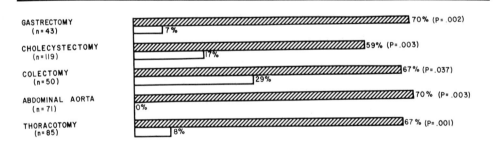

PATENTS TREATED WITH TENS
CONTROL GROUP PATIENTS

FIGURE 10-8. Following T.E.N.S. therapy, cough improved significantly in all groups. The ability to cough was noted before and after stimulation by observers who had no knowledge of whether the individuals were treated or controls. This ability to cough probably reflects a reduced sensation of pain and results in better tracheobronchial toilet. As a result, there may be fewer pulmonary complications postoperatively.

CLINICAL T.E.N.S.

compared with three patients in the control group. This difference is not significant (P = .11) within the number of patients studied.

A 70 percent improvement in cough was noted in the treated group, compared with 7 percent in the control group (P = .002). In the treated group, the nasogastric tube was removed on the average of 3.6 days following surgery, compared with 4.1 days in the control group (P = .06). All nasogastric tubes were removed when the patient expelled flatus or had a bowel movement.

BILATERAL NEPHRECTOMY AND SPLENECTOMY

Fifty-eight patients were studied: 25 treated, 33 control. Only 8 percent of those treated and 39 percent of control patients developed atelectasis. The difference is significant (P = .003). No treated patient had problems with postoperative ileus, whereas it occurred in 21 percent of the control patients (P = .005).

Observations showed that most patients treated with T.E.N.S. reported little or no reduction in the perception of pain. Most of these patients complained of a sharp burning sensation from the stimulation. However, most of these same patients were asleep within 20 minutes after treatment was instituted.

The treated patients were in the intensive care unit on the average of 2.8 days, compared with 4.4 days in the control group (P = .03). Total average hospital stay was 9.4 days for the treated group, compared with 14.2 days for the control patients (P = .08).

This unique group of patients generally received more hypnotic and tranquilizing drugs preoperatively while in a chronic dialysis program, compared with patients studied in other categories.

CHOLECYSTECTOMY

A total of 119 patients were studied: 60 treated, 59 control. Age and sex distribution were equal in both groups.

Three patients treated with T.E.N.S. developed postoperative atelectasis, compared with five patients in the control group (P = .06). No treated patients developed ileus, and only 1 of the 59 control patients developed ileus. The majority of treated patients (50 percent) improved their ability to cough postoperatively, compared with only 17 percent of the control group (P = .003).

COLECTOMY

Hemicolectomy and partial colectomy were performed primarily for carcinoma and the complications of diverticular disease. In this group, 30 patients were treated with T.E.N.S., and 20 served as controls. As noted in Figures 10-6 and 10-7, there was no significant difference in the complication rate of ileus or atelectasis in either group. However, 67 percent of the treated patients improved their cough, compared with 29 percent of the control group (P = .037).

THORACOTOMY

Of the 85 patients who underwent a thoracotomy, 42 were treated with T.E.N.S. and 43 were controls. Only 14 percent of the treated patients developed a postoperative atelectasis, compared with 56 percent for the control group (P = .001). Moreover, 67 percent of the treated patients improved their cough postoperatively, compared with only 8 percent in the control group (P = .001). An additional 100 patients were treated with T.E.N.S. but not randomized. In this group, only 11 percent developed postoperative atelectasis. In a previous study with patients serving as their own controls, the humerus was raised from an average of 90 degrees before treatment to 135 degrees after treatment (P = .001). In the present study, the treated patients raised the humerus an average of 119 degrees, compared with an average of 104 degrees in the control group (P = .03).

MISCELLANEOUS ABDOMINAL PROCEDURES

This group of 155 patients underwent one of a variety of procedures, such as lumbar sympathectomy, small-bowel resection, appendectomy, enterolysis for bowel obstructions, and pancreatectomy. All of these patients were treated with T.E.N.S. Eighteen (12 percent) of the patients in this treated group developed postoperative atelectasis, whereas six (4 percent) developed postoperative ileus.

POSTOPERATIVE ILEUS

This group of 93 postsurgical patients was referred by other surgeons for treatment of persistent or unresolving postoperative ileus. These patients were treated without randomization. The T.E.N.S. treatment was started on the average of 5.5 days postoperatively. Electrodes were placed in the paravertebral position as well as on the anterior abdominal wall. The majority of these patients had restoration of appropriate function of bowel within 48 hours as noted in Table 10-2.

For purposes of analysis, these patients were divided into two categories: 51 patients who had nasogastric suction prior to referral, and 42 patients managed without nasogastric decompression. For the most part, the patients in the second group were not as severely distended as in the first group. In the patients with nasogastric suction, following the application of T.E.N.S., 79 percent expelled flatus within 48 hours and 71 percent had a bowel movement within this time. The nasogastric tube was removed in 72 percent of these patients within 48 hours.

Of 42 patients treated without nasogastric suction, 88 percent expelled flatus within 48 hours from the onset of T.E.N.S. treatment, and 86 percent had a bowel movement.

NARCOTICS

In all of the postsurgical patients studied, there was no evident difference between the treated group and control group in the frequency or total use of narcotics. Analysis of these data in our institution showed that, for the most part, the need for narcotics was determined primarily by the attending nurse and not necessarily because the patient requested medication for pain.

LENGTH OF STAY

No difference in the length of stay in the intensive care unit or the total hospitalization was noted in any groups, except in the nephrectomy and splenectomy group.

TABLE 10-2. Postoperative Ileus Treated With T.E.N.S. (Treatment Started on Average of 5.5 Days Postoperatively)

	Day 1	Day 2	Day 3+
51 patients with nasogastric suction	21	16	14
	41%	31%	28%
Nasogastric tube removed	- 72% -		
	35	5	11
	69%	10%	21%
Flatus	- 79% -		
	25	11	15
	49%	22%	29%
Bowel movement	- 71% -		
42 patients without nasogastric suction	31	6	5
	74%	14%	12%
Flatus	- 88%		
	31	5	6
	74%	12%	14%
Bowel movement	- 86%		

DISCUSSION

These observations indicate that a complex neurophysiologic process results when T.E.N.S. is used. This therapy has demonstrated a striking reduction in postsurgical pulmonary complications and postoperative and post-traumatic ileus as well as pain. At least two obvious physiologic effects secondary to T.E.N.S. can be noted in these studies. Other effects, more subtle and not as easily measured, are also noted.

The first physiologic effect is the subjective reduction of perceptible pain. This effect is noted both directly and indirectly. The reduction of pulmonary complications perhaps can be attributed to a reduced perception of postoperative pain. Deep diaphragmatic breathing seemed easier and was more common in patients treated with T.E.N.S. Coughing was less painful for treated patients; therefore, they were able to cough more effectively, resulting in better bronchotracheal toilet and fewer pulmonary complications.

No attempt was made to control or measure narcotics use in this study. However, independent investigations[2,5,17] specifically studying use of narcotics show that T.E.N.S.

provided good pain relief for 77 percent of treated patients, compared with 17 percent of control patients.

Subjective reduction of pain in our experience was related to the position of the electrodes and area of the electrodes, with the greatest effectiveness noted when they were parallel and within 2 to 3 inches from the incision. Furthermore, better pain reduction was noted with increased frequency and pulse width. McCorkle[12] clearly demonstrated that the striking reduction in post-thoractomy pain was directly related to the amount of energy in the electrical signal transmitted to the skin. These combined observations suggest that subjective pain reduction is related to an increase in current energy, optimal electrode position near the incision, and the area covered by the electrodes.

These findings are somewhat inconsistent with the gate theory of pain[11,18] and are supported by other observations. Campbell and Taub[3] noted pain and touch thresholds to a needle stick were significantly elevated following proximal nerve T.E.N.S. They concluded that analgesia from T.E.N.S. resulted from a peripheral blockage of the A-delta fibers.

In an independent study, Ignelzi and Nyquist[10] observed that T.E.N.S. alters conduction velocity and amplitude of the A-alpha, beta, and delta waves, with the A-delta (pain conduction) component showing the greatest reduction. McCorkle's findings,[12] as well as our own, confirm both these observations. We surmise that the mechanism of pain reduction noted in our study probably is a local phenomenon in the peripheral nerves or the receptor end-organs or both.

This does not imply that no central blockage occurs with transcutaneous electrical nerve stimulation. Clearly, the experimental data demonstrate some form of inhibition of the pain signal to higher perceptive centers within the nervous system. It has been hypothesized that peripheral stimulation may potentiate endogenous production of opiate-like materials, namely endorphins, which in turn may alter pain perception in high centers.[13]

The second physiologic effect of T.E.N.S. may involve the autonomic nervous system, resulting in stimulation of persistaltic activity in the gastrointestinal tract. Early in this study, one of the investigators applied electrodes to his own back in an attempt to discover an optimal area for electrode placement. In so doing, he noted an immediate hyperperistalsis, resulting in a colonic purge. Subsequent stimulation was followed by a similar physiologic response, thereby convincing him that the observed phenomenon was, indeed, real. That same day, electrodes were applied to a patient with persistent ileus, 6 days after vagotomy and hemigastrectomy. As noted by auscultation, peristalsis was strikingly increased with T.E.N.S. and then absent when T.E.N.S. was discontinued. This patient subsequently expelled flatus and evacuated the bowel within 2 hours after application of T.E.N.S. (Although the results of this study have shown that ileus can be effectively treated as well as prevented by T.E.N.S., a few patients did not respond to this form of therapy, indicating it has some limitations.)

The mechanism by which this phenomenon occurs is not clear. To date, there has been no published basic science research on this subject or the subject of the effect of T.E.N.S. on the secretory and mobility functions of the organs of the abdominal cavity.

Perhaps T.E.N.S. decreases or inhibits sympathetic tone that results in peristaltic activity of abdominal viscus and likewise increases the blood flow to an extremity being stimulated.[4]

In some patients, skin temperature increased when a peripheral nerve on an extremity or over the lumbar sympathetic chain was stimulated. These observations were consistent with the findings of Cook and coworkers.[4] However, the findings of Dooley and Kasprak[6] conflict with these observations. We have also observed that T.E.N.S. will constrict the pupil on the ipsilateral side when applied to the stellate ganglion.

Another phenomenon secondary to T.E.N.S. is suggested by this study. Patients who had undergone nephrectomy and splenectomy subjectively disliked the skin sensation of T.E.N.S. However, most of these same patients were asleep within 10 to 15 minutes after the initial application of T.E.N.S. Similar phenomena have been personally noted by other investigators in our group. This sedative-like effect has also been reported by many patients using T.E.N.S. for chronic pain, which suggests a mechanism such as release of endorphins or other humoral agents within the central nervous system as the cause.[1,13,15,16]

CONCLUSIONS

1. T.E.N.S. subjectively reduces postsurgical pain in the majority of patients.
2. Because pain is alleviated by T.E.N.S., patients can breathe deeply and cough more effectively. Thus, T.E.N.S. indirectly reduces the incidence of pulmonary atelectasis.
3. T.E.N.S. is a noninvasive method that can prevent and may be used to treat paralytic ileus. The mechanism of this action remains unclear, but a sympatholytic effect may be caused by T.E.N.S.
4. A sedative-like effect on the central nervous system of patients has been noted secondary to T.E.N.S.

REFERENCES

1. ANDERSSON, SA: *Pain control by sensory stimulation.* Second World Congress on Pain, Montreal, Canada. Pain Abstracts 1:97, 1978.
2. BOULOS, MI, ET AL: *Neuromodulation for the control of postoperative pain and muscle spasm.* In LEROY, PL (ED): *Current Concepts on the Management of Chronic Pain—Pro Dolore Symposium.* Symposium Specialists, Miami, 1977, p 69.
3. CAMPBELL, JM AND TAUB, A: *Local analgesia from percutaneous electrical stimulation.* Arch Neurol 28:347, 1973.
4. COOK, AW, ET AL: *Vascular disease of extremities, electric stimulation of spinal cord and posterior roots.* NY State J Med 76:366, 1976.
5. COOPERMAN, AM, ET AL: *Use of transcutaneous electrical stimulation in control of postoperative pain.* Surg Forum 26:77, 1975.
6. DOOLEY, DM AND KASPRAK, M: *Modification of blood flow to the extremities by electrical stimulation of the nervous system.* South Med J 69:1309, 1976.
7. HOSOBUCHI, Y, ADAMS, J, AND LINCHITZ, R: *Pain relief by electrical stimulation of the central gray matter in humans and its reversal by naloxone.* Science 197:183, 1977.
8. HYMES, AC, ET AL: *Electrical surface stimulation for treatment and prevention of ileus and atelectasis.* Surg Forum 25:223, 1974.
9. HYMES, AC, ET AL: *Acute pain control by electrostimulation: A preliminary report.* Adv Neurol 4:761, 1974.
10. IGNELZI, RJ AND NYQUIST, JK: *Direct effect of electrical stimulation on peripheral nerve evoked activity: Implications for pain relief.* J Neurosurg 45:159, 1976.
11. MELZACK, R AND WALL, DW: *Pain mechanisms: A new theory.* Science 150:971, 1965.
12. McCORKLE, CE JR: Personal communication, 1974.
13. PERT, CB AND SNYDER, SH: *Opiate receptor: Demonstration in nervous tissue.* Science 179:1011, 1973.
14. ROBERTS, HJ: *Transcutaneous electrical nerve stimulation in the management of pancreatitis pain.* South Med J 71:395, 1978.

15. SHEALY, CN, KWAKO, JL, AND HUGHES, S: *Effects of transcranial neurostimulation upon mood and serotonin production: A preliminary report.* Il dolore 1:13, 1979.
16. SNYDER, SH: *Opiate receptors and internal opiates.* Sci Am 236:44, March 1977.
17. VANDER ARK, GO AND McGRATH, KA: *Transcutaneous electrical stimulation in treatment of postoperative pain.* Am J Surg 130:338, 1975.
18. WALL, PD: *The gate control theory of pain mechanisms: A re-examination and re-statement.* Brain 101:1, 1978.

CHAPTER 11

POSTOPERATIVE T.E.N.S. ANALGESIA: PROTOCOL, METHODS, RESULTS, AND BENEFIT

GERALD N. LAMPE, B.S., R.P.T., AND
JEFFREY S. MANNHEIMER, M.A., R.P.T.

The procedures for the use of T.E.N.S. for control of postoperative pain need not be haphazard or difficult. This has been clearly demonstrated in the case study by Hymes in Chapter 10. Previously, because of the lack of scientific data, the methods of stimulation have been largely randomized and empirical. As a result of Hymes' work, as well as our own, the following observations to standardize the principles of applications within rather common, effective, preset instrument settings can be made.

FREQUENCY

Frequency parameters can be preset within the range of 100 to 150 pulses per second so the patient may obtain optimal benefits. Our experience suggests that there is little subjective differentiation between the 100 and 150 settings; therefore, tendency is to select 100 pulses per second in an effort to improve battery life of the T.E.N.S. generator.

PULSE WIDTH

The duration of the on time of the individual pulse, or the pulse width, can be preset to produce the most significant benefit for the patients. Our experience suggests that setting between 150 and 250 μsec most frequently provides optimum benefit. Again, to preserve the battery life of the T.E.N.S. generator, we tend to begin stimulation of the 150-μsec output level and make adjustments upward only if the patient's discomfort cannot be effectively managed by adjusting the amplitude settings (see Pulse Width Adjustment, Chapter 6).

AMPLITUDE

The amplitude requirements will vary according to the thickness of the tissues where the electrodes are placed. In most instances, we found that patients first subjectively experience the sense of stimulation with approximately 14 mA of output and that the ideal, depending upon tissue thickness, usually was between 20 and 35 mA. However, the amplitude should be adjusted according to the patient's subjective needs in order to *produce a sense of stimulation within the painful region.*

ELECTRODE PLACEMENT

Large electrodes provide the best clinical results of pain management. Placing the electrodes 2 to 3 inches either side of an incision site provides the desired benefits. This also results in deeper penetration of the "current."

Initially, attention may be given to managing postoperative incisional pain only, but clinical experience has demonstrated that the pain from the incision site is not always the major painful symptom. Instead, the pain results from noxious input from many regions: the incision, the tissue "damaged" by retraction, and deeper structures. Following thoracic surgery, clinical observation dictates that when using T.E.N.S., the intent is to block all regional intercostal nerves innervating the entire surgical field. This is accomplished with one widely separated electrode channel at the incisional site and a second channel placed bilaterally at the appropriate paravertebral region. This provides electroanalgesia at the incisional site as well as the contused and bruised soft tissue and skeletal structures incised and retracted during the procedure. Similar applications to ensure stimulation of nerve structures innervating the surgical region proximally are made for many procedures within the abdominal and the lumbar spine regions. Postoperative T.E.N.S. applications following surgery of extremities include local (site) stimulation and augmentation of electroanalgesia by electrostimulation of the peripheral nerves proximal to the surgical site with a second channel.

These procedures have significantly improved postoperative analgesia and have also resulted in marked reduction in postoperative muscle spasm, which can be a secondary pain source in the postoperative phase.

STIMULATION PROTOCOL: WHEN, HOW OFTEN, HOW LONG

Whenever possible, T.E.N.S. stimulation is initiated in the recovery room. Otherwise, stimulation is instituted as soon as the patient returns to the hospital room. It is recommended that the stimulation be continuous for the first 24 to 48 hours, after which time a regimen of intermittent stimulation is pursued. To achieve intermittent stimulation periods/sessions, the patient may stimulate *up to 1 hour* (to establish a maximum per-period application) in the pain-free state and then turn the T.E.N.S. generator off. Absolute absence of pain may not be achieved, but relative comfort may be produced, thus giving a relative meaning to pain-free. Stimulation should begin again if, or when, pain returns. This establishes a dynamic, intermittent prn protocol for T.E.N.S. that:

1. Removes the guesswork as to how often stimulation should be repeated each 24-hour day
2. Allows the patient maximum benefit with minimum dependency
3. Provides an easy and accurate basis to ensure that medical necessity will determine when T.E.N.S. stimulation should be discontinued permanently.

The patient uses T.E.N.S. as often (daily) and as long (number of days) as required for effective symptomatic relief, but no more than is required (dependency avoidance) to accomplish same.

INITIATING AND SUSTAINING A T.E.N.S. PROGRAM IN A HOSPITAL

A thorough educational process emphasizing the indications and effectiveness of postoperative T.E.N.S. is the first step in establishing a postoperative T.E.N.S. program. The process should include administrators, physicians, nurses, physical therapists, and other appropriate personnel. Manufacturers of T.E.N.S. equipment have information available for individual or group instruction. When requested, they can provide personnel to assist in the educational process. Professional publications also document the indications as well as effectiveness of this therapy. After completion of this educational process, it is rare that postoperative T.E.N.S. therapy would not be evaluated and/or pursued as an adjunctive procedure to surgical practice.

With the educational procedure completed and surgeons identified who wish to evaluate the value of postoperative T.E.N.S. therapy in their practices, the second phase of the program—the program design—is initiated. The program design and the personnel to carry it out are of prime importance for a successful program. The program design is also the most significant "problem" of the program. We have found that for a postoperative T.E.N.S. therapy program to sustain itself, one individual or small group within the hospital must be designated as the central coordinator of the entire program. Any good program design will work well initially, but even a good program design will support long-term program viability only if one individual or one small group is identified as the "authority"— the team leader. Because of the variable staffing patterns and the limited hours of operation of some departments within the hospital, the need for a single, stable group or individual as the "authority" is evident. Once this "authority" is identified, then the efforts of all other personnel involved can be coordinated to bring about an effective pain management program. Responsibilities can be assigned and accountabilities established.

The following program design protocol developed by Dawn Meyer and Jerry Lampe outlines the responsibilities of the "authority" and other persons involved in the T.E.N.S. program. This guide should be used to create a detailed *task analysis* list of events that must become routine, coordinated functions for the entire team. This task analysis can then be used to make individual/group assignments. Each and every task must be formally assigned. The task-personnel assignments must be appropriately distributed so the "team" is fully cognizant of the assignments. Assignment of tasks establishes staff-line *responsibility*. It must be remembered that responsibility carries with it appropriate *authority*. Finally, the role of the "authority" (team leader) must provide the element of accountability.

CLINICAL PROCEDURE FOR TREATMENT OF POSTOPERATIVE PAIN USING TRANSCUTANEOUS ELECTRIC NERVE STIMULATION (T.E.N.S.)*

Objectives

1. To reduce postoperative pain, thereby decreasing the need for narcotics.
2. To reduce postoperative complications, that is, ileus and atelectasis.

---

*© Copyright 171-306, Pain Control Services, Inc., 1978.

3. To increase mobility for the patient.
4. To obtain a more uneventful recovery period.
5. To shorten ICU or hospital confinement.

Contraindications

1. Cardiac pacemakers.
2. Application over a pregnant uterus.
3. Senility.
4. Application over the carotid sinus.

Preoperative Procedure

1. Provide a written information/education form for the patient relative to the postoperative use of T.E.N.S.
2. Surgical shave prep should be done with extreme caution to avoid any skin abrasions or irritation that could eliminate the patient as a candidate for the T.E.N.S. program.
3. Explain the T.E.N.S. program to the patient as it relates to his or her surgery.
4. Instruct the patient in the operation of the T.E.N.S. unit, and give the patient the appropriate operational manual.
5. Inform the patient that T.E.N.S. will be used for approximately 3 to 5 days unless otherwise ordered by the physician.
6. Note the parameter settings that are comfortable to the patient, and record them on the postoperative data sheet in the chart.

Operating Room Procedure

1. The circulating nurse should observe the patient's skin very carefully before and after the surgical scrub prep. Scrubbing with a stiff-bristled brush is not recommended.
2. If an iodine-based prep is used, the skin must be thoroughly rinsed prior to the application of the sterile postoperative electrodes.
3. The circulating nurse will peel the outer package open so that the scrub nurse can receive the sterile inner package, which contains two sterile electrodes with attached lead wires.
4. The physician or the scrub nurse will place the self-adhesive electrodes parallel to the incision approximately 2 to 3 inches away from the sutures. *The electrodes should not touch each other.* Press gently around the border of pregelled electrodes to establish skin adhesion and avoid pressure on the center of the electrode. Karaya and polymer electrodes should be pressed from center to border to ensure total electrode contact and adhesions.
5. Wound dressings should be applied allowing the electrode lead wires to protrude from under the dressing.

Recovery Room Procedure

1. Plug the lead wires into the adapter, or appropriate receptacle, which is then attached to the T.E.N.S. unit.

2. Adjust the amplitude, rate, and/or pulse width (some units may have only one or two external, independent variables) to the predetermined settings indicated on the postoperative data sheet in the chart.
3. When the patient is awake and alert, readjust the amplitude within the patient's tolerance and comfort.
4. Keep the T.E.N.S. unit on continuously, unless otherwise ordered.
5. Check the settings on the generator frequently in the event they might have been inadvertently adjusted.
6. Within 8 to 12 hours, the patient's skin should be checked for rash or irritation (slight redness is normal). This is done by lifting a corner of the electrode and looking under the pad.
7. The patient should be encouraged to vary the T.E.N.S. output amplitude since the level of discomfort varies.

Postoperative Surgical Floor Procedure

1. The physician should leave a standing order for T.E.N.S. to be discontinued immediately if any complications develop.
2. Normal length of usage is 3 to 5 days.
3. The skin should be checked every 12 hours for rash or irritation. This is done by lifting a corner of the electrode and looking under the pad.
4. Depending on the sterile electrode materials employed and the conditions of the patient's skin or incision, electrodes may require replacement during recovery. If the conducting medium should dry out or the electrodes come loose, stimulation will be uncomfortable, indicating a need to secure or change the electrodes.
5. If replacing the electrodes is necessary, place each one parallel to the incision, approximately 2 to 3 inches from the sutures. If any skin irritation is present and stimulation is to be continued, place the electrodes at alternate sites parallel to the suture line to avoid the irritation.
6. The patient should reset the amplitude knob to a comfortable effective setting.
7. Increase generator output prior to coughing and increased physical activity, which may increase noxious input.
8. Chart on the postoperative analgesia record all pertinent information relative to the use of T.E.N.S. throughout the recovery period.

Results of Postoperative Program

1. The results of a good postoperative T.E.N.S. program should coincide with the objectives listed above.
2. For the program to succeed, cooperation of all personnel involved in the care of the patient is vital.
3. It is of critical importance to keep an accurate record of the patient's recovery period so that proper evaluation can be established.
   a. Narcotic use
   b. NG tube use—how many days
   c. Presence of ileus
   d. Presence of atelectasis
   e. Mobility of the patient
   f. Other

ALTERNATE ELECTRODE PLACEMENTS
FOR SPECIFIC SURGICAL PROCEDURES

Most surgery requires placement of the electrodes bilateral to the incision. Generally, 2 to 3 inches from the sutures is acceptable and will elicit the desired results.

The diagrams of alternate electrode placement indicate that in specific surgeries, equal or better results can be obtained by modifying the bilateral incisional applications.

CERVICAL ANTERIOR FUSION

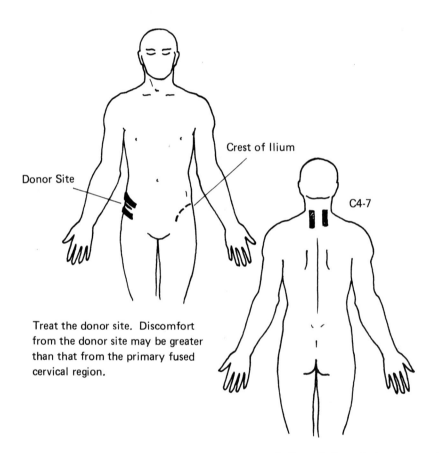

Donor Site

Crest of Ilium

C4-7

Treat the donor site. Discomfort from the donor site may be greater than that from the primary fused cervical region.

1. Do not place electrodes near the carotid sinus
2. Treat the referred pain at level of C4-7

THYROIDECTOMY

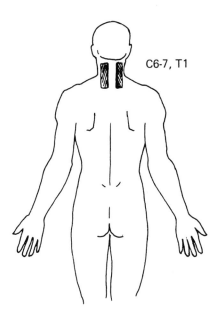

C6-7, T1

Treat referred pain C6-7, T1.
Do not place electrodes by
incision because of carotid
sinuses.

MAMMAPLASTY

Most commonly, single channel
applications provide excellent
comfort. Occasionally, paraspinal
electrodes including T3-T7 may
improve comfort.

THORACOTOMY

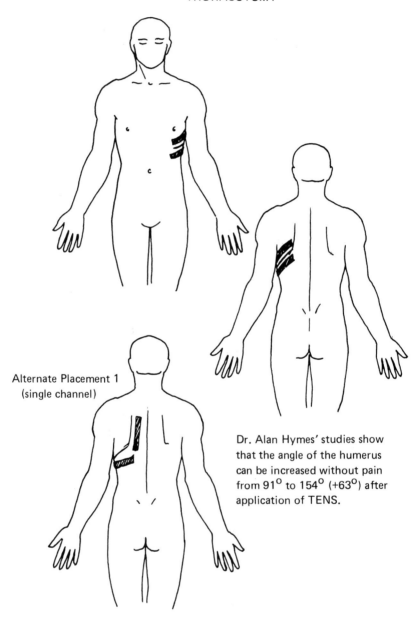

Alternate Placement 1
(single channel)

Dr. Alan Hymes' studies show
that the angle of the humerus
can be increased without pain
from 91° to 154° (+63°) after
application of TENS.

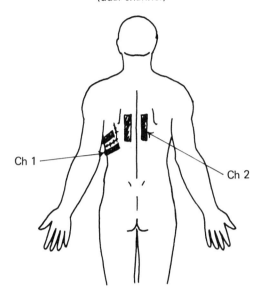

Alternate Placement 2
(dual channel)

Ch 1

Ch 2

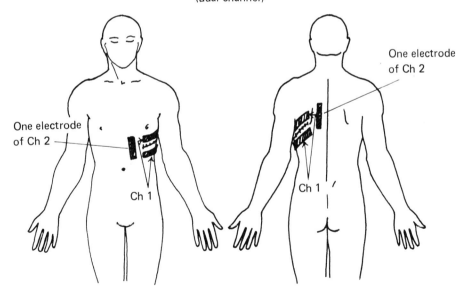

Alternate Placement 3
(dual channel)

One electrode
of Ch 2

One electrode
of Ch 2

Ch 1

Ch 1

GASTRECTOMY

ILEUS

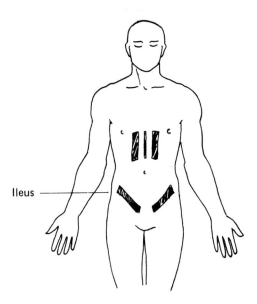

Treat both reduce discomfort
around the incision and to prevent
or reduce possible postoperative ileus.
When treating ileus, the electrodes
should extend along the ascending
or descending colon.

RECTAL SURGERY

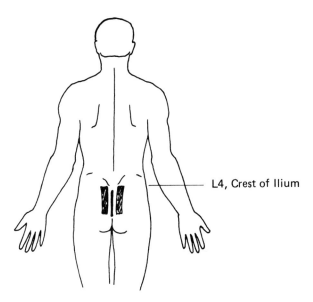

L4, Crest of Ilium

Place the electrodes from L5, S1, down over the sacrum. Do not allow electrodes to touch. Separation increases "depth of penetration" of stimulating current.

HYSTERECTOMY

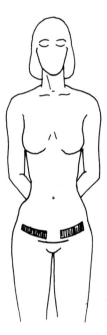

Placement of electrodes proximal to the incision provides adequate post-surgical analgesia. Electrodes may be placed in a more acute V configuration for prevention or management of postoperative ileus.

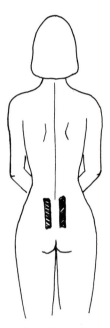

With a presurgical diagnosis of endometriosis, lumbar region discomfort is often noted post-surgically. Bilateral, paraspinal placement of electrodes from L3-4 to S1-2 while patients are in OR or RR has become routine for this patient population (nonsterile electrodes). Place electrodes at level of L4-5, S1.

CLINICAL T.E.N.S.

FOREFOOT RECONSTRUCTION

Note: No electrodes are placed at or near surgical site(s). Electrodes are placed to establish neural electrostimulation proximal to the painful region.

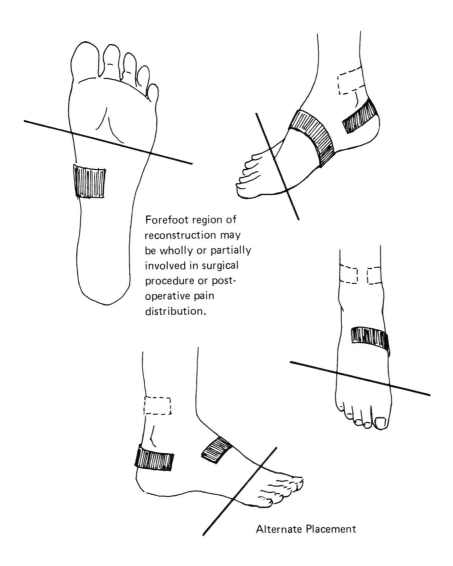

Forefoot region of reconstruction may be wholly or partially involved in surgical procedure or post-operative pain distribution.

Alternate Placement

KNEE SURGERY

Place electrodes using the collateral ligaments as surface orientation.

[2 elec] may be utilized for single channel placements

| 2 elec | commonly used for single channel placements

| 2 elec | + [2 elec] both channels, 4 electrodes may be placed concurrently as illustrated

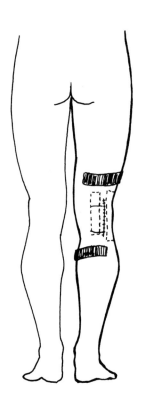
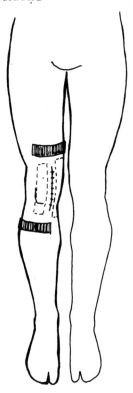

SPECIAL NOTES ON POSTOPERATIVE T.E.N.S.

1. In some instances, the analgesic effect of T.E.N.S. does not start immediately with the onset of current flow; there may be a latent period.
2. Education of the nursing personnel involved in the care of the postoperative patients should include reinforcement of the fact that *every patient does not need medication for comfort.*
3. To prevent "loss" of T.E.N.S. generators after therapy has been discontinued and the unit is removed from a patient, one individual on the nursing unit, for example, the unit supervisor, should be responsible for all discontinued units. The units should be stored in a locked area until the "authority" receives them.
4. Sterile electrodes should be used along the incisional site for obvious reasons. If augmental or primary stimulation is applied in areas remote from the surgical site, conventional types of nonsterile electrodes can be used.
5. The experiences in treating patients with postoperative pain have provided useful guidelines in management of cancer pain. As in postoperative T.E.N.S., it is beneficial to use large electrodes to "surround" the diffuse area of pain. Also, cancer patients frequently benefit from additional stimulation with electrodes placed in the somatosegmental or viscerosegmental paravertebral regions (usually several segments higher than the dermatomes).
6. Use of T.E.N.S. for open heart surgery patients and for patients in labor and delivery has sometimes been complicated by the tendency of the high-frequency T.E.N.S. generator to interfere with the telemetry monitoring process. We have found this interference can be reduced in two ways:
   a. Stimulation below 60 cycles per second does not interfere with the monitoring process; a characteristic stimulus artifact will be present and identifiable as a product of T.E.N.S. input, but it does not alter or interfere with monitored patterns
   b. Interface units that "filter" T.E.N.S. frequencies higher than 60 cycles per second can be used.
7. The patient should be properly advised that the T.E.N.S. stimulation can be discontinued at his or her direction.
8. The policy of reimbursement by third-party payers for postoperative analgesia is consistent with policies related to T.E.N.S. for management of acute clinical pain.
9. The electrode placement designs, as presented previously, may require modification such as in foot reconstruction surgery and hand surgery where placement of the electrodes near the surgical site is not possible. Stimulation proximally along the peripheral nerves innervating the foot and hand will usually offer adequate analgesia. Also, some electrodes may be trimmed to conform to particular size/shape restrictions demanded by certain surgical procedures.
10. Although there are rechargeable systems that provide adequate stimulation for 12 to 24 hours, we prefer disposable battery systems.

PREOPERATIVE PATIENT INSTRUCTION PROTOCOL

The primary emphasis of this section is preoperative patient instruction. Chapter 7 presents a thorough discussion of patient instruction protocol related to the safe, effective employment of the T.E.N.S. system during therapy.

In the preoperative interviews, we found that nearly all patients have initial emotional (affective and rational/cognitive) anxieties and fears as they anticipate surgery. From these same interviews, we concluded that patients *do not have significant fears regarding the pain during the surgery*, thus reflecting a trust and confidence in the anesthesia provided, but that their greatest fears and anxieties are regarding the *pain* expected or anticipated *following the surgery*. Therefore, part of the preoperative instruction should include a brief interview to assess the patient's anticipations, fears, and anxieties. Then these should be appropriately addressed when presenting the reasons T.E.N.S. therapy is being offered. Through these instructions, the patient should become aware that the health-care team also anticipates that the patient may experience some discomfort postoperatively and if it occurs, it will not be ignored. The patient should be made confident that safety and comfort are the primary objects of the health-care team.

The patient should recognize that appropriate analgesic medication will be available as or if required. It should be emphasized that 100 percent of the pain or discomfort may not be relieved with T.E.N.S. therapy alone or with a combination of T.E.N.S. and medication, but that a significant and major portion of the discomfort will be controlled. *Perhaps all of it will be controlled.* In this instruction phase, the patient is also advised of the active role he or she will assume in the T.E.N.S. therapy and that he or she will have the ability to exercise active control over the discomfort and will not be completely dependent on the medical and nursing staff to provide all of the interventions.

With this background information completed, electrodes are then applied to an area in close proximity to the proposed incisional site. The pulse rate and the pulse width are preset as previously outlined (see Chapter 7). The patient then turns the units on and increases the amplitude "until a sense of stimulation is perceived" in the region of the electrodes, not beneath each electrode. During this initial few minutes, while the patient is becoming acquainted with the sense of stimulation at very low levels, he or she is advised that the output controls for the rate and pulse width will be protected so the parameters will not be inadvertently adjusted. If rate or pulse width adjustment is required, the team members will assist in making this adjustment in the postoperative phase. With adequate instruction, the patient recognizes that the procedure is not complicated. The amplitude will be the only variable the patient will adjust routinely and without staff assistance. After the initial minutes of stimulation, the patient is instructed to increase the amplitude until a "moderate to strong sensory perception" is created. After several minutes, the patient will experience an analgesia between and/or distal to the electrodes. The patient is then directed to squeeze a large area of the skin with the thumb and index finger to experience that analgesia within the area is present. This regional analgesia is the object of stimulation in the postoperative phase and will occur, but the amplitude settings required to produce adequate analgesia may be higher after surgery. Therefore, the amplitude settings established during this instructional period will serve only to establish initial stimulus intensity levels.

Note: Sometimes patients do not experience the same sensation of stimulation postoperatively as preoperatively. Therefore, it is sometimes helpful in determining the proper postoperative amplitude by increasing the output intensity until the perception of stimulation "replaces" the pain.

Once the patient has become familiar with the apparatus and the sense of stimulation, he or she should increase the amplitude to *produce muscle contraction* within the region of the electrodes to demonstrate that *this response is possible but undesirable*. The patient should also increase the amplitude rapidly to a level of discomfort and then immediately return it to the comfort range. Although this is obviously not pleasant, it teaches by demonstration and experience what may occur if the amplitude knob should accidentally or inadvertently be turned to a high intensity. This also shows that although this sensation is not comfortable, it will not cause any real harm. Patients overtly or covertly harbor questions or fear of "what if . . ." when instructions omit this consideration.

The patient should be aware that electrodes may be placed at regions of the body removed from the incisional site to provide additional pain relief, if required. This initiates the instruction that the patient may have two channels of output to adjust but that channel 1 will always govern the electrodes at the incision site and channel 2 will govern the electrodes in the remote site.

The parameter settings (never strong, low-rate, acupuncture-like near incision) as established in the preoperative evaluation period are noted on the preoperative chart to be used as the optimal dial settings by the recovery room nurses to *initiate* T.E.N.S. after surgery.

After the instruction period is completed, the patient should be permitted time for questions. The patient should also be specifically directed to contact the instructing "authority" should more questions arise at a later time. Instruction should advise that daily visits (or more frequently if required) will be made by the appropriate individuals to assess the patient's general well-being, the response to T.E.N.S., and the function of the T.E.N.S. system.

If postoperative T.E.N.S. has not been anticipated preoperatively and the patient had not received preoperative instructions, it is recommended that T.E.N.S. therapy not be initiated until the patient has returned to the room. At this time, the patient is more alert and responsive to information and instructions. Instituting T.E.N.S. in the operating or recovery room without the patient's prior knowledge of T.E.N.S. can be a very disconcerting experience, and it is nearly impossible to provide an adequate explanation of T.E.N.S. to a patient who is not fully alert.

SUMMARY

T.E.N.S. provides benefits in several aspects of postoperative care:

1. Excellent patient acceptance and compliance, thus increasing patient mobility and independence.
2. Reduction of nursing services required in caring for the postoperative patient.
3. Improved functional results.
4. Diminished need for analgesic drugs.
5. Significant incidence of reduced ICU/hospital stay.

Electrode placement in the region of the incision is almost always the primary site of stimulation. Augmental, or primary, stimulation of appropriate innervating nerves proximal to the incision can be provided if necessary.

The parameters of stimulation are flexible and easily established. The mode of stimulation may vary, but only the conventional, high-rate or the brief, intense mode is applied near the incision. This is thought to produce selective recruitment of the large, coarsely myelinated peripheral fibers for pain management secondary to modulated activities in the peripheral neural structures, the spinal cord, the central neuraxis, and/or other higher nervous system structures. Although there may be definite enkephalin-related pain inhibition with either or these modes, there probably is not a primary analgesic effect from significant action of endorphin mechanisms.

In view of the evidence available at this time, the humanistic and medical benefits derived from T.E.N.S. therapy for the management of postoperative pain suggest that most patients anticipating surgery should be offered this therapy as an adjuvant/alternative analgesic.

BIBLIOGRAPHY

ALI, J AND YAFFE, C: *The effect of transcutaneous electric stimulation (TENS) on postoperative pain and pulmonary function.* Presented at Canadian Association of General Surgeons Annual Meeting, Montreal, February 5–9, 1979.

ALM, WA, GOLD, ML, AND WEIL, LS: *Evaluation of transcutaneous electrical nerve stimulation (TENS) in podiatric surgery.* J Am Podiatry Assoc 69:537, 1979.

BUSSEY, JG AND JACKSON, A: *TENS for post-surgical analgesia.* Presented at Second Annual Meeting of the American Pain Society, New York City, September 1980.

HARVIE, KW: *A major advance in the control of postoperative knee pain.* Orthopedics 2:26, 1979.

PIKE, PMH: *Transcutaneous electrical stimulation: Its use in the management of postoperative pain.* Anaesthesia 33:165, 1978.

SMITH, CM AND LaFLAMME, CA: *Managing a TENS program in the OR.* AORN J 32:411,1980.

SOLOMON, RA, VIERNSTEIN, MC, AND LONG, DM: *Reduction of postoperative pain and narcotic use by transcutaneous electrical nerve stimulation.* Surgery 87:142, 1980.

STABILE, ML AND MALLORY, TH: *The management of postoperative pain in total joint replacement: Transcutaneous electrical nerve stimulation is evaluated in total hip and knee patients.* Ortho Review 7:121, 1978.

SWEENY, SS: *OR observations: Key to postop pain.* AORN J 32:391, 1980.

TICHO, U, OLSHWANG, D, AND MAGORA, F: *Relief of pain by subcutaneous electrical stimulation after ocular surgery.* Am J Ophthalmol 89:803, 1980.

CHAPTER 12

FACTORS THAT HINDER, ENHANCE, AND RESTORE THE EFFECTIVENESS OF T.E.N.S.: PHYSIOLOGIC AND THEORETICAL CONSIDERATIONS

JEFFREY S. MANNHEIMER, M.A., R.P.T., AND GERALD N. LAMPE, B.S., R.P.T.

The effectiveness of T.E.N.S., aside from electrode placement and proper evaluation, can be hindered, enhanced, and restored by many factors. These factors are listed in Table 12-1. It cannot be claimed T.E.N.S. is effective in every patient; however, with a cooperative, legitimate patient and without clinical time restraints, we feel that satisfactory (according to the patient) efficacy can be obtained in the majority of patients.

Wolf, Gersh, and Rao have confirmed that the systematic application of electrodes and the readjustment of stimulation parameters over several sessions reduce failures and increase the success rate of T.E.N.S.[1] Their study showed that only 10 of 114 patients obtained the best result with T.E.N.S. during the first treatment session.

Cost to the patient can be minimized by having the individual (after specific instruction) evaluate other electrode arrangements and/or different modes of stimulation at home over a weekend using a "loaner" unit. If success has not been obtained after three evaluative sessions, but we feel pain relief can be obtained, the patient is advised that if he or she is willing to continue trying, we will do so without further fee. This approach is valuable in that pain relief ultimately may occur, and we in turn will gain experience and knowledge that will be of help to future patients.

PHYSIOLOGIC CONSIDERATIONS

When failures do occur, they are frequently due to hindering factors such as senility, dependency, and visual or functional impairment (see Table 12-1).

Senility obviously hinders a patient's understanding of instructions concerning T.E.N.S. as well as the clinician's ability to determine effectiveness. We experienced this with two

TABLE 12-1. Factors Influencing the Effectiveness of T.E.N.S.

Hindering	Enhancing	Restoring
Senility	Wean from medications	Tryptophan loading
Dependency	Tricyclics/tryptophan	Ice massage
"Cure syndrome"	D-phenylalanine	Change stimulation mode
↓ manual dexterity	Stimulation close to area of pain (brief, intense)	Change electrode placement sites
Visual impairment		Re-evaluate pain distribution; it may have changed
Unwillingness of patient to evaluate alternate electrode placement sites after initial failure with T.E.N.S.	Increased tolerance should result from a gradual progression to stronger stimulation parameters	Modulate current parameters
↑ pain perception after T.E.N.S.	If stronger stimulation modes cannot be tolerated at the painful region, try stimulation in segmentally related, but not painful, myotomes on ipsilateral, contralateral, or bilateral regions	
Diazepam		
Narcotics/addiction		
Corticosteroids		
Prolonged pain and stress	Pulse-train stimulation may be tolerated better than acupuncture-like with equal effectiveness	
Poor posture and/or body mechanics	Do not stimulate over areas of dry, scaly skin	
	Place electrodes over motor points when using acupuncture-like, burst, or pulse-train modes	
	Use self-adhering electrodes	
	Skin prep may enhance electrode adherence	
	Patient should perceive stimulation throughout the area of pain with conventional T.E.N.S.	
	Placement of one electrode at the proximal and distal extent of pain (conventional and brief, intense)	
	Evaluation of posture and body mechanics	

patients where the presence of a family member was required during the T.E.N.S. evaluation to inform us of changes in the patient's behavior and/or facial expression indicating increased or decreased pain. Also, this family member had to administer the T.E.N.S. to the patient.

Patients who are dependent on a spouse, relative, or friend to perform activities of daily living (ADL) most probably will not achieve success with T.E.N.S. This is illustrated in Case Study 1 in which a patient depended solely on her husband to operate the T.E.N.S. unit. Bates and Nathan reported that patients who rejected T.E.N.S. within the first week exhibited a higher proportion of psychologic and social problems than those usually seen with chronic pain.[2]

Case Study 1

An 80-year-old female with a 9-month history of cervical and thoracic spine pain was referred on 11/14/80 for physical therapy. The patient also complained of low back and left arm pain and had received previous hospital outpatient treatment consisting of moist heat and ultrasound without benefit. A history of congestive heart failure and respiratory difficulties were also reported.

Evaluation revealed the complaint of a relatively constant pain in the cervical to midthoracic region described as a "cold feeling." Pain was eased by lying supine and/or wearing a soft cervical collar. Structurally, there were profound abnormalities. The patient had a significant forward head posture with a marked thoracic kyphosis and increased lumbar lordosis that, according to the patient and her husband, had been present for a number of years. Active ROM of the cervical spine was limited by 25 percent in forward bending and 50 percent in all other directions. Pain was increased by left rotation, side bending, and backward bending of the head. The patient was taking medication for pain with no significant benefit. Active ROM of the shoulders was grossly WNL. Upper extremity reflexes were hyperactive, but the C1–T1 myotomes displayed normal strength. Passive movement testing of the cervical and thoracic spine showed significant hypomobility. Palpation revealed a generalized tenderness throughout the painful region. Overview of the patient's sitting posture uncovered the possible cause of the spinal abnormalities.

The patient specifically requested mechanical cervical traction since this had "cured" her friend. She was informed that such treatment would probably not be beneficial in light of her structural abnormalities. However, she insisted, and it was decided that 1 to 2 weeks of traction would be performed on a three-times-a-week basis and if no benefit was obtained, it would be discontinued. In addition, the patient was instructed in proper body mechanics and postural exercise, which at this point would only negate further progression of her deformities. T.E.N.S. as a means of pain control in lieu of medication was suggested but not accepted by the patient.

The traction was unsuccessful and the patient was discharged on 11/19/80. On 12/11/80, the patient called, saying she had decided to try T.E.N.S. She was evaluated and reported satisfactory pain relief in the office while the unit was on and for a 20-minute carryover. She then decided to rent a unit from the distributor. A Medtronic "comfort burst" unit was chosen because it was the simplest to use (no adjustable rate or width). She was evaluated with the unit and again reported pain relief with the conventional mode of stimulation.

The patient and her husband were instructed in the use of the unit, placement of karaya electrodes, and different electrode arrangements to try at home for further evaluation. She was also given written home instructions and evaluation forms. However, the patient wanted her husband to do everything in regard to using the unit. Her lack of desire to help herself hindered the chance of success. The patient called after 1 week to report that she was not coming in for her follow-up evaluation since she had not yet used the unit. The following week she returned the unit stating that she could not use it herself and her husband could not be depended on to help her every time. She was again instructed that once the unit and electrodes were in place in the morning she need not do anything more than simply turn the unit (amplitude controls) on and off as needed. However, she was unable to accept this, stating that she could not do this herself. At that point, it was decided not to make any further attempts at working with this patient. It was our opinion that this patient may have indeed been using her pain (pain game) to obtain attention from her husband and that if her discomfort was severe enough, she would have participated to a greater extent.

Patients who have problems with manual dexterity (possibly due to arthritis) or vision also present difficulty to the clinician.[2] Case Study 2 provides an example.

Case Study 2

A 75-year-old female was referred for evaluation with T.E.N.S. due to a history of degenerative arthritis of the spine. Pain had been intensifying for a year. She had been given a lumbar corset and was using a moist heat pad for the past 6 to 7 months without benefit.

At the time of the initial evaluation, the patient was driven to the office by a friend. The patient revealed that she was blind in one eye and lived alone. She complained of a constant toothache-like pain throughout the lumbosacral spine aggravated by housecleaning, forward bending, and ambulation. Pain was eased by sitting up straight. Structurally, there was a loss of the normal lumbar lordosis. Active ROM of the lumbar spine was severely limited by 75 percent and painful in all directions. Straight leg raise was negative, and strength of the L1–S2 myotomes was within normal limits. The patient was unable to assume a prone position, thus eliminating further testing. The patient was introduced to the role of T.E.N.S. in pain control and shown various units. She had difficulty in applying the electrodes and working the dials on the unit.

She stated she could not think of anyone who could help her in applying the electrodes each day, but would think about it and contact us in a few days. She subsequently called and said she did not feel she could use the unit satisfactorily and did not want to use it on a trial basis. This patient was not seen beyond the initial visit. An electrode placement belt* for the low back may have helped this patient. Electrodes can be placed on the belt and then worn around the abdomen like a brassiere.

It is not uncommon to have patients who consider the use of T.E.N.S. as a cure in that pain will not return. Bates and Nathan reported this as a reason for returning the stimulators within the first 3 months.[2] In addition, if the patient discovered that the effect of T.E.N.S. was similar to that of analgesia, they returned the unit.[2] This factor is discussed in Case Study 3.

Case Study 3

This patient was a 70-year-old female with a 2-year history of low back and sciatic pain. Etiology was due to a fall in which the patient landed on the left buttock. Concurrent medical history consisted of a hiatal hernia, Parkinson's disease, and previous thoracic surgery for bovine tuberculosis.

At the time of referral, the patient complained of "back spasms" and left sciatic pain occurring on an intermittent basis but persisting for 2 to 3 days at a time. Pain was present bilaterally in the lumbosacral region and referred down the left sciatic distribution to the ankle. The patient was unable to differentiate the pain distribution between medial and lateral ankle. Pain was intensified by driving and sitting and was eased by moist heat. Active ROM of the lumbar spine was limited by 50 percent in forward bending, 60 percent in backward bending, and 25 percent in side bending bilaterally. Left side bending intensified the pain, and there was a positive right straight leg raise producing left low back pain at 60 degrees, intensified by passive dorsiflexion of the ankle. Palpation revealed tenderness at the L4–5 and L5–S1 paravertebral regions on the left more than the right, a tender buttock trigger point, popliteal space, and left proximal superficial aspect of the sural nerve (B 57). There was weakness of one grade of the left extensor hallucis longus as compared with the right.

The patient was unable to lie in the supine or prone position (rib resections) for more than 2 minutes. Consequently, a program of Cyriax traction could not be performed, and she was unable to tolerate gentle joint mobilization. She was instructed in a home exercise program and proper lumbar spine mechanics and evaluated with T.E.N.S.

The initial trial with conventional-mode T.E.N.S. produced satisfactory pain relief. After being fully instructed in its use, the patient expressed a desire to obtain a rental unit. One week after obtaining the unit from the distributor, the patient reported satisfactory relief of pain when the unit was on but when the unit was turned off the pain would return after a few hours. She was again told that T.E.N.S. provided only symptomatic relief, like medication, and would not stop the pain from returning. She was instructed to turn the stimulator on whenever the pain began, not only when it got severe.

The patient decided to return the unit to the distributor after the initial month's rental. She continued to report pain relief lasting for up to 4 hours after T.E.N.S. but was convinced that the unit was not working for her because the pain always returned. We were unable to change her conviction in regard to T.E.N.S. and thus considered the patient's experience with T.E.N.S. a failure.

We have had a few patients who did not return for another session after an unsuccessful initial T.E.N.S. evaluation. We have also encountered the patient who complains of an increase in pain during and/or after T.E.N.S. This has been rare in our experience, but

---

*Tenswear automatic electrode placement belt, Wallant International Trade Inc., 41 Madison Ave., New York, NY 10010.

CLINICAL T.E.N.S.

there are reports in the literature attesting to this.[2,4] Picaza and associates reported that in one series of patients about 10 percent perceived an increase of pain during or after the use of T.E.N.S.[5] This was primarily for brief periods, but some patients experienced increased pain up to 24 hours. An analysis of these patients revealed that increased pain often accompanied stimulation with a frequency higher than 80 Hz (80 to 200 Hz), and the problem was eliminated by lowering the rate. There were also instances of pain intensification from low-rate stimulation. Changing the stimulation parameters usually stopped the increased pain.

Directly related to the findings of Picaza and associates is that by Ignelzi and Nyquist.[6] They reported that high-frequency repetitive electrical stimulation of the superficial radial nerve of the cat via an implanted cuff electrode produced a decreased excitability followed by an enhanced excitability. The fibers that demonstrated this response were larger than A-delta. The enhanced excitability after analgesia may be the phenomenon behind pain returning at a greater intensity than that which existed prior to electrical stimulation if the same mechanism also occurs with fibers mediating nociceptive input.

The perception of an increase in pain after T.E.N.S. may be misinterpreted in light of another phenomenon. A patient who has repeatedly experienced only a 25 percent reduction of pain from medication suddenly obtains a 50 percent or greater decrease as a result of T.E.N.S. When post-T.E.N.S. pain returns, it does so at a range of at least 50 percent or more as opposed to 25 percent, and this may be misinterpreted by the patient as increased pain. In actuality, pain has returned to the same level after relief with T.E.N.S. as it has after the medication wears off. The difference is that the patient now equates the return of pain with one of intensification since medication never provided a similar degree of pain relief.

Occasionally, a patient may get a transitory increase in pain due to the liberation of histamine. Nausea and vomiting after T.E.N.S. have also been reported. Patients who have been on codeine may demonstrate this phenomenon. Rao has stated that codeine will stick to opiate receptor sites and the effect of T.E.N.S. may result in displacement, causing a gastrointestinal reaction similar to that from opiate administration.[7,94]

Reports dealing with increased or decreased pain as a result of the application of T.E.N.S. should not be based solely on the findings demonstrated by one patient.[4] Increased pain may occur after any treatment regardless of the modality and can be misleading. However, if complications consistently occur in relation to a specific modality, they should be reported.

Just as there may be hindering factors, there are a number of factors that enhance and/or restore the effectiveness of T.E.N.S., for example, electrode placement, ice massage, change in stimulation mode, and modulation of current parameters (see Table 12-1).

Melzack and associates compared the effectiveness of ice massage with that of T.E.N.S. in a group of patients with chronic low back pain.[9] The stimulation parameters employed were compatible with those required to activate supraspinal inhibitory mechanisms. The results showed that both modalities produced similar effectiveness. Melzack postulated that ice massage may be employed as a means of regaining the effectiveness of T.E.N.S. by substituting it for electrical stimulation. This would have the net effect of producing a different type of afferent input to hopefully negate the effects of habituation.

Electrode placement arrangements are unlimited, yet to determine the effectiveness of each array need not be time consuming. With conventional and brief, intense modes, the electrodes are rearranged if some pain relief is not apparent within 10 to 20 minutes. Strong, low-rate (acupuncture-like) and pulse-train (burst) parameters require at least 20 to 30 minutes to assess. (The complete T.E.N.S. evaluation process is discussed in Chapter 7.)

Brief, intense T.E.N.S. seems to be enhanced by placing electrodes as close as possible to the painful region. Janko and Trontelj obtained the best results when T.E.N.S. was applied to the same finger as the noxious stimulus.[10] This also relates to the use of conventional T.E.N.S. The best results will be obtained when the current is perceived throughout the area of pain. If the effectiveness of conventional T.E.N.S. is via the gate control theory, then pain relief must occur in a segmental fashion. If small-fiber nociceptive input is entering the lumbosacral region, it will be optimally gated by large-fiber (T.E.N.S.) input entering at the same segments. Large-fiber activity entering the L1 dorsal horn will probably not be as effective in inhibiting small-fiber input entering the L5 dorsal horn.

The use of different modes of stimulation has been previously discussed. Utilizing modes other than conventional T.E.N.S. can only serve to enhance effectiveness. Tolerance to the stronger modes of stimulation can be enhanced by a process of gradual progression.[5,11,12]

Strong, low-rate (acupuncture-like) T.E.N.S. and, to a similar degree, strong, pulse-train (burst) stimulation may not be tolerated by a significant number of patients. The strong, beating contractions are uncomfortable, especially in an area of pain. The clinician is advised to try stimulation at segmentally related but not painful myotomes. For example, if a patient with chronic low back pain is unable to obtain satisfactory pain relief with conventional T.E.N.S. at the lumbosacral region and will not tolerate strong, low-rate T.E.N.S. at that area, stimulation of the calf musculature may produce benefits. The innervation of these myotomes is via the same segments as the lumbosacral spine. There is also greater muscle mass to stimulate, which will produce strong contractions in an area segmentally related to the painful region. A similar effect may occur with contralateral stimulation to the involved region when ipsilateral stimulation can not be performed. Bilateral stimulation of related myotomes should provide optimal results.

Eriksson and colleagues reported that strong pulse-train (burst) stimulation may be tolerated when strong, low-rate stimulation cannot.[13] Use of rhythmic pulse trains at high intensity can produce muscle contractions equivalent to that of the strong, low-rate mode but at one-half to two-thirds the intensity. One of the objectives when utilizing strong, low-rate or high-intensity, pulse-train T.E.N.S. is to obtain strong muscle contraction. The best site to stimulate muscle is the motor point; therefore, electrode placement should be at that site. Stimulation of the motor point will produce the strongest contraction with the least amount of current and thus may serve to enhance effectiveness. Electrode placement on superficial aspects of peripheral nerves innervating the desired muscle group is equally or even more effective. One individual muscle will be stimulated per motor point, yet an entire myotome or group of muscles can be made to contract when the related peripheral nerve is stimulated.

The use of self-adhering electrodes and their benefits were presented in Chapter 9. When self-adhering electrodes are not available and electrode tape patches are used, a substance known as skin prep can enhance the use of tape patches.* Skin prep will promote better adherence of the tape patch and may decrease skin irritation. It is best applied as a swab around the electrode placement site prior to application of the tape patch. It will not interfere to any significant extent with conduction of the electrical impulse. Adherence may also be enhanced by placing the electrodes under bra straps, stockings, socks, and girdles using an electrode placement belt.† Tape also may be placed over stockinette around an extremity to eliminate skin irritation.

---

*United Skin Prep, Howmedica Inc., Largo, FL 33540.
†Wallant International Trade Inc.

MODULATION

Nerve adaptation (accommodation) may be reversed by changing the stimulation parameters instead of the mode of T.E.N.S. Units incorporating modulating features that automatically change the frequency, duration, amplitude, or combinations thereof within a preset range may be beneficial in restoring effectiveness, increasing tolerance to the stronger stimulation modes, and delaying the possibility of accommodation.* Accommodation occurs when the initial stimulus seems to weaken or fall to a subthreshold level. This is considered to be due to a change in excitability of the nerve. The nerve membrane potential may stabilize due to a net outflow of potassium ions producing an increased threshold.[17] During an ongoing, steady application of electrical impulses, the nerve fiber membrane becomes less excitable (increased threshold) and perception can be restored only by a sudden rise or fall of the intensity (amplitude and/or pulse duration) of the stimulating current. Accommodation is more pronounced with stimulation of large myelinated fibers (conventional T.E.N.S.). These fibers contain a greater amount of protoplasm, which has the universal property of accommodation to all types of stimuli.[17]

Modulation of the electrical parameters probably represents the latest advance in the T.E.N.S unit and can be accomplished in various ways. Once the stimulation parameters have been properly adjusted to a desired stimulation mode, the modulation feature can be activated. Depending on the manufacturer, one or more individual pulse parameters can be modulated. Modulation frequency is approximately once every second, and the degree of parameter fluctuation is usually within the range of 40 to 100 percent of the preselected value, depending on the manufacturer. Therefore, if the pulse rate is initially set at 100 Hz and modulation is employed, the unit will automatically shift from a rate of 100 Hz down to one of 50 Hz (50 percent) and back to 100 Hz each second. The patient will perceive a continual fluctuation of pulse rate every second. If pulse rate is the only parameter being modulated, the intensity and pulse duration remain constant at the predetermined settings. Modulation of pulse rate is most beneficial when a high frequency is employed, such as with the conventional or brief, intense mode.

A change in the total energy of each pulse separate from the frequency (pulse rate) can also be obtained by modulating amplitude and/or pulse width parameters. Units that incorporate control of pulse width and amplitude in one control will produce modulation of both parameters simultaneously. Amplitude modulation employed by Empi (EPIX) functions in this manner.[14] Activation of amplitude modulation produces a concomitant downshift of amplitude and pulse width of 40 and 60 percent, respectively, followed by a return to preset levels within a time frame of 1 second.

Neurogar (Neurogar III) offers recurrent pulse-width modulation independent of amplitude. The pulse width increases from 200 to 400 μsec in a series of graduated pulses, then returns to the original level in a continuous fashion when the modulation feature is activated.

Biostim (BIOMOD) offers simultaneous modulation of pulse width and pulse rate (50 to 100 percent of preset levels) independent of amplitude, but in alternate directions every second.[171] Independent pulse-width controls for each channel allow the degree of pulse-width modulation to be different for each channel. Given a preset pulse rate of 100 Hz and

---

*EMPI Inc., Minneapolis, MN 55422; (Neurogar) AGar Ginosar Electronics & Metal Products, Kibbutz Ginosar 14980, Israel; Biostim Inc., Princeton, NJ 08540; Neuromedics Inc., Freeport, TX 77546.

pulse width of 100 μsec, activation of the modulation mode will produce an initial decrease in pulse rate to 50 Hz at 100 μsec, which will be followed by a return of pulse rate to 100 Hz and concomitant decrease in pulse width to 50 μsec. Pulse rate and pulse width will continue to oscillate simultaneously but in alternate directions every second not exceeding the preset levels. Simultaneous modulation of all three parameters (amplitude, pulse duration, and pulse rate) as performed by the Empi (EPIX) unit produces alteration of the amplitude by 40 percent, pulse duration by 60 percent, and pulse rate by 40 percent. Modulation of pulse energy and frequency parameters, unlike that of Biostim, occurs in the same direction. Activation of multiple parameter modulation has the net effect of making strong stimulation more tolerable, alternately recruiting high- and low-threshold nerve fibers while concomitantly inhibiting nervous system accommodation.

Modulation of energy levels is advantageous when the strong, low-rate (acupuncture-like) or brief, intense mode is used. Modulation will allow for increased tolerance by decreasing the degree of C-fiber activation. When repetitive strong and rhythmic muscle contractions are desired for a period of 30 minutes or more, the strength of the contractions can be altered each second between moderate and strong levels. Therefore, instead of having the patient perceive strong muscle contractions constantly, the strength can decrease every other second (depending on the degree of modulation). As long as the total energy per pulse is able to produce a contraction sufficient to excite all contractile units within a muscle, the effectiveness of the strong, low-rate mode should not be hindered.

The desired goal of brief, intense T.E.N.S. is to produce either muscle tetany or nonrhythmic muscle fasciculation with strong electrical paresthesia. When modulation is activated in this mode, the degree of tetany and strength of the electrical paresthesia can be altered. This is best accomplished by modulating pulse rate and the energy per pulse (width and/or amplitude) simultaneously.

The pulse-train or cycled mode whereby the number of pulses per burst can be altered also provides for a degree of modulation.[14,171] Asynchronous firing of each channel during this mode offers one type of modulation that can be built into the stimulator.[171] Basically, besides decreasing accommodation and increasing the tolerance to the stronger stimulation modes, many patients report the perception of a comfortable massaging sensation when modulation is employed. This sensation is frequently preferred to one that is unchanging and thus serves to increase patient acceptance and utilization of T.E.N.S.

Decreased benefit may be overcome by a change in electrode placement sites. Even if the distribution of pain remains the same, different electrode sites in the same region can be used. The case studies in Chapter 9 illustrate the effectiveness of changing electrode placement and mode of stimulation. The patient who begins to report decreased effectiveness with T.E.N.S. must be re-evaluated to determine if there has been a change in the actual pathology, quality of pain, or distribution of pain, or if other specific treatment is indicated. A change in the distribution of pain will necessitate a change in the electrode placement. A change in the quality of pain or the pathology may necessitate a change in the stimulation mode. A patient with superficial, acute pain who was initially managed effectively with conventional T.E.N.S. may require the acupuncture-like or high-intensity, pulse-train mode if the problem becomes chronic and/or the quality changes to a deep ache.

The use of two electrodes of uneven size for a single-channel arrangement may serve to enhance effectiveness. An array utilizing electrodes of equal size that results in perception of stimulation only at one site can be altered by changing the size of one electrode. Either the electrode at the site where stimulation is not perceived can be made smaller or the one at which stimulation is perceived can be made larger. Substitution of either a larger or smaller electrode will have the net effect of increasing current density (smaller electrode) at the site at which the current was not perceived. Prior to making this change, the clinician should first determine that electrode placement is accurate to couple the stimulation channel or increase amplitude and/or pulse duration. Both adjustments may produce proper sensation or a more even distribution of current flow throughout the area of pain.

Dry, scaly skin or edema will increase resistance under the electrode. Therefore, alternate stimulation sites should be employed.

ENKEPHALINS AND ENDORPHINS

The neuropharmacologic concepts, isolation of natural pain-relieving peptides, and mechanisms involved with T.E.N.S. were discussed in Chapter 3. In support of this, recent information sheds more light on some of the factors that interact with T.E.N.S. There are now considered to be two independent peptidergic systems:[15] one system consists of short-chain peptides called enkephalins; the other, long-chain peptides called endorphins (Fig. 12-1).

Enkephalins are composed of a 5-amino acid chain and are widespread throughout the central and peripheral nervous systems. They are weaker than the endorphins and degrade rapidly via the action of aminopeptidase and carboxypeptidase. Methionine enkephalin and leucine enkephalin are examples of short-chain opioid peptides that have half-lives of less than 1 minute.[16] Leucine enkephalin is only one half as strong as methionine enkephalin.[42] Beta-endorphin is a 31-amino acid chain peptide that is part of beta-lipotropin—a pituitary hormone. The action of beta-endorphin is centered around the hypothalamus-pituitary axis, thalamus, midbrain, medulla, and pons.[15,17] Beta-endorphin is more resistant to enzymatic degradation and thus has a half-life of at least 2 to 3 hours.[16] When injected into the brains of experimental animals, its action has been shown to be 48 times stronger than that of morphine.[18] Other neuroactive peptides have since been isolated and may even have an action more powerful than that of beta-endorphin. Neurotensin, bombesin, dynorphin, and angiotensin are examples of other such endorphins.[19–22] Pharmaceutical firms are actively involved in producing a nonaddictive synthetic endorphin, which has yet to appear.[15]

The administration of enkephalin into the spinal cord primarily results in a decreased response to noxious stimuli with little interruption to the response of non-nociceptive stimuli.[15] Neurons and/or cell bodies containing enkephalin/endorphin have been found in the dorsal horn (laminae 1, 2, and 5), the trigeminal nucleus, amygdala, the periaqueductal gray, nucleus raphe magnus, reticular gigantocellular regions, globus pallidus, limbic-hypothalamic system, and various other brainstem structures.[15–23] The amygdala has been shown to contain the greatest density of opiate receptor sites followed by the hypothalamus, thalamus, and periaqueductal gray of the midbrain and diencephalon.[24,25]

The action of system I peptides has been equated with that of neurotransmitters since they are weak and short lasting in effect. However, the action of the endorphins is so strong and widespread that they may be considered as hormones since they affect not only pain but also mood, endocrine function, respiration, and gastrointestinal motility (see Fig. 12-1).[15,19]

Various experiments have uncovered the relationship of these neuroactive peptides with the pain response and the fact that the locations of opiate receptors correspond to afferent nociceptive pathways.[24,25] It has been demonstrated via assay of the cerebrospinal fluid (CSF) that patients with nonorganic or psychogenic pain complaints have a higher level of endorphins than do patients with actual organic pathology (Fig. 12-2).[15,26,30] The CSF endorphin level of patients with psychogenic pain is either normal or elevated.[27] The

System I

- Short Chain Peptides
- Leucine - Enkephalin
- Methionine - Enkephalin
- Primarily Found in Short Interneurons in PAG, Limbic System, Basal Ganglia, Hypothalamus, and Spinal Cord
- Rapid Enzymatic Degradation
- Weak (Relatively)
- May Function as Neurotransmitters

System II

- Long Chain Peptides
- Alpha - Endorphin
- Beta - Endorphin
- Primarily Found in Amygdala, Limbic, Hypothalamic–Pituitary Axis, and Other Brainstem Structures
- ↑ Resistance to Enzymatic Degradation
- Strong (Relatively)
- May Function as Hormones

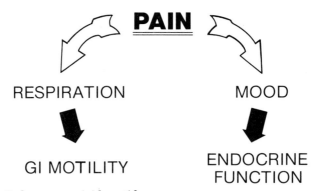

ENDORPHINS
SYSTEMIC EFFECTS

PAIN

RESPIRATION → GI MOTILITY

MOOD → ENDOCRINE FUNCTION

FIGURE 12-1. Endogenous opioid peptides.

CSF of patients with trigeminal neuralgia demonstrated a lower level of morphine-like neuropeptides as compared with CSF in normal persons.[30] Patients with high levels of endorphins demonstrated elevated pain threshold and tolerance levels. Akil and associates performed electrical stimulation of periventricular brain sites in eight patients with intractable pain.[31] Stimulation produced significant analgesia in all patients. The prestimulation (baseline) levels of endorphin in these patients were lower than normal. Von Knorring and associates found circannual variations in CSF endorphin concentration in 90 chronic pain patients. The highest concentrations occurred during January and February; the lowest, during July and August.[183] There was no noted relationship to patient age, sex, or size, or to etiology of pain.

Neurohumoral Neurotransmitter Theory

Monoamine (Neurotransmitters)

	Function
Dopamine	Parkinsonism
Epinephrine	Activation of RAS = Arousal/Alertness
Acetylcholine	Motor Function
Serotonin	Pain

1975 Endorphins/Enkephalins - Endogenous Morphine Like Substances Were Isolated

Cerebrospinal Fluid

Subnormal Endorphin Levels

Chronic Pain Patients (Organic) Such as in Trigeminal Neuralgia

Normal or Elevated Levels

Non-organic Pain States or Depression, Which Decreases Sensitivity to Pain

Pain Relief Associated with an Increase in Endorphin Levels

Experiments

NALOXONE ⇕ Increases pain perception and somatosensory evoked potential (SEP) in humans with below average pain sensitivity but not in those with above average sensitivity.

SEROTONIN ⇕ ↑ At synaptic or receptor level = Analgesia

↓ In brain or S.C. = Sensitivity and/or reactivity to noxious stimuli

Level in brain is determined by amount of Tryptophan in Diet.

FIGURE 12-2. Neurohumoral experimentation.

Experiments similar to that of Akil involving deep brain stimulation of regions such as the periaqueductal gray, which have been shown to possess concentrations of endorphins as well as opiate receptor sites, produced profound pain relief throughout the body. The pain relief induced by such stimulation has been reversible by morphine antagonists such as naloxone, which blocks the binding of morphine to opiate receptors.[32,33] Pain relief obtained by acupuncture and electroacupuncture in animals and humans has also been shown to be reversible by naloxone.[26,34–39] However, the results are not always the same. Humans with below-average pain sensitivity obtain an increase in pain perception and somatosensory evoked potentials (SEP) from naloxone, whereas pain sensitivity and SEP decrease in patients with above-average sensitivity to pain.[40,41]

STRESS

Pain and stress play important roles in endorphin liberation. The effectiveness of T.E.N.S. may be hindered by prolonged pain and stress but enhanced by short episodes of pain or stress. Guillemin and colleagues reported that ACTH and beta-endorphin are secreted concurrently by the pituitary gland and released into the bloodstream.[43,44] Other researchers have confirmed the localization of endorphin specifically to the anterior and intermediate lobes of the pituitary gland.[45,46] The anterior pituitary produces and liberates a number of hormones. One is a lipid-mobilizing hormone (beta-LPH) that may be cleaved into peptide chains such as endorphins.[184] However, there is some controversy, since Pomeranz and colleagues were unable to demonstrate acupuncture analgesia in hypophysectomized mice;[45] whereas Furui and associates infer that hypophysectomy results in an increase of CSF beta-endorphin.[95] Cheung and Goldstein state that the pituitary is not needed for such analgesia and endorphins are probably synthesized in the brain.[45,47] Rats and mice demonstrated an enhancement of endorphin release after 15 minutes of cold stress at 4°C. After 30 minutes, there was a decrease toward the control levels. After 4 hours of continued cold, the potency of morphine decreased to 50 percent of the baseline level.[48] Therefore, prolonged stress seems to deplete endorphin stores due to an increase in corticosteroid levels.[48,50] Cheng and associates used electroacupuncture on horses to demonstrate a similar mechanism.[51] After 30 minutes of electroacupuncture, blood cortisol levels of horses significantly increased; whereas horses receiving sham treatment demonstrated no significant change. ACTH, corticosterone, and dexamethasone seem to antagonize the antinociceptive action of morphine. Glucocorticoids can inhibit the synthesis of beta-endorphin.[43,48] Corticosteroids seem to have an affinity for nuclei of the amygdala and hippocampus. ACTH and beta-endorphin are contained in some neurons of the ventral portion and arcuate nucleus of the hypothalamus.[184] Prolonged use of corticosteroids may therefore trigger endorphin release, thus decreasing normal stores, and/or shunt the normal production process.

A common stressful condition is pregnancy. A study of pregnant rats showed a gradual increase in pain threshold to electric shock from 16 to 4 days prior to parturition.[52] There was an abrupt elevation of pain threshold 1 to 2 days prior to the onset of labor and delivery. The increase in pain threshold was abolished by the administration of naltrexone, a morphine antagonist. Beta-endorphin-like peptides, recently isolated in human placenta, were found to be composed of an amino-acid chain longer than the classic pituitary endorphin.[53] Long-term labor may deplete endorphin levels and thus raise the sensitivity to pain. As a result, T.E.N.S. may in fact lose its effectiveness during prolonged labor and other long-term stress-related conditions such as chronic pain unless enhanced by elevation of the neurotransmitter serotonin.

SEROTONIN

A discussion of depression and pain sensitivity cannot proceed without presenting the role of serotonin. Serotonin is a naturally occurring amino acid actively involved in temperature regulation, pain, sleep, mood, and appetite.[34,59,60,96] It is considered to be a monoamine neurotransmitter as dopamine, epinephine, and acetylcholine (see Fig. 12-2). The level of serotonin and the rate of synthesis in brain neurons are directly dependent on the amount of its precursor, tryptophan, in the diet.[59,60,96] Foods high in tryptophan are eggs, meat, poultry, and dairy products. Corn, rice, and legumes contain low levels of tryptophan.[61] Trytophan is also a precursor of niacin (vitamin B_3).[59,61] Serotonin-containing cells have been detected in the gastrointestinal tract, blood platelets, pineal gland, and mast cells of the thymus.[59] The ingestion of carbohydrates and other amino acids seems to enhance the transport of tryptophan into the CNS.[73,96] Wurtman has explained that the degree to which serotonin is synthesized depends on the relationship of protein and carbohydrates in the diet.[96] Most proteins contain a significantly lower level of tryptophan than do other amino acids. A high-protein, low-carbohydrate diet thus decreases the plasma ratio of tryptophan (resulting in decreased serotonin synthesis); whereas a high-carbohydrate, low-protein diet increases serotonin synthesis since a greater amount of tryptophan crosses the blood-brain barrier to the neurons that synthesize serotonin. Tryptophan thus must compete with other amino acids to gain attachment to carrier molecules for transportation across the blood-brain barrier. The small proportion of tryptophan to other amino acids in protein decreases its chances of getting to the neurons where it is synthesized.

Therefore, diets of patients with chronic pain should be reviewed to determine whether or not tryptophan supplements and/or a dietary change could decrease pain as well as enhance the effectiveness of T.E.N.S. The enhancement of the effects of deep brain stimulation for pain relief also occurs with an increased dietary intake of tryptophan.[74] Seltzer and associates conducted a study of 30 normal subjects after dietary manipulation with tryptophan.[180] Fifteen subjects received 2 g/day of tryptophan and 15 received a placebo. They were instructed to follow a high-carbohydrate, low-protein, low-fat diet for 7 days. Results showed no significant change between groups for pain perception threshold, but pain tolerance levels became significantly higher in the subjects receiving tryptophan. Side effects of itching, nausea, diarrhea, mood elevation, and a feeling of rest were present in some subjects receiving tryptophan. These findings are consistant with other reports concerning skin flushing and itching as a result of an increase in metabolic niacin. Tryptophan is a niacin precursor.

Numerous studies have described the relationship of serotonin and pain.[59,60,62,66] Sternbach and associates administered oral doses of a serotonin-depleting agent (reserpine) to a group of patients with chronic pain, resulting in increased depression and pain.[62] The administration of serotonin precursors increased the levels of central serotonin, resulting in decreased pain and depression.

Toomey and associates[3] performed acupuncture on 40 patients with chronic pain who were then separated into two groups on the basis of their positive and negative responses to treatment. This was followed by assessments of personality, affect, and stress for each group. Those not responding to acupuncture displayed more passivity, had conventional and stereotyped behavior and thought patterns, were highly submissive, and lacked spontaneity. These characteristics were shown to be consistent with depression. In addition, patients also suffering from a coexistent systemic disease unrelated to their specific pain complaint did not respond well to acupuncture. The possibility that these patients had altered pain thresholds due to disordered serotonin function was presented.

Johansson and Von Knorring found that the use of zimelidine, a tricyclic antidepressant that inhibits serotonin uptake, provided significantly better pain relief than placebos in a group of chronic pain patients.[63] Also noted was an improvement in well-being and a reduction in the need for pain medication. The administration of parachlorophenylalanine (PCPA), a serotonin synthesis inhibitor, partially depleted stimulation-produced analgesia.[64] Analgesia can be restored by the use of the serotonin precursor tryptophan. PCPA has been shown to block the initial hydroxylation of tryptophan, thus inhibiting serotinin synthesis.[59] When given to human subjects, PCPA resulted in increased reaction to pain stimuli so that non-noxious activity (speaking, facial expressions, skin function, etc.) produced discomfort.[59]

The cell bodies of serotonergic neurons in the brain and spinal cord are present in the midbrain raphe nuclei of the pons and brainstem (ventromedial nuclei of the pontine and reticular formation).[59,96] The axons of serotonergic cell bodies located in the median forebrain innervate cells of the hypothalamus, hippocampus, striatum septum, and cortex.[59,96] In a group of patients with chronic pain who received high-intensity electroacupuncture, platelet serotonin levels were elevated. Stimulation was at a rate of 8 to 15 Hz, pulse width was 40 msec, and intensity produced uncomfortable but not painful muscle contractions.[65] A similar group of patients receiving the same stimulation, but with a lower intensity, did not exhibit platelet serotonin elevations. The elevation in platelet serotonin level was found to be correlated with decreased pain and increased activity. Shealy and associates reported changes in mood and pain as a result of low-intensity, high-frequency transcranial stimulation, which altered serotonin output as measured in the urine and blood.[66] The serotonin changes noted by Shealy occurred only with transcranial stimulation and have not as yet been demonstrated to occur with low-intensity stimulation at peripheral sites. Low-intensity deep brain stimulation, however, has produced endorphin liberation.[97]

Serotonin does not pass through the blood-brain barrier; however, tryptophan does.[59,65,68] Omura reports that the conversion of serotonin into N-acetylserotonin, which can be converted into melatonin in the pineal gland, allows for passage through the blood-brain barrier.[68] As a result, it has been elucidated that plasma tryptophan may influence the level of central serotonin. Messing and Lytle, in their extensive review of serotonergic mechanisms, strongly support the view that pain sensitivity can be decreased by enhancing the level of serotonin[59] and concluded that an increase in serotonin neurotransmission is associated with a decrease in pain sensitivity or reactivity and an increase in the action of analgesic medication. A decrease in serotonin neurotransmission is therefore associated with hyperalgesia and decreased potency of analgesic medication. King has also noted a decrease in pain with administration of tryptophan.[69]

The actual role of serotonin, however, remains confusing. It is considered to be a pain-producing substance (excitation of tissue chemoreceptors) when liberated as a result of injury. However, at brain and spinal cord synapses, serotonin has demonstrated the ability to depress activity at cells receiving nociceptive input, possibly by enhancing the release of pain-inhibiting endogenous opiates.[59,75,76,96]

NARCOTICS

Kosterlitz and Hughes[54] and Wei and Loh[55] have researched the role of physical dependence on exogenous analgesic agents and infer that the body may stop producing its own pain-relieving peptides owing to a dependency on external administration of similar substances. This results in a decrease in the amount of enkephalins/endorphins, thus necessitating higher dosages of morphine. Higher dosages of morphine will, in turn, cause the body to produce even less endogenous opiates. The effectiveness of strong, low-rate and high-intensity, pulse-train (burst) T.E.N.S. may therefore be hindered by narcotic addiction. A recent study at John Hopkins University Medical Center on postoperative control of pain with T.E.N.S. found no significant benefit in drug-experienced patients.[56] Those patients who did use T.E.N.S. postoperatively but continued to complain of pain and demanded large amounts of narcotics also did not obtain any significant relief from the medication. The drug-naive group of patients showed a 51.8 percent mean decrease in the need for postoperative narcotic medication with the use of T.E.N.S. The authors presumed that patients who had developed some tolerance to narcotic medication also were tolerant to T.E.N.S. The relationship among endorphin levels, depression, and pain sensitivity is interesting. Ward and associates noted that pain relief obtained from administration of tricyclics was associated with improvement in depression.[57] Merskey found that depressed patients complaining of pain exhibited decreased thresholds to noxious stimuli. However, depressed patients not complaining of pain demonstrated elevated thresholds to noxious stimuli.[58] Von Knorring and associates reported that depressed patients are relatively insensitive to pain and have been found to have high levels of CSF endorphins[27] (see Fig. 12-2).

Prolonged use of diazepam, narcotics, and corticosteroids may hinder success with T.E.N.S. These factors will be present more so in the patient with chronic rather than acute pain and may be another cause of the low success rate with T.E.N.S. in the presence of chronic pain. Weaning the patient off these drugs is of primary importance and one of the first steps that should be taken in the rehabilitation of the chronic pain patient. Directly related to this are reports concerning experiments on heroin addicts. Neither 30 minutes of electroacupuncture nor pure acupuncture produced changes in the plasma of CSF beta-endorphin levels in two groups of heroin addicts.[70] Possibly, the addiction suppressed the body's natural endorphin production. Brain endogenous opiate levels were found to be reduced in rats subjected to chronic overexposure of opiate alkaloids.[108] However, another study showed an increase of methionine-enkephalin in the CSF of heroin addicts with successful electroacupuncture.[108] Salar and associates have noted a depletion of endorphin stores with continuous transcutaneous stimulation beyond 1 hour.[181] They thus recommend a suspension of stimulation for a few hours to allow a recovery of endorphins.

The effectiveness of T.E.N.S. may thus be enhanced by substituting tricyclic antidepressants or tryptophan for diazepam, weaning the patient from narcotic medication, and teaching proper nutrition and exercise. Diazepam acts as a serotonin-depleting agent, thus decreasing its effectiveness. The use of tricyclic antidepressants in place of diazepam will provide similar therapeutic effects without inhibiting but enhancing serotonin action.[57,71] Amitriptyline is a commonly prescribed medication for depression that is in the tricyclic category. Certain drugs potentiate the action of a neurotransmitter by blocking its degradation at the synaptic region where it acts.[72] Tricyclics amplify the action of norepinephrine and serotonin by blocking re-uptake at the synapse. Diazepam and other benzodiazepine drugs facilitate the action of certain neurotransmitters such as GABA (gamma-aminobutyric acid), which is an inhibitory neurotransmitter.[33]

Hosobuchi has recently reported on the use of tryptophan loading as a means of reversing tolerance to narcotic medication.[73] Five patients with chronic low back pain who had developed tolerance to morphine were given oral doses of tryptophan in the amount of 1 g 4 times a day over a 2- to 6-week period. Each patient reported increased activity and improved pain relief from opiate medication and were able to decrease the amount of narcotic that had previously been needed. Hosobuchi reported that the longer tryptophan was given, the better was the analgesic effect of morphine. Prolonged use of narcotic medication may therefore decrease the rate at which serotonin is synthesized, thus decreasing the effectiveness of morphine.

INVASIVE ELECTROACUPUNCTURE VERSUS T.E.N.S.

A great deal of the research into the physiologic mechanisms of pain relief stems from that involving clinical and experimental studies with electroacupuncture via needle electrodes. This is not the same as using a small-diameter blunt probe to stimulate acupuncture points transcutaneously, which is known as noninvasive electroacupuncture. Stimulation parameters employed with electroacupuncture are basically the same as those employed with strong, low-rate (acupuncture-like) T.E.N.S. via surface electrodes. The differences are the electrode size—needle electrode versus circular, square, or rectangular large-diameter electrode—and that the needle is percutaneous whereas the other is transcutaneous. Both the needle and surface electrodes are connected via lead wires to similar electrical pulse generators.

Studies have been conducted comparing the effects of T.E.N.S. with those of acupuncture and electroacupuncture when the same stimulation parameters and electrode placements were employed. Fox and Melzack compared the effects of pure acupuncture (no electrical stimulation) with those of T.E.N.S. in a group of 12 patients with chronic low back pain.[80] Acupuncture and T.E.N.S. were performed at the same sites. Acupuncture was given for 1 minute with strong manual needle rotation described as painful to three specific points. T.E.N.S. was given to the same points for 10 minutes each. Stimulation with 60-Hz sine wave trains at a rate of three per second was given at a painful but tolerable intensity. Results showed no significant differences in the duration and degree of relief between the two forms of stimulation.

Andersson, Holmgren, and associates obtained greater effectiveness with surface electrodes as compared with needle electrodes with similar stimulation parameters.[11,67,81,82] They concluded that the larger area of stimulation obtained with surface electrodes allowed for utilization of and greater tolerance to increased electrical intensity. The stronger and more widespread muscle contractions that occurred may have had a more profound supraspinal effect. Chapman also noted a similar effect with acupuncture-like T.E.N.S. as compared with electroacupuncture with needles.[83] Experiments conducted with peripheral electrical stimulation in rats have shown little difference in effects between T.E.N.S. and percutaneous treatment.[79]

To enhance the analgesic effect of electroacupuncture, Cheng and Pomeranz added d-phenylalanine (DPA) and d-leucine, which increased the effectiveness in mice, as compared with treatment without a combined approach. DPA blocks the action of carboxypeptidase and aminopeptidase, thus possibly enhancing the action and life span of endogenous opiates that were liberated as a result of electroacupuncture. Budd has done a similar study of patients with intractable pain who were given 250 mg of DPA three times daily for 4 weeks. Seven of 20 patients showed 50 percent or more improvement.[78]

The opposite approach was taken by Woolf and associates.[79] Experimental rats were given the serotonin-depleting agent PCPA prior to T.E.N.S. This resulted in a dampening of the effectiveness of electrical stimulation as well as the administration of morphine.

THEORETICAL IMPLICATIONS

The proliferation of research into the neurophysiologic mechanisms of acupuncture, electroacupuncture, and T.E.N.S. has led to the development of new theoretical concepts. The gate control theory has previously been utilized to explain the segmental effects of conventional T.E.N.S. (see Chapter 3). However, the advent of new and stronger stimulation modes that primarily affect the higher (supraspinal) centers requires different explanations.

In light of the comparative effects obtained with cutaneous and percutaneous electrical stimulation, it seems appropriate to use the same physiologic mechanisms to explain the action of both techniques as long as other treatment variables are consistent.

STRONG, LOW-RATE (ACUPUNCTURE-LIKE)
AND HIGH-INTENSITY, PULSE-TRAIN (BURST) T.E.N.S.

Our discussion at this point must center around the possible physiologic mechanisms and theoretical implications of the stimulation modes that produce strong, rhythmic muscle contractions. The initial question that comes to mind relative to these modes of stimulation that require muscle contraction within myotomes segmentally related or unrelated to the painful region is "How can stimulation that may be uncomfortable relieve pain?" Recent evidence seems to point to the relationship of endorphins, serotonin, and activation of the brainstem raphe system.

Ascending Supraspinal Facilitation and Descending Inhibition

The brainstem raphe system, located within the medulla, is part of the reticular activating system (RAS), which is widespread throughout all levels of the neuraxis and has numerous connections.[40,84] Afferent input to the RAS from the spinal cord is by way of the spinoreticulothalamic pathway; however, numerous other afferent tracts from different CNS areas also converge on the RAS. Descending pathways via the reticulospinal tract have a widespread influence on the ANS, and the locomotor, sleep, and limbic systems. However, the RAS is considered to be involved with just about all major functions of the nervous system.[40]

One part of the RAS is the nucleus raphe magnus (NRM). Dense projections from the NRM course to the marginal layer of the spinal cord, trigeminal nucleus caudalis, and dorsal motor nucleus of the vagus nerve, as well as to other areas.[59,86,87] Termination of descending pathways from the NRM is near neurons that receive afferent input from fibers mediating nociceptive stimuli.[85-87] The dorsolateral funiculus (DLF) is a prime pathway for bilateral descending projections from the NRM to the dorsal horn of the spinal cord.[20,40,59,63-65,67,72-74,77,84-85,87-89] Specifically, NRM fibers descend within the DLF and have been shown to terminate in laminae 1, 2, and 5 of the dorsal horn and the trigeminal nucleus caudalis.[85,91] These same regions have been shown to contain a dense grouping of opiate receptors.[20,85] The NRM thus is capable of exerting descending inhibitory influences at many areas. Studies involving ablative lesions of and electrical stimulation to the NRM and its projections support this statement.

Electrical stimulation of the NRM has resulted in a descending inhibition to the spinal cord and trigeminal nucleus caudalis, causing analgesia.[86,87,91,99] Furthermore, such analgesia is reversible by the morphine antagonist naloxone.[87,110,111] Lesions of the DLF or NRM inhibit the analgesia produced by electrical stimulation of the NRM or PAG.[87,91,109] Injection of nonadrenergic antagonists and morphine into the NRM does not result in analgesia if the NRM or the DLF has been destroyed.[91,98] Iontophoretic application of 5-hydroxytryptamine (serotonin) in animals has been shown to cause a depression of activity in lamina 1 cells that respond to noxious cutaneous stimuli. NRM fibers descend to these same neurons. Long descending fibers from the NRM within the DLF have been found to be primarily serotonergic and may represent a possible final common pathway for the effects of morphine or electrical stimulation administered to the PAG.[40,59,87,99,114]

The elements of a serotonin/endorphin pain-inhibiting system have thus been shown to exist. The serotonin-containing NRM has a direct pathway connecting it to the structures that receive noxious afferent input. Other brainstem regions such as the PAG have not been shown to have definitive connections or pathways to the dorsal horn.[87] Thus, how does the action of the endorphins come into play?

There is a direct connection between the PAG and the NRM.[85,87] Electrical stimulation invasively of the PAG not only liberates enkephalin/endorphin peptides but also activates neurons in the NRM, as does the administration of opiates.[85-88,105] Becker and associates have shown that the majority of neurons in the mesencephalic reticular formation and PAG are excited by peripheral touch, pinch, and thermal stimuli at intensities high enough to activate A-delta and C fibers as opposed to A-beta fibers.[115] Furthermore, these neurons demonstrated an increased response to intense repetitive afferent stimulation, suggesting a summation mechanism. This activation, however, has been shown to be blocked by lesions of the DLF.[100]

Invasive electrical stimulation of the NRM seems to require a pulse duration of 0.5 to 1.0 msec for maximal effectiveness.[101] A rate of no more than 3 Hz has been shown to be optimal for activation of reticular formation neurons via invasive stimulation.[102] These stimulation parameters are most conducive to the characteristics of C fibers that mediate nociception and therefore are most probably involved with raphe system excitation. Systemic opiates inhibit C-fiber activity to a greater degree than A-delta fibers and inhibit A-beta fibers the least.[161] Since chronic pain more frequently involves C-fiber pathways, opiate administration as well as strong, low-rate or high-intensity, pulse-train (burst) T.E.N.S. that liberates opiate neuropeptides should be more beneficial in the patient with chronic rather than acute pain.

Inhibition of flexor reflex afferents (FRA) on segmental motoneurons has also been demonstrated with activation of the NRM.[11,87] This inhibition has been able to be antagonized by administration of PCPA.[100–103] Invasive stimulation of the PAG has also been shown to cause inhibition of spinal dorsal horn neurons that respond to noxious stimulation.[87,112] It therefore seems appropriate that if peripheral electrical stimulation can be shown to activate the NRM, an ascending means of supraspinal facilitation could result in descending inhibition. A relay center for such afferent input is the nucleus reticularis gigantocellularis (NGC), which responds to noxious stimuli from the spinal and the trigeminal systems.[86,87,106,107] There are neural connections from the NGC to the reticular formation and NRM as well as to the hypothalamus, limbic system, and cortex.[102,116] The hypothalamic-pituitary relationship must also be explained as it relates to endogenous opiate release. The intermediate lobe of the pituitary receives some neural innervation from the hypothalamus, but the anterior lobe does not. The posterior lobe is connected to the median eminence of the hypothalamus. Hormones are released at the median eminence of the hypothalamus and enter the portal blood complex via exocytosis.[184] Nerve endings of the median eminence are situated close to capillary loops of the portal blood complex, which reaches the anterior pituitary. Thus, the release of beta-LPH from the anterior lobe may occur from chemical stimulation via releasing hormones produced by its posterior lobe or the hypothalamus. This, however, is not true of the poorly vascularized intermediate lobe, which is probably activated by neural stimulation. Neurohumoral peptide release is profound and widespread. The dorsal motor nucleus of the vagus nerve contains a dense plexus of enkephalin neurons, and there is a projection to it from the hypothalamus. Connections among the amygdala, NRM, reticular formation, and limbic system and the hypothalamus also exist, accounting for regulation of autonomic functions.[184]

Activation of the NRM seems to occur from electroacupuncture as well as strong, low-rate (acupuncture-like) or high-intensity, pulse-train (burst) T.E.N.S. Peripheral noxious stimulation has produced an increased firing of NRM serotonergic neurons in the medulla of the cat.[93] Resultant inhibition of spinal cord dorsal horn neurons in laminae 1, 2, and 5 was demonstrated. It has also been demonstrated that focal electrical stimulation in the NRM inhibits the activity of spinal cord dorsal horn neurons that mediate nociception.[103,104] Enkephalinergic cell bodies and terminal elements have been found in the PAG and NGC.[113] Acupuncture-like T.E.N.S. is specifically designed to activate the smaller pain fibers, and electrical parameters are within the acceptable range to excite NRM neurons. As previously presented, proper usage of strong, low-rate (acupuncture-like) or high-intensity, pulse-train (burst) T.E.N.S. requires the production of strong, visible muscle contractions optimally in segmentally related myotomes. Therefore, if muscle contraction is obtained, activation of flexor motoneurons also occurs. When activated, the flexor motoneurons can result in the flexor withdrawal response. This response is easily demonstrated when high-intensity noxious electrical stimulation, extreme heat, cold, or mechanical pressure is applied.[11,82,88] However, if such stimulation is kept just below the pain threshold level, flexor withdrawal can be prevented, but FRA would still be activated. Included within the FRA group are cutaneous afferent fibers, group II and III muscle afferents, and high-threshold joint afferents that may synapse on common interneurons in the dorsal horn of the spinal cord.[11,82]

The flexor withdrawal response and pain perception are considered to have similar dorsal horn neural mechanisms.[88] Electrical stimulation of the sural nerve in humans gives rise to a two-part reflex response of the lower limb flexors. An initial, short-latency (RII) component occurs from activation of low-threshold, large-diameter myelinated cutaneous fibers. A longer latency (RIII) occurs from stimulation of small-diameter fibers at higher intensities. There is a close relationship between the RIII reflex and pain sensation.[174] Therefore, activation of FRA could also result in an ascending nociceptive input to the supra-spinal centers. Figure 12-3 represents a hypothetical schematic of supraspinal activation of neurohumeral peptides, their subsequent widespread activity, and proposed neural pathways.

Endogenous Opiate Liberation

Experiments dealing with strong, low-rate (acupuncture-like) T.E.N.S. demonstrated the need for a long induction period (20 to 20 minutes). Such a long induction period is concomitant with summation mechanisms of peripheral noxious stimulation necessary to cause endogenous opiate liberation, the effects of which are generally reversible by naloxone.[26,35–39] Morphine has resulted in the inhibition of polysynaptic nociceptive flexion reflexes, which were reversible by naloxone.[118] Pomeranz is of the opinion that acupuncture activates deep muscle receptors that excite an afferent system to release endorphins from the pituitary gland.[119,120] Thus, the modes of T.E.N.S. that best seem to activate the NRM system and release endogenous pain-relieving substances are the strong, low-rate (acupuncture-like) and high-intensity, pulse-train (burst) modes.[35] Experiments comparing the results of conventional and acupuncture-like T.E.N.S. have not been able to demonstrate reversibility of response (a return of pain by naloxone administration) with conventional T.E.N.S.[117,121] A study of 20 patients with chronic pain was conducted by Sjolund and Erikson to compare the influence of naloxone on different stimulation modes.[117] One group of 10 patients received high-rate T.E.N.S. (0.2-msec duration, 50 to 100 Hz, and an intensity of two to three times perception threshold); the other group of 10 received pulse-train stimulation (70-msec duration, 100-Hz internal frequency with a 2-Hz carrier wave, and an intensity three to five times perception threshold). Results showed that 6 out of 10 patients who received high-intensity, pulse-train stimulation (similar to acupuncture-like) obtained inhibition of pain relief with intravenous injections of naloxone. The 10 patients who received high-rate (similar to conventional or brief, intense) T.E.N.S. did not demonstrate naloxone reversibility. Abrams, Reynolds, and Cusick recently demonstrated in a double-blind experiment that pain relief produced by conventional T.E.N.S. was not reversible by naloxone or saline injection.[121]

A related study performed in 10 patients with chronic pain demonstrated that the CSF level of beta-endorphin but not methionine-enkephalin was increased above baseline after electroacupuncture.[122] Electroacupuncture that results in pain relief has been shown to be reversible by naloxone.[122,123,125]

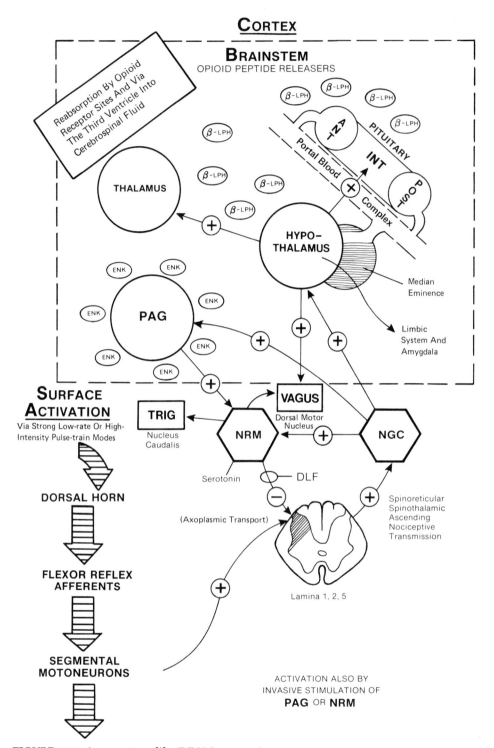

FIGURE 12-3. Acupuncture-like T.E.N.S.

The electrical parameters equated with conventional T.E.N.S. do not activate FRA due to the low intensity of stimulation and high rate.[102] Andersson and Holmgren state that the intensity of stimulation must be as close as possible to the painful level to activate the FRA.[11,82] The use of noxious but not unbearable stimulation levels requires a long latency or induction period but results in a prolonged aftereffect.[72] The long latency period prior to the onset of analgesia thus requires repetitive somewhat noxious stimulation to produce a sustained neuronal discharge to the NRM, which in turn activates the descending inhibitory mechanism.[85,87,120] The use of low-intensity stimulation (below muscle contraction threshold) with a low frequency (1 to 5 Hz) has also not been able to produce the effects of low-rate, high-intensity stimulation.[12] Pertovaara and colleagues found that low-frequency stimulation that was not considered painful by healthy volunteers but produced an increase in the dental pain threshold was not antagonized by intravenous administration of 0.8 mg of naloxone.[177] Trains of five pulses of 0.2-msec duration at 100-msec intervals at a frequency of 2.5 Hz were delivered transcutaneously to both cheeks. Subjects were instructed to raise the intensity to the highest nonpainful level. Unpleasant but not painful muscle twitches were elicited. The pain threshold level as tested by tooth pulp stimulation was raised from 20 to 150 percent (35 percent median). Stimulation was applied for 1 hour. Thus, in this study, it seems apparent that stimulation at a low frequency must also be significantly painful for excitation of an endogenous opioid mechanism. Specific stimulation parameters thus seem to be required for neuropeptide liberation. In a study dealing with stress-induced analgesia in animals, Grau and associates concluded that the pattern (frequency), amount (intensity), and duration (time or length of stressful stimulation) are critical to the production of analgesia.[125] Prolonged stress was needed. They inferred that such stimulation may make the endogenous opioid system hypersensitive. In a related experiment, Lewis and associates demonstrated that naloxone blocked analgesia produced by 30 minutes of intermittent foot shock but not analgesia obtained by 3 minutes of continuous foot shock.[50] However, it should be remembered that previous discussion has inferred that prolonged stress may deplete endorphin stores. Therefore to use the terms high-rate and low-rate T.E.N.S. to describe two distinct stimulation modes is not specific enough. We feel that the terms conventional and strong, low-rate (acupuncture-like) are more descriptive of the different types of stimulation.

A recent study concerning the possible neurohumoral mechanism of T.E.N.S. was conducted by Salar, Iob, and Mingrino.[126] Percutaneous electrical stimulation of the median nerve at the wrist was performed on six normal male subjects. Electrical parameters consisted of a square wave of 0.1-msec duration, frequency of 1.5 Hz, and an intensity of 20 mA. The level of stimulation was tolerable but not pleasant. T.E.N.S. was applied near the percutaneous needle electrode at a rate of 60 Hz, duration of 0.2 msec, and intensity between 40 and 80 mA for 15 minutes (brief, intense parameters). T.E.N.S. produced an immediate decrease in the pain elicited by the percutaneous median nerve stimulation. Naloxone hydrochloride (0.8 mg) was administered intravenously to each subject after 15 minutes of T.E.N.S. Results showed that four subjects had an immediate return of pain, whereas two perceived a decrease in pain beyond that brought about by T.E.N.S. Although the result of this experiment may seem to point to a possible endorphin-enkephalin liberation via brief, intense T.E.N.S., the percutaneous stimulation alone may have caused the response. The percutaneous median nerve stimulation parameters were consistent with those equated with acupuncture-like T.E.N.S.; unfortunately, the experimenters failed to state the length of time that this painful stimulation was given. Thus, the return of pain produced by naloxone could be totally misleading.

The action of naxolone does not always cause a return of pain after successful analgesia, thus implicating dose-dependent effects. Salar and associates cite the work of Buchsbaum, Davies, and Bunney, who reported on the possibility that certain patients are more or less responsive to pain than others. Such responsiveness, they inferred, may be linked to an inherent capacity to release greater or lesser amounts of endorphins.[41]

Salar and associates also reported changes in the cortical evoked response (CER) of each patient, which was decreased during T.E.N.S. The CER returned to baseline levels in the four subjects who were naloxone-responsive, which was statistically significant. The other two subjects showed no significant change in the CER after naloxone administration. Intravenous administration of saline solution also failed to cause a return of pain after T.E.N.S. or a change in the CER.[126]

The degree of a patient's responsiveness to pain and concomitant endorphin release relate well to the placebo response, but there are conflicting reports.[127] A neurohumoral mechanism has been postulated to explain pain relief with placebo administration. Levine and associates experimented with 50 dental patients who underwent extractions of impacted mandibular third molars.[128] Placebo, as medication, was given postoperatively 3 to 4 hours after surgery. The initial test drug given to all patients was a placebo, and those who experienced a decrease or increase in pain were classified as positive or negative placebo responders, respectively. The subsequent administration of naloxone resulted in pain intensification among positive placebo responders but not among negative placebo responders. It was thus hypothesized that the naloxone-induced pain enhancement occurred as a result of endorphin release by the positive placebo responders.

The possibility of endorphin liberation to account for the placebo response has, however, been challenged by others. Mihic and Binkert subjected healthy volunteers to cold pressor pain and then administered 1 ml of 0.9 percent sodium chloride intravenously with the suggestion that it was an analgesic.[129] Placebo responders obtained pain relief from the sodium chloride; however, the subsequent intravenous administration of 0.4 mg of naloxone (described as another dose of the same analgesic) failed to antagonize the analgesia but in fact seemed to enhance the effect of the placebo. Naloxone was also given prior to the placebo, but analgesia was still able to be obtained via a placebo effect. Mihic and Binkert thus concluded that clinical doses of naloxone do not reverse or prevent placebo analgesia and that the placebo effect does not mediate an endorphinergic mechanism.

Chen demonstrated that cognitive activities effected the placebo response more than endorphin mechanisms in experimental conditions.[130] The placebo effect was increased when positive beliefs as to potency of the placebo were present. No placebo effects were demonstrated in the presence of negative beliefs. Naloxone did not reverse the placebo effects.

Goldstein stated that experimental evidence relating to endorphin-induced placebo mechanisms is far from conclusive. Furthermore, experimental results are still fragmentary as to the definitive role of the endorphins in pain modulation.[131]

Mechanism of Action at the Synapse

The physiologic mechanism at the synaptic level in the dorsal horn, thalamus, or trigeminal nucleus caudalis, where inhibition of nociceptive input occurs, involves neurotransmitter mechanisms. Morphine can be injected or applied iontophoretically at various afferent nociceptive pathways in the neuraxis to produce pain relief. It can also travel through the body via the CSF and circulatory system and be reabsorbed by various brainstem and peripheral nervous system structures. Circulatory neuropeptides may be able to gain access to the brain by way of the choroid plexus and CSF, pituitary, and the third ventricle, which divides the hypothalamus.[165] Invasive or strong, low-rate modes of transcutaneous electrical stimulation have previously been shown to increase the CSF concentration of opiate neuropeptides, conceivably allowing for its action at any segmental level of the central nervous system.

Axoplasmic Transport

Opiate neurotransmitters may also arrive at specific or segmentally related afferent nociceptive synaptic junctions by a process known as axoplasmic transport. Axoplasmic transport is the physiologic mechanism that allows for the movement of proteins, neurotransmitters, and other constituents of the nerve down the axon to the region at which they act.[33,132–138] Neuroplasmic transport is another term that has been suggested since the mechanism involves not only axons but other neuronal processes. The axoplasm, a fluid with the consistency of jelly, flows in both directions within the axon between the neuronal cell body and terminal elements. Slow axonal transport at a rate of 1 to 3 mm a day moves constituents involved in growth and regeneration of the axon away from the cell body.[182] Fast axonal transport occurs in both directions between 12 and 300 mm a day and in part involves neurotransmitters. Presently about 20 to 30 different substances are suspected of being neurotransmitters.[33] Other than serotonin, dopamine, and endorphins, substance P, somatostatin, GABA (gamma-aminobutyric acid), glycine, cyclic GMP, and glutamic acid are among those also believed to be neurotransmitters.[22,33] The relative speed of axoplasmic transport may possibly be related to the need for an induction period up to 30 minutes before analgesia occurs with the strong, rhythmic, muscle-contraction stimulation modes.

The receptor sites for the neurotransmitters are large protein molecules embedded in the semifluid matrix of the cell membrane. The actual physiologic binding involves a lock-and-key mechanism.[33]

Substance P

The actual mechanism at the synapse is thought to be related to the action of afferent neurotransmitters such as substance P. Substance P is an 11-amino acid chain peptide that has been found in neuronal pathways in the brain, in primary sensory fibers of peripheral nerves, the nucleus caudalis, and tooth pulp.[33,139,141–142] Substance P is believed to be produced in the cell bodies of dorsal root ganglia and transported in both directions to central and peripheral axon terminals.[173] Serotonin, stored in the cytoplasm of NRM cell bodies, axons, and nerve fibers, may be mobilized by neuroplasmic transport. Substance P has been found to be present with serotonin in NRM neurons.[148] The action of substance P as a neurotransmitter for noxious input is considered to be dose related. When present in high doses, substance P results in excitation of neurons that are sensitive to nociceptive stimuli, thus promoting propagation of pain impulses. In low doses, substance P seems to facilitate endorphin release, resulting in nociceptive inhibition.[139,140] Substance P may possibly be a regulatory peptide since it could result in a normalization of the response to pain.[140] Small doses of substance P have produced analgesia in mice, which can be blocked by naloxone. When naloxone was administered after a high dose of substance P, the analgesic action of substance P diminished, resulting in hyperalgesia.[140]

Enkephalin and opiate drugs are considered to suppress the release of substance P from sensory neurons.[33,143–144] A hypothetical mechanism of action believed to be presynaptic can be demonstrated. It is presumed that at afferent synapses, interneurons that contain enkephalin/endorphin exist. These interneurons may synapse with axon terminals of neurons that respond to nociceptive input. These nociceptive neurons require the liberation of substance P to facilitate nociceptive transmission. Therefore, as substance P is released from the terminal elements of the axon, the pain impulse continues to be propagated. High-intensity electrical stimulation of the mammalian sciatic nerve has produced substance P release, the effect of which has been antagonized by opiate administration.[149] However, if enkephalin is liberated, it will conceivably inhibit substance P liberation. A lack of substance P will mean dampening of the nociceptive impulse. The enkephalinergic neurons are considered to be presynaptic and thus are capable of inhibiting the release of substance P from the small-diameter fibers. This will result in dampening of nociceptive stimuli (Fig. 12-4).

Presynaptic membranes of axon terminals release various transmitter substances that have either an inhibitory or excitatory action on the postsynaptic membrane.[17,145] If the action is one of excitation, a decrease in the postsynaptic membrane potential occurs, which will increase the rate of conduction. Stabilization of the postsynaptic membrane will occur if the transmitter action is one of inhibition. Depolarization of the postsynaptic neuron is thus rendered more difficult, thereby blocking (inhibition of Na^+ influx) or dampening the propagation of further transmission.[18,145] The degree of receptor binding of opiates and antagonists is in part controlled by the amount of Na^+ concentration.[146] Na^+ enhances the degree of antagonist or enkephalin binding to the receptor sites, thus blocking substance P activity.[147]

Exocytosis is the mechanism of transmitter release at the synapse.[75] Transmitter substances are believed to be released in multimolecular (several thousand molecules) packets called "quanta," which may be stored in the organelles or synaptic vesicles of the axon. A minute excitatory postsynaptic potential is produced by each quanta, and pain transmission is facilitated.[75] The presence of calcium ions (Ca^{++}) seems to be required for the proper release of the quanta.[17] Depolarization of the presynaptic neuronal membrane allows calcium ions to pass. An action potential is produced by this passage, which is accomplished by a release of neurotransmitter (substance P).[172,173] If the concentration of Ca^{++} at the synapse decreases (possibly due to the presence of opiate neuropeptides), a concomitant decrease will also occur in relation to released quanta.[75,136–138,143] It has been implicated that exogenous and endogenous opioid peptides presynaptically prevent substance P liberation by decreasing the concentration of calcium ions. Another possibility is that the lack of proper calcium prevents substance P from binding to the presynaptic neuronal terminals.[166]

The lack of a sufficient amount of Ca^{++} has been shown to also block axoplasmic transport, possibly inhibiting the movement of enkephalin and serotonin to the terminal elements at the synapse.[136–138] The level of Ca^{++} can be disturbed by various events such as toxicity, genetic disease, compressive trauma, ischemia, and possibly the presence of prostaglandins and other pain-producing substances.

In summary, a proper mixture of chemical, electrical, and neural events must take place at the synapse for inhibition or facilitation of nociceptive impulses to occur. Inhibition will presumably occur if substance P can be prevented from being released at the synapse. Substance P can be blocked if the Ca^{++} concentration is decreased. Release of opiate neuropeptides seems to accomplish this. Other than the administration of morphine or deep brain stimulation, strong, low-rate (acupuncture-like) or high-intensity, pulse-train T.E.N.S. performed transcutaneously or invasively can result in ascending facilitation of enkephalin/endorphin neurons and activation of the inhibitory NRM-descending serotonergic system. Na^+ has been shown to facilitate opiate binding at afferent nociceptive receptor sites and along with serotonin should enhance the action of enkephalin/endorphin to decrease the calcium current and hinder substance P release.

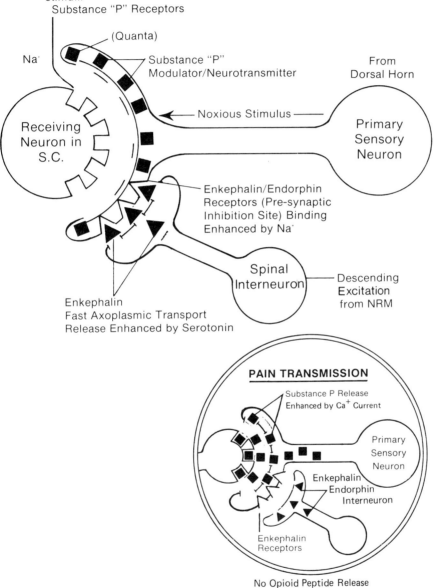

PRESYNAPTIC INHIBITION via opioid peptide release from adjacent interneurons decreases the release of substance "P" from small diameter primary afferents causing dampening of the transmission of nociceptive stimuli.

Substance "P" Receptors

(Quanta)

Na˙

Substance "P"
Modulator/Neurotransmitter

From
Dorsal Horn

Receiving
Neuron in
S.C.

Noxious Stimulus

Primary
Sensory
Neuron

Enkephalin/Endorphin
Receptors (Pre-synaptic
Inhibition Site) Binding
Enhanced by Na˙

Spinal
Interneuron

Descending
Excitation
from NRM

Enkephalin
Fast Axoplasmic Transport
Release Enhanced by Serotonin

PAIN TRANSMISSION

Substance P Release
Enhanced by Ca^+ Current

Primary
Sensory
Neuron

Enkephalin
Endorphin
Interneuron

Enkephalin
Receptors

No Opioid Peptide Release

FIGURE 12-4. Opioid peptide action at nociceptive synapse. (Adapted from Snyder.[18])

BRIEF, INTENSE T.E.N.S.

The explanation of the action of brief, intense T.E.N.S. utilizing a high rate, wide pulse width, and intensity to tolerance is different from that of conventional T.E.N.S. (gate control) and strong, low-rate (acupuncture-like) T.E.N.S. (opiate neuropeptide activation). Early reports concerning the use of this mode of stimulation were explained in terms of producing a peripheral blockade of transmission.[150]

Campbell and Taub utilized percutaneous stimulation of the digital branches of the median nerve.[118,151] A 50-V, 100-Hz, 1-msec stimulus was able to raise the threshold to touch and pain, producing analgesia. They demonstrated a decrease in A-delta fiber transmission and inferred on this basis that nociceptive input was blocked. A-delta waves were reported as being absent when stimulation was performed continuously. An intensity of 22 V raised the threshold to touch and pain, whereas 10 to 12 V elevated only the threshold to touch. An antidromic block of the palmar digital nerves was hypothesized.

Conduction Block

Torebjork and Hallin noted a marked decrease in A-delta and C fiber activity and a slowing of conduction velocity during high-intensity, high-frequency percutaneous stimulation.[152] They also noted similar effects with stimulation at a frequency as low as 0.5 Hz. Blocking of conduction velocity was most pronounced at 10 Hz, however. Nyquist and Ignelzi used an implantable cuff electrode to demonstrate that repetitive (200 Hz) stimulation for 5 to 20 minutes influenced peripheral nerve conduction velocity.[153] They concluded that a transient decrease of conduction velocity and increase in electrical threshold involved all fibers as a result of repetitive electrical stimulation. Nyquist studied the effects of repetitive electrical stimulation on isolated cutaneous peripheral nerves of the toad and again demonstrated an alteration of conduction velocity that was most prominent with high-frequency stimulation.[133,154]

Continuing with their series of experiments, this time on isolated radial nerve fibers from the cat, Ignelzi and Nyquist again used high-frequency, 180 to 200 Hz electrical stimulation.[6] Stimulation was applied via a peripheral nerve cuff (percutaneous). Results again demonstrated a transient decrease in conduction velocity with a concomitant increase in electrical threshold of both large and small fibers.

Ignelzi and Nyquist also studied the effects of repetitive peripheral nerve stimulation on fast axoplasmic transport.[132] The sciatic nerve of the cat was stimulated percutaneously at a rate of 200 Hz, 1.3 mA for 5 to 6 hours. No alteration in fast axoplasmic transport was noted. Conduction block may therefore be frequency related. High-frequency stimulation may produce an accumulation of potassium in the periaxonal space, thus inhibiting sodium conductance and propagation of the action potential. C fibers might be more susceptible to this type of block because of their greater surface to volume ratio.[179]

One of the theories that can be employed to explain the action of this form of brief, intense T.E.N.S. is a peripheral nerve antidromic block of conduction velocity. This effect has been noted to be very transient. We obtained a relatively fast analgesic effect (5 to 15 min), but this dissipated quite rapidly (usually does not exceed the length of stimulation) once the stimulator was turned off. However, the analgesia produced by this mode is quite profound. The best results have been obtained when the electrodes were applied proximal to, surrounding, or crisscrossing over the painful region (Fig. 12-5).

The physiologic effects of brief, intense T.E.N.S. resulting in a profound and rapid onset of analgesia thus seem to be best explained in terms of a conduction block, as has

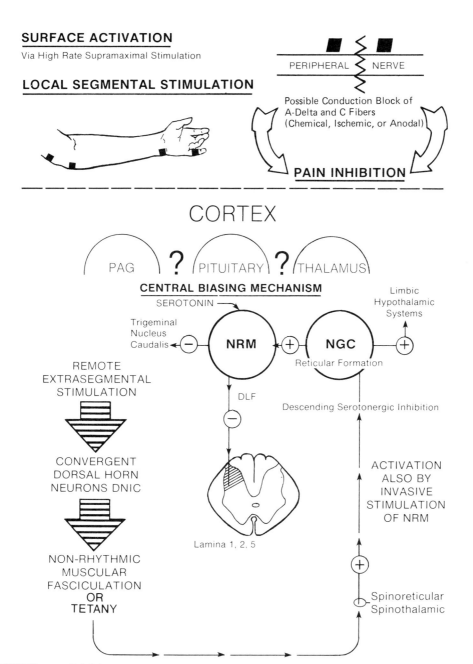

SURFACE ACTIVATION
Via High Rate Supramaximal Stimulation

LOCAL SEGMENTAL STIMULATION

PERIPHERAL NERVE

Possible Conduction Block of
A-Delta and C Fibers
(Chemical, Ischemic, or Anodal)

PAIN INHIBITION

CORTEX

PAG ? PITUITARY ? THALAMUS

CENTRAL BIASING MECHANISM

SEROTONIN

Limbic
Hypothalamic
Systems

Trigeminal
Nucleus
Caudalis ← (−) **NRM** (+) **NGC** (+)

Reticular Formation

REMOTE
EXTRASEGMENTAL
STIMULATION

DLF

(−)

Descending Serotonergic Inhibition

CONVERGENT
DORSAL HORN
NEURONS DNIC

ACTIVATION
ALSO BY
INVASIVE
STIMULATION
OF NRM

Lamina 1, 2, 5

NON-RHYTHMIC
MUSCULAR
FASCICULATION
OR
TETANY

(+)

Spinoreticular
Spinothalamic

FIGURE 12-5. Brief, intense T.E.N.S.

recently been demonstrated by Pertovaara and Kemppainen.[155,156] The clinician can easily demonstrate this effect by placing one electrode on the volar surface of the fifth finger proximal to the distal phalanx and a second at the volar aspect of the wrist over the flexor carpi ulnaris tendon (ulnar nerve below). Stimulation in the brief, intense mode with this electrode array will result in a significant decrease to pinprick at the volar surface of the distal phalanx within 1 to 5 minutes. The analgesic action can be enhanced by use of a second electrode channel above and below the olecranon overlying the ulnar nerve (see Fig. 12-5). Janko and Trontelj have also demonstrated a quick onset of analgesia with brief, intense T.E.N.S.[10] Pertovaara and Hamalainen demonstrated that high-frequency (100 Hz) and high-intensity T.E.N.S. (muscle activity elicited) when applied at a proximal site produced a marked elevation to vibrotactile stimuli.[175] The effects of conduction blocking should be enhanced by placing the positive electrode proximal to the cathode. The anodal effects of an electrical current occurs only with strong stimulation that decreases nerve irritability.[178] Brief, intense T.E.N.S. can also cause ischemia by producing vascular blockage via muscle tetany. The resultant nutrient deficit to the peripheral nerve could also decrease conduction velocity.

Since the brief, intense mode does not result in an alteration of fast axoplasmic transport as noted by Ignelzi and Nyquist and since stimulation parameters are not conducive to a release of endogenous opiates, explanation via a conduction block currently seems to be a likely physiologic explanation. Another possibility is that the noxious high-rate stimulation in some way causes a release of enkephalin at afferent synaptic sites in the dorsal horn and not at all from supraspinal centers.[157] This mechanism has not as yet been demonstrated but could be plausible in light of the close proximity of enkephalin interneurons at afferent synapses that receive noxious input and the speed at which the analgesia occurs. The short-lived analgesic effect (fast dissipation after the stimulation is stopped) is also in line with the short half-lives of the enkephalins.

Diffuse Noxious Inhibitory Controls

LeBars, Dickinson, and Besson have recently proposed another explanation to account for the effects of noxious peripheral stimulation.[158,159] They discovered a group of dorsal horn neurons that respond to noxious as well as non-noxious and proprioceptive stimuli via both C and A-alpha afferent input from cutaneous, muscular, and visceral structures. This characteristic seems consistent with that of lamina 5 neurons. These neurons were able to be strongly inhibited by peripheral noxious stimulation, which was applied primarily at regions remote from the receptive field. The term diffuse noxious inhibitory controls (DNIC) was thus given to this neuronal group.

The location of DNIC in the dorsal horn was in the lamina near the origins of the spinothalamic and spinoreticular tracts. Supramaximal stimulation by various means including T.E.N.S., when applied to remote peripheral areas, depressed DNIC activity in the lumbar spinal cord. T.E.N.S. was performed at a rate of 50 Hz. Stimulation of the tail, contralateral hind paw, forepaws, ears, muzzle, and viscera were all effective. The aftereffect of this remote noxious stimulation persisted for up to 4 times the length of the stimulation period. The prolonged aftereffect with brief, intense stimulation applied to areas remote from pain is quite different from that observed when similar stimulation is applied close to the painful region. There is no explanation for this, but it may be related to a supraspinal effect. Stimulation that was non-noxious was found to be totally ineffective. The effectiveness of this type of stimulation was enhanced by electrode placement over highly innervated large myotomes. LeBars, Dickenson, and Besson also demonstrated that when noxious stimulation is applied simultaneously at two distinct body regions, inhibition will occur in the convergent neuron group responding to the weaker stimulus. The mechanism behind DNIC may also explain the pain relief that has been demonstrated by stimulation of areas unrelated to the source of pain.

The DNIC effect was not achieved in the spinal animal. It was concluded that the mechanism of action cannot occur at the local segmental level but must be mediated by the higher centers and may be related to the descending serotonergic system. In a more recent study it was demonstrated that bilateral high-intensity (painful) stimulation of the sciatic nerve triggers the DNIC system and induces a release of serotonin in the CSF of the cat.[176]

Serotonin Liberation

Cheng and Pomeranz recently demonstrated a serotonergic mechanism with similar stimulation.[100,124] They experimented with electroacupuncture at three frequencies—0.2, 4, and 200 Hz—for 20 minutes. Intensity was at muscle contraction level and just below pain threshold. Results showed that the 200-Hz current produced the greatest degree of analgesia and 0.2 Hz the least. Naloxone reversed the 4-Hz electrical analgesia but did not affect the 200-Hz stimulation. However, PCPA partially reversed the 200-Hz analgesia. Cheng and Pomeranz concluded that high-frequency noxious stimulation did not activate endorphins but may result in serotonin liberation. Mao and associates demonstrated a similar effect with high-intensity electroacupuncture at a rate of 8 to 15 Hz.[65]

Melzack postulated that activation of a brainstem inhibitory mechanism resulted from brief, intense T.E.N.S. This would be in line with the results of Cheng and Pomeranz. Acupuncture-like; brief, intense; and high-intensity, pulse-train parameters exert some type of supraspinal effect. The mechanisms of higher center activities involve neurohumoral substrates and excitation of the midbrain raphe system. However, a distinct differentiation of the exact areas of supraspinal activation between high- and low-rate parameters (along with a wide pulse width and intensity to tolerance) does not seem clearcut at this time (see Figs. 12-3, 12-5).

Walker and Katz recently demonstrated that analgesia produced by subcutaneous electrical nerve stimulation (SCNS) was not reversible by naloxone.[160] They used needle electrodes subcutaneously in the median and radial nerves (2 inches proximal to the volar wrist crease as well as at the metatarsal-cuneiform junction and below the medial malleolus, saphenous nerve). Stimulation was performed daily for at least 1 hour with a 20-Hz sine wave at an intensity of 200 μa. Results showed that all patients reported 40 percent or more analgesia by the fourth treatment. Neither naloxone (0.4 mg) nor saline administered intravenously was able to reverse the analgesic effect.

Walker and Katz thus concluded that SCNS mediates analgesia by a nonopioid mechanism or pathway. The stimulation frequency that they used was 20 Hz, which is significantly higher than that causing neuropeptide liberation (1 to 4 Hz). Noxious high-rate stimulation has been shown to be reversible by PCPA, implying a serotonin liberation. Walker and Katz raised the issue that a descending serotonergic pathway may be involved.

CHANGING THE THALAMIC PAIN CODE

In trying to analyze, discuss, or make specific hypotheses about the mechanisms behind electroanalgesia with T.E.N.S., we arrive at more questions than answers. However, one factor seems to stand out—that each stimulation mode produces different physiologic effects in the CNS. Therefore, the same theory or explanation cannot be applied indiscriminately to each stimulation mode.

A recent theory by Emmers based on numerous experiments seems to tie up a lot of loose ends and intertwine the hypotheses proposed by other theories. Emmers explains the action of electrical stimulation as one of changing the spike-interval code of thalamic neurons. He has determined that pain and other stimulus modalities produce a specific spike-interval coded message in the brain and that changes in this code can lead to analgesia or hyperalgesia.

Emmers performed electrical stimulation of the sciatic nerve of the rat and recorded the evoked potentials via microneurography elicited by neurons in the periaqueductal gray (PAG). He initially supports the previous tenets of afferent input ascending in the lateral spinothalamic tract (paleospinothalamic and neospinothalamic divisions) to the centrum-medianum-parafascicular nuclear complex (CM-PF) of the thalamus and then to the second somasthetic region of the thalamus (SII). In addition, ascending input from the lateral spinothalamic tract (LSTT) also synapses on neurons in the lateral cervical nucleus (see Chapters 8 and 9), which provides a second degree of facilitation to the SII region. Descending input from the PAG to the nucleus raphe magnus (NRM) and then via the DLF to the dorsal horn of the spinal cord completes the feedback mechanism of ascending facilitation and descending inhibition. When excited by descending PAG neurons, input neurons of the NRM send spike potentials via the DLF to the terminals of A-delta and C fibers. Emmers stated that the poststimulation analgesia produced by increased activity of PAG neurons might possibly occur due to a release of endorphins that promoted continued excitation of PAG neurons and an ongoing descending NRM (serotonergic) excitation with resultant dorsal horn nociceptive inhibition.

Emmers' recordings indicated that single PAG neurons emit spontaneous spike potentials at a rate of 4 to 12/sec, indicative of pain. Low-frequency stimuli applied directly to these neurons or ascending peripherally from sciatic nerve excitation lower the activity of PAG neurons, thus slightly increasing the spontaneous firing of SII neurons. This gave rise to hyperalgesia. An increase in excitation via continuous high-frequency stimuli of 20, 50, or 70 Hz, especially at inappropriate intervals, produced significant agitation of CM-PF or SII neurons, producing analgesia. Increasing the duration of the pulse train provided prolonged poststimulation activity and longer-lasting analgesia. The best results were obtained with sciatic nerve stimulation using 400-msec trains of 0.5-msec pulses at 70 Hz interrupted at 2-Hz intervals (pulse-train mode). A duration greater than 80 msec is required. Emmers theorized that the increased firing of PAG neurons disrupted the apparent timed firing (spike-interval code) of SII neurons, producing analgesia.

Recordings obtained from narcotic application showed that PAG neurons were excited slightly above a rate of 4/sec. At a frequency of 8 Hz, the histograms representing electroanalgesia and narcotic analgesia were very similar. Another conclusion by Emmers, which is related to the cortical inhibitory surround theory and thalamic neuron theory of Lee (see Chapters 3 and 8), is that the suppression of pain arising from direct stimulation of pain pathways results from neural excitation rather than inhibition. Examination of thalamic neurons revealed a significant projection of the somatotopic orientation of the head of the rat onto the entire PAG. Neurons responding to the foot and legs crouch below the head and extend anteromedially within the most ventral site of its projection. A small thoracic representation, hind legs, and very small tail are situated at the ventral margin of the head. Tactile stimulation of the rat's head produced excitation of all PAG neurons. Emmers concluded that stimulation of cutaneous receptors and low-threshold sensory neurons of the head should be effective in influencing the spike-interval code evoked by stimulation of any other body part.

Perhaps optimal results with T.E.N.S. would occur with placement of one electrode or circuit on the head, jaw, or neck and another on the painful region of the body. Pain Suppression Labs recommends transcranial stimulation when stimulation at the site of pain is unsuccessful. Bilateral stimulation at the C2 levels is also a recommended secondary technique when all else fails (see Chapters 8 and 9).

The information obtained from the work of Emmers also points to utilization of the pulse train or modulation mode to disrupt the timed spike-interval code firing of SII neurons. Pulse-train and modulation modes often use high-frequency potentials (50 to 100 Hz) that are interrupted at 2-Hz (pulse train) or 1-Hz (modulation) intervals. Figure 12-6 illustrates the proposed stimulation pathways of Emmers.

SUMMARY

The overwhelming majority of clinical and experimental reports concerning T.E.N.S. do not contain adequate information relative to stimulation parameters and electrode placement sites. Clinicians who use different modes of stimulation, try various means of electrode placements, and pay close attention to the factors that influence effectiveness will obtain higher success rates with both acute and chronic patients than clinicians who solely use conventional T.E.N.S. The employment of a comprehensive approach to the rehabilitation of the patient with pain plays a highly important role in guaranteeing success.

The majority of the research concerning T.E.N.S. deals with conventional and acupuncture-like T.E.N.S. It should be noted that published research and clinical reports relative to brief, intense and high-intensity pulse-train (burst) T.E.N.S. are very sparse. Table

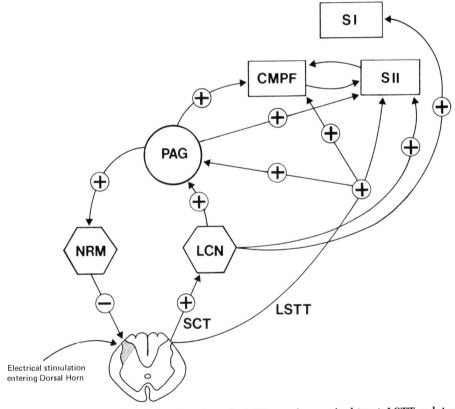

FIGURE 12-6. Changing the thalamic pain code. SCT = spinocervical tract; LSTT = lateral spinothalamic tract; LCN = lateral cervical nucleus; PAG = periaqueductal gray; CMPF = centrum medianum parafascicular nuclear complex; S I = first somasthetic region of thalamus; S II = second somasthetic region of thalamus; NRM = nucleus raphe magnus. (Adapted from Emmers.[184])

12-2 summarizes the possible neurophysiologic mechanisms of each mode based upon the reports in the literature.

Many questions, however, remain unanswered concerning the neurophysiologic mechanisms behind T.E.N.S. Another possible explanation for conventional and brief, intense T.E.N.S. is that of counterirritation. The sensation produced by these modes, if perceived throughout the area of pain, may mask the pain sensation. This is supported by the earlier work of Gammon and Starr.[164] They determined that the most effective site for counterirritation was over the painful area. However, remotely applied counterirritation was by no means ineffective. Considerable relief was obtained when counterirritating stimuli were applied 6 inches proximal to the area of pain on the related peripheral nerve. Pain relief was less effective when applied distal to the painful area. Gammon and Starr reported that maximal pain relief was obtained when the intensity of the counterirritant stimulus was close to the threshold that augments pain. This would implicate the brief, intense mode more than the conventional mode. These authors also reported that this strong stimulation may produce a temporary increase in pain that briefly precedes the onset of relief. They studied stimulation frequencies within the 1- to 300-Hz range and found 50 to 60 Hz to be most effective and 1 Hz least effective. Counterirritation applied repeatedly in a cycled mode 5 seconds on and 5 seconds off provided increased effectiveness.

Evidence is not sufficient to determine if enkephalins and endorphins are liberated simultaneously by noxious stimulation or if just the endorphins are liberated. Is serotonin liberated simultaneously with the endorphins, and what is its exact role? Does the brief, intense stimulation mode also activate supraspinal centers (PAG, pituitary) other than the NRM as the strong, low-rate (acupuncture-like) and high-intensity, pulse-train modes seem to do? Many other brainstem regions or structures that contain a high density of opiate receptors may be involved in stimulation-produced analgesia. Two such structures are the locus coeruleus and the nucleus raphe pallidus.[162,163] There is at present no clearcut mechanism to determine exactly where or which specific structures peripheral electrical stimulation activates. Many mechanisms may be activated, and more than one analgesic effect can occur simultaneously. The best example is the high-intensity, pulse-train (burst) mode using high-frequency potentials emitted via low-rate bursts or trains. This type of stimulation may produce a concomitant serotonin/endorphin liberation and involve more than one mechanism of action.

What role does frequency play in supraspinal activation and pain relief? Is intensity (noxious or muscle contraction level) the important factor, or must a concomitant low rate of stimulation also be employed with T.E.N.S. for neurohumoral liberation? Results obtained by Shealy with transcranial stimulation via very low intensity (4 mA) subthreshold, very high frequency (15,000 Hz) demonstrated a serotonin elevation.[66] This is in direct contrast to serotonin liberation via peripheral high-intensity (to tolerance), high-rate (100 to 200 Hz) stimulation. The difference may be the stimulation site (transcranial). Present evidence points to both a high-intensity and low-frequency repetitive stimulation as being necessary for endorphin liberation, yet high frequency noxious stimulation has resulted in an apparent serotonin elevation.[65,100,124] Salar and associates tested endorphin liberation in 13 patients who did not have pain.[181] Six patients had ventricular CSF shunt for obstructive hydrocephalus, and seven had lumbar drainage for CSF fistulae. Stimulation of 0.2-msec duration, 40 to 60 Hz at 40 to 80 mA was utilized to obtain paresthesia without pain. They found a statistically significant increase in CSF endorphin levels after 20 to 45 minutes of stimulation. The results of this study are in direct contrast to previous experiments, which have demonstrated endorphin elevation only with low-rate, high-intensity stimulation. Salar and associates theorized that such differences may occur between chronic pain patients and those without pain. We would like to see this study repeated with subjects who did not have CSF shunts.

TABLE 12-2. Neurophysiologic Action of T.E.N.S.

	Conventional and Low-intensity, Pulse-Train (Burst)	Brief, Intense	Strong, Low-rate (Acupuncture-like)	High-intensity Pulse-Train (Burst)
Rate	High	High	Low	High + Low Carrier
Width	Narrow	Wide	Wide	Wide
Amplitude	Low	High	High	High
Site	Primarily segmental at dorsal horn	Segmental and extrasegmental at dorsal horn (DNIC), peripheral nerve, and brainstem	Segmental and extrasegmental at supraspinal and dorsal horn	Segmental and extrasegmental at supraspinal and dorsal horn
Reversibility	Not reversible by neurohumoral antagonists	Yes, parachlorophenylalanine (PCPA) . . . a serotonin antagonist	Yes, naloxone	Yes, naloxone
Mechanisms	Gate control theory Counterirritation Cortical inhibitory surround theory Disruption in thalamic pain pattern	Chemical, ischemic, or anodal conduction block Counterirritation Cortical inhibitory surround theory Disruption in thalamic pain pattern Serotonergic	Neurohumoral Serotonergic	Neurohumoral Serotonergic Cortical inhibitory surround theory Disruption in thalamic pain pattern

Omura states that the optimal benefits of electroacupuncture and acupuncture-like T.E.N.S. occur with significant muscle contractions at a low frequency. When testing human ulnar nerve fibers as well as the tooth in the determination of the minimal and maximal pain threshold, pulse rate was found to be a significant factor when pulse duration and amplitude were relatively constant.[170]

At frequencies below 5 Hz, Omura found it took 30 seconds to 40 minutes for some pain relief to occur, and 5 minutes to 1 hour before the maximal elevation in pain threshold was evident. Pain relief would then persist for a few hours to several days. The best results were obtained with a rate between 1.2 and 3 Hz. When pulse rates between the range of 20 and 200 Hz were tested, there was a much faster rise in pain threshold, which reached maximum within 30 seconds to 15 minutes. However, aftereffect began to decrease within 30 minutes. Pulse rates between 40 and 80 Hz provided maximal comfort and benefit.

There was an almost instantaneous disappearance of pain when very high-frequency pulses, 10 kHz and 500 kHz, were tested. Pain threshold reached its maximal elevation almost immediately, but there was a very short aftereffect with quick return of pain. We have also noted a very short carryover of analgesia with brief, intense T.E.N.S.

Pain relief produced by high-frequency stimulation may occur because the cell membrane has been rendered relatively unexcitable.[170] Stimulation occurring within the absolute refractory period of the change in transmembrane potential may cause the nerve to become unable to respond or depolarize in the presence of such ultra-high-frequency stimulation.

The determination of length of pain relief post-T.E.N.S. is easily influenced by the activity that the patient engages in after T.E.N.S. If pain can be reduced or alleviated, allowing for increased physical activity, resultant large-fiber afferent input may balance or counteract the return of pain for longer periods of time. This process can occur with any mode of T.E.N.S. We clinically observe periods of pain relief after conventional T.E.N.S. that are equal to or greater than those obtained with acupuncture-like T.E.N.S. Directly related to ADL are posture and body mechanics, which are often overlooked. If patients assume an abnormal, pain-producing posture during or after T.E.N.S., the degree of pain relief and its duration will be decreased. Proper instruction in posture, specifically for patients with neck and back pain, should be provided.

Duration of pain relief is also influenced by the length of stimulation, the extent of pain prior to the advent of stimulation, strength of the stimulation parameters, and postural considerations. Strong, low-rate or high-intensity, pulse-train (burst) T.E.N.S. applied for 30 minutes conceivably should produce longer-lasting pain relief than 20 minutes of stimulation. Patients with lower degrees of pain may obtain better and longer-lasting relief than those with higher degrees of pain. Patients who can tolerate stronger muscle contractions should obtain greater and longer-lasting pain relief due to increased neuropeptide liberation. Our clinical experience with noninvasive electroacupuncture treatments at times demonstrates a quick onset of pain relief that is frequently faster than that seen with acupuncture-like T.E.N.S. At present, there are no published studies dealing specifically with this analgesic technique, which has been compared with other methods that are not entirely the same.[168,169] Noninvasive electroacupuncture performed at a rate of 4 Hz with intensity to maximal tolerance is delivered via a very small (pinhead) blunt metal probe to stimulate acupuncture or trigger points. The degree of muscle contraction observed is thus very little when compared with the large T.E.N.S. electrodes that activate a greater number of muscle fibers. Surface stimulation with T.E.N.S. electrodes was more effective than invasive stimulation with needles when similar electrical parameters were employed. However, a number of electrodes and sites (two to four) are stimulated simultaneously with acupuncture-like T.E.N.S., which is not the case with noninvasive electroacupuncture. Noninvasive electroacupuncture devices use long pulse duration (10 msec), monophasic (DC) currents that allow for tolerance to the internal stimulation without the discomfort of strong muscle contraction.[167] Studies are needed to determine the neurophysiologic effect of surface stimulation with small blunt, probes using the aforementioned parameters when applied to acupuncture/trigger points specifically for 30- to 60-second periods. When this technique is performed, only one point is stimulated at a time, and the clinician subsequently stimulates other points (distal then proximal to area of pain), contralateral, ipsilateral, or bilateral and may also add treatment to spinal and ear points. This noninvasive electroacupuncture technique has also been termed hyperstimulation analgesia.[167-168]

Our clinical experience with hyperstimulation analgesia via noninvasive electroacupuncture devices has been quite successful. The onset of pain relief at times is relatively quick, occurring after only a few points are stimulated. Melzack feels that hyperstimulation analgesia interrupts reverberatory neural circuits that cause pain memory. Pain relief produced by this technique, breaking up the pain cycle, could be followed by increased activity levels, resulting in a greater degree of large afferent fiber input, yielding prolonged pain relief. Indeed, hyperstimulation analgesia has been shown to produce pain relief lasting for several hours and sometimes days.[80,168,169] Whether or not hyperstimulation analgesia results in endogenous opioid peptide release cannot be truly stated, but we feel that this may occur. Hyperstimulation analgesia is more noxious and less tolerable than acupuncture-like T.E.N.S. Strong stimulation may be needed, since deep joint and muscle afferents are not as easily activated by one small-diameter surface electrode as with larger surface electrodes. Acupuncture-like or high-intensity, pulse-train stimulation does not have to be completely noxious to be effective, but strong muscle contractions are required for its optimal benefit. A combination of the two treatment techniques may be the best approach for the relief of chronic pain.

When utilizing acupuncture-like and pulse-train (burst) modes, the number of muscle contractions obtained during an average 30-minute stimulation period may also be significant. A greater number of muscle contractions (as long as they are strong) may produce a more profound summated input at the brainstem and yield a more significant neuropeptide activation.

The physiologic action of T.E.N.S. can no longer be explained solely by the gate control theory or by neuropeptide liberation. T.E.N.S. is a general pain-modulating technique, but it can be administered in many different modes. Each mode uses a distinct stimulation pattern different from one another, and each may activate different CNS structures and nerve fibers. Aspirin and morphine are both pain-relieving medications, yet each has a distinctly different mode of action. Therefore, the neurophysiologic mechanisms and theories must relate to the specific stimulation parameters.

REFERENCES

1. WOLF, SL, GERSH, MR, AND RAO, VR: *Examination of electrode placements and stimulating parameters in treating chronic pain with conventional transcutaneous electrical nerve stimulation (T.E.N.S.).* Pain 11:37, 1981.
2. BATES, JAV AND NATHAN, PW: *Transcutaneous electrical nerve stimulation for chronic pain.* Anaesthesia 35:817, 1980.
3. TOOMEY, TC, ET AL: *Acupuncture and chronic pain mechanisms: The moderating effects of affect, personality, and stress on response to treatment.* Pain 3:137, 1977.
4. GRIFFIN, JW AND McCLURE, M: *Adverse response to transcutaneous electrical nerve stimulation in a patient with rheumatoid arthritis.* Phys Ther 61:354, 1981.
5. PICAZA, JA, ET AL: *Pain suppression by peripheral nerve stimulation: Part I. Observation with transcutaneous stimuli.* Surg Neurol 4:105, 1975.

6. IGNELZI, RJ AND NYQUIST, JK: *Excitability changes in peripheral nerve fibers after repetitive electrical stimulation: Implications in pain modulation.* J Neurosurg 51:824, 1979.

7. RAO, VR: *Clinical transcutaneous electrical nerve stimulation seminar*, Emory University, March 14–16, 1980.

8. KAHN, J: *Low Volt Technique Supplement.* J Kahn, Syosset, NY, 1981, p 44.

9. MELZACK, R, ET AL: *Ice massage and transcutaneous electrical stimulation: Comparison of treatment for low-back pain.* Pain 9:209, 1980.

10. JANKO, M AND TRONTELJ, JV: *Transcutaneous electrical nerve stimulation: A microneurographic and perceptual study.* Pain 9:219, 1980.

11. ANDERSSON, SA AND HOLMGREN, E: *On acupuncture analgesia and the mechanism of pain.* Am J Chin Med 3:311, 1975.

12. ANDERSSON, SA, HOLMGREN, E, AND ROOS, A: *Analgesic effects of peripheral conditioning stimulation II. Importance of certain stimulation parameters.* Acupunct Electrother Res 2:237, 1977.

13. ERIKSSON, MBE, SJOLUND, BH, AND NEILZEN, S: *Long term results of peripheral conditioning stimulation as an analgesic measure in chronic pain.* Pain 6:335, 1979.

14. MAURER, D: *Stimulation modulation and the control of pain.* Empi Tech Notes 3(2), 1981.

15. KOSTERLITZ, HW: *Endogenous opioid peptides and the control of pain.* Psychol Med 9:1, 1979.

16. IGNELZI, RJ AND ATKINSON, JH: *Pain and its modulation: Part II efferent mechanisms.* Neurosurg 6:584, 1980.

17. BLOOM, FE: *Neuropeptides.* Sci Am 245:148, 1981.

18. SNYDER, SH: *Opiate receptors and internal opiates.* Sci Am 236:44, 1977.

19. MILLER, RJ AND DEYO, SN: *Pain physiology, opiate receptors and endorphins.* In *Postgraduate Medical Communications.* Ricker Labs, Northbridge, Calif, 1980, p 5.

20. BASBAUM, AI: *The anatomy of pain and pain modulation.* In KOSTERLITZ, HW AND TERENIUS, LY (EDS): *Pain and Society.* Life Science Research Report #17, Weinheim, Deerfield Beach, Fla, 1980, p 93.

21. ZIEGLGANSBERGER, W: *Pharmacological aspects of segmental pain control.* In KOSTERLITZ, HW AND TERENIUS, LY (EDS): *Pain and Society.* Life Sciences Research Report #17, Weinheim, Deerfield Beach, Fla, 1980, p 141.

22. WILSON, PR AND YAKSH, TL: *Pharmacology of pain and analgesia.* Anaesth Intensive Care 8:248, 1980.

23. NEALE, JH AND BARKER, JL: *Enkephalin-containing neurons visualized in spinal cord cell structures.* Science 201:467, 1978.

24. KUHAR, M, PERT, C, AND SNYDER, S: *Regional distribution of opiate receptor binding in monkey and human brain.* Nature 245:447, 1973.

25. PERT, A AND YAKSH, T: *Sites of morphine induced analgesia in the primate brain: Relation to pain pathways.* Brain Res 80:135, 1974.

26. SJOLUND, BH, TERENIUS, L, AND ERIKSSON, MBE: *Increased cerebrospinal fluid levels of endorphin after electro-acupuncture.* Acta Physiol Scand 100:382, 1977.

27. VON KNORRING, L, ET AL: *Pain perception and endorphin levels in cerebrospinal fluid.* Pain 5:359, 1978.

28. ALMAY, BGL, ET AL: *Endorphins in chronic pain I. Differences in CSF endorphin levels between organic and psychogenic pain syndromes.* Pain 5:153, 1978.

29. ALMAY, BGL, ET AL: *Relationship between CSF metabolites in chronic pain patients.* Psychopharmacology (Berlin) 67:139, 1980.

30. TERENIUS, L AND WAHLSTROM, A: *A morphine-like ligand for opiate receptors in human CSF.* Life Sci 16:1759, 1975.

31. AKIL, H, ET AL: *Enkephalin-like material elevated in ventricular cerebrospinal fluid of pain patients after analgetic focal stimulation.* Science 201:463, 1978.

32. HOSOBUCHI, Y, ADAMS, JE, AND LINCHITZ, R: *Pain relief by electrical stimulation of central gray matter in humans and its reversal by naloxone.* Science 197:183, 1977.

33. INVERSEN, LL: *The chemistry of the brain.* Sci Am 241:134, 1979.

34. MAYER, DJ, PRICE, DD, AND RAFFII, A: *Antagonism of acupuncture analgesia in man by the narcotic antagonist naloxone.* Brain Res 121:368, 1977.

35. ERIKSSON, MBE AND SJOLUND, BH: *Acupuncturelike electro-analgesia in TNS resistant chronic pain.* In ZOTTERMAN, Y (ED): *Sensory Functions of the Skin.* Pergamon Press, Oxford, 1976, p 575.

36. SJOLUND, BH AND ERIKSSON, MBE: *Electroacupuncture and endogenous morphines.* Lancet 2:1035, 1976.

37. SJOLUND, BH AND ERIKSSON, MBE: *Endorphins and analgesia produced by peripheral conditioning stimulation.* In *Pain Abstracts.* Second World Congress on Pain, IASP, Seattle, 1978, p 15.

38. ANDERSSON, SA: *Pain control by sensory stimulation.* In *Pain Abstracts.* Second World Congress on Pain, IASP, Seattle, 1978, p 97.

39. SJOLUND, BH AND ERIKSSON, MBE: *Stimulation techniques in the management of pain.* In KOSTERLITZ, HW AND TERENIUS, LY (EDS): *Pain and Society.* Life Sciences Report #17, Weinheim, Deerfield Beach, Fla, 1980, p 415.

40. SHERMAN, JE AND LIEBESKIND, JC: *An endorphinergic centrifugal substrate of pain modulation: Recent findings, current concepts and complexities.* In BONICA, JJ (ED): *Pain.* Raven Press, New York, 1980, p 191.

41. BUCHSBAUM, MS, DAVIS, GC, AND BUNNEY, WE JR: *Naloxone alters pain perception and somatosensory evoked potentials in normal subjects.* Nature 270:620, 1977.

42. HUGHES, J, ET AL: *Identification of two related pentapeptides from the brain with potent opiate agonist activity.* Nature 258:577, 1975.

43. GUILLEMIN, RT, ET AL: *B-endorphin and adrenocorticotropin are secreted concomitantly by the pituitary gland.* Science 197:1367, 1977.

44. CHECK, WA: *Old hormones reveal new surprises: Complex connections link brain, pituitary.* JAMA 243:499, 1980.

45. POMERANZ, B, CHENG, R, AND LAW, P: *Acupuncture reduces electrophysiological and behavior responses to noxious stimuli: Pituitary is implicated.* Exp Neurol 54:172, 1977.

46. BLOOM, F, ET AL: *Endorphins are located in the intermediate and anterior lobes of the pituitary gland, not in the neurohypophysis.* Life Sci 20:43, 1977.

47. CHEUNG, A AND GOLDSTEIN, A: *Failure of hypophysectomy to alter brain content of opioid peptides (endorphins).* Life Sci 19:1005, 1976.

48. SCHLEN, H AND BENTLEY, GA: *The possibility that a component of morphine induced analgesia is contributed indirectly via the release of endogenous opioids.* Pain 9:73, 1980.

49. LEWIS, JW, ET AL: *Stress activates endogenous pain-inhibitory system: Opioid and non-opioid mechanisms.* Proc West Pharmacol Soc 23:85, 1980.

50. LEWIS, JW, CANNON, JT, AND LIEBESKIND, JC: *Opioid and non-opioid mechanisms of stress and analgesia.* Science 208:623, 1980.

51. CHENG, R, ET AL: *Electroacupuncture elevates blood cortisol levels in naive horses; sham treatment has no effect.* Int J Neurosci 10:95, 1980.

52. GINTZLER, AR: *Endorphin mediated increases in pain threshold during pregnancy.* Science 210:193, 1980.

53. HOUCK, JC, ET AL: *Placental b-endorphin-like peptides.* Science 207:78, 1980.

54. KOSTERLITZ, HW AND HUGHES, J: *Some thoughts on the significance of enkephalins, the endogenous ligand.* Life Sci 17:91, 1975.

55. WEI, E AND LOH, H: *Physical dependence on opiate-like peptides.* Science 193:1262, 1976.

56. SOLOMON, RA, VIERNSTEIN, MC, AND LONG, DM: *Reduction of postoperative pain and narcotic use by transcutaneous electrical nerve stimulation.* Surgery 87:142, 1980.

57. WARD, NG, BLOOM, VL, AND FRIEDEL, RO: *The effectiveness of tricyclic antidepressants in the treatment of coexisting pain and depression.* Pain 7:331, 1979.

58. MERSKEY, H: *The effect of chronic pain upon the response to noxious stimuli by psychiatric patients.* J Psychosom Res 8:405, 1965.

59. MESSING, RB AND LYTLE, LD: *Serotonin containing neurons: Their possible role in pain and analgesia.* Pain 4:1, 1977.

60. SELTZER, S, MARCUS, R, AND STOCK, R: *Perspectives in the control of chronic pain by nutritional manipulation.* Pain 11:141, 1981.

61. PFEIFFER, CC: *Mental and Elemental Nutrients: A Physician's Guide to Nutrition and Health Care*. Keats Publishing, New Canaan, Conn, 1975.

62. STERNBACH, RA, ET AL: *Effects of altering brain serotonin activity on human chronic pain*. In BONICA, JJ AND ALBE-FESSARD, D (EDS): *Advances in Pain Research and Therapy*, Vol 1. Raven Press, New York, 1976, p 601.

63. JOHANSSON, F AND VON KNORRING, L: *A double blind controlled study of a serotonin uptake inhibitor (Zimelidine) versus placebo in chronic pain patients*. Pain 7:69, 1979.

64. AKIL, H AND MAYER, DJ: *Antagonism of stimulation-produced analgesia by P-CPA, a serotonin synthesis inhibitor*. Brain Res 44:692, 1972.

65. MAO, W, ET AL: *High versus low intensity acupuncture analgesia for treatment of chronic pain: Effects on platelet serotonin*. Pain 8:331, 1980.

66. SHEALY, CN, KWAKO, JL, AND HUGHES, S: *Effects of transcranial neurostimulation upon mood and serotonin production: A preliminary report*. IL Dolore 1:13, 1979.

67. ANDERSSON, SA AND HOLMGREN, E: *Pain threshold effects of peripheral conditioning stimulation*. In BONICA, JJ AND ALBE-FESSARD, D (EDS): *Advances in Pain Research and Therapy*, Vol 6. Raven Press, New York, 1976, p 761.

68. OMURA, Y: *Acupuncture (with possible roles of serotonin and melatonin) and related unorthodox methods of diagnosis and treatment: Non-invasive spheno-palatine ganglionic block, abrasion of naso-pharyngeal mucosa, and applied kinesiology*. Acupunct Electrother Res 4:69, 1979.

69. KING, RB: *Pain and tryptophan*. J Neurosurg 53:44, 1980.

70. WEN, HL, ET AL: *Immunoassayable beta-endorphin level in the plasma and CSF of heroin addicted and normal subjects before and after electroacupuncture*. Am J Chin Med 8:154, 1980.

71. FALK, D: *Antidepressants for pain*. Aches and Pains 3:8, 1982.

72. TUNG, CH: *Integrative action of the thalamus in the process of acupuncture for analgesia*. Am J Chin Med 2:1, 1974.

73. HOSOBUCHI, Y, LAMB, S, AND BASCOM, D: *Tryptophan loading may reverse tolerance to opiate analgesics in humans: A preliminary report*. Pain 9:161, 1980.

74. HOSOBUCHI, Y: *Central gray stimulation for pain suppression in humans*. In *Pain Abstracts*, Vol 1. International Association for the Study of Pain, Seattle, 1978, p 169.

75. KANDEL, ER: *Small systems of neurons*. Sci Am 241:66, 1979.

76. HANDWERKER, HO: *Pain producing substances*. In KOSTERLITZ, HW AND TERENIUS, LY (EDS): *Pain and Society*. Life Sciences Report # 17, Weinheim, Deerfield Beach, Fla, 1980, p 325.

77. CHENG, RSS AND POMERANZ, B: *A combined treatment with D-amino acids with electro-acupuncture produces a greater analgesia than either treatment alone, naloxone reverses these effects*. Pain 8:231, 1980.

78. BUDD, K: *The use of D-phenylalanine, an enkephalinase inhibitor, in the treatment of intractable pain*. Pain [Suppl I]: 95, 1981.

79. WOLF, CJ, MITCHELL, D, AND BARRETT, D: *Antinociceptive effect of peripheral segmental electrical stimulation in the rat*. Pain 8:237, 1980.

80. FOX, EJ AND MELZACK, R: *Transcutaneous electrical stimulation and acupuncture: Comparison of treatment for low back pain*. Pain 2:141, 1976.

81. ANDERSSON, SA, ET AL: *Electroacupuncture: Effect on pain threshold measured with electrical stimulation of teeth*. Brain Res 63:393, 1973.

82. HOLMGREN, E: *Increase of pain threshold as a function of conditioning electrical stimulation: An experimental study with application to electroacupuncture for pain suppression*. Am J Chin Med 3:133, 1975.

83. CHAPMAN, CR, WILSON, ME, GEHRIG, JD: *Comparative effects of acupuncture and transcutaneous stimulation of the perception of painful dental stimuli*. Pain 2:265, 1976.

84. WARWICK, R AND WILLIAMS, PL: *Gray's Anatomy*, ed 35. WB Saunders, Philadelphia, 1973, p 888.

85. FIELDS, HL AND BASBAUM, AI: *Brainstem control of spinal pain transmission neurons*. Annu Rev Physiol 40:217, 1978.

86. BAUSBAUM, AI AND FIELDS, HL: *Endogenous pain control mechanisms: Review and hypothesis.* Ann Neurol 4:451, 1978.
87. FIELDS, HL AND ANDERSSON, SD: *Evidence that raphe-spinal neurons mediate opiate and midbrain stimulation produced analgesia.* Pain 5:333, 1978.
88. MAYER, DJ AND PRICE, DD: *Central nervous system mechanisms of analgesia.* Pain 2:379, 1976.
89. LOVICK, TA AND WOLSTENCROFT, JH: *Inhibiting effects of nucleus raphe magnus on neuronal responses in the spinal trigeminal necleus to nociceptive compared with non-nociceptive inputs.* Pain 7:135, 1979.
90. BOWSHER, D: *Pain pathways and mechanisms.* Anesthesia 33:935, 1978.
91. OLESON, TD, TWOMBLY, DA, AND LIEBESKIND, JC: *Effects of pain-attenuating brain stimulation and morphine on electricity activity in the raphe nuclei of the awake cat.* Pain 4:211, 1978.
92. CLANTON, CH AND FIELDS, HL: *Three bulbospinal pathways from the central medulla of the cat: An autoradiographic study of pain modulating systems.* J Comp Neurol 178:209, 1978.
93. ANDERSSON, DS, BASBAUM, AI, AND FIELDS, HL: *Response of medullary raphe neurons to peripheral stimulation and to systemic opiates.* Brain Res 123:363, 1977.
94. YAKSH, TL: *Spinal opiate analgesia: Characteristics and principles of action.* Pain 11:293, 1981.
95. FURUI, T, KAGEYAMA, N, AND KUWAYAMA, A: *Increase of B-endorphin in cerebrospinal fluid after removal of ACTH-secreting pituitary adenomas.* Pain 11:127, 1981.
96. WURTMAN, RJ: *Nutrients that modify brain function.* Sci Am 246:50, 1982.
97. HOSOBUCHI, Y, ET AL: *Stimulation of human periaqueductal gray for pain relief increases immunoreactive B-endorphin in ventricular fluid.* Science 203:279, 1979.
98. HAMMOND, DL, LEVY, RA, AND PROUDFIT, HK: *Hypoalgesia following microinjection of non-adrenergic antagonists in the nucleus raphe magnus.* Pain 9:85, 1980.
99. ANDERSSON, SA AND HOLMGREN, E: *Analgesic effects of peripheral conditioning stimulation III. Effect of high frequency stimulation; segmental mechanisms interacting with pain.* Acupunct Electrother Res 3:23, 1978.
100. CHENG, RSS AND POMERANZ, B: *Monoaminergic mechanism of electroacupuncture analgesia.* Brain Res 215:77, 1981.
101. WEST, DC AND WOLSTENCROFT, JH: *A comparison of strength-duration curves for slow and fast raphe spinal axons.* J Physiol (Lond) 269:39, 1977.
102. BOWSHER, D: *Role of the reticular formation in responses to noxious stimulation.* Pain 2:361, 1976.
103. BEALL, JE, ET AL: *Inhibition of primate spino-thalamic tract neurons by stimulation in the region of the nucleus raphe magnus.* Brain Res 114:328, 1978.
104. FIELDS, HL, ET AL: *Nucleus raphe magnus inhibition of spinal cord dorsal horn neurons.* Brain Res 125:441, 1977.
105. POMEROY, SL AND BEHBELANI, MM: *Physiologic evidence for a projection from periaqueductal gray to nucleus raphe magnus in the rat.* Brain Res 176:143, 1979.
106. JORDON, LM, ET AL: *Depression of primate spinothalamic tract neurons by iontophoretic application of 5-hydroxytryptamine.* Pain 5:135, 1978.
107. PEARL, GS AND ANDERSON, KV: *Response patterns of cells in the feline caudal nucleus reticularis gigantocellularis after noxious trigeminal and spinal stimulation.* Exp Neurol 58:231, 1978.
108. CLEMENT-JONES, V, ET AL: *Acupuncture in heroin addicts: Changes in met-enkephalin and B-endorphin in blood and cerebrospinal fluid.* Lancet 2:380, 1979.
109. BASBAUM, AI, ET AL: *Reversal of morphine and stimulus-produced analgesia by subtotal spinal cord lesions.* Pain 3:43, 1977.
110. OLIVERAS, JL, ET AL: *Opiate antagonist, naloxone, strongly reduces analgesia induced by stimulation of a raphe nucleus (centralis inferior).* Brain Res 120:221, 1977.
111. RIVOT, JP, CHAOUCH, A, AND BESSON, JM: *The influence of naloxone on the C fiber response of dorsal horn neurons and their inhibitory control by raphe magnus stimulation.* Brain Res 176:355, 1979.
112. BENNETT, GJ AND MAYER, DJ: *Inhibition of spinal cord interneurons by narcotic microinjection and focal electrical stimulation in the periaqueductal gray matter.* Brain Res 172:243, 1979.

113. UHL, GR, ET AL: *Immunohistochemical mapping of enkephalin containing cell bodies, fibers and nerve terminals in the brainstem of the rat.* Brain Res 166:75, 1979.

114. YAKSH, TL: *Direct evidence that spinal serotonin and noradrenalin terminals mediate the spinal antinociceptive effects of morphine in the periaqueductal gray.* Brain Res 160:180, 1979.

115. BECKER, DP, ET AL: *An inquiry into the neurophysiological basis for pain.* J Neurosurg 30:1, 1969.

116. LIPMAN, J; Personal communication, 1980.

117. SJOLUND, BH AND ERIKSSON, MBE: *The influence of naloxone on analgesia produced by peripheral conditioning stimulation.* Brain Res 173:295, 1979.

118. TAUB, A: *Percutaneous local electrical analgesia: Origin, mechanism and clinical potential.* Minn Med 57:172, 1974.

119. POMERANZ, B: *Do endorphins mediate acupuncture analgesia.* In COSTA, E AND TRABUCCHI, M (EDS): *Advances in Biochemical Psychopharmacology,* Vol 18. Raven Press, New York, 1978, p 351.

120. POMERANZ, B: *Brain's opiates at work in acupuncture?* New Scientist 12-12, 1/16/77.

121. ABRAM, SE, REYNOLDS, AC, AND CUSICK, JF: *Failure of naloxone to reverse analgesia from transcutaneous electrical stimulation in patients with chronic pain.* Anesth Analg (Cleve) 60:81, 1981.

122. JONES, VC, ET AL: *Increased B-endorphin but not met-enkephalin levels in human cerebrospinal fluid after acupuncture for recurrent pain.* Lancet 2:946, 1980.

123. CHENG, RSS AND POMERANZ, B: *Electroacupuncture analgesia could be mediated by at least two pain-relieving mechanisms: Endorphin and non-endorphin systems.* Life Sci 25:1957, 1979.

124. CHENG, RSS AND POMERANZ, B: *Electroacupuncture is mediated by stereospecific opiate receptors and is reversed by antagonists of type I receptors.* Life Sci 26:631, 1980.

125. GRAU, JW, ET AL: *Long term stress-induced analgesia and activation of the opiate system.* Science 213:1409, 1981.

126. SALAR, G, IOB, I, AND MINGRINO, S: *Cortical evoked responses and transcutaneous electrotherapy.* Neurology 30:663, 1980.

127. FINER, B: *Mental mechanisms in the control of pain.* In KOSTERLITZ, HW AND TERENIUS, LY (EDS): *Pain and Society.* Life Sciences Report #17, Weinheim, Deerfield Beach, Fla, 1980, p 223.

128. LEVINE, JD, GORDON, NC AND FIELDS, HL: *Evidence that the analgesic effect of placebo is mediated by endorphins.* In *Pain Abstracts,* Vol 1. Second World Congress on Pain, International Association for the Study of Pain, Seattle, 1978, p 18.

129. MIHIC, D AND BINKERT, E: *Is placebo analgesia mediated by endorphin?* In *Pain Abstracts,* Vol 1. Second World Congress on Pain, International Association for the Study of Pain, Seattle, 1978, p 19.

130. CHEN, ACN: *Behavioral and brain evoked potentials (BEP) evaluation of placebo effects: Contrast of cognitive mechanisms and endorphin mechanisms.* In *Program Abstracts.* Second General Meeting of the American Pain Society, New York, 1980, p 12.

131. GOLDSTEIN, A: *Endorphins as pain regulators: Reality or fantasy?* In *Program Abstracts.* Second General Meeting of the American Pain Society, New York, 1980, p 1.

132. IGNELZI, RJ AND NYQUIST, JK: *Observations on fast axoplasmic transport in peripheral nerve following repetitive electrical stimulation.* Pain 7:313, 1979.

133. IGNELZI, RJ AND NYQUIST, JK: *Direct effect of electrical stimulation on peripheral nerve evoked activity: Implications for pain relief.* J Neurosurg 45:159, 1976.

134. SAMSON, F: *Axonal transport: The mechanisms and their susceptibility to derangement: Anterograde transport.* In KORR, IM (ED): *The Neurobiologic Mechanisms in Manipulative Therapy.* Plenum Press, New York, 1978, p 291.

135. THOENEN, H, SCHWAB, M, AND BORDE, YA: *Transfer of information from effector organs to innervating neurons by retrograde axonal transport of macro-molecules.* In KORR, IM (ED): *The Neurobiologic Mechanisms in Manipulative Therapy.* Plenum Press, New York, 1978, p 311.

136. SJOSTRAND, J: *Discussion and short reports on axonal transport.* In KORR, IM (ED): *The Neurobiologic Mechanisms in Manipulative Therapy.* Plenum Press, New York, 1978, p 333.

137. SJOSTRAND, J, ET AL: *Impairment of intraneural microcirculation, blood–nerve barrier and axonal transport in experimental nerve ischemia and compression.* In KORR, IM (ED): *The Neurobiologic Mechanisms in Manipulative Therapy.* Plenum Press, New York, 1978, p 337.

138. OCHS, S, CHAN, SY, AND WORTH, R: *Calcium and the mechanism of axoplasmic transport.* In KORR, IM (ED): *The Neurobiologic Mechanisms in Manipulative Therapy.* Plenum Press, New York, 1978, p 359.

139. HENRY, JL, ET AL: *Effects of substance P on nociceptive and non-nociceptive trigeminal brain-stem neurons.* Pain 8:33, 1980.

140. OEHME, P, ET AL: *Substance P: Does it produce analgesia or hyperalgesia.* Science 208:305, 1980.

141. OLGART, L, ET AL: *Localization- of substance P-like immunoreactivity in nerves in the tooth pulp.* Pain 4:153, 1977.

142. HOKFELT, T, ET AL: *Substance P: Localization in the central nervous system and in some primary sensory neurons.* Science 190:889, 1975.

143. MUDGE, AW, LEEMAN, FE, AND FISHBACH, GD: *Enkephalin inhibits release of substance P from sensory neurons in culture and decreases action potential duration.* Proc Natl Acad Sci (USA) 76:526, 1979.

144. JESSELL, T AND INVERSEN, LL: *Opiate analgesics inhibit substance P release from rat trigeminal nucleus.* Nature (Lond): 268:549, 551, 1977.

145. HUBEL, DH: *The brain.* Sci Am 241:44, 1979.

146. PERT, C, PASTERNAK, G, AND SYNDER, S: *Opiate agonists and antagonists discriminated by receptor binding in brain.* Science 182:1359, 1973.

147. SIMON, E, ET AL: *Further properties of stereospecific opiate binding sites in rat brain: On the nature of the sodium effect.* Pharmacol Exp Ther 192:531, 1976.

148. LAKOSKI, JM, MOHSLAND, JS, AND GEBHART, GF: *The effect of morphine on the content of serotonin, 5-hydroxyindoleacetic acid and substance P in the nuclei raphe magnus and reticularis gigantocellularis.* Life Sci 27:2639, 1980.

149. YAKSH, TL, ET AL: *Intrathecal morphine inhibits substance P release from mammalian spinal cord in vivo.* Nature (Lond) 286:155, 1980.

150. CHAHL, LA AND LADD, RJ: *Local oedema and general excitation of cutaneous sensory receptors produced by electrical stimulation of the saphenous nerve of the rat.* Pain 2:25, 1976.

151. CAMPBELL, JN AND TAUB, A: *Local analgesia from percutaneous electrical stimulation.* Arch Neurol 28:347, 1953.

152. TOREBJORK, HE AND HALLIN, RG: *Responses in human A and C fibers to repeated electrical intradermal stimulation.* J Neurol Neurosurg Psychiatry 37:653, 1974.

153. NYQUIST, JK AND IGNELZI, RJ: *Repetitive electrical stimulation of peripheral nerve: A peripheral mechanism underlying electrical analgesia.* In *Pain Abstracts,* Vol 1. Second World Congress on Pain, International Association for the Study of Pain, Seattle, 1978, p 125.

154. NYQUIST, JK AND IGNELZI, RJ: *The electro-physiological behavior of single peripheral nerve fibers of amphibian sciatic nerve in response to various frequencies of repetitive electrical stimulation: Implications for electroanalgesia.* In *Scientific Program Abstracts.* First Annual Meeting of the American Pain Society, San Diego, 1979, p 60.

155. PERTOVAARA, A: *Experimental pain and transcutaneous electrical nerve stimulation at high frequency.* Appl Neurophysiol 43:290, 1980.

156. PERTOVAARA, A AND KEMPPAINEN, P: *The influence of naloxone on dental pain threshold elevation produced by peripheral conditioning stimulation at high frequency.* Brain Res 215:426, 1981.

157. O'BRIEN, W: *Personal communication,* 1981.

158. LE BARS, D, DICKENSON, AH, AND BESSON, JM: *Diffuse noxious inhibitory controls (DNIC) I. Effects on dorsal horn convergent neurons in the rat.* Pain 6:283, 1979.

159. LE BARS, D, DICKENSON, AH, AND BESSON, JM: *Diffuse noxious inhibitory controls (DNIC). II Lack of effect on non-convergent neurons, supraspinal involvement and theoretical implications.* Pain 6:305, 1979.

160. WALKER, JB AND KATZ, RL: *Non-opioid pathways suppress pain in humans.* Pain 11:347, 1981.

161. JURNA, I AND HEINZ, A: *Differential effects on morphine and opioid analgesics and A and C fiber evoked activity in ascending axons of the rat spinal cord.* Brain Res 171:573, 1979.

162. BIRD, SJ AND KUHAR, MJ: *Iontophoretic application of opiates to the locus coeruleus.* Brain Res 122:523, 1977.

163. PROUDFIT, HK: *Effects on raphe magnus and raphe pallidus lesions on morphine induced analgesia and spinal cord monoamines.* Pharmacol Biochem Behav 13:705, 1980.

164. GAMMON, GD AND STARR, I: *Studies on the relief of pain by counterirritation.* J Clin Invest 2:13, 1941.

165. RAPOPORT, SI, ET AL: *Entry of opioid peptides into the central nervous system.* Science 207:84, 1980.

166. NORTH, RA: *Opiates, opioid peptides and single neurons.* Life Sci 24:1527, 1979.

167. CASTEL, JC: *Pain Management, Acupuncture and Transcutaneous Electrical Nerve Stimulation Techniques.* Pain Control Services, Lake Bluff, Ill, 1979.

168. MELZACK, R; *Prolonged relief of pain by brief, intense transcutaneous electrical stimulation.* Pain 1:357, 1975.

169. MELZACK, R: *Myofascial trigger points: Relation to acupuncture and mechanisms of pain.* Arch Phys Med Rehabil 62:114, 1981.

170. OMURA, Y: *Electro-acupuncture: Its electro-physiological basis and criteria for effectiveness and safety—Part I.* Acupunct Electrother Res 1:157, 1975.

171. BIOSTIM INC: *The Theory of Pain and the Role of Biostimulation.* Book 1 of Informative Series. Biostim Inc, Princeton, NJ, 1982.

172. LLINAS, RR: *Calcium in synaptic transmission.* Sci Am 247:56, 1982.

173. YASPHAL, K, WRIGHT, DM, AND HENRY, JL: *Substance P reduces tail-flick latency: Implications for chronic pain syndromes.* Pain 14:155, 1982.

174. WILLER, JC: *Comparative study of perceived pain and nociceptive flexion reflex in man.* Pain 3:69, 1977.

175. PERTOVAARA, A AND HAMALAINEN, H: *Vibrotactile threshold elevation produced by high frequency transcutaneous electrical nerve stimulation.* Arch Phys Med Rehabil 63:597, 1982.

176. CHITOUR, D, DICKENSON, AH, AND LEBARS, D: *Pharmacological evidence for the involvement of serotonergic mechanisms in diffuse noxious inhibitory controls (DNIC).* Brain Res 236:329, 1982.

177. PERTOVAARA, A, ET AL: *Dental analgesia produced by nonpainful, low frequency stimulation is not influenced by stress or reversed by naloxone.* Pain 13:379, 1982.

178. SHRIBER, WJ: *A Manual of Electrotherapy*, ed 4. Lea & Febiger, Philadelphia, 1977.

179. CAMPBELL, JN: *Examination of possible mechanisms by which stimulation of the spinal cord in man relieves pain.* Appl Neurophysiol 44:181, 1981.

180. SELTZER, S, ET AL: *Alteration of human pain thresholds by nutritional manipulation and L-tryptophan supplementation.* Pain 13:385, 1982.

181. SALAR, G, ET AL: *Effect of transcutaneous electrotherapy on CSF β-endorphin content in patients without pain problems.* Pain 10:169, 1981.

182. SINCLAIR, D: *Mechanisms of Cutaneous Sensation.* Oxford University Press, Oxford, 1981, p 46.

183. VON KNORRING, L, ET AL: *Circannual variations in concentrations of endorphins in cerebrospinal fluid.* Pain 12:265, 1982.

184. ISAACSON, RL: *The Limbic System*, ed 2. Plenum Press, New York, 1982.

185. EMMERS, R: *Pain: A Spike-Interval Coded Message in the Brain.* Raven Press, New York, 1981.

APPENDIX

Illustrations of various electrode systems and T.E.N.S. units follow. Each manufacturer should be contacted for information pertaining to features and parameter specifications.

Standards for the manufacture and marketing of transcutaneous electrical nerve stimulators (T.E.N.S.) have been developed by the Neurosurgery Committee of the Association for the Advancement of Medical Instrumentation (AAMI).* AAMI has established standards governing labeling of the devices, electrical safety and performance requirements of the unit, lead wires and electrodes, testing methods, and terminology for the T.E.N.S. industry. Included for the manufacturer is specific information pertaining to the maximum charge per pulse as well as contraindications, warnings, and precautions that should be included in instructional manuals for patients and clinicians.

---

*Association for the Advancement of Medical Instrumentation, 1901 North Ft. Meyer Dr., Suite 602, Arlington, VA 22209.

ELECTRODE SYSTEMS

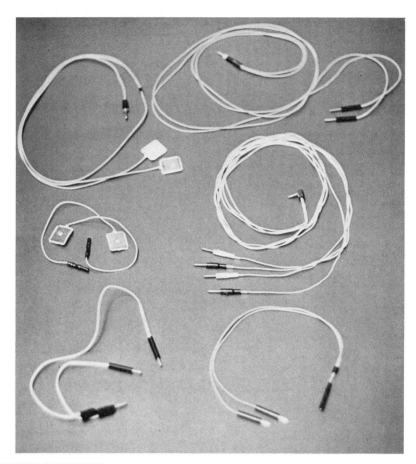

ELECTRODE LEAD WIRES

Velcro attachments (upper left); Velcro adapters (middle left); piggyback leads (lower left); single connector with dual leads (upper right); single connector with four leads (middle right); "Y" adapter (lower right). Available from most manufacturers.

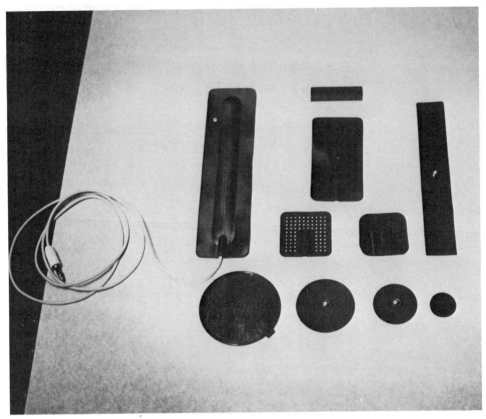

SILICONE-CARBON ELECTRODES

Standard electrodes require tape and gel or karaya for adherence and activation, respectively, and are available in different sizes and shapes from all manufacturers. The perforated electrode* is designed for use with a karaya pad. Depending on the electrode, a snap or pin lead will be needed. Foam and paper adhesive tape patches can be obtained in required sizes from the manufacturers.

*Perforated electrode available from Stim-Tech, c/o Codman & Shurtleff, Randolph, Mass 02368.

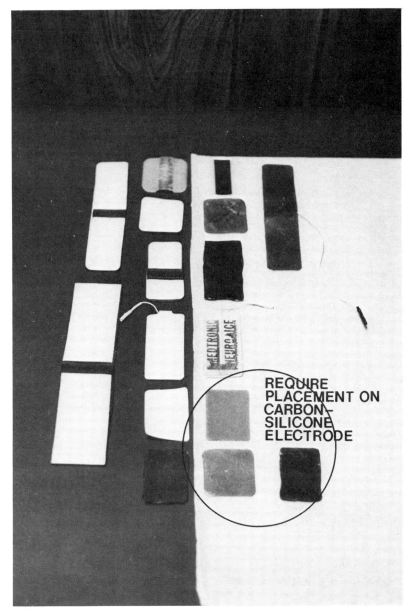

REUSABLE SELF-ADHERING ELECTRODES THAT REQUIRE WATER FOR ACTIVATION

Various sizes of karaya and synthetic polymer electrodes that do not require placement on a standard silicone-rubber electrode. Karaya pads with inner mesh to prevent deformity. Some require placement on a silicone-carbon electrode, as indicated.

Manufacturers:
Lee-Tec Inc., 10205 Crosstown Circle, Eden Prairie, Minn 55344
Medtronic, Inc., 3055 Old Highway Eight, Minneapolis, Minn 55440
3M Inc., St. Paul, Minn 55101
Stim-Tech, c/o Codman & Shurtleff, Inc., Randolph, Mass 02368 (Dermaforms)
Rodel Products Corp., 7100 East Lincoln Dr., Suite D-222, Scottsdale, Ariz 85253

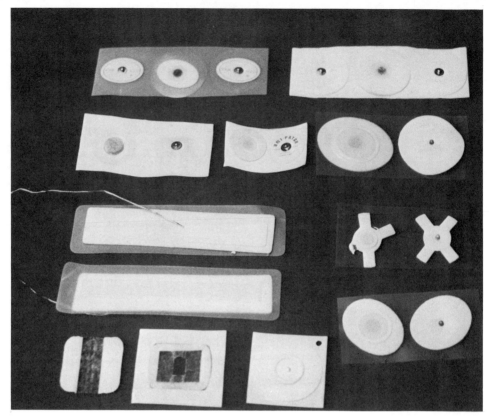

PRE-GELLED SHELF-ADHERING ELECTRODES

Available in various sizes and shapes, these electrodes can be left in place and used for 2 to 5 days before discarding. The two electrodes in the lower left-hand corner require water for activation; they are not pre-gelled.

Manufacturers:
Vermont Medical Inc., Bellows Falls, Vt 05101 (Silver-Silver Chloride Disposable).
Uni-Patch Inc., P.O. Box 1001, Burnsville, Minn 55337
INS-TENS, c/o Codman & Shurtleff, Inc., Randolph, Mass 02368
Consolidated Medical Equipment, Inc., 10 Hoffer Street, Utica, NY 13501
3M Inc., St. Paul, Minn 55101
Staodynamics, Inc., P.O. Box 1379, Longmont, Colo 80501

3M gel pads, foam, and tape patches.

3M Inc., St. Paul, Minn 55144

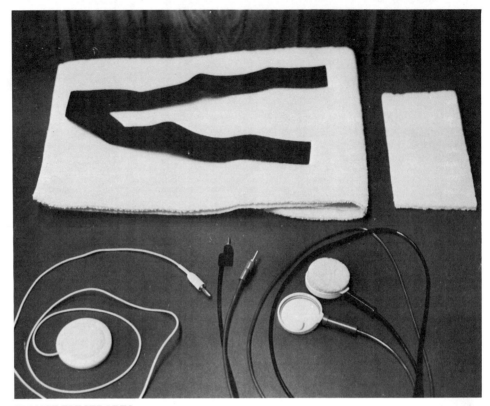

SPONGE ELECTRODES

Carbon impregnated circumferential sponge. Piggyback leads with sponge electrodes. Sponge electrode with banana plug.

Manufacturers:
Stim-Tech, c/o Codman & Shurtleff, Inc., Randolph, Mass 02368
Pain Suppression Labs, Inc., 559 River Road, Elmwood Park, NJ 07407

DISPOSABLE ELECTRODE PADS

Premoistened paper pads (Spectra Pad). Parker Labs Inc., Orange, NJ 07050
TENS gel pad. 3M, St. Paul, Minn 55101
Skin-prep wipe (acts to decrease skin irritation from electrode tape). United Division of
Howmedica Inc., 11775 Starkey Road, Largo, Florida 33540

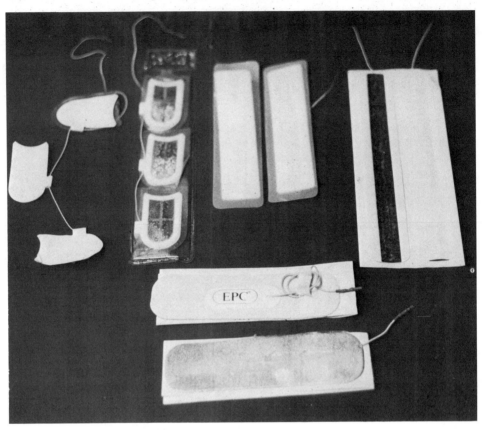

POSTOPERATIVE SELF-ADHERING ELECTRODES

Available in different lengths, some of which can be trimmed down. The serpentine electrode on the left can be adapted to curved incision sites.

Manufacturers:
Medical Devices Inc., 833 Third Street, SW, St. Paul, Minn 55112
Consolidated Medical Equipment, Inc., 10 Hoffer Street, Utica, NY 13501
Stim-Tech, c/o Codman & Shurtleff, Inc., Randolph, Mass 02368
3M, St. Paul, Minn 55101

T.E.N.S. UNITS

STIM-TECH DUAL-CHANNEL T.E.N.S.

Stim-Tech, c/o Codman & Shurtleff, Inc., Randolph, Mass 02368

Stim-Tech Stimburst Model 6077 dual-channel with pulse-train (burst) mode.

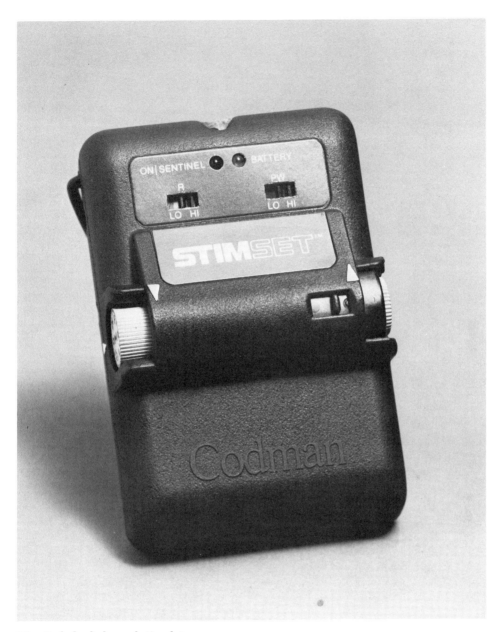

Stim-Tech dual-channel stimulator.

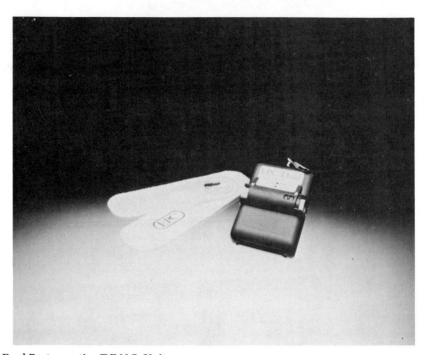

EPC Dual Postoperative T.E.N.S. Unit.

Stim-Tech, c/o Codman & Shurtleff, Inc., Randolph, Mass 02368

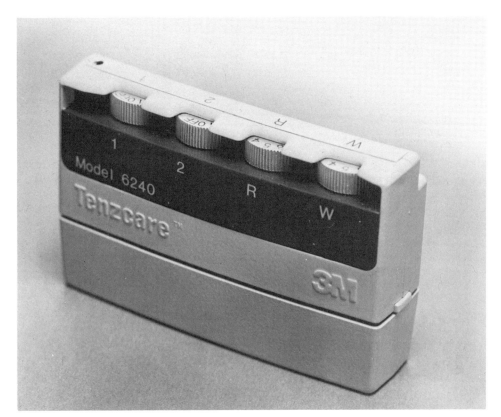

3M Dual-channel Tenzcare unit with pulse-train (burst) mode.

3M Inc., St. Paul, Minn 55144

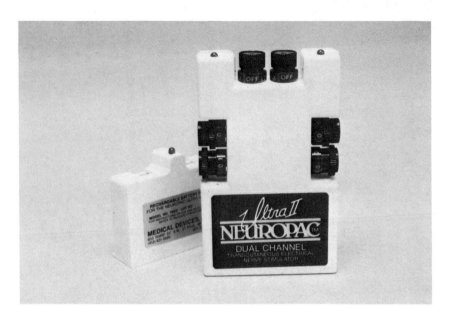

Ultra II dual-channel unit.

Medical Devices Inc., 833 Third St., SW, St. Paul, Minn 55112

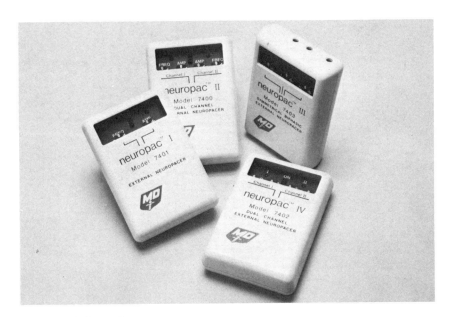

Single- and dual-channel neuropacers.

Medical Devices Inc., 833 Third St., SW, St. Paul, Minn 55112

Mentor Dual-Channel 150 with pulse-train (burst) mode.

Mentor Corporation, 1499 West River Road North, Minneapolis, Minn 55411

Staodyn Dual-Channel Model 4500.

Staodynamics Inc., PO Box 1379, Longmont, Colo 80501

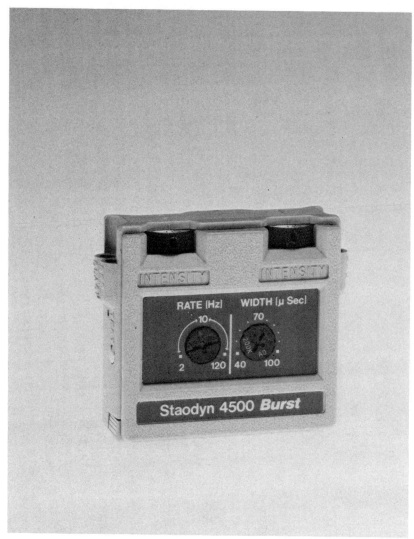

Staodyn model 4500 (dual-channel) with pulse-train (burst) mode.

Staodynamics Inc., PO Box 1379, Longmont, Colo 80501

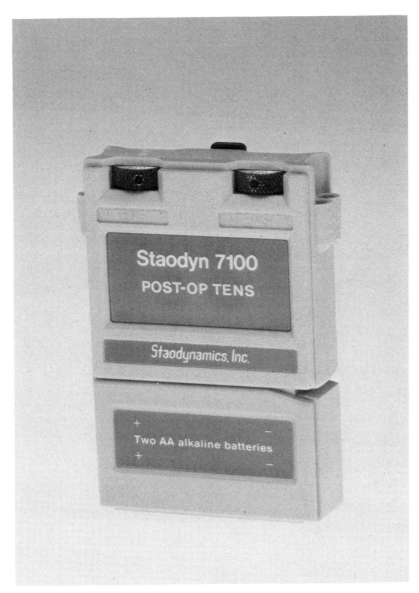

Staodyn Model 7100 Post-Op T.E.N.S. (dual-channel).

Staodynamics Inc., PO Box 1379, Longmont, Colo 80501

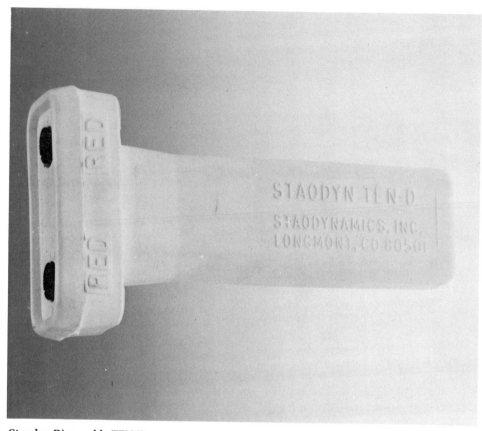

Staodyn Disposable TEN-D

Staodynamics Inc., PO Box 1379, Longmont, Colo 80501

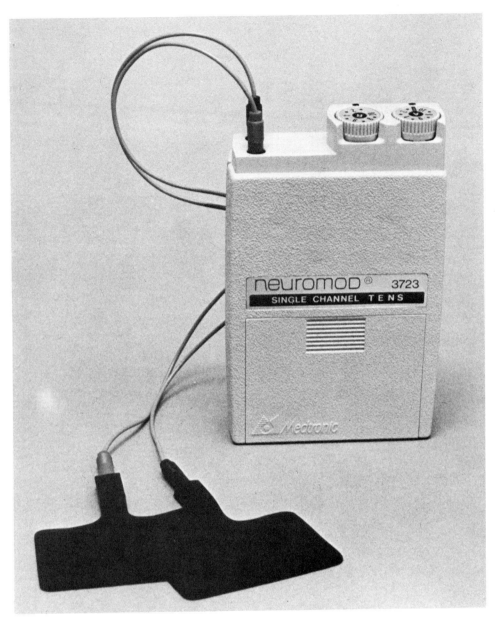

Neurmod Single-Channel T.E.N.S. Also available in dual-channel model.

Medtronic Inc., 2199 N. Pascal, Roseville, Minn 55113

Medtronic: Comfort Burst Dual Channel (upper right)
Selectra Dual-Channel (middle)
Complement Dual-Channel (bottom)
All with pulse-train (burst) mode.

Medtronic Inc., Neuro Division, 6951 Central Avenue, NE, PO Box 1250, Minneapolis, Minn 55440

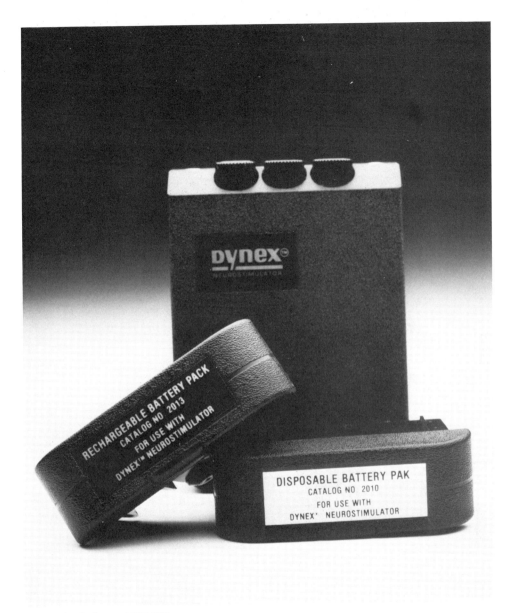

Dynex dual-channel T.E.N.S.

La Jolla Technology Inc., 11558 Sorrento Valley Road, San Diego, Calif 92121

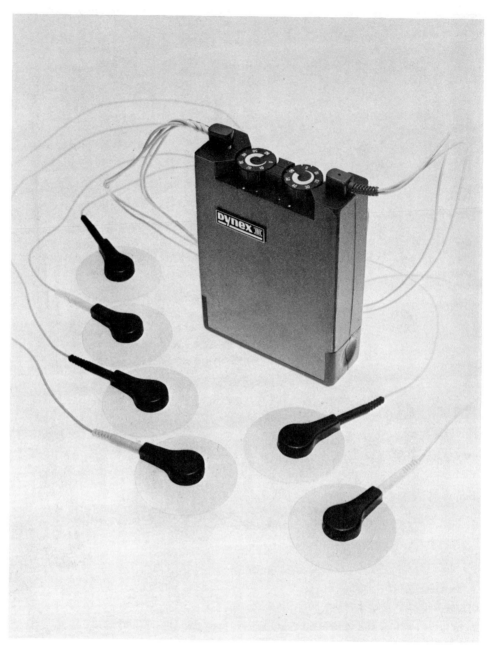

Dynex II dual-channel T.E.N.S. with pulse-train (burst) and modulation modes.
La Jolla Technology Inc., 11558 Sorrento Valley Road, San Diego, Calif 92121

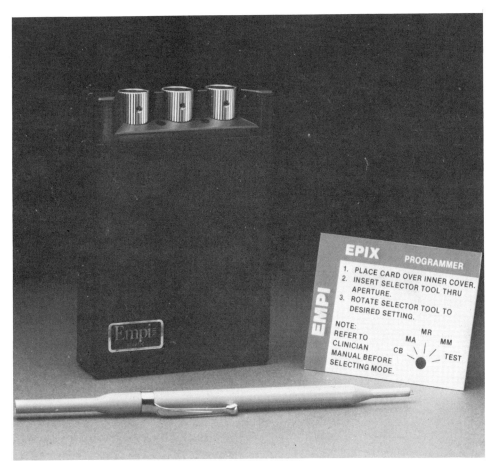

Empi EPIX dual-channel programmable with pulse-train (burst) and modulation modes.

Empi Inc., 261 South Commerce Circle, Fridley, Minn 55432

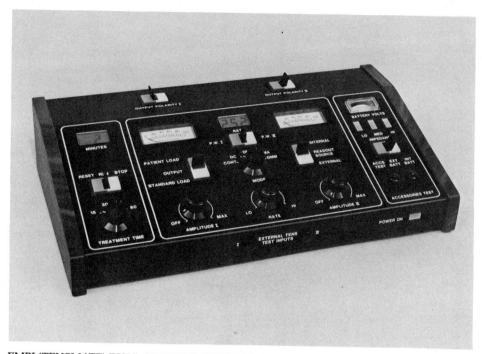

EMPI (TENSMATE) DUAL-CHANNEL CLINICAL EVALUATION SYSTEM

Empi, Inc., 261 South Commerce Circle, Fridley, Minn 55432

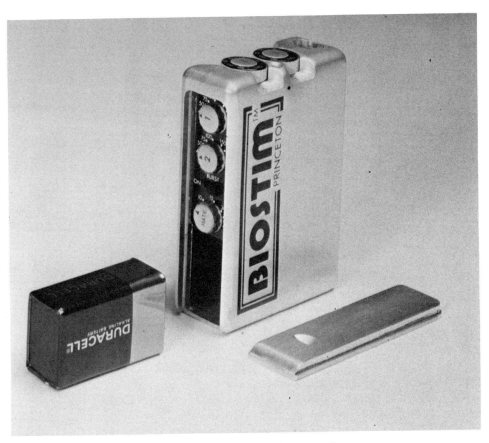

BIOSTIM System 10 Dual-Channel with pulse-train (burst) mode.

Biostim Inc., Clarksville Road & Everett Drive, PO Box 3138, Princeton, NJ 08540

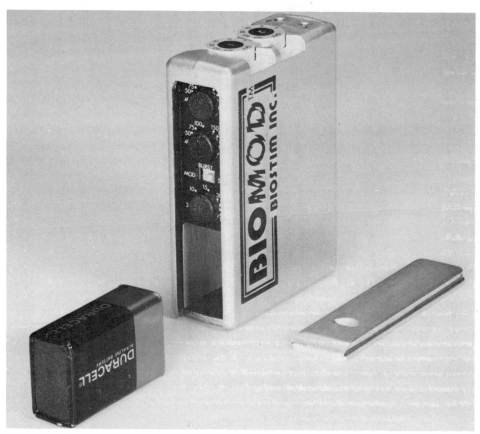

BIOSTIM BIOMOD dual-channel with pulse-train (burst) and modulation modes.

Biostim Inc., Clarksville Road & Everett Drive, PO Box 3138, Princeton, NJ 08540

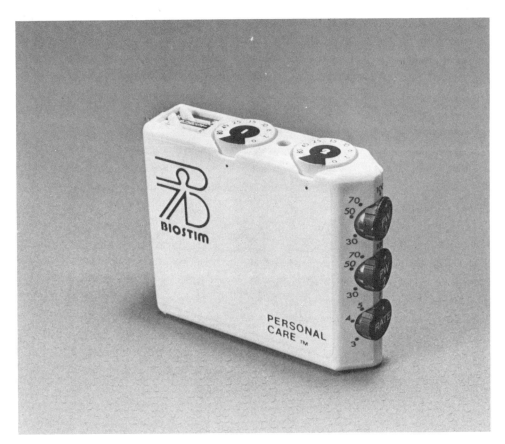

BIOSTIM Personal Care dual-channel with pulse-train (burst) mode.

Biostim Inc., Clarksville Road & Everett Drive, PO Box 3138, Princeton, NJ 08540

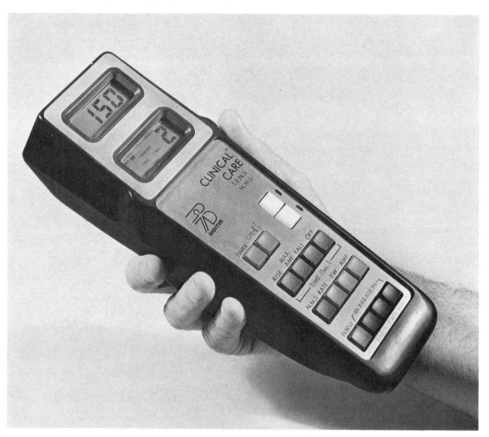

Biostim (Clinical Care) dual-channel T.E.N.S. INMS evaluation system.

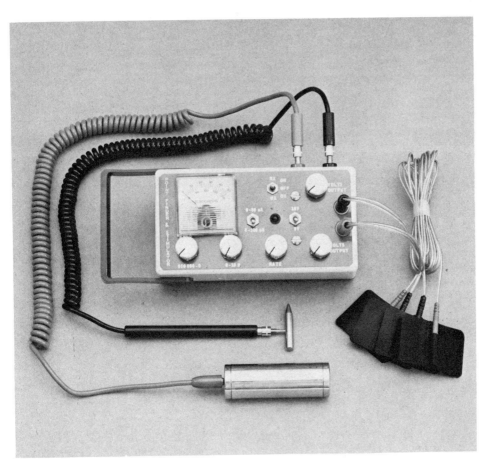

Joanco Model 4 point locator and dual-channel T.E.N.S. stimulator.

Joanco Medical Electronics Ltd. #704, 145 East 13th Street, North Vancouver, BC, Canada V7L2L4

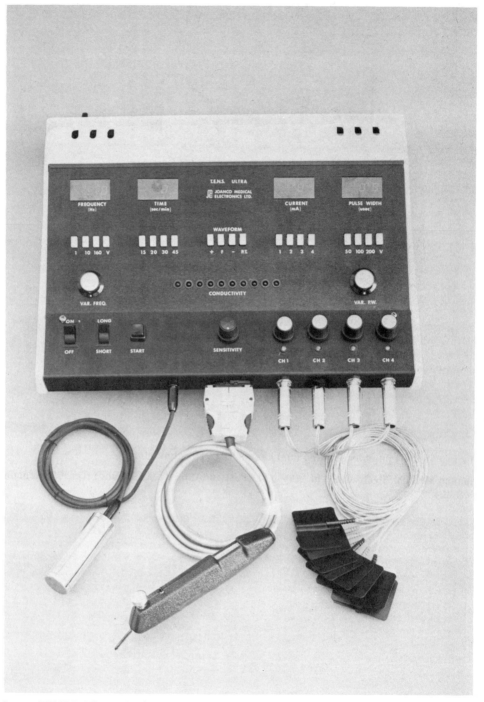

Joanco T.E.N.S. Ultra point locator/stimulator/evaluation system, 4-channel T.E.N.S. clinical unit.

Joanco Medical Electronics Ltd. #704, 145 East 13th Street, North Vancouver, BC, Canada V7L2L4

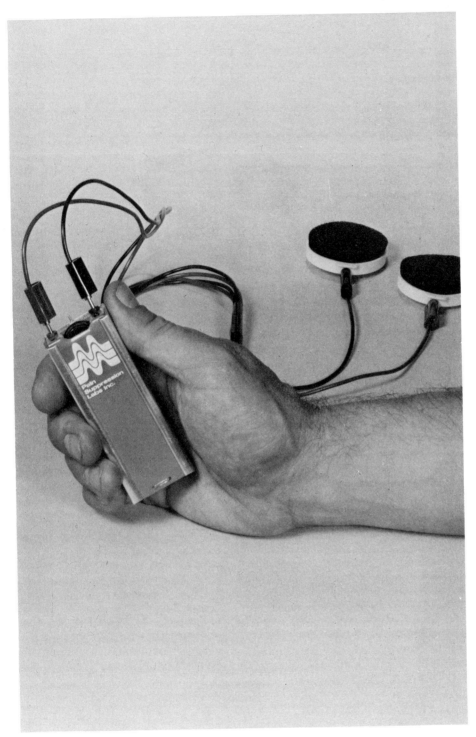

Pain Suppressor Model 106A.

Pain Suppression Labs, 559 River Road, Elmwood Park, NJ 07407

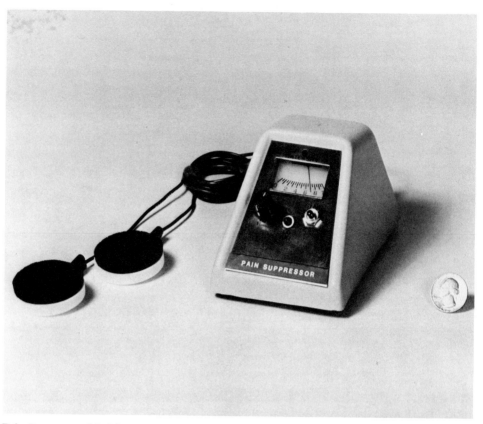

Pain Suppressor Model 105C.

Pain Suppression Labs, Inc., 559 River Road, Elmwood Park, NJ 07407

Neuroprobe System II point locator and stimulator.

Medical Research Labs, Inc., 1 Armour Court, Lake Bluff, Ill 60044

INDEX

A t following a page number indicates a table. A page number in *italics* indicates a figure.

Cerebrospinal fluid (CSF)
  endorphin levels in, 537–538, *539*, 540
  pressure changes in, headache due to, 134
Cerebrovascular accident (CVA), precaution on
    T.E.N.S. in, 58
Cervical anterior fusion, alternate electrode
    placement after, *516*
Cervical disk pathology, tenderness in, 86
Cervical doorbell pushbutton sign, anterior, 86
Cervical myotomes, quick scan of, 97, 98, 99t
Cervical radiculopathy, T.E.N.S. and, 385–393
Cervical spine
  headaches due to dysfunction of, 138–140
    seven signs of, 140
  pain in
    example of patient with, 287
    electrode placement for, 352, 366–368, *367,*
      368, 372, 378, 378–385, *386, 387,* 391–
      393, *394,* 395t
    postlaminectomy, *386, 387,* 389–392
  pain referred from, 385–393, *389–391*
Cervical spondylosis, 105–106, 108–110
Cervical strain. *See also* Cervical syndrome,
    chronic
  acute, T.E.N.S. with joint mobilization for, 462–
    463
  chronic, 378–385, *378, 379*
    T.E.N.S. with articulation techniques for,
      463, *470*
  headache due to, 366, *367*
Cervical sympathetic syndrome, posterior, 140
Cervical syndrome, chronic, *382. See also* Cer-
    vical strain
Changing the thalamic pain code, 557–559, *559*
Chapman's reflexes, 282
Chemical reactions to T.E.N.S., 60
Chemical substances, migraine related to, 130
Chemoreceptor, *65*
Chest
  pain in, T.E.N.S. for postoperative, 411–417,
    414–416
  trigger points of, *117*
  wall of, precaution on electrodes on, in car-
    diac patients, 58
Children
  migraine in, 129
  T.E.N.S. for, 457
Cholecystectomy, T.E.N.S. after, 505
Cholecystitis, 95
Chondromalacia, trigger points in, 120
Chronic headache, 126
Chronic pain syndrome, 11, *12*
  interview with patient, 220
  psychological aspects of, 31–32. *See also* Pain
    game

tenderness in, 86–87
T.E.N.S. for, 226
Chronic paroxysmal hemicrania, 133
Cimetidine (Tagamet), as placebo, 33–34
Circadian rhythm, 90
Circuit(s)
  emotional, 12
  Livingstone's theory of self-sustaining rever-
    berating, 147
Classic migraine headache, 129
Clinical pain level, 87, 90
Cluster headaches, causes of, 130, 132–133, 132t
Cluster responses, 227, *228,* 229
Coban, electrodes held in place with, 62
Codeine, and diminished response to T.E.N.S.,
    23
Colectomy, T.E.N.S. after, 505
Cold, application of. *See* Cryotherapy
Colles' fractures, reflex sympathetic dystrophy
    (RSD) after, 145–147
Comfort Burst Dual Channel unit (Medtronic),
    598
Common migraine headache, 129
Complement Dual-Channel unit (Medtronic), *598*
Compliance, psychologic aspects of, 37–38
Compression. *See* Spinal cord, compression of
Conceptualizations, present neurophysiologic,
    T.E.N.S. and, 51, 52
Conditioning, operant, 34
Conduction block, 554–556
Constant current, versus constant voltage, in skin
    burns, 59
Contract-relax stretching, 470–478, 484t
Convergence-facilitation theory of referred pain,
    103–104
Convergence, modality, 44
Convergence-projection theory of referred pain,
    103, *109*
Conversion cephalalgia, 126
Cord. *See* Spinal cord
Cordectomy, 148
Corpuscles
  Meissner's, 43, 43t
  Pacinian, 43t
Cortex
  in modulating pain perceptions, 49
  sensorimotor, 47, *47*
  somatosensory, 46, 102
Cortical evoked response (CER), 550
Cortical inhibitory surround theory, 273
Corticosteroids, 540
  effect on T.E.N.S., 543
Cost
  of T.E.N.S. therapy, 233–235
  of T.E.N.S. units, 201–202

Costopleural syndrome, 110
Cough, after T.E.N.S. therapy, *504*
CPI. *See* California Psychological Inventory
Cranial nerves, 261, 263
Craniomandibular dysfunction, headaches due to, 138–139
"Cross-talk" of impulses, 143
Cryotherapy
  at Delaware Valley Physical Therapy Associates, 334
  indications for, 334
  in pain management, 18, 20, 21
  physiologic effects of, 20
  types of, 20, 21
Cultural factors, in pain threshold, 30
Current
  constant, versus constant voltage, in skin burns, 59
  from electrode to nerve, 207
  stimulating, pulse width of, measurements of, 338, 339
Cutaneous nerves, 261
Cutaneous pain, 92, 99. *See also* Superficial pain
Cutaneovisceral reflex points, 272
Cycle of pain
  chronic, 11, 12
  classification of, *8*
  guarding response in, 7–10, *9*
  internal changes associated with, 8, *9, 10*
  interventions in, 20–23, *21*
  muscle spasms in, 7, *10*
  primary, *10*
  soft tissue dysfunction in, 7–9, *9, 10*
Cyriax traction, at Delaware Valley Physical Therapy Associates, 334

Deep pain, 99–100, *100*
  characteristics and mechanisms of, visceral, *100*
  definition of, 99
  somatic, 78t, 99–101
  versus superficial, 99–102
  transmission through ascending system, 101t
  visceral versus somatic, 99–101
Deep somatic structures, in pain patterns, *67*, 94
Deep unilateral syndrome, 110
Delaware Valley Physical Therapy Associates (DVPTA), 173
  clinical objectives at, 333
  procedures followed at, 332–338
Dental application, temporomandibular joint syndrome and, 353–366
Dental pain. *See also* Tooth pulp pain threshold
  electrode placement techniques for TMJ syn-

drome and, 353, 359–362, *361, 363, 364,* 366t
  ice massage for, 355
Depression
  endorphins in pain and, 542–543
  serotonin in pain and, 541
DeQuervain's syndrome, electrode array for, 403, *404*
Dermaforms, *337*
Dermatomal mappings, 258, *260,* 261–264
Dermatomal pain, *163,* 165
Dermatome(s), 69, 70
  anatomic and clinical factors in development of, 257t
  development of, in limb bud, *258, 259*
  innervation of, 250
  in locating pain, 94
  in spinal cord segment anatomy, 256–260
  sympathetic, 94
Dermomyotome, tendon pain referred through, 68
Descending inhibition, 545
Diabetic neuropathy, foot and ankle pain in, 438–440, *439–441*
Diaphragm, pain referred from, 77
  to shoulder, 105–106, *106, 107,* 108–110
Diathermy
  microwave, 20
  shortwave, 20
  ultrasound, 20
Diazepam, 23, 95, 543
Diet. *See also* Nutritional habits
  headaches due to, 131t
  in pain modification, 95
  protein and carbohydrate in, 541
  tryptophan in, 540–541
Diffuse noxious inhibitory controls (DNIC), 556–557
Digits. *See* Fingers
Disk(s), intervertebral
  annulus and nucleus pulposus of, *67, 71, 73*
  derangement of, 165, 167
  in embryological development, 250, 252
  facet joints and, differentiating involvement of, 161, 161t, 162
  herniation of, 162, *163, 164,* 165, *419, 420*
  lesion of, differentiated from malignancy, 97–98
  Merkel's, 43t
  pain arising from, *67, 71, 73,* 166t
  signs of pathology of, versus sacroiliac pathology, 168t
  surgery on, in U.S., 155
Diskogenic pain, *67, 71, 73, 163,* 166t
Disposable electrode pads, *581*

Headaches—*continued*
>   characteristics of, 128t
>   childhood, 129
>   common or classic, 129
>   diet and, 95
>   facial or lower-half, 128–129
>   hemiplegic, 128
>   menstrual, 129
>   ophthalmoplegic, 128
>   relaxation training and, 16
>   retinal, 128
>   stages of, 127–128
>   substances causing, 130, 131t
>   types of headaches related to, 129t
>   triggering of, 130
>   muscle-contraction (tension), 126
>   biofeedback for, 16
>   characteristics of, 127t
>   electrode placement for, 353–355, 353, 355, 356
>   post-traumatic, 126
>   psychogenic, 125, 126
>   sex, 134
>   substances causing, 131t
>   due to temporomandibular joint (TMJ) syndrome, 134–136, 136, 137, 138
>   T.E.N.S. for, 124–126
>   electrode placement techniques in, 366–369, 367–372, 380t, 371, 373–378
>   toxic, 125
>   traction, 125
>   vascular, 125, 127–130, 128t, 129t
Healing, of bone and T.E.N.S., 459
Heart. *See* Cardiac disease; Cardiac pain
Heat. *See* Hyperthermia, pain management and
Heat tests, radiant, on pain threshold, 91
Hemicrania, 129
Hemiplegic migraine headache, 125, 128
Hemorrhage, subarachnoid, as cause of headache, 133
Hernia, of intervertebral disk, T.E.N.S. in, electrode placement techniques in, 420. *See also* Low back pain
Heroin addicts, 543
Herpes zoster, neuralgia due to, 141t, 143, 144, 441–445, 446
5-HIAA. *See* Serotonin
High-intensity pulse-train (burst) T.E.N.S., studies of uses of, 343–344
High-rate T.E.N.S., 210, 211
High-voltage galvanic stimulation, indications for, 335
Hilton's law, 258
Histamine, 102
>   migraine due to, 130, 131t

History, in pain evaluation, 82–83t
"Hoku" point, 271
>   in temporomandibular joint pain, 355
>   in tooth pain, 360
Home instructions, for T.E.N.S. therapy, 237–245
Hopelessness scale, 31
Horner's syndrome, 105, 132
Horton's headache, 130
Hospital, T.E.N.S. program in, 513–515
>   contraindications, 514
>   length of stay in, 506
>   objectives, 513–514
>   operating room procedures, 514
>   postoperative surgical floor procedures, 515
>   preoperative procedure, 514
>   recovery room procedures, 514–515
>   results of postoperative program, 515
Hump, Dowager's, 68
Hyaline cartilage, 67, 70
Hyperabduction, test for, 150
Hyperalgesia, 80t, 85
Hyperesthesia
>   definition of, 80t
>   versus tenderness, 85
>   T.E.N.S. for, 478–485, 482, 483, 486
>   ulnar nerve lesion with, 467–469
Hyperpathia, 80t, 143
Hypersensitive teeth, desensitization of, 359
Hyperstimulation analgesia, 563
Hyperthermia, pain management and, 18, 20, 21
Hypoalgesia, 80t
Hypoesthesia, 80t
Hypothalamus, 47
Hysterectomy, alternate electrode placement after, 522

ICE massage, 355, 533. *See also* Cryotherapy
Ileus
>   alternate electrode placement after, 520
>   postoperative, 498, 503, 504, 504
>   T.E.N.S. for, 502, 506, 507t
Iliac crest, 281
Iliac spine, locating pain in, 93
Ilium, in sacroiliac joint dysfunction, 169, 169t, 170
Imagery, 11–13
>   guided, therapeutic application of, 18
>   jungian guided, 36
>   negative, 12–13, 13
>   positive, 11–12, 13
>   visual techniques of, 13
Impedance, electrode, 205, 349
Implant(s)

Ligament(s)—*continued*
  pain produced by, 67, 70, 72t
  trigger points associated with, 120
Limbic forebrain structures, 47
Limbic system, in pain imagery, 12
Linear pathway of pain, 386
Lissauer's tract, 274, 280
Livingstone's theory of self-sustaining reverberatory circuits, 147
Long-sitting test, 169
Lorazepam, 95
Low back pain, 155–173
  causes of, 156, *156*, 157
  change in location of, 93
  chronic
    electrode placement in T.E.N.S. for, *152, 153, 417–436, 419–423, 425, 427, 428, 430, 432, 433, 435*
    patient with, example of, 287
    post–lumbar laminectomy, *427, 430, 433*
  discrepancies in delineation of, 159t
  examples of patients with acute, chronic, and bilateral, 286–288
  exercises for, 335
  psychological tests of patients with, 31
  referred, 165–166, *167,* 169–170
  referred to lower extremities, *429, 430*
  symptoms of common syndromes, 159, 160t
  T.E.N.S. for, 173
  of visceral origin, 171, *171*
Lower extremities
  changes in length of, due to sacroiliac joint torsion, 169, *170*
  chronic low back pain referred to, *429, 430*
  optimal stimulation sites for, *318,* 319t, *320,* 321t, *322,* 323t, *324,* 325t
Lower-half migraine headache, 128, 129
Low-intensity direct current (LIDC), 458
Low-rate acupuncture-like T.E.N.S., 211, 212, *212*
Low resistance areas (LRA), 279, 280
Lumbar lordosis
  loss of normal, 162
  posture and, 96
Lumbar myotomes, quick scan of, 97, 98, 99t
Lumbar pain postlaminectomy, *386, 387*
Lung cancer
  arm pain due to, 105, *106*
  six pain syndromes in, 110

McGill-Melzack Pain Questionnaire (MPQ), 87, 88–89
Malignancy, pain in, 97–98
Malingerer, 31, 83t, 171

Mammaplasty, alternate electrode placement after, *517*
Mandible. *See* Craniomandibular dysfunction, headaches due to; Temporomandibular joint (TMJ) syndrome
Mandibular device, orthopedic, TMJ syndrome patient with, *359*
Manipulation, definition of, 463
Mapping, dermatomal, 257, 258, *258–264*
Marginal zone, of spinal cord, 45, 48
Massage, and pain management, 18, 21
  ice, 355, 533
  soft tissue friction, 21
  transverse friction, and contract-relax stretching, 334, 470–478, 484t
Mechanical skin reactions, 61–62
Mechanoreceptors, in pain perception, 64, *65*
Mechanosensitive nociceptors, 42
Median nerve, post-surgical decompression of, 447, *448*
Medical Devices, Inc., 362
Medication. *See also* Analgesics; Drugs; Narcotics
  in pain management, 23, *24*
  refraining from, before T.E.N.S., 331
Medtronic T.E.N.S. units, *598*
Medulla, 47, *47,* 50, 51
Meissner's corpuscles, 43, 43t
Membrane potential, 206
Meningeal blood vessels, 127
Menisci, intra-articular, 67, 70
Meniscoids, 70
Menstrual migraine headache, 129
Mentor Dual-Channel 150 unit, *592*
Mercaptobenzothiazole, 60
Meridian system, 275
Merkel's disks, 43t
Mesodermal somites, 249
Metabolites, production of, due to guarding, 8, 9
Metamere, 249
Methionine, 49
Microelectrode recordings, 42
Microneurographic recordings, 42
Micropunctate burns, 59
Microwave diathermy, 20
Midbrain, 47, *47,* 49, *50*
Migraine headache. *See* Headache(s), migraine
Minnesota Multiphasic Personality Inventory (MMPI), 31
Minimal intervertebral derangement (MID), 165, 167
Mobility exercises, 21–22
Mobilization. *See also* Movement(s)

definition of, 463

joint, T.E.N.S. with, 462–469, *465, 467–470,*
484t

principal characteristics of stimulation modes
and, 347t, 348

transverse friction massage and, 470–478

types of, 463

Modality convergence, 44

Modulation of pain, 535–537

T.E.N.S. and, 462–486, 484t

Morphine analgesia, 49, 50t, 550

Morphine-like pentapeptides, 49

Motor line, 264–265

Motor points, 263–265, 266t

specific points and, 268–273, 269t

Movement(s). *See also* Range of motion (ROM)

effects of, on pain, 96–97

in physical evaluation, 83–84t

active, 83t

passive, 84t

resistive, 84t

testing, 97

MSG (monosodium glutamate), 131t

Multiple sclerosis (MS), T.E.N.S. for, 148, 452

Muscle(s)

atrophy of, 97

nociceptors of, 42

pain arising from, *67,* 69, 72t

referred, 69

in quick bilateral myotome scan, 97–98, 99t,
100t

rigidity and tenderness of, due to visceral lesion, *112*

spasms of

in guarding, 7, 8, *10*

trigger points in, 118, 124

Muscle-contraction headaches. *See* Head-
ache(s), muscle-contraction

Muscle spindle, hyperactive, 266

Muscular rheumatism, 113

Musculoskeletal system. *See also* Neuromusculoskeletal system

pain arising from structures of, 72t

Mushroom phenomenon, 165

Myalgia, 112, 113

Myelogenic pain, 162, *163*

Myocardial infarction, *112*

Myofascial pain, 111–124

causes of and predisposing factors in, 115–
116, 118t

Myofasciitis, 112, 113

Myogenic pain, 166t

Myo-Monitor, 361–362

Myositis, 112, 113

Myotomes

cervical, 97, 98, 99t

innervation of, 250

in locating pain, 94

lumbar, 97, 98, 99t

segmentally related, 351

in spinal cord segment anatomy, 258–259

NALOXONE, *539,* 547, 549, 550

acupuncture blocked by, 51, 539

serotonin and, 557

Narcotics

effects of

on endogenous opiates, 542–543

on pain, 95

on T.E.N.S., 23, 542–543

postoperative, with T.E.N.S., 506, 507–508

Neck

optimal stimulation sites for, *304,* 305t

pain referral pattern of muscles of, *137*

trigger points of, *114*

Negative feedback loop, 50, *51*

Neospinothalamic tract (NSTT), 46, *47*

Nephrectomy, T.E.N.S. after, 505

Nerve(s)

damage to

categories of, 76

in Colles' fracture, 146

paratendinous, 68

peripheral. *See* Peripheral nerves

regeneration of, 101

of spinal complex, 157

Nerve action potential (NAP), 206, *206, 207,*
207

Nerve endings

encapsulated, 70

free

in hair follicle, 43t

in pain perception, 64, *65*

Paciniform, 43t

in pain transmission, 43, 43t

Ruffini, 43, 43t

sensory, 66

in skin, 66

in viscera, 77, 78

unencapsulated, 70

Nerve fibers. *See* Fibers

Nerve roots, 254, 255, *256. See also* Dorsal root

in diskogenic, myogenic, and neurogenic pain,
166t

entrapment of, 149t, 150

pain from, 73, 74t, 75

Nerve sheaths, vascularity of, 76

Nerve structures, sensory, as T.E.N.S. target, 200

Nerve trunk, pain from, 74t, 75–76
Nervous system. *See also* Autonomic nervous
    system (ANS); Central nervous sys-
    tem (CNS)
  excitability of, 200–207
  structures of, pain from, due to noxious stim-
    uli, 74t
Neuralgia, 142–144
  atypical facial, 141t, 144
  characteristics of, 141t
  definition of, 81t
  geniculate, 143
  glossopharyngeal, 143
  intercostal, 413, 415, *415, 416*
  periodic migrainous, 130, 132
  post-herpetic, 141t, 143, 144
    T.E.N.S. for, 441–446, *446*
  superior laryngeal, 144
  trigeminal, 93, 141t, 142–143
    cluster headaches similar to, 132
Neurapraxia, 76
Neuraxis, 44, 46–47, *47*, 50, 545
Neuritis
  definition of, 81t
  leprous, 449
Neuro-Aid, 335
Neurogar III T.E.N.S. unit, 535
Neurogenic pain, 163, 165, 166t
Neurohumoral mechanisms of T.E.N.S., 549–
    550
Neurohumoral neurotransmitter theory, 537–539,
    539
Neurologic evaluation, 84t, 98
Neurolymphatic points, 270
Neuromod Single-Channel unit, *597*
Neuromuscular stimulation, 200, 361–362
Neuromusculoskeletal system
  examination of, 96–98, 98t, 99t
  pain-producing structures in, 64, *67*, 66–68,
    72t, 74t, 78t, 79t
Neuroskeletal system, 96–98, 98t, 99t
Neurons
  of dorsal horn, 103
  high-threshold, 103
  in neuralgia, 143
  nociceptive, 46, 143. *See also* Nociceptors
  trigeminothalamic, 143
  wide-dynamic, 143
Neuropacers, single- and dual-channel, *591*
Neuropathy, definition of, 81t. *See also* Diabetic
    neuropathy, foot and ankle pain in
Neuropharmacology, in pain modulation, 49, 50
Neurophysiologic effects of T.E.N.S., 559–560,
    561t, 562–563
  postoperative, 507–509

Neurophysiologic research, 2
Neuroprobe, 125
Neuroprobe System II point locator and stimu-
    lator, *611*
Neurosurgery, for pain management, 18
Neurotmesis, 76
Neurotransmitters
  mechanism of action, 550, 551
  opiate, 551
Neurovascular bundles, 66
Neurovascular compression syndrome, 150–151,
    152, 153, 153t, 154
Neurovascular hilus, 263–264
Nickel, allergic reaction to, 60
Nociceptive neurons, 46, 143
Nociceptive synapse, opioid peptide action at,
    552, *553*
Nociceptors, 64, *65*,
  in afferent input, 42, *67*
  definition of, 81t
  mechanosensitive, 42
  muscle, 42
  polymodal, 42
  somatic and visceral structures with and
    without, *67*
  thermal, 42
Nodes, Schmorl's, 165
Noninvasive electroacupuncture, 289, 290
Nonsuppurative nodular panniculitis, 68
Notochord, 252
Noxious, definition of, 81t
Noxious information, ascending projections of
    pathways conveying, 46–46, *47*
Noxious input, central processing of, 44–46
Noxious mechanisms, transmission of, 123
Nucleus
  posterior thalamic, 46, *47*
  pulposus, *67*, 71, 73, *251*, 252
  raphe magnus (NMR), 50, *50*, 51, 545, 546
  reticular gigantocellularis (RGC), 50, *50*, 546
  reticularis magnocellularis (RMC), *50*, 51
  ventrolateral posterior, 46, *47*
Numbness. *See* Paresthesia
Nutritional habits. *See also* Diet
  behavior influenced by, 35

OBSERVATION of patient. *See* Patient
Occipital headache, 138
Occipital nerves, headache due to irritation of,
    95
Occiput, optimal stimulation sites for, *306*, 307t
Olecranon, open reduction of fracture of, *402*
Operant conditioning, 34
Operating room procedures, in T.E.N.S. pro-
    gram, 514

Ophthalmic headache, 125, 128
Opiate analgesia, 50, 51
Opiate neurotransmitters, 550, 551
Opiate receptors, 49
Opiates. *See* Endogenous opiates; Narcotics
Opioid peptides, *538*
  at nociceptive synapse, 552, *553*
Optimal stimulation sites (OSS)
  for face, *302*, 303t
  for forehead and lateral neck, *304*, 305t
  for lower extremity, *318*, 319t
  for major joints, 326t
  for shoulder and volar region, *310*, 311t, 312t
  specific guidelines to selection of, 285–268
  for T.E.N.S. electrodes, 283–289
Orthotron, 333
Osteoporosis, 145

PACEMAKERS, T.E.N.S. contraindicated in patients with, 57
Pacinian corpuscles, 43t, 77
Paciniform endings, 43t
PAG. *See* Periaqueductal gray (PAG)
Pain. *See also* specific anatomic parts
  acute versus chronic, 10–13, 11t
  assessment of
    forms for, 173, 190–197
    scale for, 227, *228*
  cancer, and T.E.N.S., 456, 457
  characteristics of, 78t, 79–98
  chronic, 10–13, 11t, 18. *See also* Chronic pain syndrome; Pain cycle
  chronology of, 79
  classification of causes of, 7, *8*
  confusing nature of, 79t
  cultural factors and, 30, 90
  cycle of
    chronic, 11, *12*
    classification of, *8*
    guarding response in, 7–9, *9*, *10*
    internal changes associated with, 8, 9, *10*
    interventions in, 20–23, *21*
    muscle spasms in, 7, *10*
    physical interventions in, 20–23
    primary, *10*
    soft tissue dysfunction in, 7–9, *9*, *10*
  deep. *See* Deep pain
  definitions of, 29, 80t
  definitions in study of, 80–81t
  endurance of, 29. *See also* Pain tolerance, maximum; Pain tolerance level
  enhancing treatment of, 37, 38
  evaluation of patient, 78–79, 82–84t. *See also* Pain, assessment of; Patient
  grading of, by patient, 91

hysterical component of, 31
  as indicator of pathology, 63–64
  intensity of, 30
  life style of, 32–33. *See also* Pain game
  lateralization of, 93
  linear pathway of, 386
  location of, 93–94
  management of. *See also* Pain, modulation of
    acupuncture in, 18
    autogenic training in, 18
    autogenic/biogenic techniques in, 15, 16
    behavior modification in, 17, 34, 35
    biofeedback techniques in, 15, 16, 18
    cryotherapy in, 18, 20, 21
    electrical stimulation in, 18
    hyperthermia in, 18, 20, 21
    massage in, 18
    neurosurgery in, 18
    physical therapy in, 18–23
    protocol for, 7
    psychologic considerations in, 29–40
    psychotherapy in, 17
    relaxation techniques in, 17
    relaxation training programs in, 16
    stress management techniques in, 18
    therapeutic applications of guided imagery in, 18
  measurement of, 87, 90–91, *92*
  modifying factors in (diet, drugs, movement, posture), 30, 95–98
    muscles for quick bilateral myotome scan, 98t
    muscles for quick lumbar myotome scan, 99t
  modulation of, 41–52, 64, *65*. *See also* Pain, management of
    afferent input, 41–47
    present, and T.E.N.S., 51–52
    theories of, 48–51
  neuromusculoskeletal structures producing, 64, 66–78
  neurophysical mechanisms in modulation of, 41–52
  pathophysiology of, 46, 47, *47*, 386
  perception of, 29–30, 64, *65*
    learning theory and, 30
  phantom limb, *141*, 147, 148
    hyperesthesia and, 478–486
  postoperative. *See* Postoperative T.E.N.S.
  psychology of. *See* Psychological aspects of pain
  quality, nature, and intensity of, 64, *65*, 85–87
  questionnaires on, 87, *88–89*. *See also* Pain, assessment of, forms for

Pain—continued
    referred versus radiating, 102–105. See also
        Referred pain
    relief of. See Pain, management of
    statistics on, 16, 16t
    subjective nature of, 91, 228
    substances producing, 131t
        endogenous, 8
    superficial versus deep, 99–102. See also Deep
        pain; Superficial pain
    syndromes of, 66, 124
    "taking away" and symptomatic relief of, in
        T.E.N.S. therapy, 225–227, 228, 229
    visceral, 78. See also Viscera
Pain clinics, 14–16
    biofeedback, 15
    comprehensive, 15, 15t
        psychologic aspects, 33
        single-modality and, 14–15
    types of, 14 14
Pain cycle, 7–9, 9, 10, 11, 12, 20, 21
Pain game, 11, 18–20, 19, 32–33, 220
Pain and Health Rehabilitation Center, 36
Pain level
    clinical, 87, 90
    just-noticeable difference in, 90
Pain-modulating mechanisms, 48–51
Pain-pressure endings, 43t
Pain-spasm pain cycle, 124
"Pain spots," 43
Pain Suppressor, 352–353, 353, 358, 366, 373,
        375
Pain Suppressor Model 105C, 610
Pain Suppressor Model 106A, 609
Pain syndrome. See Chronic pain syndrome
Pain threshold, 30
    cultural factors in, 30
    definition of, 81t
    studies on, 90–91
        cutaneous, 90
Pain test, torniquet (TPT), 87, 88
Pain tolerance, maximum, 90
Pain tolerance level, 81t
Paleospinothalamic tract (PSTT), 46, 47
Palpation
    deep, between transverse processes, 279
    to determine tenderness of peripheral motor
        points, 281
    in examination, 84t, 86
    of peripheral nerves, 282
Palsy, Bell's, 143
Pancoast syndrome, 110
Pancreatic cancer, 169–170
Pancreatitis, T.E.N.S. for, 454
Panniculitis, 66, 68, 447, 447

nonsuppurative nodular, 68
Parachlorophenylalanine (PCPA), 541
Paramedian posterior point, 86
Parameter adjustment, T.E.N.S., 205–207, 206–
        208
Paratendinous nerves, 68
Paresthesia
    definition of, 81t
    due to dorsal root irritation, 75
    in lower extremities, 85
    due to nerve trunk irritation, 75–76
    sensory loss differentiated from, 75, 85
Parietoskeletal reflex, 77
Patella
    referred pain to, 120
    subluxations of, post-surgical T.E.N.S. for, 476–
        478, 480, 481
Pathways, 46–47, 47, 386
Patient
    assessing suitability of, for T.E.N.S., 234–235
    assessment forms for
        pain, 173, 190–197
        wellness, 235, 236, 237
    attitudes of. See also Psychological aspects of
        pain
        anger, 220
        fear of electricity, 221
        compliance related to, 37–38
        healing process and, 38
        on pain, 30–33
    evaluation of. See Evaluation, T.E.N.S.
    incompetent, precautions on T.E.N.S. in, 58
    observation of, 82t, 172
        to estimate pain, 91
    pain descriptions by, 82t, 87, 88–89
    pain location indicated by, 93
    preoperative instruction protocol for, 525–527
    scale to use, for indicating magnitude of per-
        ceived discomfort, 227, 228
    T.E.N.S. and, 219–247
        amplitude advancement by, 221–224
        assessing suitability for, 234–235
        follow-up for, 237
            questionnaire for, 238, 246–247
        home instructions for, 237–238
        initial interview, 219–224
        issues in, 225–237
            perceived sensation changes by, accord-
                ing to intensity, pulse width, and pulse
                rate, 222, 222t, 223t
Patterns of pain referral, 113, 114, 137. See also
        Referred pain
Pattern theory, 44
Pectoralis minor syndrome, 150–151
Pectoralis trigger point, 151

Primary ramus, anterior (APR), 253
Professional Pain Management Seminars, 81
Progressive relaxation training, 36
Proprioceptors, 43
Propylene glycol, irritation due to, 61
Prostaglandins, 8, 129–130
Prostatitis, 170
Protopathic pain, 101
Protopathic system, 44
Psychogenic headaches, 126
Psychogenic pain
  endorphins in, 537
  T.E.N.S. for, 459, 461–462
Psychological aspects of pain, 8, 29–38
  of chronic pain, 11–13, 13, 87. See also Pain
    game
  in pain cycle, 8
Psychologic testing, in treating pain, 30–32
Psychology of pain, 30–31
Psychophysiologic balancing, 36
Psychotherapy, 17
Pulse rate, 222, 223t
Pulse-train (burst) T.E.N.S., 213, 224t, 276, 338t,
    343–344, 347t, 348, 534
  acupuncture-like T.E.N.S. and, 544–553
  single pulse versus, 211–212, 212, 213
Pulse width, 222, 223t, 511
  knob for, 217
  lack of international standardization on, 338–
    339

QUANTA, 552, 553
Quasivisceral pain, 77
Questionnaire
  on pain, 87, 88–89
    follow-up, 238, 246–247
  on stress, 32

RADIAL nerve, decompression of superficial, 447,
    447
Radiant heat tests, 91
Radiating pain, referred pain versus, 102–105
Radiculopathy, 383–393
Rami communicantes, 253
Ramsey-Hunt syndrome, 145
Range of motion (ROM)
  active, 96, 97
  assessing, 96–97
  joint mobilization to increase, 333
  loss of active, due to posture, 96
  in low back pain, 172
  passive, 97
Rapid eye movements (REM), 130, 132
Raynaud's disease, 154, 455–456

Raynaud's phenomenon, 455–456
Reactions. See Skin reactions
Receptors. See also Nociceptors
  axons and, 41–47. See also Afferent input
  behavior patterns of, 42, 42t
  characteristics of, 43, 43t
  definition of, 41
  end-organ, 43
  opiate, 49
  in transmission, modulation, and perception
    of pain, 64, 65
Recording, microelectrode, 42
Recovery room procedures, 514–515
Rectal surgery, alternate electrode placement
    after, 521
Referral patterns
  in muscle pain, 69
    of head and neck, 137
  trigger points in, 114, 114–117
Referred pain
  after chronic pain, 11
  convergence-facilitation theory of, 103–104
  convergence-projection theory of, 103, 109
  definition of, 103
  mechanisms of, 103
  versus radiating pain, 102–105
  sclerotomes in, 94
  in skin pain, 66
  trigger points in, 111–114, 114–117
  from viscera, 94, 105–106, 106–109, 108–
    111
Reflex sympathetic dystrophy (RSD), 94, 145–
    147, 406–411, 407–411, 465
Relaxation
  headache due to, 128
  for headache patients, 16, 125
Relaxation response
  in biofeedback, 35–36
  in biogenics, 36
Relaxation training, 16, 354, 355
Release phenomenon, 75
REM sleep, 130, 132
Resistance, accommodating and progressive, 333
Resistive testing, 97
Response pattern, peak-and-valley, 22, 23
Reticular activating system (RAS), 545
Reticular formation, 47
Retinal migraine headache, 128
Reusable electrodes, 557
Rheumatism, as term, 113
Rhythm, circadian or diurnal, 90
Rib cage pain, 413, 415, 415, 416
Root avulsion injury, 448–449
Rotator cuff surgery, shoulder pain after, 399